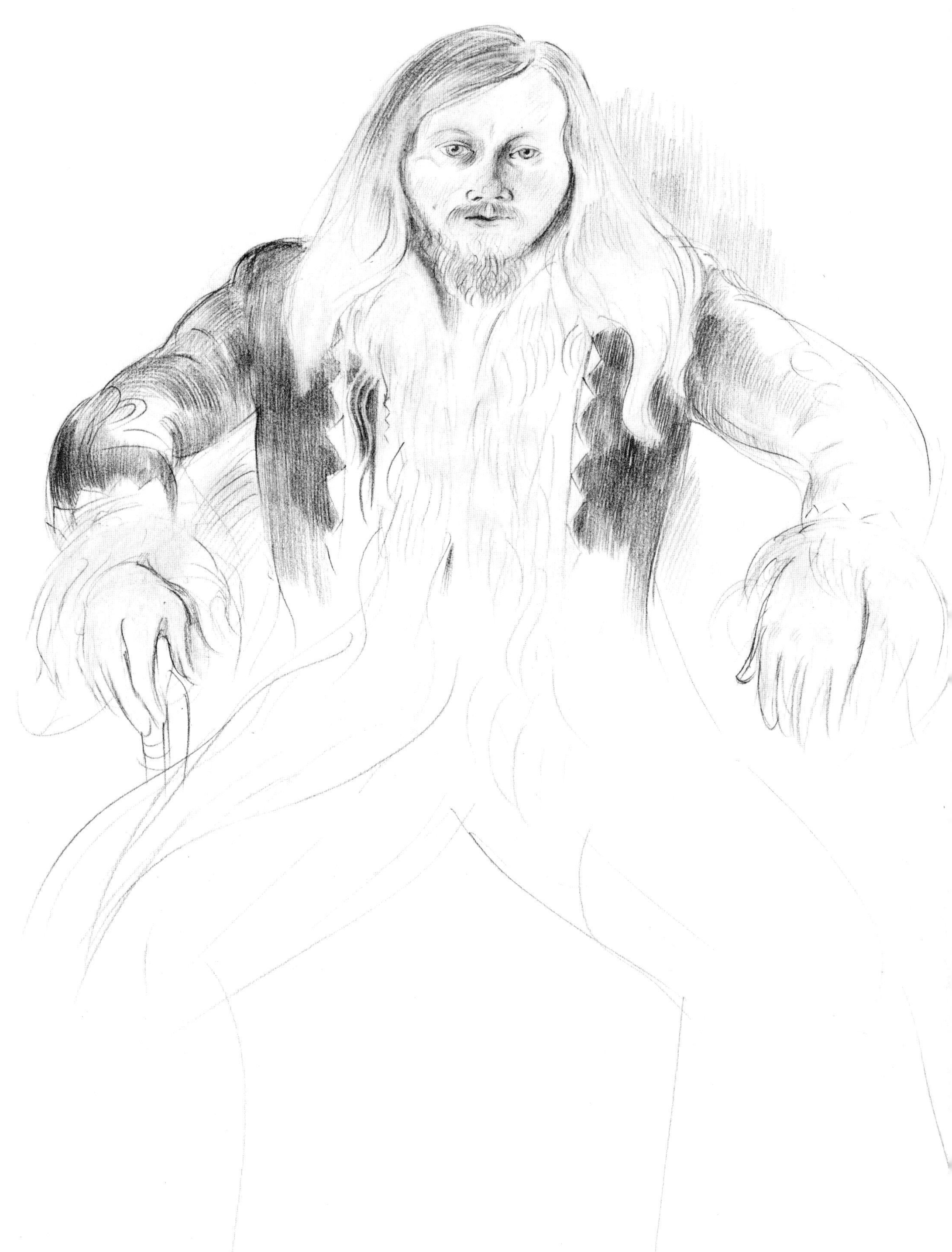

ANNA KEEL

Bilder und Zeichnungen

Mit einem Vorwort
von Federico Fellini

Diogenes

Die Originale der in diesem Katalog versammelten 133 ›Bilder und Zeichnungen‹ sind in einer gleichnamigen Ausstellung im Spätherbst 1976 in der Galerie Daniel Keel in Zürich zu sehen, mit deren Erlaubnis sie hier erstmals veröffentlicht werden als

51. Werk im ›Club der Bibliomanen‹

30/76/AT-B/I
ISBN 3 257 00471 0

Als kleiner Junge war ich sehr mager. Eben wegen meines dürren Hampelmannkörpers und meines leicht verstörten Blicks hatte der Maler Bonfante Bonfantoni es sich in den Kopf gesetzt, daß ich ihm um jeden Preis Modell stehen müßte für das große Fresko, das er in der neuen Kirche der Kapuzinermönche malte.

Das Bild stellte ein biblisches Thema dar, eine Szene, die etwas mit den zehn ägyptischen Plagen zu tun hatte. Trotzdem traute meine Mutter dem Bonfantoni nicht recht; sie fürchtete, auf dem Bild könnte es nackte Frauen geben, allenfalls mit großen Engelsflügeln, aber doch mit entblößten Bäuchen und Brüsten. Sie sagte, ›das Kind‹ könnte eine schwere seelische Erschütterung davontragen.

Der Bischof, ein sehr alter, gelähmter Herr, der im Geruch der Heiligkeit stand, mußte eingreifen. Durch den Mund des Pater Guardian ließ der fromme Mann verlauten, bei aller Hochachtung für die edlen Befürchtungen meiner Mutter, übernehme er persönlich die Verantwortung. Er fügte hinzu, die Bereitschaft, sich auf einem von göttlichen Dingen handelnden Gemälde abbilden zu lassen, wenn auch nur als Symbol einer der zehn ägyptischen Plagen, würde dem Menschen sicher früher oder später irgendwie angerechnet; lang ist das Leben, und wer säet, der wird ernten. An diesem Punkt wurde meine Mutter weich. Sie putzte mir die Ohren, kämmte mich und übergab mich der Großmutter, die mich zu der neuen Kirche bringen sollte, wo der Maler seine Arbeit wieder aufnahm, sobald die Mönche ihren Gottesdienst beendet hatten.

Bisher hatte ich abends noch nie eine Kirche von innen gesehen. Sie kam mir riesig und ungeheuer hoch vor. Das Geräusch der Schritte hallte oben in den dunklen Wölbungen wider. Bonfantoni arbeitete ganz hinten, neben dem Altar, in einem Kranz brennender Kerzen, die er so ziemlich überall hatte anbringen lassen, ich weiß nicht, ob des Lichtes oder der Wärme wegen.

Mit großem Gepolter kletterte er über ein paar Holztreppchen hinauf und hinunter, zu den langen hölzernen Planken, die vor der Wand mit dem Fresko im leeren Raum hingen. Man sah einen weiten, von schwarzen Wolken geblähten Himmel, durchzuckt von Blitzen und Feuerzungen. Darunter war ein geborstener Berg, Herden, Hirten und Hunde stürzten in den Abgrund. Weiter unten schleuderten die Wogen eines wild aufgewühlten Meeres Boote und ganze Schiffsmannschaften in die Luft...

Ich muß durch dieses Übermaß an Katastrophen sichtlich betroffen gewesen sein, denn einer der Mönche, der daneben saß und gemeinsam mit seinen Mitbrüdern Litaneien murmelte, stand auf und schenkte mir eine Nuß.

Meine Tätigkeit als Modell bestand darin, auf dem Bauch zu liegen und einen Arm in die Höhe zu strecken, als wollte ich mich vor etwas schützen, was auf mich herabsauste (vielleicht die Herden oder die Hirten). Das Gesicht mußte ich zu einer Grimasse des Schreckens verziehen. Neben mir lag gleichfalls ausgestreckt Giudizio, ein einäugiger Bettler, der um seiner verschiedenen Absonderlichkeiten willen in der ganzen Gegend bekannt war. Auch er war wegen seinem klapperdürren Gerippe auserwählt worden, doch um ihn zum Modellstehen zu bewegen, mußte Bonfantoni ihm jedesmal einen halben Liter Wein spendieren. Giudizio, der ein Trinker war, genügte ein Fingerhut Alkohol, um in Fahrt zu kommen, und jetzt, weiß Gott, masturbierte er vor den Augen der Mönche mit affenartiger Geschwindigkeit, während er mit schallender Stimme die Frau des Zahnarzts anrief. Bonfantoni warf ihm eine Büchse an den Kopf und hob so gewaltig zu fluchen an, daß die Kerzenflämmchen flackerten und die Mönche in lauteren Tönen psalmodieren mußten, damit der Himmel den Lärm nicht zu hören bekäme.

Niemand hat je das fertige Gemälde erblickt, denn plötzlich starb der Bischof, und sein Nachfolger hatte nichts für die Mönche mit ihrer neuen Kirche übrig. So zahlte niemand mehr, und Bonfantoni ließ alles stehen und liegen und ging nach Brasilien. Als einziges Zeugnis meiner freiwillig geleisteten Dienste blieb im untersten Winkelchen eine Hand zurück, die sich in einem weitläufigen, schwarzen Durcheinander von Schafen, Booten, Wolken und Blitzen emporstreckte.

In späteren Jahren passierte es mir noch einmal, daß ich Modell stand, aber nun handelte es sich um ein Porträt, ein Porträt von mir, diesmal angezogen, mit einem großen Halstuch und leicht zerzaustem Haar, weil der ›berühmte Porträtmaler‹ unbeirrt behauptete, ich hätte einen Beethovenkopf.

Er hieß Ghiglia, der Maler, und wir sind Freunde geblieben.

Beim Malen sang er aus vollem Hals komplette Opernarien. Mitten in einem schrillen Ton verstummte er auf einen Schlag und starrte mich durchbohrend an, worauf er zum Zeichen des Widerwillens und Abscheus langsam den Kopf schüttelte. Oder er zog die Augenbrauen unwahrscheinlich hoch, während er den Mund aufriß, daß er sich schier die Kinnlade ausrenkt oder ihn zu einem Rosenknöspchen spitzte. Dabei ließ er seinen Blick matter werden oder ganz erlöschen, bis sein Gesicht völlig stumpfsinnig aussah. Ich begann zu befürchten, daß er mir mit all diesen irren Grimassen einen anderen Gesichtsausdruck suggerieren wollte. Ich hatte nie bemerkt, daß Beethoven so ausgesehen hätte. Die Sache beunruhigte und beleidigte mich.

Auch seine Art, sich von dem Bild zu entfernen, um dessen Wirkung zu prüfen, verblüffte mich. Er zog sich mit unterseeischer Langsamkeit von der Leinwand zurück, ein tückisch-verschlagenes Lächeln um die Lippen, als wollte er sagen: ›Du wirst schon sehen, was dir passiert!‹ So durchquerte er, rückwärts gehend, das ganze Zimmer, bis zur Tür. Oft war ich überzeugt, daß er jetzt gehen würde, und stand auf, um mich zu verabschieden. Doch dann kehrte er zischend und puffend wie eine alte Lokomotive wieder zum Bild zurück und arbeitete weiter, während er unverständliche Drohungen vor sich hinmurmelte und mir finstere Blicke zuwarf.

Eines Tages, bei der vierten oder fünften Sitzung, ergriff Ghiglia einen dicken Pinsel, den allerdicksten, tauchte ihn in eine Büchse mit kackegelbem Lack und rührte lange darin herum. Worauf er damit, ohne ein Wort zu sagen, wie rasend über die Leinwand zu streichen begann, bis das ganze Bild mit der infamen Farbe bedeckt war. Schließlich ließ er, zum Ausdruck seiner Freude und Wut, ein lautes Furzgeräusch hören, stieß einen mächtigen Seufzer der Erleichterung aus, und dann gingen wir in die nächste Bar trinken. Vom ›Porträt à la Beethoven‹ war nie wieder die Rede.

Ich weiß nicht recht, warum ich diese unwahrscheinlichen Erinnerungen eines verhinderten Modells erzählt habe. Vielleicht sind sie mir in den Sinn gekommen, als ich das vertrauensvolle Sichgehenlassen, die entspannte Haltung, die natürliche Ruhe der Menschen sah, die in diesem Buch abgebildet sind.

Die erste Empfindung des Betrachters ist Vergnügen. Die Bilder versetzen euch in gute Laune, und ihr bekommt Lust, euch auch von einer Künstlerin porträtieren zu lassen, bei der man sich so wohl fühlt. Welch friedliche Atmosphäre, welch heitere Vertraulichkeit! Man meint beinahe zuhören zu können, die Gespräche zu hören, die Porträtistin und Porträtierte ein ums andere Mal miteinander geführt haben müssen. Denn um mit solcher Eindringlichkeit und Zartheit einen Charakter, eine Geschichte wiedergeben zu können, um einzig mit einem leichten Bleistiftstrich den Hauch eines verlegenen Lächelns anzudeuten; um auf so vielen Menschengesichtern den Ausdruck resignierter Trauer, pathetischer Eitelkeit oder leerer Grübelei zu erhaschen, sie zu beseelen mit einem weisen Radiergummi, der das Zeichen nicht auswischt, sondern in das hauchfeine Zwielicht gewisser alter Fotografien entrückt; um das zu erreichen, um Langeweile, Melancholie, Gleichgültigkeit, Zufriedenheit, Stumpfheit, Bescheidenheit, Dünkel, Unschuld so meisterhaft darzustellen – dazu muß man von liebevoller Neugier bewegt sein und die anderen brauchen, sich mit ihnen einlassen und mit ihnen reden, ein wenig an ihrer Freude und ihrem Kummer teilhaben. Und die Malerin amüsiert sich, manchmal ist sie auch ergriffen, aber immer diskret und zurückhaltend. Ich glaube, auch der grimmigste Gegner figurativer Kunst muß vor dem Charme dieser so überaus persönlichen Malerei die Waffen strecken; schon um der Form willen, wenn man den Inhalt wirklich ignorieren will (aber warum denn den Inhalt ignorieren?).

Man findet heute selten einen Künstler, der den Mut hat, eine so umfassende und eigenwillige Ausdrucksfähigkeit nicht zu verbergen. Im allgemeinen beherrscht der ›Nichtausdruck‹ das Feld; mit lachhafter Unverschämtheit und ideologischem Terror stellt sich der ›non-sense‹ zur Schau, der ›behaviourism‹ und die ›land art‹, die arme Kunst. Nicht einmal um dem Pluralismus zu huldigen, läßt man zaghafte Versuche einer figürlichen Darstellung zu. Wie sollte man sich nicht mit dieser Malerin solidarisch fühlen, die sich wieder auf die im Wesen der Kunst liegenden ästhetischen und hedonistischen Zielsetzungen besinnt, die ernsthaft etwas ausdrückt, darstellt, abmalt und, natürlich mit modernem, zeitgenössischem oder, um den Modeausdruck zu gebrauchen, ›historischem‹ Bewußtsein, zeichnet und erzählt? Der Inhalt ihrer Bilder ist deutlich bestimmt, klar ausgeführt, aber immer aufgelockert und in seinem formalen Ausdruck poetisch erhöht. Ihre oft nackten Frauen, ihre Männer und manchmal auch ihre landschaftlichen ›Ausblicke‹ sind mit sicherem Strich, wenn auch nicht naturalistisch, in ihrer objektiven Wahrheit dargestellt, jedoch stets in jener Verklärung, die eben das Kennzeichen des echten Künstlers ist. Dies gilt für die Bilder, die Aquarelle und für die wunderschönen Zeichnungen, in denen der Bleistift überraschende Effekte erzielt. Die Farben sind nie schreiend; das Ganze ruht in einer gelassenen dämmerigen Tönung, einem diskret gefilterten Licht, einer Atmosphäre, die an mitteleuropäische Verhältnisse oder an manche nachimpressionistische französische Bilder erinnert.

Aber ich möchte noch von den Modellen sprechen und von der Art, in der die Malerin sich mit ihnen unterhält. Anna Keel ist eine Psychoanalytikerin, die euch nicht erschrecken will. Sie ist gern mit euch zusammen und erzählt euch von euch selbst, ohne zu entmutigen. Tragödien – soweit es sie gibt – werden stillschweigend wahrgenommen und durch Ironie und liebevolles ›Auf-den-Arm-Nehmen‹ gemildert, was immer notwendig ist, wenn man wirklich Freunde werden will. Manche Modelle scheinen sogar zu merken, daß die Malerin sich eben ein bißchen über sie lustig macht, und wenn ihr genau hinschaut, seht ihr, daß Anna Keel auch das noch aufzeichnet – im Blick der Augen, der plötzlich ein leises Mißtrauen spiegelt, oder im Lächeln, das in einem soeben erwachenden Verdacht steckenbleibt.

Und alle Bilder haben noch etwas, was einen zum Lachen reizt und gleichzeitig rührt: das ist der noch schwankende, halb selbstgefällige, halb ängstliche Ausdruck eines Menschen, der sich im nächsten Moment selbst erblicken und wiedererkennen wird, im vornherein stolz auf sich ist und sich gleichzeitig schon auf eine Enttäuschung gefaßt macht oder auf die demütig hingenommene Erkenntnis, daß er eben doch nicht schön genug ist, um eines Porträts würdig zu sein.

In diesem Buch blättern – das ist, als läse man die Geschichten von Maupassant und Simenon, als streifte man durch Bahnhöfe, Straßen, Cafés; im Grunde ist es, als fändest du deine Freunde, deine Verwandten wieder, Menschen, denen du in deinem Leben begegnet bist. Und plötzlich entdeckst du, daß ja von dir die Rede ist, während du geglaubt hast, nur die Bilder einer Malerin aus einem andern Land zu betrachten, die eine andere Sprache spricht, eine andere Erziehung genossen, eine andere Geschichte hat. Mir scheint, das ist einer der zahllosen Reize jener Art von Kommunikation, die wir Kunst nennen. Wenn sie echt ist. Und dann ist sie unverwechselbar und man vergißt sie nicht.

FEDERICO FELLINI

Inhalt

63 rechts Peter Weber mit Cowboyhut und Jeansjacke
Bleistift 66 x 50 1974

64 oben Stilleben mit Sendak-Postkarte und Zitrone
Farbige Kreide 34 x 25 1971

64 unten Stilleben mit Dürrenmatt-Kritik und Nasentropfen
Bleistift 21,5 x 27 1973

65 Monika Weber mit Cowboyhut
Bleistift 66 x 50 1975

66 Stilleben mit Teetasse und Zimmerpflanze und Zitronen
Bleistift 46 x 32 1975

67 Peter Weber mit Daisys Hut
Bleistift 66 x 50 1973
Eigentum des Kantons Zürich

68 Schneelandschaft mit Nebel
Bleistift 32,5 x 46 1976

69 Schneelandschaft mit Nebel
Bleistift 46 x 32,5 1976

70 Monika Augschöll
Bleistift 66 x 50 1975

71 Maggi mit Philipp
Bleistift 50 x 33,5 1973

72 Kellner in Sabaudia
Bleistift 46 x 32 1975

73 Maggi mit Pelzjacke
Bleistift 66 x 50 1974

74 Maggi mit Zigarette und Felljacke
Bleistift 50 x 33,5 1974

75 Maggi mit aufgestütztem Arm
Bleistift 34 x 25 1974

76 links Philipp daumenlutschend
Bleistift 30,5 x 24 1973

76 rechts Maggi am Telephon
Bleistift 34 x 24 1973

77 links Daisy mit Pelzjacke und Zigarette
Bleistift 66 x 50 1973

77 rechts Maggi am Küchentisch mit aufgestütztem Arm
Bleistift 34 x 24 1974

78 Kellner in Sabaudia
Bleistift 34 x 25 1975

79 Kellner in Camogli
Bleistift 66 x 50 1972

80 Monika Augschöll mit Serviette
Bleistift 46 x 32 1975

81 Fräulein Klara von der Kronenhalle
Öl 100 x 66 1970
Privatbesitz Rudolf C. Bettschart, Meilen

82 Gian Carlo Cappellini, Kellner in Camogli
Bleistift 66 x 50 1972

83 Kellner in Saturnia
Bleistift 34 x 25 1976

84 Jean Goldiger, ehemaliger Koch von Omar Bradley, genannt Bunker-Picasso
Öl 70 x 55 1973

85 Daisy und Silviane
Öl 159 x 121 1972

86 David und Mia
Bleistift 66 x 50 1975

87 Slim
Bleistift 66 x 50 1975

88 Martin Bruggmann
Öl 81 x 60 1970
Eigentum der Stadt Zürich

89 Daisy mit Hut und Zigarette
Öl 68 x 50 1972

90 Mädchen mit Pelzjacke
Bleistift 66 x 50 1975

91 Kellner in Locarno
Bleistift 48 x 34 1970

92 Sebastian Schroeder
Öl 70 x 55 1972

93 Aldo Ferrari, Kellner in Zürich
Öl 104 x 76 1972

94 Marlies Fischer, Schauspielschülerin
Bleistift 66 x 51 1975

95 Der Maler Karl Madritsch II
Bleistift 66 x 51 1973

96 Giuseppe Calgagni mit Töchterchen Pierina
Öl 125 x 115 1975

97 Lino, Kellner in Sabaudia
Bleistift 34 x 25 1975

98 links oben Slim
Bleistift 15 x 10,5 1975

98 rechts oben Stilleben mit Frankenstein-Shampooflasche und Picasso-Postkarte
Bleistift 34 x 25 1975

98 links unten Stilleben mit Rembrandt-Postkarte und Pinseln
Bleistift 27 x 20 1974

98 rechts unten Stilleben mit Christusfigur und Jongleur
Bleistift 23 x 20 1974

99 Ram
Bleistift 66 x 50 1975

100 Jill, Akt
Bleistift 66 x 51 1976

101 Jean Goldiger, ehemaliger Koch von Omar Bradley, genannt Bunker-Picasso
Bleistift 46 x 32 1975

102 Anita, Akt
Bleistift 66 x 51 1975

103 Anita
Bleistift 34 x 25 1975

104 Marisa, Akt mit Hund I
Bleistift 51 x 66 1976

105 Pesche als Rocker
Bleistift 66 x 50 1974

106 Massimo, Matrose in Sabaudia
Bleistift 34 x 25 1975

107 oben Marisa, Akt mit Hund II
Bleistift 50 x 66 1976

107 unten Marisa, Akt mit Zigarette
Bleistift 50 x 66 1976

108 Pesche mit Pekinese
Bleistift 66 x 50 1975

109 André Steiger mit Schäferhund
Bleistift 66 x 50 1975

110 Pesche mit Parisiennemütze
Bleistift 46 x 32 1976

111 Pesche mit Schäferhund
Bleistift 66 x 51 1976

112 Der Maler Karl Madritsch III
Bleistift 66 x 51 1974

113 Taffy zurück aus Amsterdam
Bleistift 66 x 51 1975

114 Ram mit aufgestütztem Arm
Bleistift 66 x 50 1976

115 Meine Mutter Héloise da Cunha
Bleistift 66 x 50 1975

116 Meine Bremer Großmutter auf dem Totenbett
Bleistift 29,7 x 21 1972

117 Barbara
Bleistift 66 x 50 1976

118 links Nach Picasso ›El sastre Soler‹ 1903 Musée de l'Erémitage Leningrad
Bleistift 27 x 20 1973

118 rechts Nach Rembrandt ›Brustbild einer jungen Frau‹
Bleistift 17,5 x 10,5 1972

119 Nach Hieronymus Bosch ›Dornenkrönung‹, National Gallery London
Bleistift 51 x 66 1976

120 Tommy Bodmer
Bleistift 66 x 50 1975
Privatbesitz Zürich

121 Barbara mit aufgestütztem Fuß
Bleistift 66 x 51 1976

122 Carmelina
Bleistift 37 x 34 1975

123 Pina
Bleistift 66 x 50 1976

124 Susi Weber mit aufgestütztem Arm
Bleistift 34 x 25 1975

125 Der Schauspieler Jean Schlegel
Bleistift 66 x 50 1975

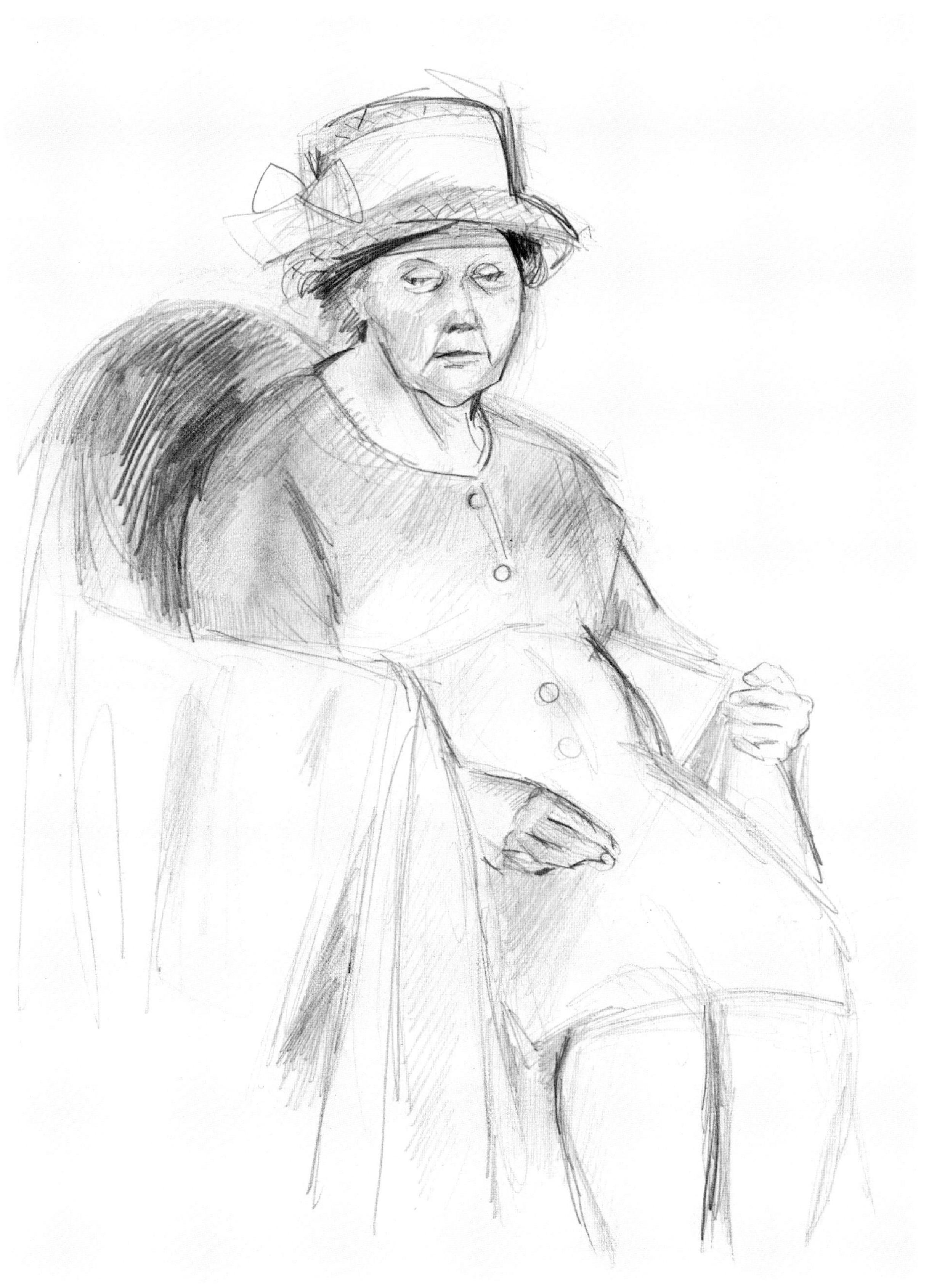

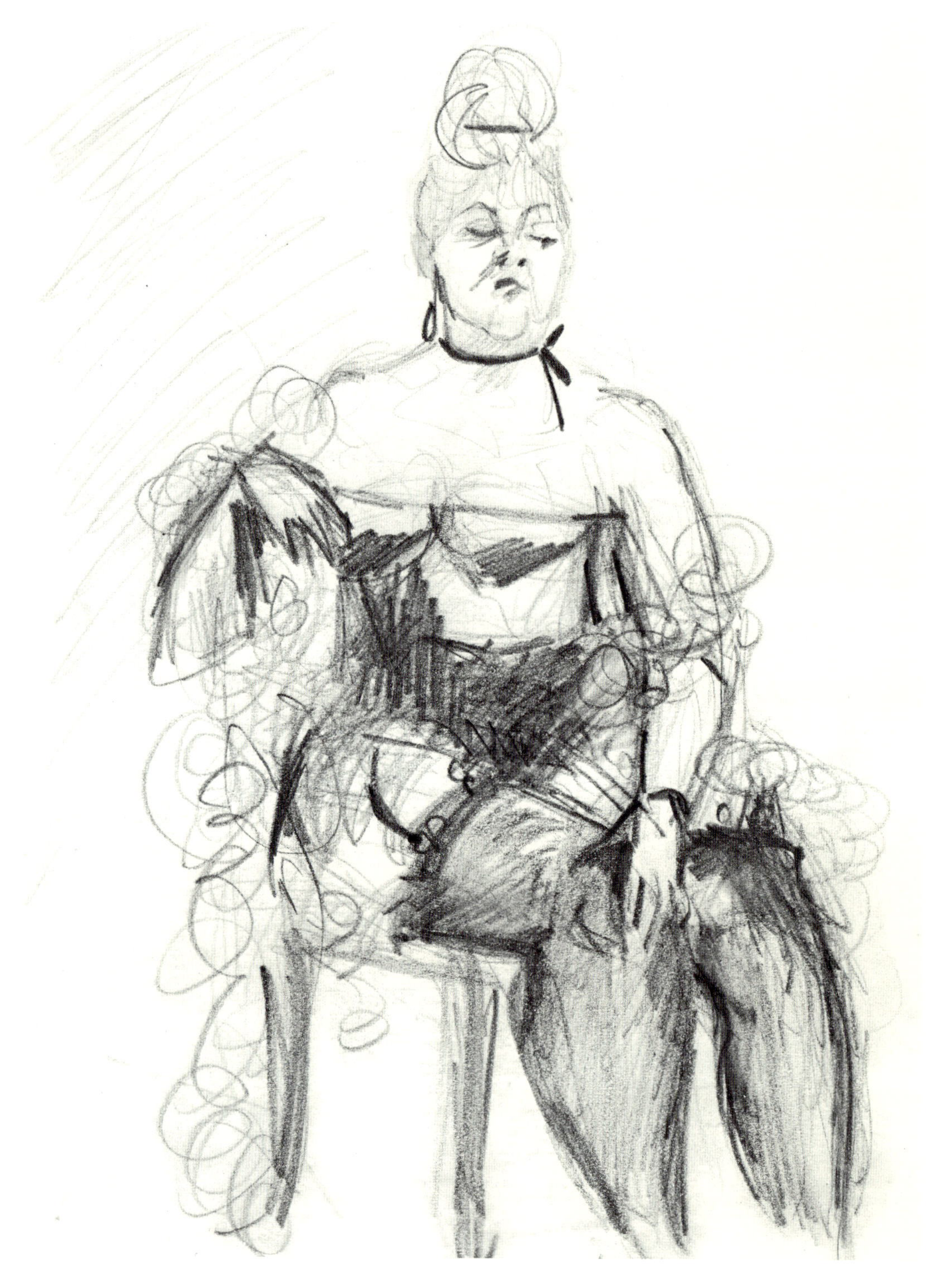

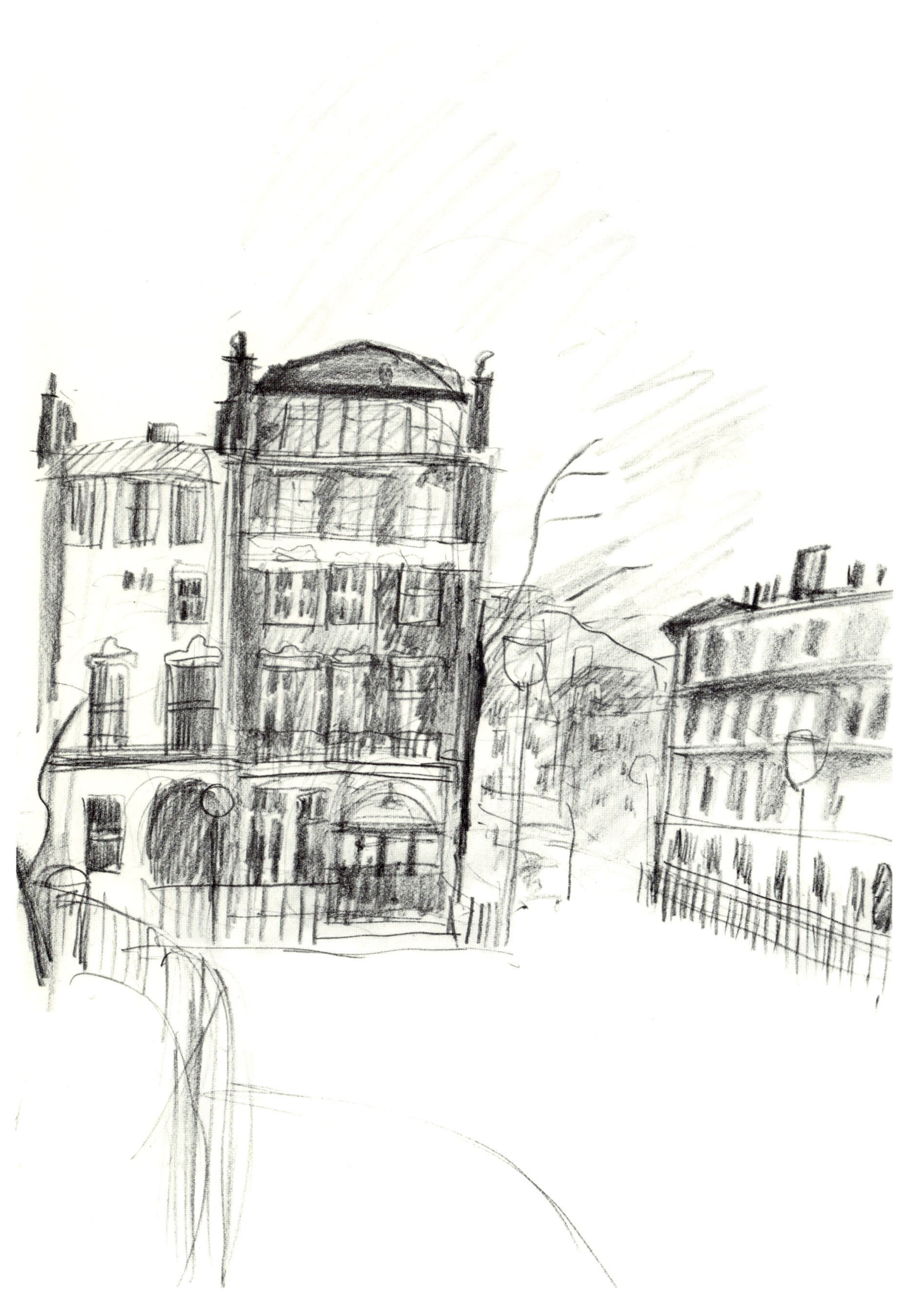

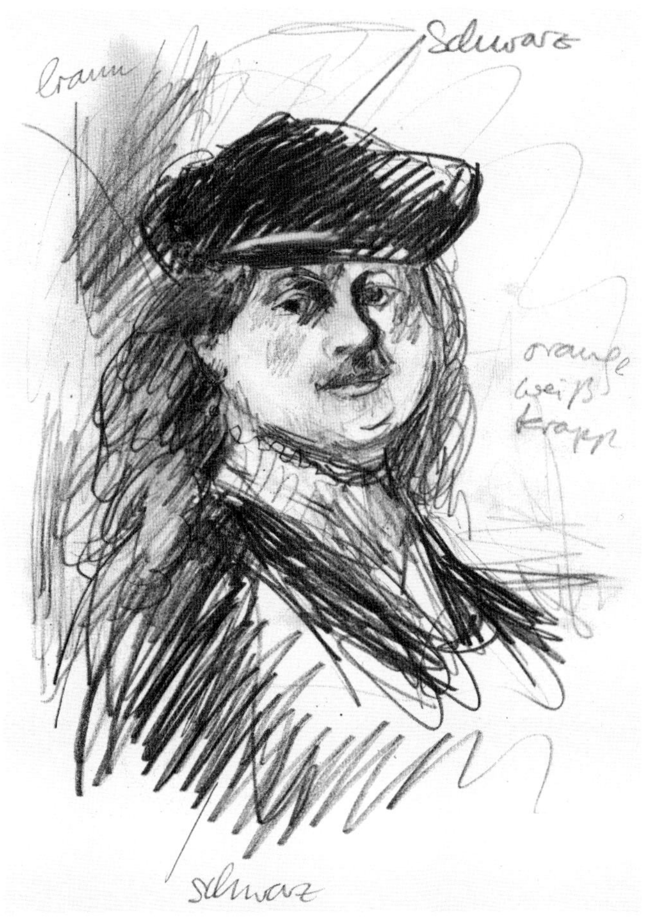
Schwarz
braun
orange
weiß
Krapp
schwarz

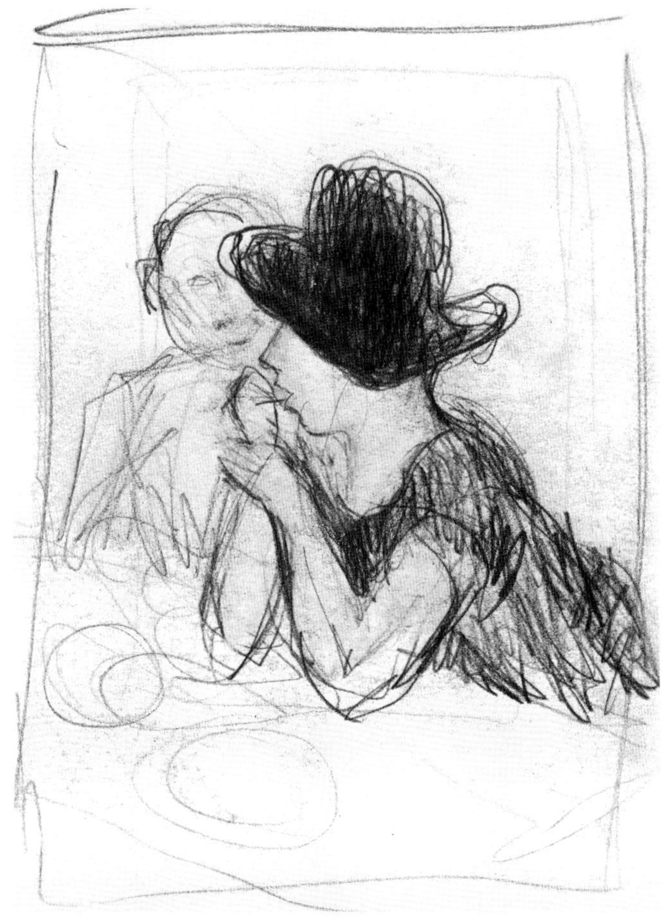

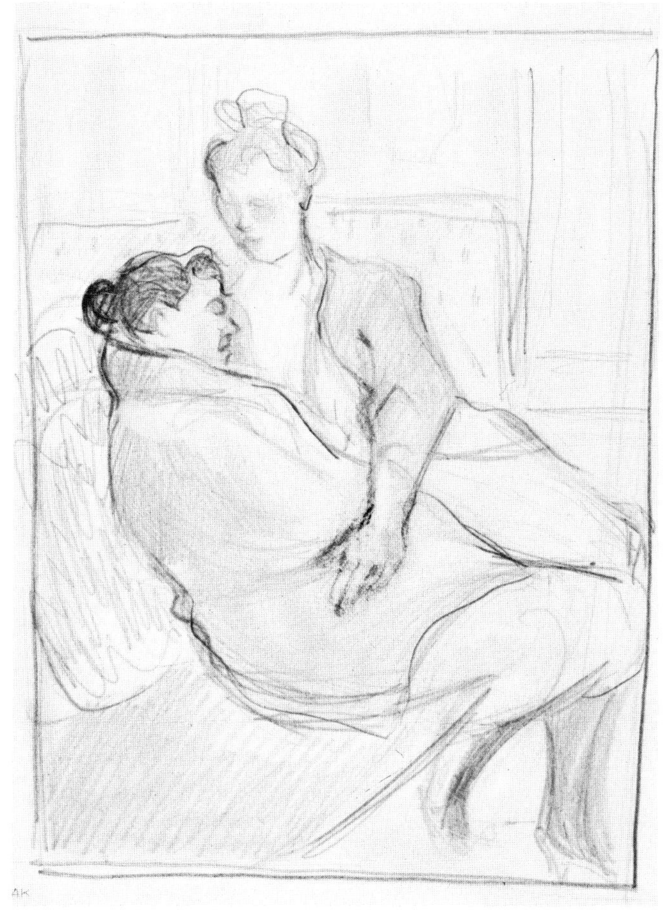

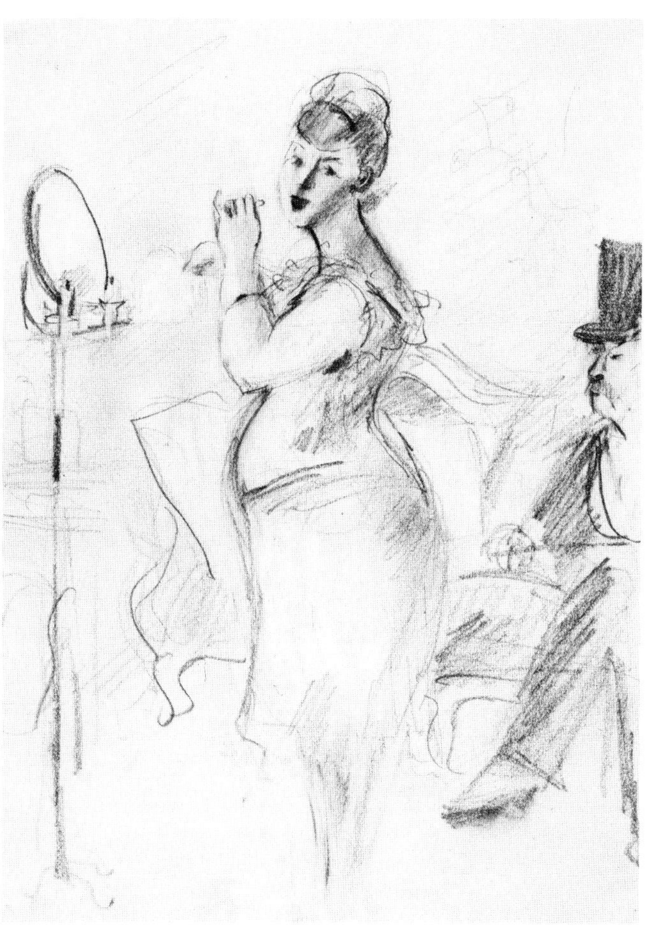

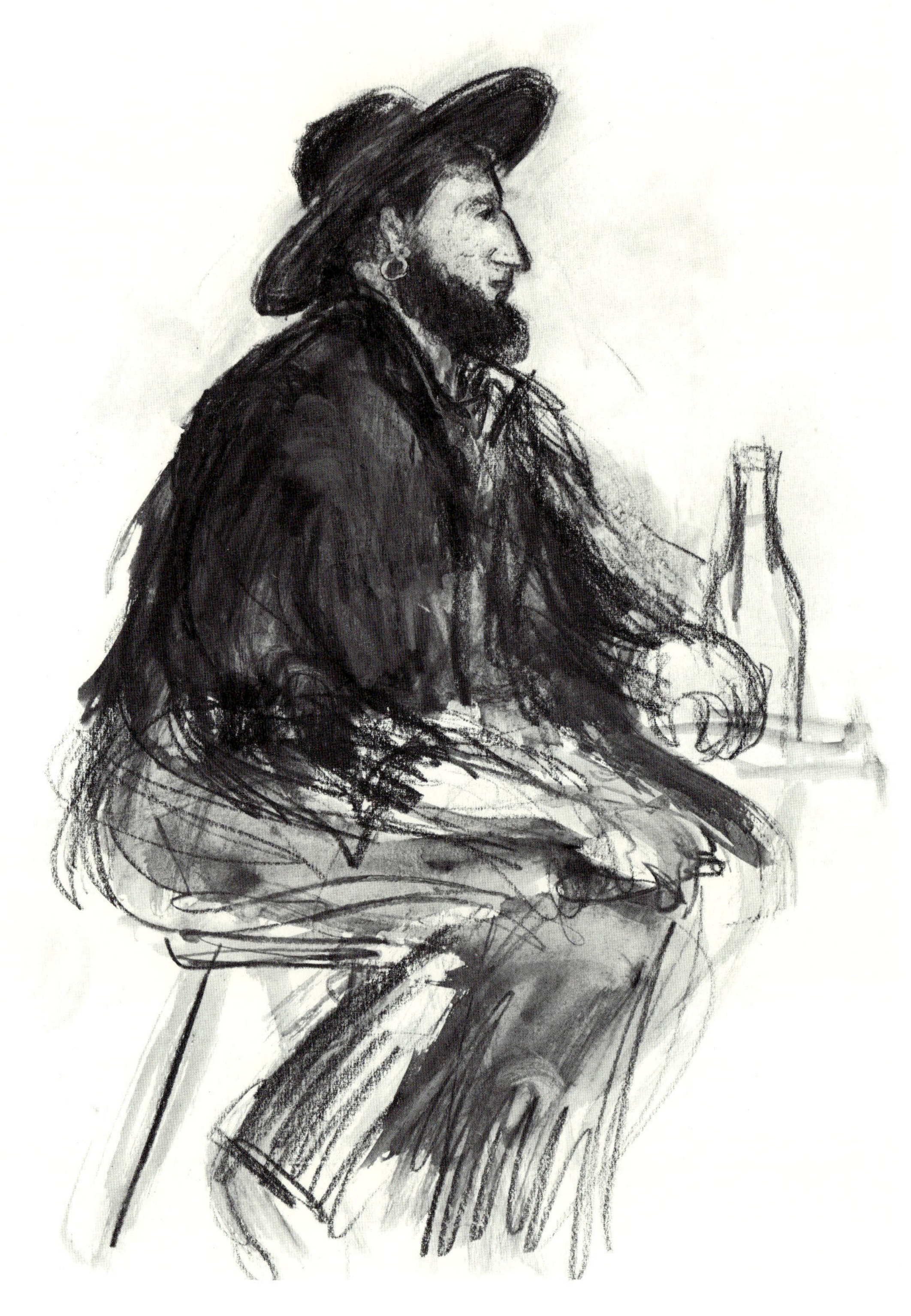

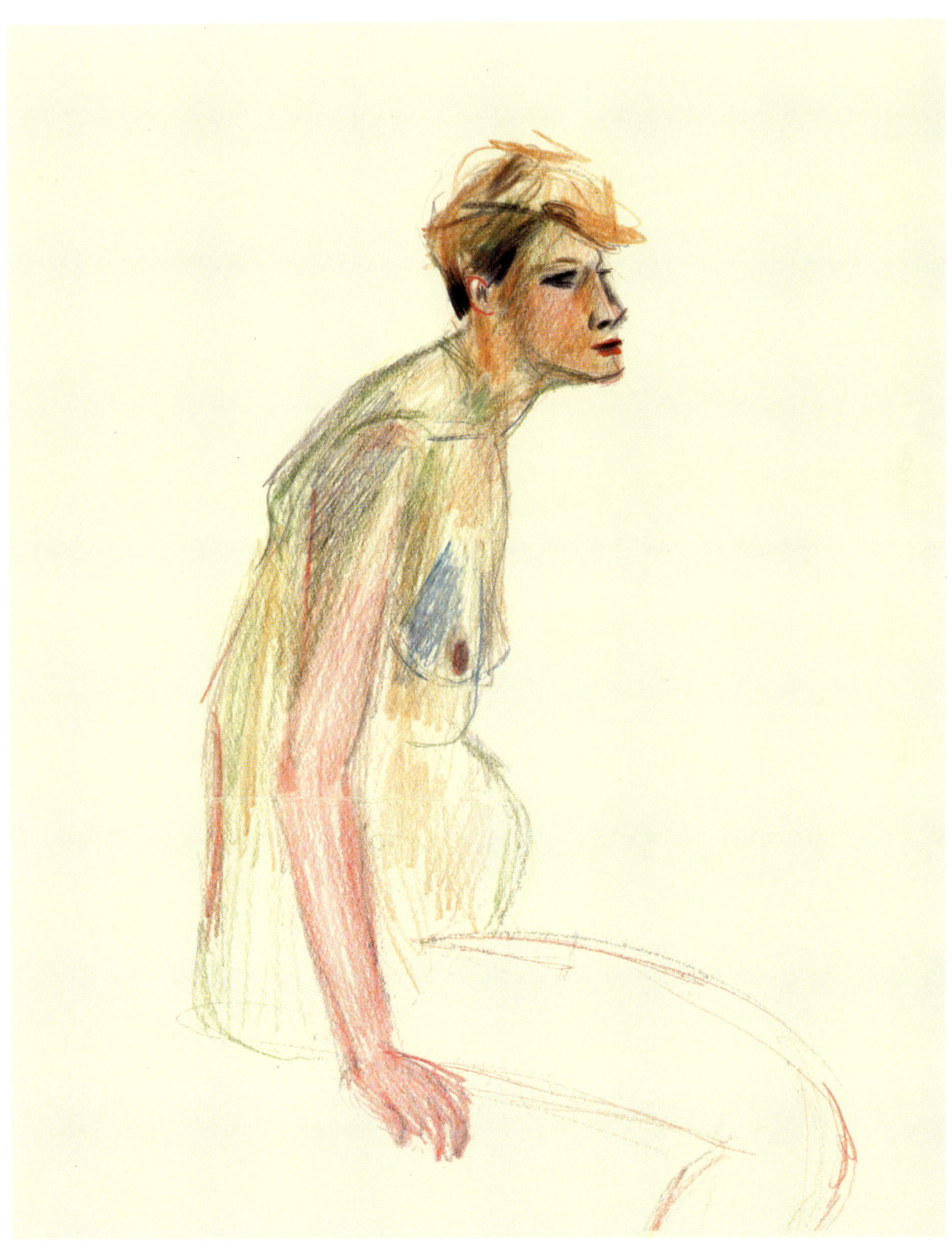

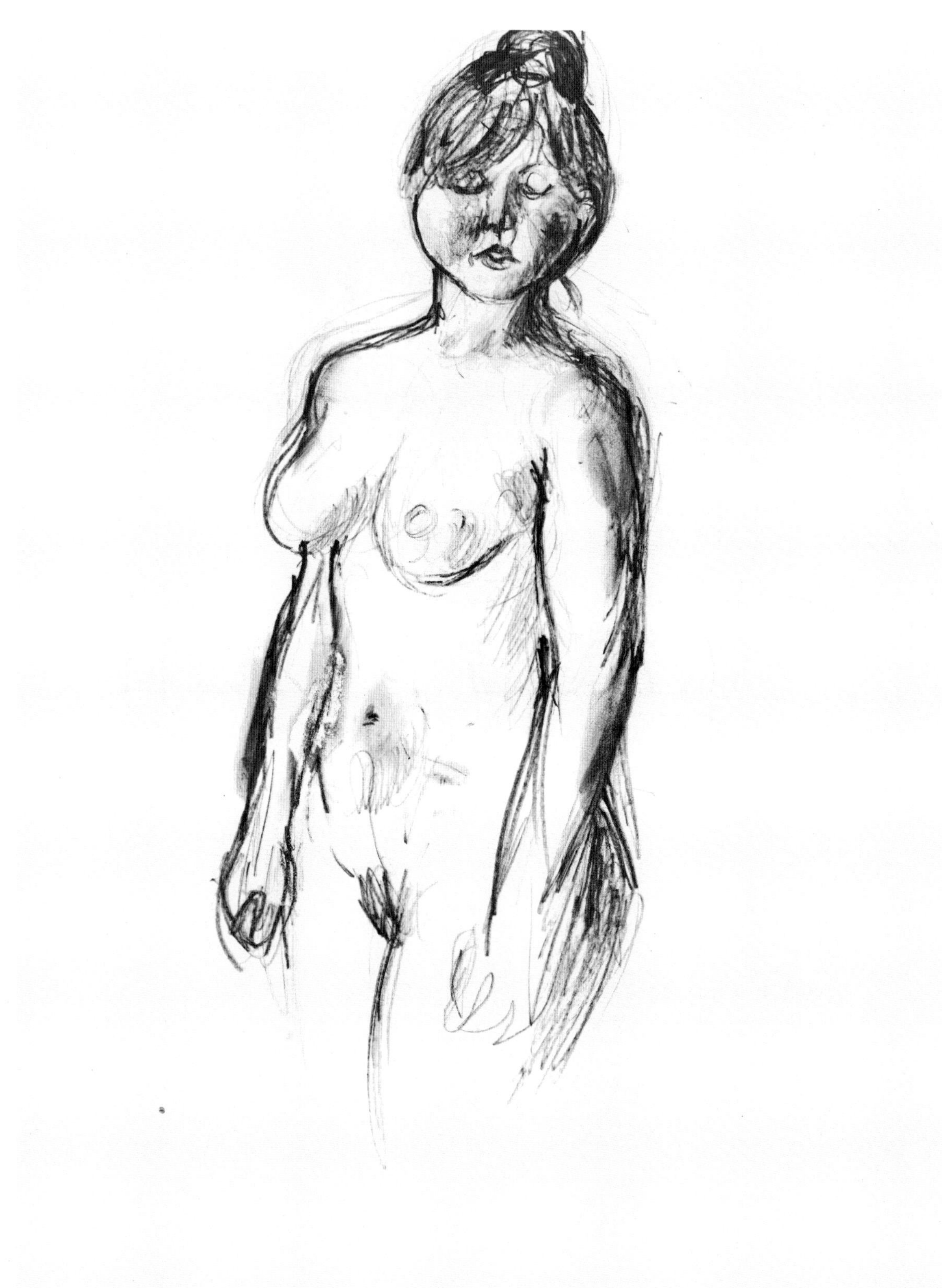

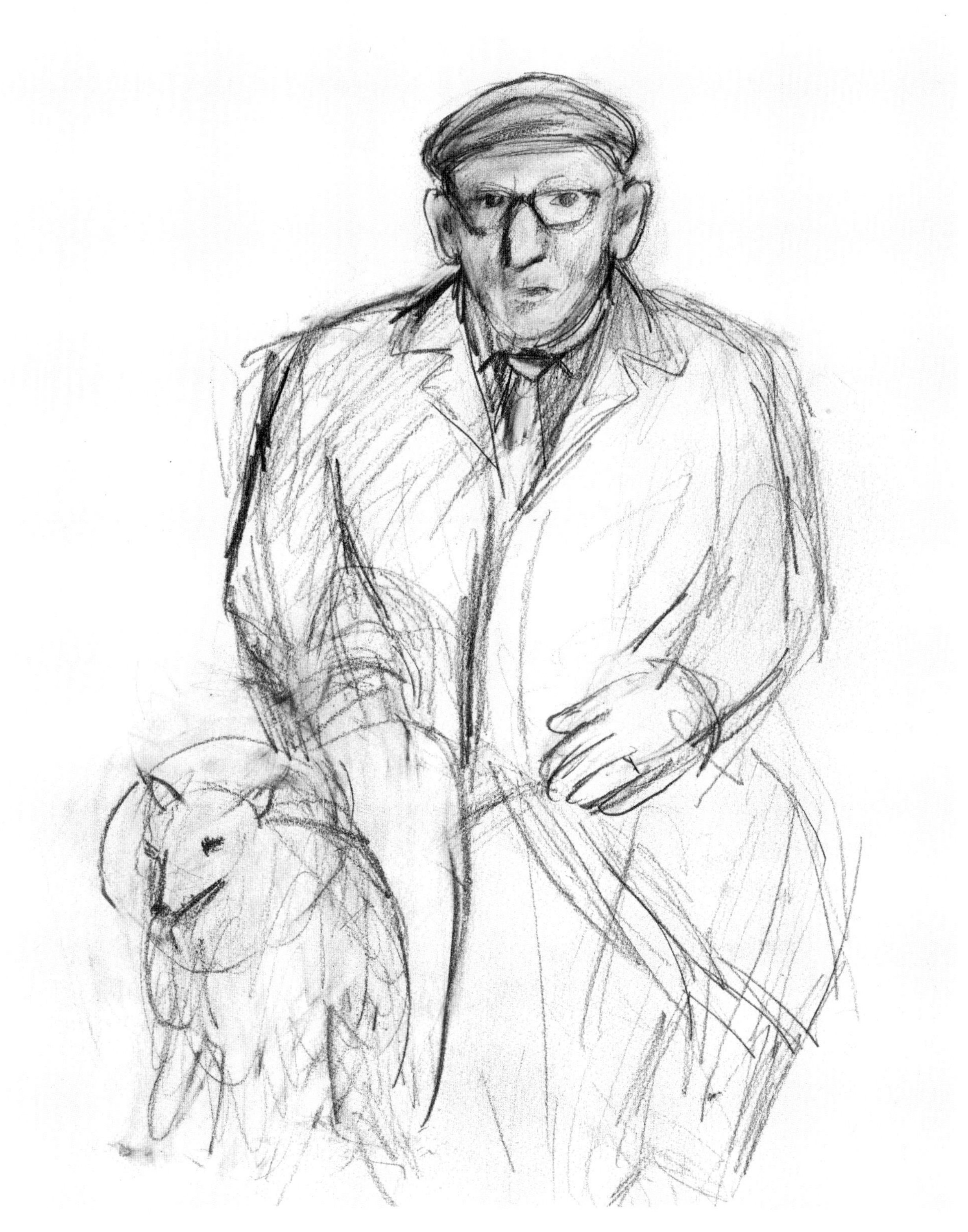

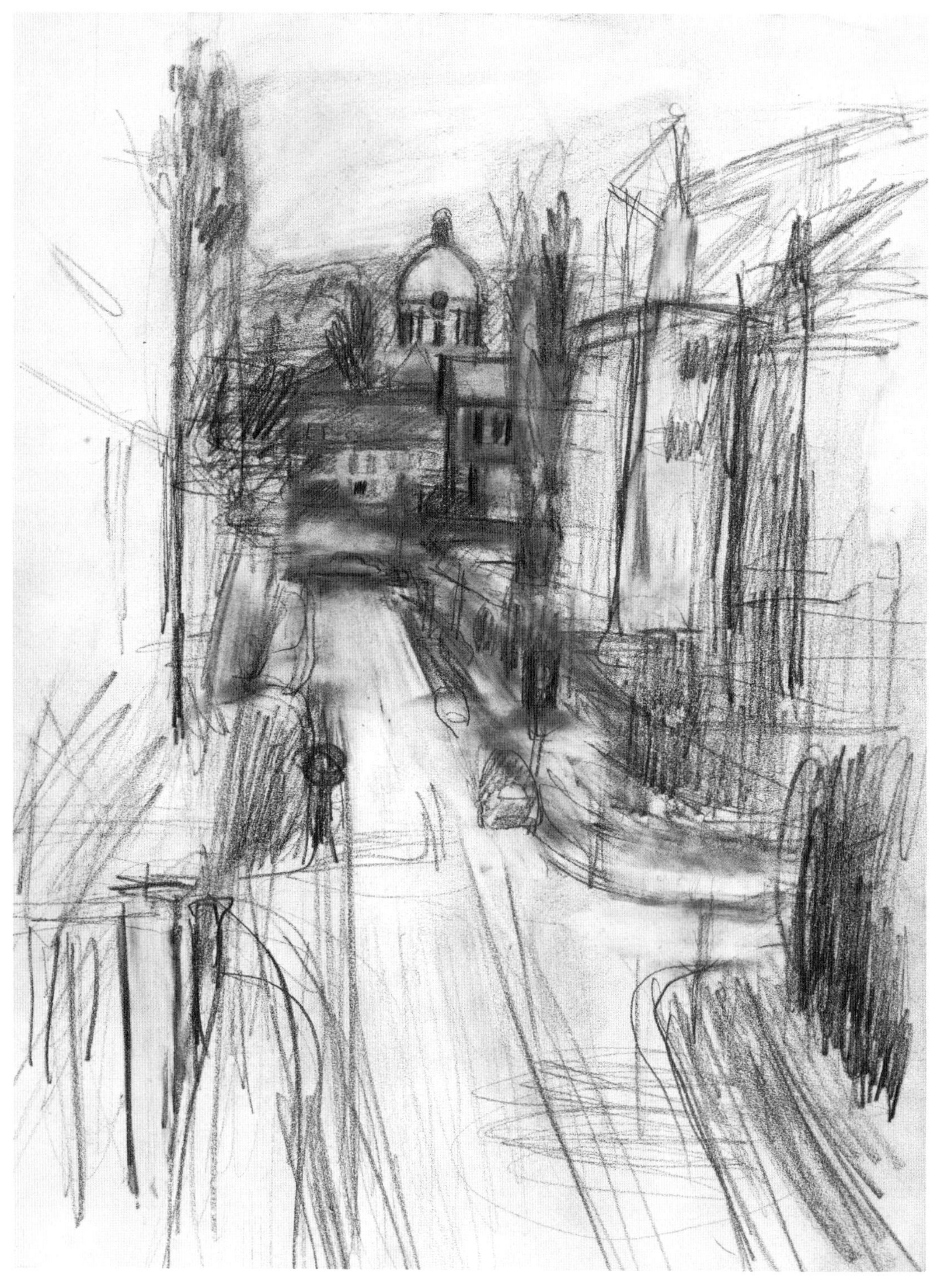

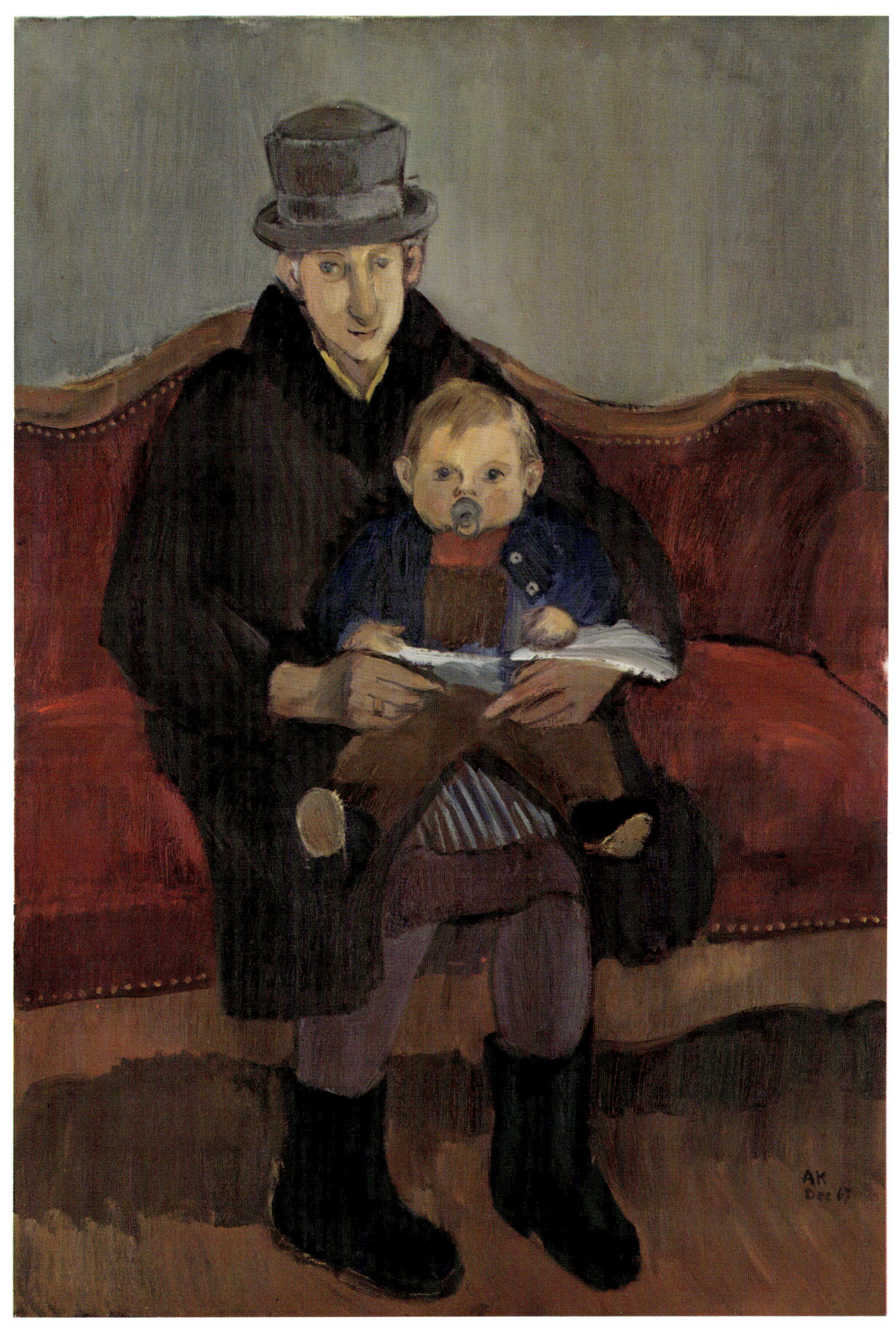
AK
Dec 67

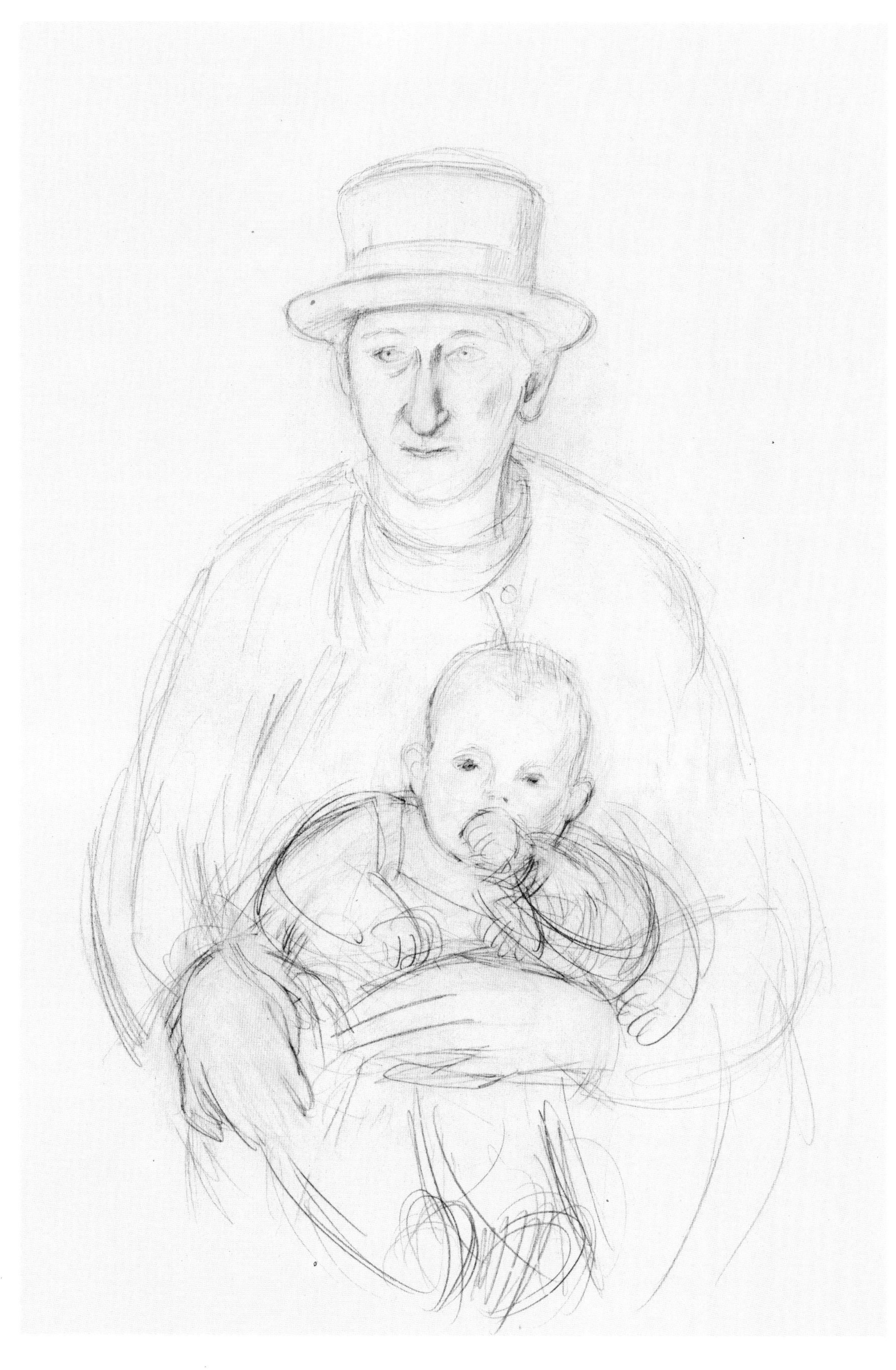

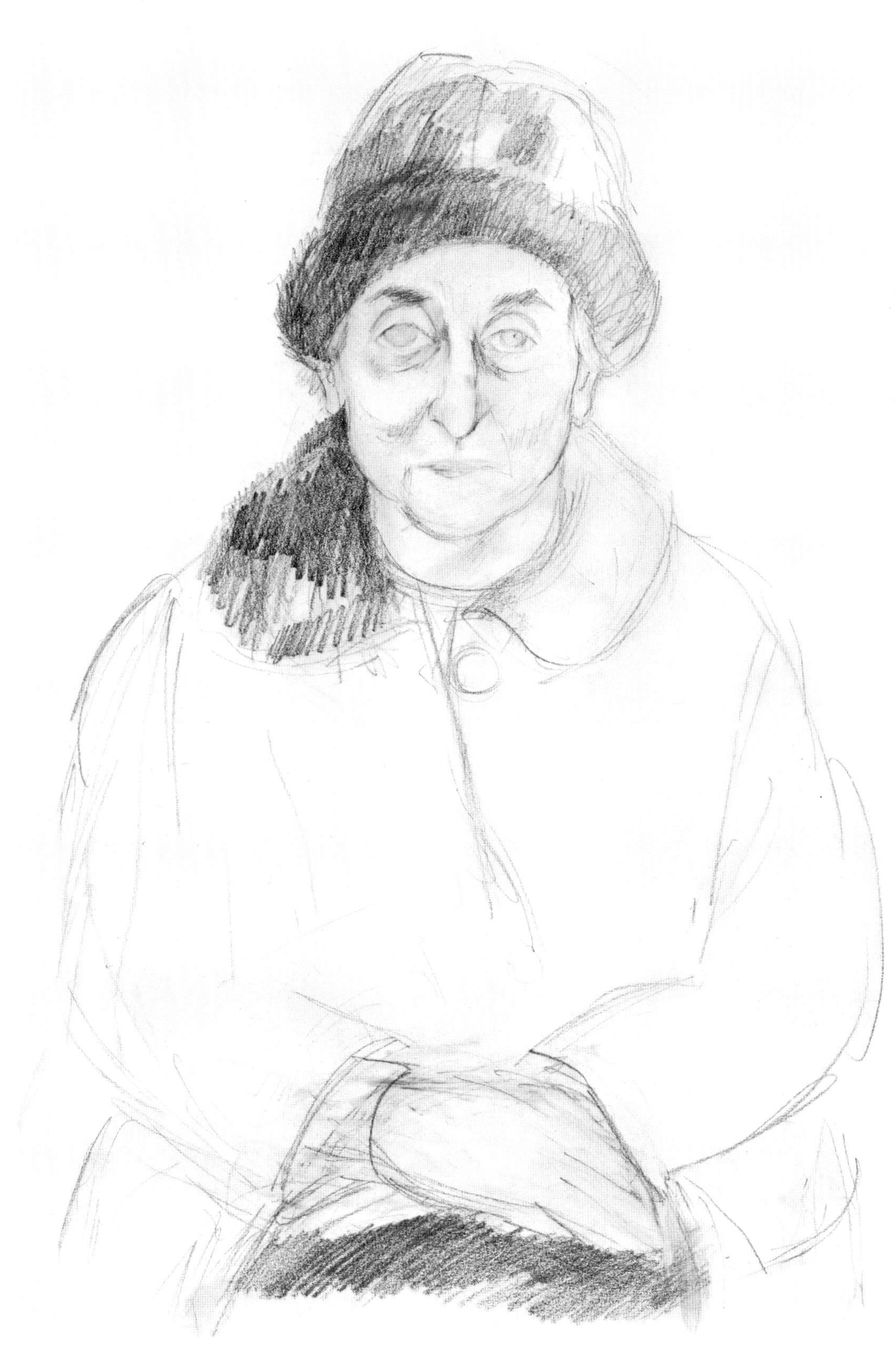

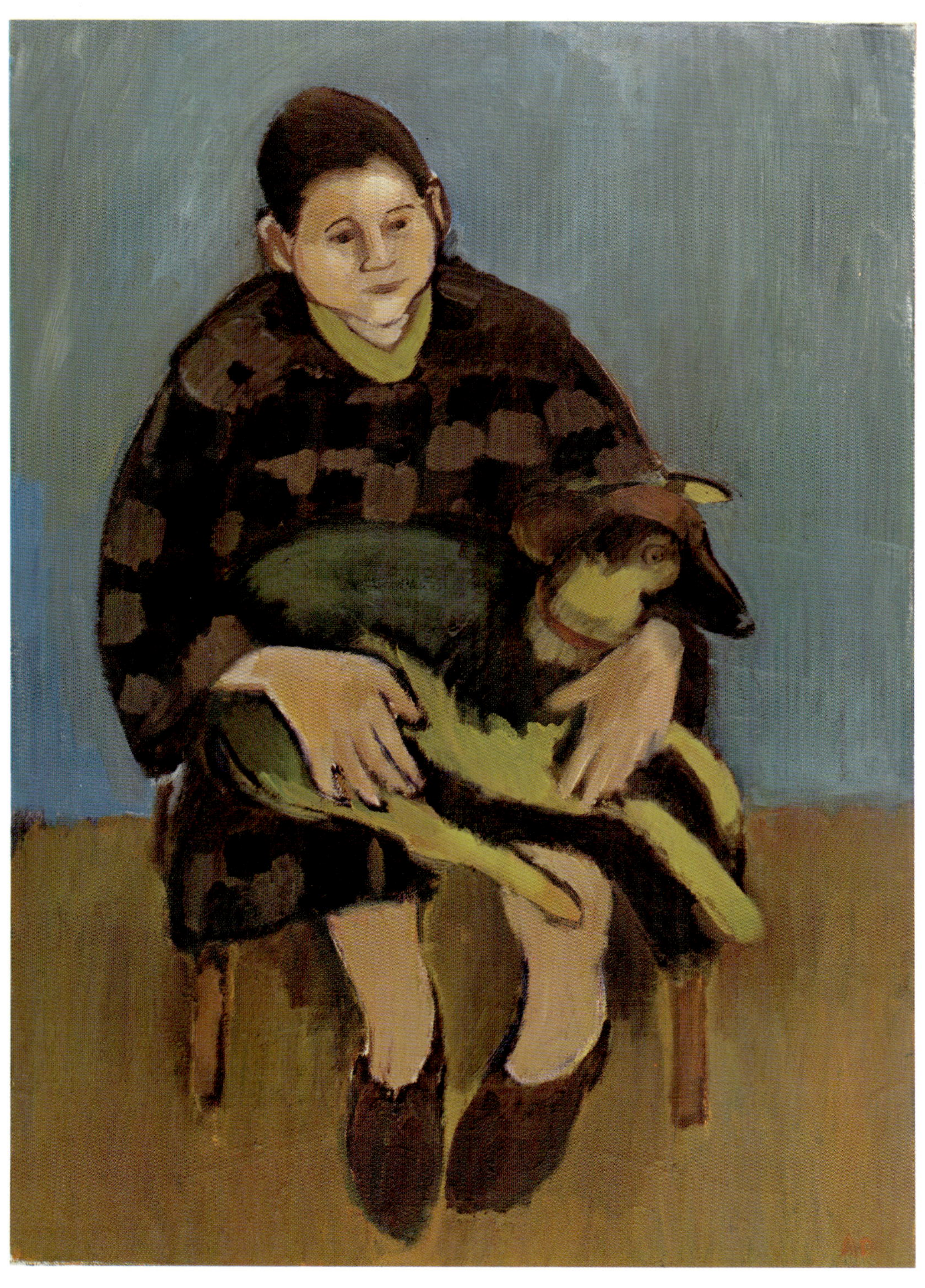

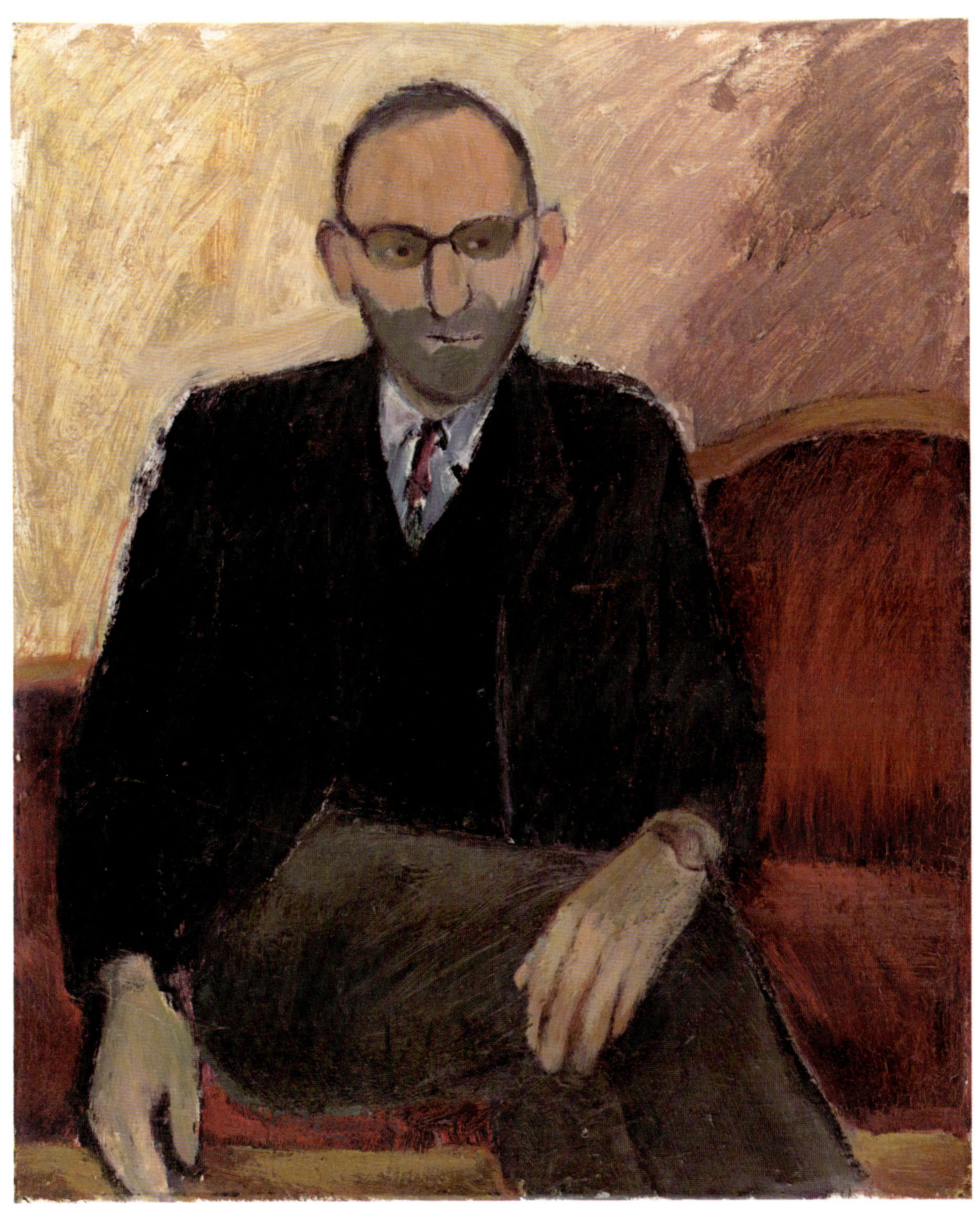

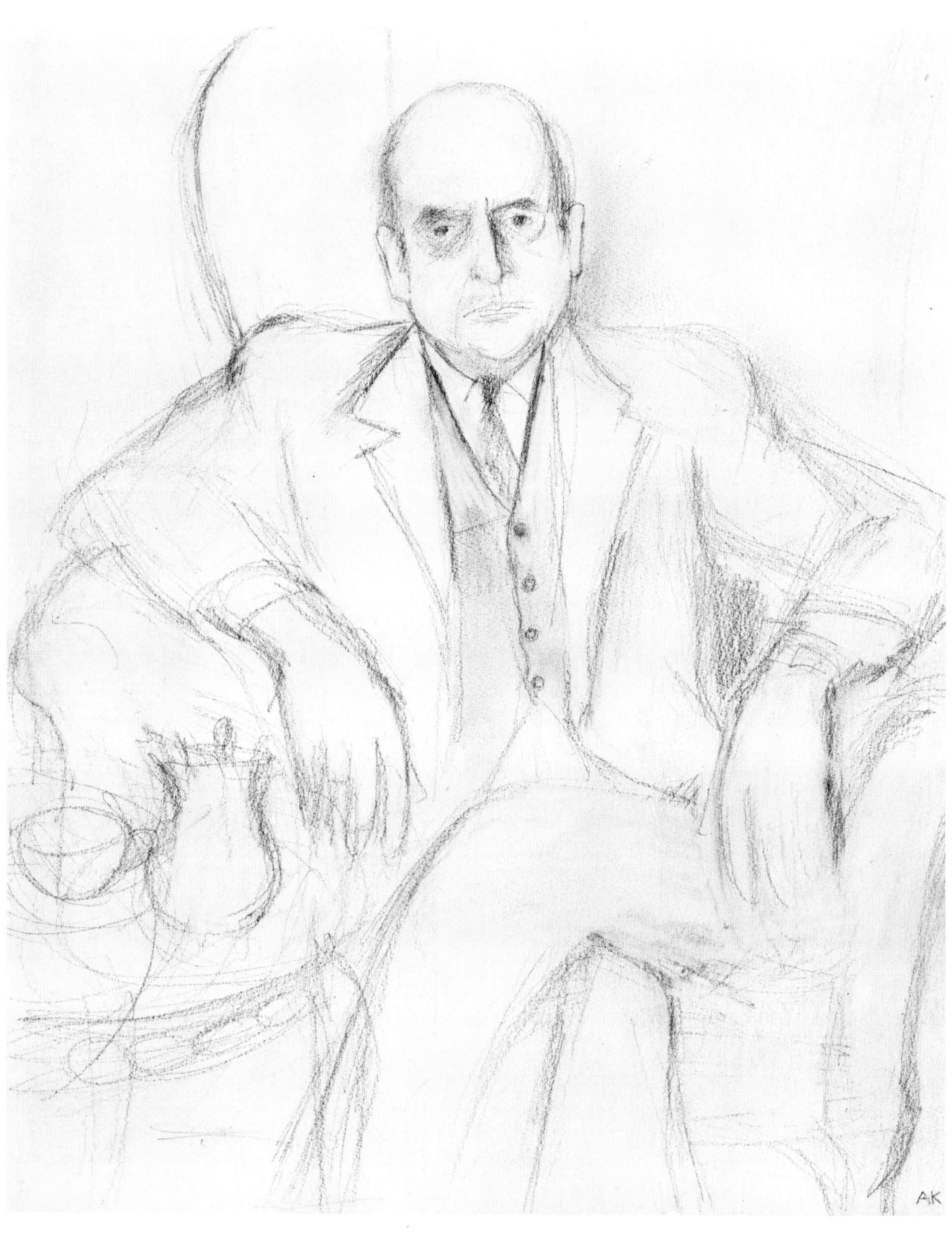
AK

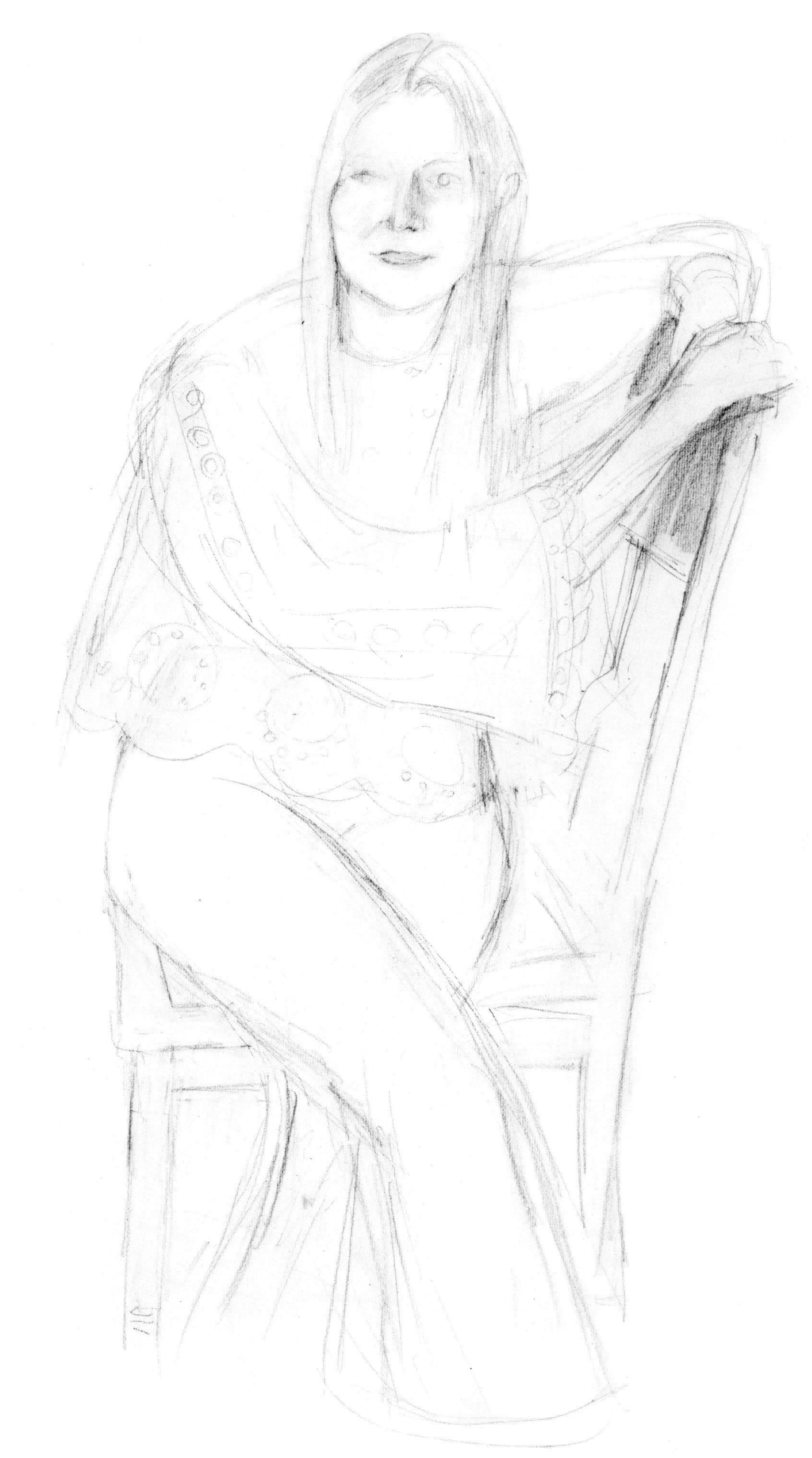

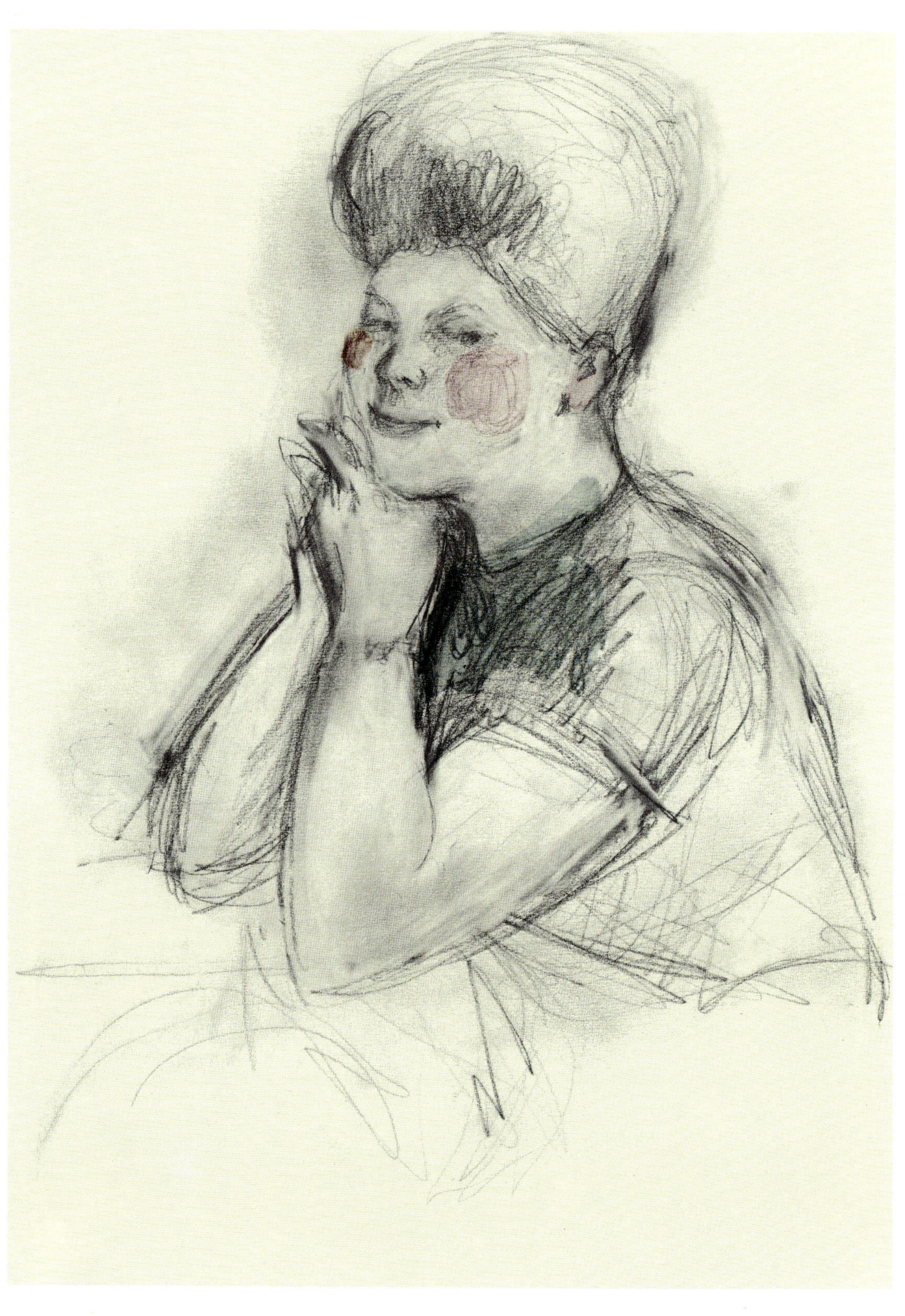

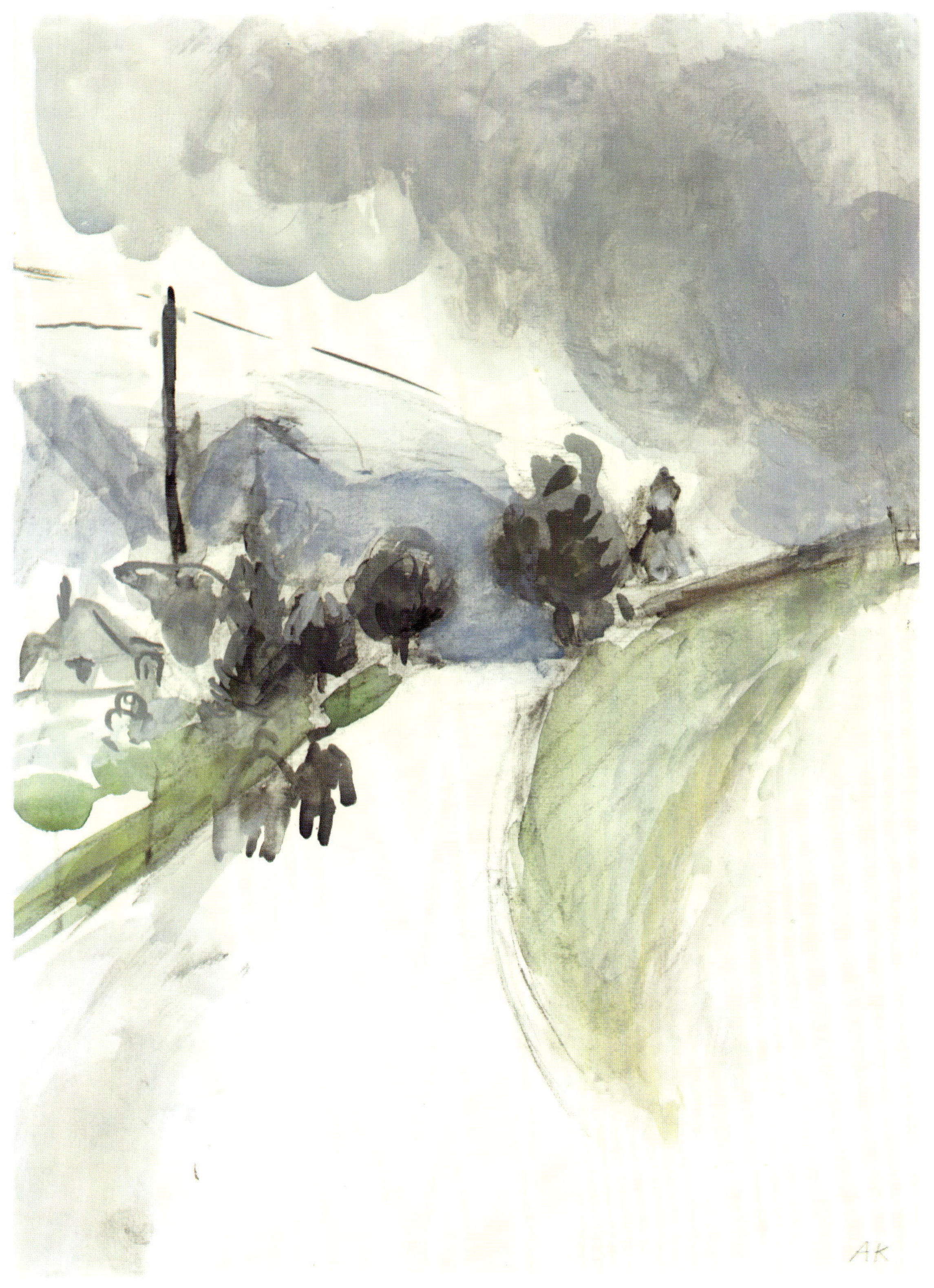

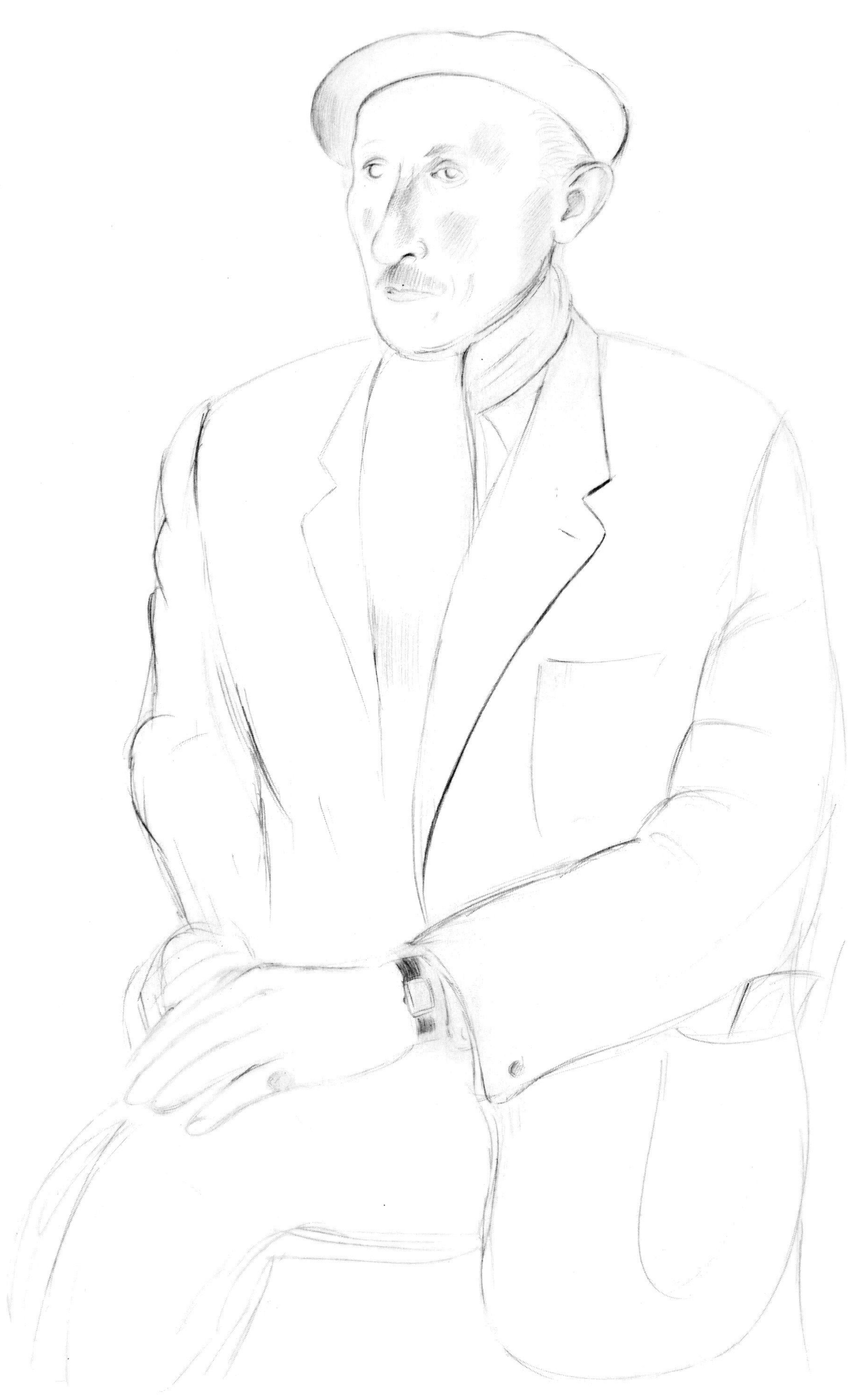

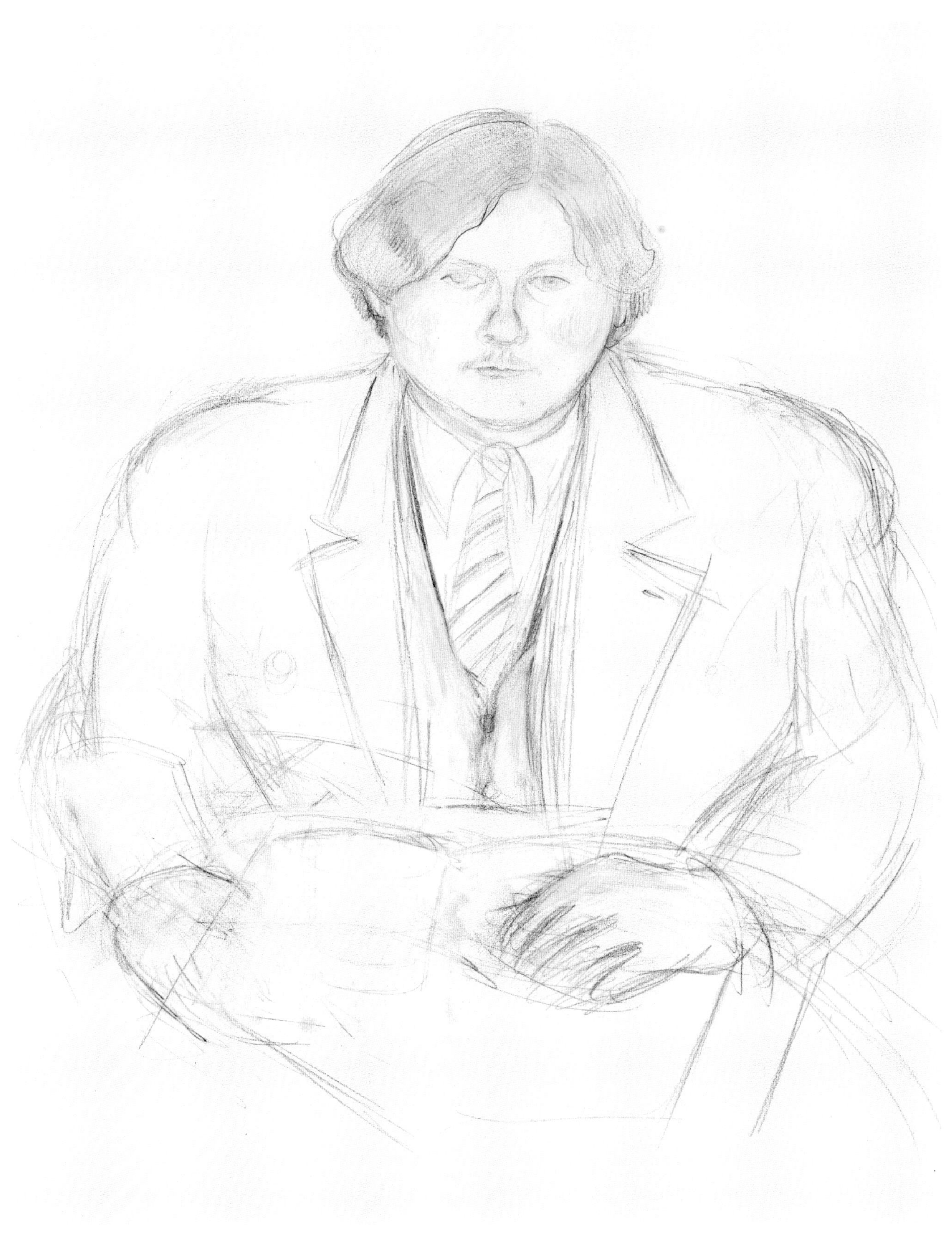

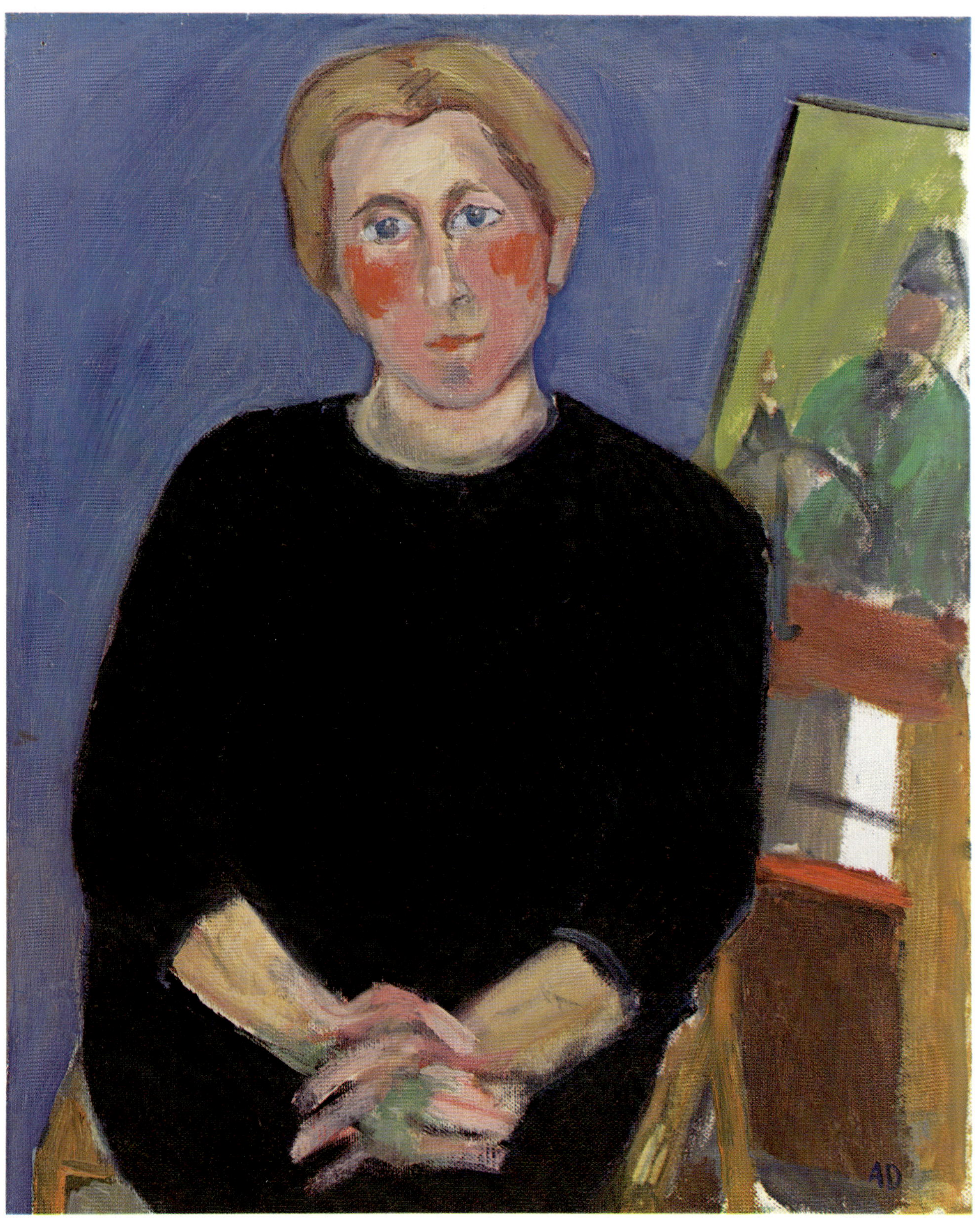
AD

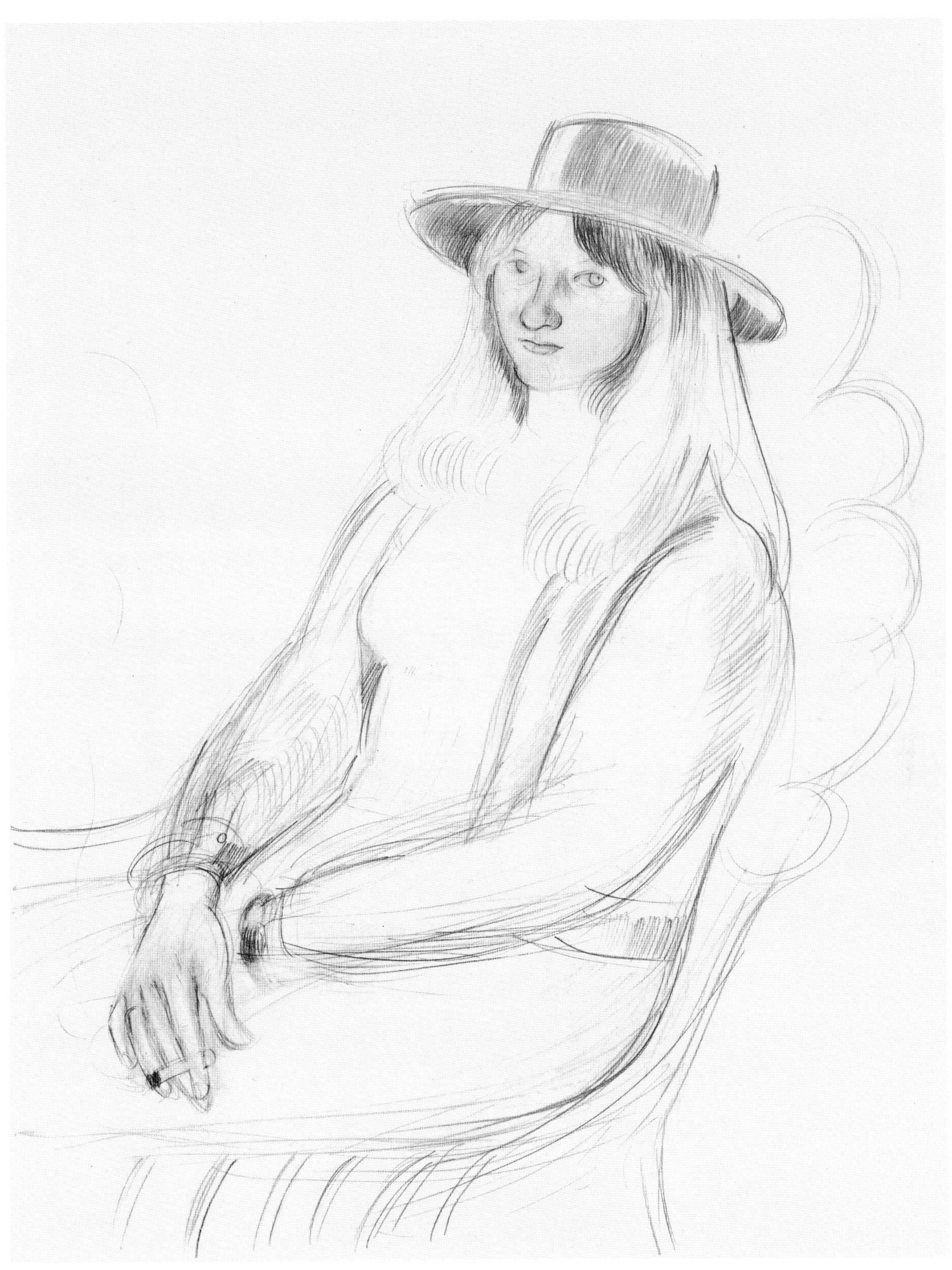

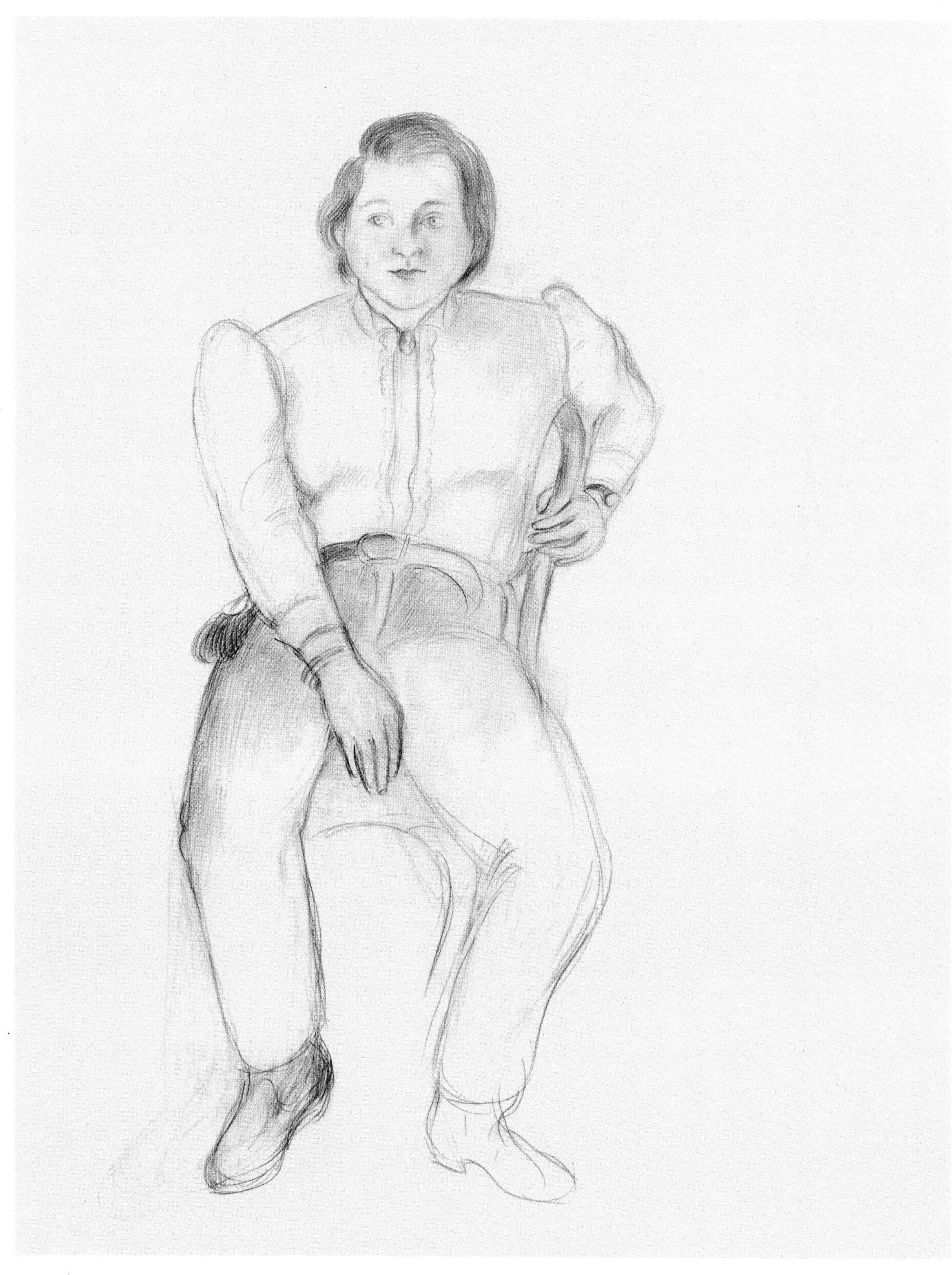

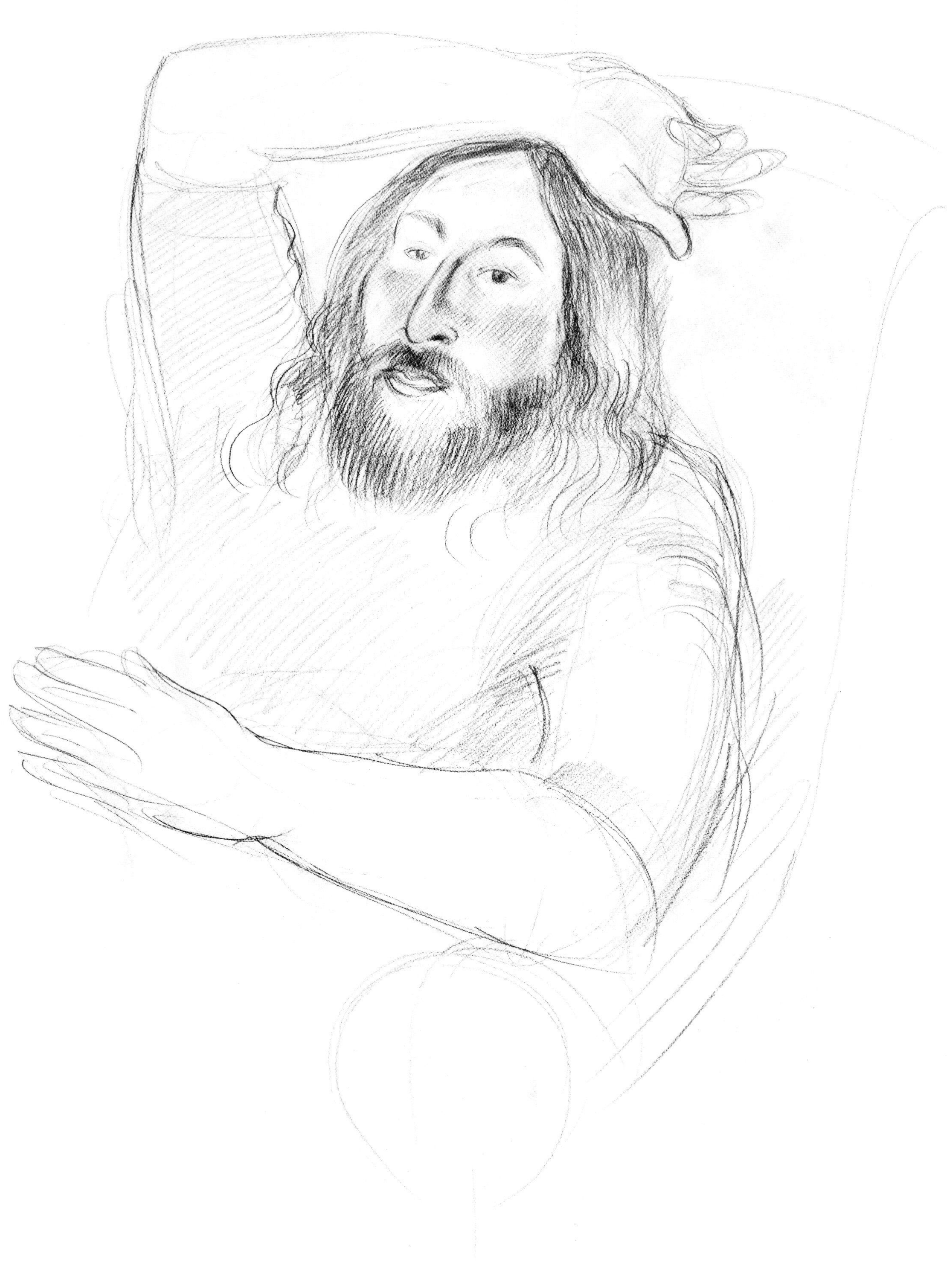

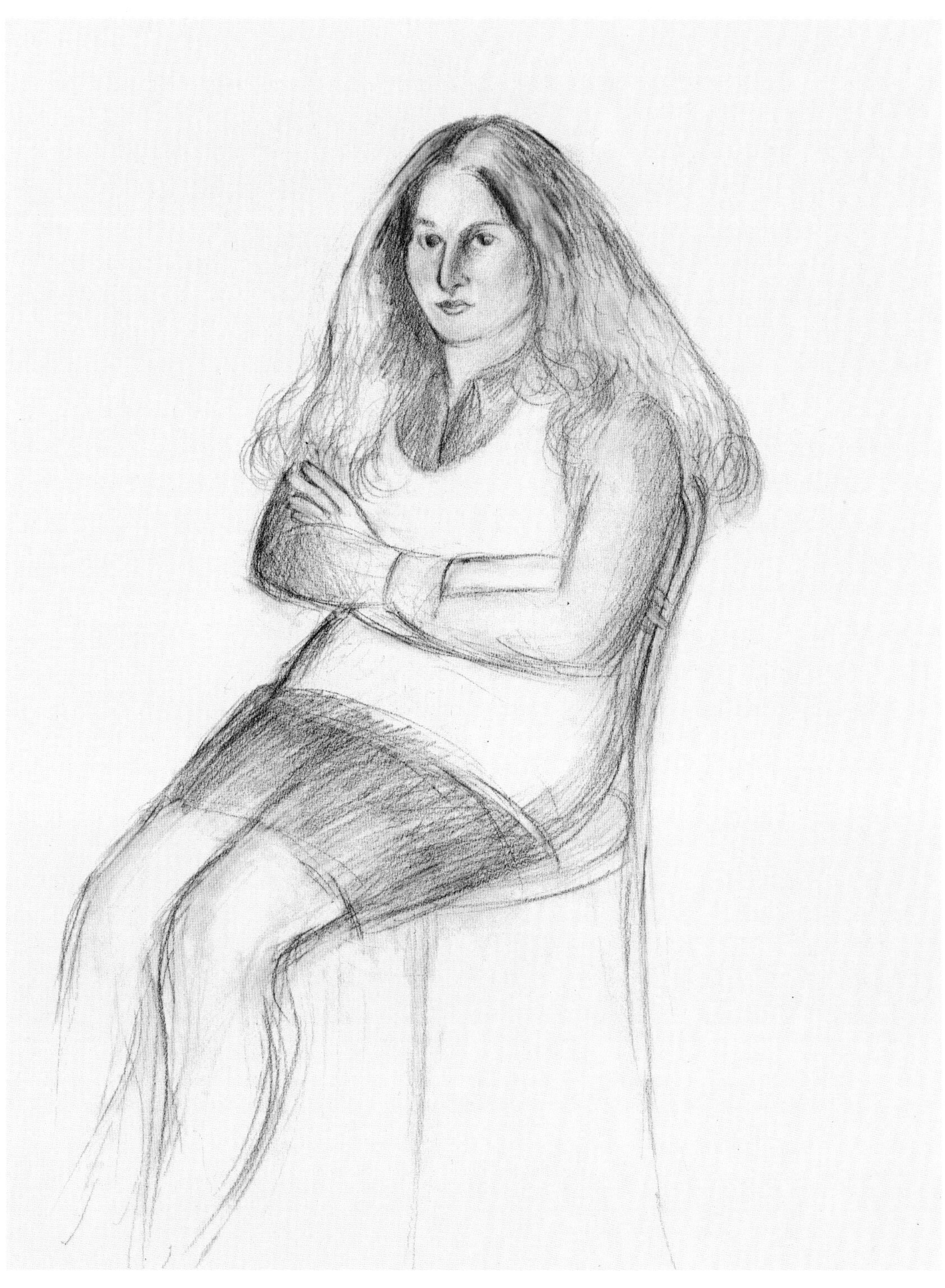

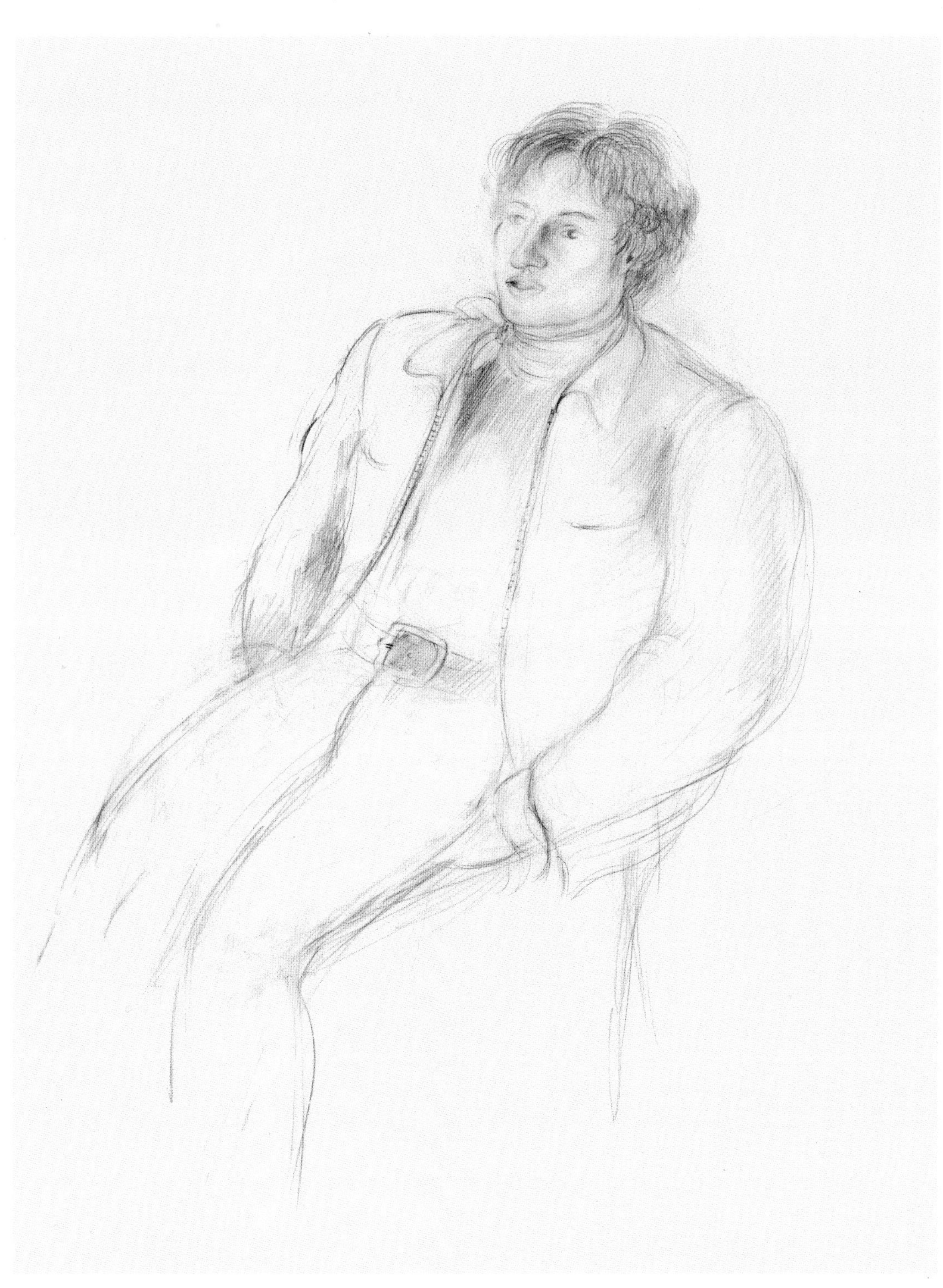

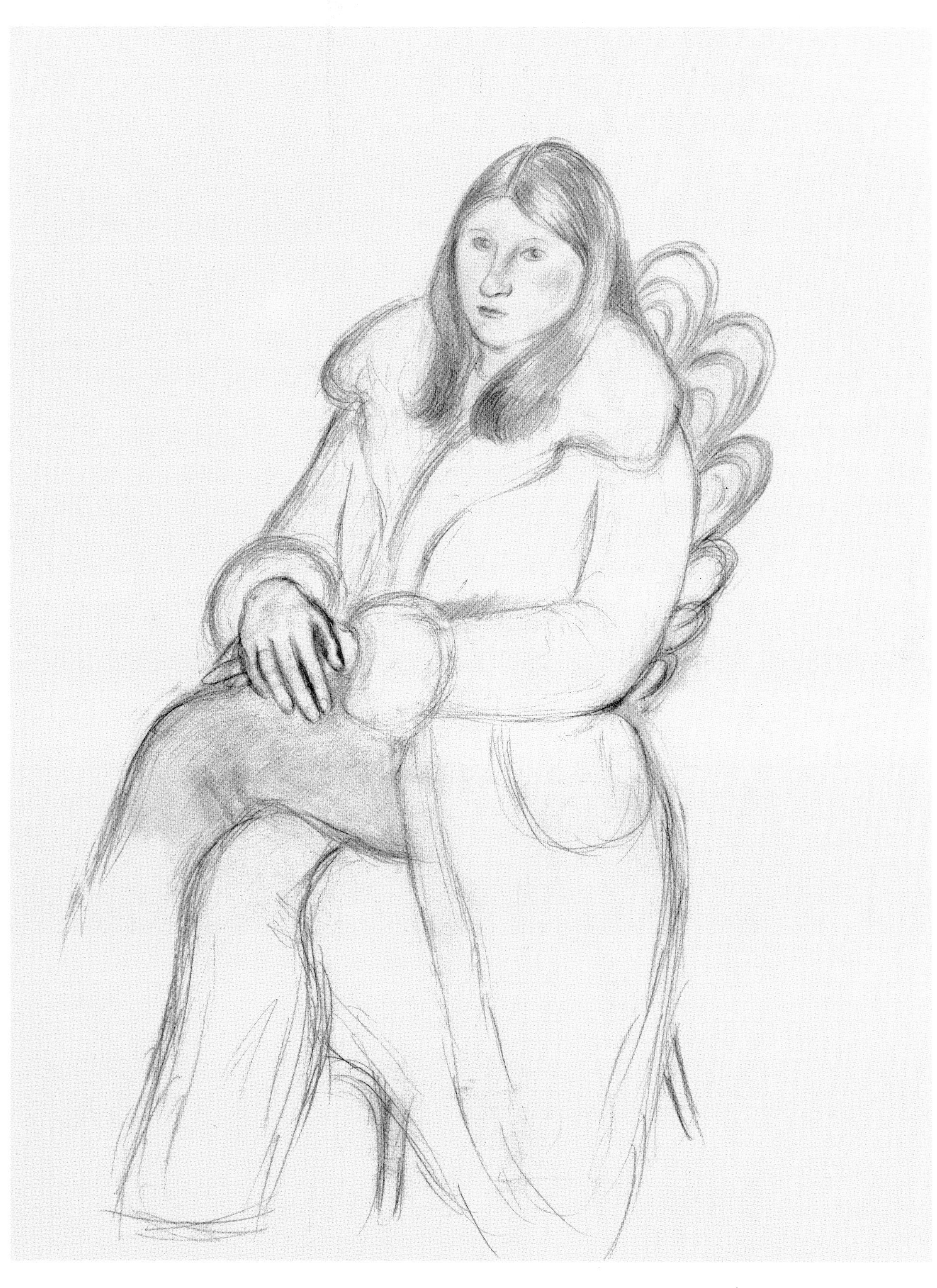

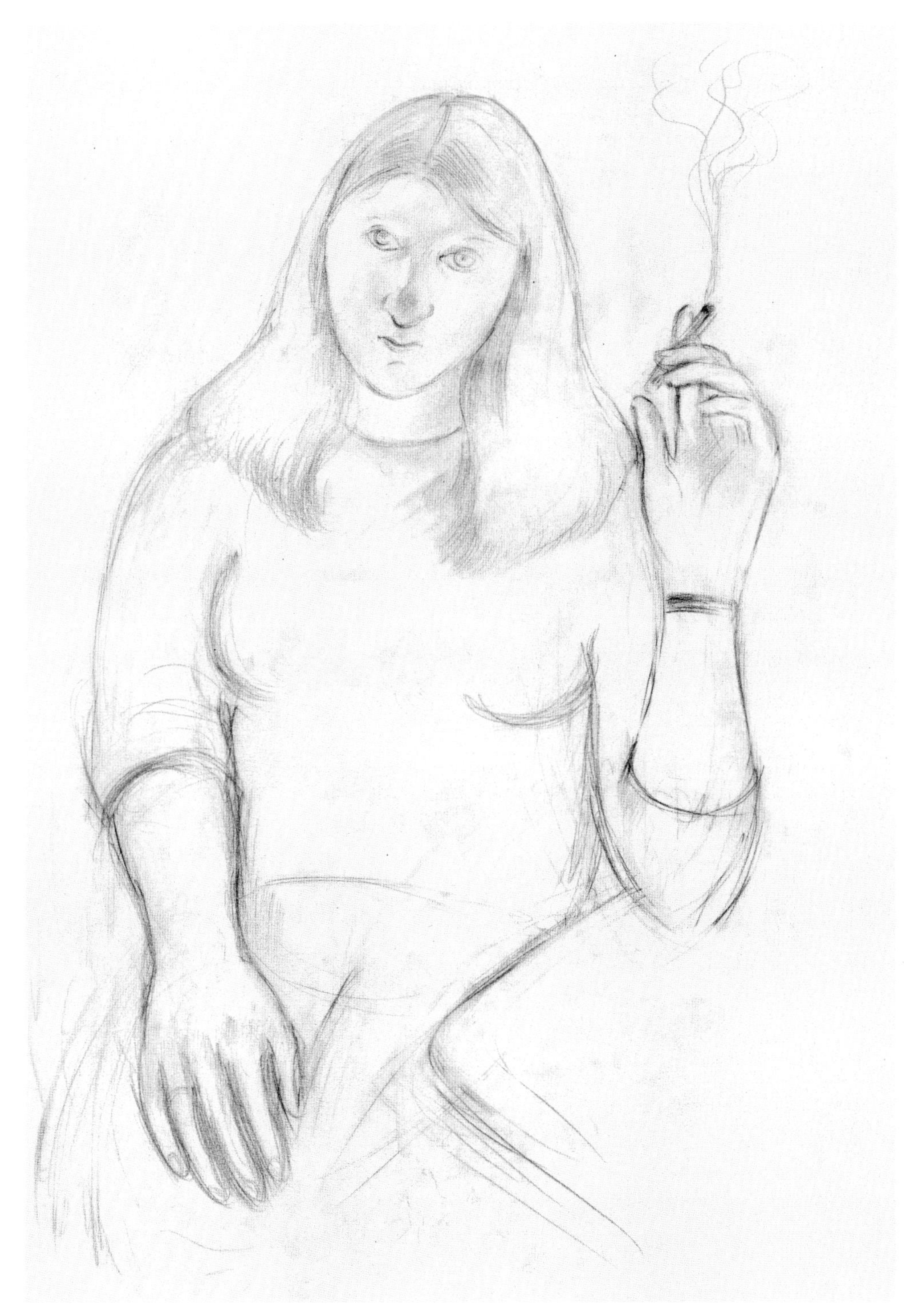

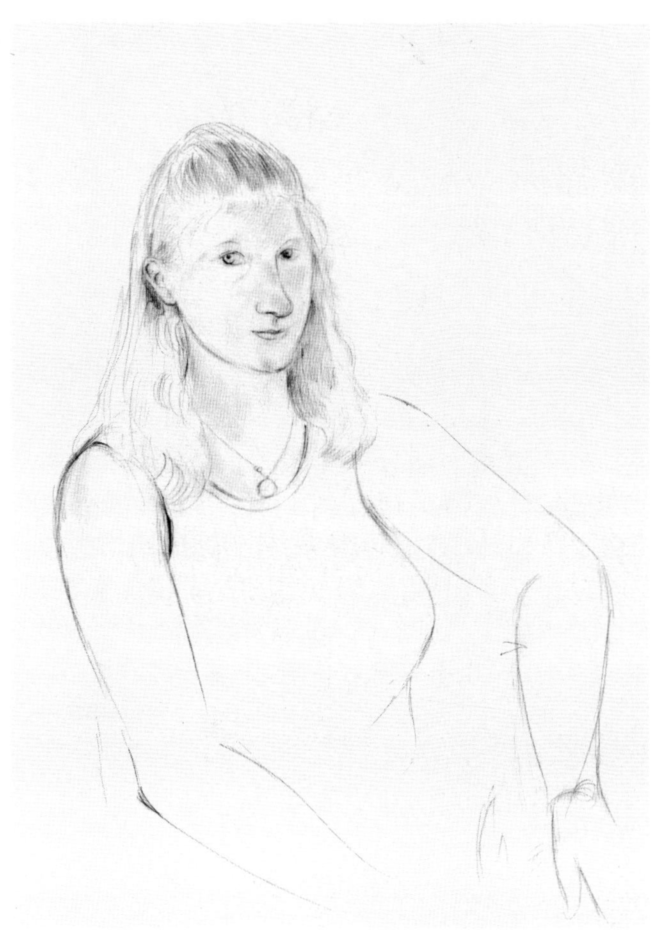

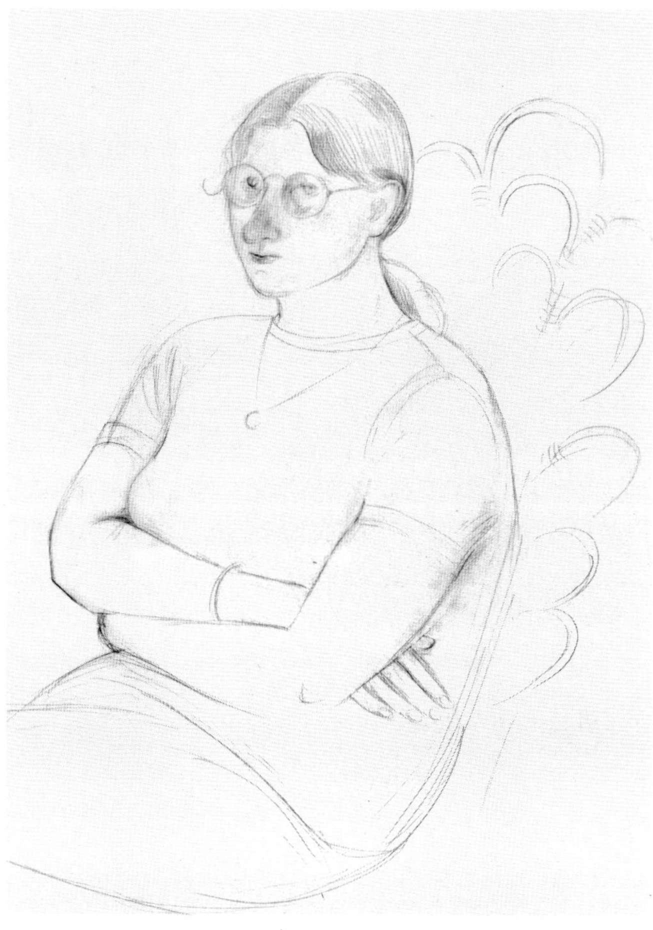

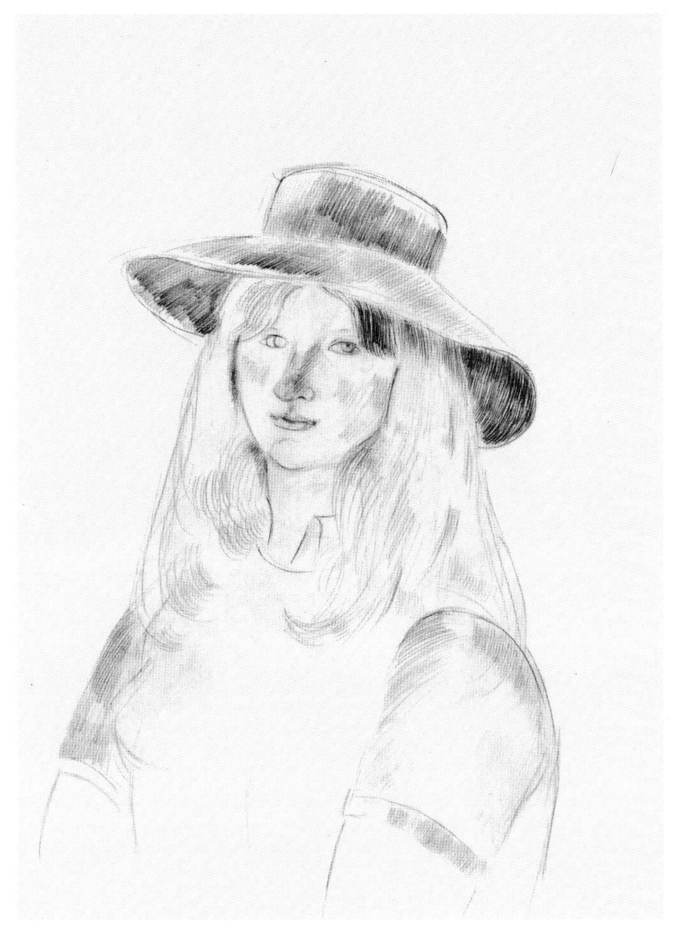

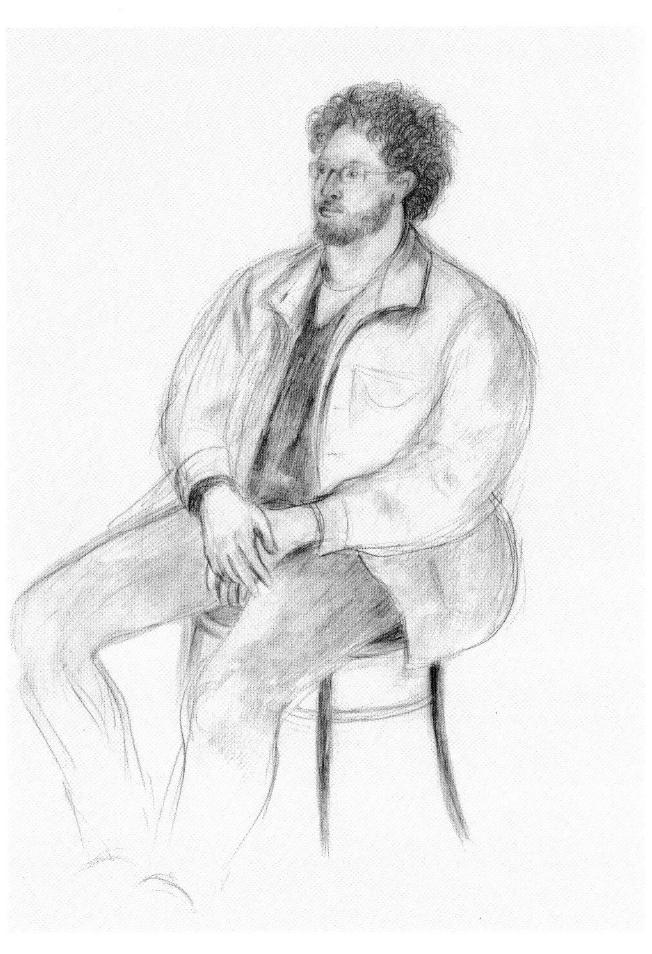

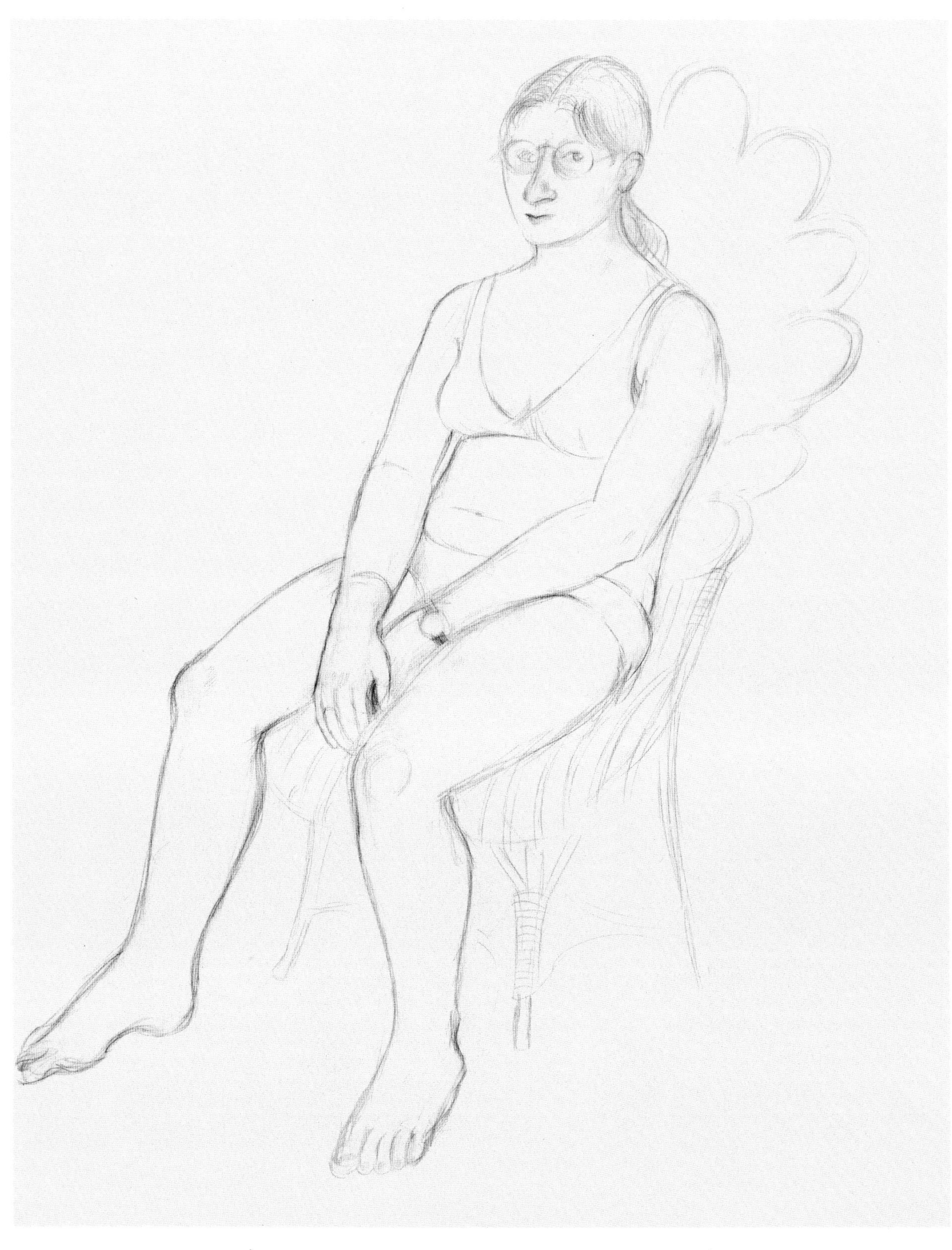

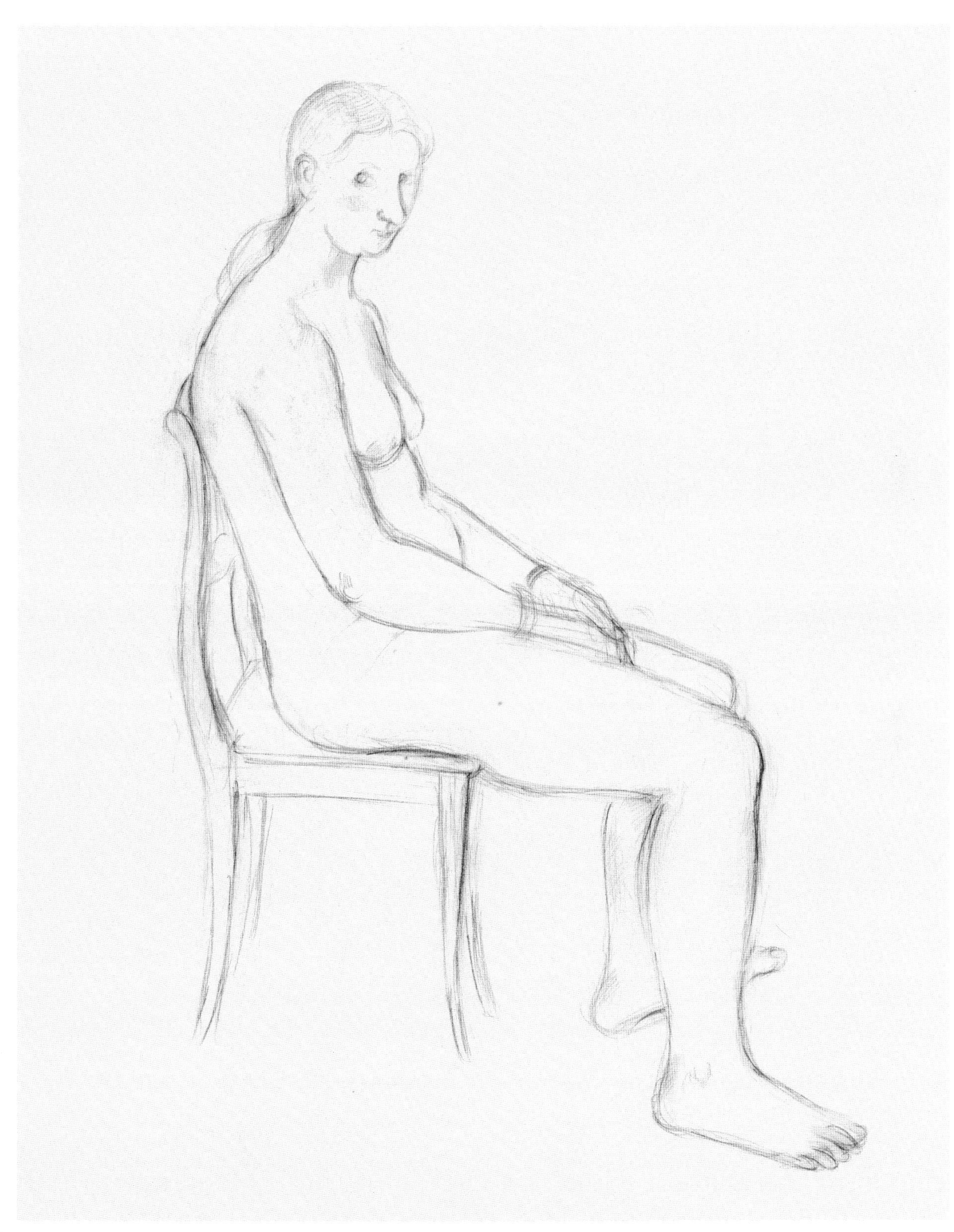

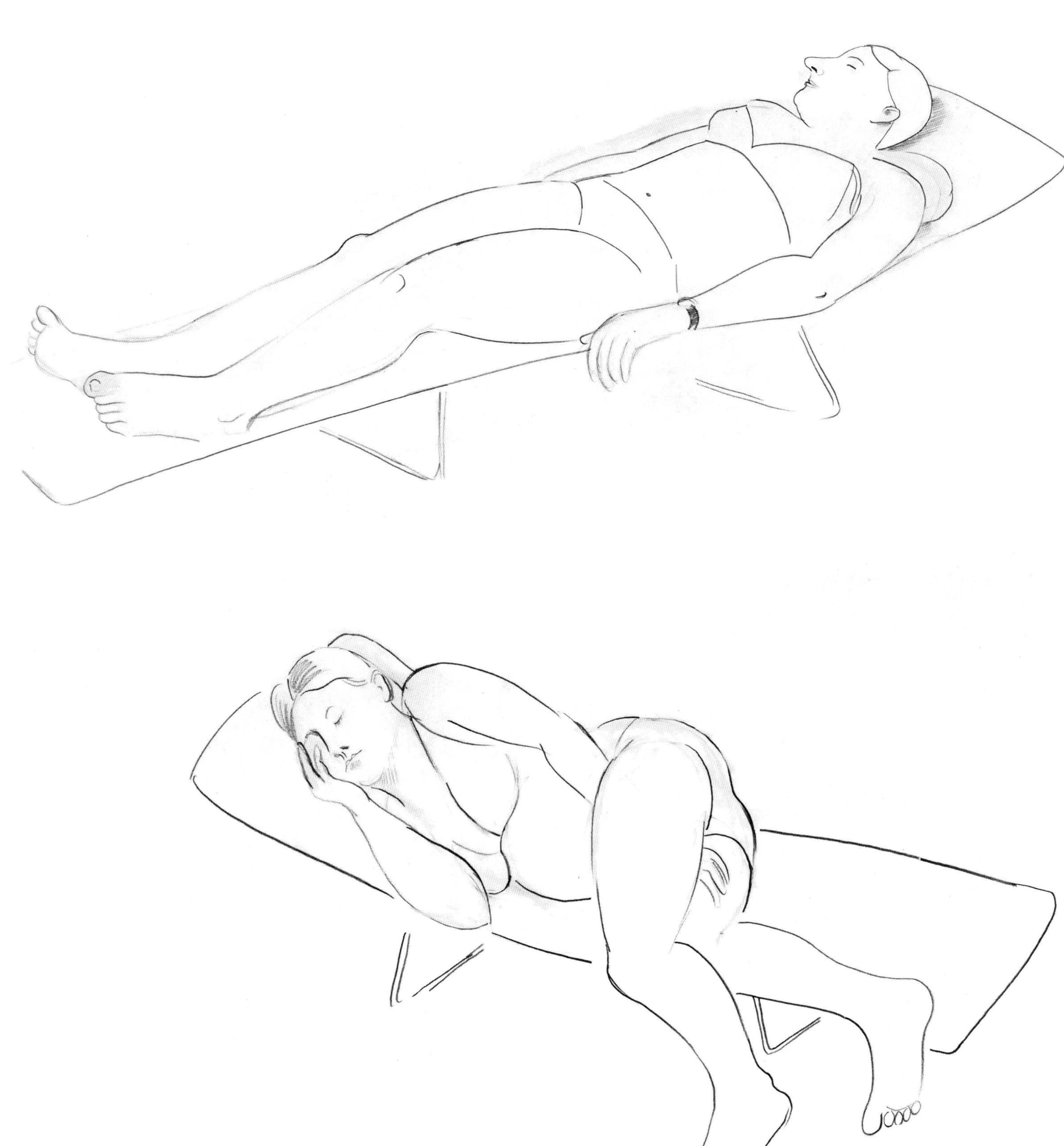

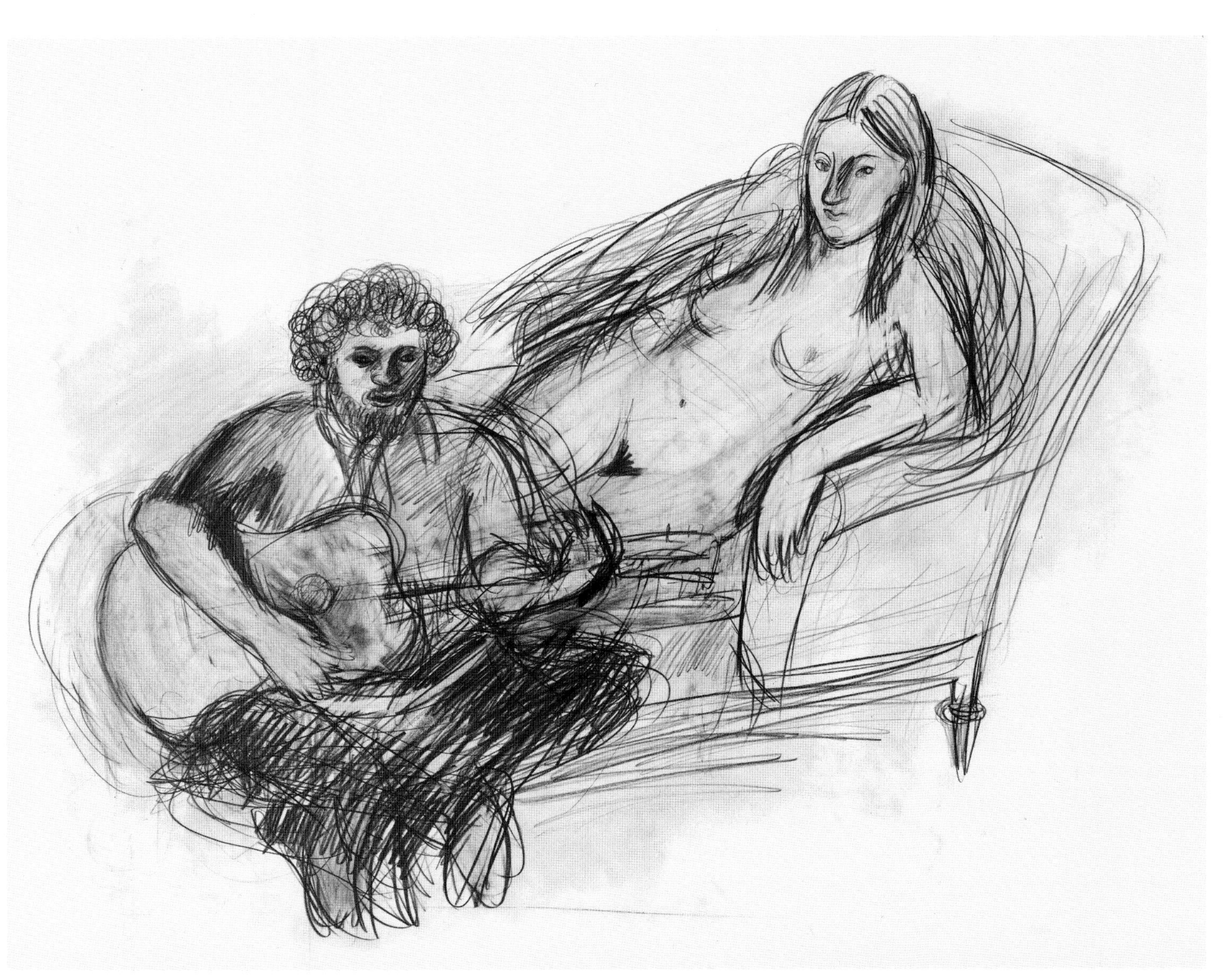

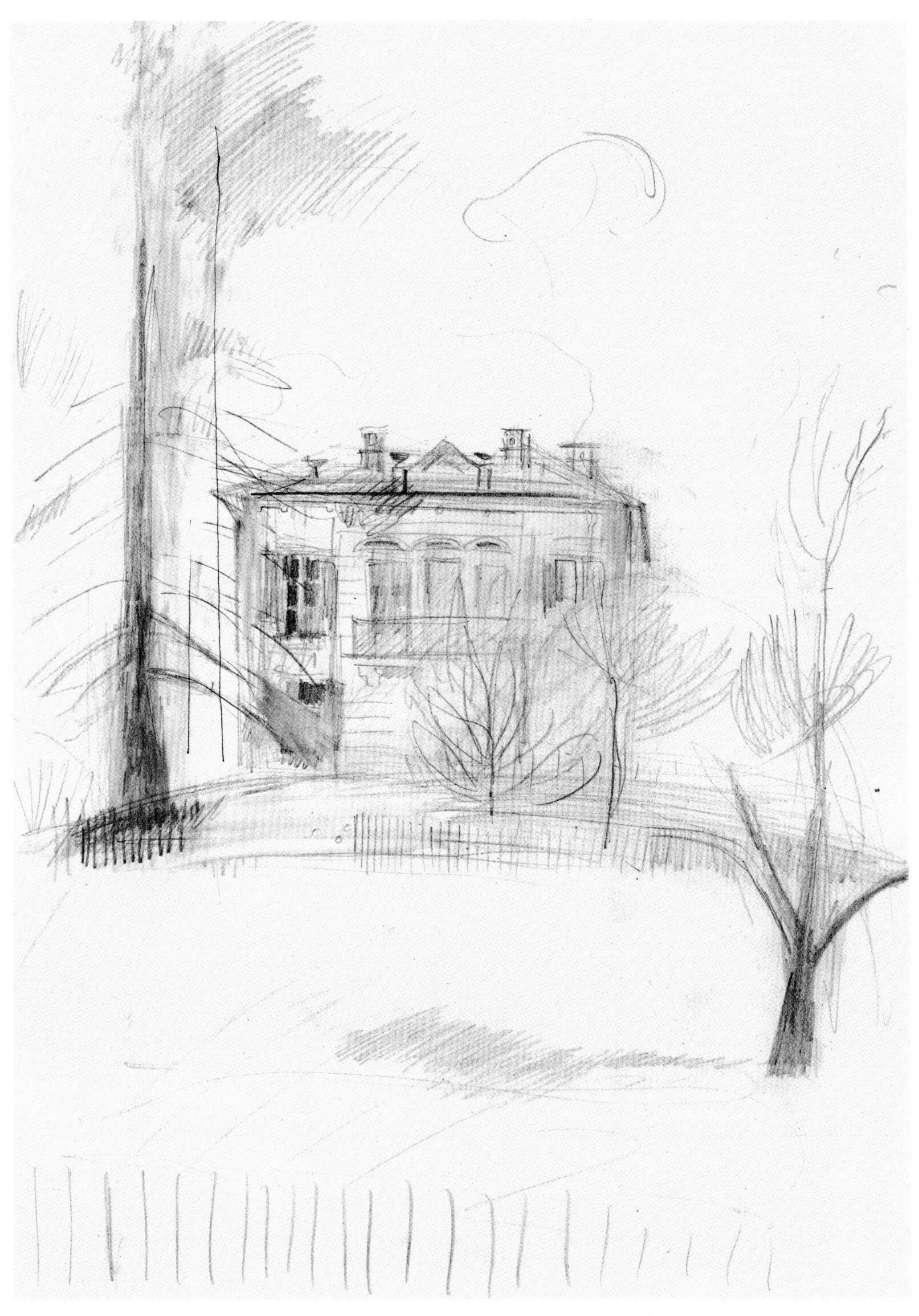

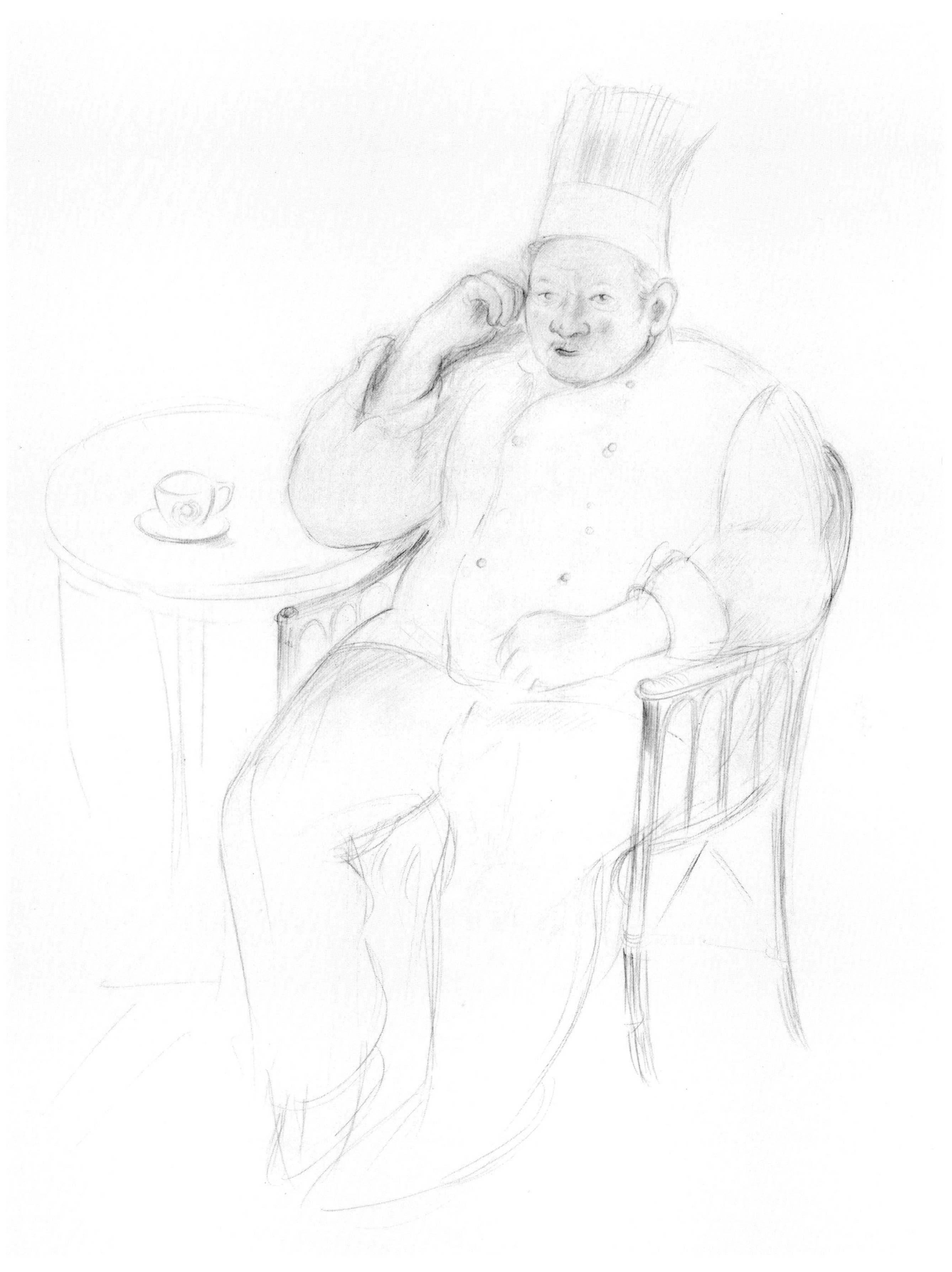

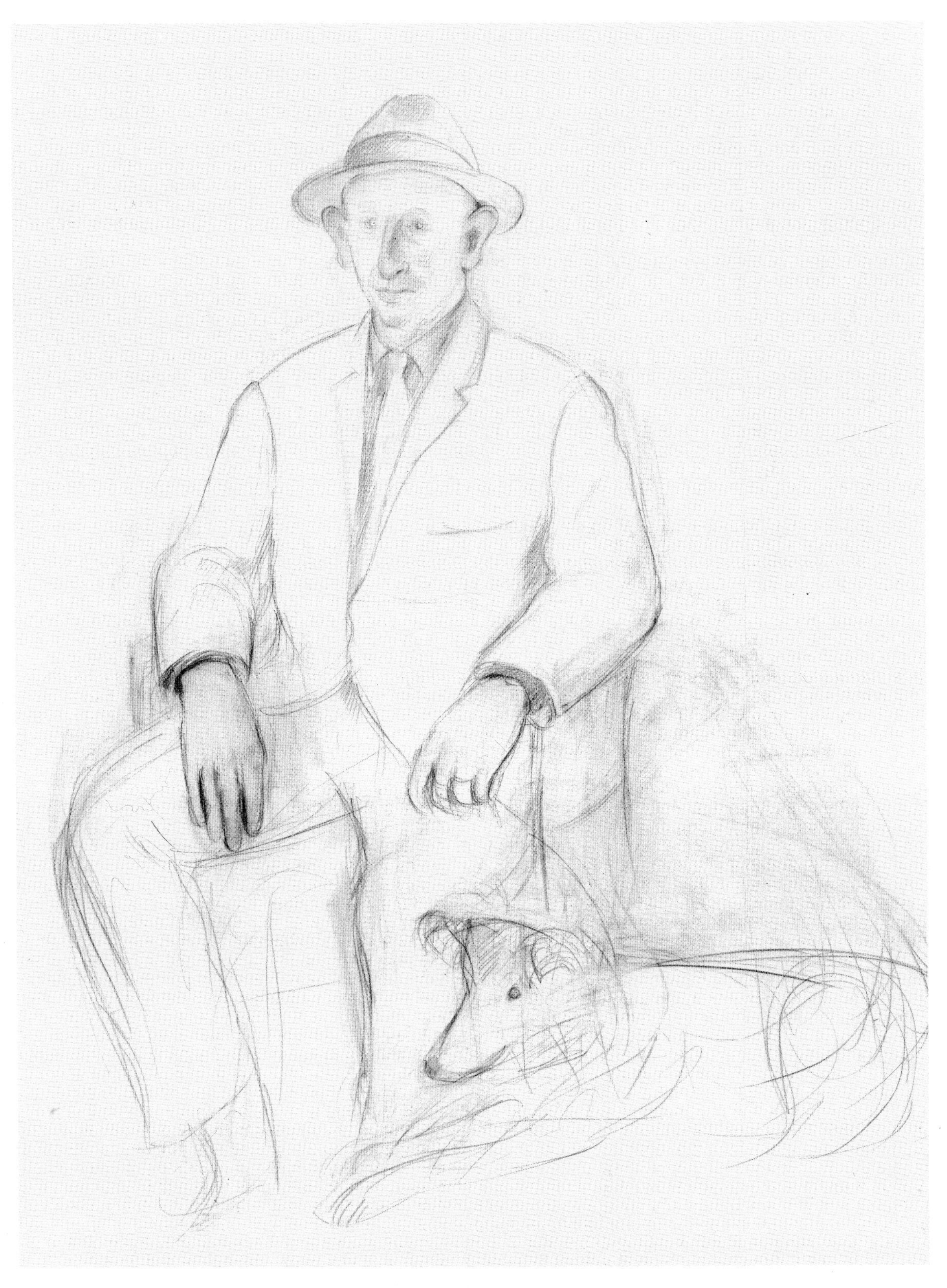

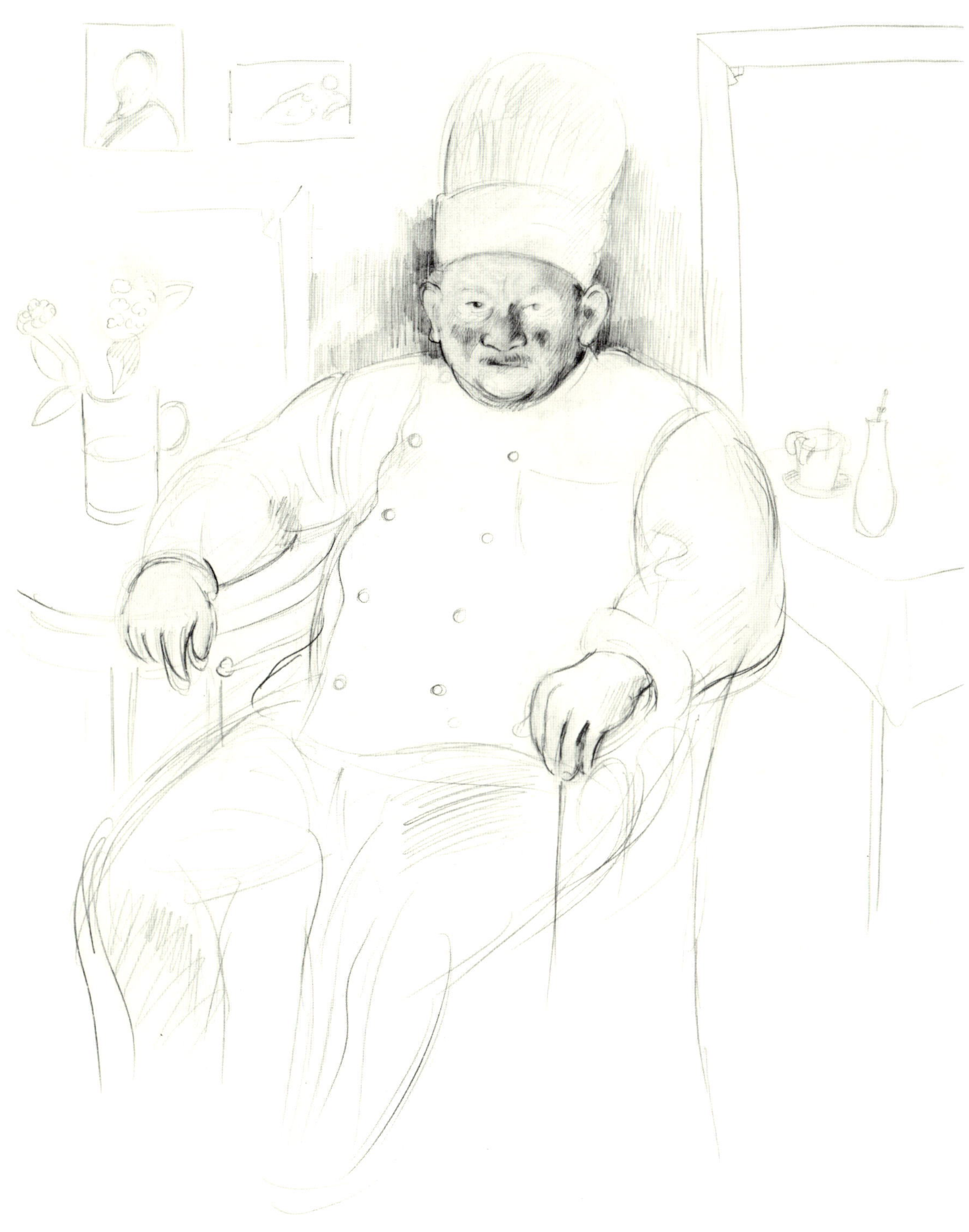

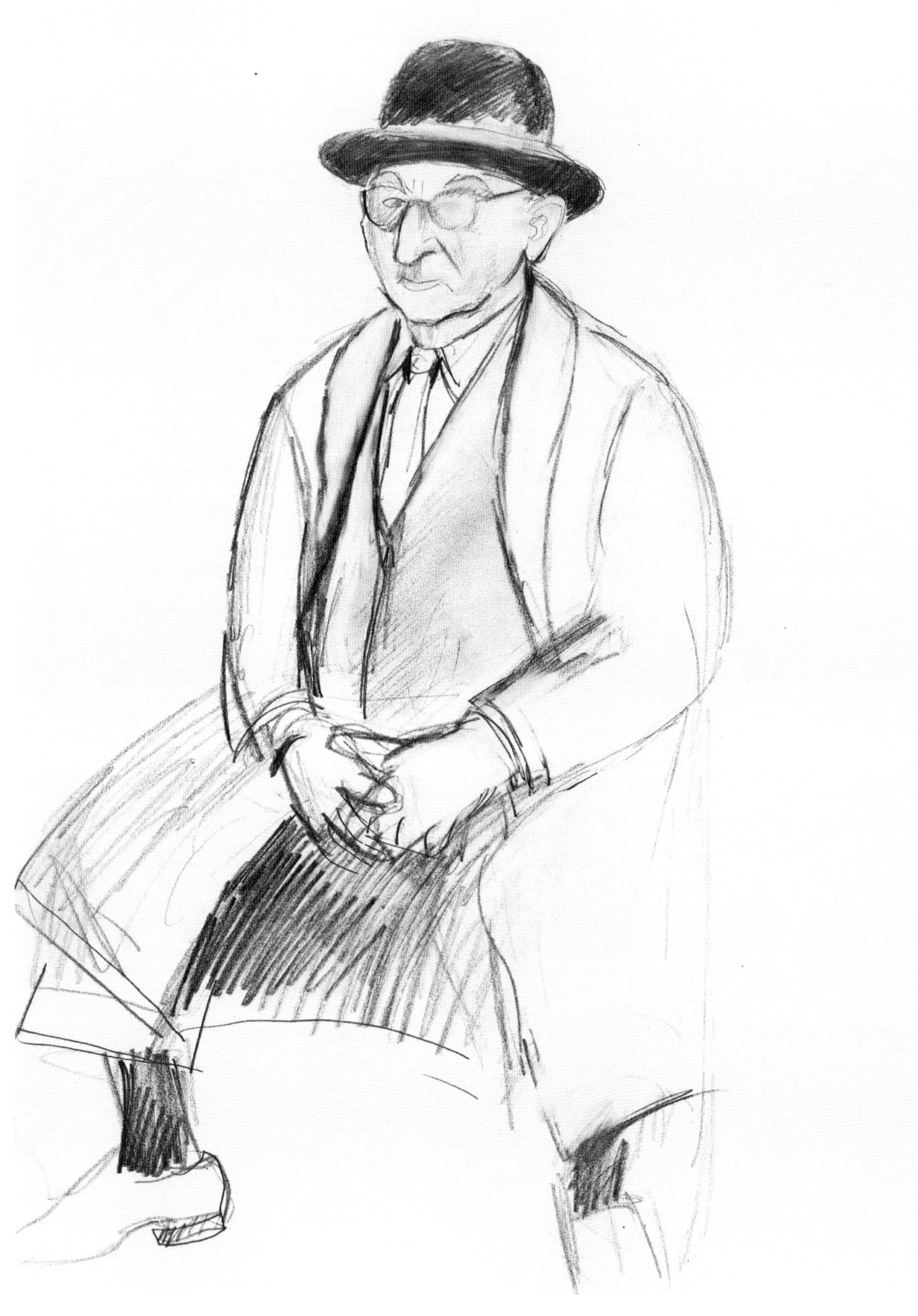

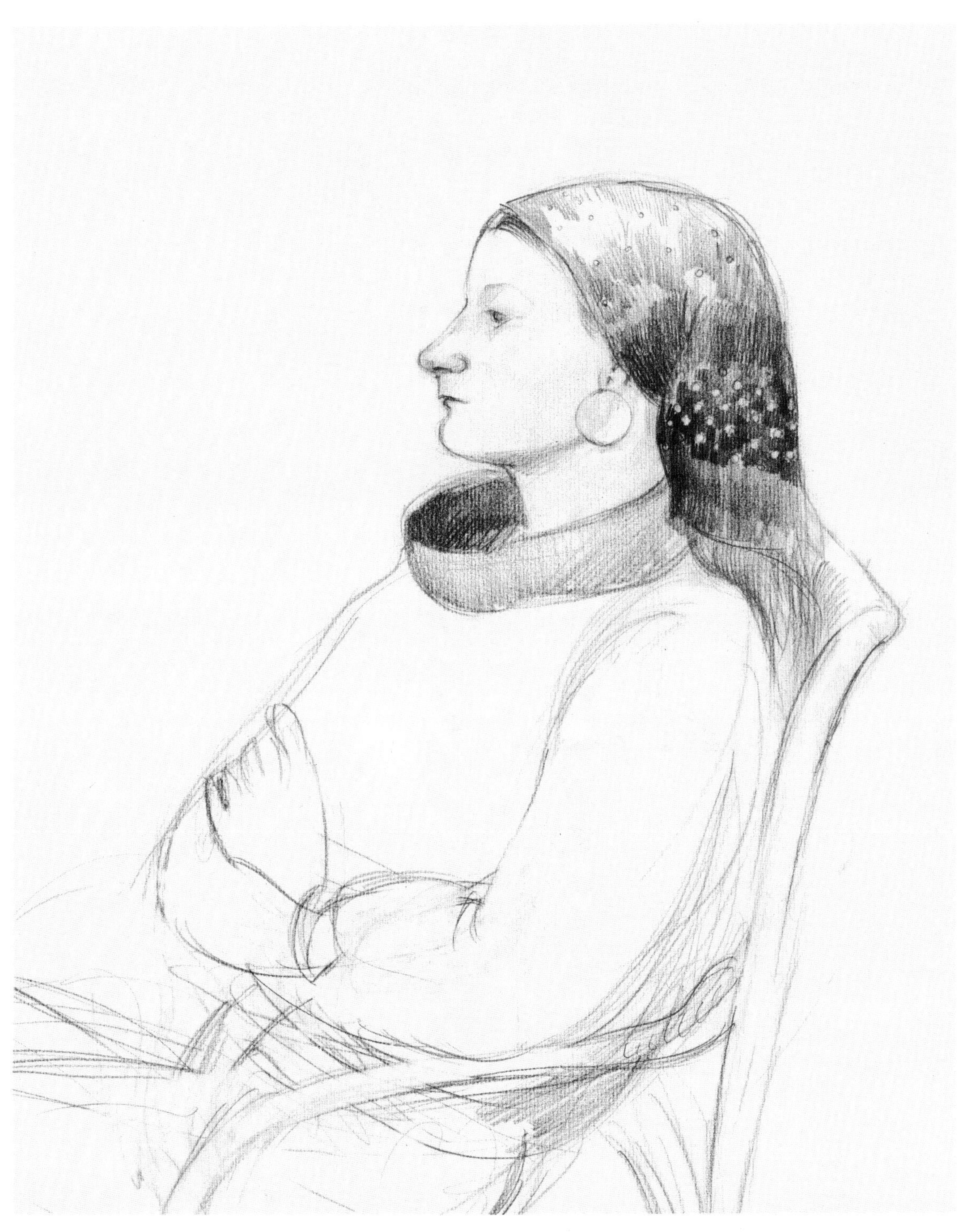

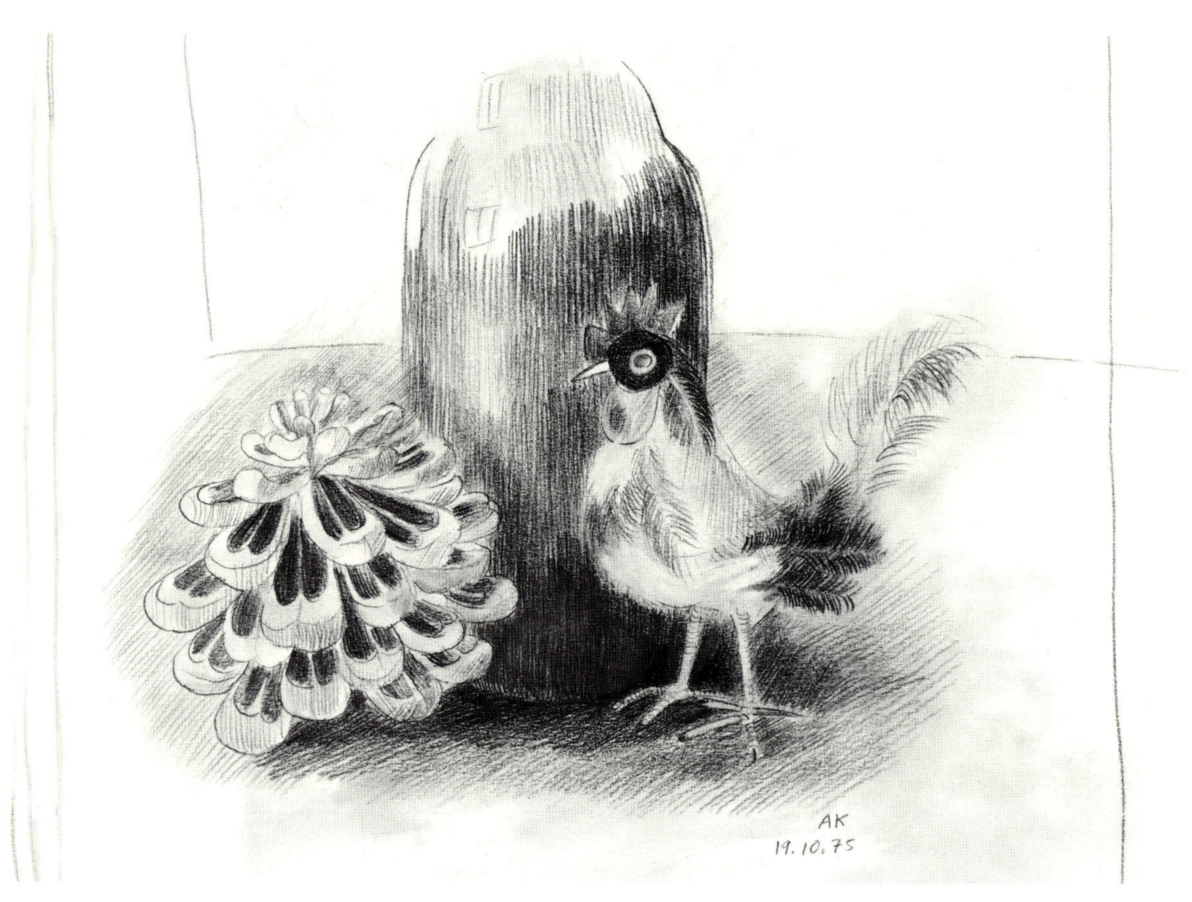
AK
19.10.75

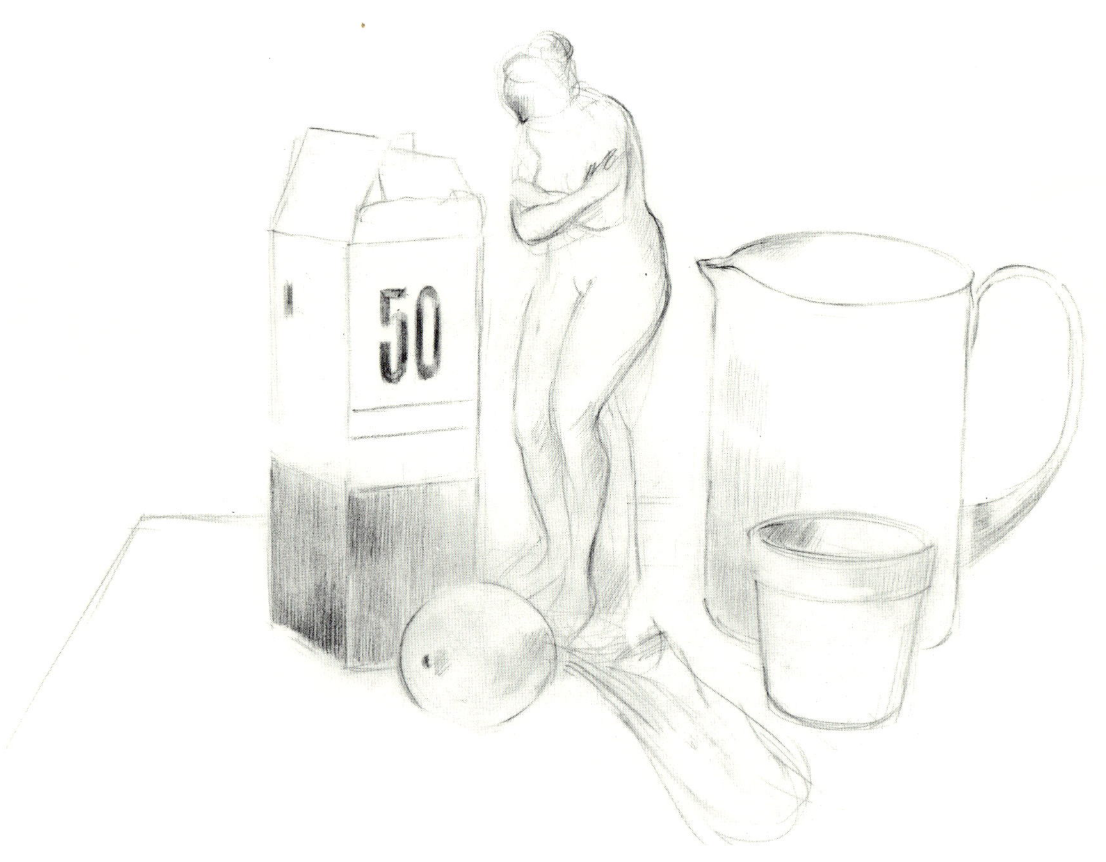
50

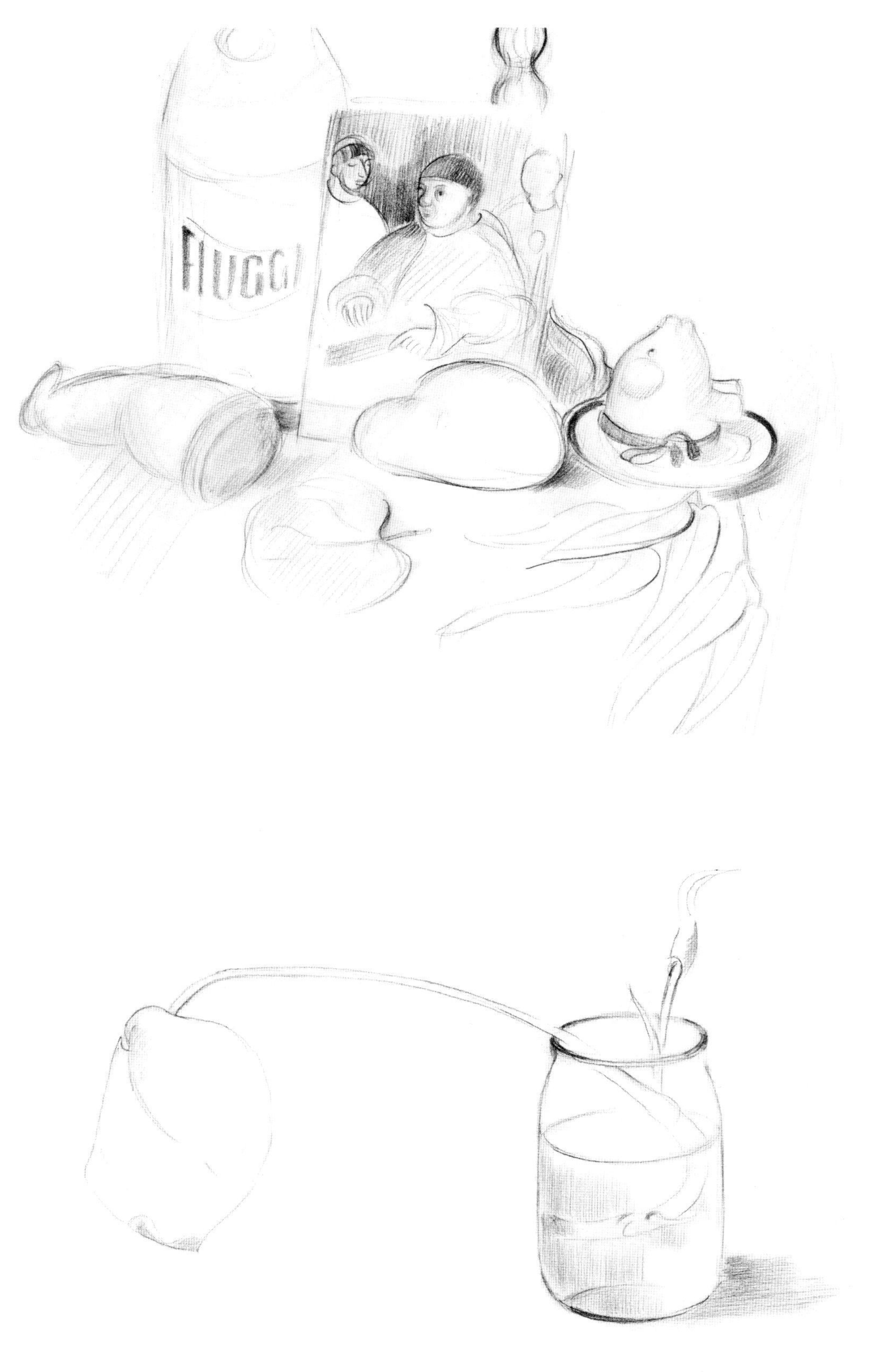
FIUGGI

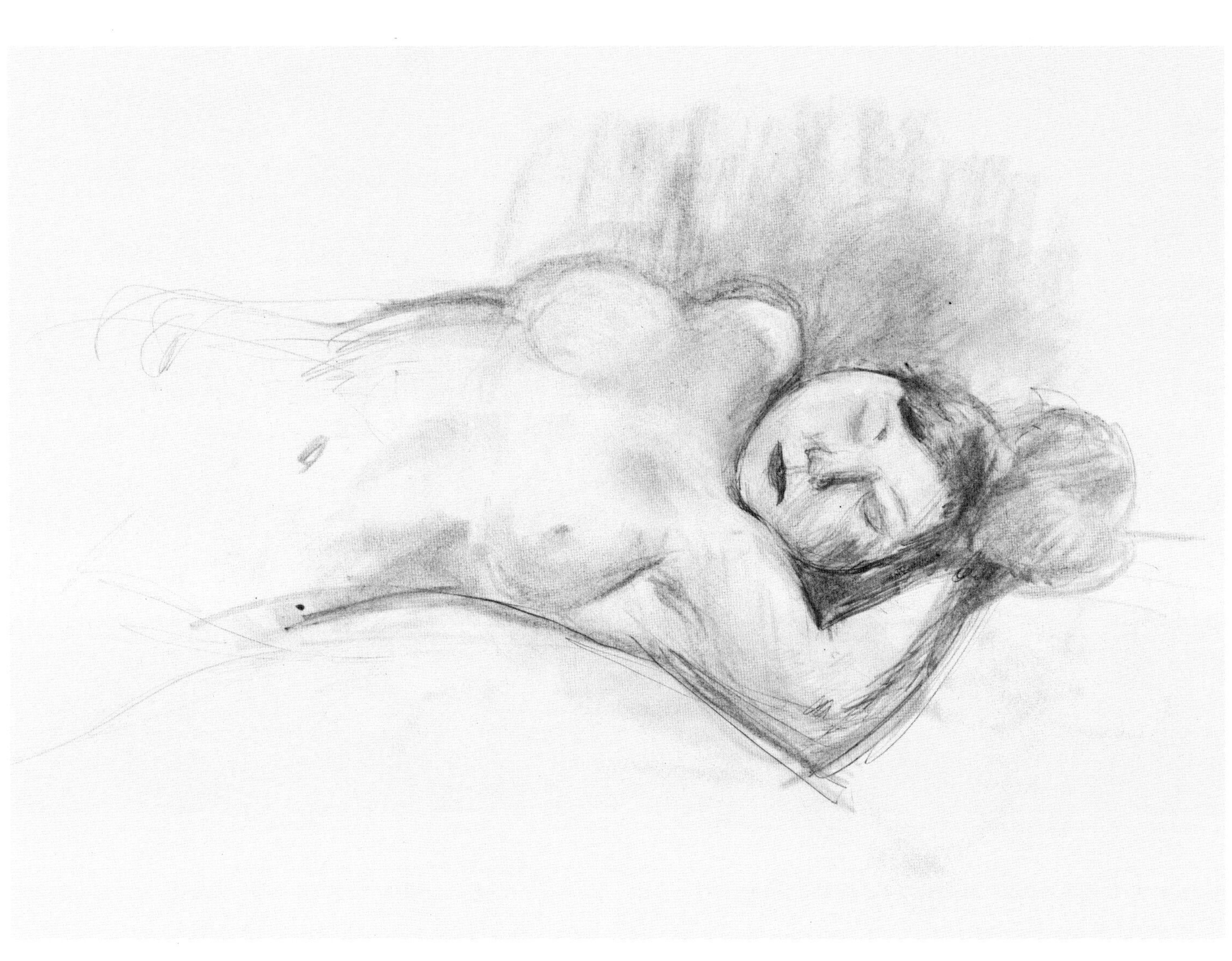

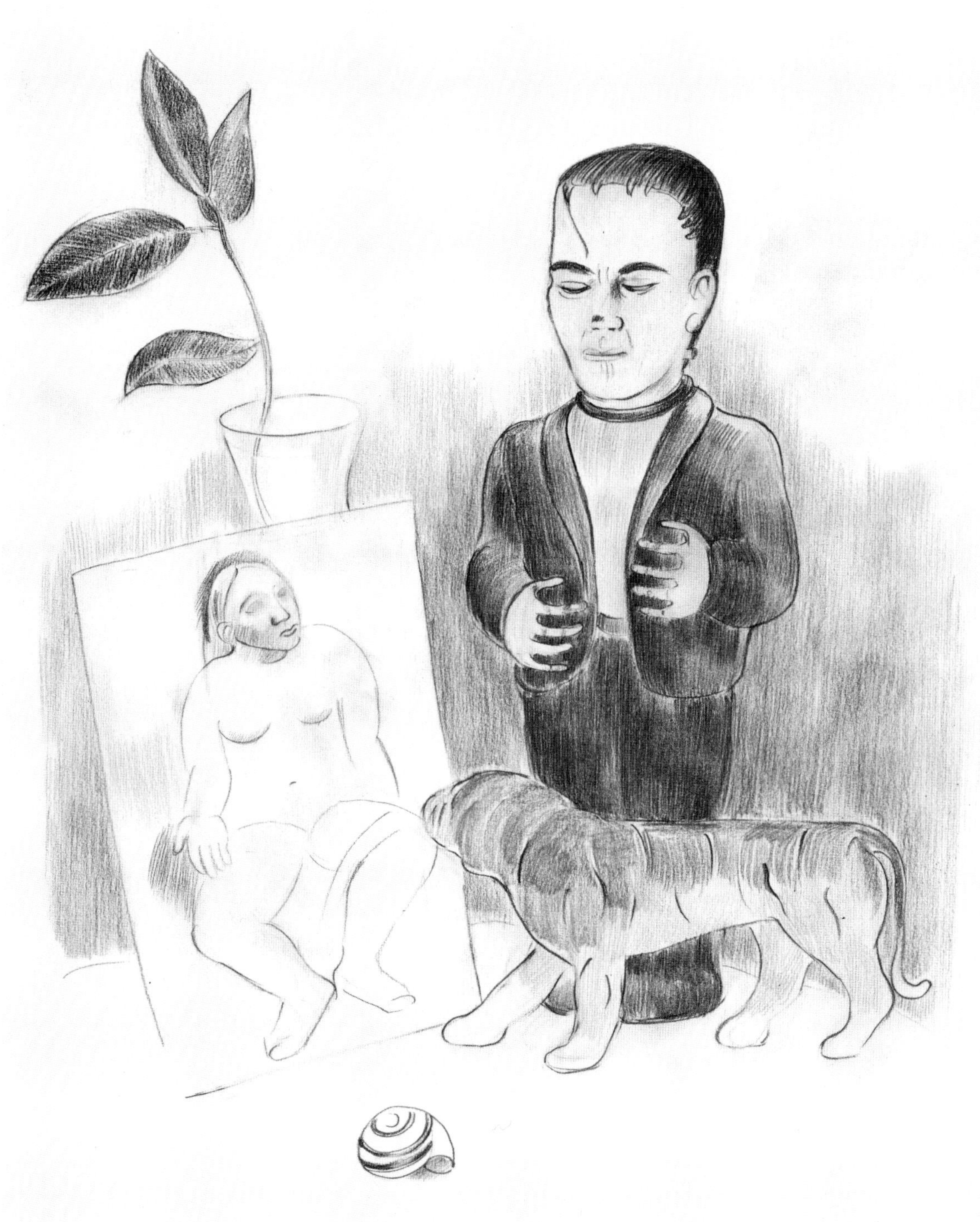

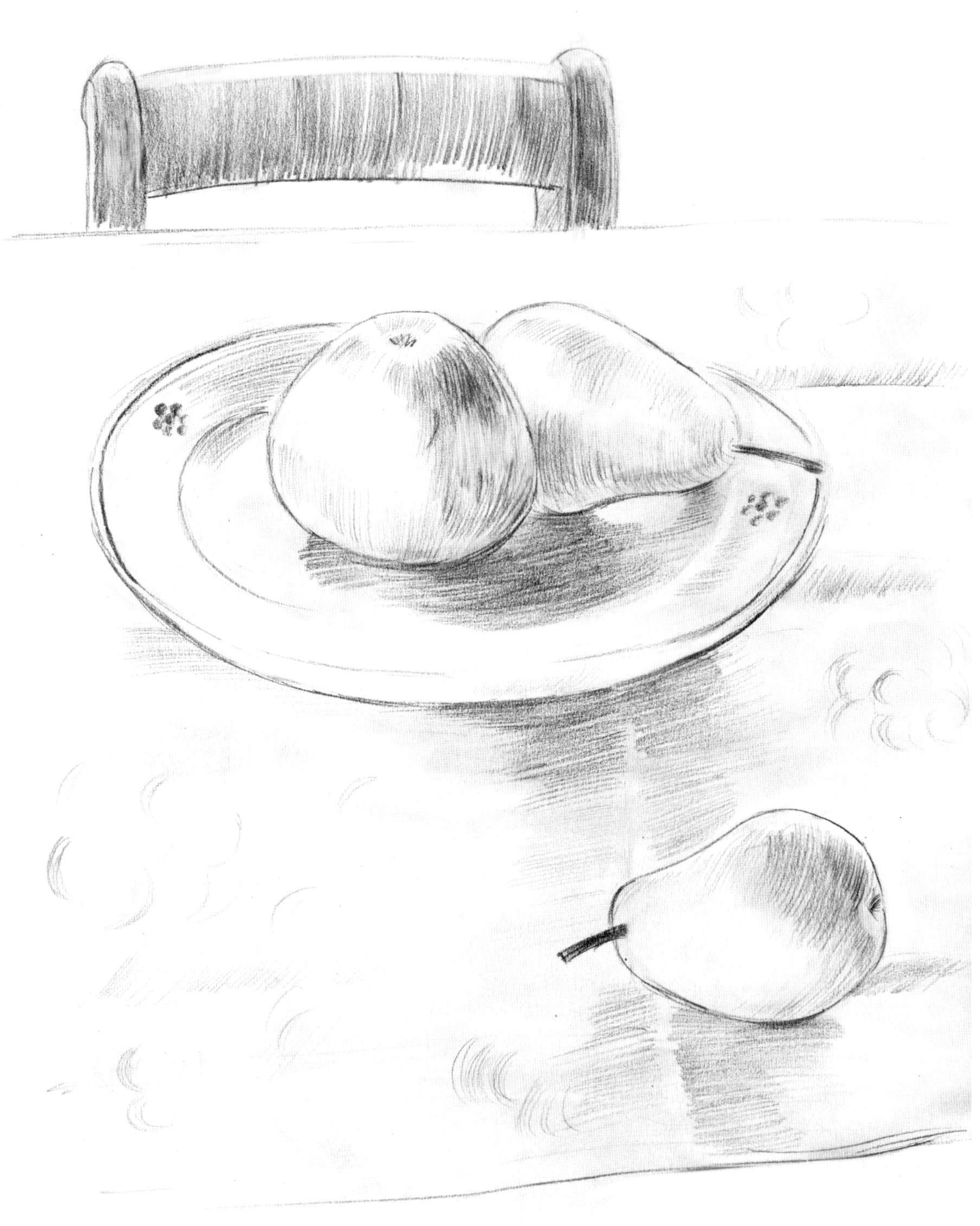

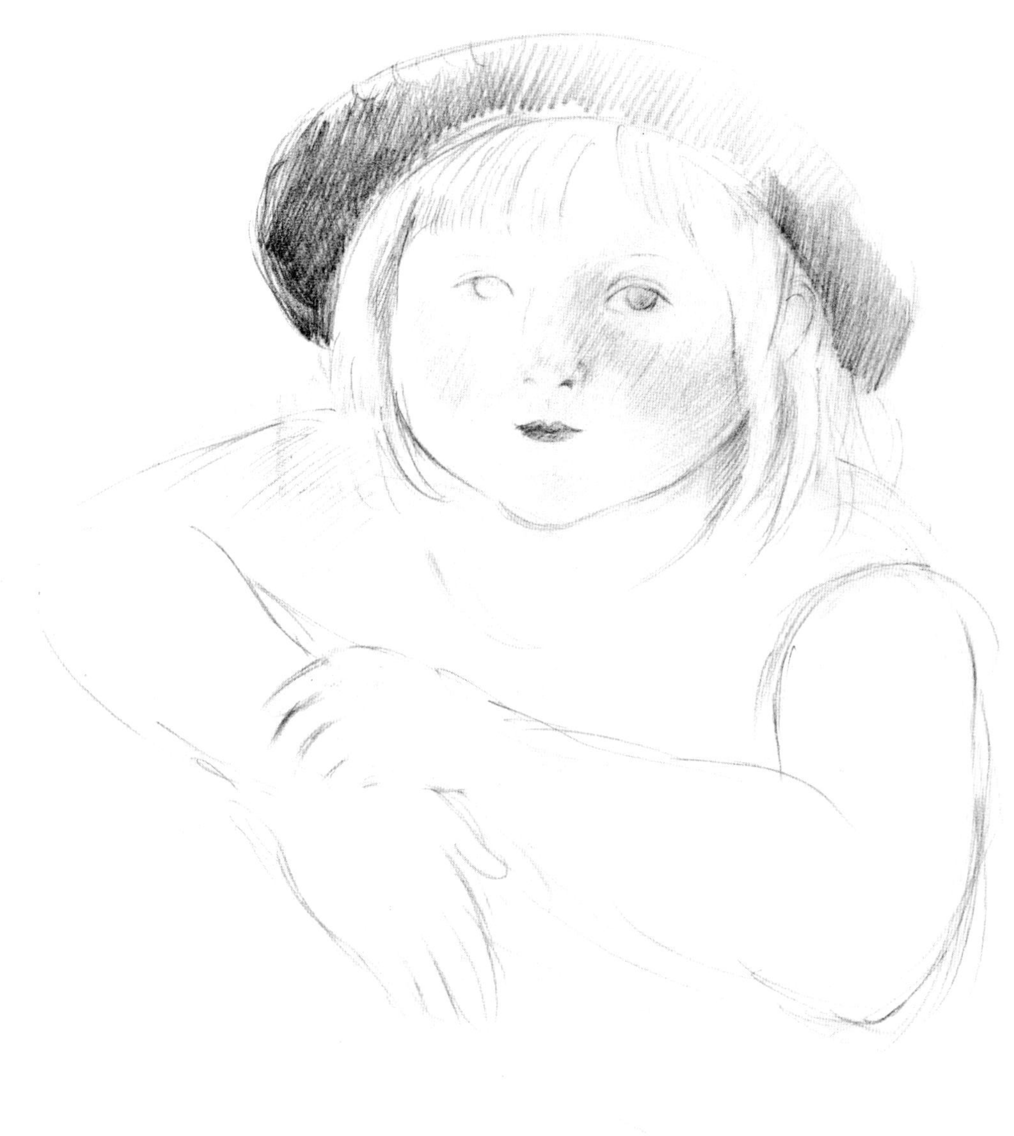

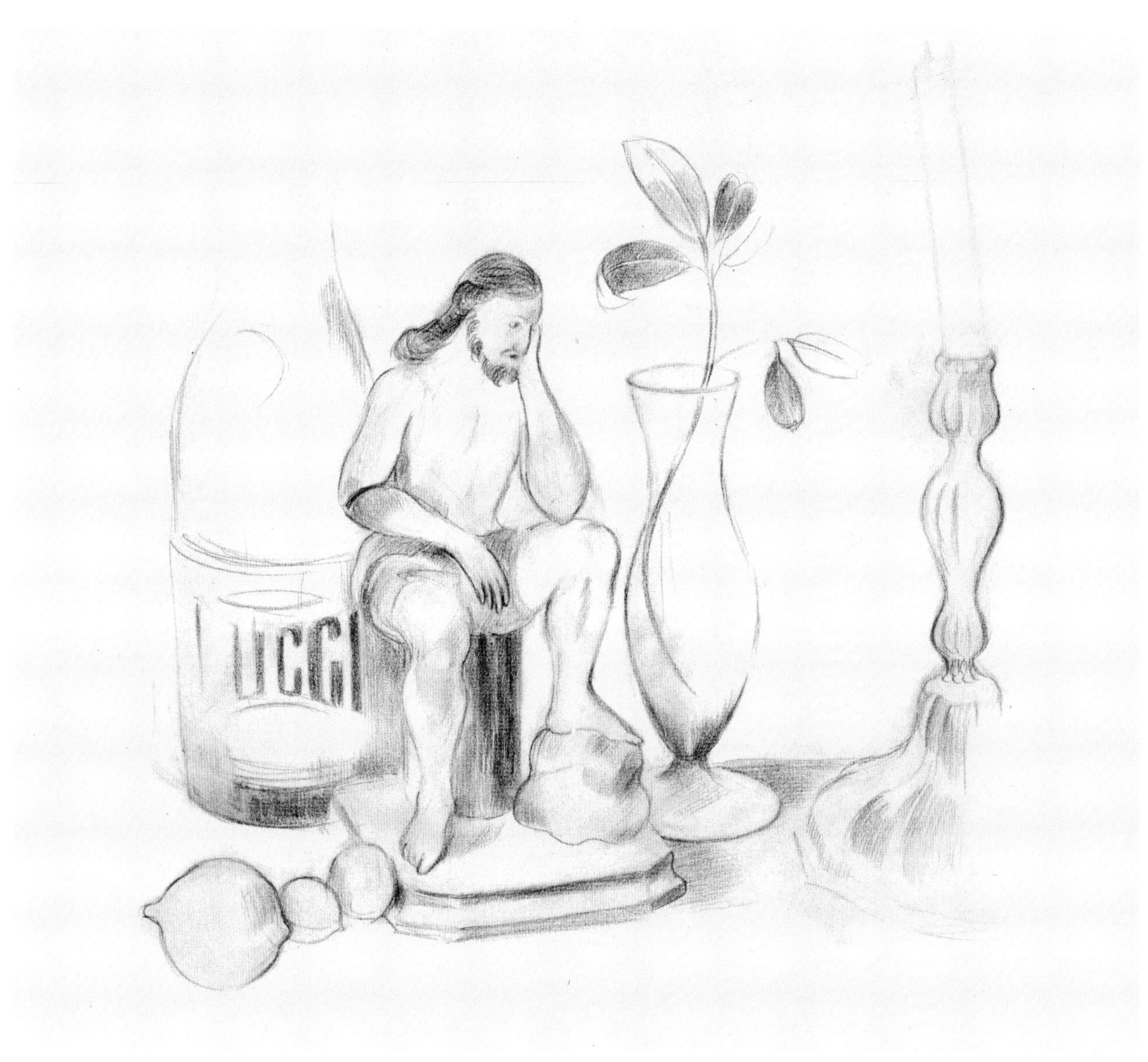

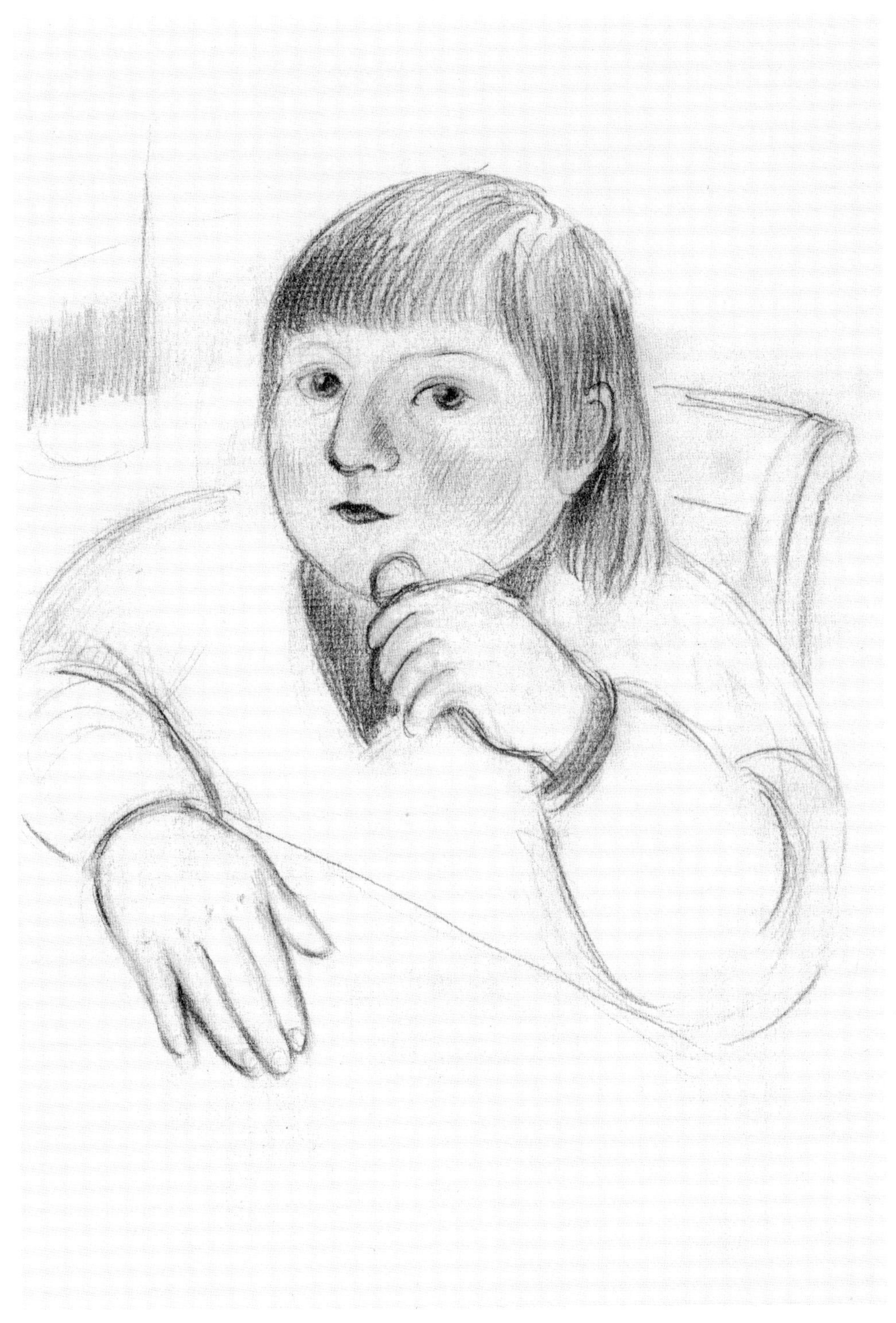

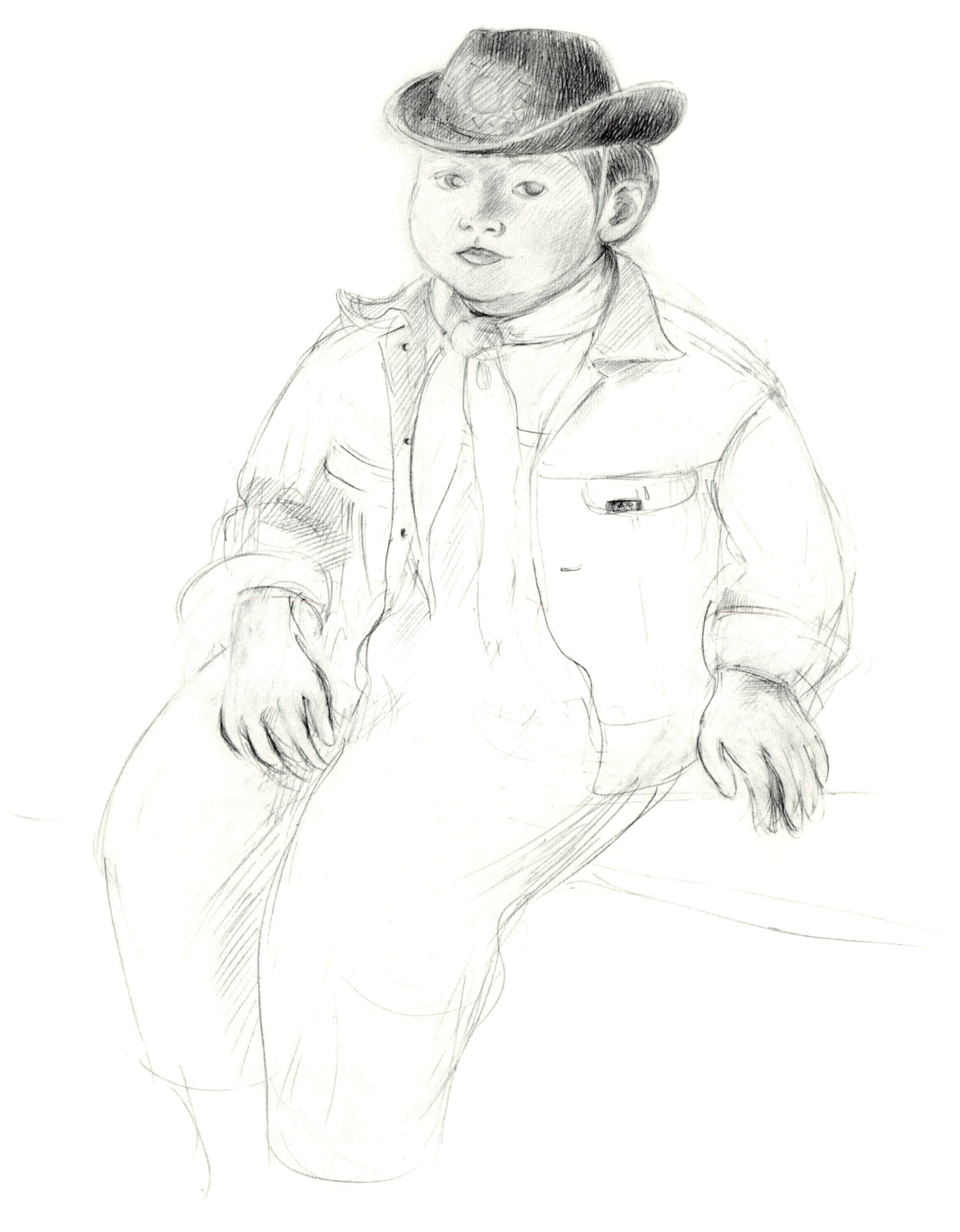

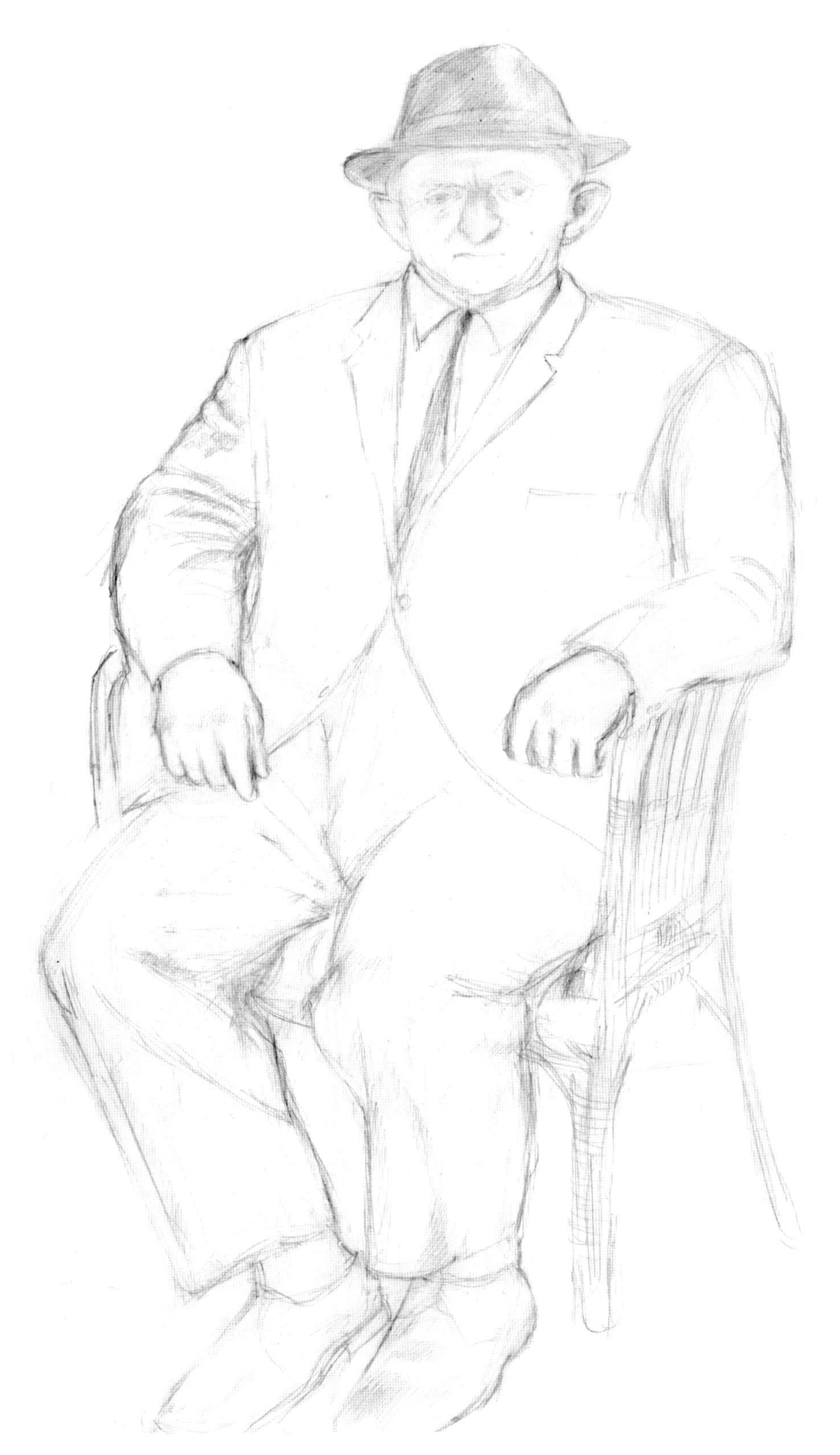

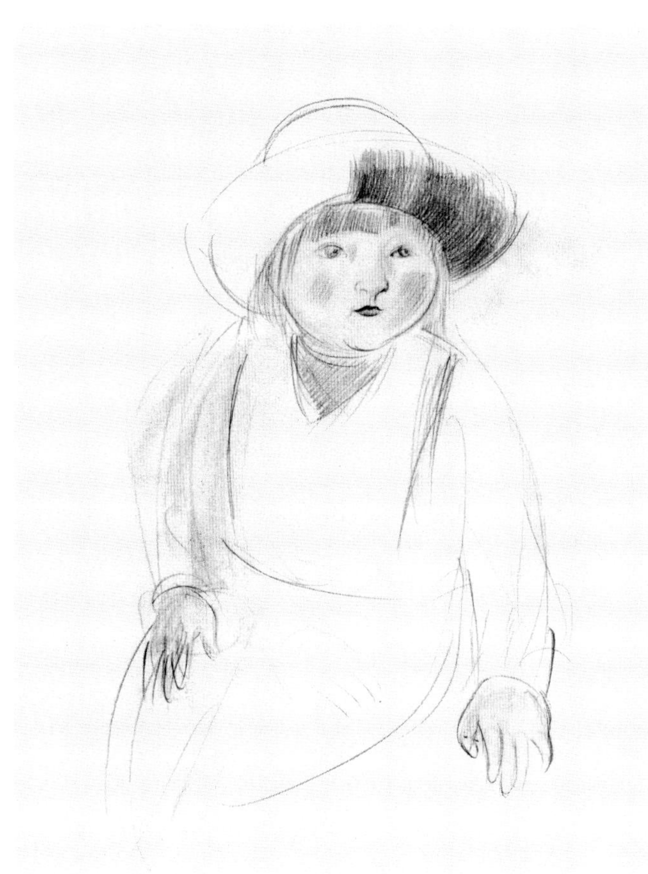

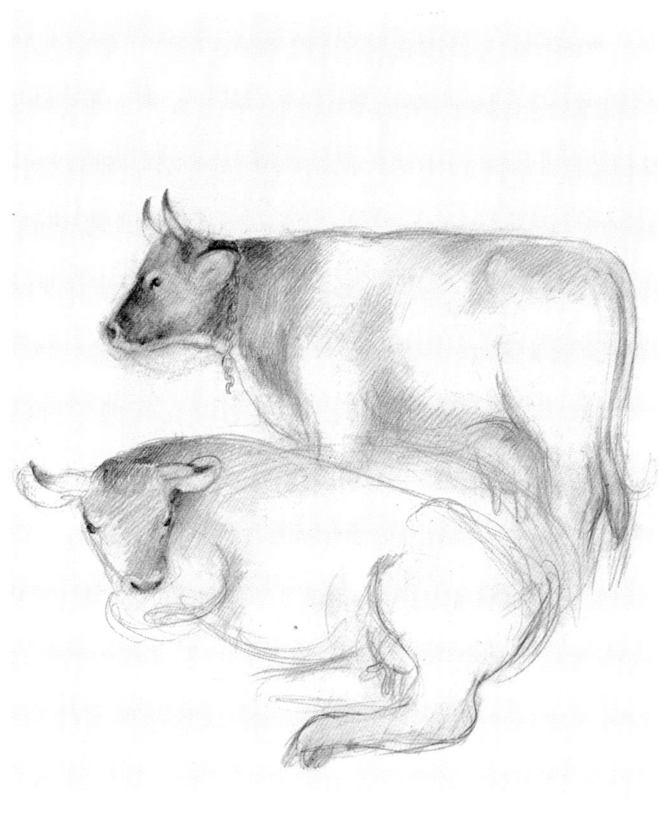

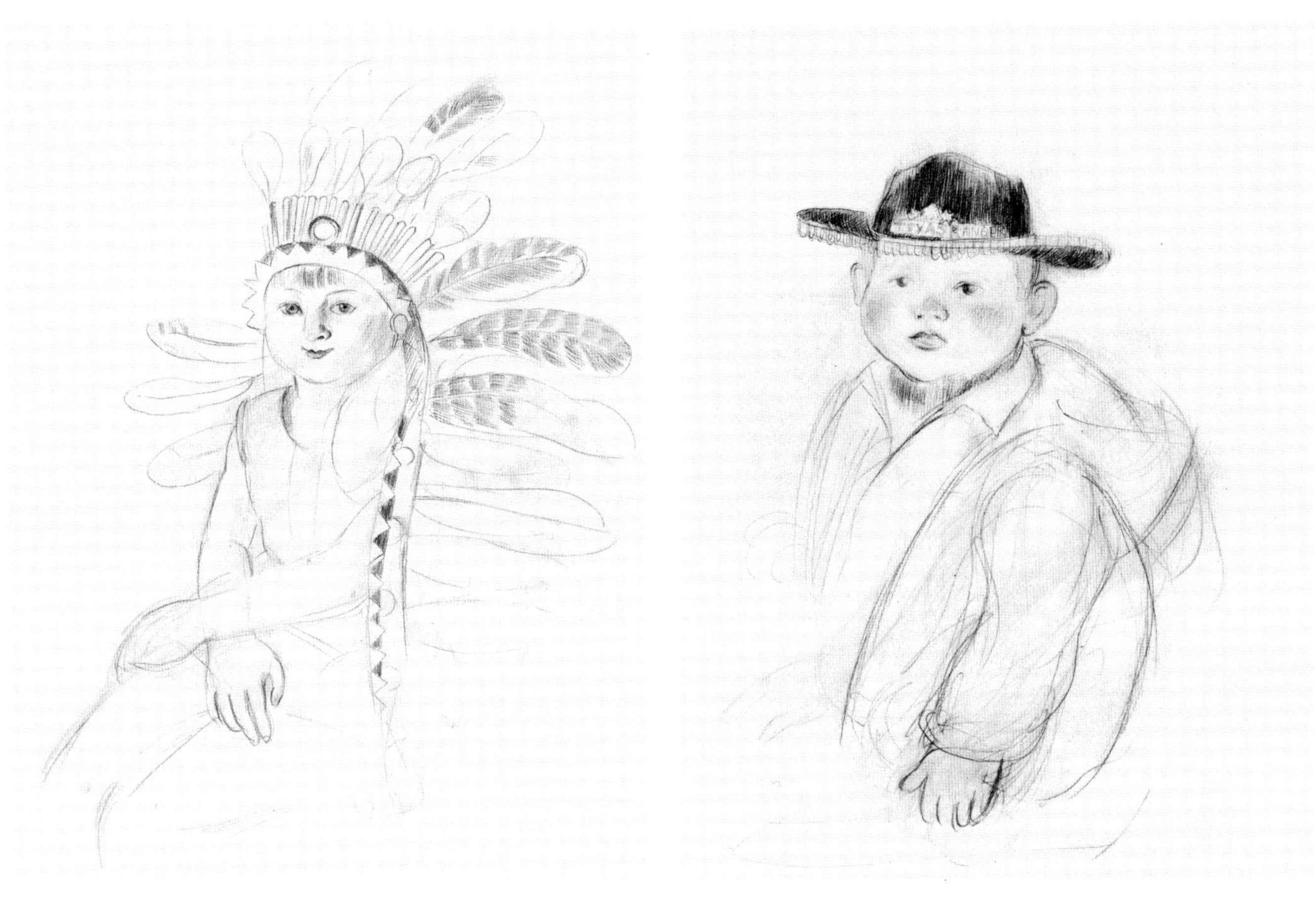
TEXAS RANGER

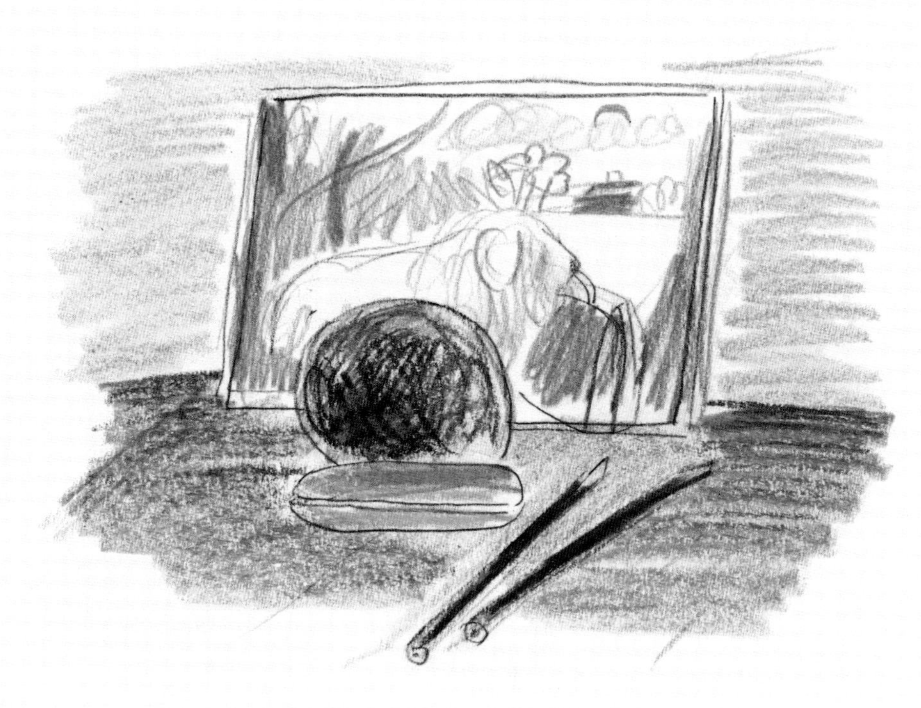

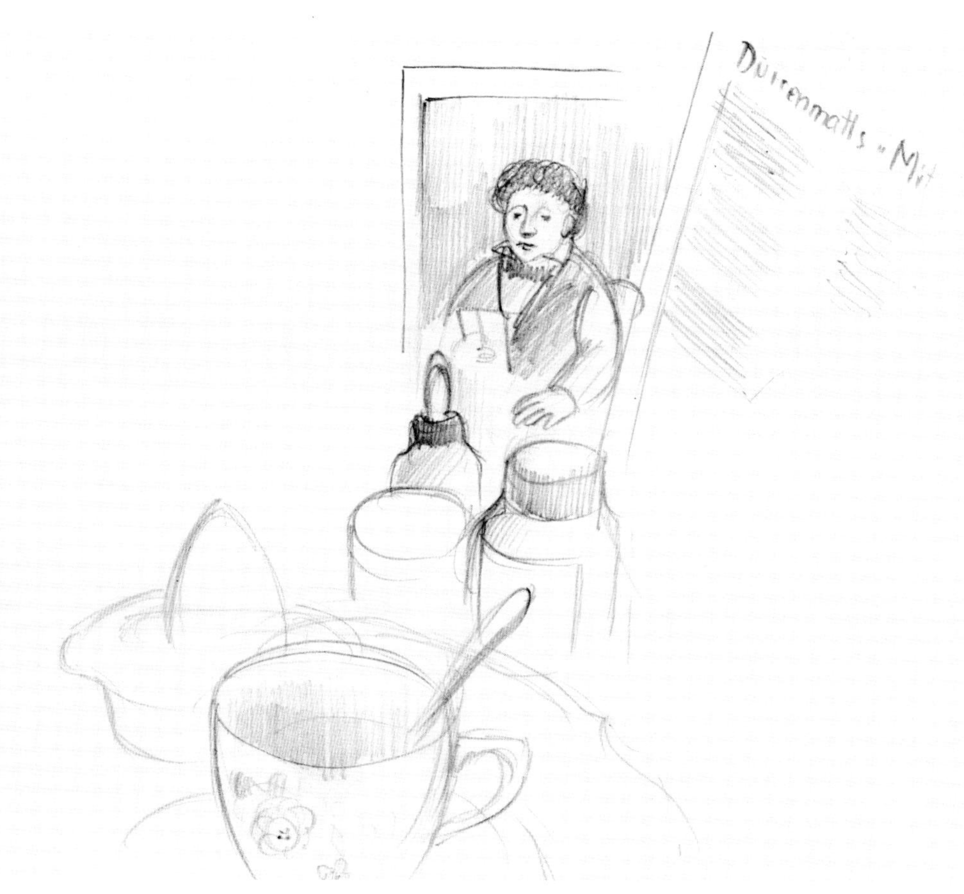
Dürrenmatts „Mit

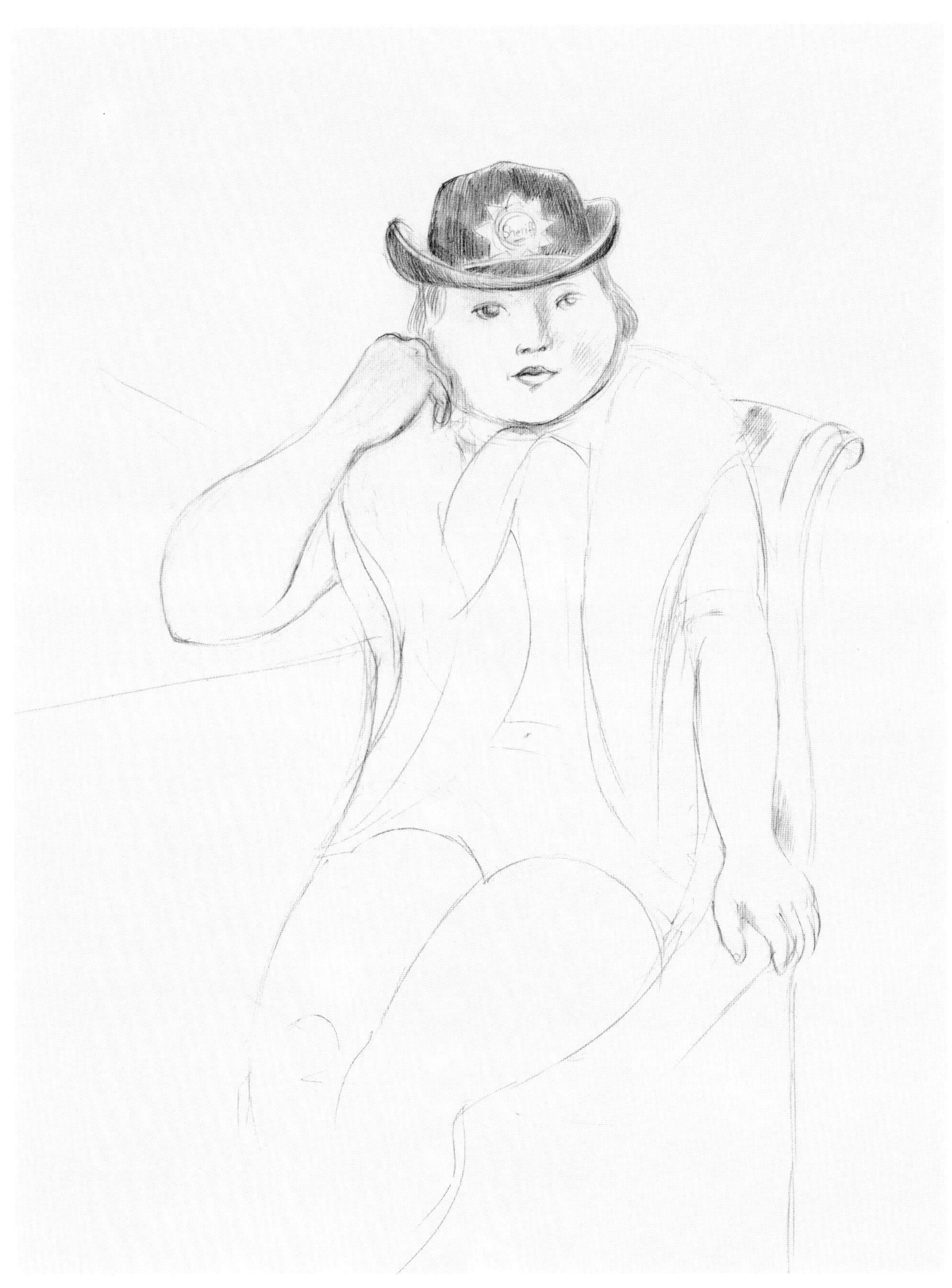
Sheriff

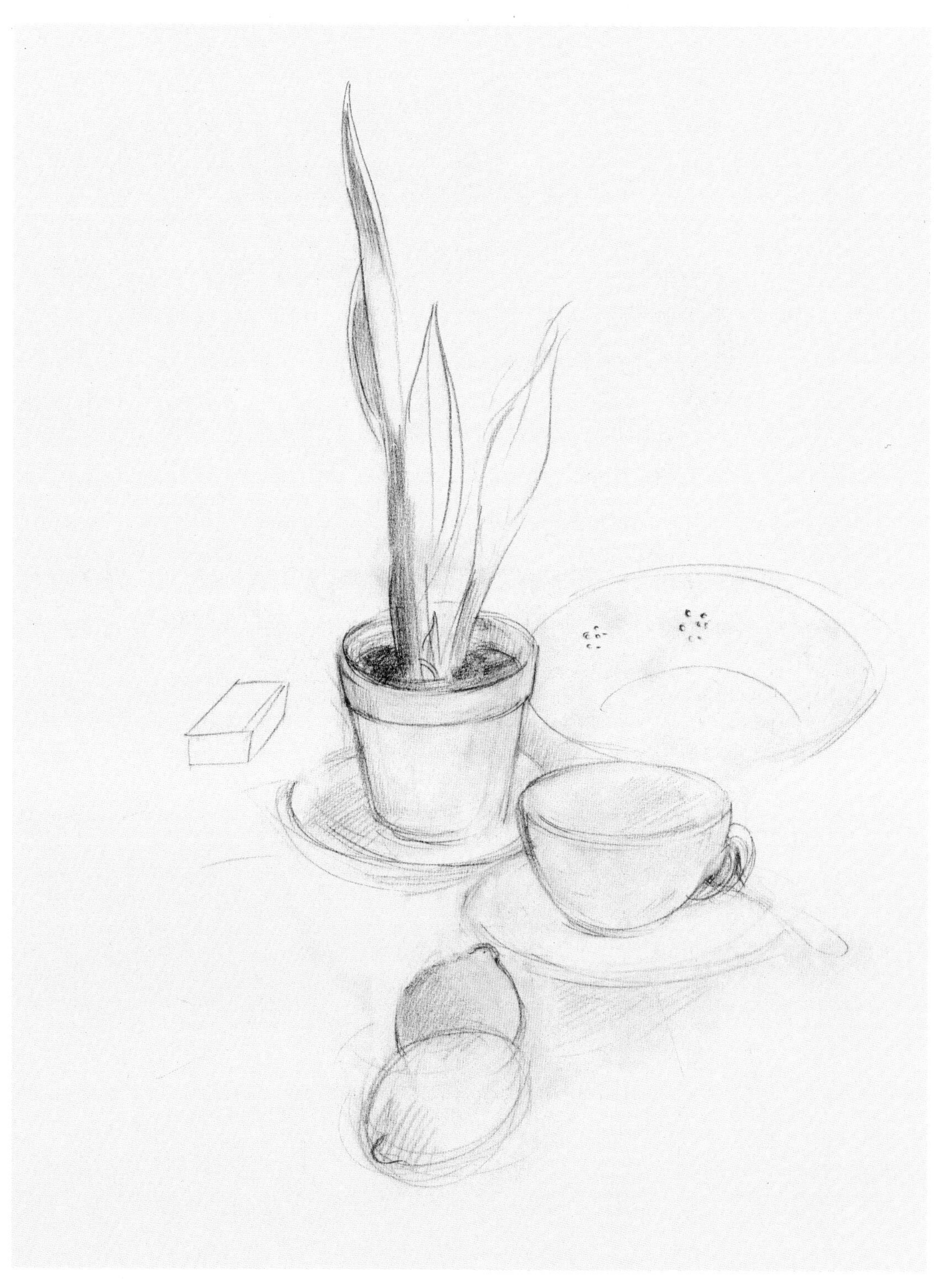

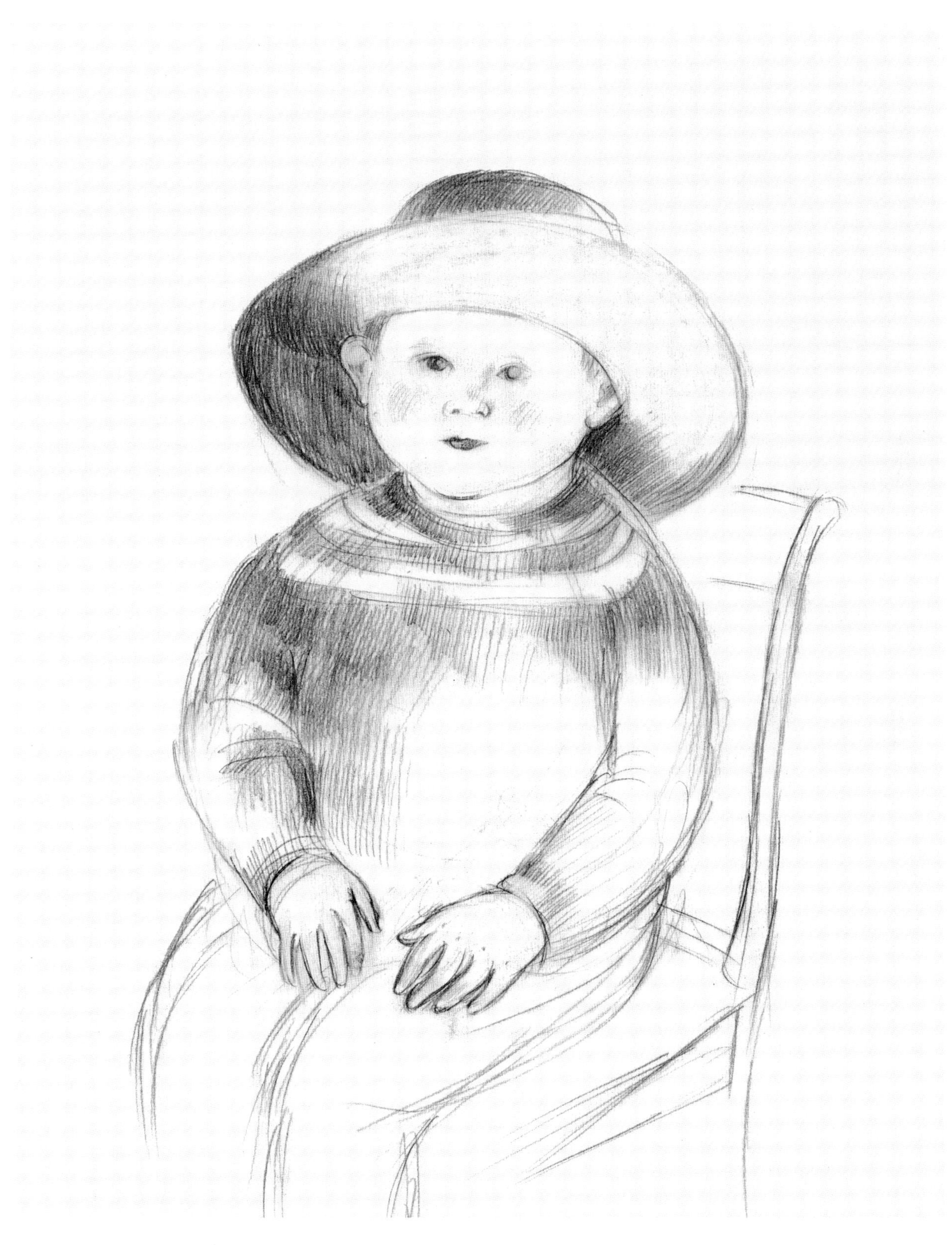

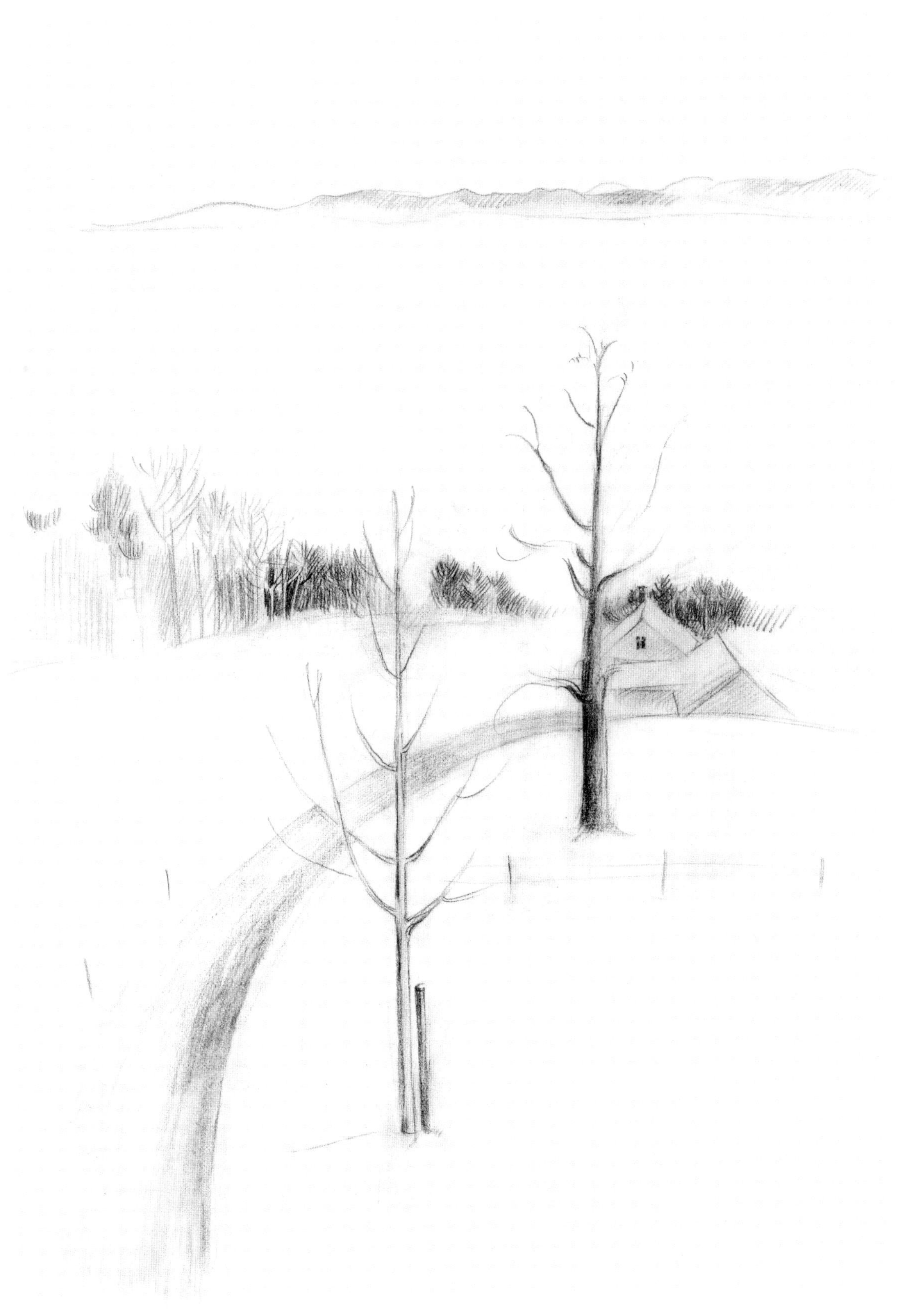

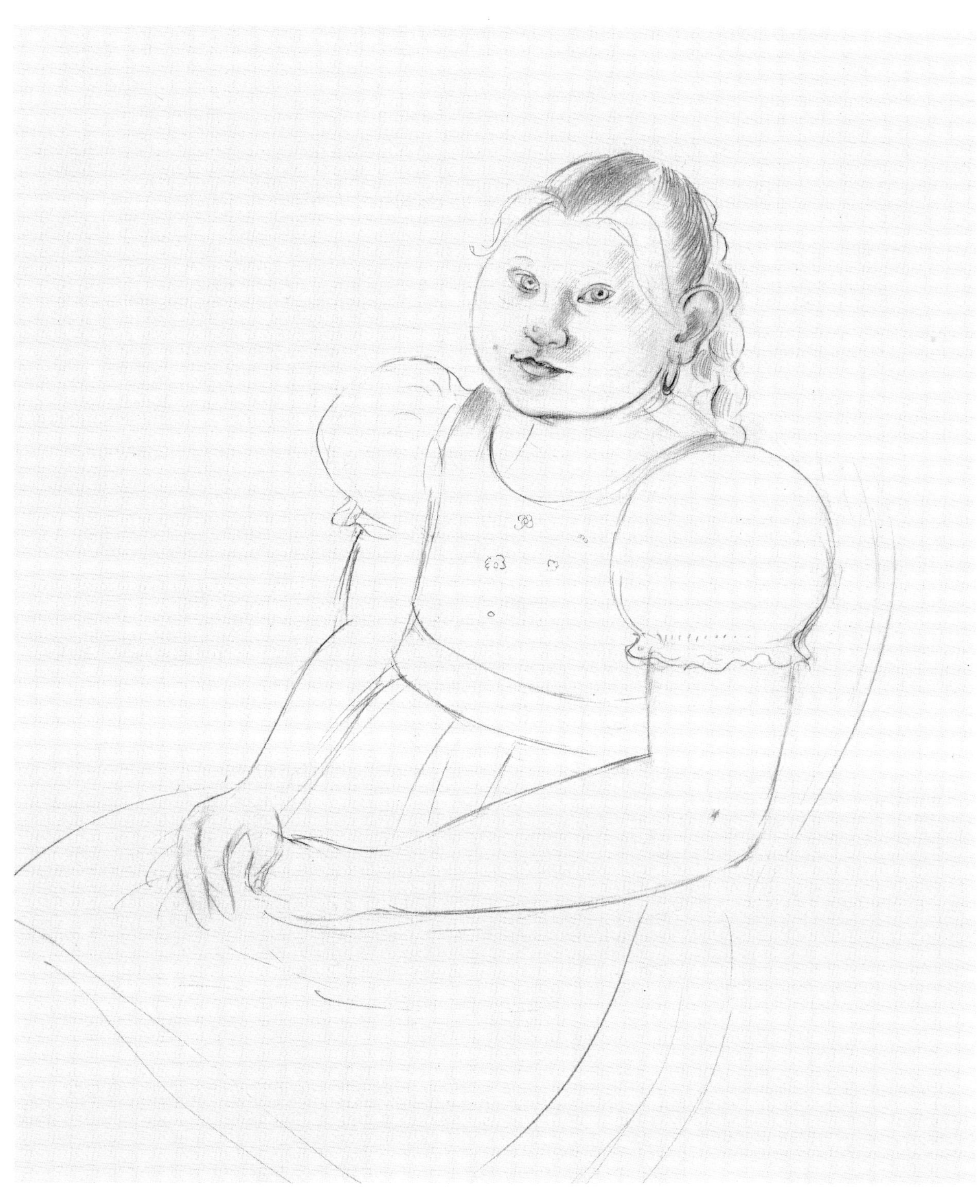

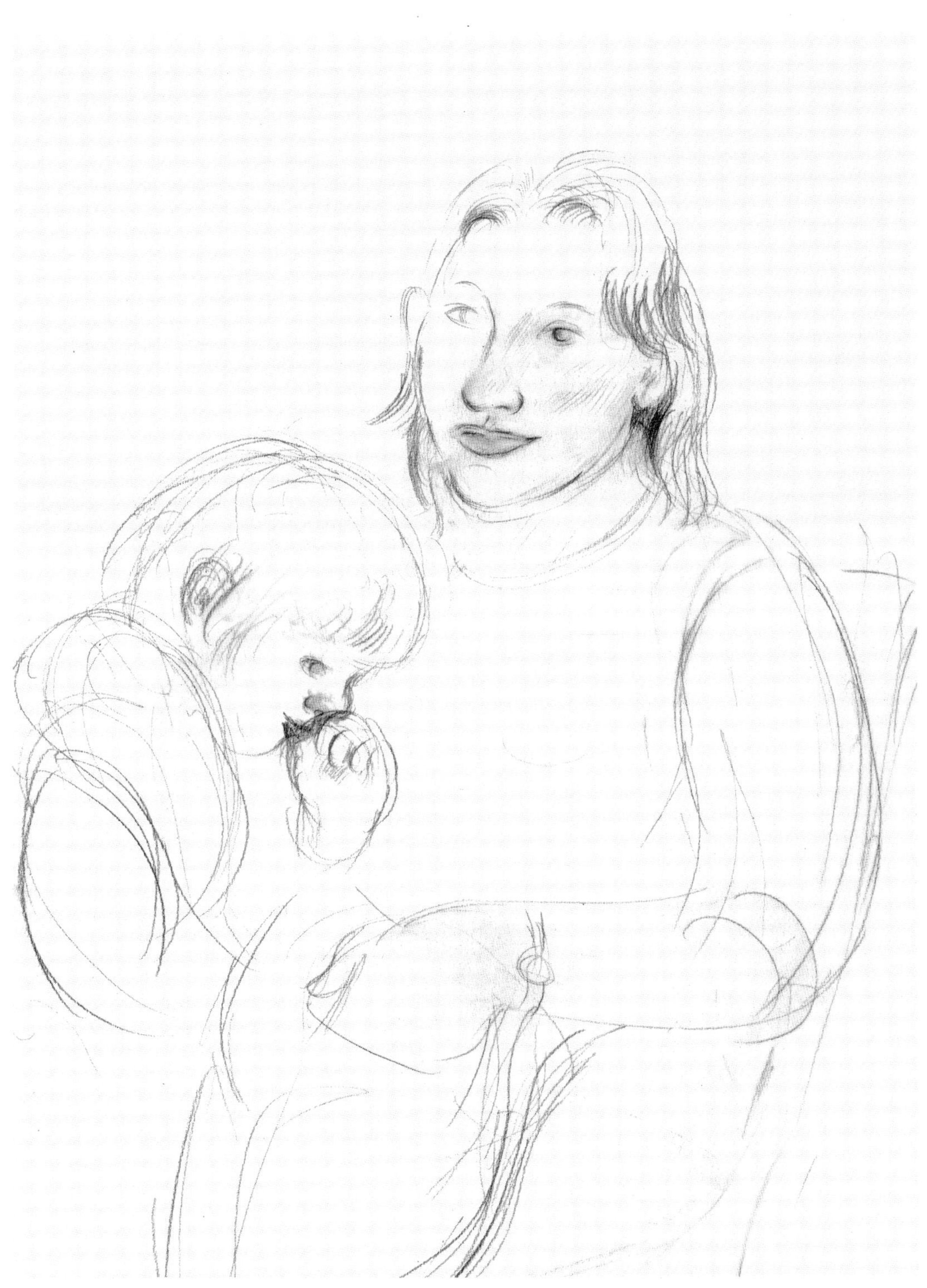

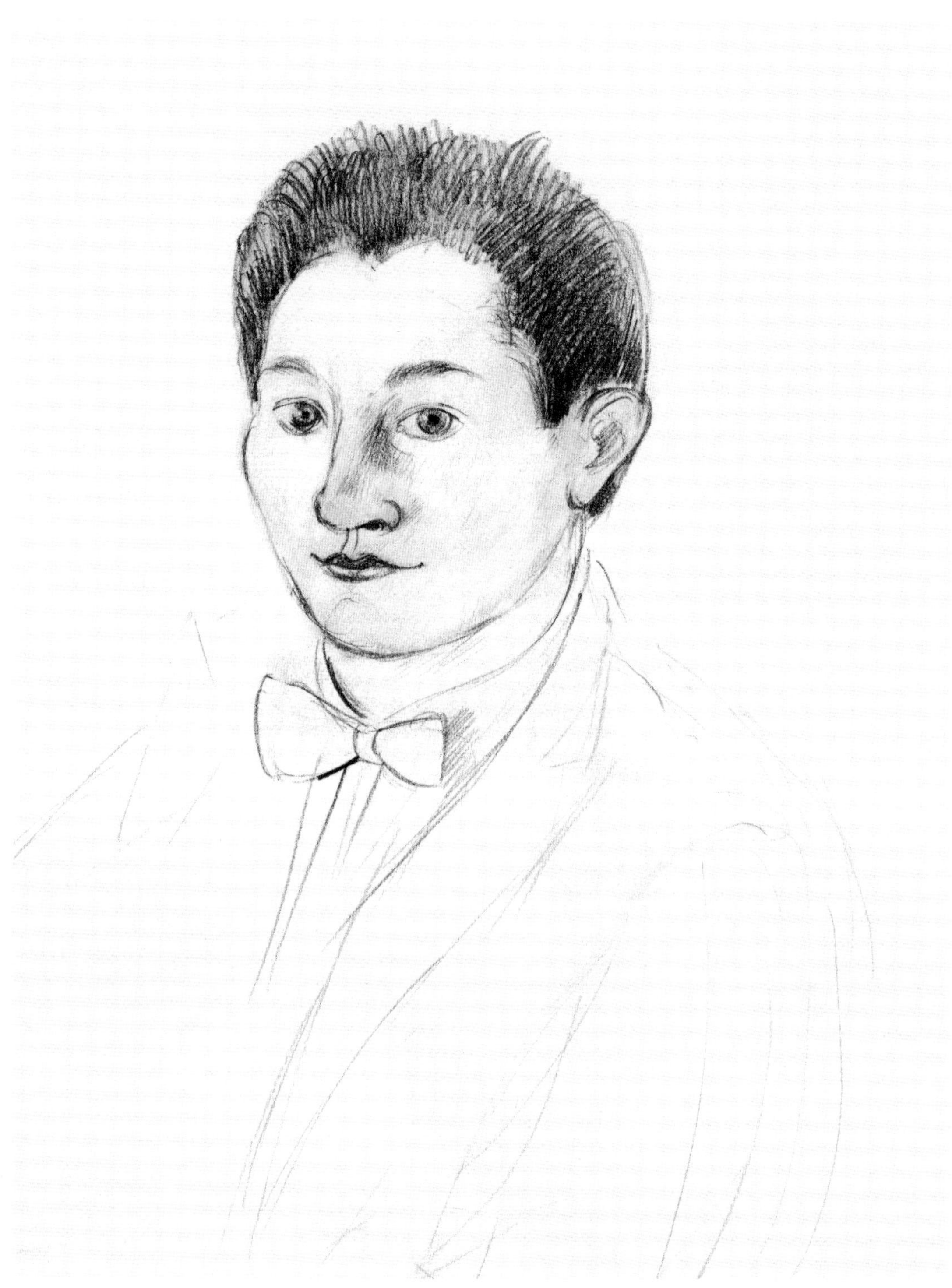

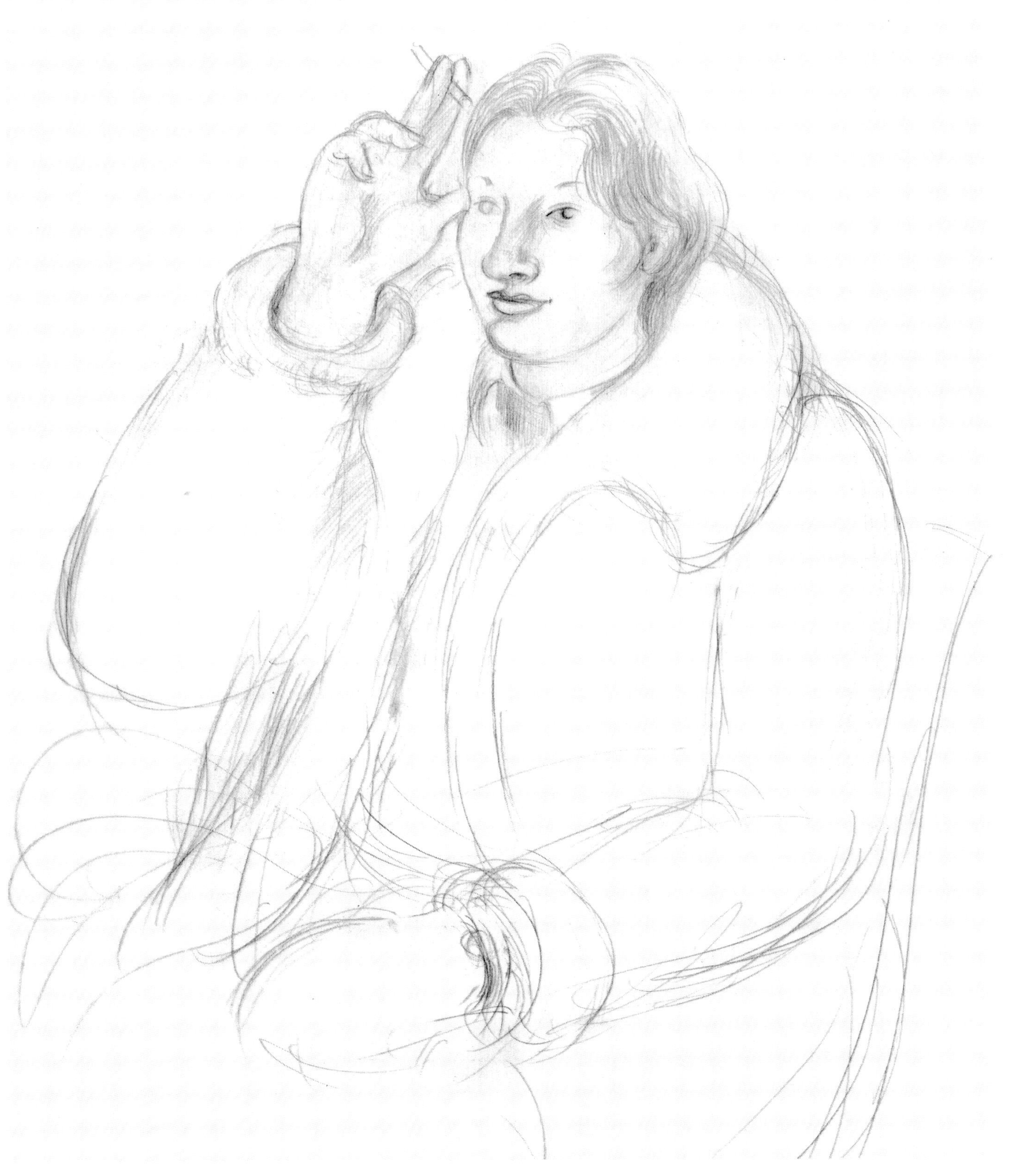

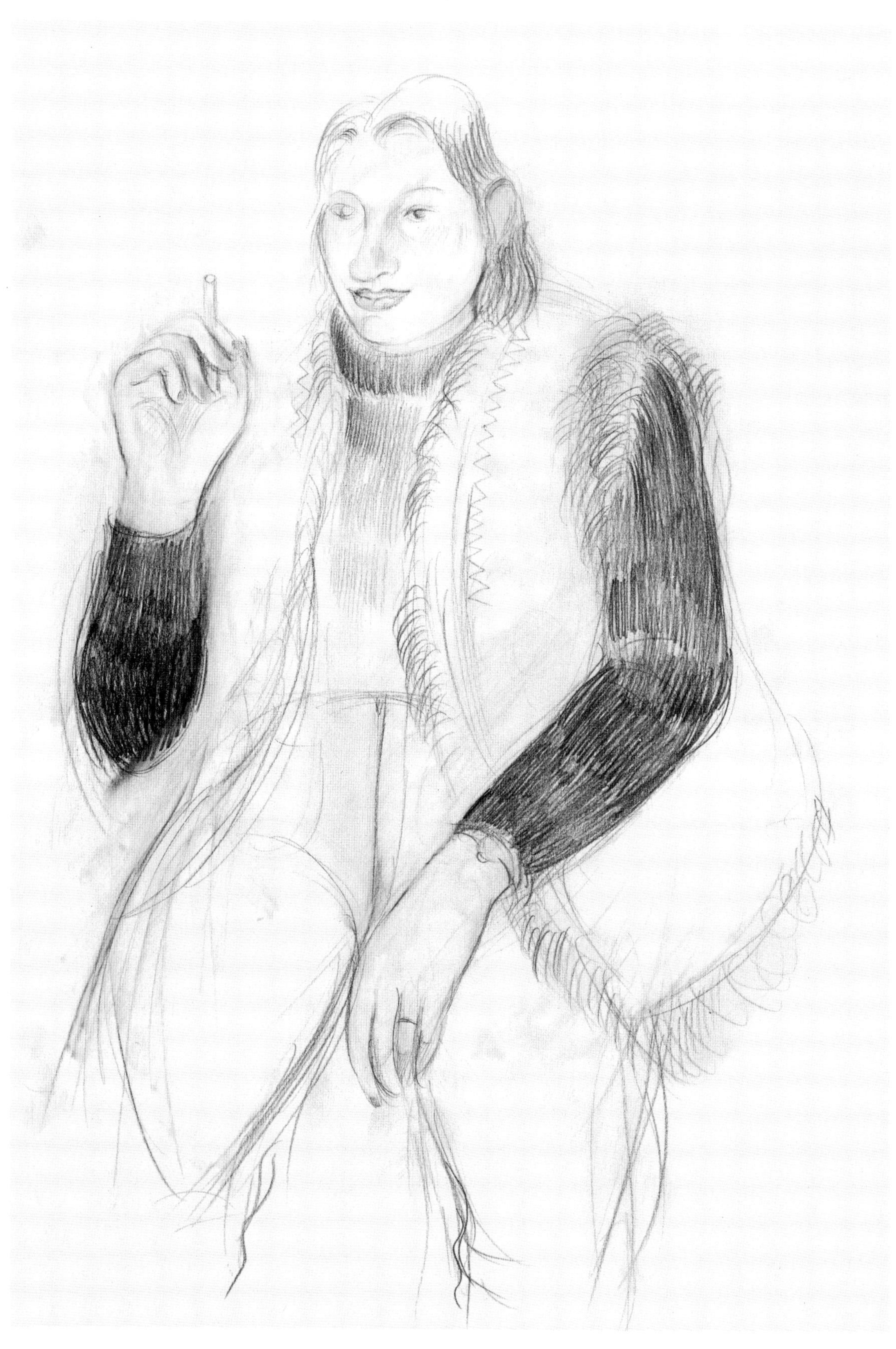

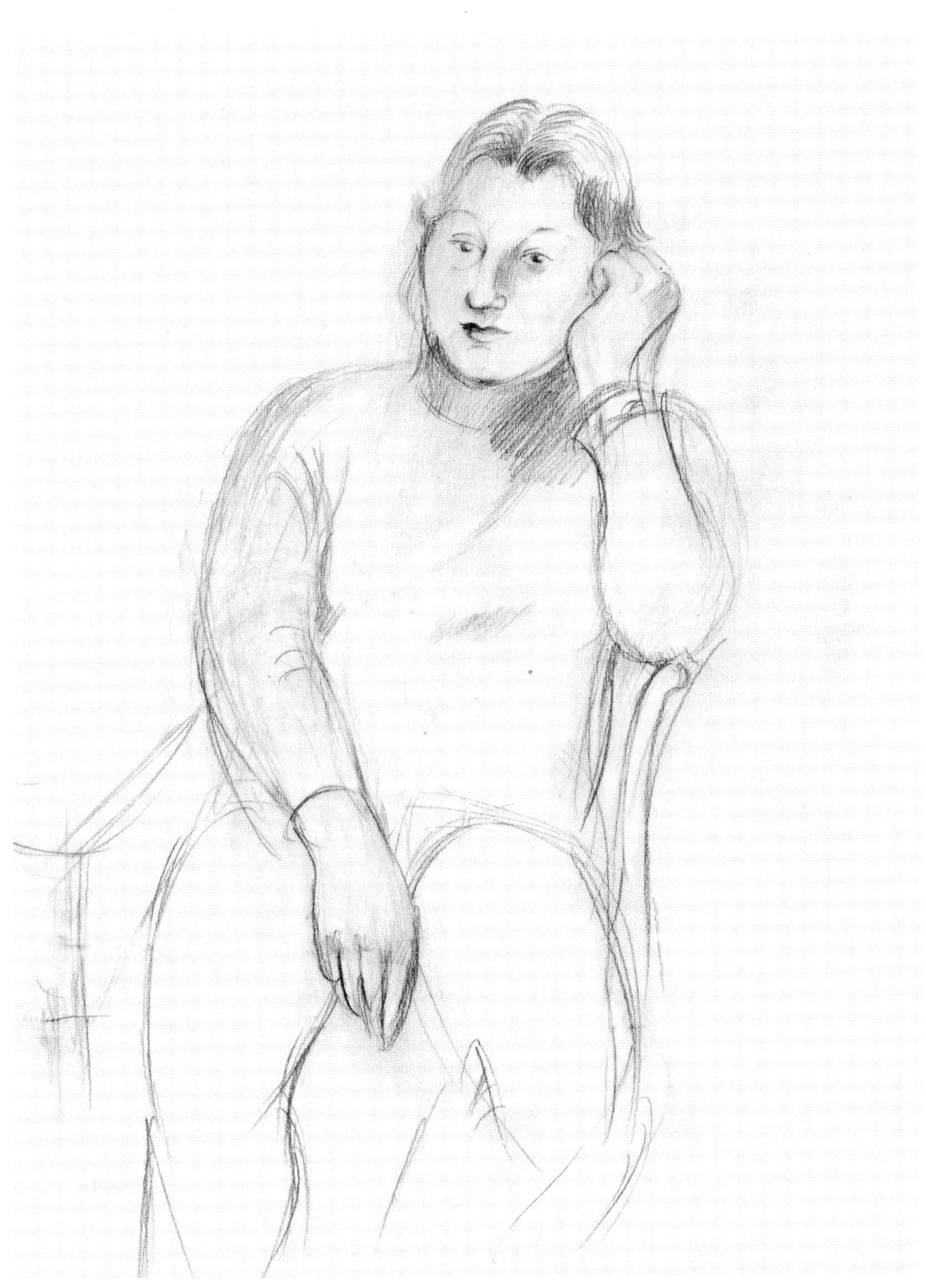

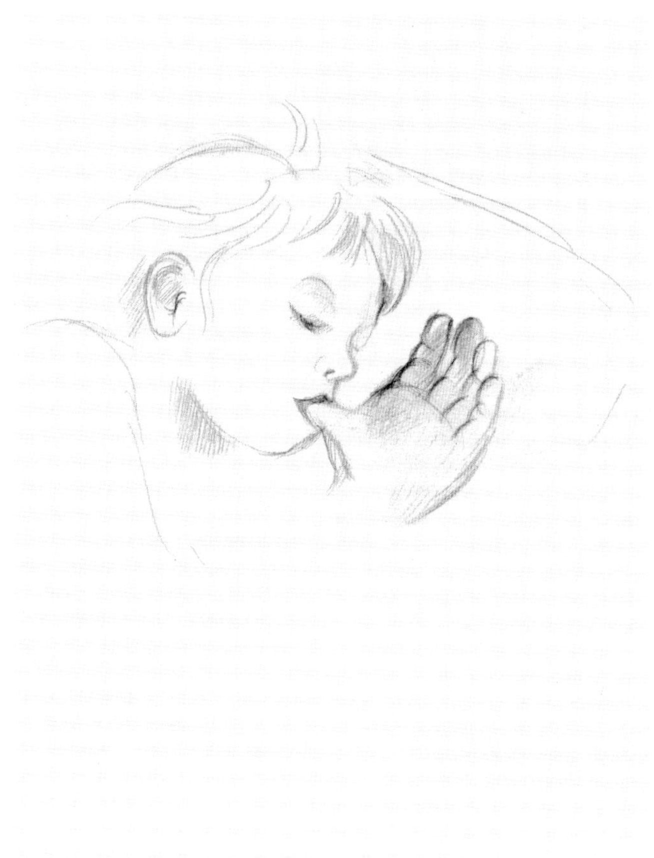
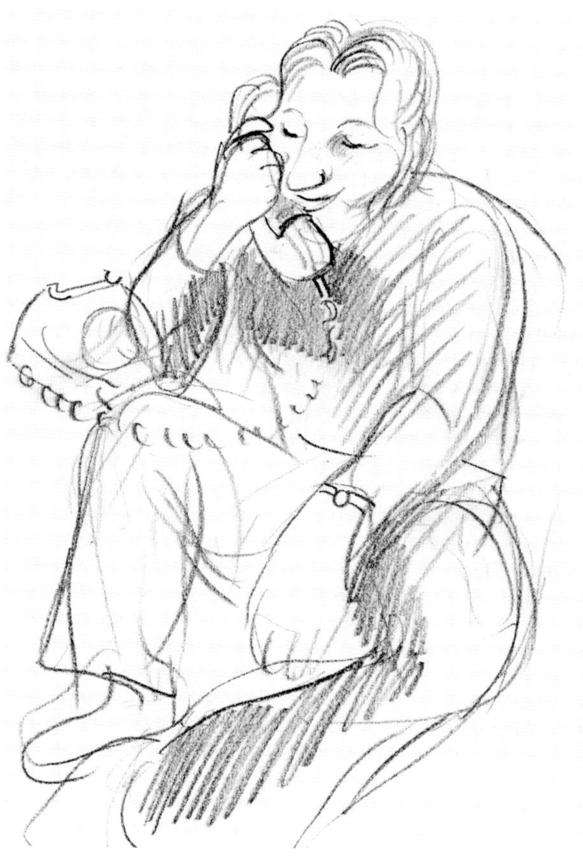

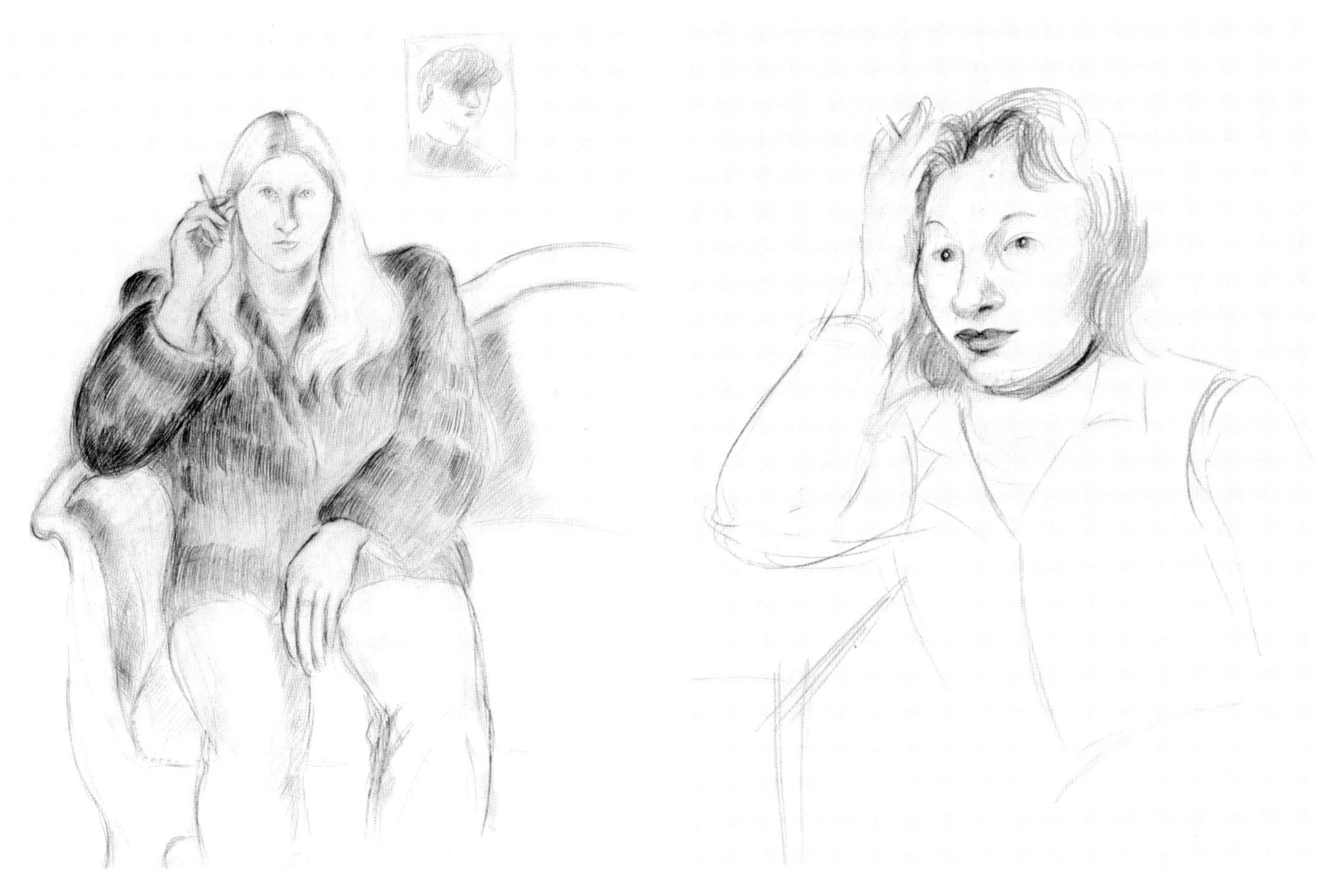

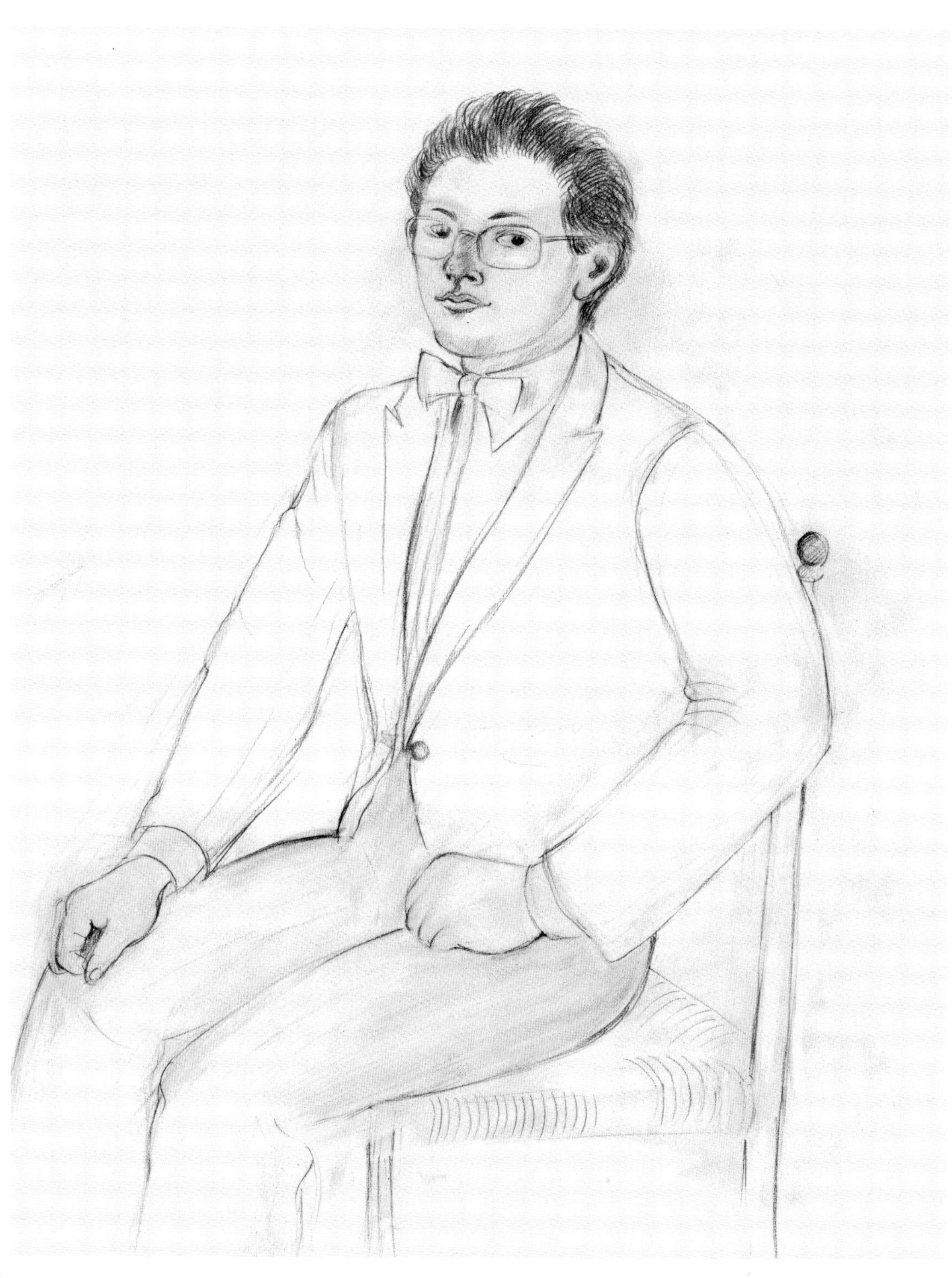

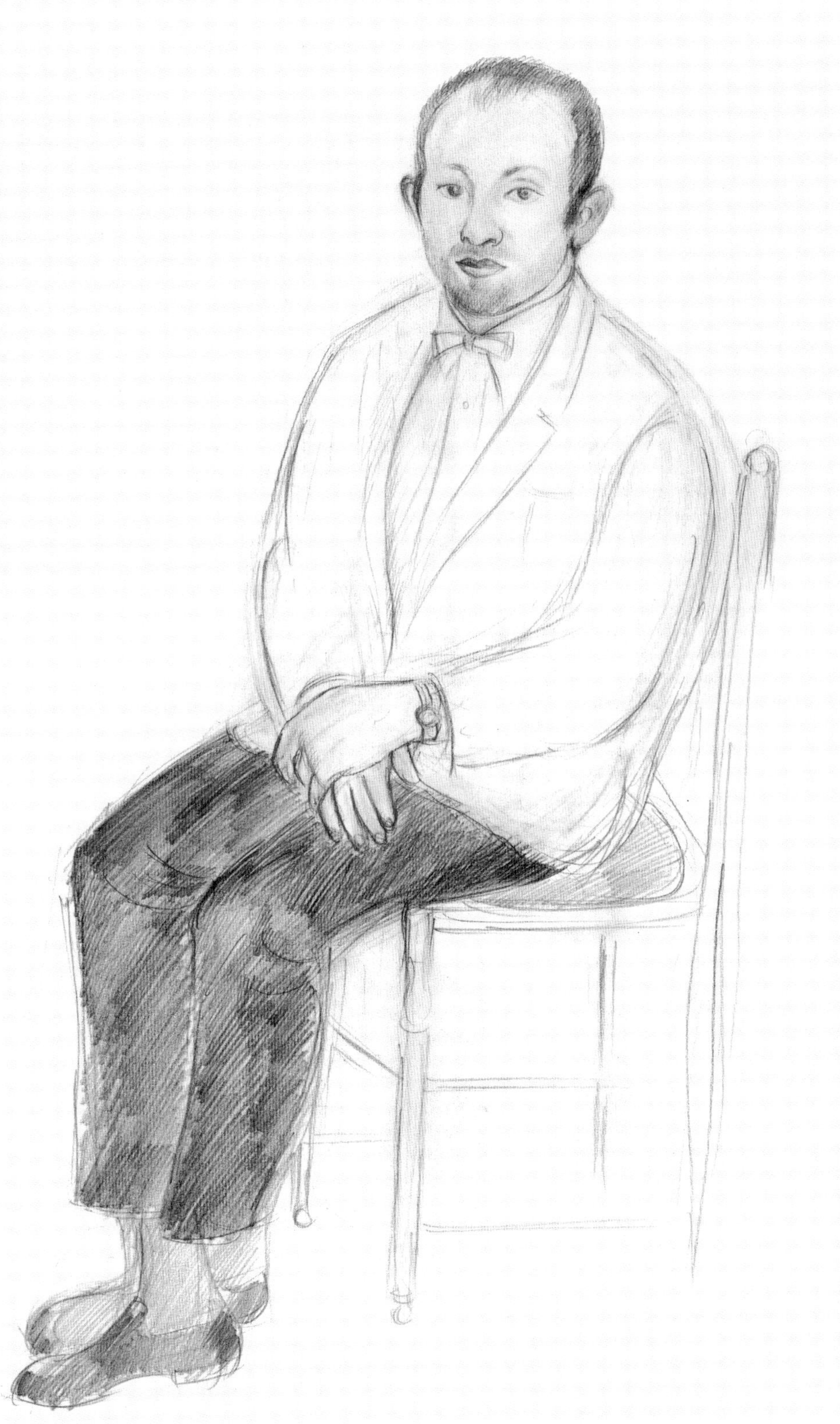

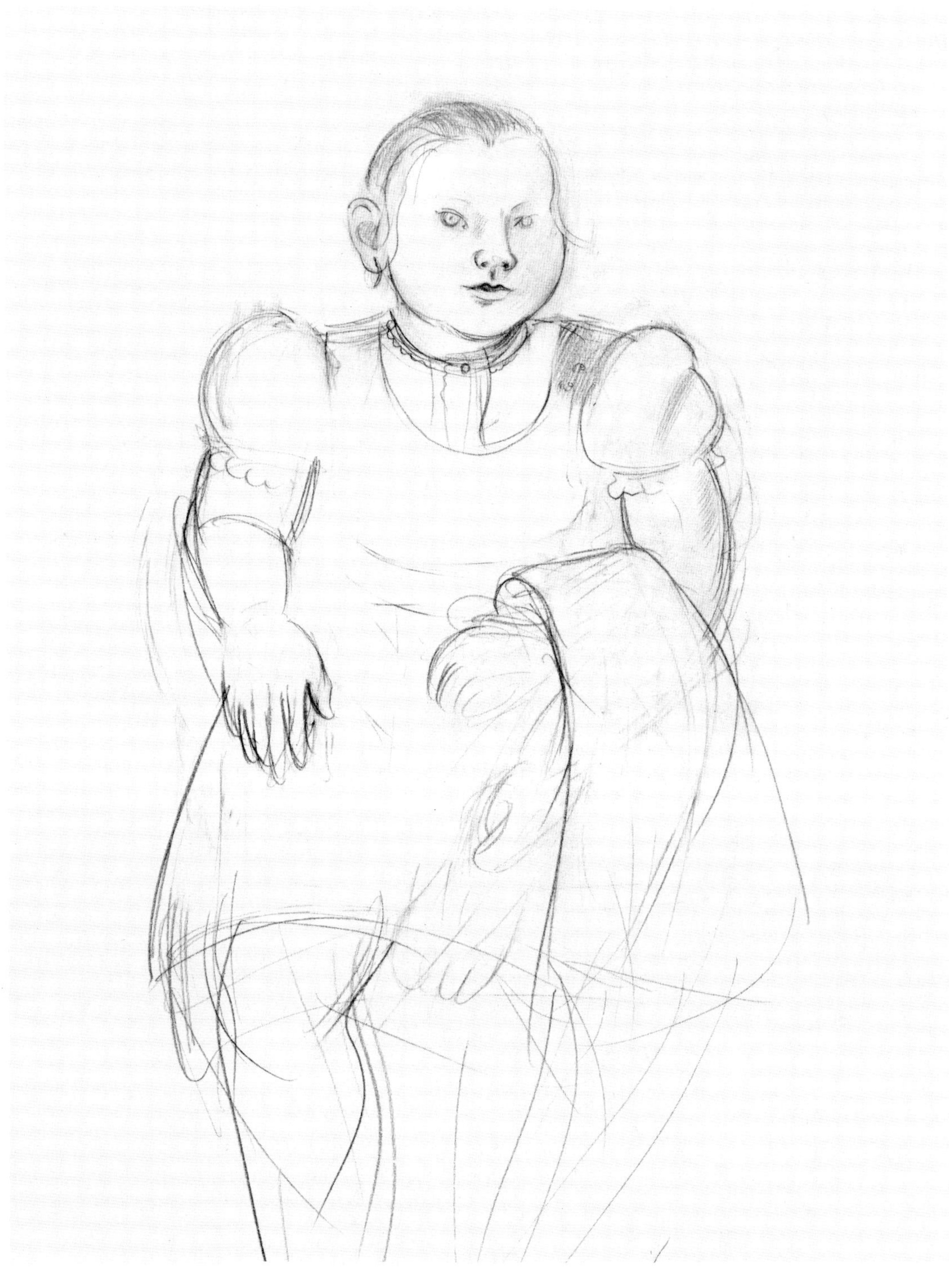

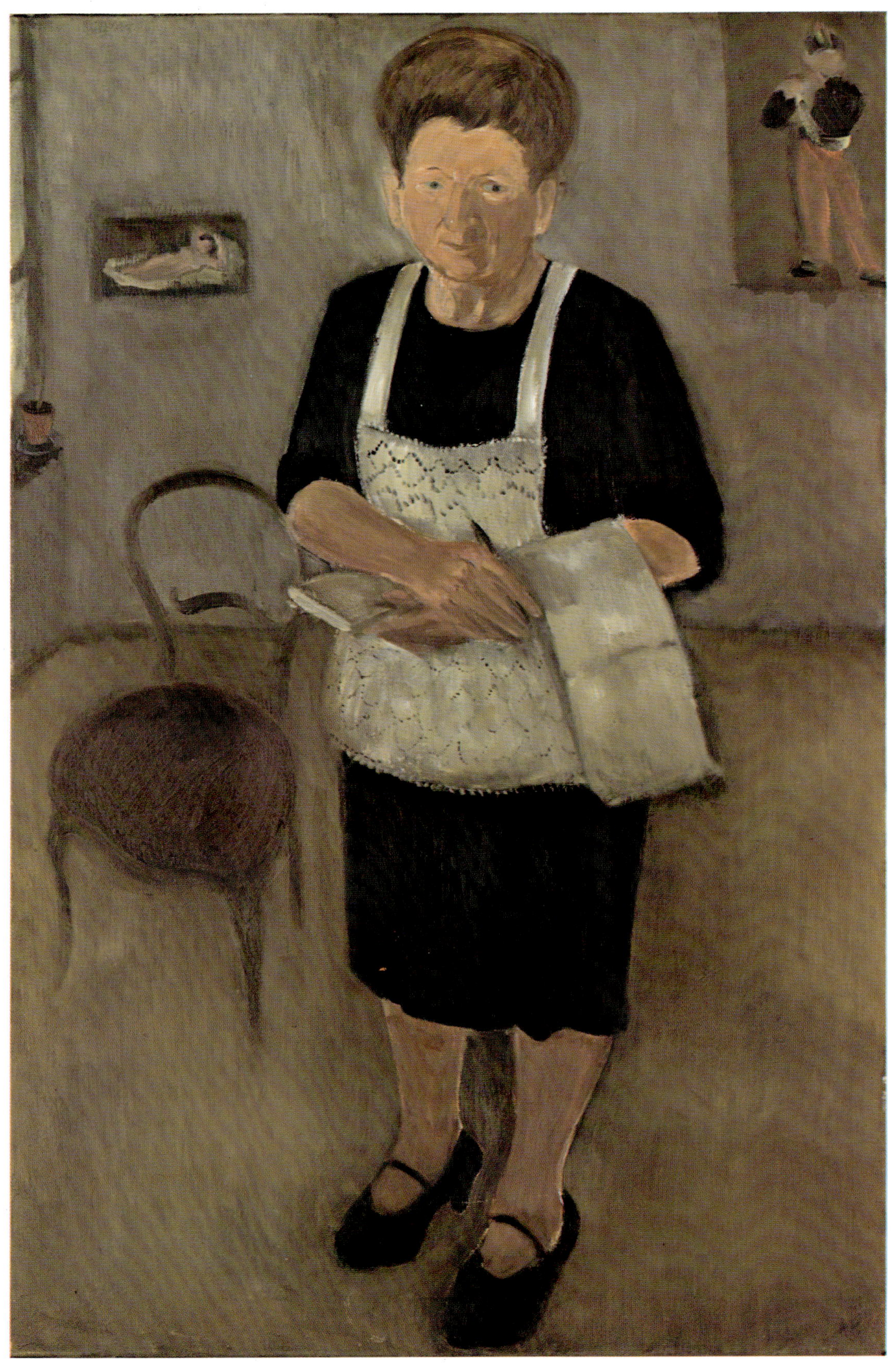

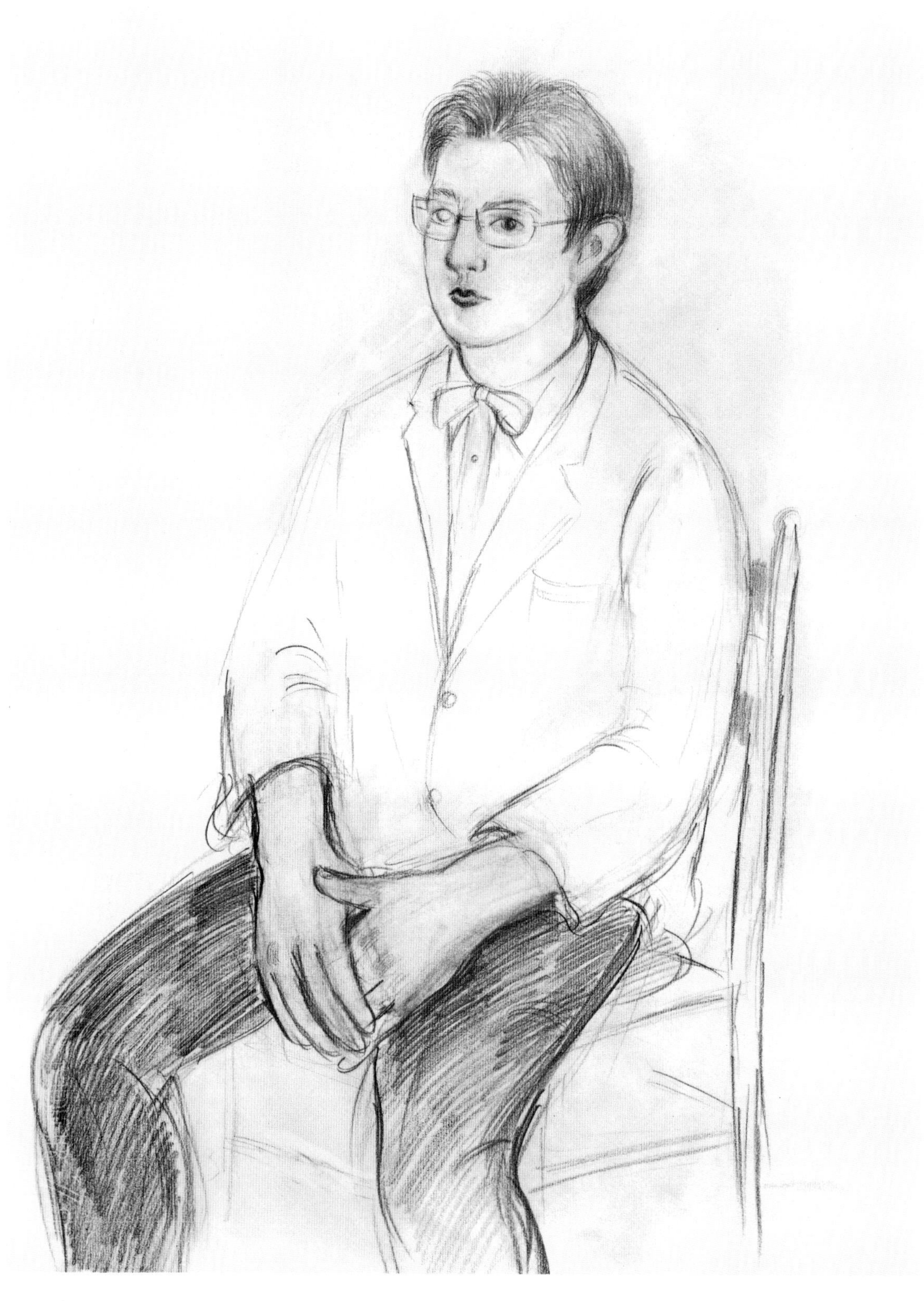

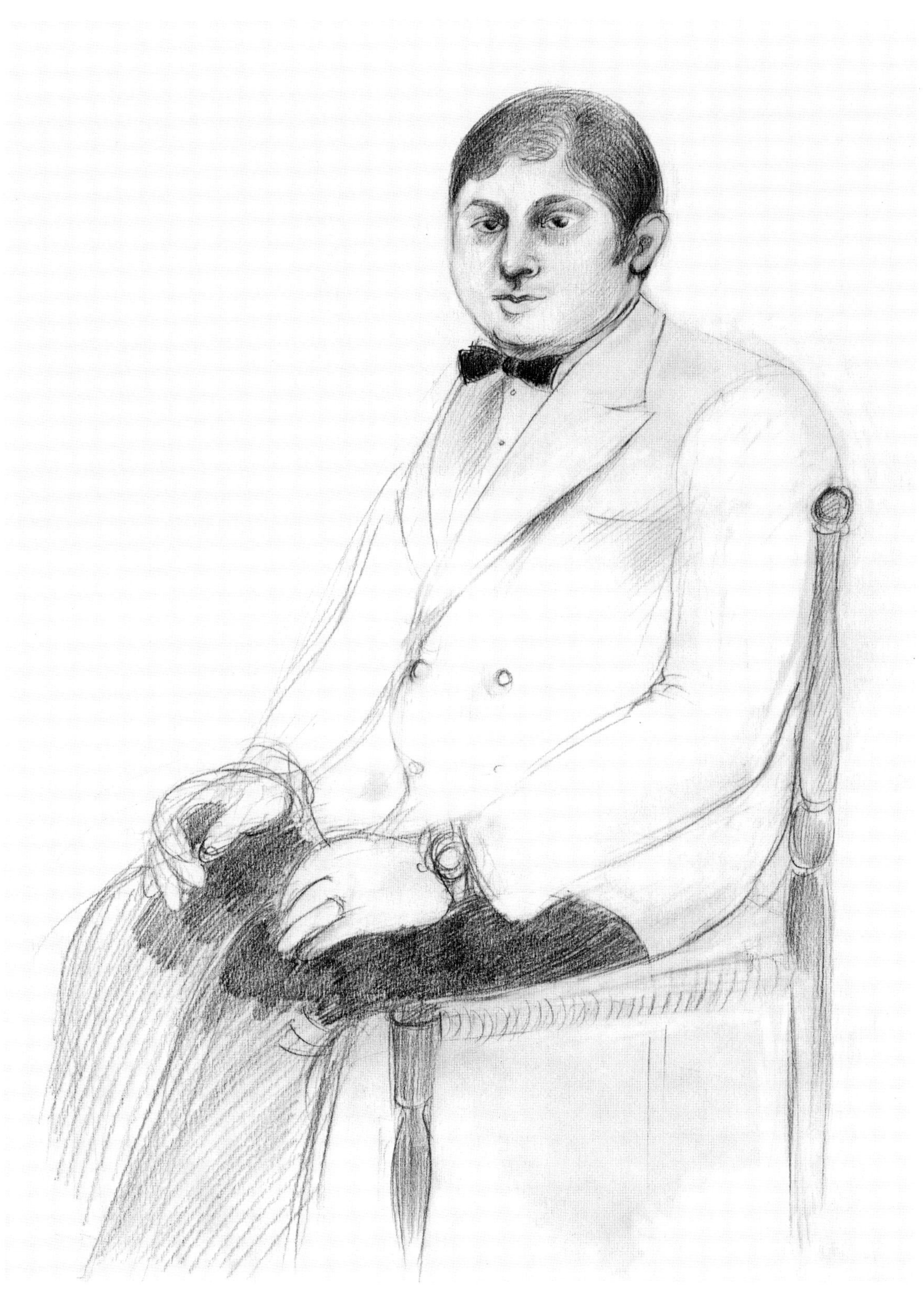

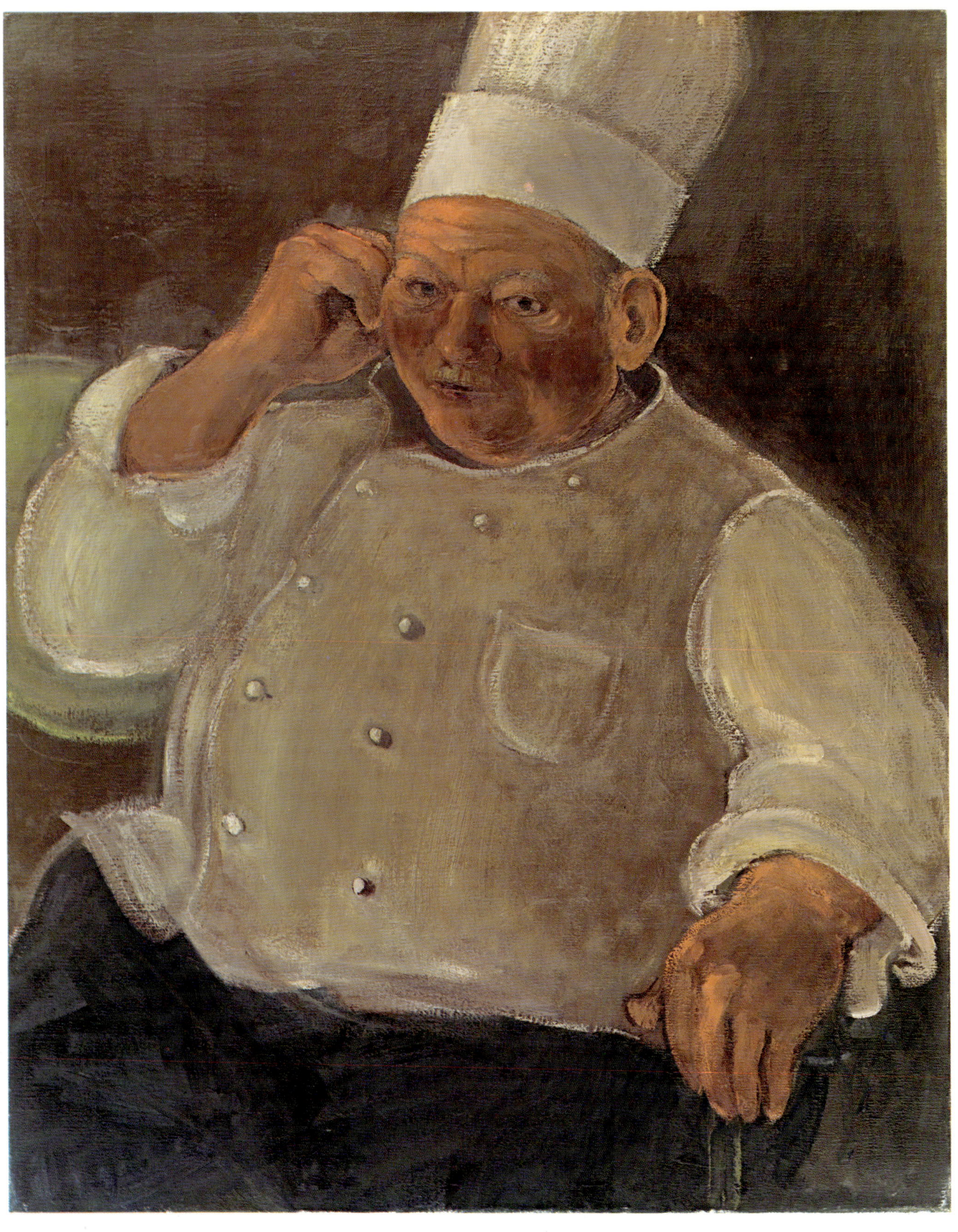

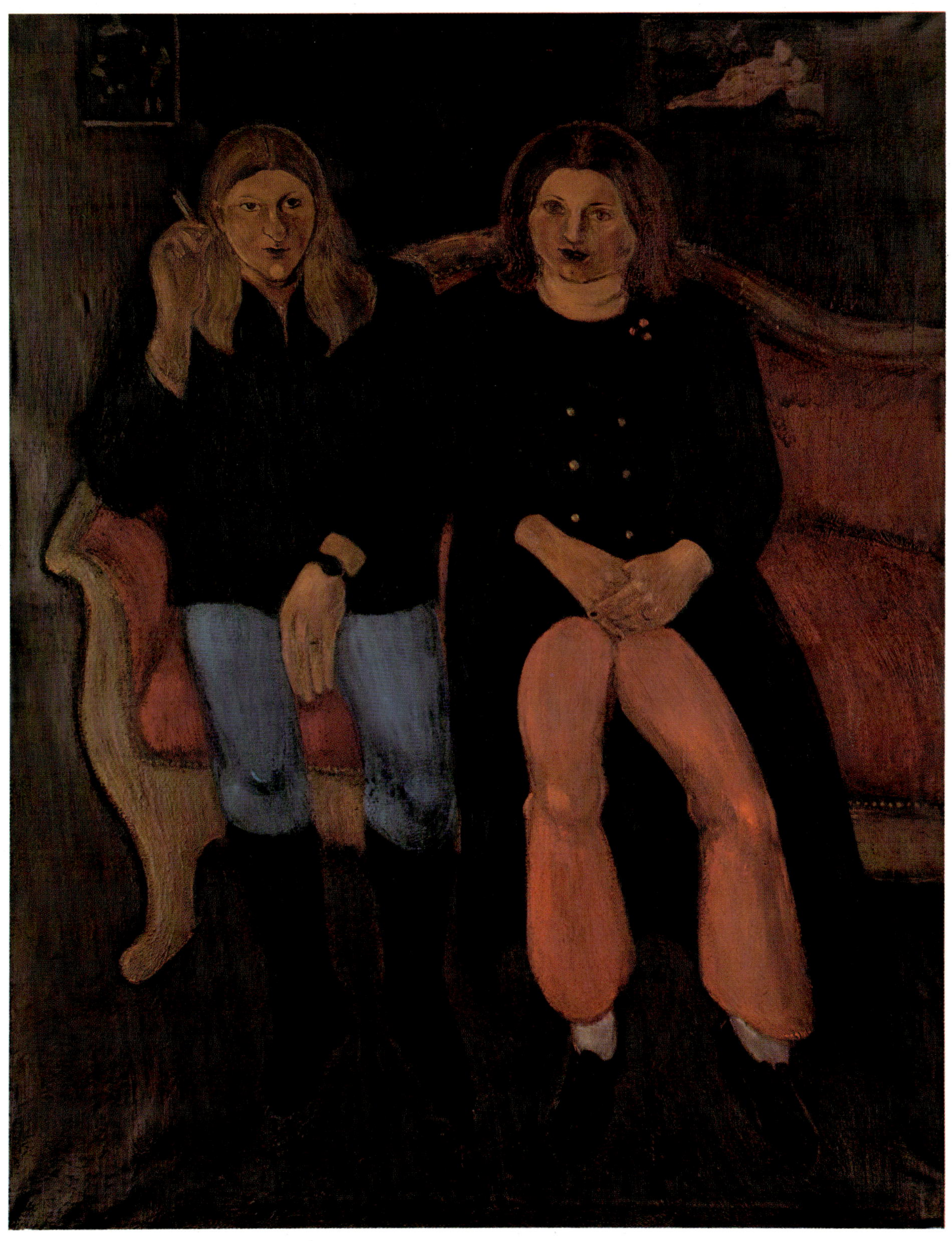

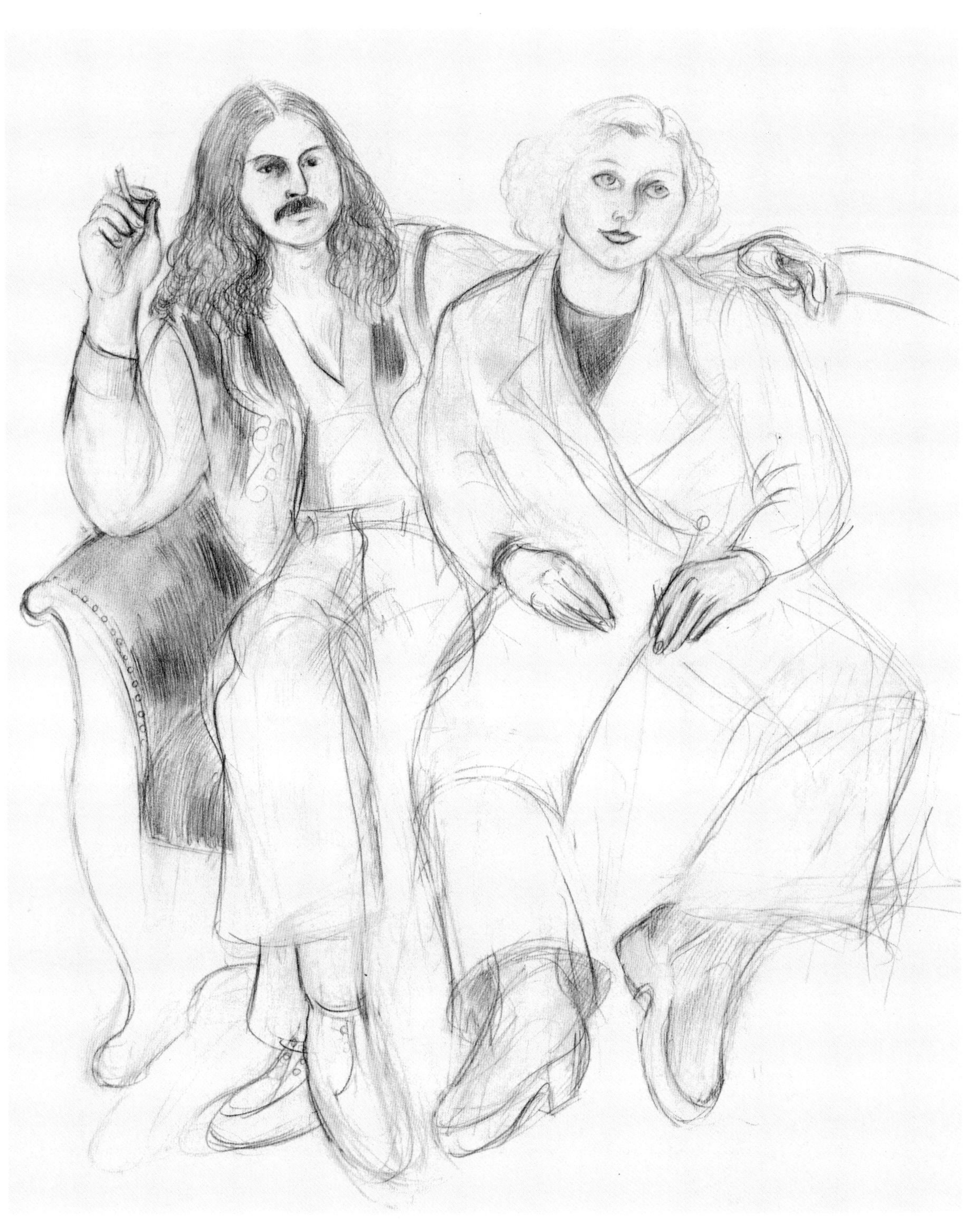

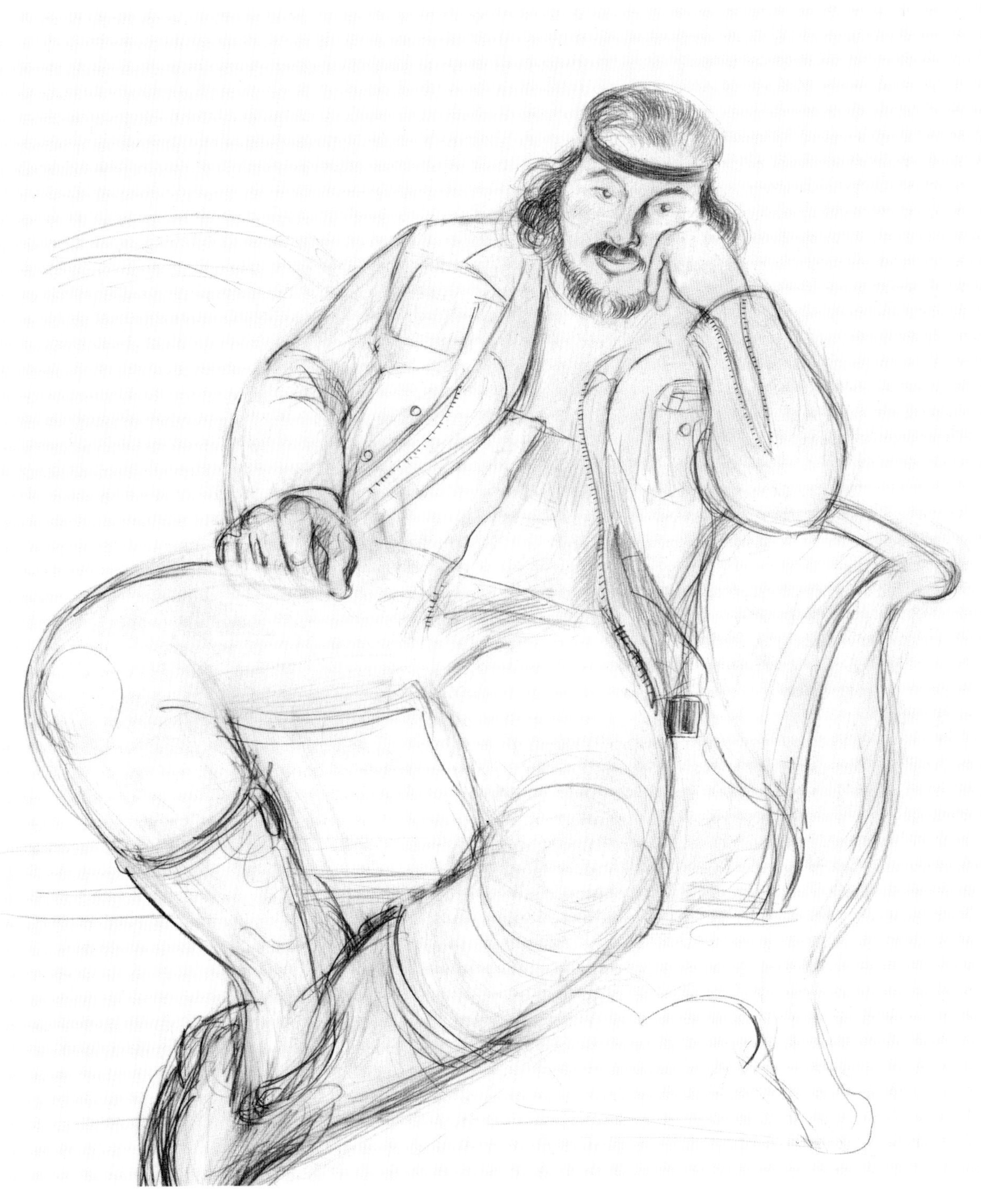

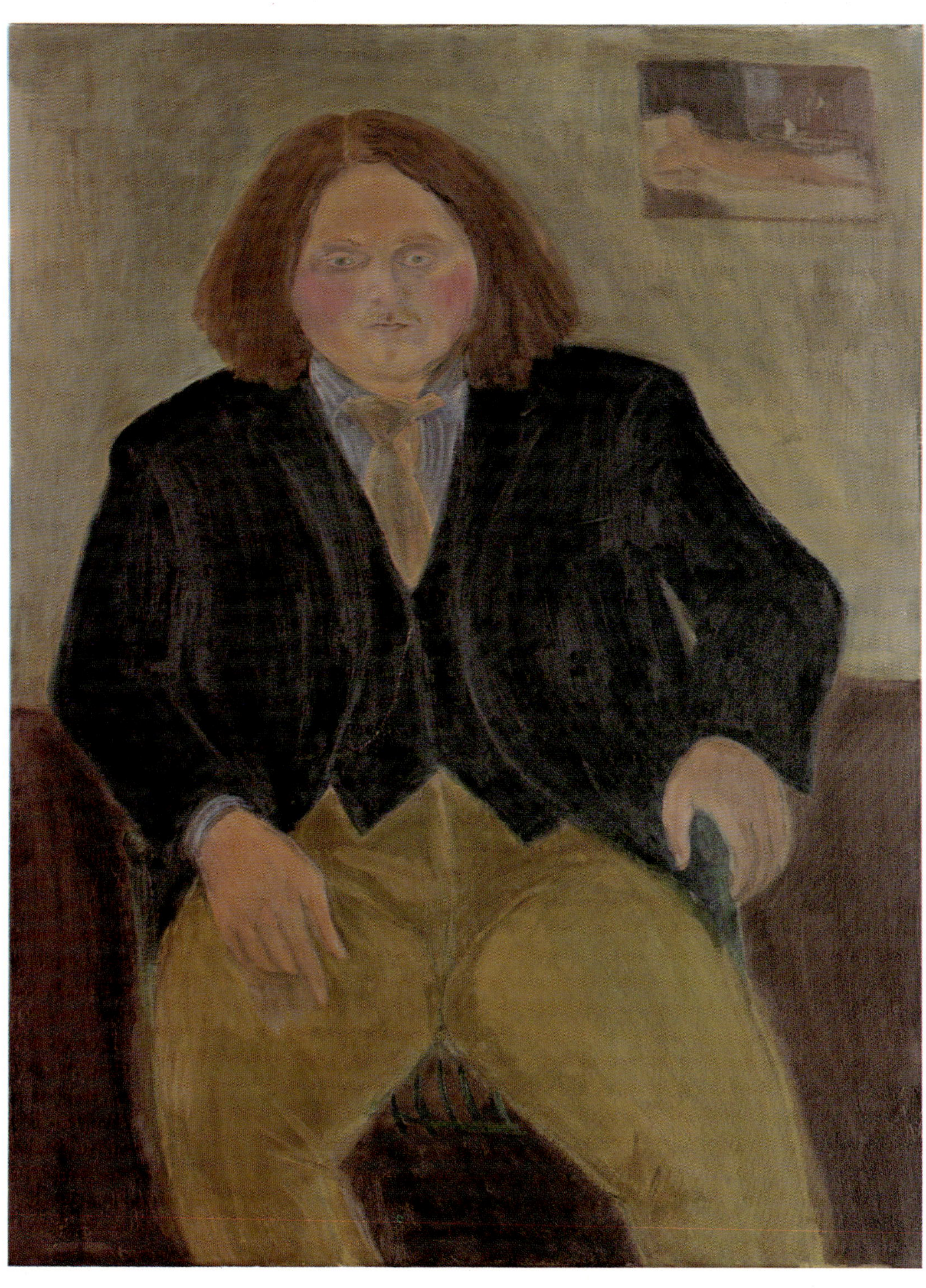

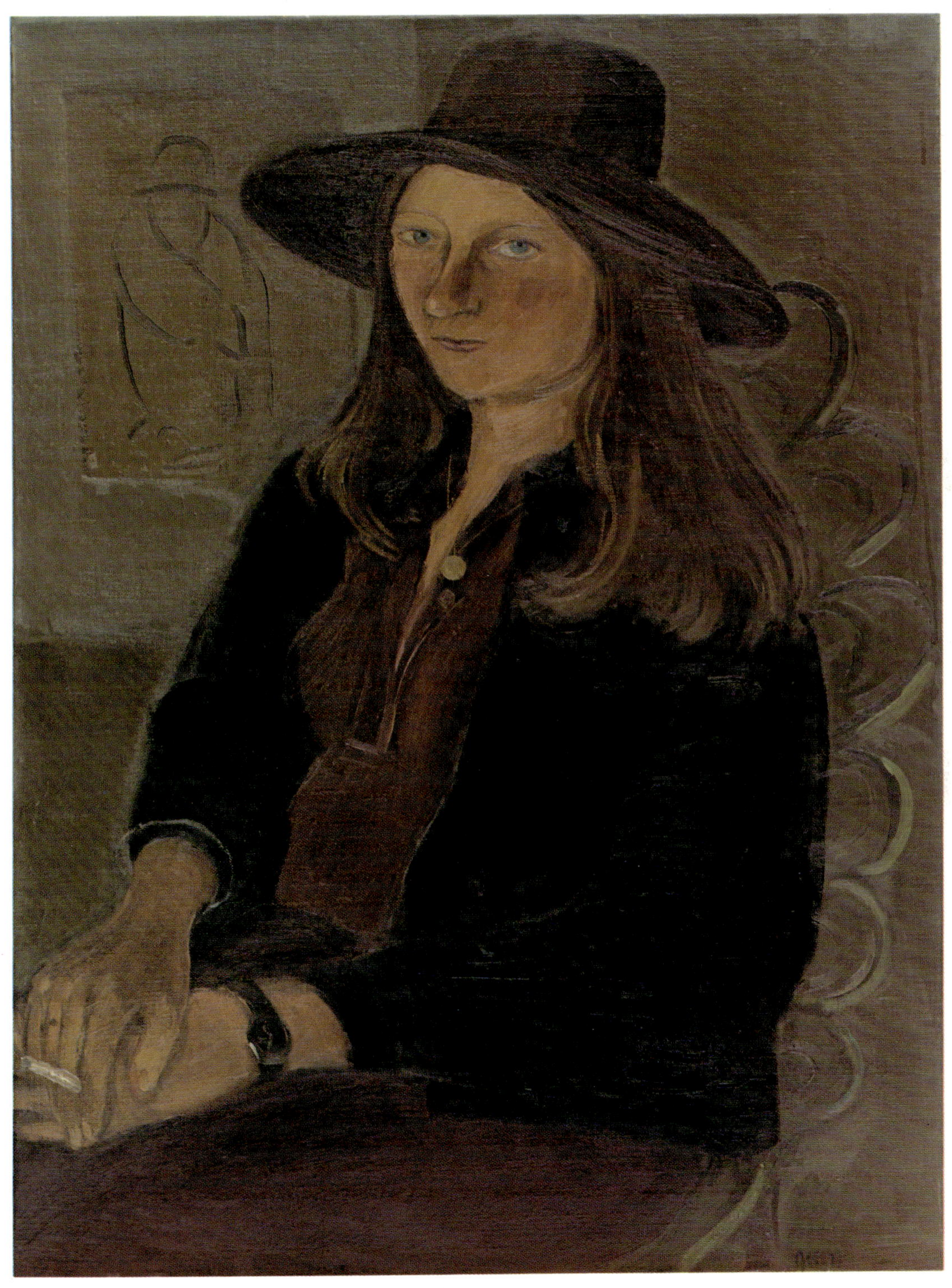

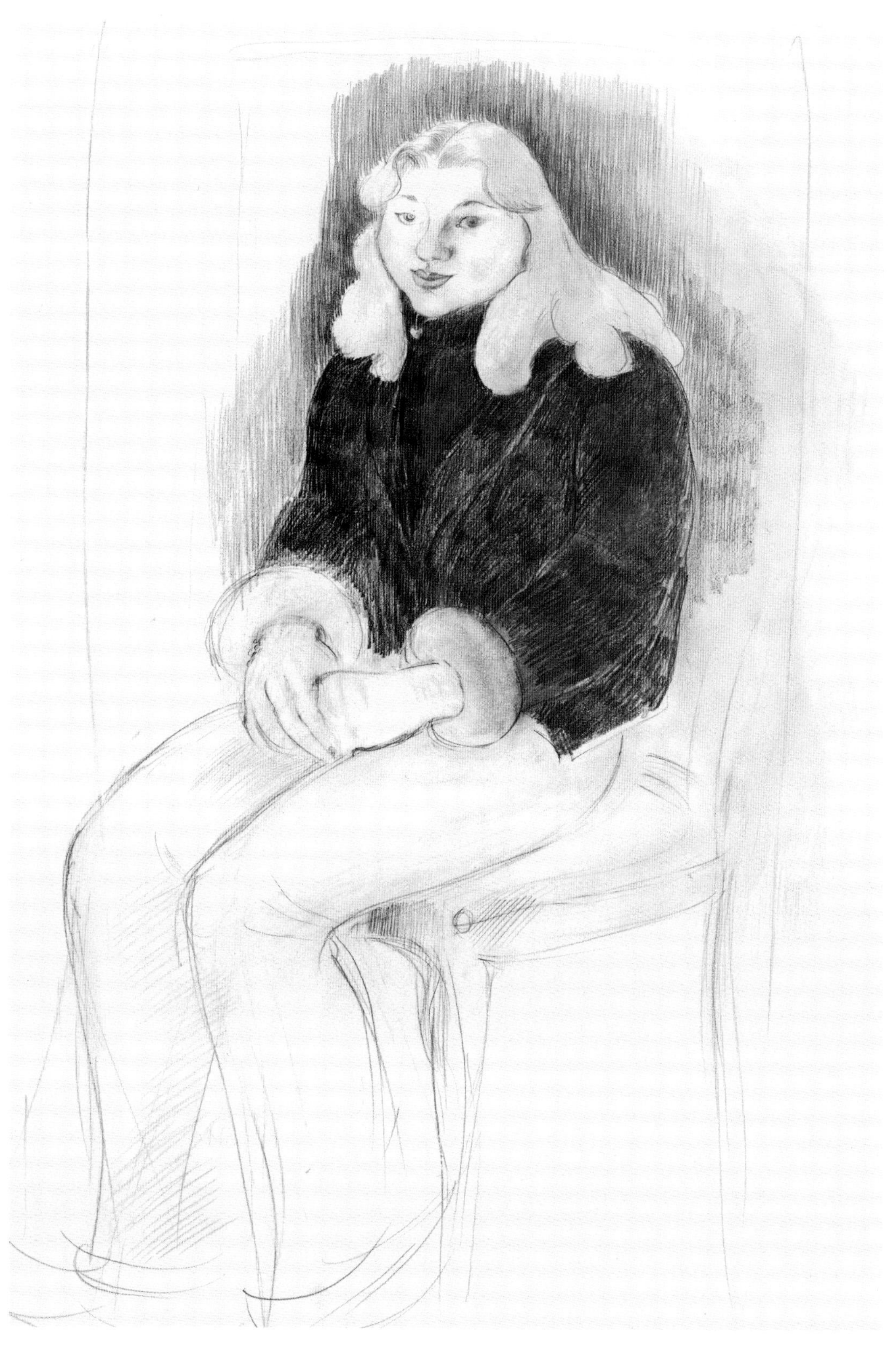

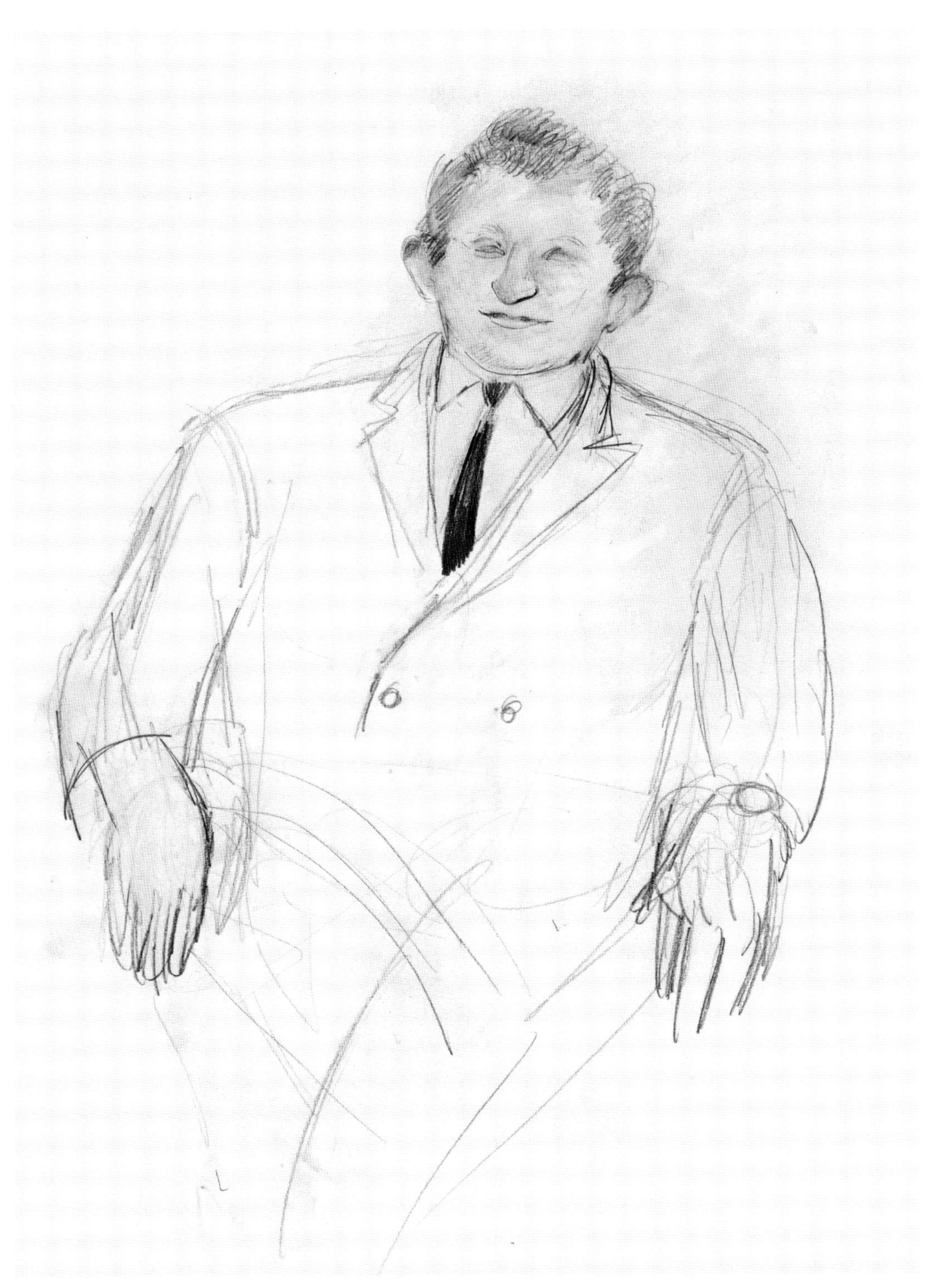

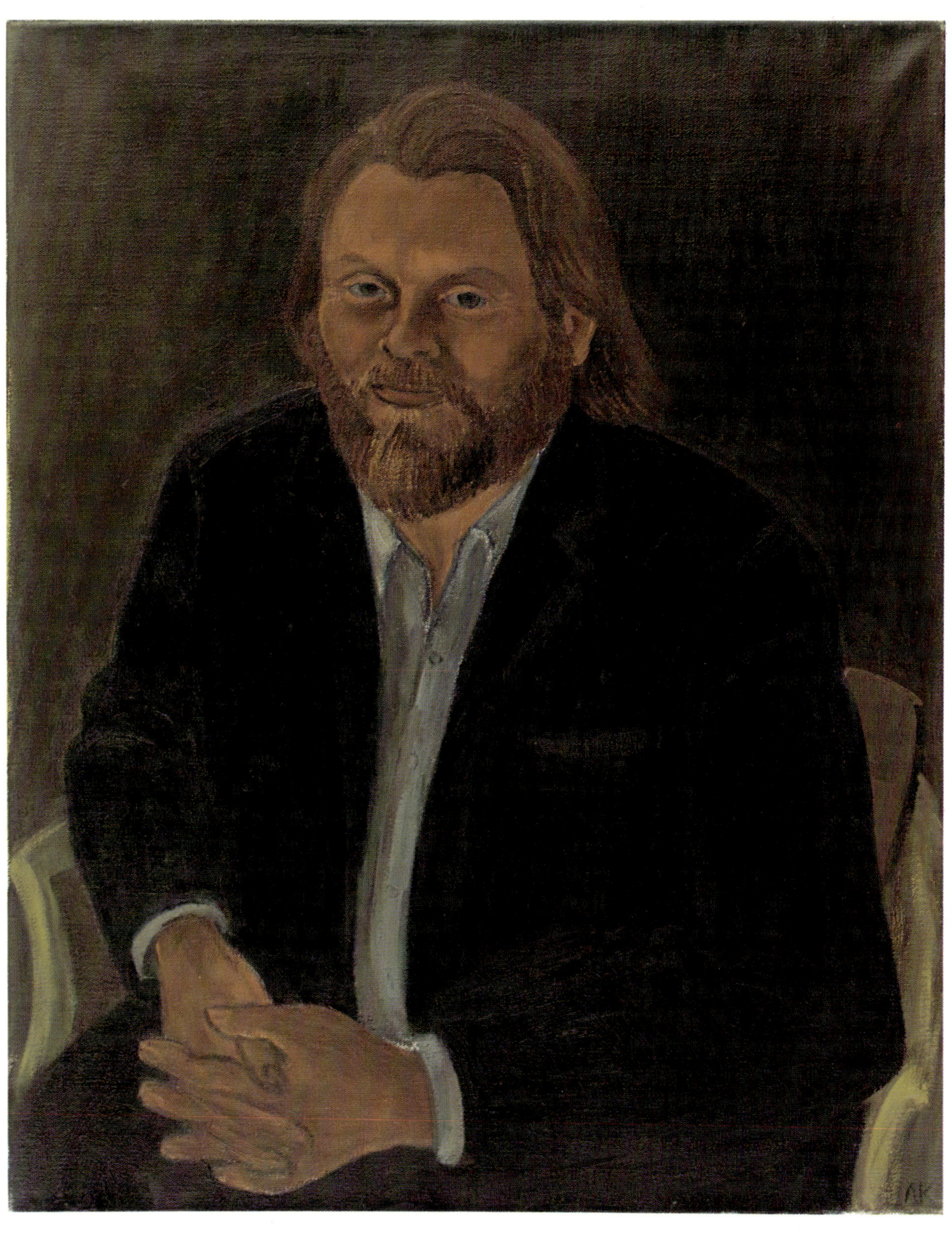

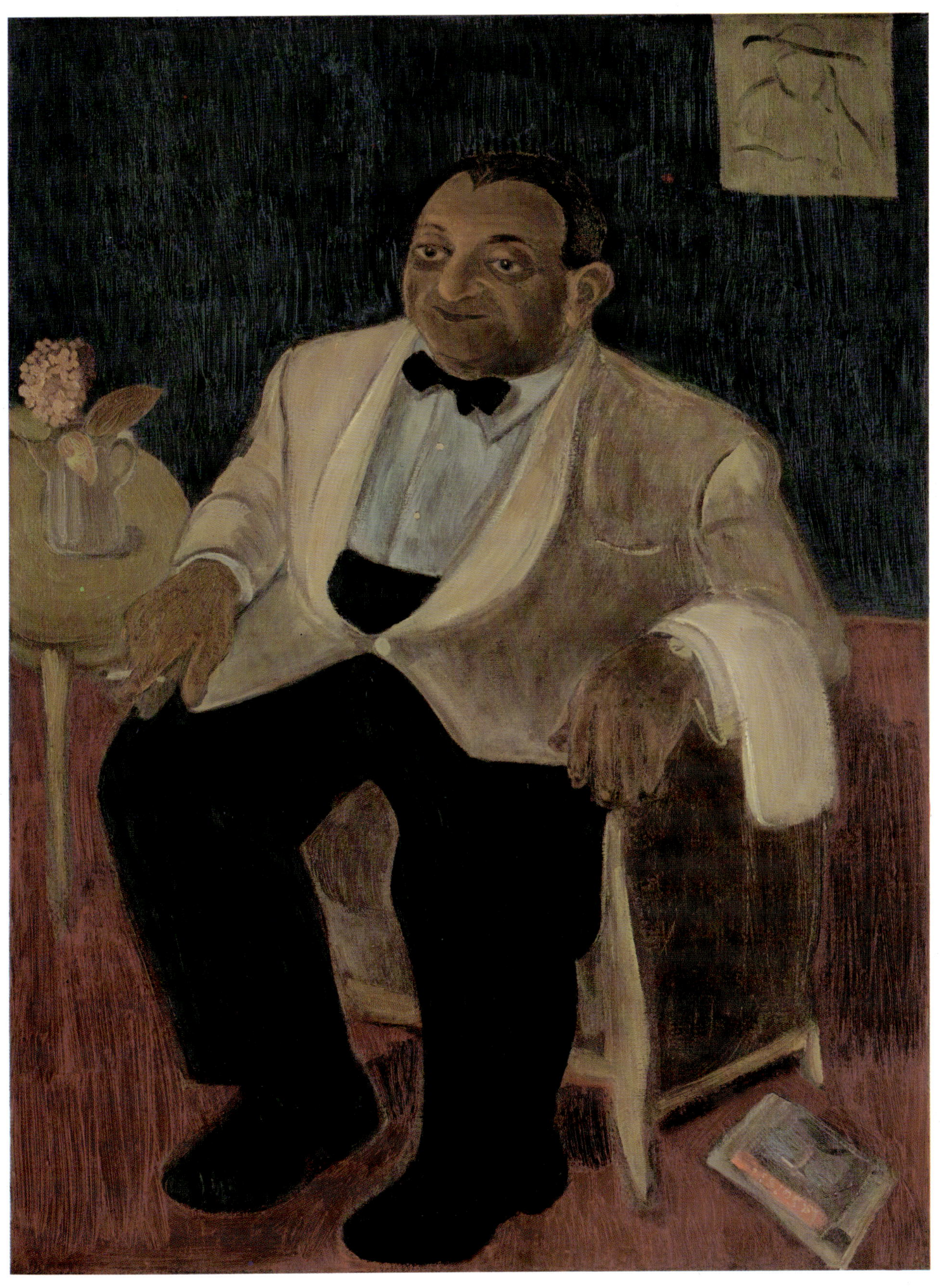

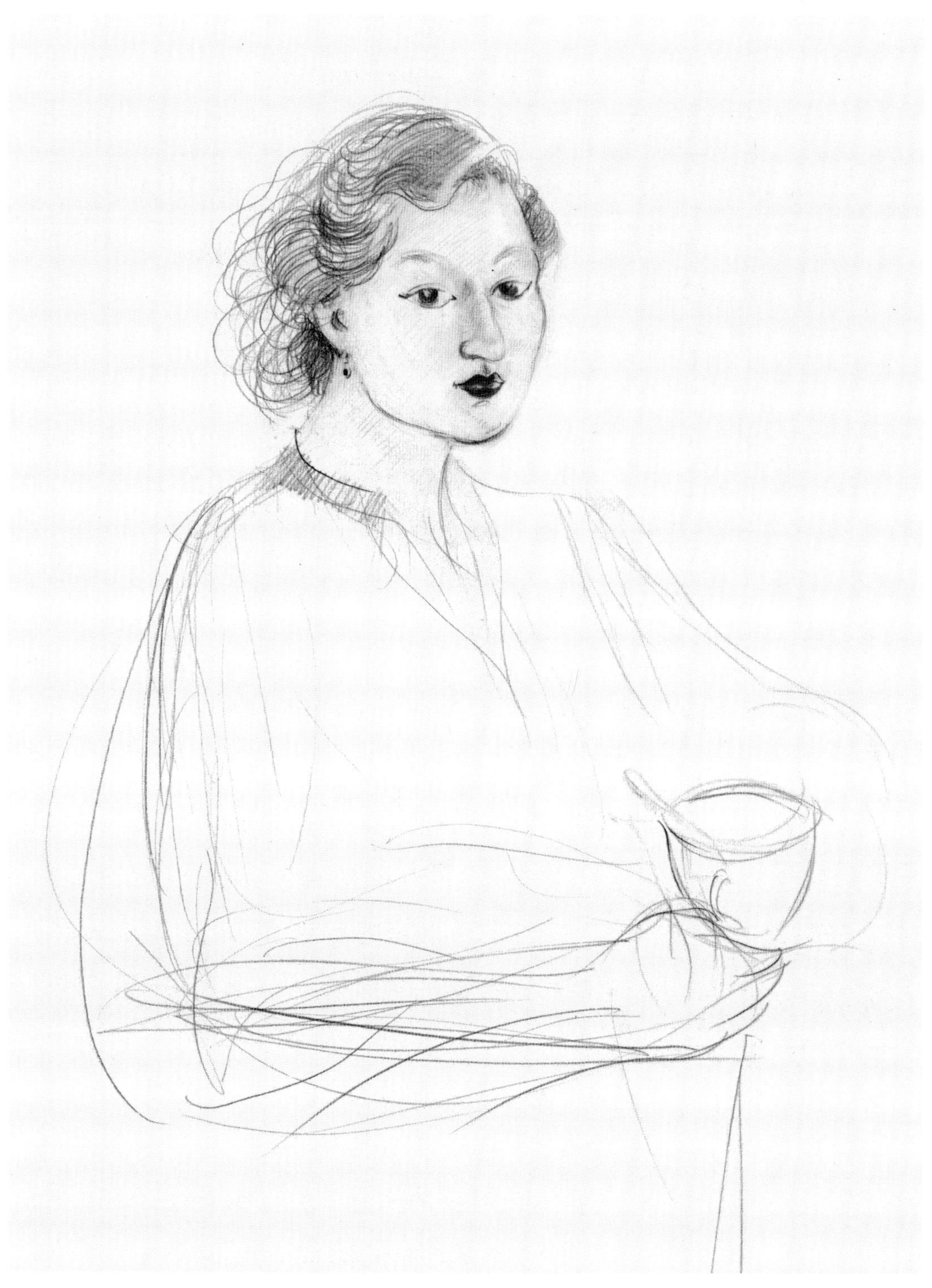

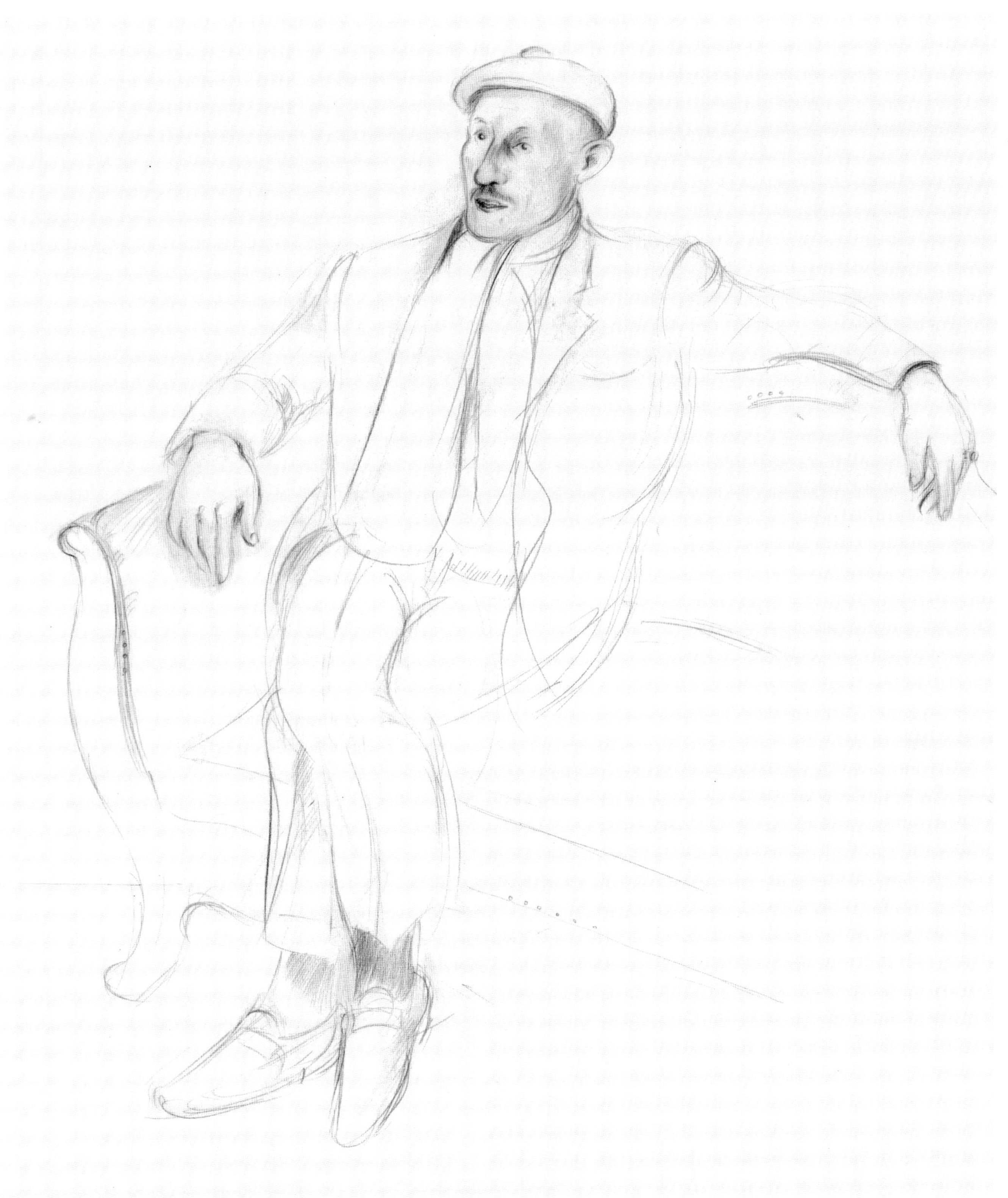

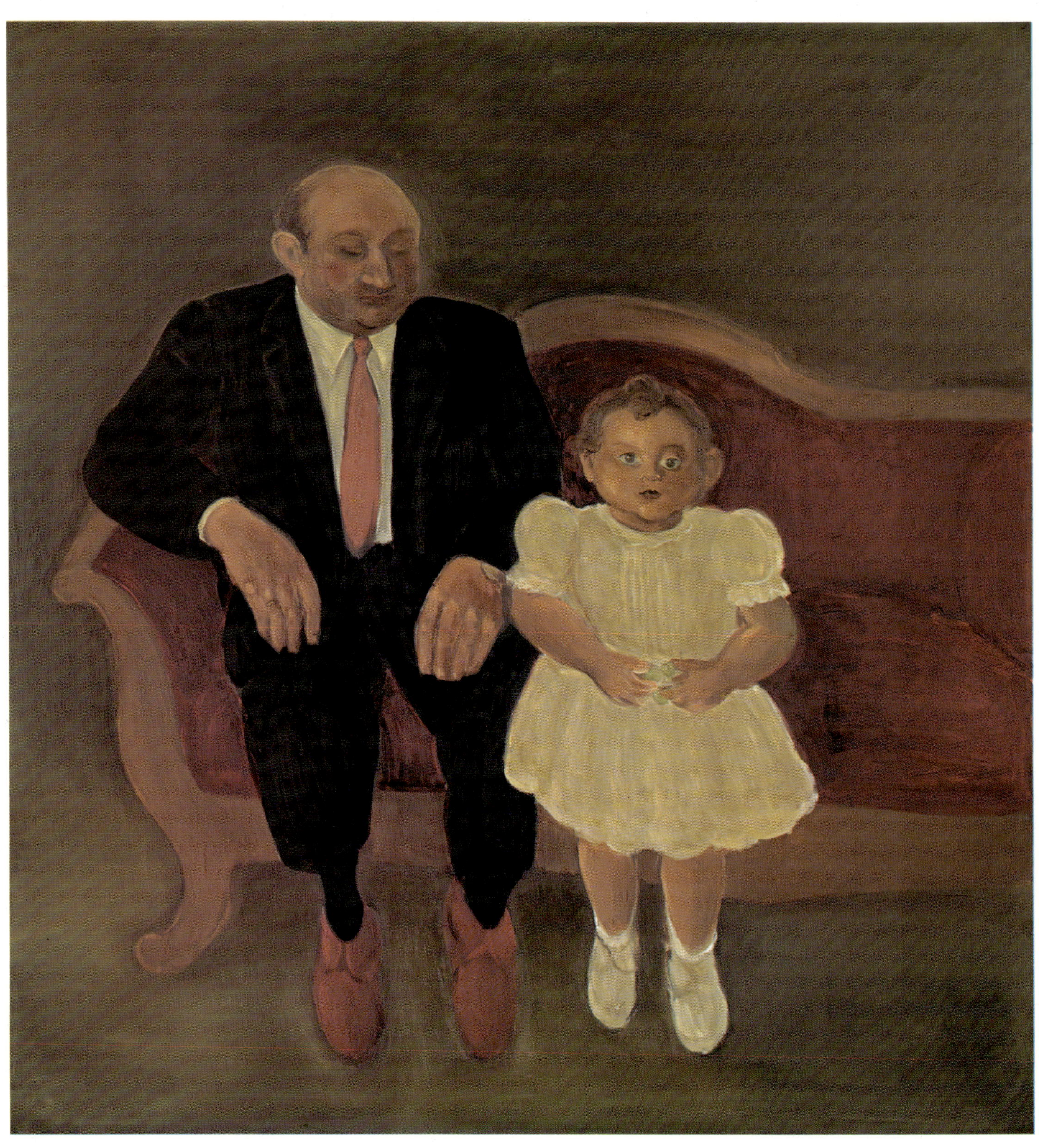

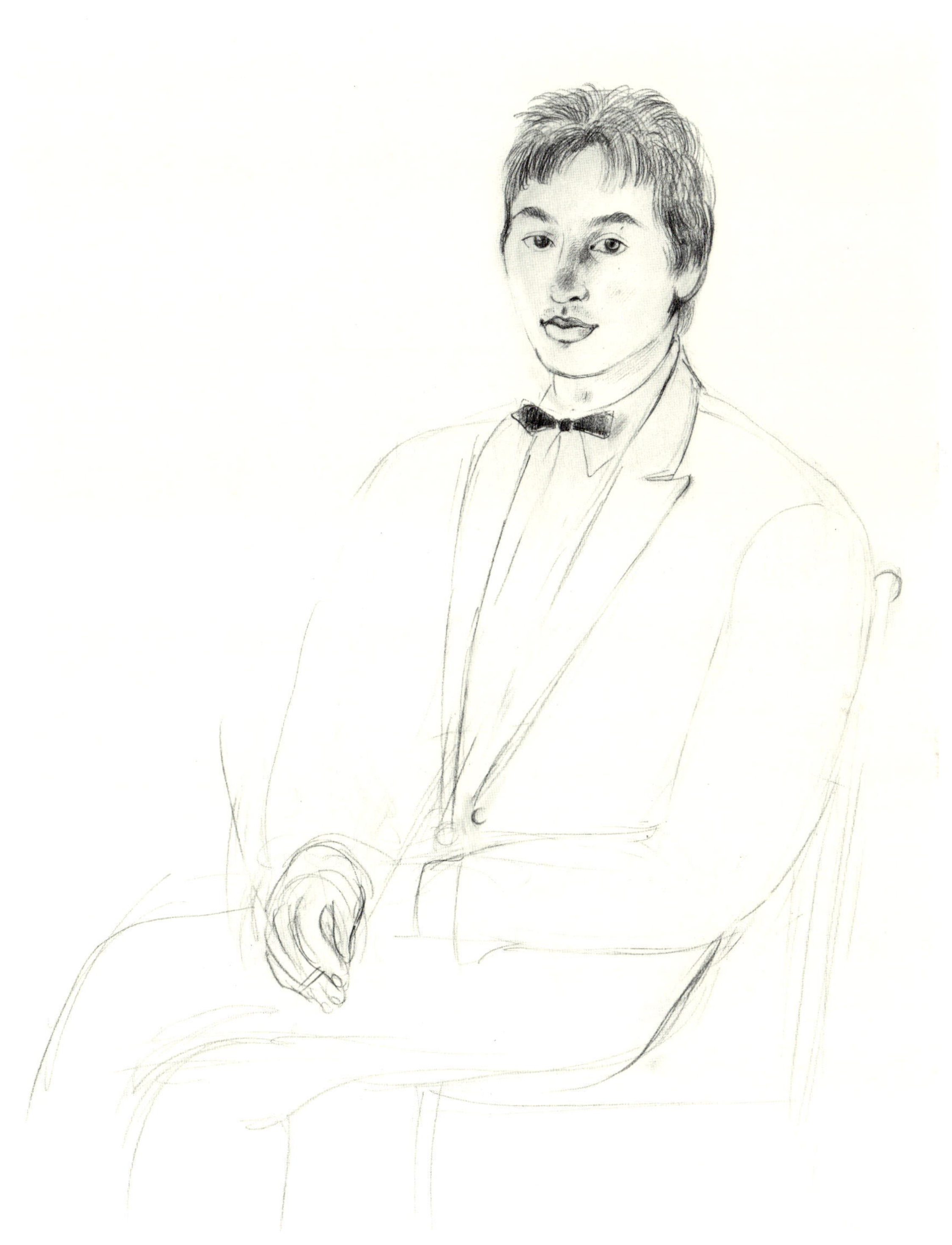

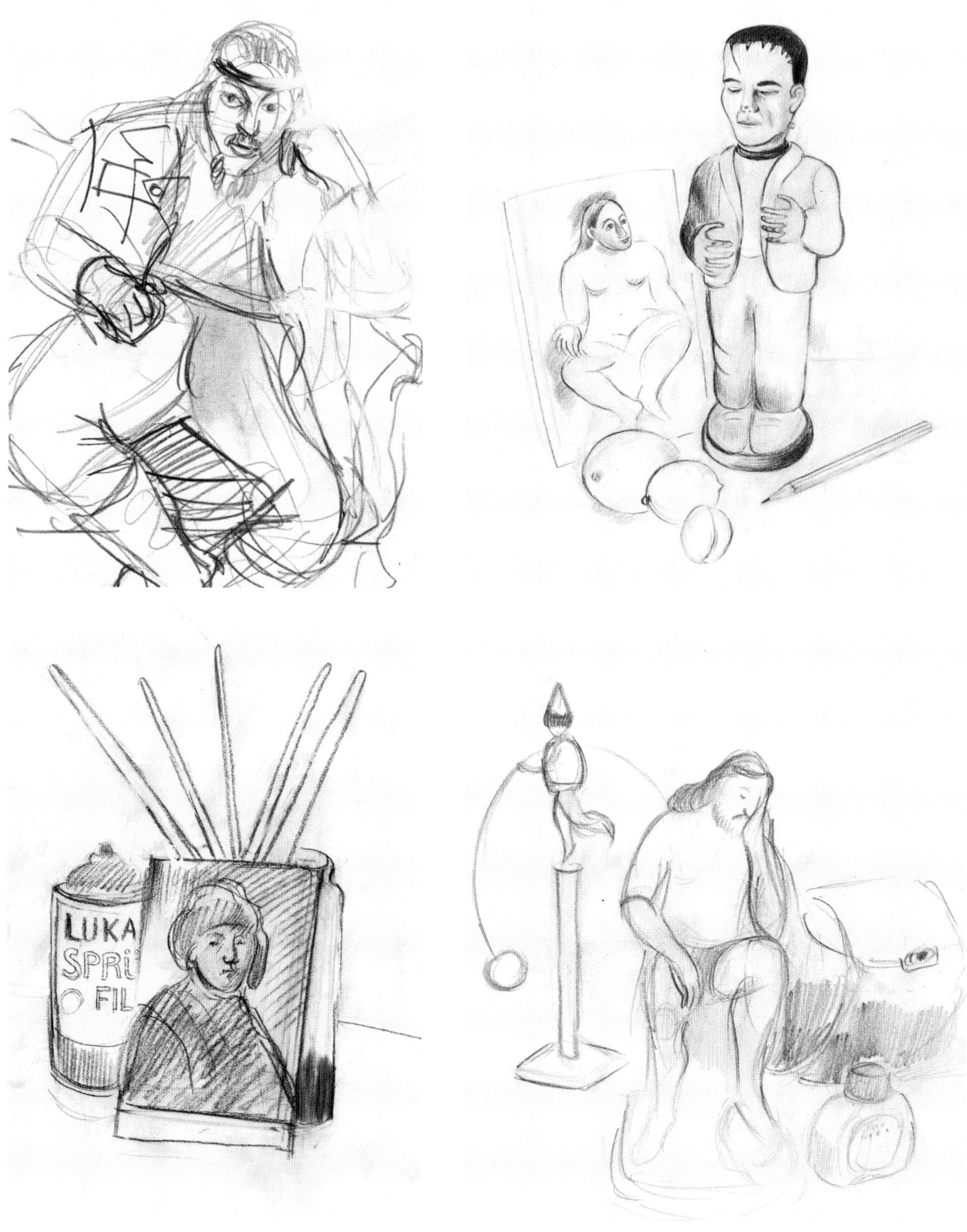
LUKA
SPRÜ
FIL

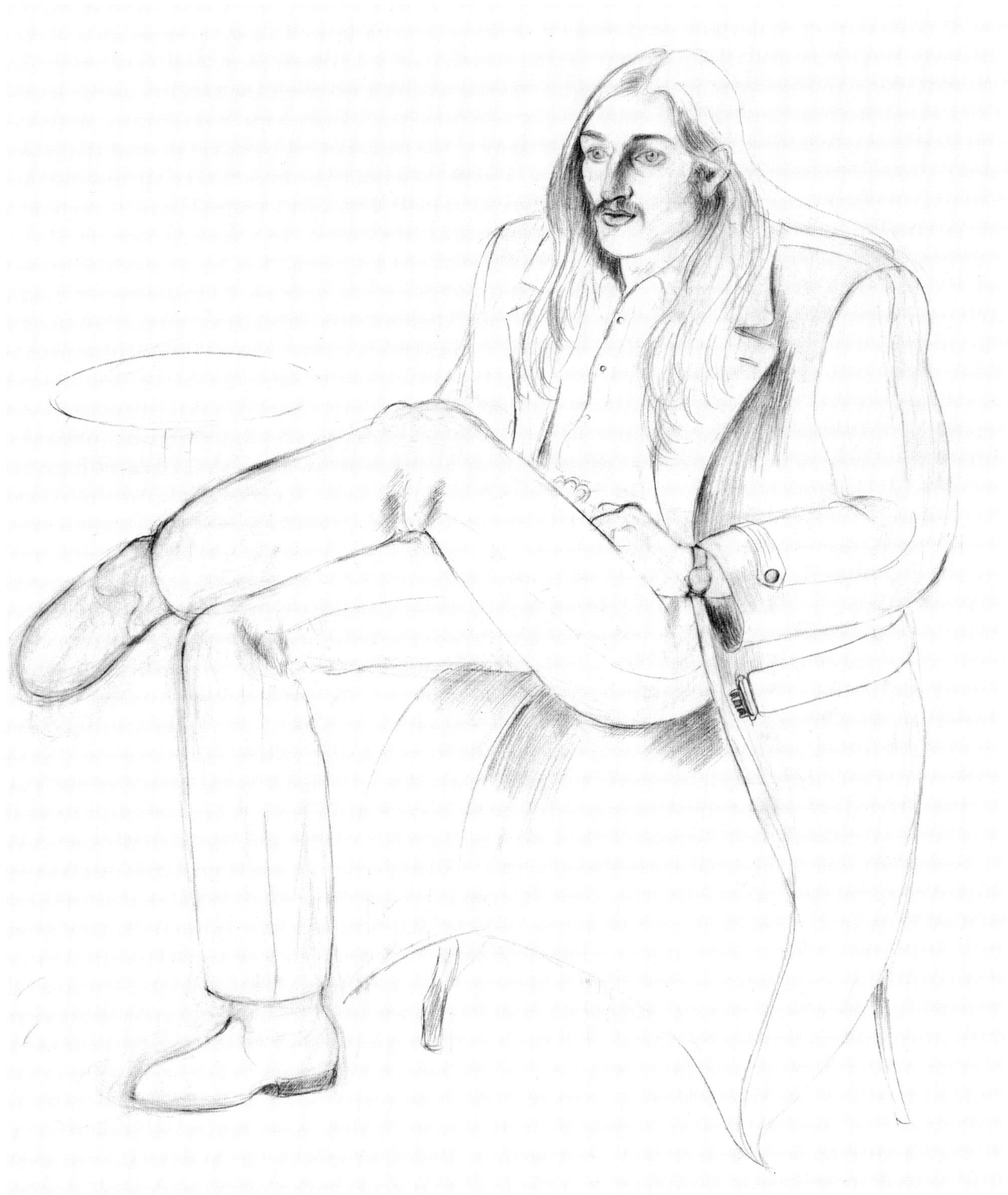

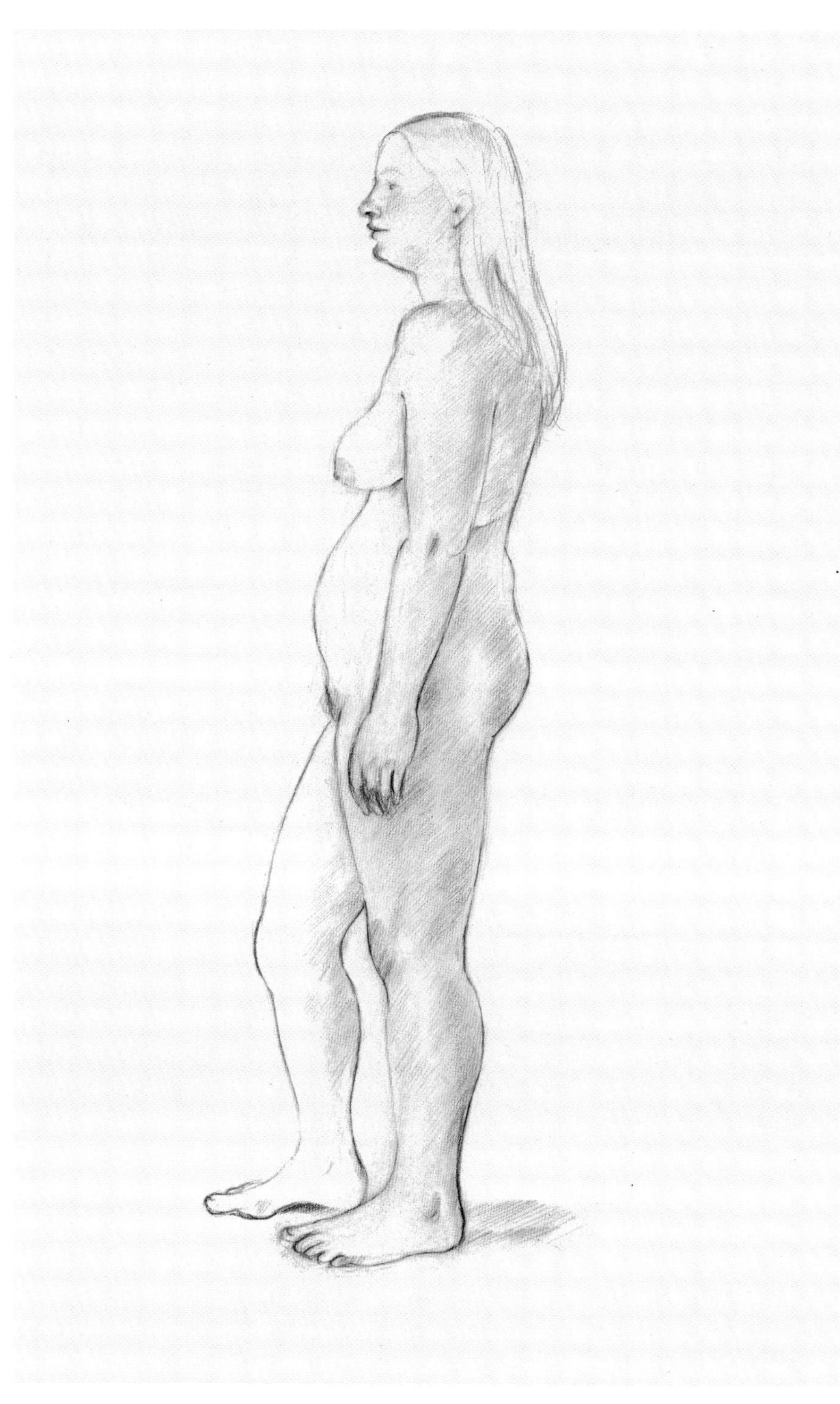

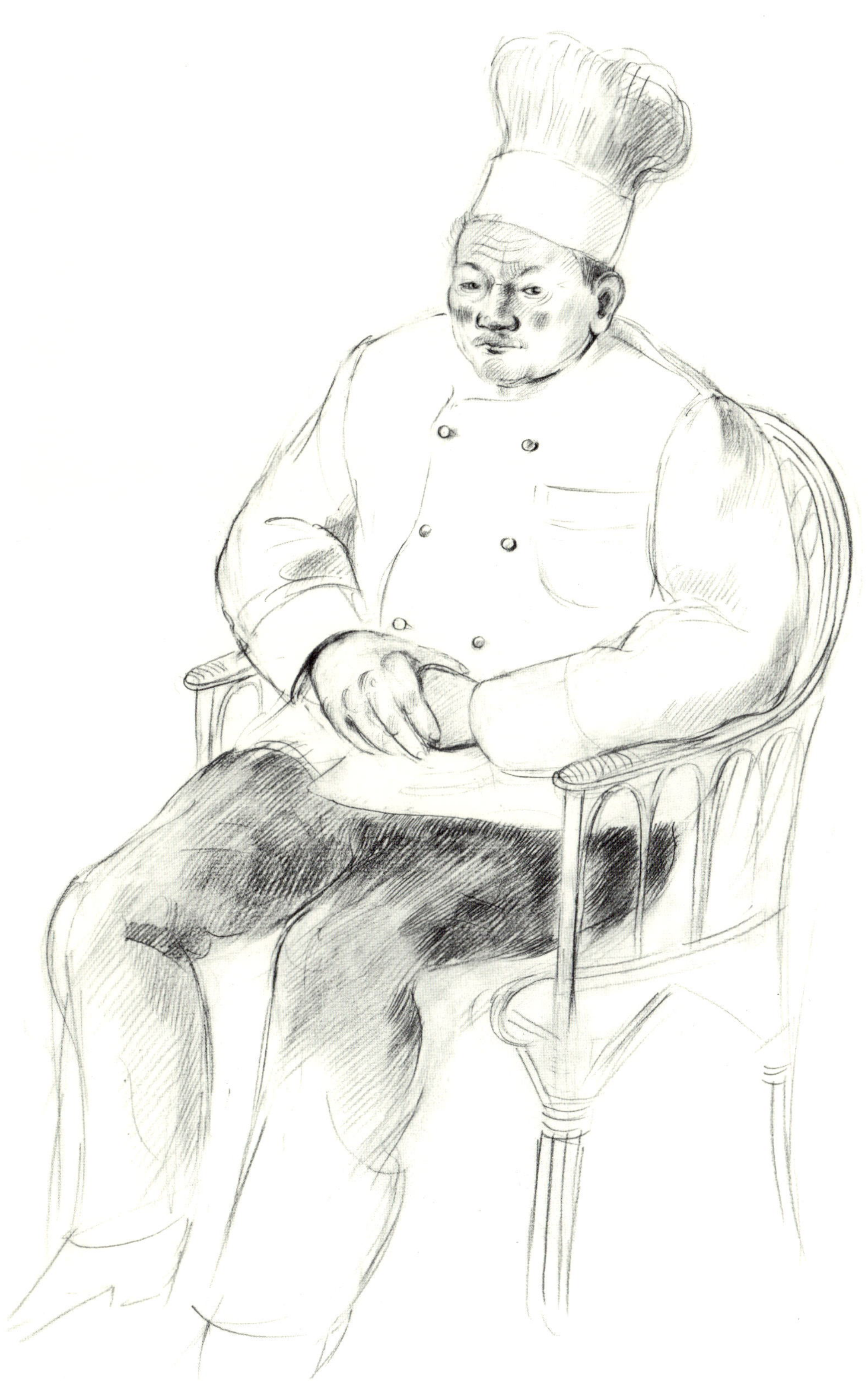

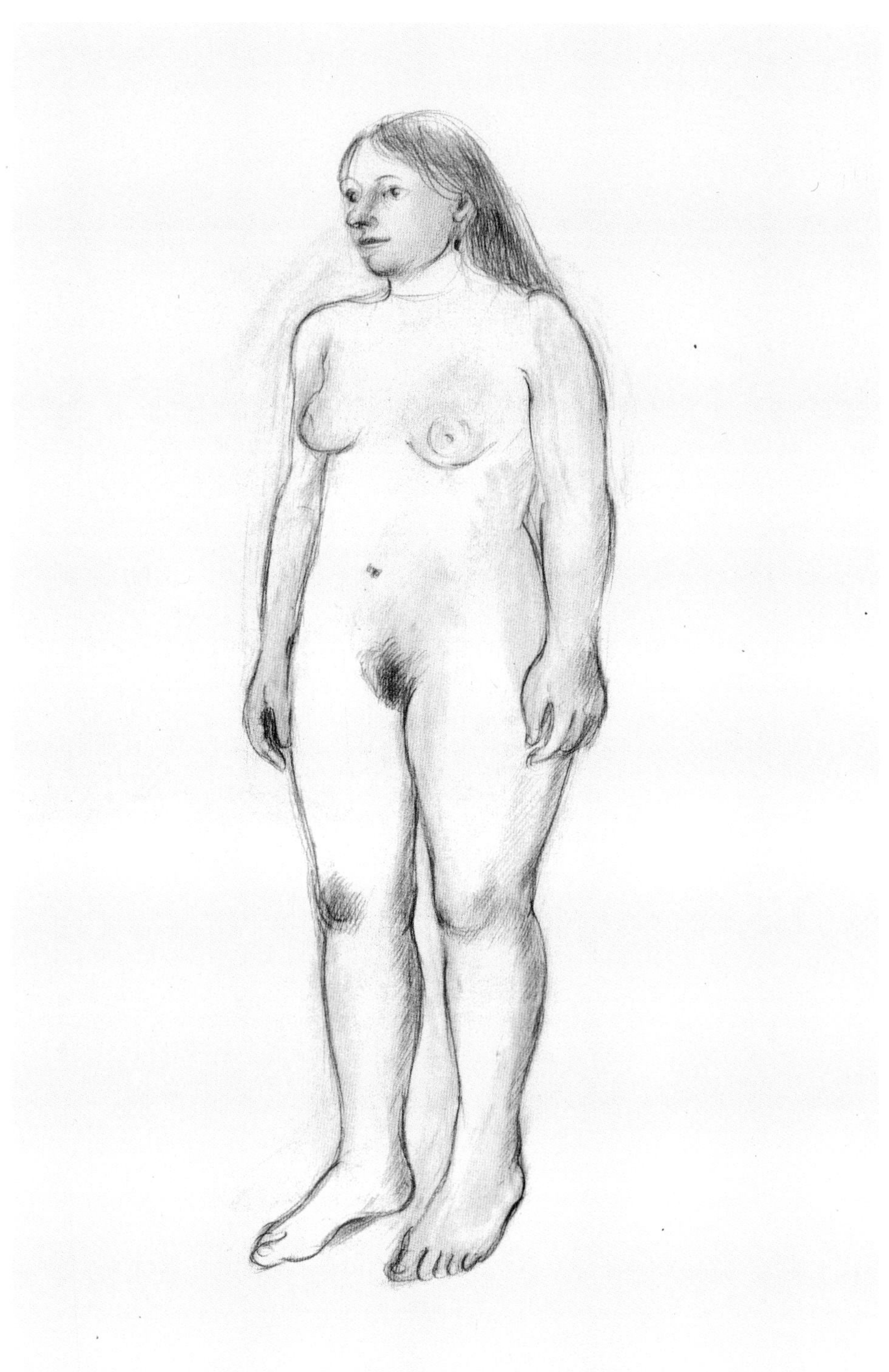

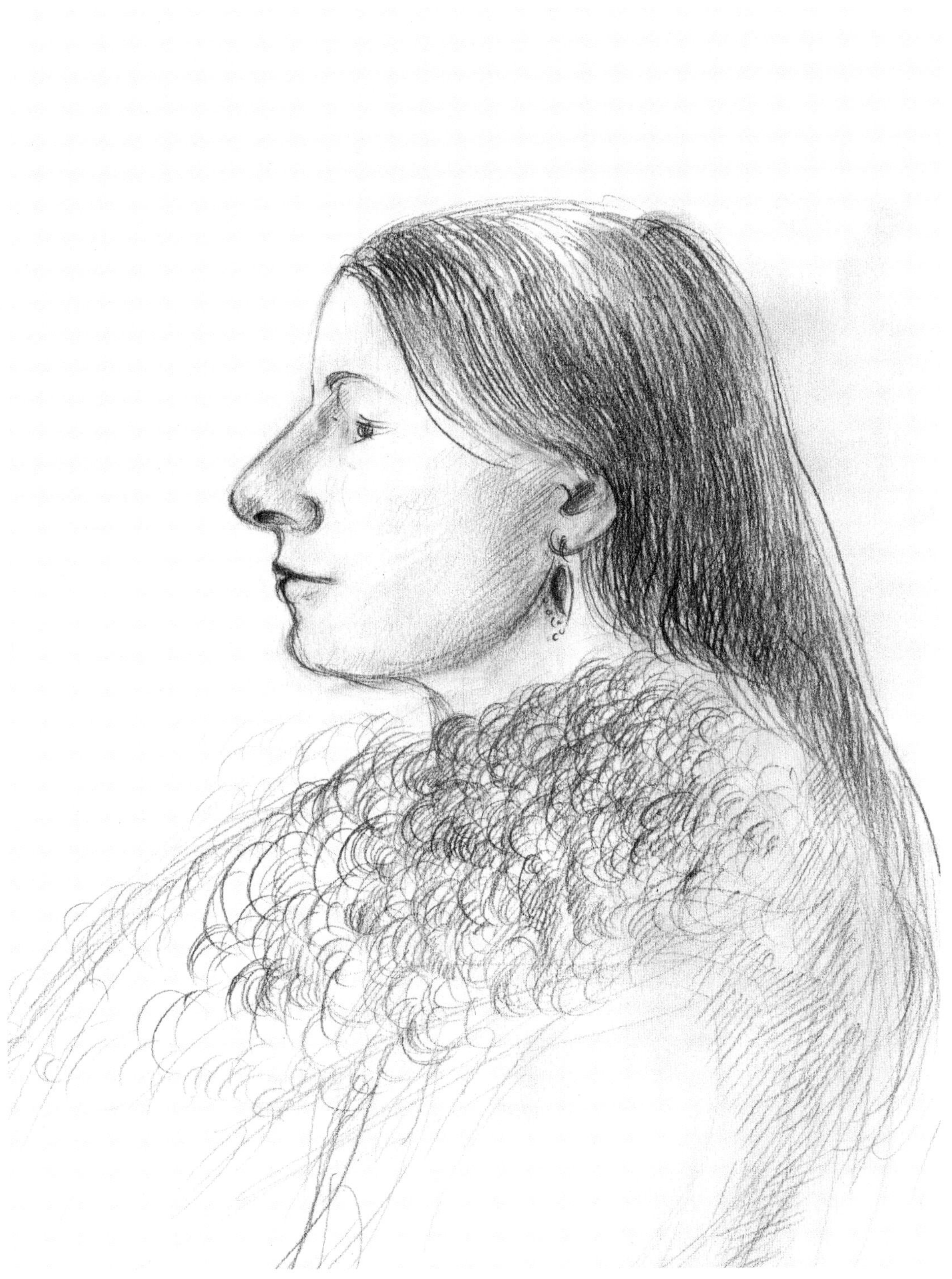

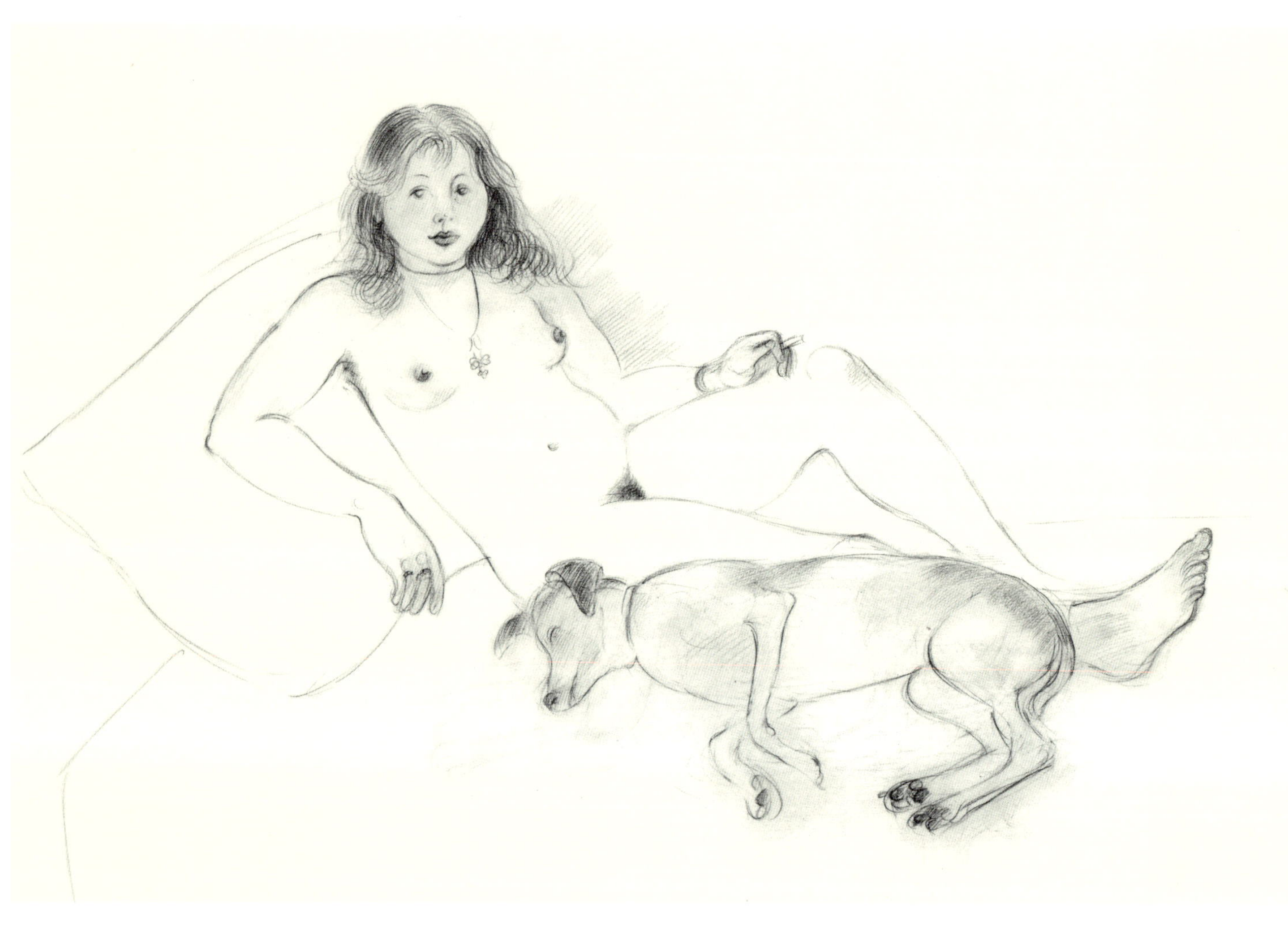

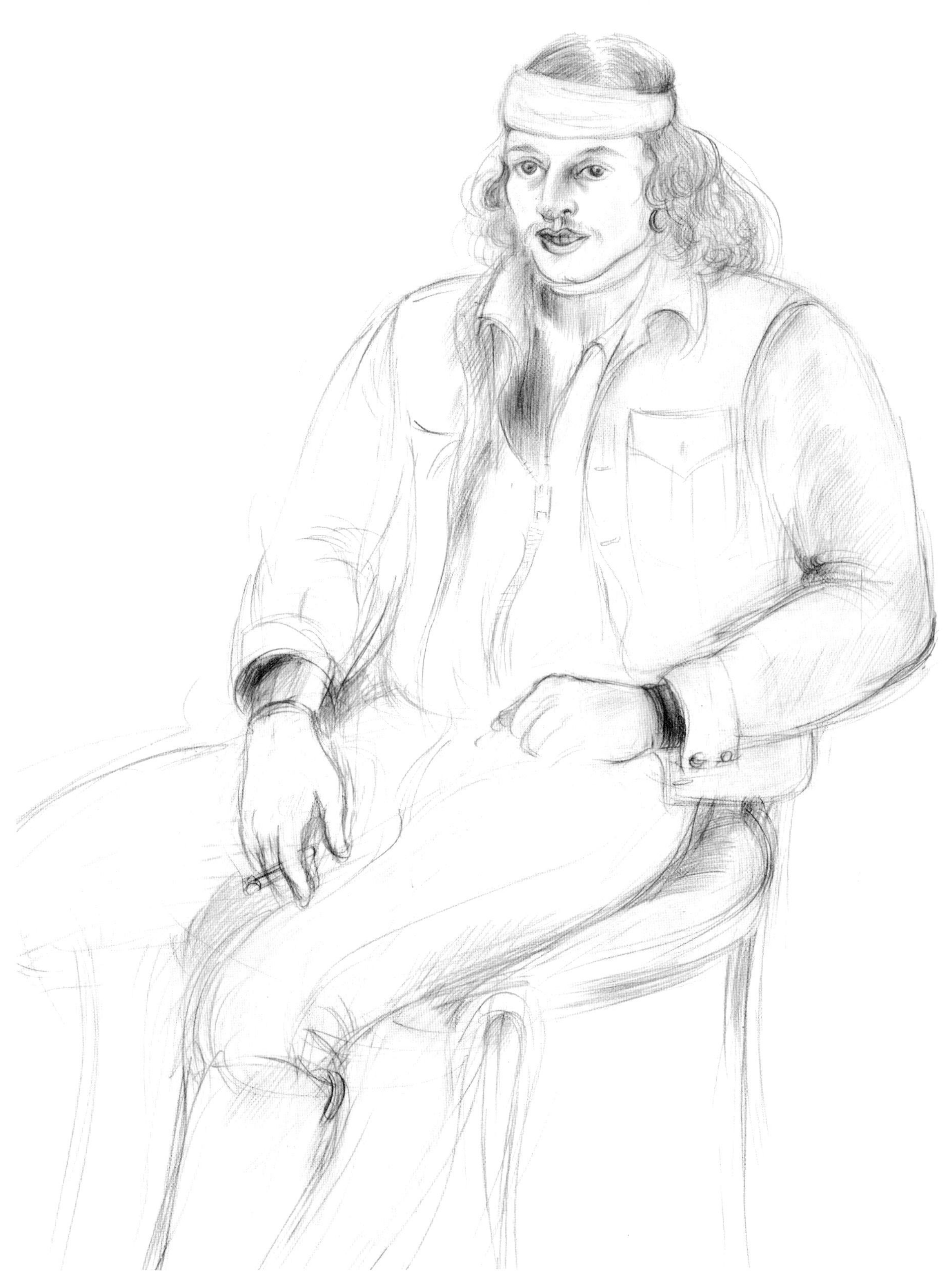

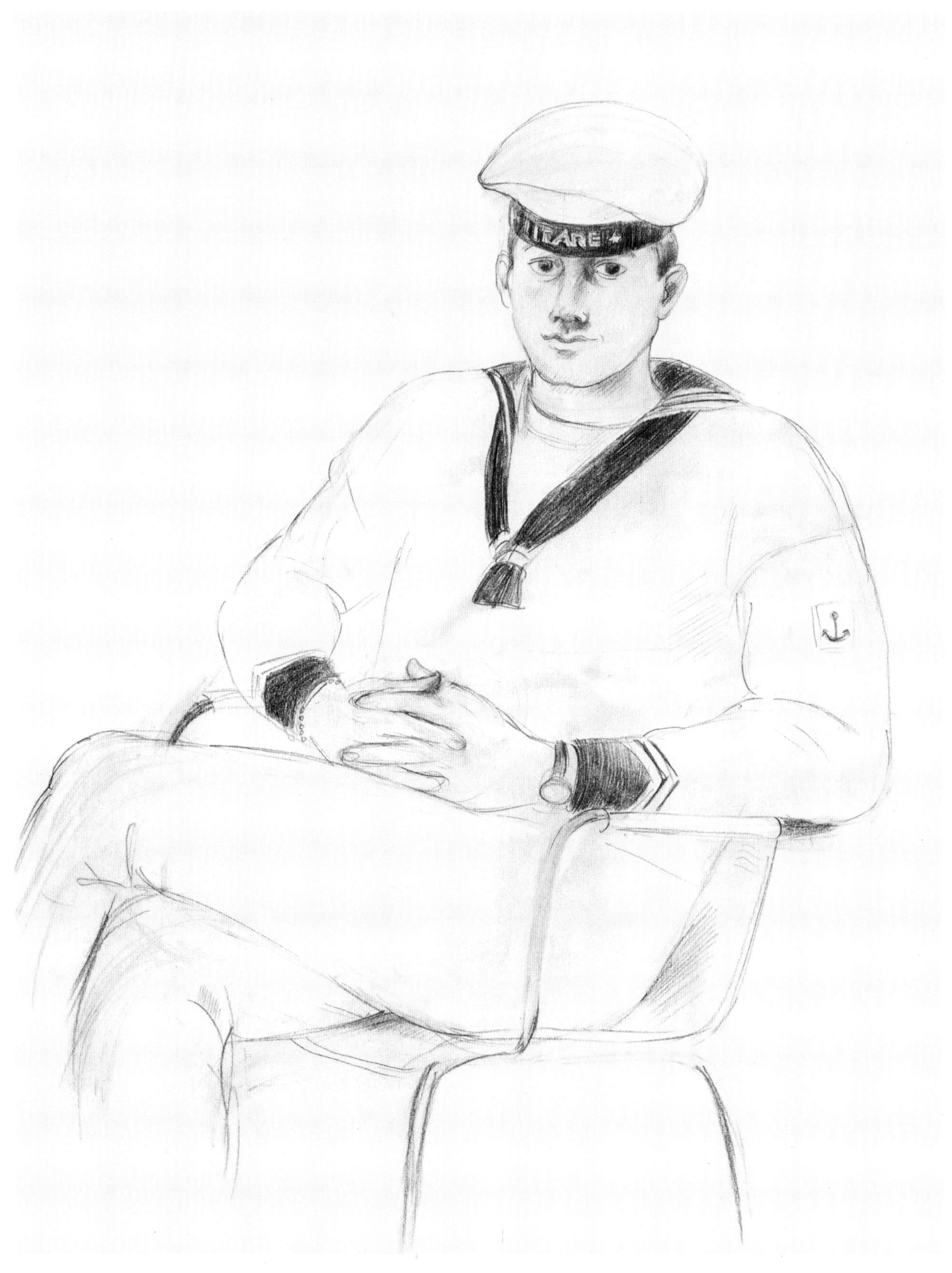

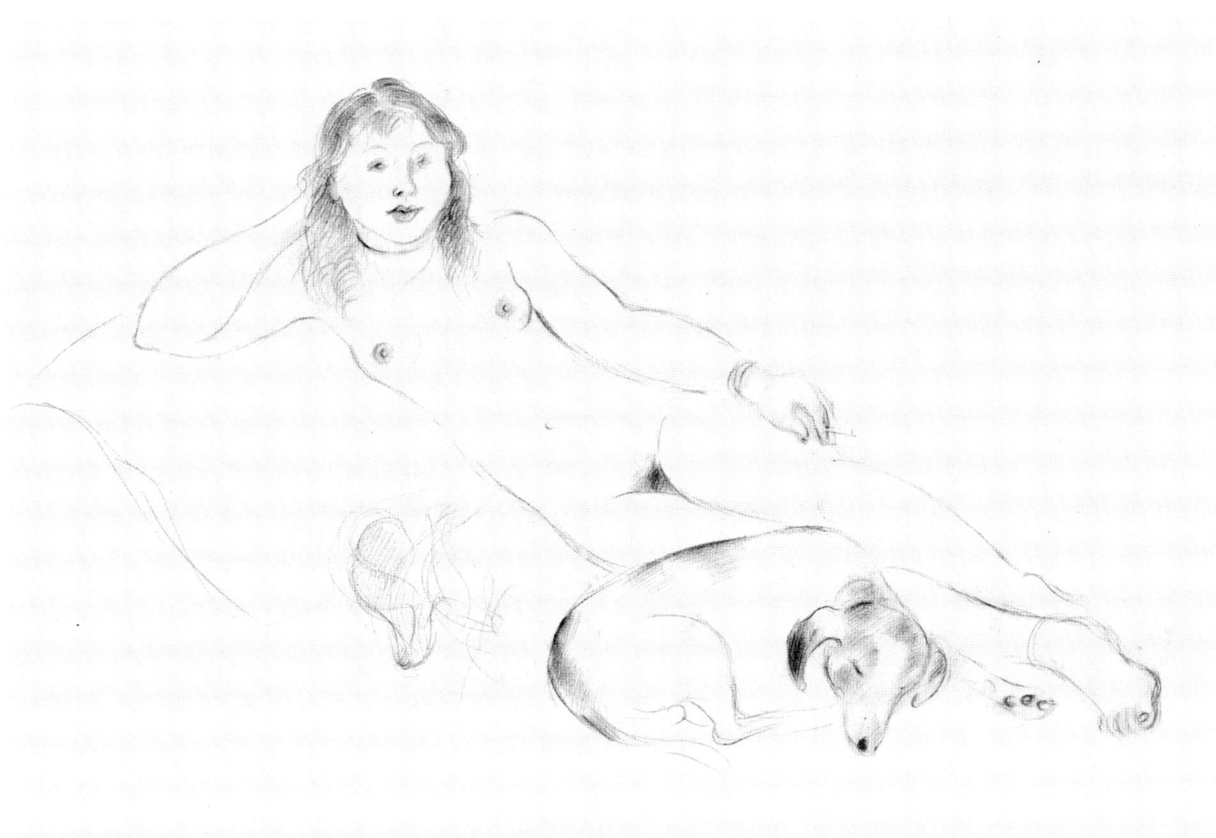

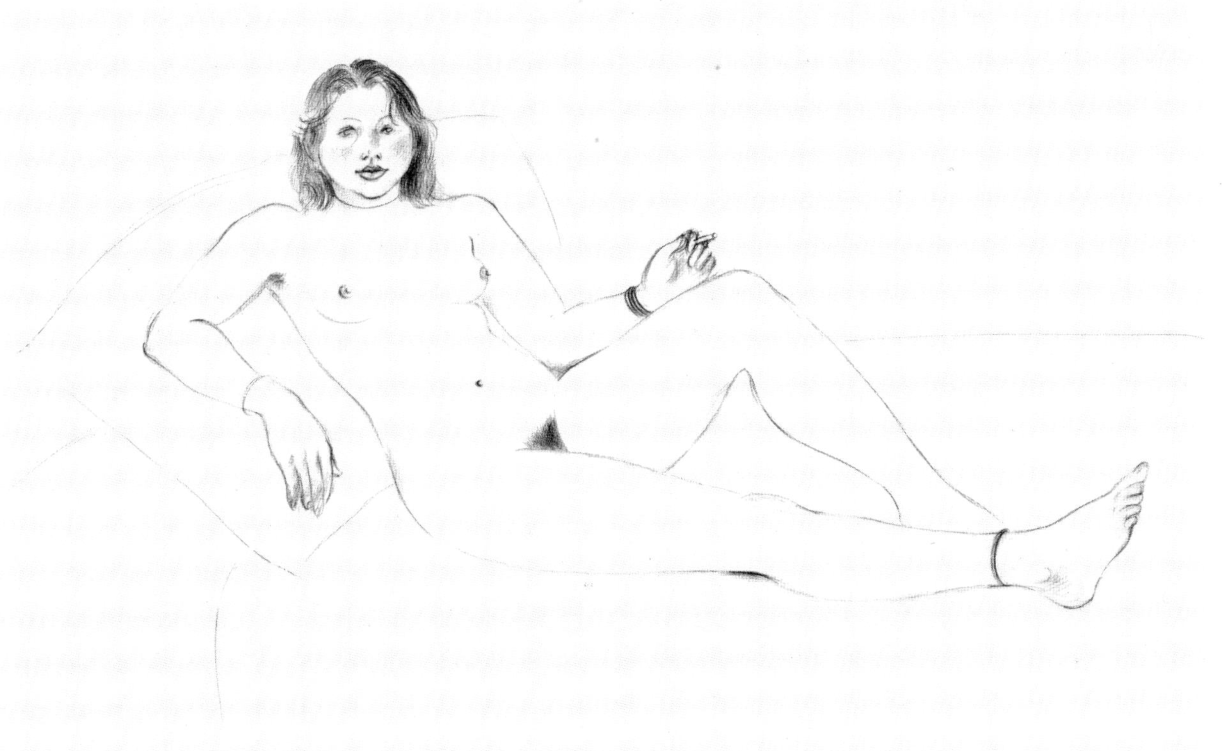

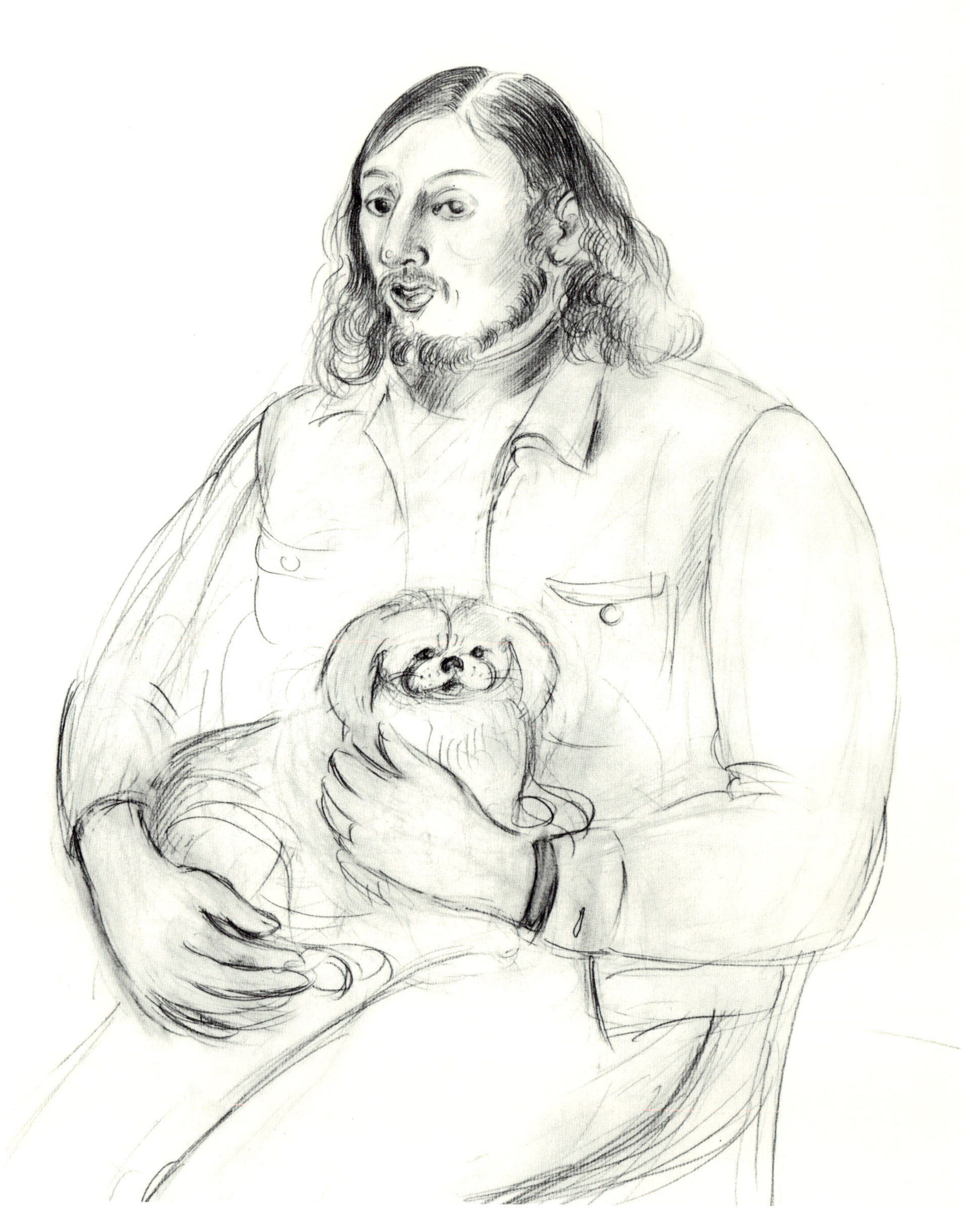

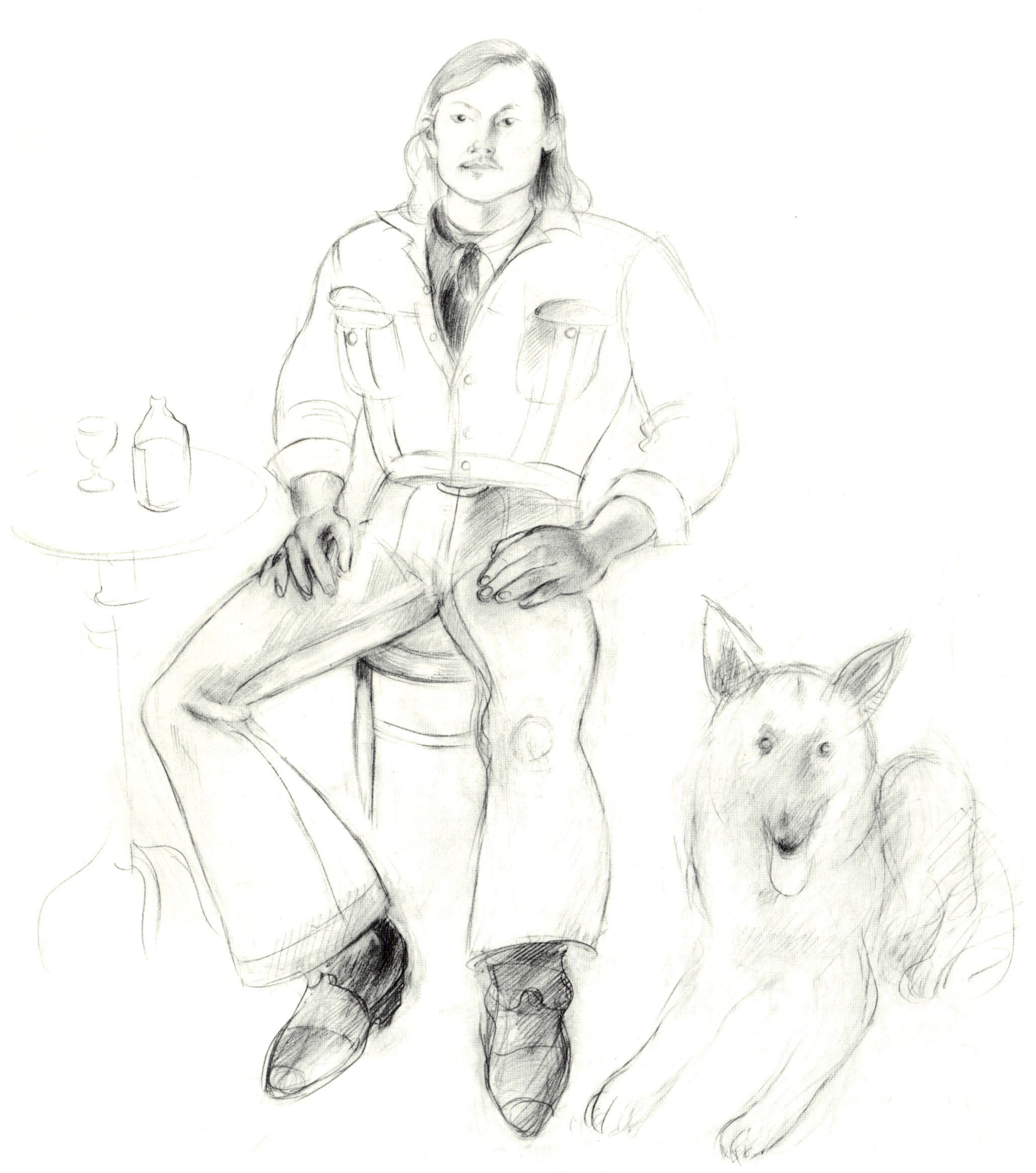

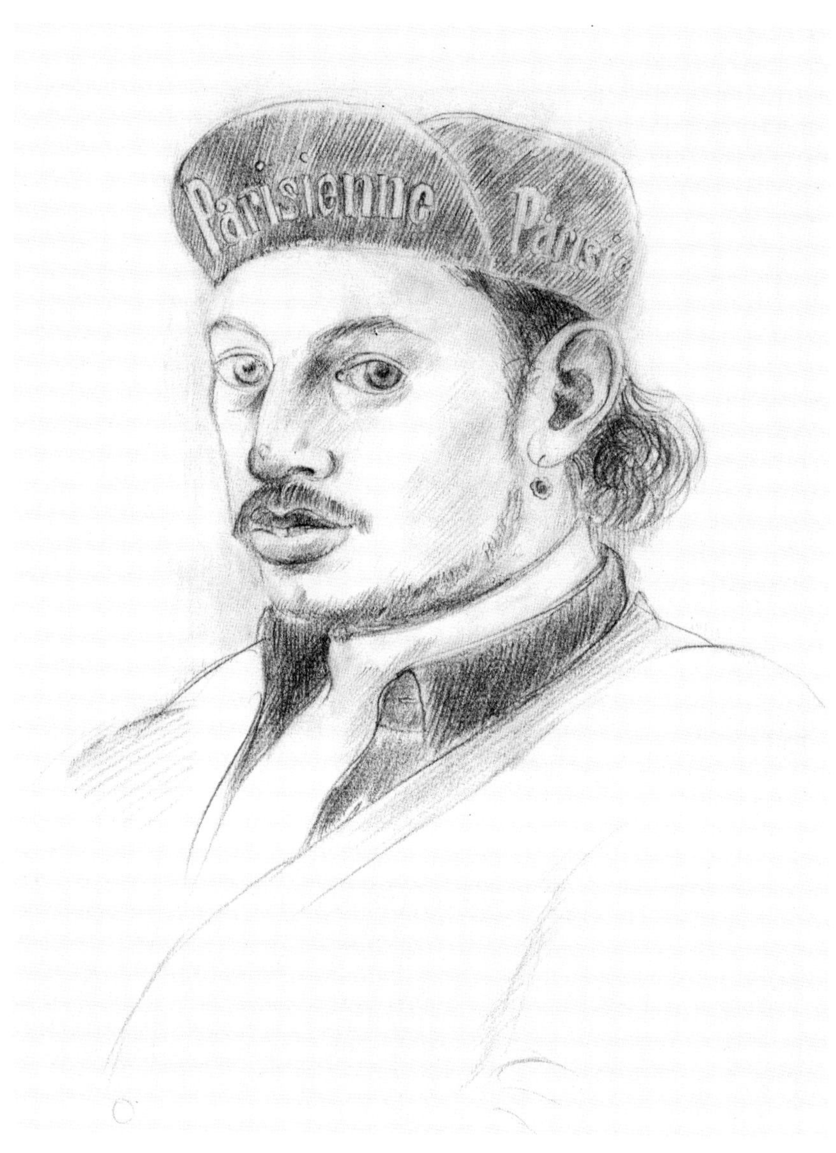
Parisienne
Parisie

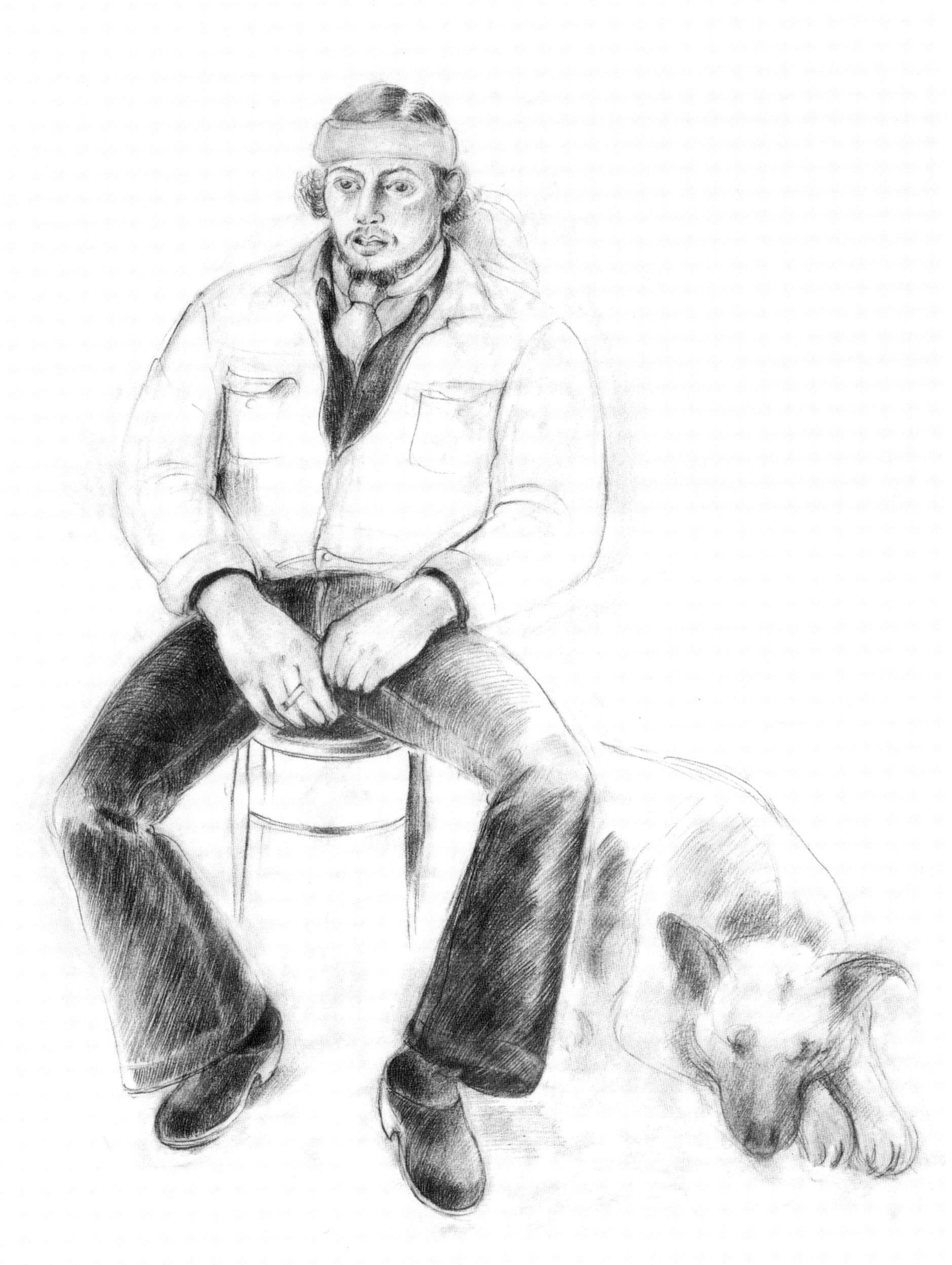

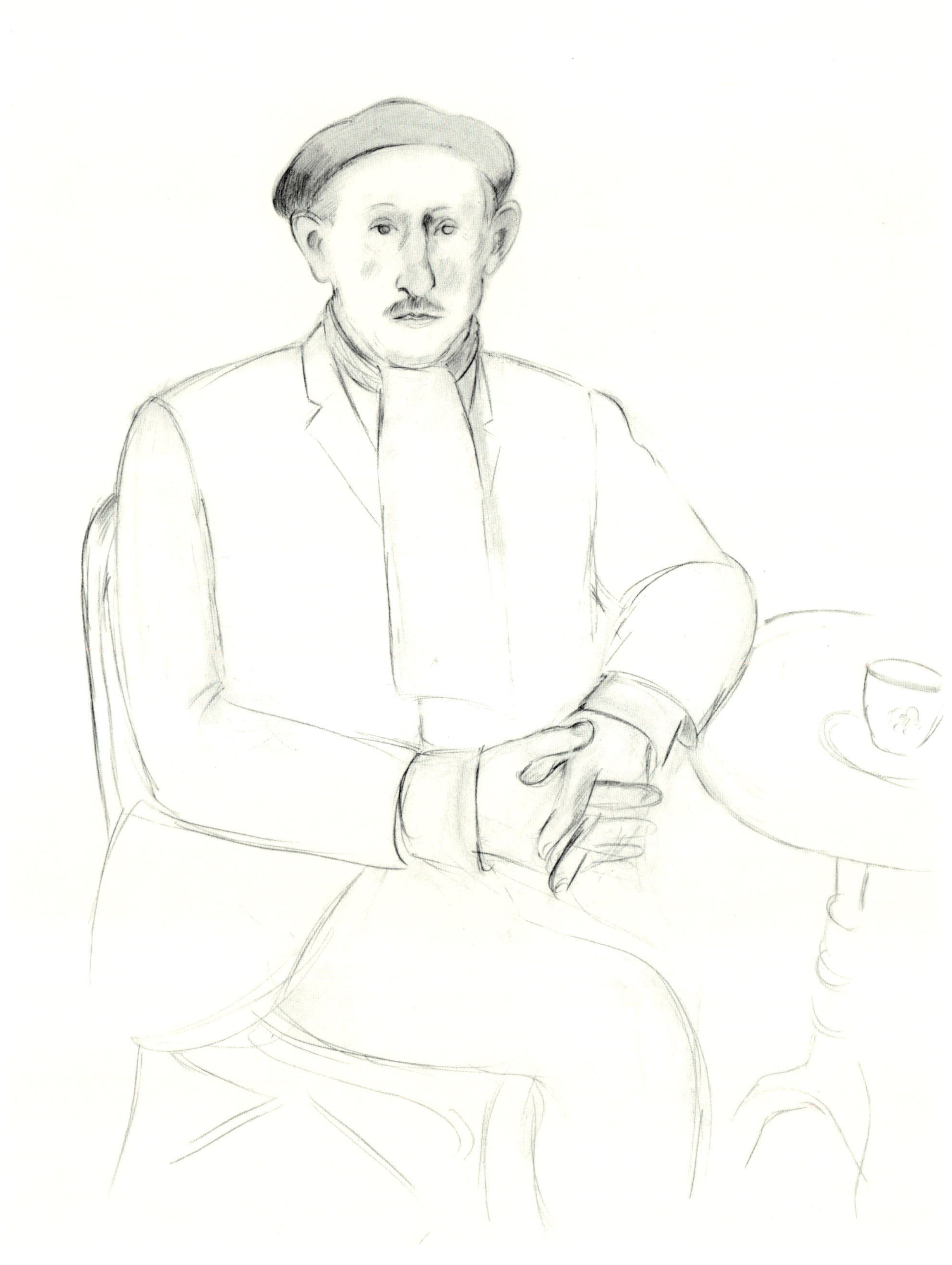

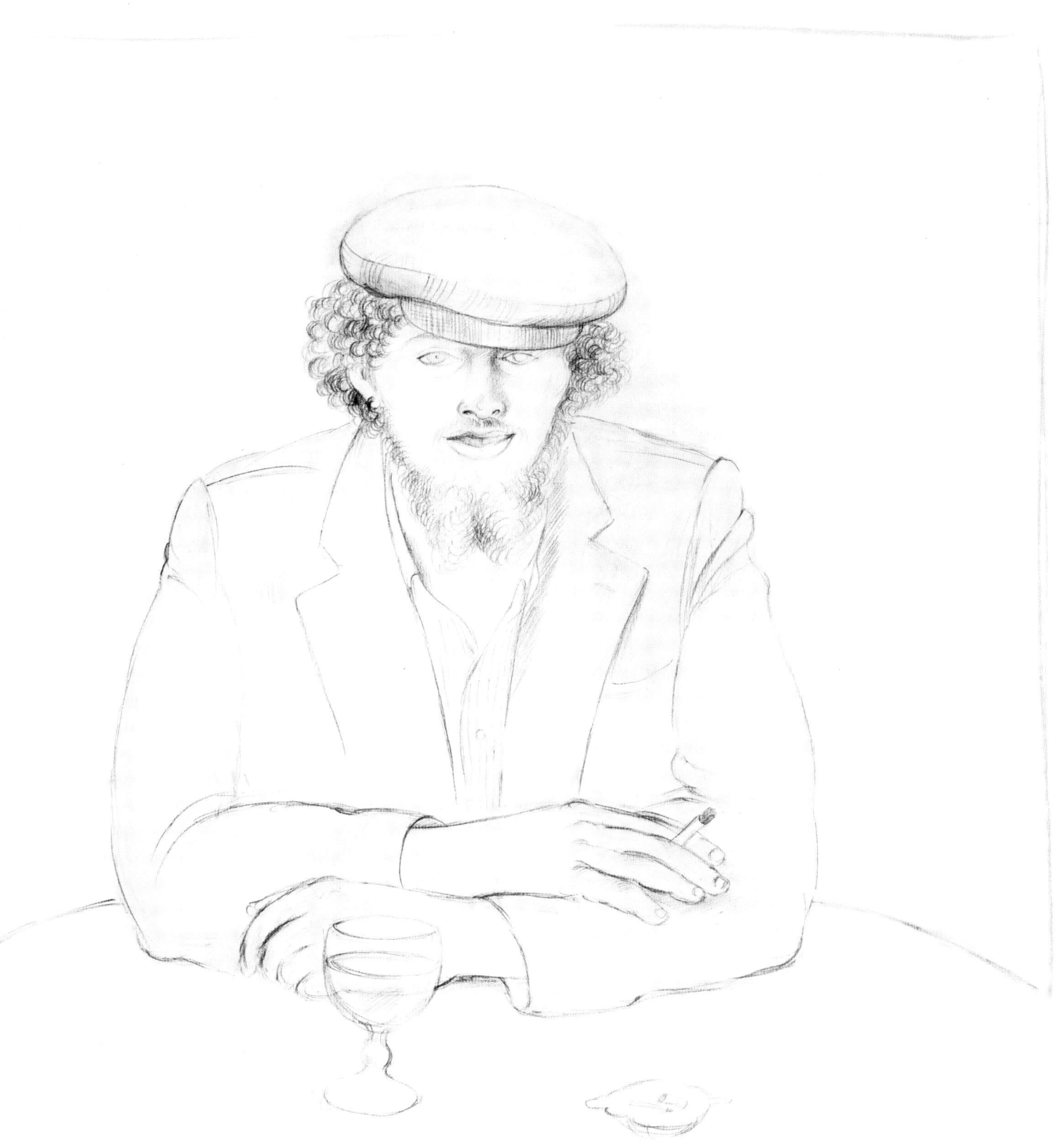

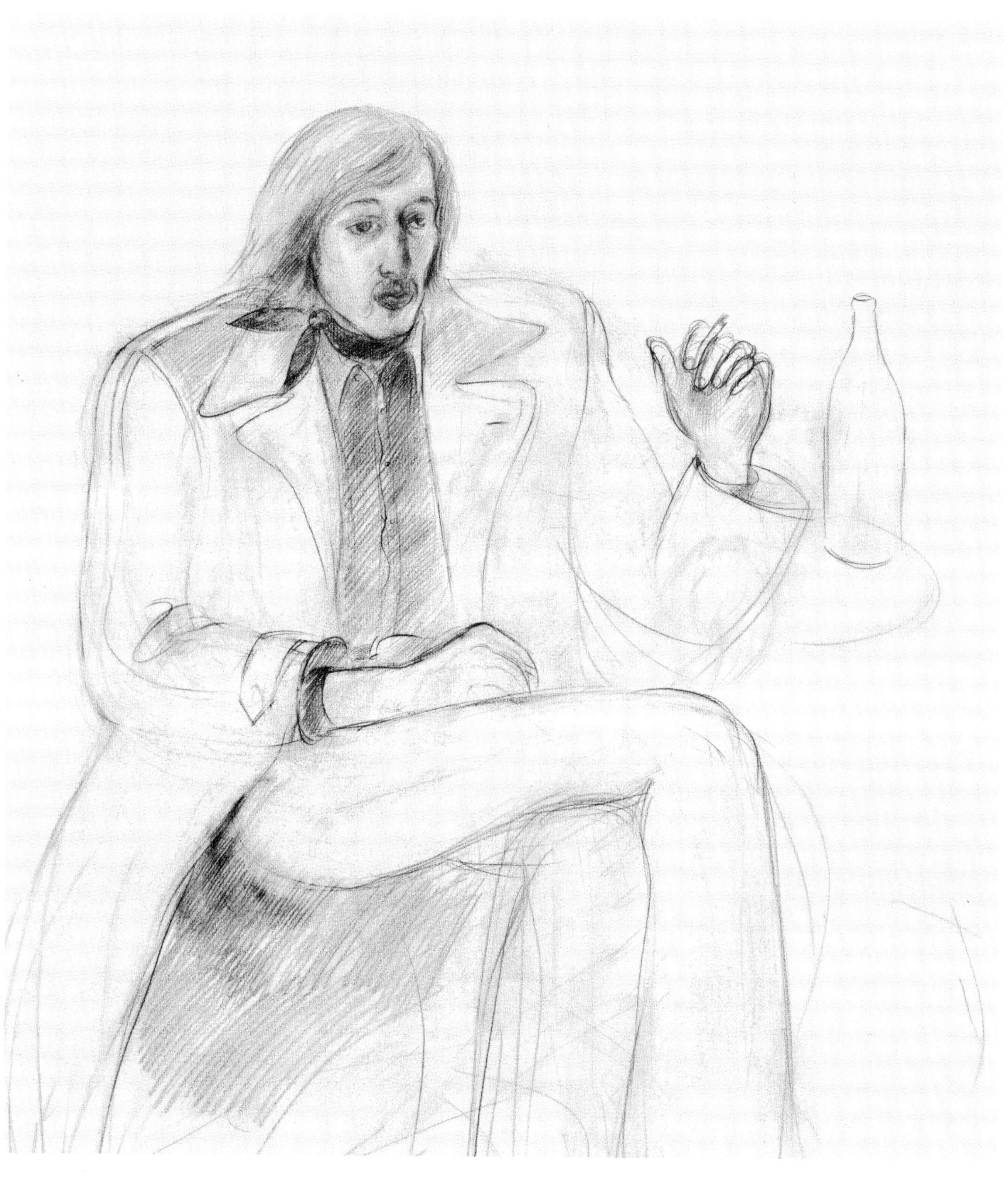

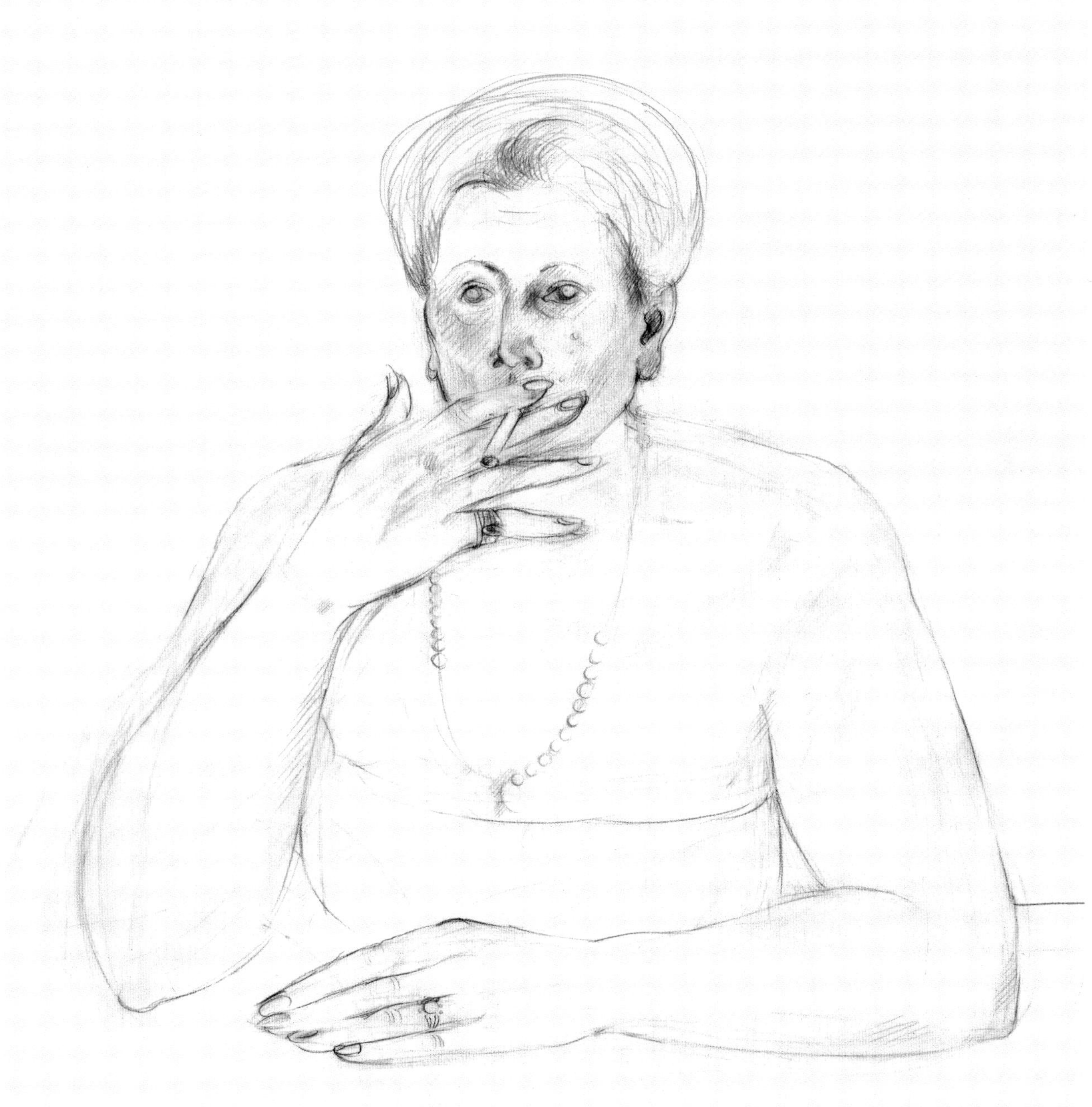

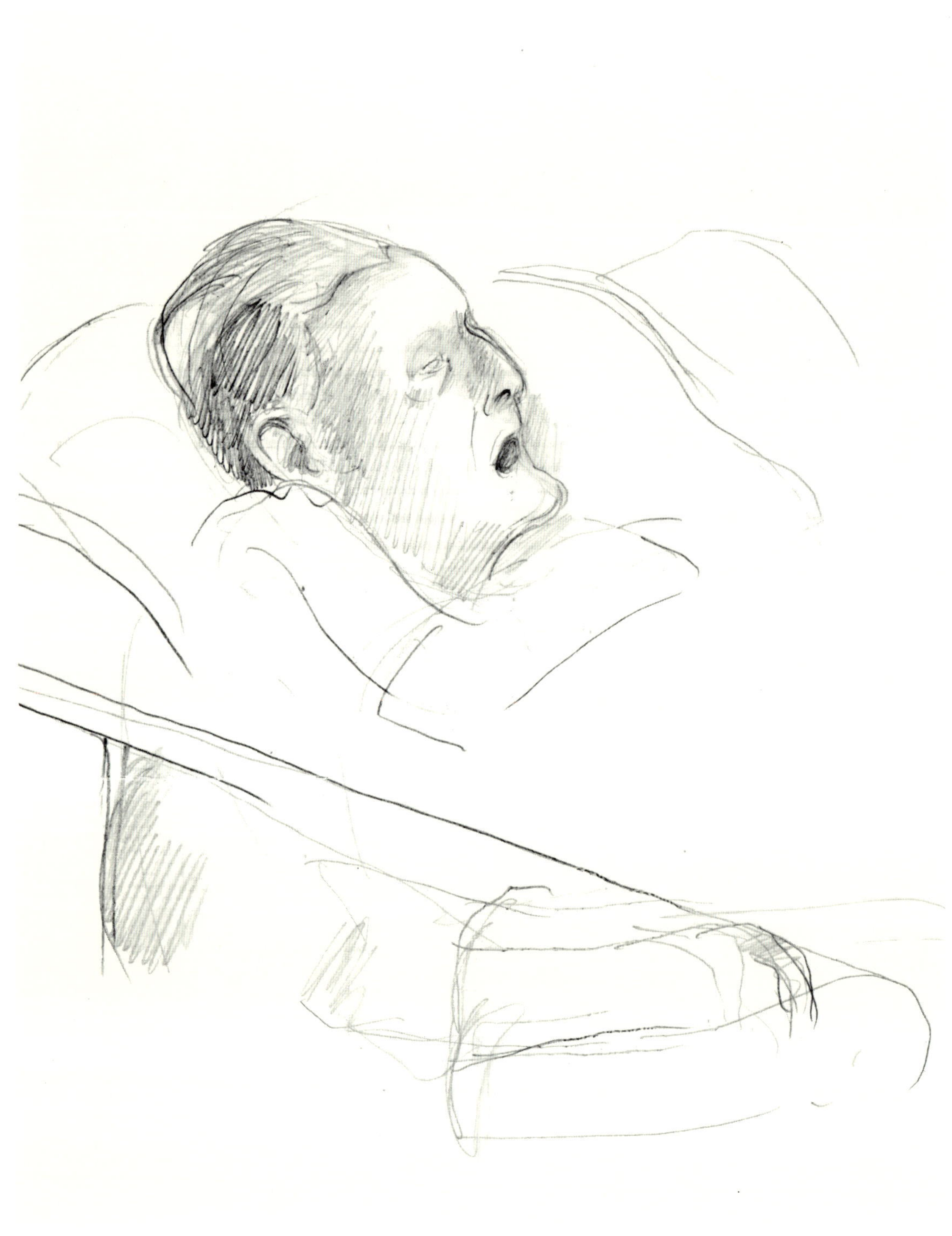

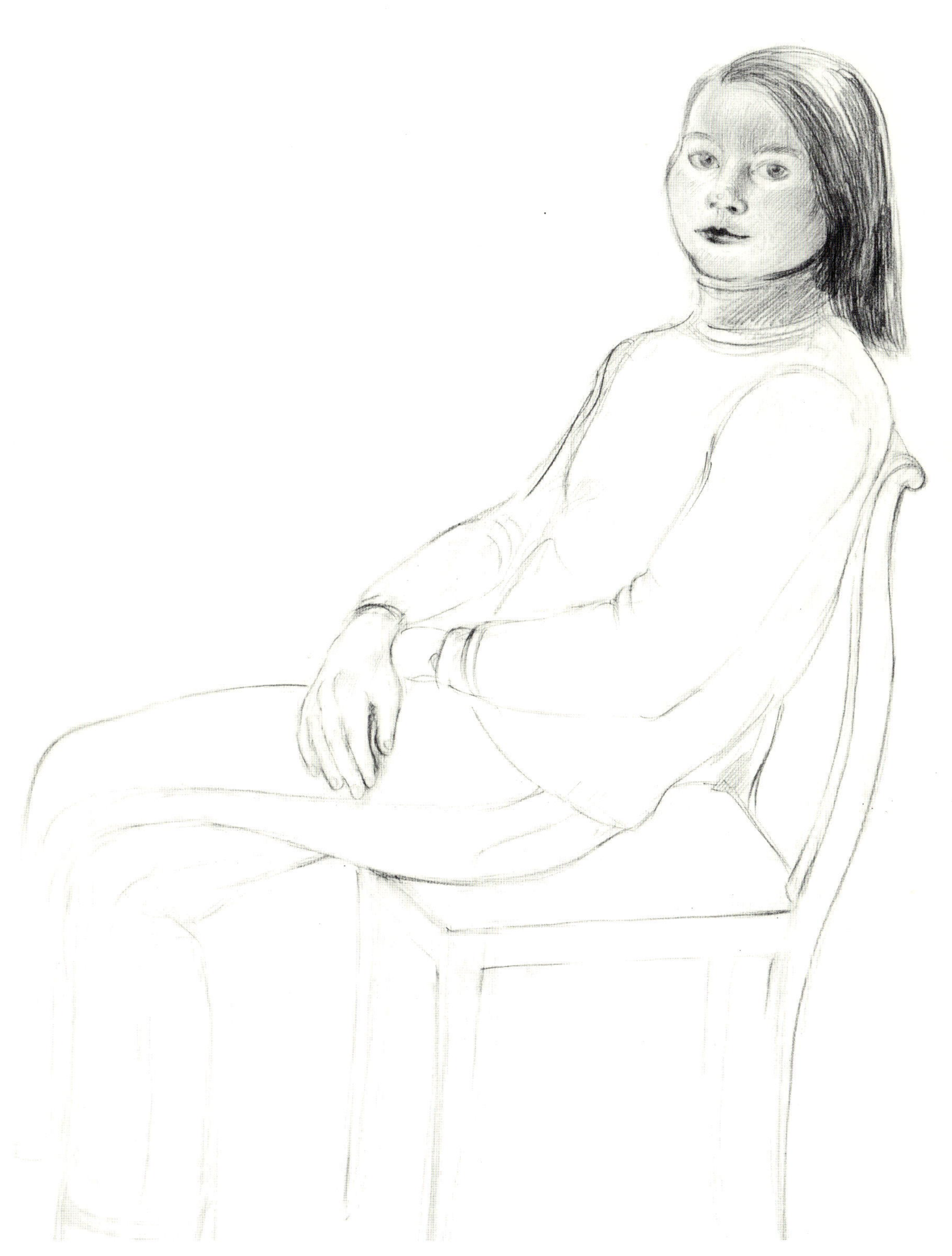

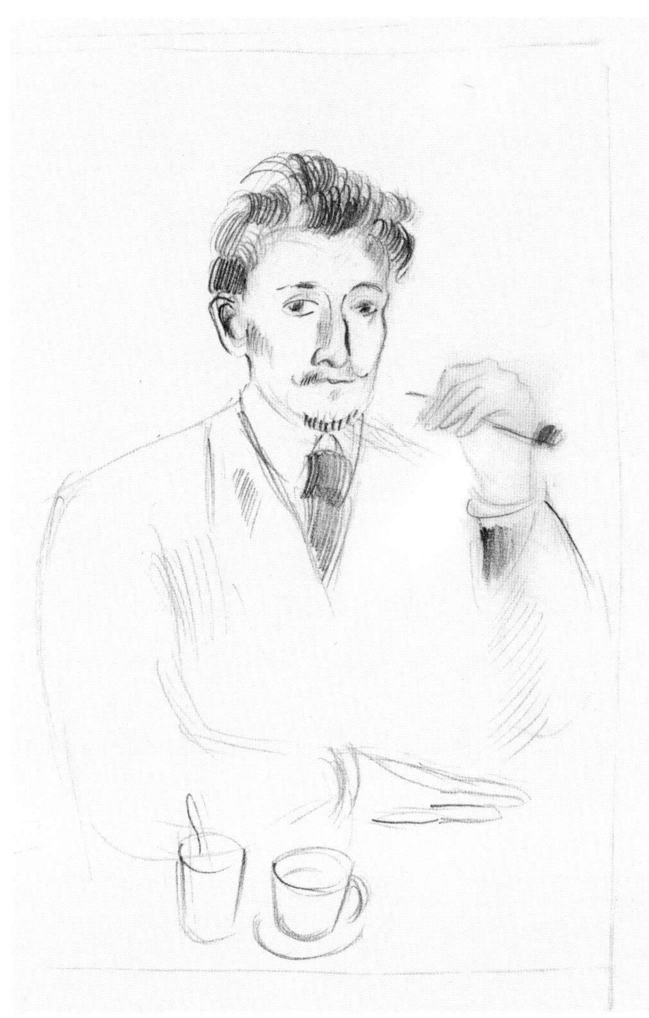

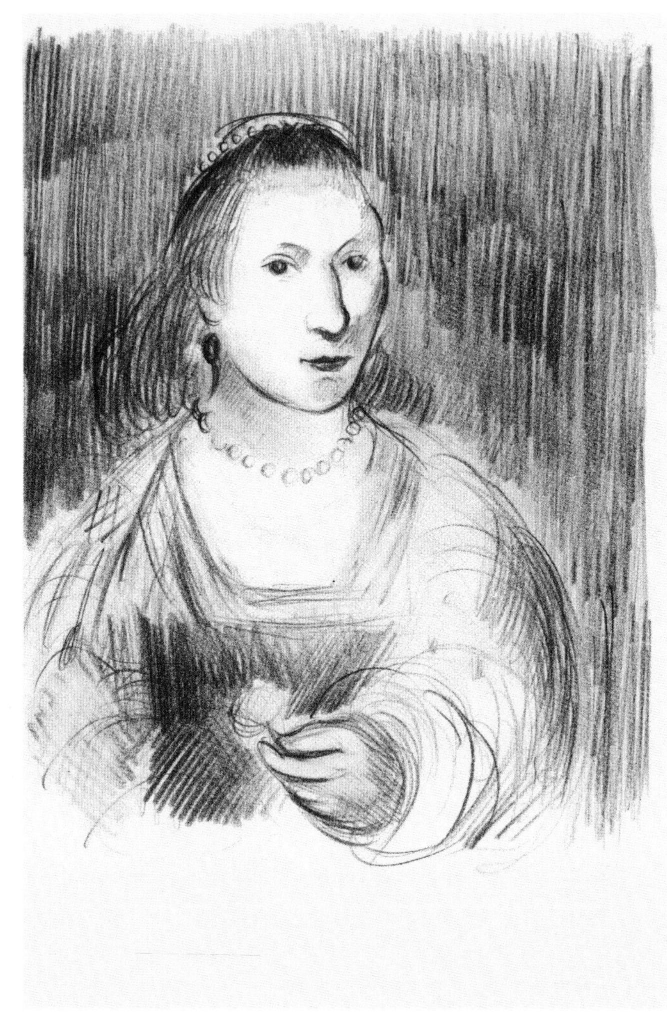

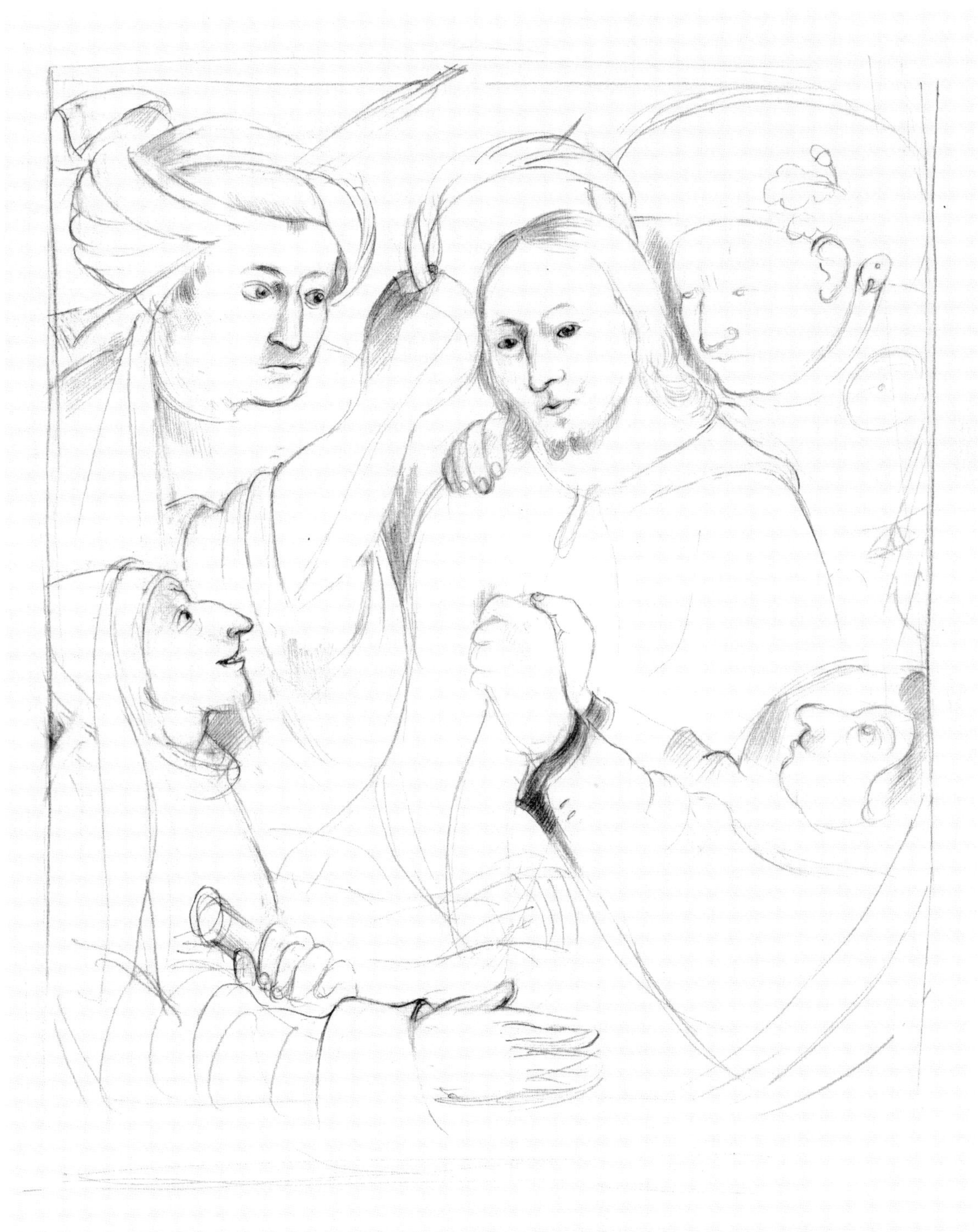

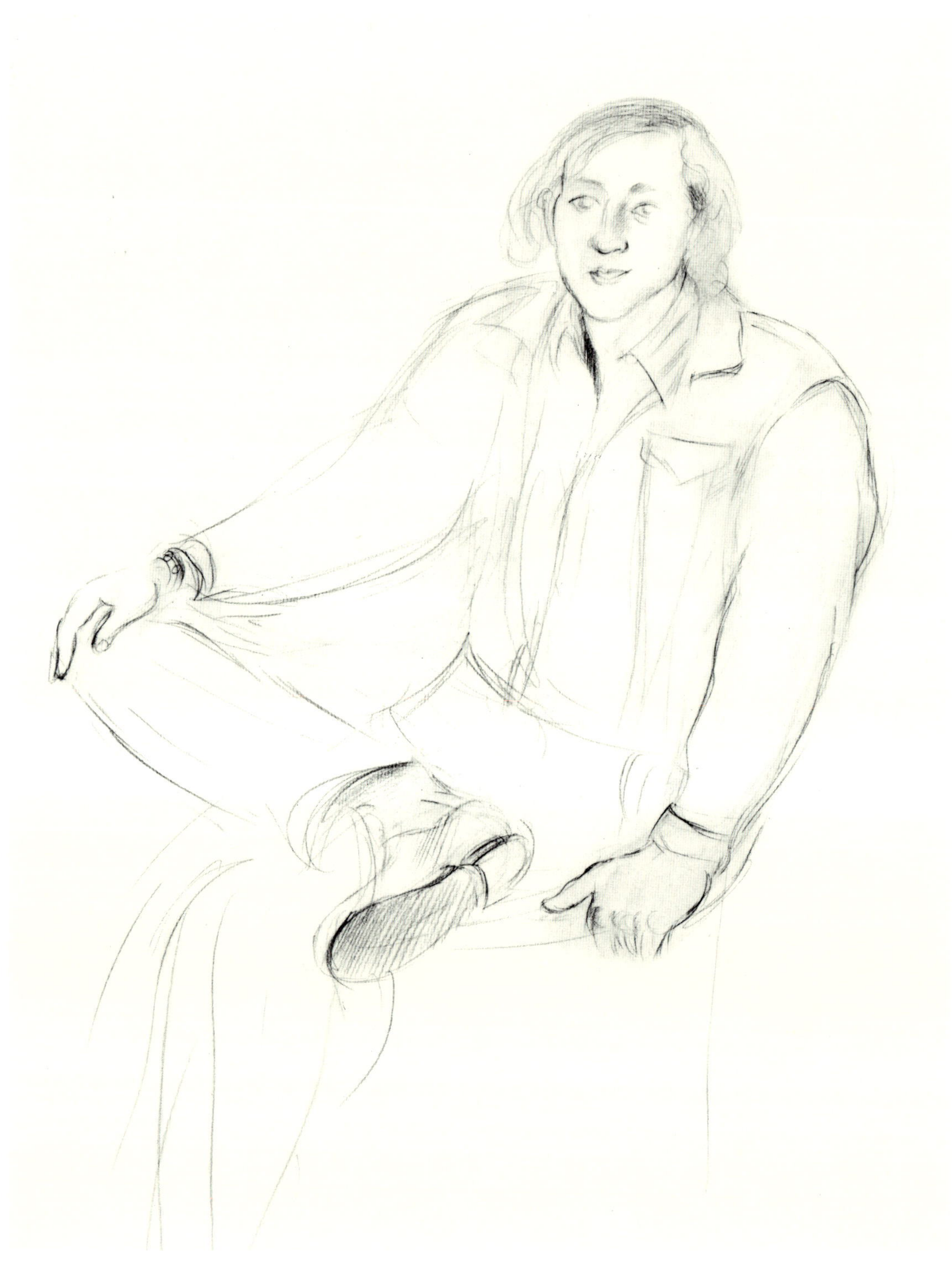

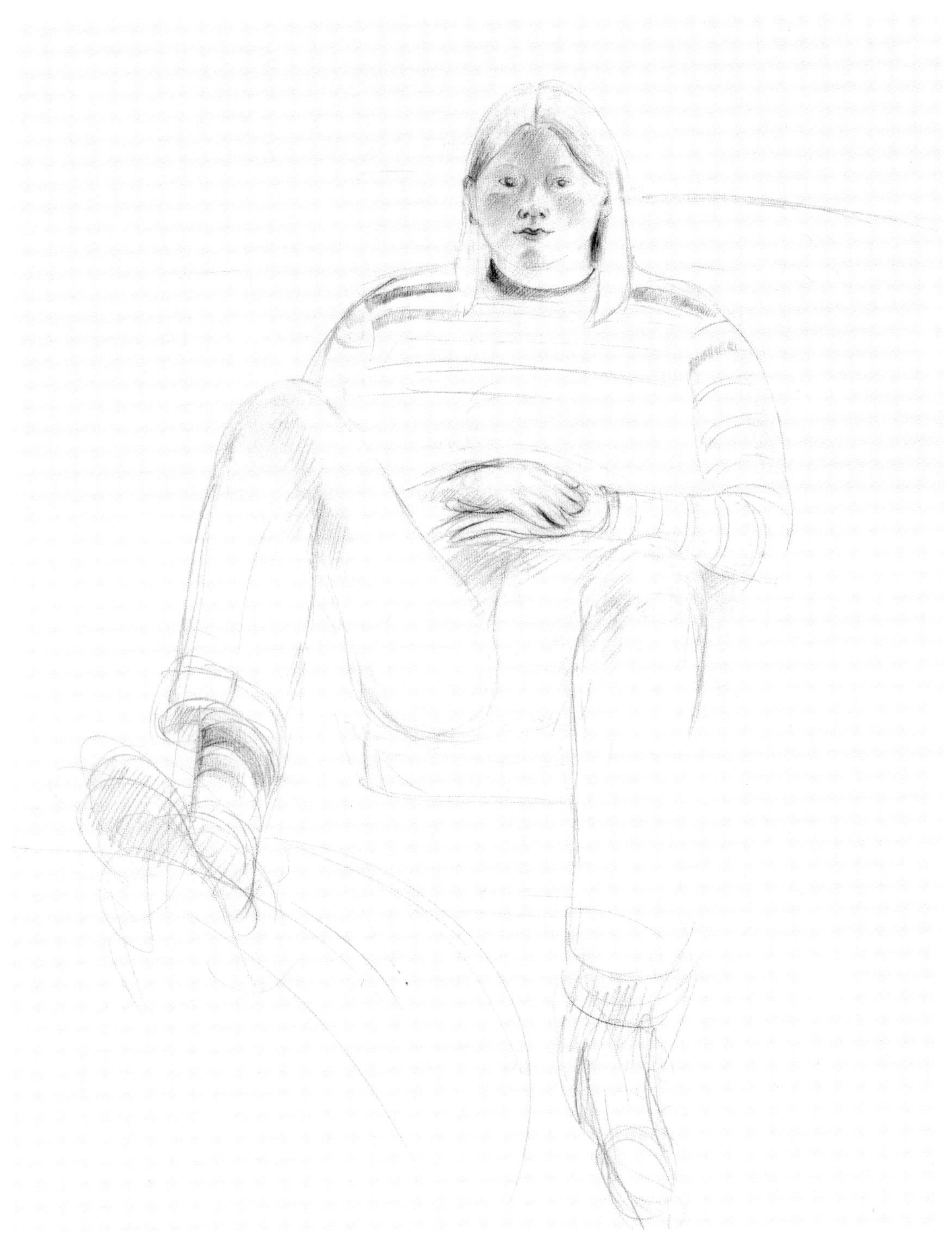

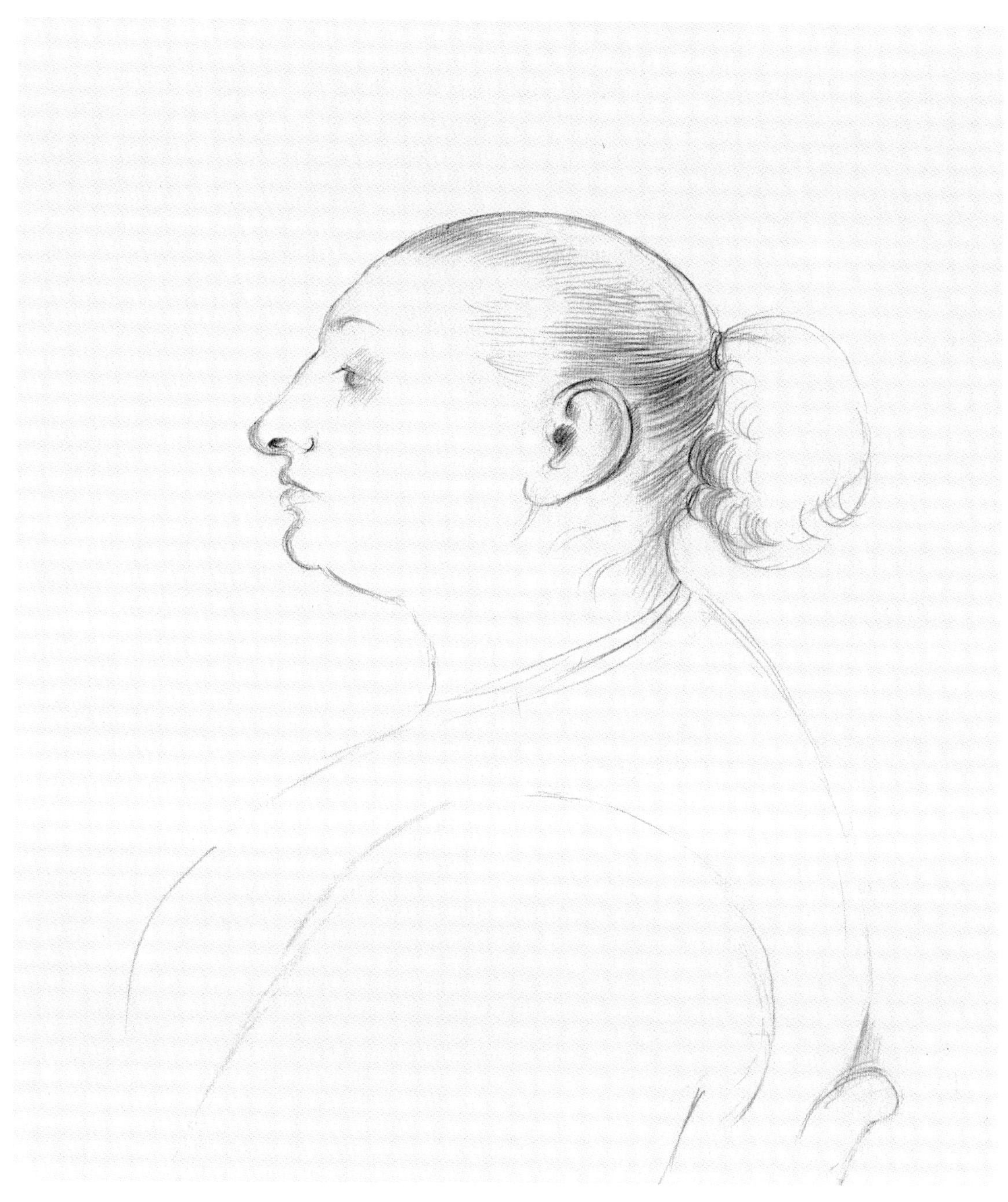

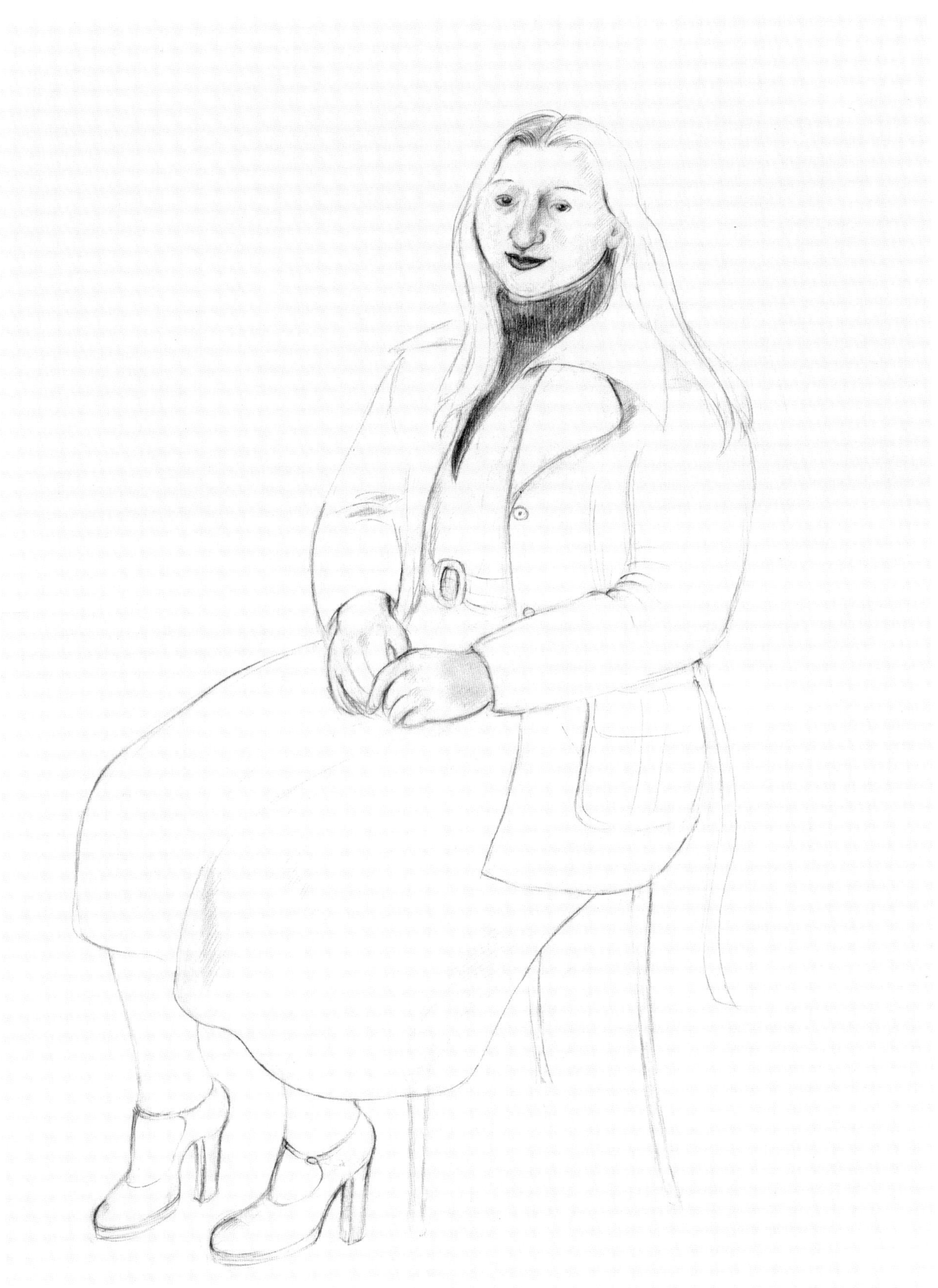

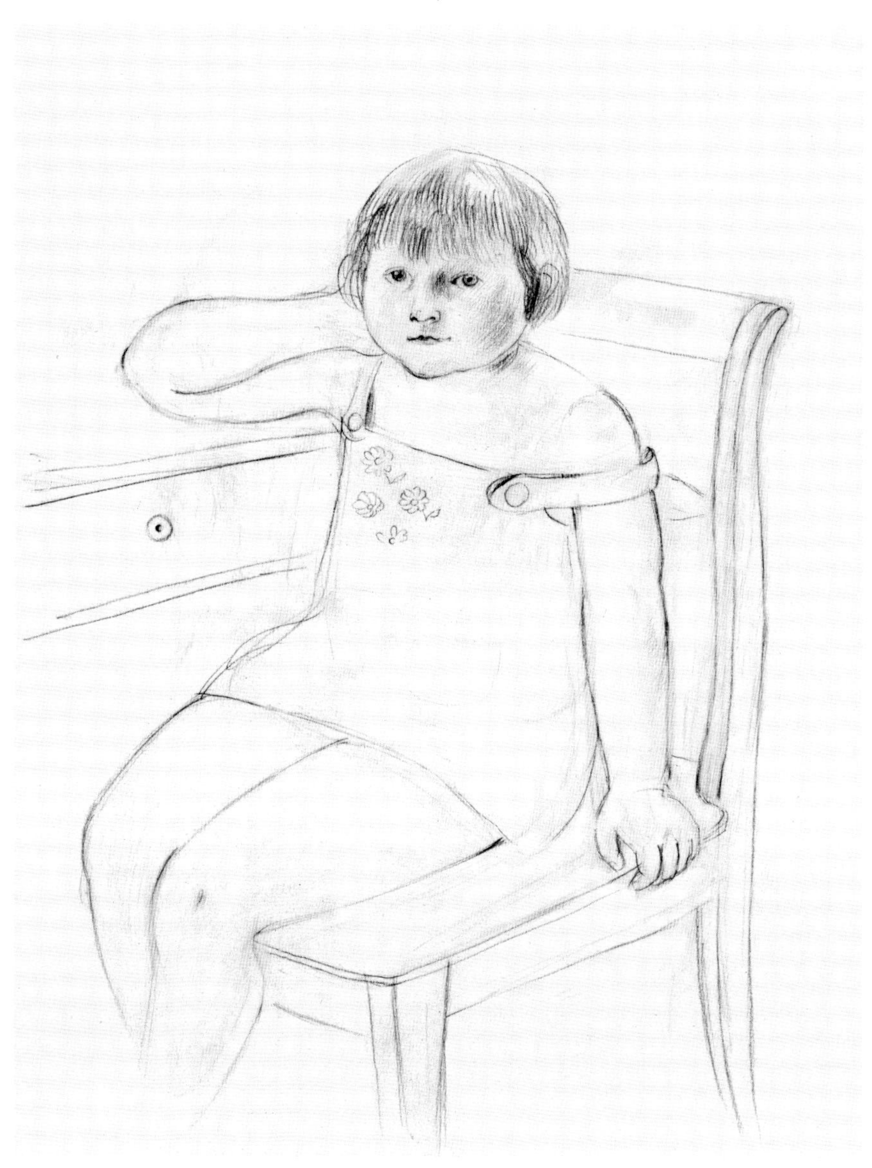

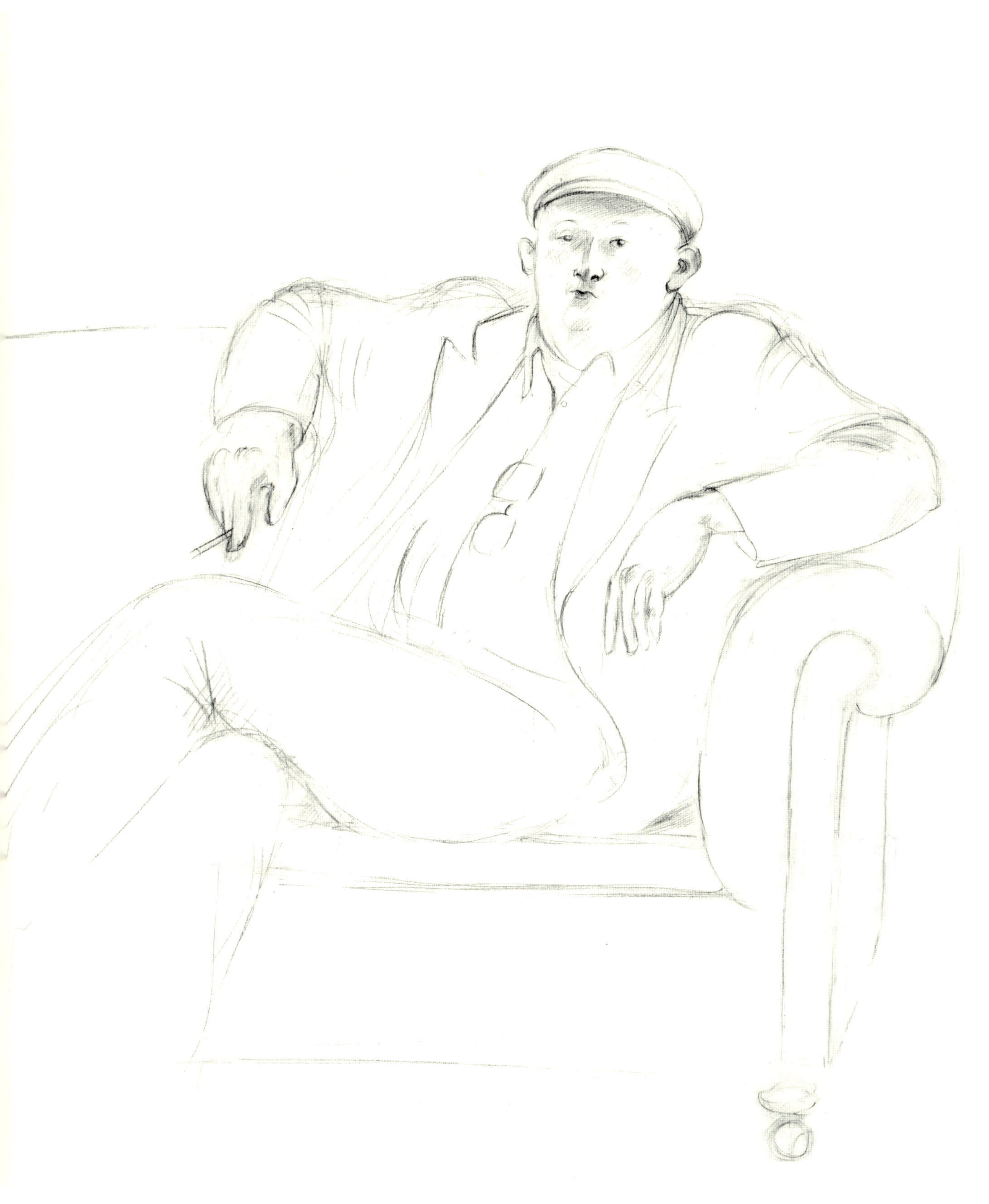

Originale
der in diesem Buch abgebildeten
Werke finden Sie in der

GALERIE DANIEL KEEL
am Kunsthaus Zürich
CH-8001, Rämistraße 45, Tel. (01) 32 31 82

die sich auf Originalzeichnungen,
Originalgraphik, Bücher,
Drucke, Poster und Portfolien
folgender Künstler spezialisiert:

BAYROS · BEARDSLEY

CHAGALL · DAUMIER · ENSOR

FLORA · GAVARNI · GOYA

GRANDVILLE · GROSZ

KUBIN · LAUTREC · PASCIN

PICASSO · SEMPÉ

SENDAK · STEINBERG

STEINLEN · TOPOR · UNGERER

VALLOTTON · VAN DEN BORN

ZIMNIK u.a.

Reshaping the Field: Arts of the African Diasporas on Display

Edited by Nana Adusei-Poku

With contributions by Nana Adusei-Poku, Mora J. Beauchamp-Byrd, Bridget R. Cooks, Abby R. Eron, Amber Esseiva, Cheryl Finley, Languid Hands (Imani Mason Jordan and Rabz Lansiquot), Julie L. McGee, Derek Conrad Murray, Serubiri Moses, Senam Okudzeto, Richard J. Powell, Jamaal B. Sheats, Howard Singerman, Marlene Smith with Claudette Johnson, Lucy Steeds and Brittany Webb.

Exhibition Histories

Exhibition Histories

Afterall's *Exhibition Histories* book series, published since 2010, addresses what happens when art becomes public. Research led, it is committed to presenting a plurality of voices and critical perspectives, while bringing archival and other primary materials to bear on current and future practice. The series to date has focused on curatorial experimentation; exhibitionary activity led by artists; and contested articulations of the 'global' and the 'located'. Complementing the books are online publications at afterall.org, discussion events and a research-based masters course in Exhibition Studies at Central Saint Martins, University of the Arts London. As researchers, publishers and teachers at Afterall, we will continue to explore situations that productively challenge and refine our understandings of 'art', 'exhibition' and 'history', mindful of what those terms might mean for the present. This would not be possible without the collaboration of our project partners: Asia Art Archive, based in Hong Kong; the Center for Curatorial Studies at Bard College, New York; and the Faculty of Fine, Applied and Performing Arts, University of Gothenburg.

Reshaping the Field: Arts of the African Diasporas on Display
Edited by Nana Adusei-Poku

First published 2022 by Afterall in association with Asia Art Archive, the Center for Curatorial Studies, Bard College and the Faculty of Fine, Applied and Performing Arts, University of Gothenburg

Exhibition Histories Series Editors
Lauren Cornell, Tom Eccles, Charles Esche, Sanne Kofod Olsen, Pablo Lafuente, Sneha Ragavan, Lucy Steeds, John Tain and Mick Wilson

Managing Editor
David Morris

Assistant Editor
Wing Chan

Copy Editor
Deirdre O'Dwyer

Design
Andrew Brash

Printed and bound by
die Keure

Distributed by
Verlag der Buchhandlung Walther und Franz König (Europe: verlag@buchhandlung-waltherkoenig.de); Cornerhouse Publications Ltd. – HOME (UK & Ireland: publications@cornerhouse.org); and D.A.P. / Distributed Art Publishers, Inc. (outside Europe: orders@dapinc.com)

Afterall
Central Saint Martins
Granary Building
1 Granary Square
London N1C 4AA
www.afterall.org

Afterall is a Research Centre of University of the Arts London and was founded in 1998 by Charles Esche and Mark Lewis.

Director
Mark Lewis

Associate Directors
Charles Esche and Chloe Ting

Project Coordinator
Camille Crichlow

ISBN 978-3-7533-0238-6 (Verlag der Buchhandlung Walther und Franz König)
ISBN 978-1-84638-263-5 (Afterall Books)

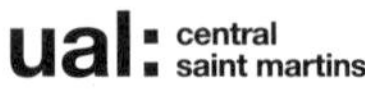

III CCS BARD

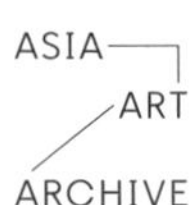

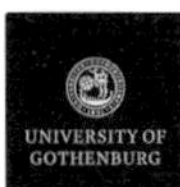

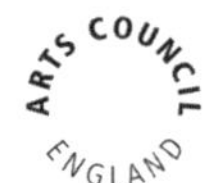

Reshaping the Field: Arts of the African Diasporas on Display

Exhibition Histories

Contents

Introduction: Reshaping the Field – Nana Adusei-Poku

Reshaping the Field: Arts of the African Diasporas on Display is the first publication to focus exclusively on African diasporic art in the US and UK through the histories of Black art exhibitions.[1] Combining perspectives from art historians, theorists, artists and curators – including a number of historical protagonists and contemporary witnesses – we had the opportunity to gather knowledge that traverses art historical research and oral histories while generating primary resources. *Reshaping the Field* aims to reflect on the sociopolitical circumstances essential to the emergence of a field of study and mode of exhibition that constantly reshapes itself and challenges normative orders.

The idea for this book, and the conference that preceded it, emerged out of my teaching practice at the Center for Curatorial Studies at Bard College (CCS Bard), which has a strong focus on exhibition histories. More than a decade after the publication of Bridget Cooks's *Exhibiting Blackness: African Americans and the American Art Museum* (2011), a seminal publication in directly addressing historic exhibitions focusing on African diasporic (or more precisely, African American) art, it is still necessary to consider the record of exhibitions that have told the story of Black art and its networks. Furthermore, it is urgent that we create fresh resources for art historians, curators, artists and researchers in the fields of exhibition studies, museum studies, cultural studies and beyond, in order to spark new research that will highlight emerging histories not necessarily considered in relation to modern art history.

Reshaping the Field stresses the profound role of Historically Black Colleges and Universities (HBCUs) – and their artist networks – which articulates itself in the book's first section, 'Marginalized Legacies and Networks'. HBCUs exhibited Black artists and collected their work during times when the quality of the work was often undermined; these institutions fostered a dialogue that spanned across the United States and to the African continent. The contributions by Richard Powell, Abby Eron, Cheryl Finley and Jamaal B. Sheats map the rich networks that established the foundations for the flourishing of Black art, art education and artists, and its ongoing importance to exhibition-making today. Although HBCUs were foundational for African American art, the essays in this anthology prioritize thinking about the dialogical nature of the Black diaspora, considering Blackness in its multiplicity instead of binding it to nationality.

When I emphasize multiplicity in this introduction, I also wish to ask: What do Black audiences want and need to see in an exhibition to feel connected and affirmed? This question challenges the ways we think through Blackness in exhibitions in different contexts – New York, Los Angeles, London, Chicago, Berlin, Paris, Stockholm, Salvador de Bahia, Port-au-Prince, Nassau, Accra, Cape Town or New Orleans. As a person who has lived, studied and worked on different continents – Africa, Europe and, now, North America – and in a range of countries – Ghana, Germany, Netherlands, the UK and the US – I am particularly sensitive to the ways in which the Black diaspora is informed by diverse perspectives and context-specific experiences. I argue that it has never been possible to connect artists only through a racial signifier, and I advocate that we be attuned to the distinctiveness of practices, formal expressions and cultural frameworks. And yet, nothing is more exciting than looking at the contemporary spectrum from various historical perspectives in order to identify commonalities despite differences in form and subject positions, which are often shaped through relationality.

Reshaping the Field builds on a long history of scholarship addressing the diversity of practices and aesthetic impact that African diasporic artists have had on global cultures, as manifested in book publications such as Alain Locke's *The Negro in Art* (1940), James A. Porter's *Modern Negro Art* (1943), Cedric Dover's *American Negro Art* (1960), Judith Wragg Chase's *Afro-American Art and Craft* (1971), Samella Lewis's *African American Art and Artists* (1972), Harry Henderson and Romare Bearden's *A History of African-American Artists: From 1972 to the Present* (1993), Deborah Willis's *Picturing Us: African American Identity in Photography* (1994), Richard Powell's *Black Art and Culture in the 20th Century* (1997) and Sharon F. Patton's *African-American Art* (1998); for the British context, I want to also mention Kobena Mercer's *Welcome to the Jungle: New Positions in Black Cultural Studies* (1994), David A. Bailey, Ian Beacom and Sonia Boyce's *Shades of Black: Assembling Black Arts in 1980s Britain* (2005) and Eddie Chambers's *Black Artists in British Art: A History Since the 1950s* (2014).

Building on this exciting scholarship allows exhibition histories to expand the ways in which we consider art and its publics. This is seen in the way that contributors to 'Marginalized Legacies and Networks' articulate the connections between different HBCUs, the African continent and wider Black diasporas. It is further developed in the section on 'Dialogics of Diaspora', which engages with Black British art and the relational nature of Black artistic and curatorial practices. One articulation of such expansive practice is Mora J. Beauchamp-Byrd's reflection on 'Transforming the Crown', which she curated in 1997; the essay gives insight into how the exhibition came into being and how we might consider it today. Marlene Smith, in conversation with Claudette Johnson, uses the 1982 exhibition 'The Pan-Afrikan Connection: An Exhibition by Young Black Artists' as a starting point for an exploration of the energetic Black British arts scene of the 1980s that fostered Smith's practice. And Lucy Steeds engages with two of the collectives that emerged from this milieu, Black Audio Film Collective and Sankofa Film/Video Collective, following their works' presentation across cinema, television and exhibition contexts to evoke multiple resonances and publics.

In the section 'Between Inclusion and Making Space', Brittany Webb contributes a succinct revisitation of Bridget Cooks's *Exhibiting Blackness* and its argument that Black artworks (and artists) are often caught between anthropologically organized exhibitions versus exhibitions aimed at establishing a universal art. For Webb, the pages of *Exhibiting Blackness* offer a history of the present. Webb highlights the protests activated in New York by the Metropolitan Museum of Art's 1969 exhibition 'Harlem on My Mind', and she identifies the reflection of this critique in recent activism against institutional exhibition practices, and how the perception of such critique often remains ahistorical. Howard Singerman's contribution stresses how Black artists have insisted on inclusion by organizing exhibitions and institutions outside of mainstream museums by strategically creating Black spaces, with particular reference to the historical examples of Cinque Gallery and Acts of Art in New York City.[2] Julie McGee shows how Black artists including David C. Driskell strategically utilized the museum to highlight their achievements in major projects such as 'Two Centuries of Black American Art' (1976). Driskell, in particular, transformed the field by drawing upon his rootedness in artistic, educational and curatorial practice; his professional and personal networks; and the institutional network of HBCUs.[3]

Such a transformation becomes especially apparent in the section titled 'Ruptures', with particular reference to 'Freestyle' at the Studio Museum in Harlem in 2001. Senam Okudzeto, one of the participating artists in 'Freestyle', provides a reflection on the experience of that project in light of the current state of the art field and new problematics that have emerged for Black practitioners: 'Is the same market that sold the ancestors in fact actively commodifying white guilt? Is there a process at hand, which is in fact colonizing the discourse of decolonization?' In my contribution, I situate 'Freestyle' and explore the complex tensions and possibilities that it introduced via the concept of *post-black* and how it ruptured the arts. Derek Conrad Murray extends these questions through a deep theoretical engagement with the question of Black representation.

These chapters show the necessity of Black group exhibitions and their networks, which have secured, collected, archived and preserved cultural histories for present generations. They are explored here with the hope that they may influence and serve as case studies for exhibitions to come. Students of colour at CCS Bard, where I work, are often confronted with the question of identity signifiers for curatorial frameworks. As the present volume reflects, this is not a new problem. While students often want to work with artists in creating group shows based on artists' shared identity categories, they are reluctant to use these markers for fear of marginalization; or the critique of oversimplification of artistic practice; or the feeling of being pigeonholed as 'curators of colour'. However, the history and necessity of exhibitions that use a racial signifier has been contested since its beginning. In 1946, Romare Bearden stated: 'The work of Negro artists reflects all the artistic trends of the time.'[4] Bearden emphasized Black art as a part of the American narrative – and yet the quality of Black art is consistently questioned and excluded from the dominant narrative of art history and exhibition-making. In 1968, painter and art educator Charles Alston equally emphasized the bias by art critics reviewing Black shows in an oral history interview.[5] This legacy of bias can be traced back to one of the first Black group exhibitions in an art museum in the US, which was supposed to give African American artists a larger platform and visibility: 'The Negro in Art Week: Exhibition of Primitive African Sculpture, Modern Paintings, Sculpture, Drawings, Applied Art, and Books', organized by the Chicago Woman's Club in consultation with Alain Locke at the Art

Institute of Chicago in 1927. The museum's director, Robert B. Harshe, noted to the white curators that the exhibition should 'conform as near as possible to standards set by regular art museum exhibitions and exhibition galleries'.[6] Here, 'regular' in this sentence may be interchanged with 'white', which highlights that whiteness, however lucid, was used as a measurement of quality as well as of the constraints under which Black artists and curators had to exhibit.

When we look at the history of Black exhibitions, we look at more than just the intricacies of artistic display and inclusion or exclusion. The reason why Black art exhibitions in particular are a tremendously rich resource to understand artistic movements, political shifts and aesthetic developments is that Black exhibitions tell cultural histories and allow for revelatory debates to emerge about our current moment and potentially moments to come. This notion of futurity has a special focus in this book's section 'Curating Black Futures', which foregrounds the voices of contemporary Black curators and practitioners as they articulate their visions, experiences and hopes for the field. As part of this dialogue, which features contributions by Amber Esseiva, Languid Hands, Brittany Webb and Serubiri Moses, the shared yet often isolating experience of being Black in predominantly white institutions is problematized, especially as a historical through line.

Institutions are reminded by social justice movements such as Black Lives Matter that they are intrinsically founded in White Supremacy – that gratuitous violence against Black people is not necessarily new. Bridget Cooks's opening essay in this anthology highlights the profound anxiety that Blackness provokes and how understanding this anxiety can help us in rethinking art history, museums and institutional practice. As Richard Powell expressed so eloquently in a recent interview, BLM's demands are

> *a reverberation of other moments in time where people have stood up and said, 'enough is enough'. Black Lives Matter is in some ways a twenty-first-century reverberation of 'Black Is Beautiful' and 'Black Power', and 'Black Power' was a reverberation that hearkened back to the 1920s and 30s, to the Jazz Age and the Harlem Renaissance. So, we've always had these periods in Black America, intermittently, where a particularly vocal and expressive movement says, 'I matter, I exist.'*[7]

Black artists' works are now achieving record sales at international auctions as collectors are focusing on expanding their collections with pieces by artists of African descent.[8] Educational and art institutions are forced, again, to reflect on their legacies and to make significant structural changes. With each reverberation of the existence and mattering of Black Life comes a wave of exhibitions focusing on Black art.

I hope this publication will serve as a resource for how we can make connections to the past, and how we can gather materials and knowledge to support and enable artists, curators, critics and art historians in making well-informed and nuanced curatorial decisions and writing art histories that tell stories of multiplicities beyond historical bias.

Notes

[1] Editors' Note: Across this publication there are various approaches to the capitalisation of 'Black'/'black'; rather than apply a universal rule, in each essay we have followed the usage of individual authors.

[2] This debate continues to be important today, in projects such as Titus Kaphar's NXTHVN in New Haven; Yinka Shonibare's Guest Projects in London; and Noah Davis's Underground Museum in Los Angeles, to name just a few. See also the contribution of Languid Hands to this volume.

[3] 'Two Centuries of Black American Art' opened at the Los Angeles County Museum of Art (LACMA) in 1976, before travelling to Atlanta's High Museum of Art, the Dallas Museum of Fine Arts and the Brooklyn Museum.

[4] Nicholas Miller, 'The History of the Group Exhibition from the Harmon Foundation to Black Male', in Eddie Chambers (ed.), *The Routledge Companion to African American Art History*, New York: Routledge, p.301.

[5] See Bridget R. Cooks, *Exhibiting Blackness: African Americans and the American Art Museum*, Amherst: University of Massachusetts Press, 2011, p.43.

[6] N. Miller, 'The History of the Group Exhibition from the Harmon Foundation to Black Male', *op. cit.*, p.303. Emphasis mine.

[7] Folasade Ologundudu, 'Decades Ago, Richard J. Powell Was Once Among Only a Handful of Scholars Dedicated to Black Art History. Here's How He Has Seen the Field Change', *Artnet*, 18 February 2021, https://news.artnet.com/art-world/richard-j-powell-interview-1944754.

[8] Nate Freeman, 'Black Artists Shatter Multiple Records in $392.3 Million Sotheby's Sale', *Artsy*, 17 May 2018, https://www.artsy.net/article/artsy-editorial-black-artists-shatter-multiple-records-3923-million-sothebys-sale. During my time at CCS Bard the collection has grown exponentially with regard to Black artists.

Art, Museums and the Fear of a Black Planet – Bridget R. Cooks

I cannot stop thinking about the discourses of Blackness, art and museums.[1] My thoughts come from my experiences working in art museums as an educator and curator – ideas that I discuss in my book *Exhibiting Blackness*, which has the following premise:

> *Exhibitions of African American art in American art museums have been curated through two guiding methodologies: the anthropological approach, which displays the difference of racial Blackness from the elevated White 'norm', and the corrective narrative, which aims to present the work of significant and overlooked African American artists to a mainstream audience. The former methodology reflects an institutional curiosity concerning the presence of racial otherness, commonly coupled with a desire to perpetuate the superiority of Eurocentric culture through its contrast to a Black difference defined as inherently inferior. The latter methodology was formed out of the necessity to present the art by African Americans and correct for its historical absence and misrepresentation in mainstream art museums.*[2]

The book provides a context for contemporary exhibitions of art by Black people.

In what follows, I will consider the anxieties that Blackness provokes for art museums in the United States and how understanding that anxiety can aid us in rethinking art history and art museums. I am particularly interested in illuminating the ongoing pressures museums have faced since the publication of *Exhibiting Blackness*, in their efforts to decolonize their spaces and rethink their functions.[3] I will posit that a key part of the exhibition process is our responsibility as students of the arts, viewers, researchers, writers and critics to engage and respond to the work that museums do.

Although problems at the heart of questions regarding the future of Blackness in the art world today are tethered to those in my book, where we are right now reflects a unique set of anxieties. The Covid-19 pandemic and the spectacular set of recorded violences against Black people in the US have brought issues of mortality and survival to the doorsteps of institutions that have enjoyed the privilege of authoritarian positions. Thinking through the recent failures of museums to address these issues brought me back to the title of Public Enemy's infinitely influential album *Fear of a Black Planet*, which I've taken for the title of my talk. In 1990, *Fear of a Black Planet* amplified Black voices through hip-hop by setting a new bar for turntablism, eclectic sampling and danceable rhythms combined with humour and politically astute rhymes. With this album, Public Enemy returned to the charts energized by their 1989 anthem 'Fight the Power', made popular through Spike Lee's film *Do the Right Thing* (1989). The plot of Lee's work resonated with many Black viewers' frustrations with police surveillance, police brutality, economic injustice and everyday anti-Black disrespect. Together Public Enemy and Lee made the summer of 1990 very hot, and very pro-Black. Public Enemy's follow-up, *Fear of a Black Planet*,

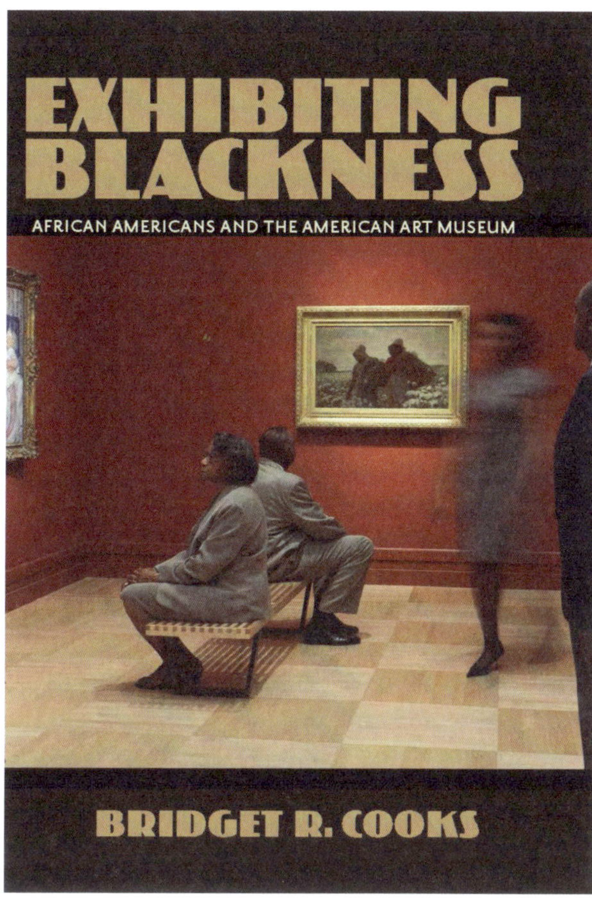

Cover of Bridget R. Cooks's *Exhibiting Blackness: African Americans and the American Art Museum*, Amherst: University of Massachusetts Press, 2011

gave us classics such as 'Welcome to the Terrordome', '911 Is a Joke', 'Who Stole the Soul?', 'Burn Hollywood Burn' and the eponymous title track.

As a collection, the album testifies to a Black presence that exists on a different plane, outside of the legal protections of liberty and justice for all. The Black planet is a nation within a nation. It describes Black communities that become terrordomes when under attack from white supremacy, communities in which emergencies are not regarded by those who profess to protect and serve those in need. The Black planet is a place that suffers through white appropriation and the superficial misrepresentations of Black culture most evident in fashion, music and language created by Black people, but quickly re-labelled 'urban', a term used to free an idea from Blackness and extend proprietary rights to all city dwellers, including non-Black people who rush to emulate Black trends.[4] Public Enemy's album insists on Black political resistance and creativity as the antidote to anti-Black pain and loss.[5]

Fear of a Black Planet preceded the discovery of WASP-12b by NASA's Hubble Space Telescope by nearly two decades. Known as the oddball exoplanet, the

Installation view, 'The Facade Commission: Wangechi Mutu, *The NewOnes, will free Us*', The Metropolitan Museum of Art, New York, 2019–20. Photo © The Metropolitan Museum of Art/ Art Resource/Scala, Florence

pitch-black planet WASP-12b lies outside of our solar system and, according to NASA, is 'black as fresh asphalt because it eats light rather than reflecting it back to space'.[6]

I cannot help but draw parallels between the force of Blackness in these two realms. The characterization of the aggressive black planet that 'eats light' resonates with the way in which anti-Black rhetoric describes Black Lives Matter activism as terrorism that threatens white supremacy as the norm.[7] The cry against white supremacy and the institutions that uphold racial hierarchies permeates *Fear of a Black Planet*. Now, over thirty years later, that call against anti-Blackness resounds again in response to the persistence of racism and superficial gestures in the name of diversity, inclusion and equity. Concerns about the absence of light, and more poignantly the presence of darkness, socially and astronomically, reveal deep anxieties around new ways of perception that threaten to distort previous laws of vision. Indeed, the art world crises around Blackness involve issues of racial parity and mixing that would force the reconfiguration of categories such as American art, Modernism and fine art – distinctions on which the authority of museums rests.

I will offer some examples of events that demonstrate the historic moment we are living in now concerning art museums and the discourses of ethics, decolonization, historical truth and community engagement.[8] Although struggles over power and representation have been ongoing since the early twentieth century, I will focus on the recent past (2017–21) in order to bring perspective to our current situation. In 2019, the Metropolitan Museum of Art in New York unveiled four bronze sculptures created by Kenyan American artist Wangechi Mutu. The sculptures filled four architectural alcoves on the outside of the museum building that had sat as empty platforms since the building's completion in 1902. The commission was the first in a series of annual commissions planned for artists to make new work in response to the Met's collection.[9] The sculptures are reimagined from ancient caryatids – female forms used to hold up the weight of a structure. Here, Mutu's forms sit independently, with authority and without the burden of supporting something else. Each woman-figure is made of long, draped, elegant coils that create the regal contours of their form. With narrowed eyes, hair pulled back and a sun-reflecting disc placed on the front or back of the head, each woman faces forward with hands resting on knees. The symbolism here is magnificent. The sculptures in *The NewOnes, will free Us* (2019–20) show the Black female form as goddess. They mark a terrific step towards making changes to the long-troubled history of colonization at the Met. However, we as viewers must make the museum accountable, so that the artwork does not sit as a gesture, but signals the reverent treatment of Black artists, staff and visitors inside the galleries.

Also in 2019, the International Council of Museums (ICOM), an organization that represents twenty thousand museums across the globe, met in Japan for its annual conference. On the agenda was the vote to officially revise its definition of a museum. The proposed definition has divided its membership – some of whom reject a new mission to promote justice in multiple forms for the planet and its people. The new definition claims an active function for

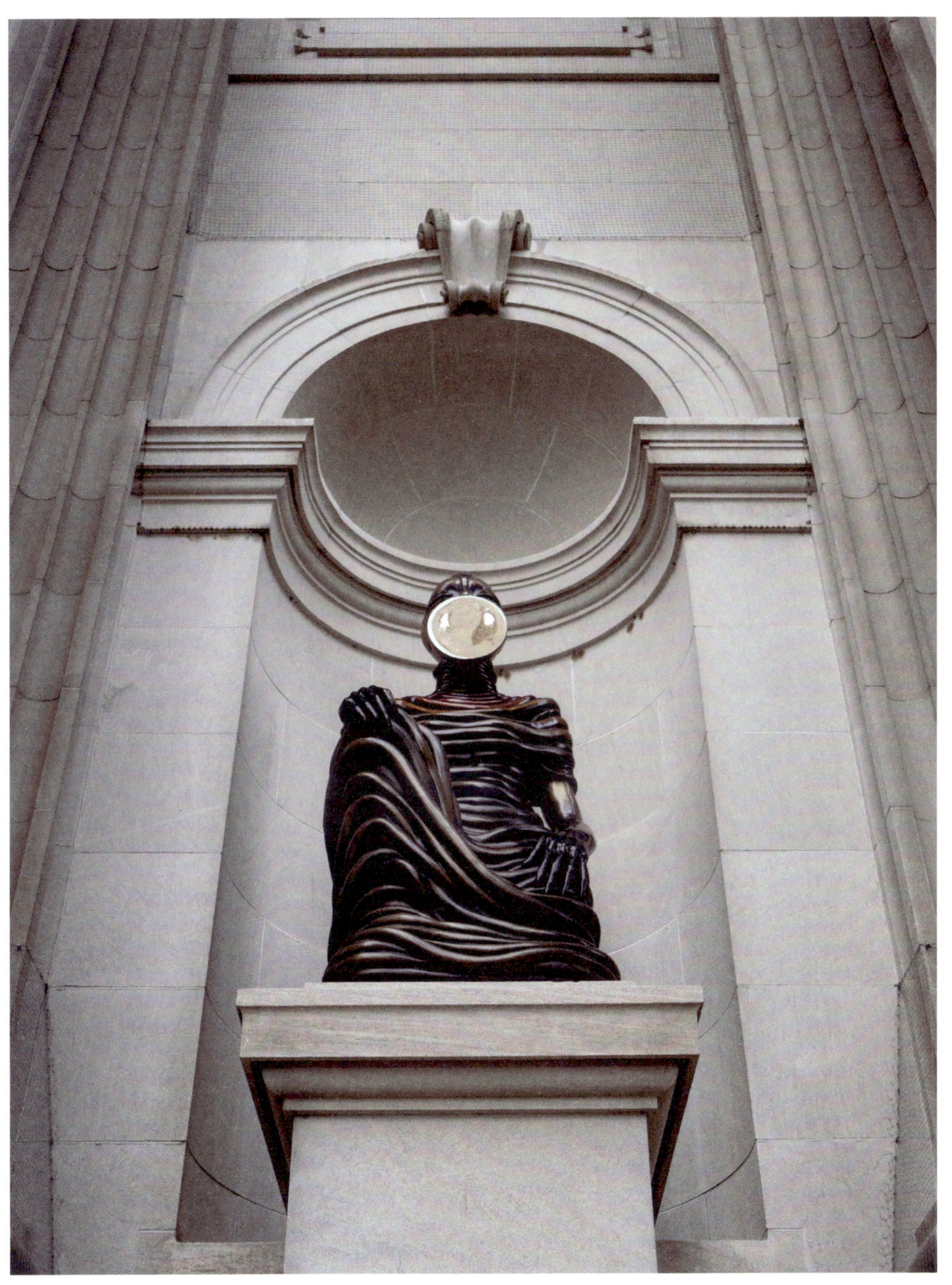

museums. It states: 'Museums are democratizing, inclusive and polyphonic spaces for critical dialogue about the pasts and the futures.' It also states that the museum should guarantee 'equal rights and equal access to heritage for all the people'.[10] The definition was considered too radical by many members, and ICOM decided to postpone the vote.[11]

In May 2019, the Whitney Museum of American Art in New York faced organized and persistent protest because of the investments of Warren B. Kanders, who was serving as vice chairman of the museum's board of directors. The protestors, including activists in the group Decolonize This Place, objected to Kanders's ownership of Safariland, a company that manufactures tear gas used against migrants along the Mexico-US border.[12] Many of the artists in the biennial called for Kanders's resignation, which came in July.[13]

In February 2021, Newfields, a campus of gardens and art spaces that houses the Indianapolis Museum of Art, faced community backlash against the museum's posted job description for a new director. The ad doubled down on white supremacy, saying that the museum was interested in 'maintaining the Museum's traditional, core, white audience'.[14] While likely true, the statement conflicted with other pronouncements by the museum that it is committed to diversity. In the face of institutional pressure, the president of Newfields, Charles L. Venable, resigned. This latest scandal followed the 2020 resignation of the museum's only African American curator, Kellie Morgan, who has gone on record to make public the anti-Black conditions she suffered as a museum employee.[15]

In June 2020, Neal Benezra, director of the San Francisco Museum of Modern Art, apologized for deleting comments by Taylor Brandon, a Black woman and former communications associate who called out SFMOMA for its poor handling of anti-Black activity within the museum, and for its lack of response to the murder of George Floyd, one of five men killed by police across the US on May 25, 2020. Pushback from Benezra's censorship prompted an apology and may be related to the resignation of Nan Keeton, who was deputy director of external relations at SFMOMA.[16]

The assertations of the #BlackLivesMatter, #DecolonizeThisMuseum and #MuseumsAreNotNeutral movements challenge and generally perplex mainstream museum leadership. Few museum directors or curators have acted to address the legacy of white supremacy and social hegemony in their institutions or disrupted regular acquisition and exhibition procedures in order to claim that Black Lives Matter in their institutions. Their efforts have been lauded and criticized. In April 2018, Christopher Bedford, director of the Baltimore Museum of Art at the time, announced that the museum would deaccession seven works by white men in their collection, in order to fund the accession of works by white women and artists of colour. As a result, Bedford stated that 'the BMA acquired 11 major works of art by women and artists of color purchased in full or in part with funds from the objects that were deaccessioned last spring. This is just one aspect of the museum's strategy to broaden the historical narrative of art and build a more diverse and inclusive art experience for Baltimore.'[17]

In October 2020, a second round of deaccessioning was planned in the attempt to diversify the collection. The auction was called off a mere few hours before it began. The museum faced dissent from former trustees and board members who opposed the sale, and two board member rescinded promised gifts based on Bedford's deaccessioning plan. In February 2019, SFMOMA followed the BMA's lead with the sale of a Mark Rothko work to purchase works by makers of different racial and gender identities. These are bold gestures by these museums, but they are also unsustainable. I am hoping that the boards and donors of these museums and others will understand the seriousness of changing their permanent collections and that they will commit to funding transformational collection and exhibition practices. This would mean increasing the number of objects in collections and rethinking how narratives can be told with a more expansive selection of artworks used to represent American art.

In 2017, New York City mayor Bill de Blasio formed a committee to consider what should be done about several statues in the city that promote white supremacy. One of these was the troubling *Equestrian Statue of Theodore Roosevelt* by James Earle Fraser, which was commission by the American Museum of Natural History and installed in front of the building in 1940.[18] In 2019, the museum opened an exhibition called 'Addressing the Statue' and invited visitors to share their thoughts about the promotion of demeaning representations of Indigenous and Black people through Fraser's work. The statue shows an Indigenous man and a Black man walking on either side of the president, who rides above them on horseback. A month after public protest against anti-Black violence was sparked by the video recording of Minneapolis police officers murdering George Floyd on May 25, 2020, de Blasio ordered the removal of the statue. The statue remained in place for much longer, and was only removed in January 2022.

In 2020, the directors of all four venues of the retrospective exhibition 'Philip Guston Now' agreed to postpone the project over concerns that they had not communicated appropriately with Black constituents in preparation for it. In particular, the museum directors worried over the potential response to Guston's paintings that feature cartoonish Ku Klux Klan figures. The exhibition was planned to debut at the National Gallery of Art, Washington DC in June 2020 before travelling to the Museum of Fine Arts, Houston; the Tate Modern, London; and the Museum of Fine Arts, Boston.[19] Suffice it to say, these museum leaders agreed to pause their actions for a time of reflection and reconsideration. It was unclear at the time how the museum directors expected the anti-Black climate in museums to change, or why they believed it had improved enough to open the show in 2022.[20]

The museum trouble that is going on now is not new. The history of conflict between upholding white supremacy, on the one hand, and representing people of colour as equal peers, on the other, is older than the museum itself. For African American people, it has a specific, traceable history through exhibitions. In fact, it was my experiences of visiting and working in museums such as the National Gallery of Art, Washington DC and the Los Angeles County Museum of Art (LACMA) that encouraged me to write *Exhibiting Blackness.*

In mainstream museums, I found the regular omission of art created by Black artists from the works on view. When there was an exhibition with work by Black artists, I noticed a few other things: First, Black artists were featured within group exhibitions about Black identity. They were not regularly shown in thematic exhibitions organized around a style of art or specific topic, and rarely were their works shown alongside artists who were not Black. Second, the object labels for works by Black artists stated that the artists were Black; however, labels for works by white artists did not identify them as white. Third, when an exhibition of work by Black artists was on view, the majority of museum visitors who commented about the exhibition stated that they had never seen an artwork by a Black artist before; that they believed that the exhibition was the first of its kind; and that they wanted to know more.

There are many examples that precede the recent ones I have recounted, some of which can be found in *Exhibiting Blackness*. The most notorious example is, doubtless, 'Harlem on My Mind: Cultural Capital of Black America, 1900–1968' (1969), organized by the Metropolitan Museum of Art. It was an exhibition that sought to trace the history and value of the predominantly Black community of Harlem in New York City. In organizing one of the most controversial exhibitions in United States history, the Met decided to exclude people from Harlem from participating in the planning and to exclude artworks by Harlem's thriving artist community. The museum justified these decisions by arguing that Harlem itself was a work of art and the inclusion of artworks in 'Harlem on My Mind' would only detract from the overall exhibition.[21]

Another example of the continuation of the anthropological, and really sociological, approach to showing art by Black artists involves Jacob Lawrence. Every decade, the Museum of Modern Art in New York and the Phillips Collection in Washington DC exhibit Lawrence's complete sixty-panel artwork *The Migration of the Negro* (1940–41). Lawrence's tempura-on-panel paintings chronicle the push-and-pull factors that led to the Great Migration in the United States. Shared interest by MoMA and the Phillips Collection led to the awkward split of the artwork into odd and even panels acquired by both institutions. Its exhibition at MoMA in 1942 was the first solo exhibition by an African American artist at the museum.[22] Its most recent presentation was in 2015, when MoMA displayed Lawrence's work in an exhibition called 'One-Way Ticket'. Basic elements of art – colour, line, shape, composition – and common sources for analysis – artistic style, influences and innovation – were not part of the curatorial presentation through wall texts or object labels. Although the work has strong narrative content, there is a thoughtful formal relationship between the messages in the work and its medium. At MoMA, *The Migration of the Negro* was presented less as an artwork and more as documentary illustration. The curators made a bank of computers central to the presentation. Through digital content, the exhibition presented a team of experts of African American culture: history professors, authors, curators and performers provided what the title wall called 'other visions of the great movement north'. They formed a supplement to Lawrence's art; an informative source on the Great Migration; and ultimately a distraction from the focus – the art that was in the room.

Art historian Elizabeth Berkowitz offers an astute analysis of the exhibition:

> *[D]espite seemingly universal critical praise, MoMA's show failed to avoid the difficulty endemic to art historical emphasis on a non-white – and therefore noncanonical – artist. In a painstaking attempt to showcase and laud Lawrence and his work (a parade of good intentions), MoMA's 'One-Way Ticket' inadvertently accomplished the opposite. 'One-Way Ticket' fell into the trap of artistic pigeonholing, as the exhibition classified Lawrence as a painterly-historian of African-American history, rather than an* American artist *who used the visual and political interests of an interwar, international art scene to create works which focused on African-American subjects.*[23]

MoMA treated Lawrence as an anthropological native informant. It reinscribed racial hierarchy within its collections and, in turn, its exhibitions. In other words, the museum was doing a lot of contextualization to present art by a Black artist about Black people.

I want to return to this fear and share more examples of anxieties around activating and owning Blackness as a way of seeing. One example begins with artist Anish Kapoor's 2016 purchase of the exclusive rights to Vantablack, known as 'the world's blackest black substance'.[24] The substance was developed by Surrey NanoSystems for satellite-borne blackbody calibration systems. It abs-orbs 99 per cent of light, making an object completely invisible in darkness. Vantablack has been used in the defence and space industries in the UK and in the US for stealth weaponry and detection systems. Described as having the ability to make the experience of looking at any object like looking into a black hole, the liquid became appealing to visual artists interested in appropriation for illusionist possibilities. It also engendered hostility from artists who resented Kapoor's exclusive right to the blackest black, particularly from white British post-Pop artist Stuart Semple, who started a successful Kickstarter campaign to make a blacker black substance that would be available to all artists.[25] Pitched as 'the blackest, the mattest paint in the known universe. Like a black hole or void in a bottle', the blackest black wasn't something that only Semple wanted.[26] He exceeded his Kickstarter funding goal after 38 hours and went on to manufacture Black 3.0 in 2019.[27]

In August 2020, the colour development company Pantone announced Ultra Black, a colour inspired by a song of the same name by hip-hop icon Nas. Here is an extended quote from the company, describing the project:

> *A testament of the times, Ultra Black is a statement to being unapologetically Pro-Black, and thus pro-humanity. While the color black often connotes feelings of darkness, Nas reimagines the term to represent its richness, complexity, and profound beauty. An electrifying phrase honoring the Black community as the life force of culture, the term extends beyond race, class or creed. It is symbolic of the fortitude, power, legacy and interconnectedness of all people worldwide. Just as black absorbs all light, Ultra Black represents the unification of all people, spotlighting Black joy and the promising future ahead.*[28]

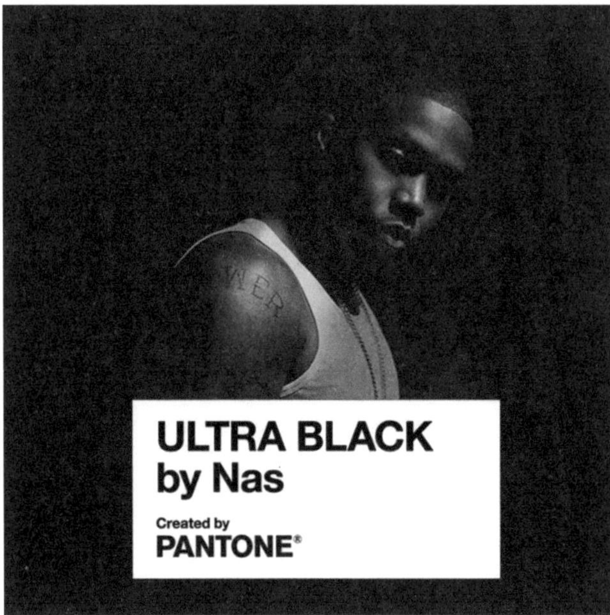

Left:
Publicity image for Pantone 'Ultra Black', 2020

Right:
Stuart Semple, Black 3.0 promotional graphic, 2019. Courtesy the artist

What's immediately remarkable is how, at every turn of phrase that focuses on Blackness, the text moves away from the colour to an emphasis on the way it represents humanity. Pantone creates Blackness in order to disarm its darkness and transform it into something for everyone. Proceeds from the sales of Ultra Black swag by Nas are designated for charity, and charity seems to be a code for Black organizations. What is this rush to own Blackness – its colour, its optical abilities to change perception of physical dimensions, its association with Black excellence? How can we characterize this interest in manifesting and owning the purest black – a black that changes vision and defies the perception of dimensionality in space? As I've just indicated through my interpretation of Pantone's Ultra Black, part of the answer is the desire to own Blackness, to appropriate it, and ultimately the desire to destroy it, by redefining it through white appropriation.

At the heart of this and other answers to the question of the lust for Black possession is the key relationship between black as pigment and black as form.[29] This articulation is something that artists have been wrestling with in visual language for generations. In 2015, a joke was discovered underneath Kazimir Malevich's 1915 Suprematist painting *The Black Square*. Described in *The New Yorker* as 'the most famous, most enigmatic and most frightening painting known to man', the revelation of the hidden text offers new interpretations of the black monochromatic.[30] In the white border of the painting is a message that translates into English as 'Negroes battling in a cave.'[31] The racist joke transforms the painting into an image of Black flesh in conflict and equates the colour black as a representation of people of African descent. As film-maker Arthur Jafa explains, the implications of accessing the embodiment of Black people through Modernist abstraction demands:

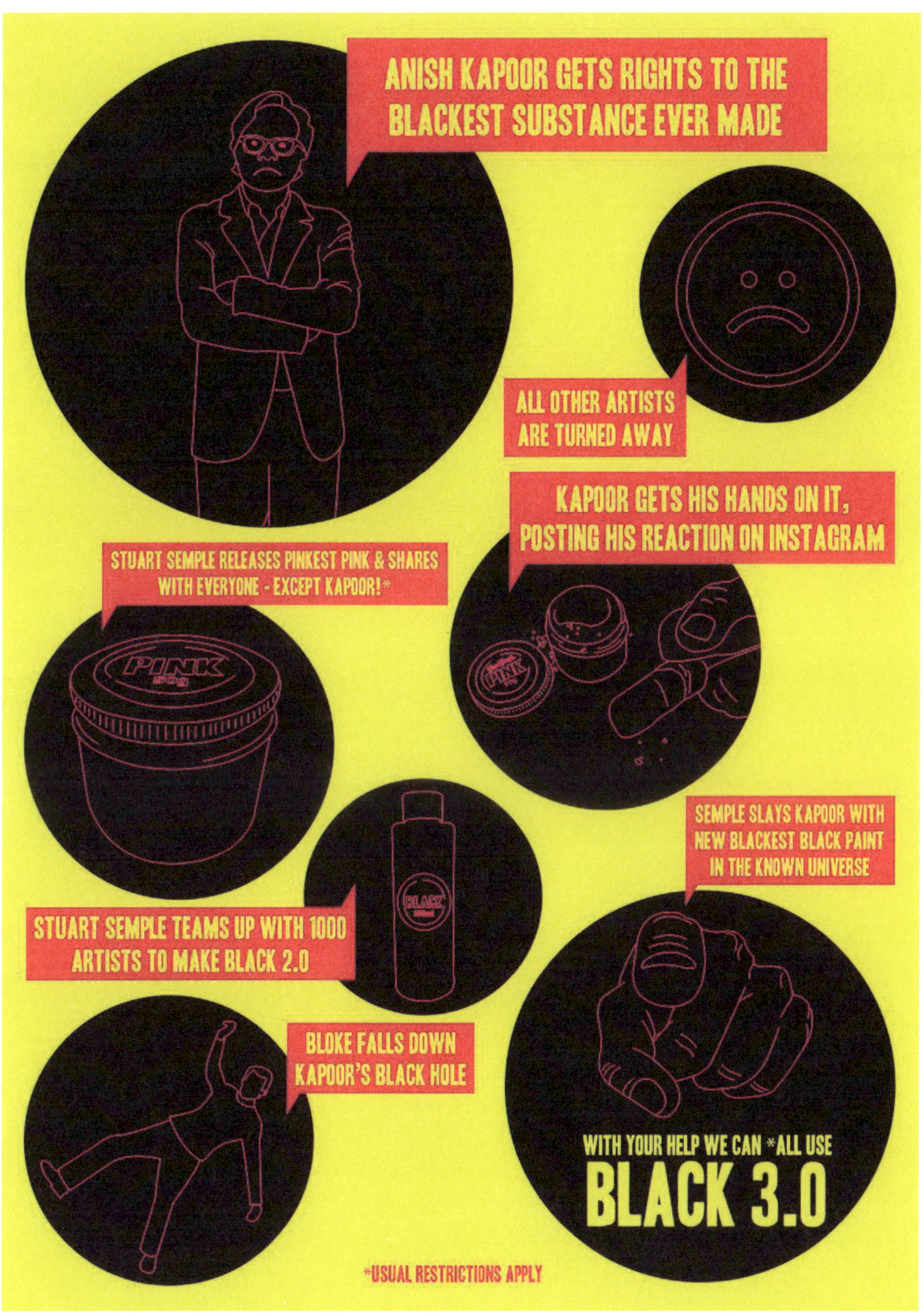
ANISH KAPOOR GETS RIGHTS TO THE BLACKEST SUBSTANCE EVER MADE
ALL OTHER ARTISTS ARE TURNED AWAY
KAPOOR GETS HIS HANDS ON IT, POSTING HIS REACTION ON INSTAGRAM
STUART SEMPLE RELEASES PINKEST PINK & SHARES WITH EVERYONE - EXCEPT KAPOOR!*
PINK
SEMPLE SLAYS KAPOOR WITH NEW BLACKEST BLACK PAINT IN THE KNOWN UNIVERSE
BLACK
STUART SEMPLE TEAMS UP WITH 1000 ARTISTS TO MAKE BLACK 2.0
BLOKE FALLS DOWN KAPOOR'S BLACK HOLE
WITH YOUR HELP WE CAN *ALL USE
BLACK 3.0
*USUAL RESTRICTIONS APPLY

some major reconsiderations of the conceptual origins and parameters of modernism: how black bodies activate space, or the volumetric intensity of black bodies, of cities; the attraction of the entropic; modernism as a substrand of black aesthetics; the black body as the premier anti-entropic figure of the twentieth century. The trauma provoked by the introduction of the black body into white space is profound.[32]

Regardless of whether Malevich wrote it, the description of his painting references Blackness in social space and opens up another understanding of the debt that Modernism owes to Black people and the phantasm of Blackness in the white imaginary.[33]

In matters of perception, experience and force, Blackness shows its relevance for art and visuality. Its interpretation demonstrates the facts that Black lives matter and Black art matters. As viewers, we engage with artworks on at least two registers, which we can call *presentation* and *representation*.[34] There is the visual presentation of the object that has a presence and takes up space in the gallery. It is hung, lit, visible and presented. Then there is representation, which is how we perceive and understand what we see. What do we perceive as the subject matter? What is depicted in the pictures? And how is it depicted? Our job in viewing, thinking and writing is to pay attention to both registers. We should let the art signify and be challenged by it, not in fear, but because it offers new ways of seeing. We will only see Black futures in museums that are different and more dimensional than what we have seen in the past, once curators and directors confront their fears of a Black planet. It is an inevitable place created by white supremacy that they are scrambling to deny and control. The foundations of art history are at stake, and the evidence of Black brilliance blinds the gatekeepers who are afraid of the dark.

Notes

1 Editors' Note: This text is adapted from the author's presentation at the online conference 'Reshaping the Field: Arts of the African Diasporas on Display', hosted by the Center for Curatorial Studies, Bard College, 4–6 November 2021.

2 Bridget R. Cooks, *Exhibiting Blackness: African Americans and the American Art Museum*, Amherst: University of Massachusetts, 2011, p.1.

3 The idea of decolonizing a museum involves addressing the violence of nation-building and its supporting institutions. The colonial philosophies that justified the force used to dominate land, people and cultures are the foundation of many museums in the United States. The colonial mindset still exists in the acquisition of art, institutional definition of aesthetics and the presentation of objects in exhibitions.

4 For an intellectually astute and richly informed discussion of the ongoing appropriation of Black cultural production, see Greg Tate (ed.), *Everything But the Burden: What White People are Taking From Black Culture*, New York: Broadway Books, 2003.

5 Anti-Blackness is the ideology that Black people's lives do not matter coupled with the expression of white supremacy. People who subscribe to anti-Blackness are not limited to people who identify as white. Anti-Black attitudes express the hatred of Black people, their efforts to assert belonging in the world, their insistence that their lives matter and their expressions of joy and celebration of life.

6 Donna Weaver, Ray Villard and Taylor Bell, 'NASA's Hubble Captures Blistering Pitch-Black Planet', 14 September 2017, https://www.nasa.gov/feture/goddard/2017/hubble-captures-blistering-pitch-black-planet.

[7] For a first-hand account of this interpretation of Black life as a threat to white life, see Asha Bandele and Patrice Khan-Cullors, *When They Call You a Terrorist: A Black Lives Matter Memoir*, New York: St. Martin's Griffin, 2019.

[8] As explored, for instance, in Aruna D'Souza, *Whitewalling: Art, Race & Protest in 3 Acts*, New York: Badlands Unlimited, 2018.

[9] See 'The Façade Commission: Wangechi Mutu, *The NewOnes, will free Us*', Metropolitan Museum of Art website, https://www.metmuseum.org/exhibitions/listings/2019/facade-commission-wangechi-mutu.

[10] Kate Brown, 'Are Art Institutions Becoming Too "Ideological"? A Debate Breaks Out at the International Council of Museums Over Politics in the Galleries', *Artnet*, 20 August 2021, https://news.artnet.com/art-world/icom-museum-definition-debate-1630312; and Vivienne Chow, 'Should Art Museums Be More or Less Ideological? After Pushback, a Gathering of Museum Leaders Refuses to Address the Question', *Artnet*, 9 September 2019, https://news.artnet.com/art-world/museums-icom-ideological-definition-1645387.

[11] A revised and decidedly more generic version, which omits the above-quoted phrases, finally went to the vote in 2022. See https://icom.museum/en/news/museum-definition-process-the-two-final-proposals/.

[12] See, for instance, '"You Can't Hide": Protesters March From Whitney To Warren B. Kanders's Home During Biennial Opening', *Artforum.com*, 18 May 2019; https://www.artforum.com/news/you-can-t-hide-protesters-march-from-whitney-to-warren-b-kanders-s-home-during-biennial-opening-79854; and 'Artists Withdraw From Whitney Biennial as Backlash Builds Against Warren Kanders', *Artforum.com*, 19 July 2019, https://www.artforum.com/news/artists-withdraw-from-whitney-biennial-as-backlash-builds-against-warren-kanders-80360.

[13] See Helen Holmes, 'Warren Kanders Resigns From the Whitney Board After Months of Artist and Activist Protests,' *The Observer*, 25 July 2019, https://observer.com/2019/07/warren-kanders-whitney-board-resignation-biennial-protests/.

[14] Valentina De Liscia, 'Indianapolis Museum of Art President Resigns After Facing Backlash for Offensive Job Posting', *Hyperallergic*, 17 February 2021, https://hyperallergic.com/622740/indianapolis-museum-of-art-president-resigns/.

[15] Domenica Bongiovanni, 'Curator Calls Newfields Culture Toxic, Discriminatory in Resignation Letter', *Indianapolis Star*, 18 July 2020, https://www.indystar.com/story/entertainment/arts/2020/07/18/newfields-curator-says-discriminatory-workplace-toxic/5459574002/.

[16] See Tony Bravo, 'SFMOMA Official Resigns Amid Uproar Over Deletion of Comment by Black Ex-employee', *San Francisco Chronicle*, 2 July 2020. See also Neal Benezra, 'An Apology to Taylor Brandon', SFMOMA Press Office, 4 June 2020, quoted in *ibid.* Benezra has since stepped down as director and has been replaced by former Baltimore Museum of Art director Christopher Bedford.

[17] The acquired works include Melvin Edwards's installation *Scales of Injustice* (2017), Meleko Mokgosi's painting *Acts of Resistance I* (2018), Senga Nengudi's installation *R.S.V.P. Reverie-I* (2015) and Carrie Mae Weems's photograph *May Flowers* (2002). See Nate Freeman, 'A Controversial Deaccessioning has allowed the Baltimore Museum of Art to Buy New Works', *Artsy*, 20 December 2018, https://www.artsy.net/news/artsy-editorial-controversial-deaccessioning-allowed-baltimore-museum-art-buy-new-works.

[18] Watch artist Titus Kaphar critically address the statue in his TED talk 'Can Art Amend History?', April 2017, https://www.ted.com/talks/titus_kaphar_can_art_amend_history?language=en.

[19] See Kaywin Feldman, Director, National Gallery of Art; Frances Morris, Director, Tate Modern; Matthew Teitelbaum, Ann and Graham Gund Director, Museum of Fine Arts, Boston; and Gary Tinterow, Director, The Margaret Alkek Williams Chair, Museum of Fine Arts, Houston, '"Phillip Guston Now": Statement from the Directors', 21 September 2020, https://www.nga.gov/press/exh/5235.html; and Gareth Harris, 'Directors of Tate and the National Gallery of Art defend controversial decision to delay Philip Guston show', *The Art Newspaper*, 4 October 2020, https://www.theartnewspaper.com/2020/10/04/directors-of-tate-and-the-national-gallery-of-art-defend-controversial-decision-to-delay-philip-guston-show.

[20] The Museum of Fine Arts, Boston opened 'Philip Guston Now' on 1 May 2022. The museum's webpage includes 'A Message from the Curators' that addresses the postponement taken in order to 'look and reckon' with the paintings. See https://www.mfa.org/exhibition/philip-guston-now.

[21] B.R. Cooks, *Exhibiting Blackness*, *op. cit.*, p.14.

[22] For more on the exhibition of Lawrence's *The Migration of the Negro*, see the chapter 'Negro Art in the American Art Museum', in *ibid.*, pp.17–51; and John Ott, 'Battle Station MoMA: Jacob Lawrence and the Desegregation of the Armed Forces and the Art World,' *American Art*, vol.29, no.3, Fall 2015, pp.59–89.

[23] Elizabeth Berkowitz, 'With All Good Intentions: Jacob Lawrence at the Museum of Modern Art', *Culture, Theory and Critique*, vol.58, no.3, 2017, pp.294–95.

[24] Sarah Cascone, 'Anish Kapoor Owns the Rights to the Blackest Color Ever Made. So Another Artist Made His Own Superblack – and Now It's Even Blacker', *Artnet*, 30 January 2019, https://news.artnet.com/art-world/stuart-semple-blackest-black-anish-kapoor-1452259. Kapoor presented works made with Vantablack, such as *Void Pavilion V*, at the Venice Biennale in 2022. See Dorian Batycka, 'Into the Void: Anish Kapoor Reveals His Works Using Vantablack, the World's Darkest Color, in Venice,' *Artnet*, 21 April 2022, https://news.artnet.com/art-world/anish-kapoor-unveils-vantablack-in-venice-2102896.

[25] S. Cascone, 'Anish Kapoor Owns the Rights to the Blackest Color Ever Made', *op. cit.*

[26] *Ibid.*

[27] Others outside of the arts have also created their own 'superblack' paint, including NanoLab in Massachusetts, who created Singularity Black in 2017.

[28] Marcie Foster, 'Nas Partners with Pantone to Create "Ultra Black By Nas" Color Inspired by the Rap Legend', Pantone website, 25 August 2020, https://www.pantone.com/articles/press-releases/nas-partners-with-pantone-to-create-ultra-black-by-nas-color-inspired-by-the-rap-legend.

[29] Curator Adrienne Edwards addresses embodied and conceptual expressions of Blackness in Western art in her essay 'Blackness in Abstraction,' *Art in America*, 5 January 2015, https://www.artnews.com/art-in-america/features/blackness-in-abstraction-3-63053/.

[30] Tatyana Tolstaya, 'The Square', *The New Yorker,* 12 June 2015, https://www.newyorker.com/culture/cultural-comment/the-square. It is worth noting that experts such as Aleksandra Shatskikh have strongly contested the context and conclusions of the original research upon which the coverage in *The New Yorker* and other international outlets was based. See A. Shatskikh, 'Inscribed Vandalism: *The Black Square* at One Hundred', *e-flux*, issue 85, October 2017, https://www.e-flux.com/journal/85/155475/inscribed-vandalism-the-black-square-at-one-hundred/.

[31] The inscription likely references another painting of a black square, by Alphonse Allais, *Combat des nègres dans une Cave* (1897).

[32] Arthur Jafa, 'My Black Death', in G. Tate (ed.), *Everything But the Burden*, *op. cit.*, p.246.

[33] For a fuller discussion of the complexity of the underpainting and the symbolism of black monochromatism, see Jared Sexton, 'All Black Everything', *e-flux*, issue 79, February 2017, https://www.e-flux.com/journal/79/94158/all-black-everything/; and Fred Moten, 'The Case of Blackness', *Criticism*, vol.50, no.2, Spring 2008, pp.177–217.

[34] I owe this thought to visual studies scholar Keith Moxey. See K. Moxey, 'Visual Studies and the Iconic Turn', *Journal of Visual Culture*, vol.7, no.2, 2008, pp.131–46.

Marginalized Legacies and Networks

Founded upon the efforts of a network of Black artists, Historically Black Colleges and Universities (HBCUs) not only collected and exhibited Black art but also fostered a rich dialogue across the United States. In 1931, the artist Hale Woodruff established the art department at Atlanta University in Georgia – the first art department at a Southern Black university – where he taught alongside the sculptor Nancy Elizabeth Prophet until 1946. Woodruff also established the Atlanta Annuals (1942–70), which showed exclusively African American artists. A point of connection between artists of the Harlem Renaissance such as Jacob Lawrence and Romare Bearden, and influential art educators such as J. Eugene Grigsby, Woodruff also taught at New York University, from 1946 until his retirement in 1967. Through their teaching, exhibition programmes and collections, HBCUs have created a foundation for the flourishing of Black art, art education and exhibition-making.

Introduction to Marginalized Legacies and Networks – Richard J. Powell

What I thought I would do as an introduction is to say a little bit about, well, two things.[1] One, about the creation of collections at Historically Black Colleges and Universities (HBCUs). And secondly, I want to say something very specific about an exhibition that Nana Adusei-Poku mentioned I was involved with at the end of the twentieth century, called 'To Conserve a Legacy: American Art from Historically Black Colleges and Universities' (1999–2001). I'm going to do this very briefly.

I think it's important to remember that when we think about the creation of art collections, this will be a phenomenon that precedes the names and the moments that we're most familiar with. I think this is a phenomena that goes back to the nineteenth century, and I see two interesting polarities here, polarities that many of you are aware of as you think of the debates that were going on at the end of the nineteenth century, in particular between the president of Tuskegee University, Booker T. Washington, and the Black intellectual W.E.B. Du Bois, who was connected for a number of years to Atlanta University.

What I'm thinking about here is the idea of industrial education in the curriculum of HBCUs, particularly institutions like Hampton University, institutions like Tuskegee University. For all of the debates back and forth about whether this emphasis on industrial education gave short shrift to African American students and the like, one cannot ignore the fact that this idea of handicrafts, of developing skills, of using one's hands to produce and create that a Booker T. Washington promoted, was extremely, extremely important. It's also interesting that at both of these institutions, Hampton and Tuskegee, a part of the industrial education was photography. One doesn't want to lose sight of the fact that this was, in some ways, one of the earliest ways that these institutions were beginning to think about collections and visual culture as a part of the curriculum. On the other hand, we don't want to lose sight of W.E.B. Du Bois and his emphasis on a higher education – often an education and a curriculum that would incorporate the humanities. And thinking about the humanities at these institutions compelled faculty to move quickly into ideas around the arts and letters, and in particular, the visual arts. These are, in some ways, the very, very beginnings for the idea of a collection at an HBCU.

I think the other thing that's important to remember is time and the timing of the emergence of these collections, and how that time intersected with other major events taking place in Black America. I'm thinking in particular of the Harlem Renaissance or the New Deal initiatives during the 1930s, or other kinds of mid-twentieth-century statements and actions revolving around Black culture. It's no surprise that HBCUs are growing and their art collections are evolving in the context of those times. There's a real intersection there.

I also think that one doesn't want to lose sight of what I call the 'proactive human resources'. I'm thinking here not only of faculty people like James Herring and David Driskell and Hale Woodruff, but also I'm thinking about

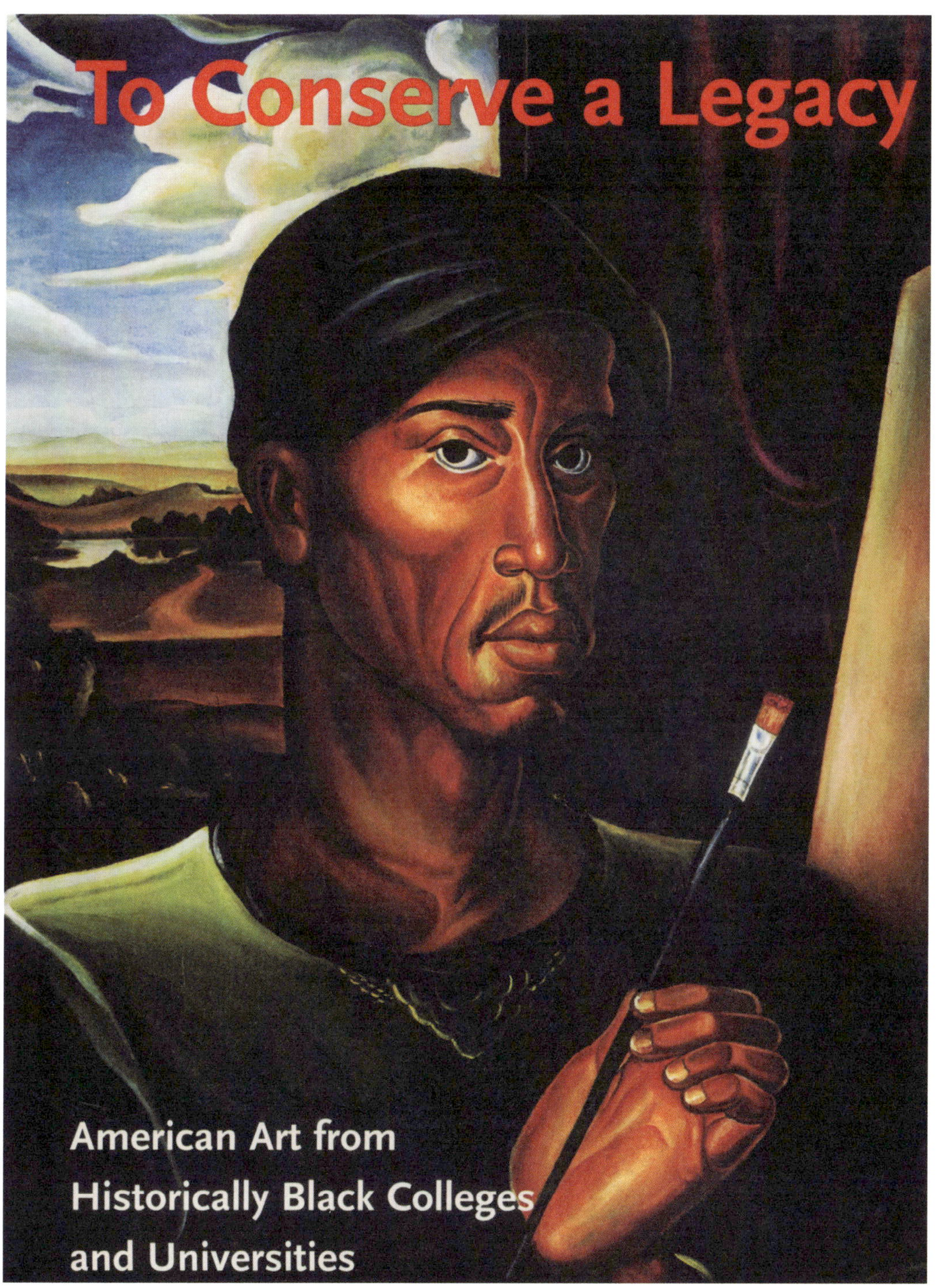
To Conserve a Legacy
American Art from
Historically Black Colleges
and Universities

Previous page: Exhibition catalogue for 'To Conserve a Legacy: American Art from Historically Black Colleges and Universities', the Studio Museum in Harlem, New York and Addison Gallery of American Art, Andover, Massachusetts, 1999–2001, showing Frederick C. Flemister's *Man with a Brush*, 1940

benefactors, people like Carl Van Vechten, who supported Fisk University in really, really important ways; the Harmon Foundation; also the Stern family, which helped support that incredible mural (*Harriet Tubman*, 1931) that's at Bennett College, by Aaron Douglas. The idea that there are people who have a vision and insist on that vision being a part of these institutions cannot be ignored.

Finally, I'll say two more things about the creation. One has to do with the mid-twentieth-century infrastructure of HBCUs really solidifying and expanding on their campuses, which allowed for galleries and buildings that could be dedicated to art to come into existence. This is very much a mid-twentieth-century phenomenon. We find this across these institutions.

And, I would say that the other big thing that looms over all of this is institutional racism and a culture that was not willing to recognize and celebrate the achievements of artists of African descent, so that these institutions became the patrons and the supporters and the places where artists like Elizabeth Catlett, William H. Johnson, Aaron Douglas – the list goes on and on – were able to thrive and produce extraordinary work.

Those are just some thoughts on that front.

I also want to say a little bit – I'm going to do this very quickly – about 'To Conserve a Legacy: American Art from Historically Black Colleges and Universities', an exhibition that took place at the end of the twentieth century, moved into the twenty-first century and was a really significant show. It opened so many people's eyes as to the treasures that these institutions have. I want to talk about the evolution of this exhibition, which in some ways began when I was director of programmes for the Washington Project for the Arts (WPA) in Washington DC.

I worked closely with the director at the time, Jock Reynolds, and we had been in conversation around projects at Howard University that we were involved with. That conversation evolved into thinking about other institutions. Jock knew that I was a graduate of Morehouse College, that I was familiar with the Atlanta University collections. He also knew that I had taught ever so briefly in the Norfolk, Virginia area and that I was connected, at least spiritually, to Hampton University. We began to have conversations about what if we put a big exhibition together that would highlight not all of these institutions, but certainly some of them.

What was so great about this collaboration was that it was not only with Jock, who at that point shifted from WPA to be the director of the Addison Gallery of American Art in Andover, Massachusetts. We also collaborated with the Williamstown Art Conservation Center, because part of our project was not just exhibiting and celebrating this material but trying to develop an initiative within these institutions around conservation, around really creating environments that would sustain these objects for, let's say, another hundred years. We were very grateful to Williamstown for helping us put this together.

And we had great benefactors of support: the John S. and James L. Knight Foundation, AT&T and all sorts of institutions were really on board for this project. Also, in terms of collaboration, I should add, the Studio Museum in Harlem, which at that time was under the leadership of Kinshasha Holman Conwill. She and her staff worked very closely with us on organizing this show. And of course, the six institutions of Clark Atlanta University, Fisk University, Hampton University, Howard University, North Carolina Central University and Tuskegee University.

Anyone who has been involved with collaboration knows that there's a lot of give and take. There's a lot of kind of ups and downs and debates and discussions, and – I'll be frank with you – arguments about how something might come to fruition. I guess the stars aligned for us, because things really came together and the show was a really, really, really big success. It also jump-started within these institutions serious reflections on their collections and on their facilities as to how to maintain and preserve and think about the future. The other part of this that I think I've got to mention, because people often lose sight of this, is that you need institutional buy-in, and it's fine to have the aim in corner, the choir as a part of your story, the faculty, the students, the artists, what have you. But part of the success of 'To Conserve a Legacy' had to do with serious conversations with administrators, with presidents, with provosts, with deans – really getting them to understand and to see that these collections were valuable and important resources that were part of the educational mission, and they needed to be preserved and needed to be expanded and taken care of and used actively in the teaching, and that there was a future for this. I think that really helped tremendously with the launch of this exhibition.

I want to leave you with that as a brief introduction around this idea of institutions and HBCUs and their collections, and as a prelude to these three amazing presentations that we're going to have today.

Notes

[1] Editors' Note: This text is adapted from the transcript of the author's presentation at the online conference 'Reshaping the Field: Arts of the African Diasporas on Display,' hosted by the Center for Curatorial Studies, Bard College, 4–6 November 2021.

Mapping Art History at the Atlanta University Center – Cheryl Finley

The project 'Mapping Art History at Historically Black Colleges and Universities' proposes to pioneer a new mode of writing art history from an African diasporic and African American–centred focus using the archives and collections of visual and material culture at historically Black colleges and universities (HBCUs) in the United States.[1] Overlooked by hegemonic histories of art and hidden in plain sight, the archives and museum collections of HBCUs tell a different history of art: one that starts before the end of the Civil War and before the beginning of the first institutions of higher education established to educate freedmen and freedwomen. Documenting safe spaces for Black artists, educators and museums through the study of archives, pedagogy and exhibitions, this project maps the unfolding of social justice movements throughout the global Black diaspora. Using geographic information systems, geotagging and cognitive mapping models as well as traditional archival research methods and digital humanities platforms, 'Mapping Art History at Historically Black Colleges and Universities' aims to be a model for future art histories that seek to uncover, privilege and centre unspoken and underrepresented narratives, archives, movements, artists and practices. Its central programme of rewriting American, African American and African diasporic art histories seeks to combine innovative technologies and digital public history platforms with interdisciplinary modes of analysis – such as global migration theory and critical race theory – and to recast the way art history is written, theorized, presented and accessed.

The questions I ask are: What would the history of art look like – how might it be different – if these stories had been included all along? How might art history as a discipline change if we look at histories of American art, African art, diasporic art and African American art more inclusively to think about how these stories are intersecting and overlapping?

I also want to foreground just a couple of ideas. The first is conservation, and the urgency with which we need to really begin to think about the preservation and care of our objects of study. Especially when we're talking about curatorial practice – it's there in the word *curator* itself, to care. Secondly, how to think about technology as something that's always on our side, that's always moving us forward, and how might we be able to think about using emerging technologies in the work that we do, either as curators or as art historians? And how to think about the work of registrars, how it too can be enhanced by technology; and also how to think about some of the emerging technologies I've been working with alongside my students, including things like blockchain, smart contracts and non-fungible tokens (NFTs) – how these might help our museums and institutions in moving forward.

'Mapping Art History at Historically Black Colleges and Universities' encompasses a larger project that is probably going to take another five to ten years to complete. It is looking at how technologies like geographic information systems (GISs) and global tagging can help us in thinking about enhanc-

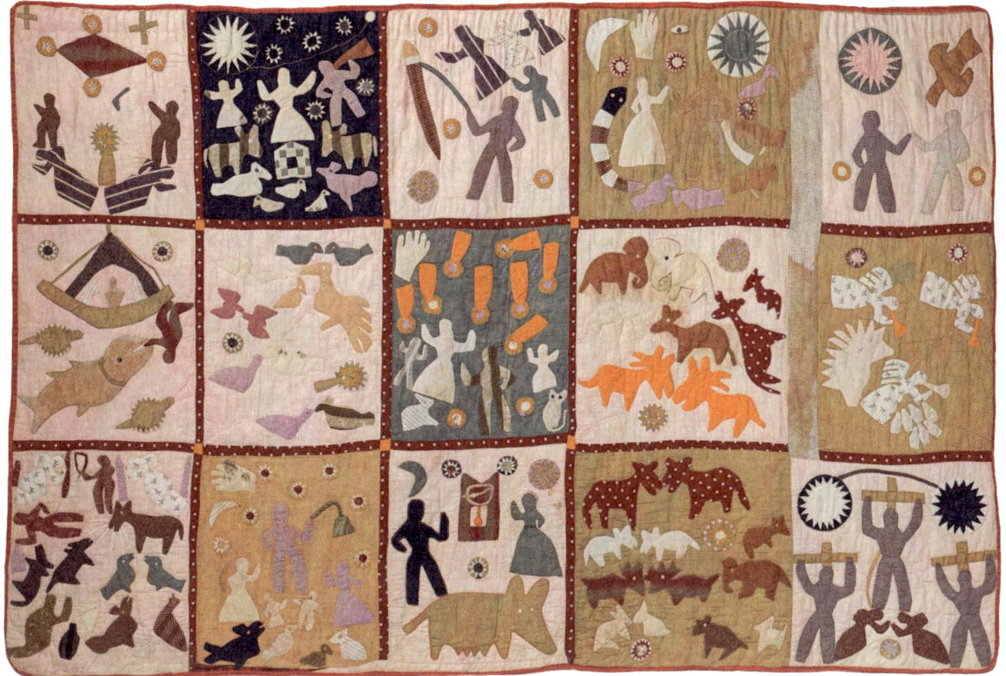

Harriet Powers, *Pictorial Quilt*, 1895–98, cotton plain weave, pieced, appliquéd, embroidered, and quilted, 175 × 266.7cm. Photo © 2022 Museum of Fine Arts, Boston

ing, rediscovering and sharing the narratives of art histories at HBCUs. I'm going to focus on the Atlanta University Center (AUC) today. Often when we talk about art history at the AUC, the story revolves very closely around Hale Woodruff and Nancy Elizabeth Prophet – as it should – and the work they did in establishing the art department at the AUC in the early 1930s. I thought that I would share instead, as a sort of a beginning point, an image of one of Harriet Powers's very famous quilts. Even in the nineteenth century, the faculty wives of the Atlanta University would have commissioned Harriet Powers quilts, and I take this as a starting point to think about art and art history, craft and technological innovation. I appreciated Richard Powell's earlier reference to the struggle between intellectualism versus technical training,[2] and how that has not only enhanced our collections in terms of having documentary photographs, but also enhanced understandings of the kinds of images and projects that were ultimately embarked upon, including W.E.B. Du Bois's transformational research. Henry Ossawa Tanner's *Banjo Lesson* (1893) is a work that was collected at Hampton University – or Hampton Normal and Agricultural Institute, as it was called at the time – and it offers a way in to talking about the very early stages of collecting art at HBCUs. I'm thinking more broadly about some of our colleges and universities. There are also the works by Thomas E. Askew that Du Bois commissioned for the 1900 Paris Exposition – 'The Exhibit of American Negroes' – again thinking about the role of photography in documenting progress and documenting Black life, but also in spreading the word of progress in local, national and international exhibitions.

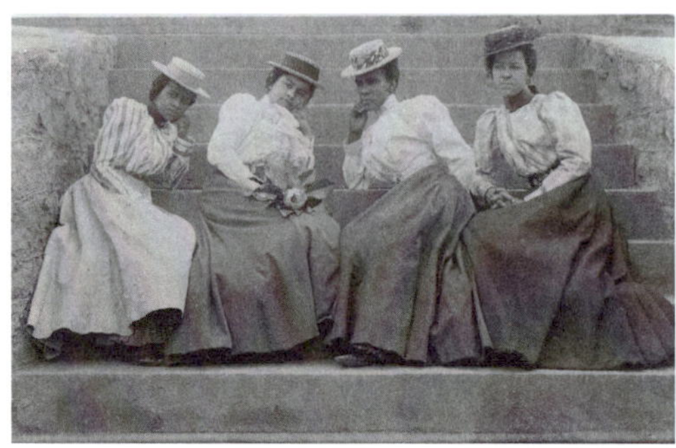

Photographs by Thomas Askew of young African American women and men, compiled by W.E.B. Du Bois in *Types of American Negroes, Georgia, U.S.A.* and *Negro life in Georgia, U.S.A.*, exhibited at the 1900 Paris Exposition. The women in the image on the right are pictured at Atlanta University, late 1890s. Courtesy Daniel Murray Collection, Library of Congress, Washington DC

Below, from left:
Mural by Aaron Douglas in Cravath Hall, Fisk University, 1930. Special Collections, Nashville Public Library; *Spelman Messenger*, vol.51 no.1, November 1934, announcing painting exhibition from the Whitney Museum of American Art and hiring of Nancy Elizabeth Prophet. Atlanta University Center Robert W. Woodruff Library, Clark Atlanta University. Courtesy Spelman College Archives

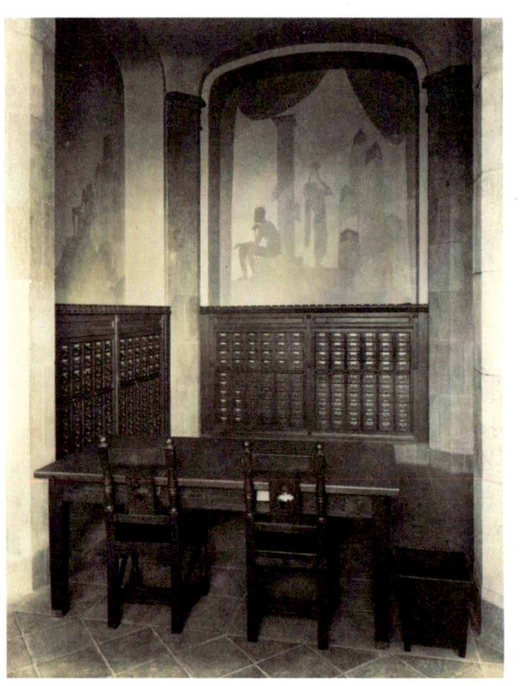

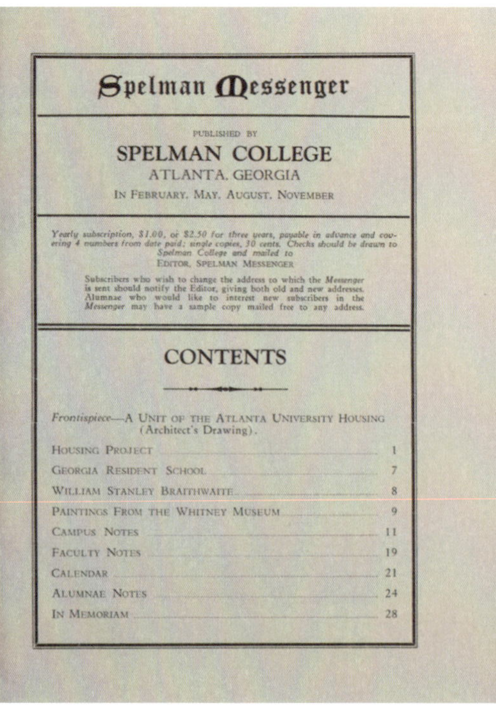

Spelman Messenger

PUBLISHED BY

SPELMAN COLLEGE

ATLANTA, GEORGIA

IN FEBRUARY, MAY, AUGUST, NOVEMBER

Yearly subscription, $1.00, or $2.50 for three years, payable in advance and covering 4 numbers from date paid; single copies, 30 cents. Checks should be drawn to Spelman College and mailed to
EDITOR, SPELMAN MESSENGER

Subscribers who wish to change the address to which the *Messenger* is sent should notify the Editor, giving both old and new addresses. Alumnae who would like to interest new subscribers in the *Messenger* may have a sample copy mailed free to any address.

CONTENTS

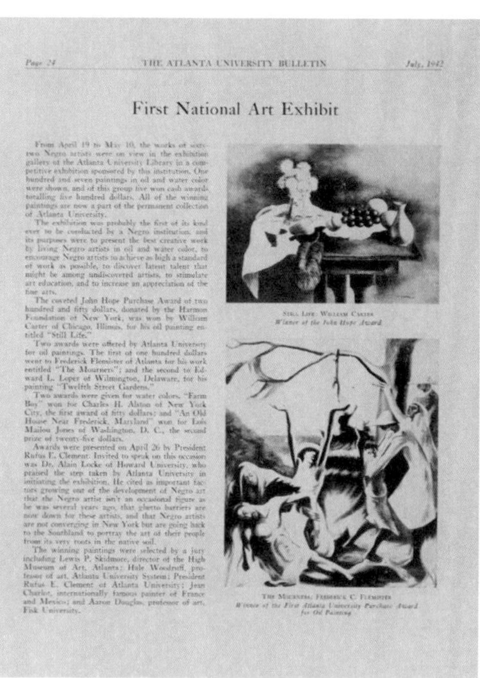

Page 24 THE ATLANTA UNIVERSITY BULLETIN July, 1942

First National Art Exhibit

From April 19 to May 10, the works of sixty-two Negro artists were on view in the exhibition gallery of the Atlanta University Library in a competitive exhibition sponsored by this institution. One hundred and seven paintings in oil and water color were shown, and of this group five won cash awards totalling five hundred dollars. All of the winning paintings are now a part of the permanent collection of Atlanta University.

The exhibition was probably the first of its kind ever to be conducted by a Negro institution, and its purposes were to present the best creative work by living Negro artists in oil and water color, to encourage Negro artists to achieve as high a standard of work as possible, to discover latent talent that might be among undiscovered artists, to stimulate art education, and to increase an appreciation of the fine arts.

The coveted John Hope Purchase Award of two hundred and fifty dollars, donated by the Harmon Foundation of New York, was won by William Carter of Chicago, Illinois, for his oil painting entitled "Still Life."

Two awards were offered by Atlanta University for oil paintings. The first of one hundred dollars went to Frederick Flemister of Atlanta for his work entitled "The Mourners"; and the second to Edward L. Loper of Wilmington, Delaware, for his painting "Twelfth Street Gardens."

Two awards were given for water colors. "Farm Boy" won for Charles H. Alston of New York City, the first award of fifty dollars; and "An Old House Near Frederick, Maryland" won for Lois Mailou Jones of Washington, D. C., the second prize of twenty-five dollars.

Awards were presented on April 26 by President Rufus E. Clement. Invited to speak on this occasion was Dr. Alain Locke of Howard University, who praised the step taken by Atlanta University in initiating the exhibition. He cited as important factors growing out of the development of Negro art that the Negro artist isn't an occasional figure as he was several years ago, that ghetto barriers are now down for these artists, and that Negro artists are not converging in New York but are going back to the Southland to portray the art of their people from its very roots in the native soil.

The winning paintings were selected by a jury including Lewis P. Skidmore, director of the High Museum of Art, Atlanta; Hale Woodruff, professor of art, Atlanta University System; President Rufus E. Clement of Atlanta University; Jean Charlot, internationally famous painter of France and Mexico; and Aaron Douglas, professor of art, Fisk University.

STILL LIFE: WILLIAM CARTER
Winner of the John Hope Award

THE MOURNERS: FREDERICK C. FLEMISTER
Winner of the First Atlanta University Purchase Award for Oil Painting

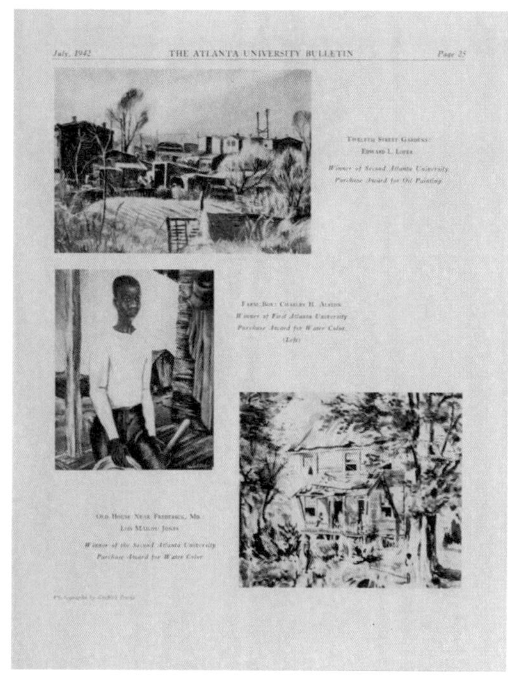

July, 1942 THE ATLANTA UNIVERSITY BULLETIN Page 25

TWELFTH STREET GARDENS:
EDWARD L. LOPER
Winner of Second Atlanta University Purchase Award for Oil Painting

FARM BOY: CHARLES H. ALSTON
Winner of First Atlanta University Purchase Award for Water Color
(Left)

OLD HOUSE NEAR FREDERICK, MD.:
LOIS MAILOU JONES
Winner of the Second Atlanta University Purchase Award for Water Color

Pages from *The Atlanta University Bulletin*, 75th Anniversary Edition, July 1942. Atlanta University Printed and Published Materials Collection, Atlanta University Center Robert W. Woodruff Library, Clark Atlanta University

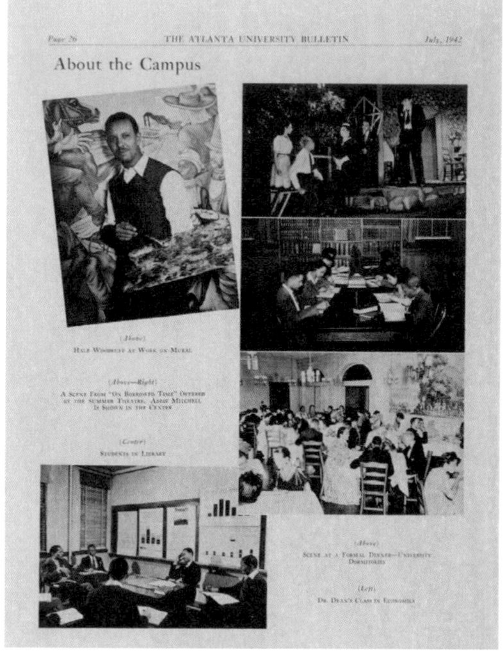

Page 26 THE ATLANTA UNIVERSITY BULLETIN July, 1942

About the Campus

(Above)
HALE WOODRUFF AT WORK ON MURAL

(Above—Right)
A SCENE FROM "ON BORROWED TIME" OFFERED BY THE SUMMER THEATRE. ABBIE MITCHELL IS SHOWN IN THE CENTER

(Center)
STUDENTS IN LIBRARY

(Above)
SCENE AT A FORMAL DINNER—UNIVERSITY DORMITORIES

(Left)
DR. DEAN'S CLASS IN ECONOMICS

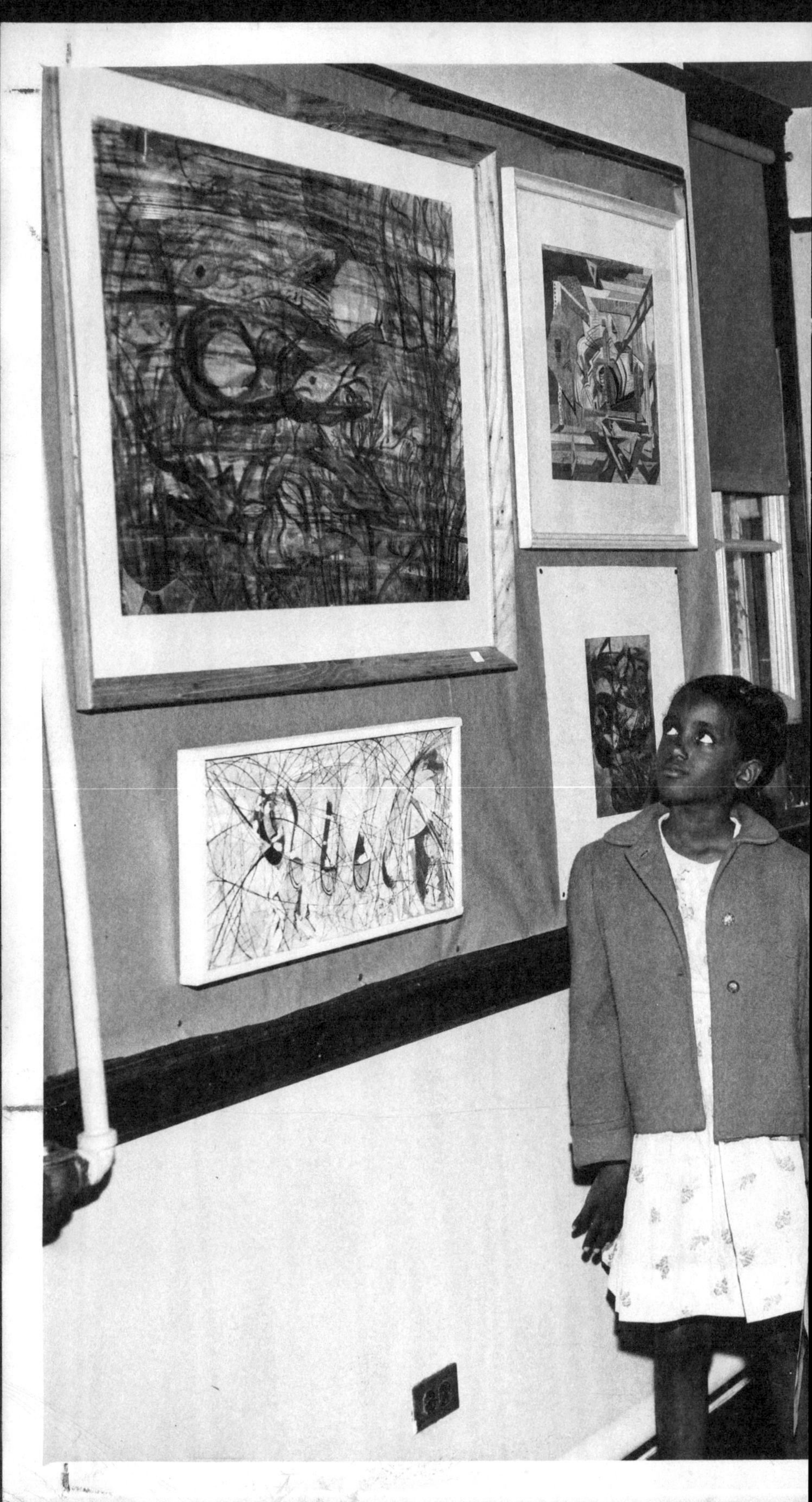

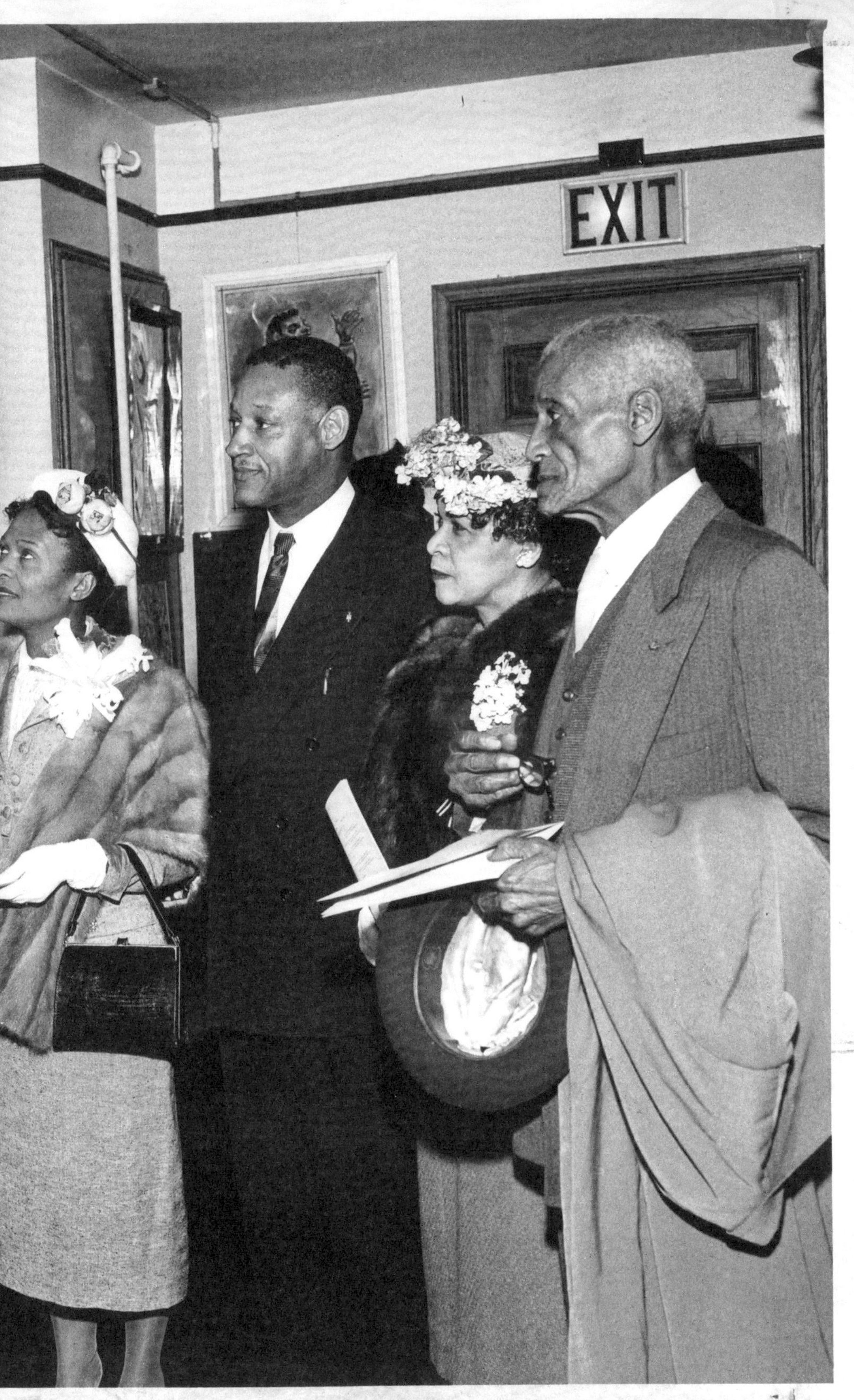
EXIT

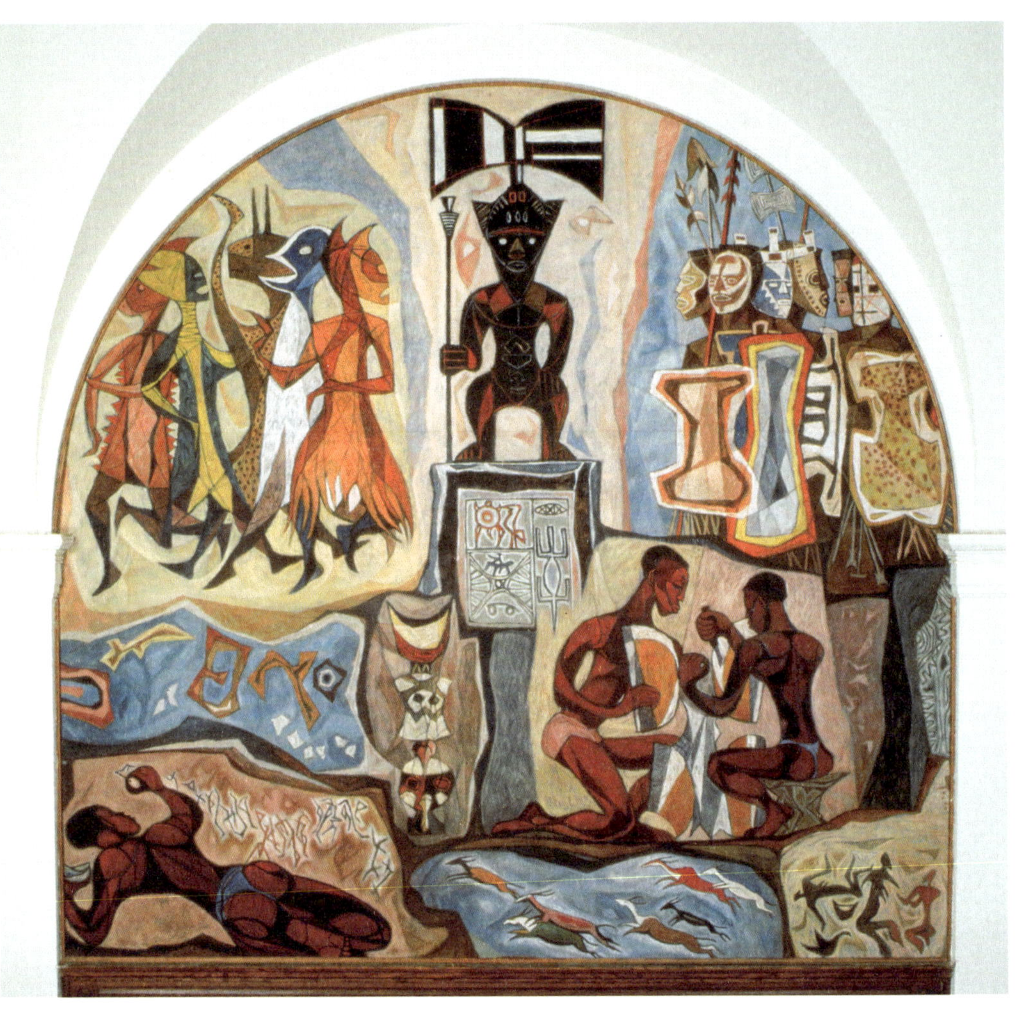

Above and opposite:
Hale Woodruff, *Art of the Negro* mural series, 1952, oil on canvas panels, 366 × 366cm each. Clark Atlanta University Art Collection

Previous spread:
Opening, 16th Annual Art Exhibition, 7 April 1957. Atlanta University Photographs Collection, Atlanta University Center Robert W. Woodruff Library, Clark Atlanta University

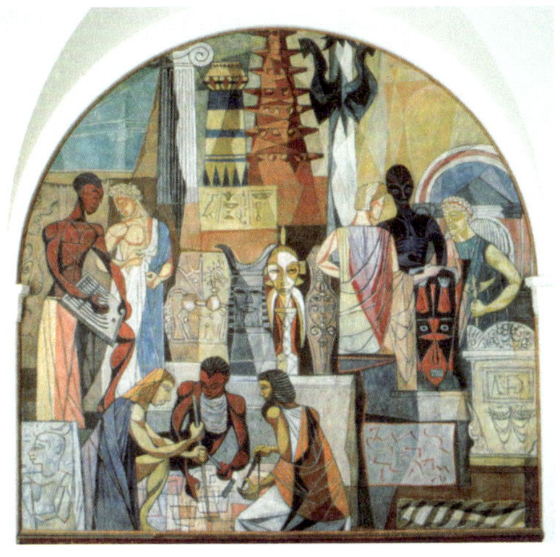

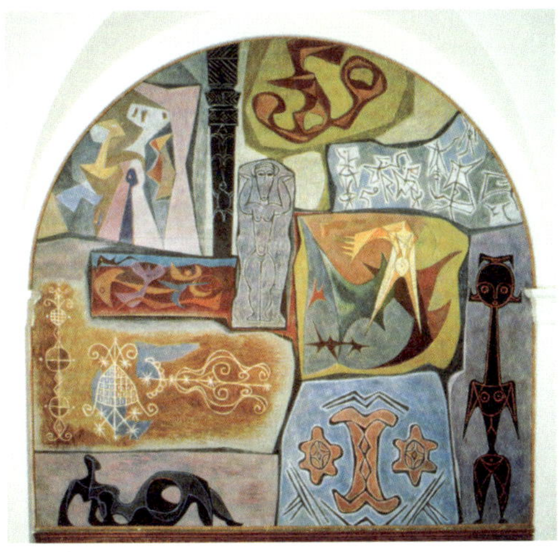

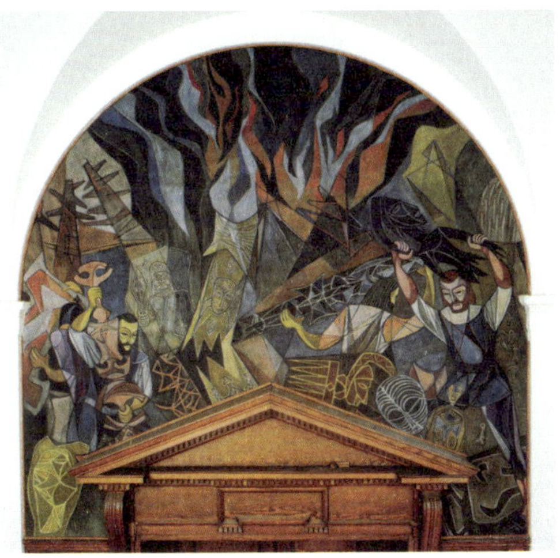

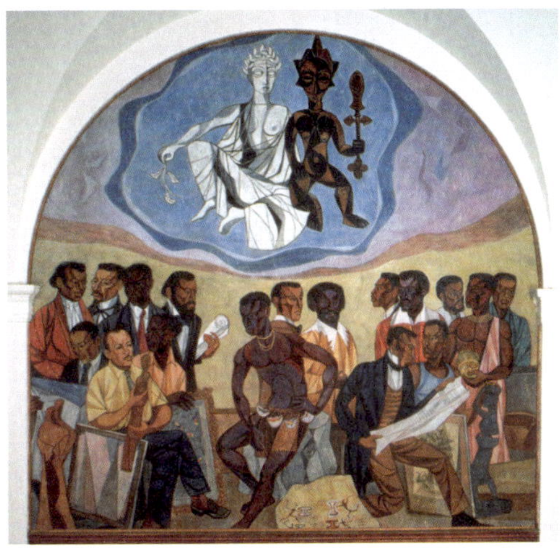

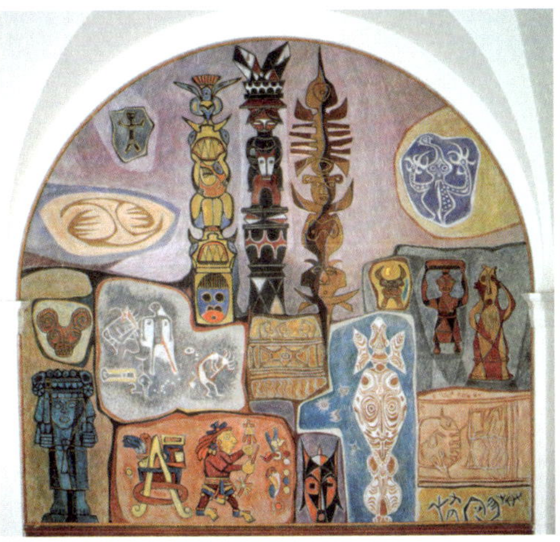

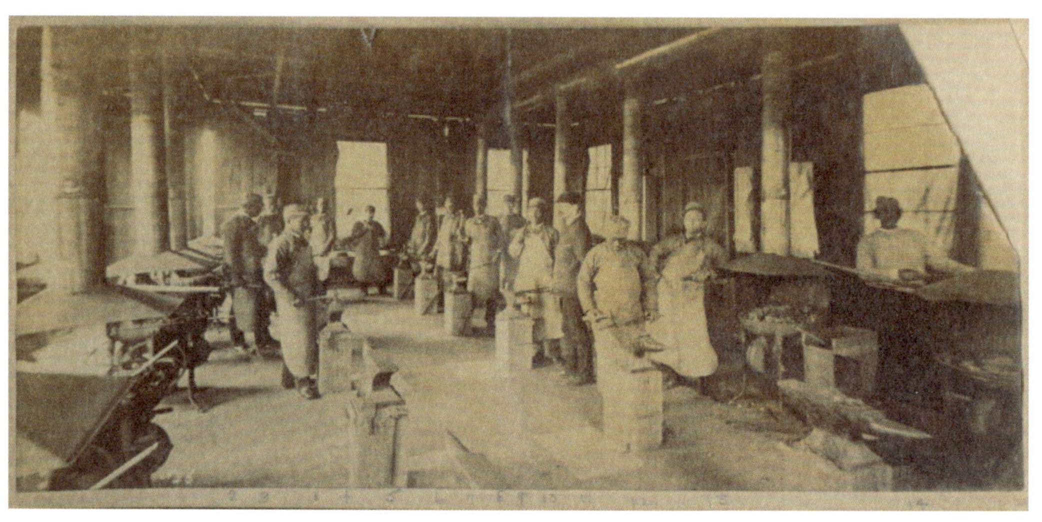

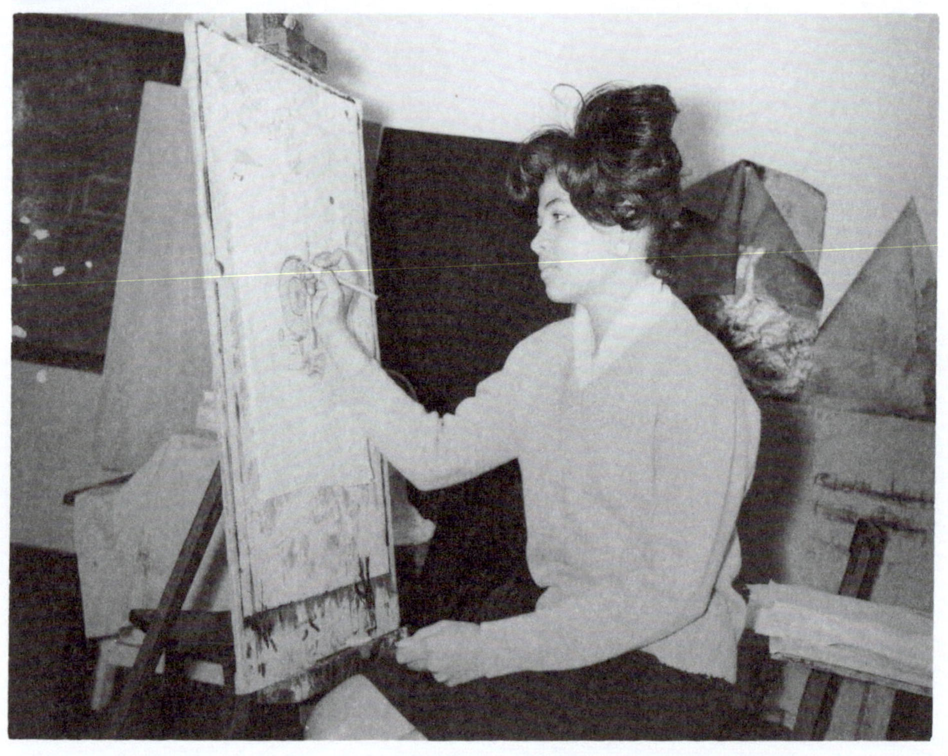

'Mapping Art History at Historically Black Colleges and Universities' began when I arrived in 2019 on the ground to begin the AUC Art Collective in Atlanta. As Rick Powell mentioned, I'm a graduate of Wellesley College, which is not an HBCU, but my sister and brother were at Spelman College and Morehouse College, respectively. My grandfather was at Morehouse, and I really wanted to get to know the campuses where I was going to be working, and the relationship between art and art history and those campuses. That's one of the places where this project began. I was thinking about people like Edmonia Lewis, whose work I knew about growing up in Washington DC, having gone frequently to places like the Howard University art galleries – and people like Alain Locke, who would have influenced many of the artists who were graduates or became teachers at HBCUs and across networks in the United States. I wanted to think about mapping and how to draw connections between artists and those who influenced them, and intellectuals; their travels to different institutions within HBCU networks and beyond, to other centres of intellectual and artistic innovation; and how this would have been a way to continually infuse new ideas, new techniques, new ways of being, new thoughts about art and social movements.

Above: Blacksmithing class at Atlanta University, c.1890. Atlanta University Photographs Collection, Atlanta University Center Robert W. Woodruff Library, Clark Atlanta University

Below: Unidentified student in Clark College's art department, c.1965. Clark College Photographs Collection, Atlanta University Center Robert W. Woodruff Library, Clark Atlanta University

Alain Locke proposed, in the 1920s, the idea of *The New Negro*.[3] It was not just his work at Howard University but his travels that would have informed his writing and the field shift he proposed for us all in this very influential book. Of course, we can talk about how artists were also influenced by Diego Rivera and other muralists who worked in Mexico. Many artists who trained at HBCUs travelled to places like Mexico City, especially in the earlier part of the twentieth century – Aaron Douglas, for example – or to Accra or other parts of the African continent, or even to Europe. But I'm going to take us back to Atlanta and another one of the things that this project grew out of. At one point I had to give a tour to someone who was visiting campus, and I began to think about how we might craft a tour of our campus that would highlight how important the arts have been at Spelman, at Atlanta University, at Clark Atlanta University and at Morehouse College. One of the things that I found out about Hale Woodruff, who arrives in the 1930s along with Nancy Elizabeth Prophet, is that his very famous *Amistad Murals* (commissioned in 1938) were actually painted in a studio he had in Laura Spelman Hall on Spelman College's campus.

So these are the kinds of things I was interested in thinking about in the literal sense of mapping. How can we understand our relationship to the spaces where art has been created, where art history has been taught on campus? How can we understand the way in which these spaces have been utilized by our artists? I was also looking at the work of Nancy Elizabeth Prophet, who was written up in the *Spelman Messenger* upon her arrival in Atlanta from Providence, Rhode Island to teach. As we all know, Prophet was a sculptor who primarily worked in wood and, together with Hale Woodruff, she founded the art department at the AUC. I discovered that her studio was in this really amazing building on campus that I pass by every day when I go to teach.

Arthur D. Shurrid in Clark College's art department, c.1965. Clark College Photographs Collection, Atlanta University Center Robert W. Woodruff Library, Clark Atlanta University

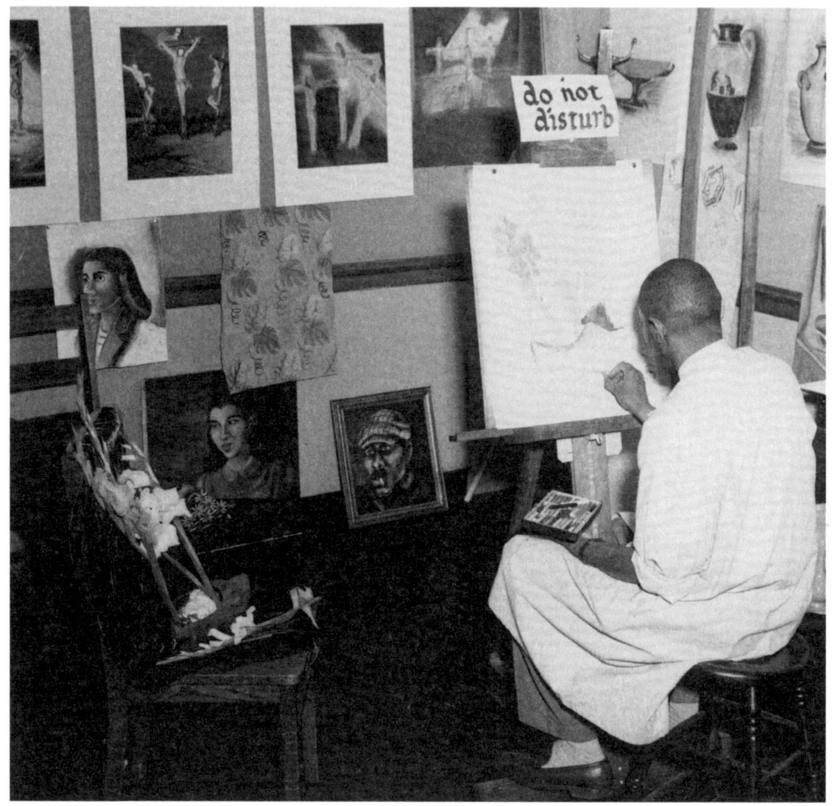

Another thing that's exciting about doing a project that looks closely at mapping at the AUC is thinking about the influence of the Atlanta Annuals, which were begun by Woodruff in the early 1940s. The Atlanta Annuals were a way to enable Black artists across the country to submit their works in a competition. This coincided with the popular Whitney Annuals and other annual competitions or other places where mainstream artists were presenting the work – but this was a way for Black artists to have their work on view, especially in the South, and also for the work to be collected and to be awarded prizes. Among the different prizes were: the John Hope Prize; a prize for oil painting; for watercolour; graphics; sculpture; and so on. And the artists included people like Charles White, Richmond Barthé, Elizabeth Catlett and Joseph Delaney. There's a lot of really amazing information that's already been researched and compiled by Tina Dunkley that's available about this series of exhibitions.

Hale Woodruff was invited back to the AUC to paint *The Art of the Negro* (1950–51) – a powerful series of murals at the entrance to the Clark Atlanta University Art Museum. If you haven't seen it, please do come to see it. It's a moving series of six panels. This is the history of art that he successfully tells, on display here, and one that continues to move and signal to subsequent artists who work in different media. For instance, Griff Davis, who also befriended

Langston Hughes and photographed him in different places in New York City and notably on the campus of Morehouse when he was in residence.

And then again, thinking back to what Rick said in his introductory remarks about the idea of different types of industrial training that would have taken place – this is a slide of a blacksmithing class from 1890 at Atlanta University; and this is a slide of artists in their studios working at Art Department in 1965.

I want to quickly acknowledge current and past presidents of Spelman College including Dr Mary Schmidt Campbell, Dr Johnnetta B. Cole, and Donald Stewart, who were great champions of the arts at Spelman College. I'd be remiss if I didn't mention Mabel Murphy Smythe-Haith, a Spelman alumna who donated her quite large collection of African art that's now being studied by my curatorial classes at the Spelman College Museum of Fine Art. We're learning about blockchain and smart contracts to think about cultural heritage and shared legacies. That collection was the subject of an exhibition, 'Art by Metamorphosis' (1988), that took place on the inauguration of Dr Johnnetta B. Cole. Finally, I want to conclude by mentioning some of the preeminent scholarly works that have already been written on this subject: Dr Powell's *To Conserve a Legacy: American Art from Historically Black Colleges and Universities* (1999) and Tina Dunkley's *In the Eye of the Muses: Selections from the Clark Atlanta University Art Collection* (2012).

Notes

[1] Editors' Note: This text is adapted from the author's presentation at the online conference 'Reshaping the Field: Arts of the African Diasporas on Display', hosted by the Center for Curatorial Studies, Bard College, 4–6 November 2021.

[2] See Richard Powell, 'Introduction to Marginalized Legacies and Networks', in this volume.

[3] See Alain Locke (ed.), *The New Negro: An Interpretation*, New York: Atheneum, 1925.

Fisk University Galleries – Jamaal B. Sheats

Fisk University, a private Historically Black University located in Nashville, Tennessee, was founded in 1866.[1] Today, Fisk University Galleries are home to over 4,500 works of art, including important holdings by Romare Bearden, Elizabeth Catlett, Aaron Douglas, David C. Driskell, Ben Enwonwu, William H. Johnson, Jacob Lawrence, Suzanne Ogunjami, Martin Puryear, Henry O. Tanner, Alma Thomas and many others. Our collections continue to expand with recent gifts of works by Alicia Henry, Dread Scott and Terry Adkins. The visual and performing arts have continued to play a critical part in the cultural and intellectual fabric of the university. Fisk University collections have a long legacy of aiding in the development of the next generations of arts leaders and advocates. This presentation highlights the impactful history of Fisk University Galleries through exhibitions and programmes.

I am going to unpack and discuss the history of Fisk University Galleries. This is a subject I would normally introduce over the course of a semester – one and a half hours a day, two to three days a week. I am going to attempt to condense it. Fisk University has been a collecting institution since the 1870s, and our early collections include gifts from Samuel Insull, Jr, Abby Aldrich Rockefeller, the Carnegie Corporation, the Federal Art Project and the Rosenwald Fund. The university's first permanent art gallery was established in 1949, when Georgia O'Keeffe donated the Alfred Stieglitz Collection. The gallery was named in honour of Carl Van Vechten, the American novelist, critic, photographer and philanthropist, who played a key role in securing the collection for Fisk. The building itself was a house that W.E.B. Du Bois built. Du Bois and the class of 1888 would secure the funds to build the first gymnasium on an HBCU campus, and this building would be converted into the gallery after the receipt of the Stieglitz Collection. In 1994, the university established the Aaron Douglas Gallery to honour the Harlem Renaissance artist and founder of the art department.

Now, it is important to note the collecting history of HBCUs. Our part of our collection history is often overshadowed because of the Stieglitz Collection, which I find interesting. But one thing that comes up often – especially now, being that the Stieglitz Collection was recently on view – is *why* did O'Keeffe donate it to Fisk? We do not know the impetus for the gift. However, the institution had developed a reputation – through preceding gifts and its use and recruitment of faculty – as a repository for cultural material. In 1929, Fisk established the Spring Arts Festival, which has since included luminaries such as Harry Belafonte, J. Mason Brewer, Countee Cullen, Ossie Davis, Ralph Ellison, Robert Hayden, Langston Hughes, Martin Luther King Jr, Sidney Poitier, Margaret Walker, Quincy Jones and Cannonball Adderley; it has also featured exhibitions from the Harmon Foundation, the Metropolitan Museum of Art and the Smithsonian, and solo exhibitions by artists such as Richmond Barthé, Elizabeth Catlett, Richard Hunt, Sam Middleton and Martina Washington. In 1930, the university commissioned Aaron Douglas to develop the murals located in Erastus Milo Cravath Memorial Library. Douglas participated in many of the Springs Arts Festivals. He also came back

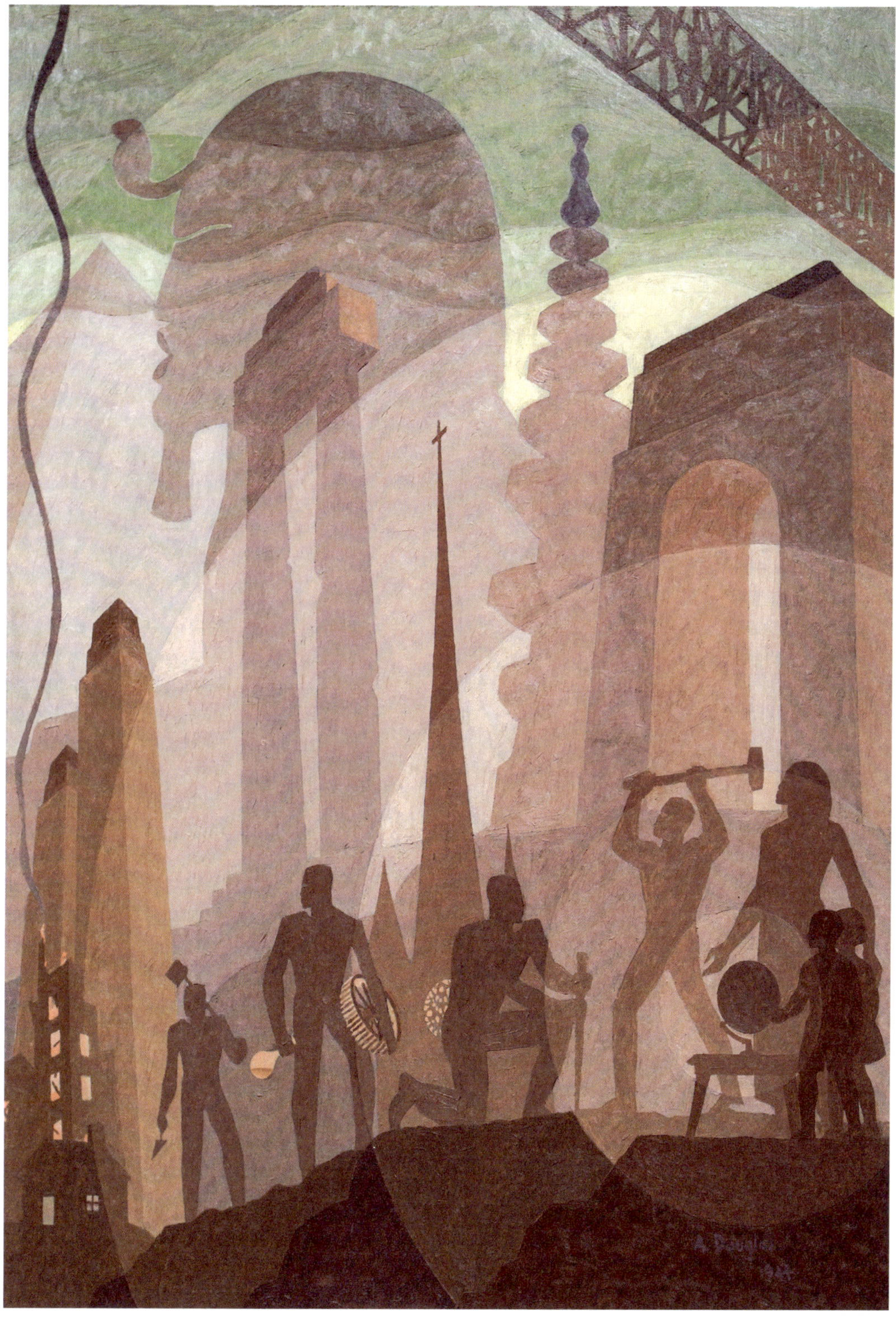

Group portrait in front of Aaron Douglas's *Building More Stately Mansions*, 1944, in the International Student Center, Fisk University, Nashville, Tennessee, undated. Special Collections, John Hope and Aurelia E. Franklin Library, Fisk University

Previous page: Aaron Douglas, *Building More Stately Mansions*, 1944, oil on canvas, 137.2 × 106.7cm. Fisk University Galleries

to Fisk in the late 1930s to teach once a semester, and by 1944 he had founded the art department. Also in 1944, Douglas was commissioned to create the painting *Building More Stately Mansions* (1944) for the International Student Center at Fisk. The International Student Center (completed in 1945) was a place where scholars would come to have discourse and conversations; it was a place in the segregated South that was open to all peoples. Exhibitions, foreign films and lectures by artists, writers and poets happened there, including prior to the gift of the Stieglitz Collection.

Charles Spurgeon Johnson is another figure who was instrumental to Fisk's art collections and its receipt of the Stieglitz Collection. Johnson was a sociologist, diplomat, educator, race relations leader and arts advocate, and one of my favourite figures in Fisk's history. He was the first African American President of Fisk University and he served in that capacity from 1946 to 1956. As President, Johnson recruited the foremost thought leaders of the period – faculty that included Harlem Renaissance luminaries Arna Bontemps, Aaron Douglas and James Weldon Johnson. He believed that the arts can change the hearts and minds of people. That perspective informs the work we do today – it alludes to what art has the capacity to do and the role it can play in the academy or at an institution like this.

Aaron Douglas was not just a prolific artist and educator, he was also an incredible administrator. He brought in exhibitions from the Metropolitan Museum of Art, from the Brooklyn Museum, from the Harmon Foundation and other institutions. He was not just looking at American or European artists, he was also looking across the African diaspora. We are preparing an exhibition that will open October 2022 titled 'African Modernism in America, 1947–1967', which will speak to the exchanges of artists at HBCUs and artists on the continent, American patrons and cultural organizations in the backdrop of the civil rights movement in the US, decolonization and the Cold War. After the receipt of the Stieglitz Collection, we saw a kind of windfall. We saw objects from institutions like the Art Institute of Chicago transferred to Fisk. One example is Henry O. Tanner's *Three Marys* (1910). In 1967, Douglas retired and became Chairman Emeritus. He and Arna Bontemps, who was a Harlem Renaissance poet, novelist and librarian, would go on to recruit David C. Driskell.

When Driskell came to Fisk, there was an explosion of activity. It was like the passing of the baton. Driskell had fresh legs to continue running the race. You see this in the number of exhibitions that were happening on campus, and not just in the art gallery – exhibitions were happening in Bennett Hall, in Livingston Hall and in the library on campus. Fisk also received gifts from the Harmon Foundation, including works by Beauford Delaney, Ben Enwonwu, Malvin Gray Johnson, William H. Johnson, James A. Porter, Betsy Graves Reyneau, James Lesesne Wells and Hale Woodruff. Also during this time, Driskell developed an artist-in-residence programme. And so, during his era, you would have artists like Martin Puryear coming to Fisk to teach (between 1971–72). You would have artists such as William T. Williams and Walter Williams coming to Fisk; or Alma Thomas exhibiting at Fisk, before going to the Whitney Museum of American Art in New York. During Driskell's

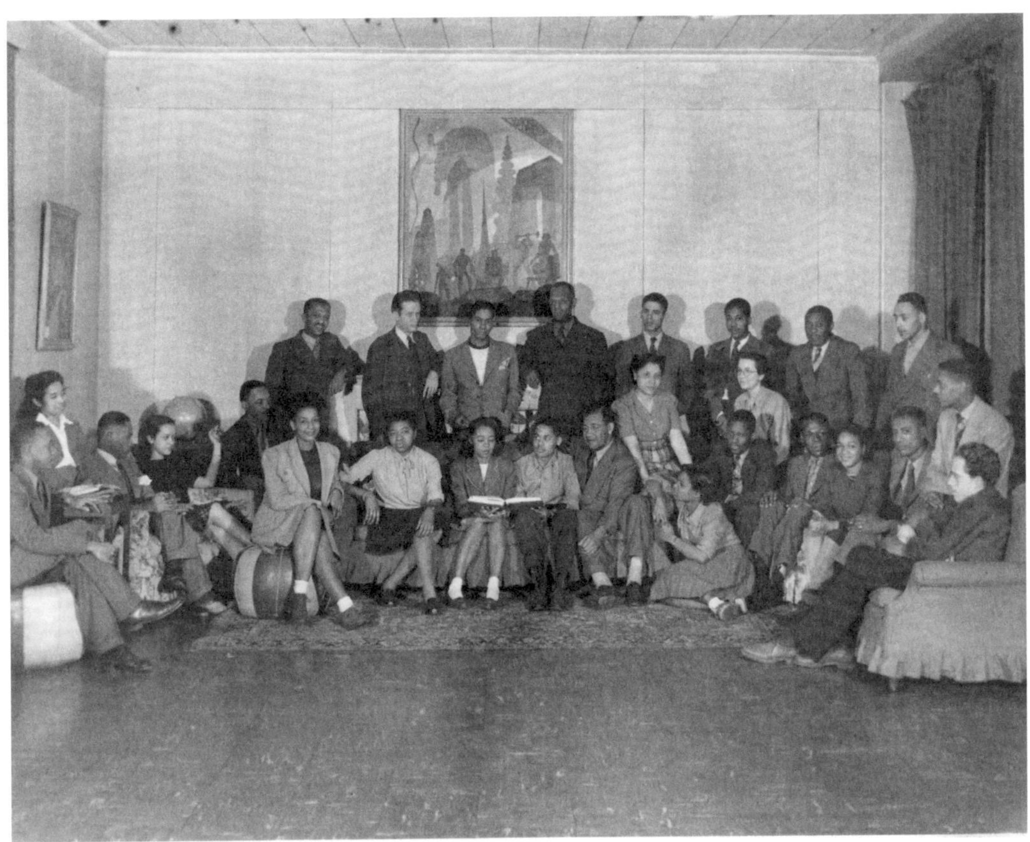

era, he would build what I call a 'dream team' of artists teaching in the art department – people like Earl Hooks, Stephanie Pogue and Greg Ridley.

I am going to pause just a moment to really talk about Earl Hooks. In my role, one of my goals is to build advocacy – to highlight artists that we should ask scholars to shift the gaze onto and reinsert into the canon. Earl Hooks is one of those artists. Hooks was a noted sculptor and ceramicist, and also an artist that worked in multiple mediums. I talked with Driskell in 2019 about what was happening at Fisk during this era, and he talked about Hooks as being the spirit of experimentation. Hooks was always challenging the faculty to try new things and to push things further. I think it is interesting to look back at the faculty who shaped a generation of artists.

During both Aaron Douglas's and Driskell's tenures, they were committed to shaping the field and integrating the collections into all academic disciplines. The same mission drives the work of the Fisk University Galleries today. Its holistic approach has produced artists like Terry Adkins, whose work we brought back home to Fisk in 2020 for the exhibition 'Terry Adkins: Our Sons and Daughters Ever on the Altar'.[2] We started the presentation at Fisk with the original plates from W.E.B. Du Bois's book *The Souls of Black Folks* (1903),

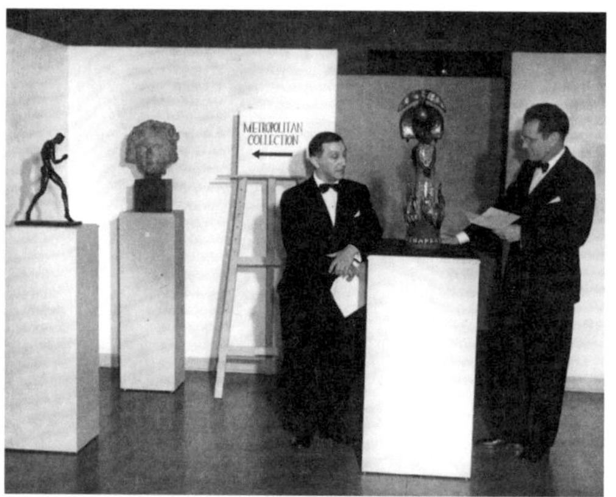

Installation view of artworks from the Metropolitan Museum of Art, New York at the Carl Van Vechten Gallery, Fisk University, 1951. Courtesy Fisk University Galleries

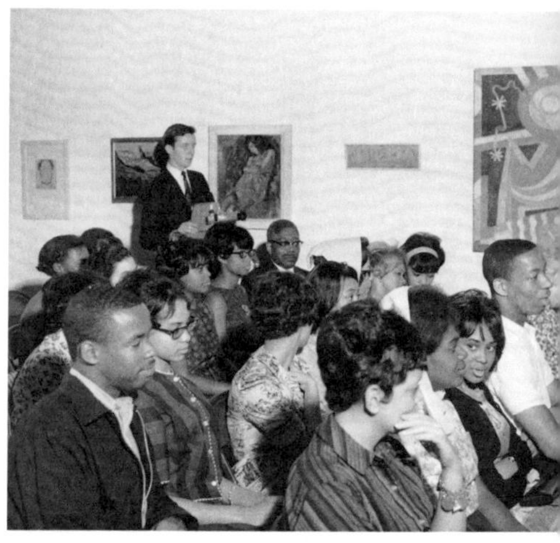

Students attending event at the 35th Spring Arts Festival, Fisk University, 1964. Special Collections, John Hope and Aurelia E. Franklin Library, Fisk University

Cover of exhibition pamphlet for the Spring Arts Festival, Fisk University, 1944. Special Collections, John Hope and Aurelia E. Franklin Library, Fisk University

CATALOGUE

ART EXHIBITIONS

FESTIVAL OF MUSIC AND FINE ARTS

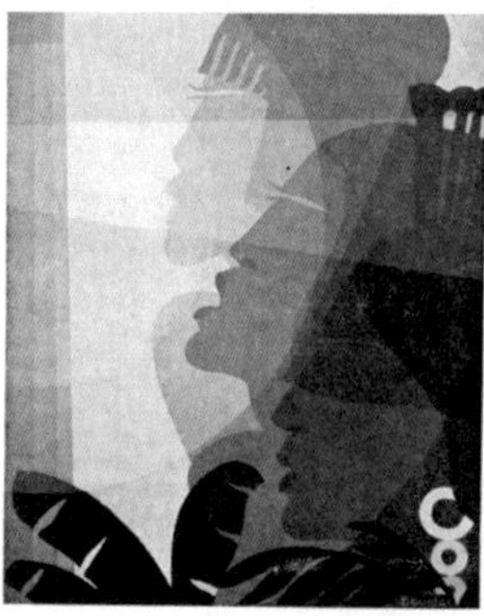

FISK UNIVERSITY
Livingstone Hall
April 19, 1944
4:00 P.M.

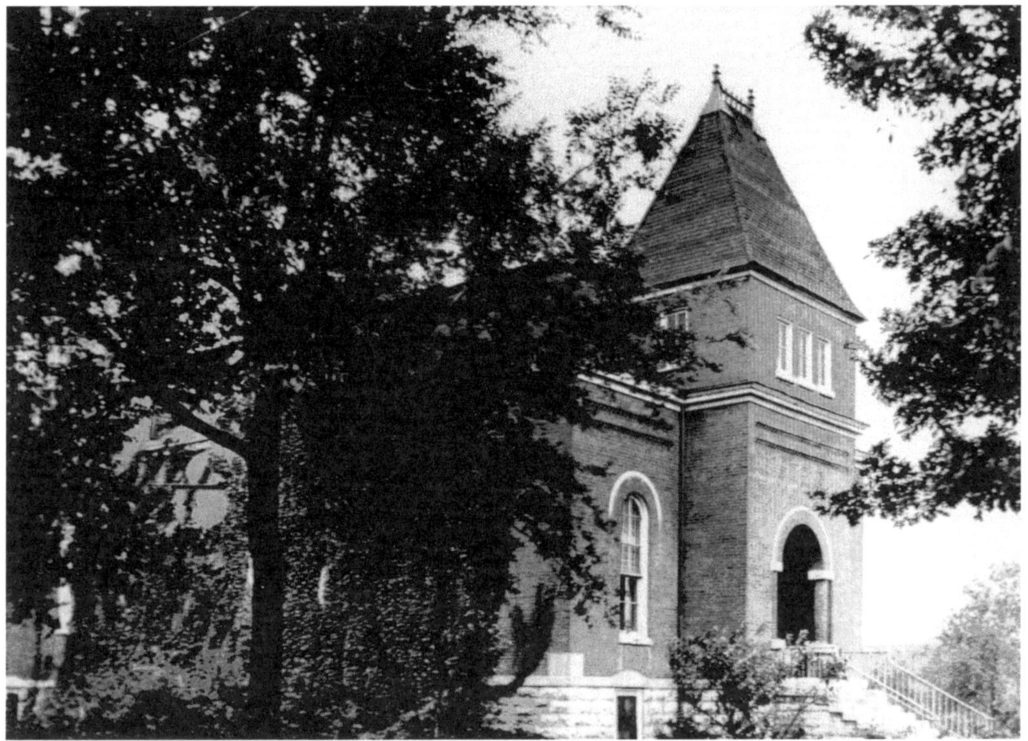

Carl Van Vechten Gallery, Fisk University, c.1950s. Special Collections, John Hope and Aurelia E. Franklin Library, Fisk University

and this exhibition was centred around artists and individuals who came out of HBCUs.

We continue to aid in the development of the next generations of arts leaders and advocates through programmes and exhibitions. The Fisk University Museum Leadership Initiative is a group of innovative, practiced-based programmes designed to educate, train and advance the careers of underrepresented groups in the field of museum management. This includes the Fisk Museum Leadership Program (FMLP); Assessment, Recruitment and Training in Conservation and Collections (ART-CC); the Bank of America Conservation Intensive; and the Gallery Ambassador Program. FMLP is a two-year, practice-based certificate programme designed to educate, train and advance the careers of minorities in the field. The programme consists of four modules followed by a one-year fellowship: 1) Conservation; 2) Curatorial; 3) Museum Education; 4) Development; and 5) Collection Management. ART-CC is a two-year fellowship in partnership with the Los Angeles County Museum of Art (LACMA) that provides full-time on-the-job training in addition to developing a pipeline of undergraduate students who, upon graduation, are ready to work with collection managers and fellows on campus. Through Fisk's Bank of America Conservation Intensive, our students have had the opportunity to work alongside conservators Ian McClure and Kathy Hebb on our collections of African modernists. Since 2015, our Gallery Ambassadors have developed programmes, led tours, coordinated events and curated exhibitions. Through

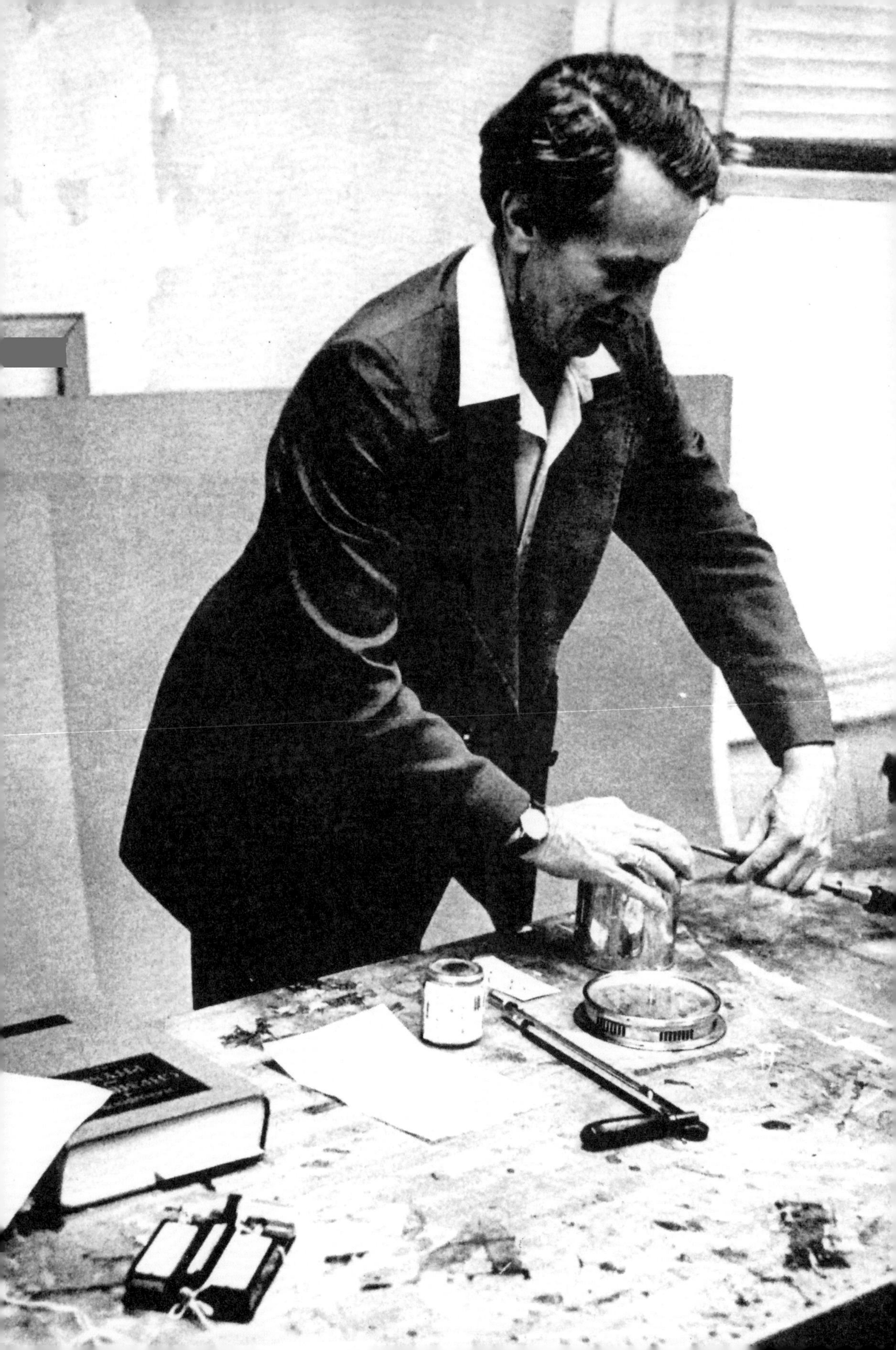

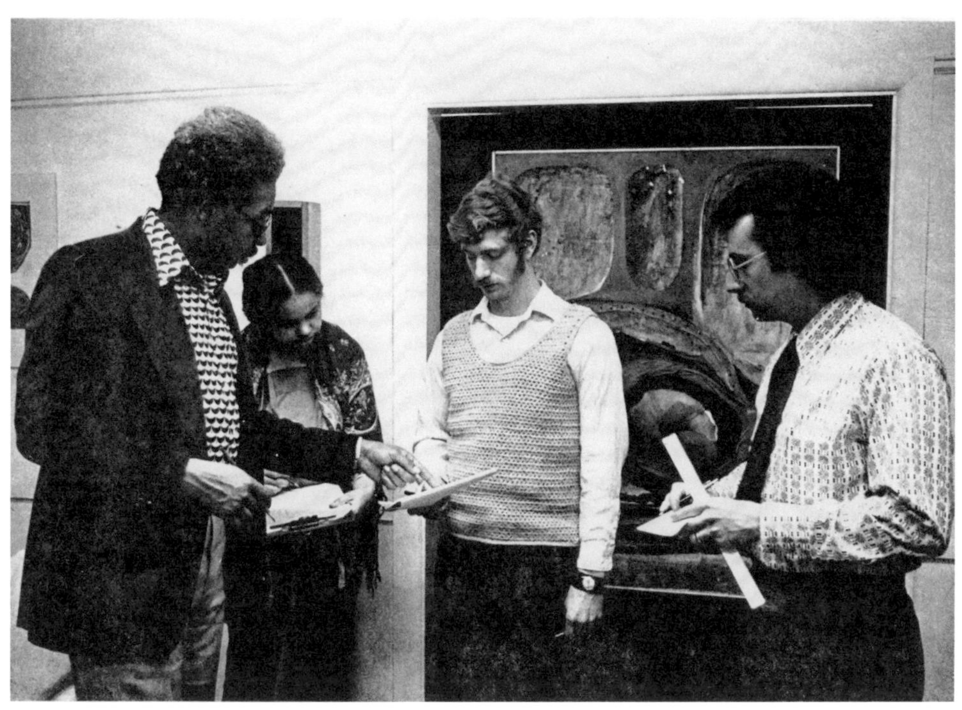

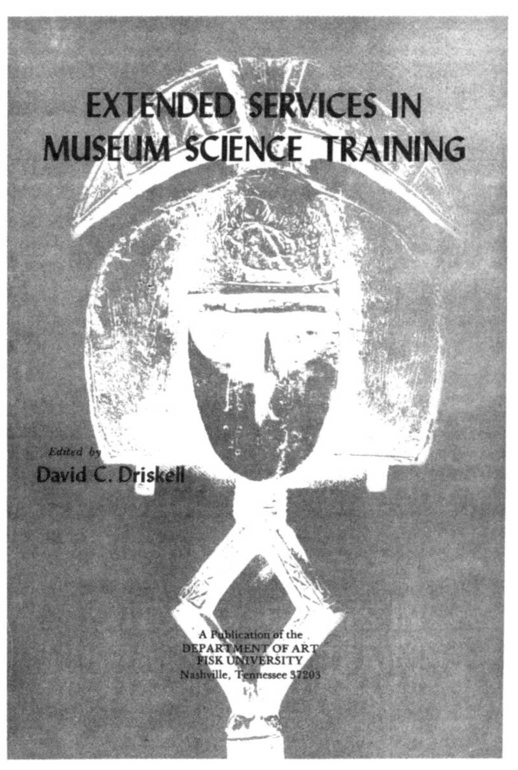

Opposite:
Nelson Fuson, professor of physics at Fisk University, conducting a workshop on museum maintenance and climate control at Extended Services in Museum Science Training conference, 1972–73. Courtesy Fisk University Galleries

Above:
Kenneth Young of the Smithsonian Institution conducting a workshop on exhibition design at Extended Services in Museum Science Training conference, Fisk University, 1972–73. Courtesy Fisk University Galleries

Left:
Cover of *Extended Services in Museum Science Training*, edited by David C. Driskell for Fisk University, 1973. Courtesy Fisk University Galleries

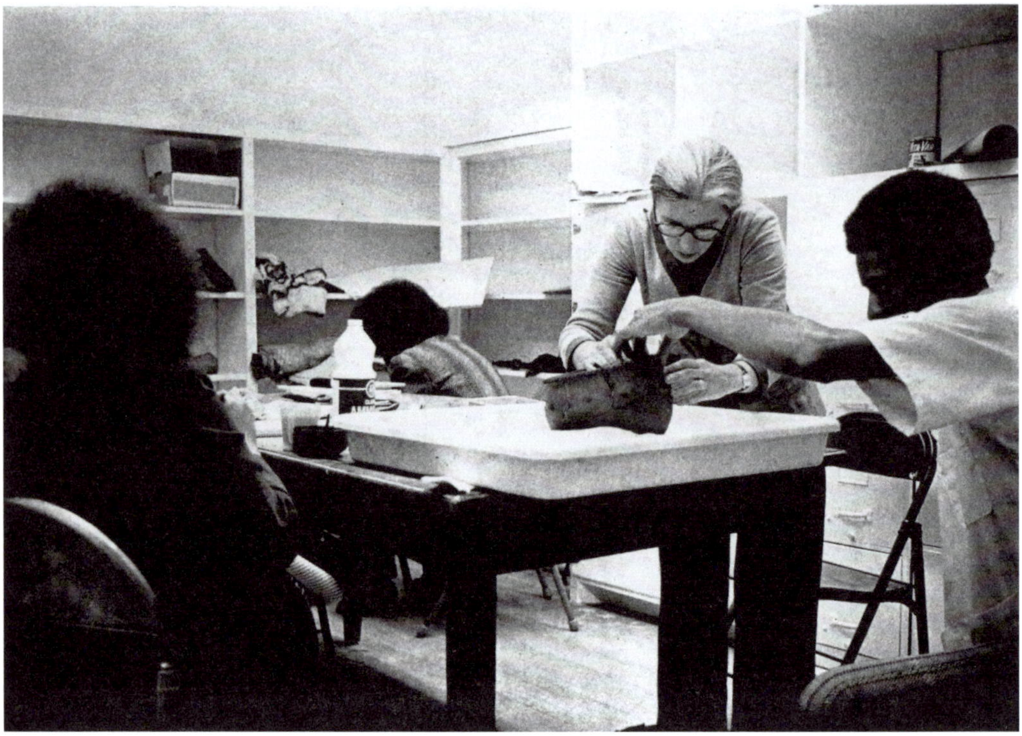

Mary Thieme (centre), lecturer in museum science at Fisk University, conducting a conservation workshop at Extended Services in Museum Science Training conference, Fisk University, 1972–73. Courtesy Fisk University Galleries

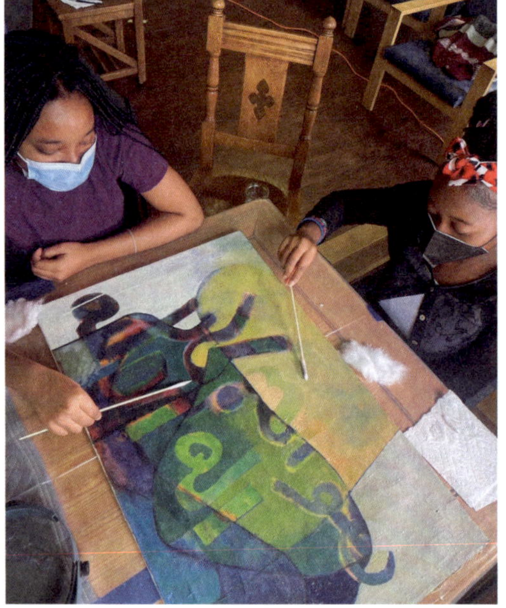

Freshman computer science majors Ayomide Adewale (left) and Esther Ogundele (right) cleaning the surface of Mohammad Omer Khalil's *Inno*, 1966, at Bank of America Conservation Intensive, Fisk University, 2022. Courtesy Fisk University Galleries

this programme we have trained over seventy students from all academic disciplines in career pathways into the field. Our collections are central to the Fisk experience.

I want to finish by asking: As we think about reshaping the field, how can we build advocacy? How can we develop sustainability? How can we think about institutions? How can we think about artists who were or continue to be marginalized or underrepresented in the institutions that house artists? How can we support those institutions as well? I leave you with these questions.

Notes

[1] Editors' Note: This text is adapted from the author's presentation at the online conference 'Reshaping the Field: Arts of the African Diasporas on Display', hosted by the Center for Curatorial Studies, Bard College, 4–6 November 2021.

[2] The Terry Adkins exhibition was co-presented in Nashville at Frist Art Museum and Fisk University Galleries.

Paving the Way: Exhibition History of African American Art at the Howard University Gallery of Art
– Abby R. Eron

Howard University's art programme has been lauded for its role in sparking generations of Black artists. In the documentary *Black Art: In the Absence of Light*, scholar and artist David C. Driskell – once acting director of the Howard University Gallery of Art and an alumnus of the Washington DC university – joined other commentators in praising the patronage by Historically Black Colleges and Universities (HBCUs) of African American artists, offering overdue credit to these institutions.[1] Howard, an HBCU, was established in 1867, in the wake of the Civil War and the abolition of slavery, to serve African American students. The Gallery of Art's affiliation with the university distinguishes it from many other art institutions, as it has always been geared towards benefiting the university's primary constituents, the students. Its exhibition history therefore reflects competing and evolving opinions about what it means to best serve Howard students, who often experience shows during formative years of early adulthood. The development of the university's eminent permanent art collection is intertwined with the gallery's exhibition history, making the impact of the gallery's exhibitions particularly long-lasting. Exhibitions at Howard have contributed to the crystallization of African American art history, while also reflecting competing visions of it. This essay examines exhibitions at two junctures: the formative years of early gallery history in the 1930s, and a period of transformation in the 1960s and 70s.

The First Decade

The Howard Gallery opened in the basement of the Andrew Rankin Memorial Chapel in April 1930 thanks to the efforts of the gallery's first director, James V. Herring, an alumnus who also founded the university's art department.[2] His leadership and connections brought in exhibitions organized by the College Art Association of America (the source of the gallery's first show), the American Federation of Arts, the Harmon Foundation, external museums and galleries, and additional private foundations and public entities. Student shows were essential from the beginning.[3]

In 1931, student exhibitors joined thirteen architects or architectural firms for 'Exhibition of the Work of Negro-Architects', which was presented by the university's department of architecture at the Howard Gallery. The show's run was short (12–28 May), typical of the gallery's first decades, when there could be over a dozen shows per year.[4] Herring, whom Howard had initially hired to teach drawing to architecture students, was on the show's jury, as was Albert I. Cassell, a professor of architecture and the university's architect. Cassell had designed the basement gallery in Rankin, and he would go on to design Howard's Founders Library, one of the gallery's later homes. Cassell's designs were included in the exhibition, as were those of Paul R. Williams, the Los Angeles–based 'architect to the stars'. *Opportunity* magazine announced this show as the first-ever exhibition of African American architects' work.[5] This exhibition is significant as such a first, as an example of interdisciplinary

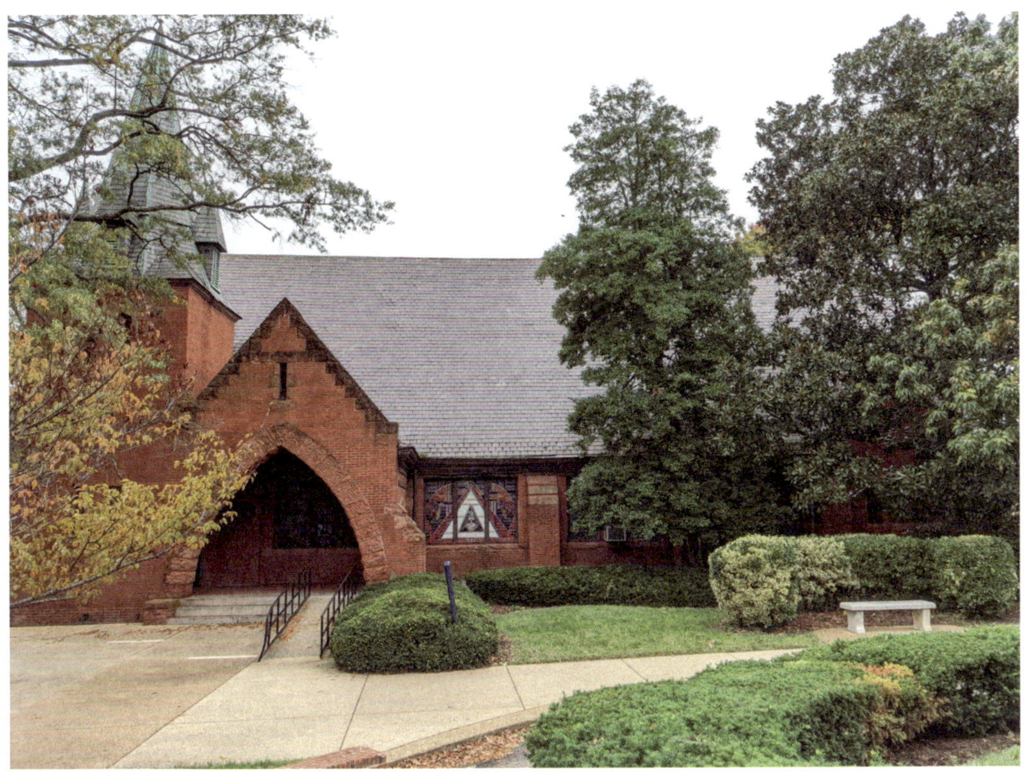

Andrew Rankin Memorial Chapel, Howard University, Washington DC. Photo: the author

collaboration at the university and as a demonstration of pathways and possibilities for Howard students with aspirations in the field.

Later that decade, Herring's foreword to the pamphlet for a 1937 exhibition, 'The Art of the American Negro', lays out some of the intra-university debates around the gallery's programme, the trajectory of African American art and student learning. In this text, Herring sets out the position of Alain Locke. Known as the 'dean' of the Harlem Renaissance, and serving as chair of the university's philosophy department, Locke was a prominent voice in art criticism. With his 1925 essay 'The Legacy of the Ancestral Arts', Locke encouraged African American artists to look to the arts of Africa as their rightful heritage and as a set of classics from which to draw inspiration.[6] In 1931, Locke published 'The American Negro as Artist' in *The American Magazine of Art* (Howard's student newspaper, *The Hilltop*, summarized his argument for a campus readership).[7] Locke again emphasized the centrality of African art to African American artists, stating, 'for them ... African art should act with all the force of a rediscovered folk-art'.[8]

Herring countered that an artist can learn from Greek, Chinese or Indian art just as well as African.[9] The schedule of exhibitions in the gallery's early decades reflects Herring's belief in global variety and its usefulness to those studying art, with shows including Dutch seventeenth-century painting, *ukiyo-e* woodblock

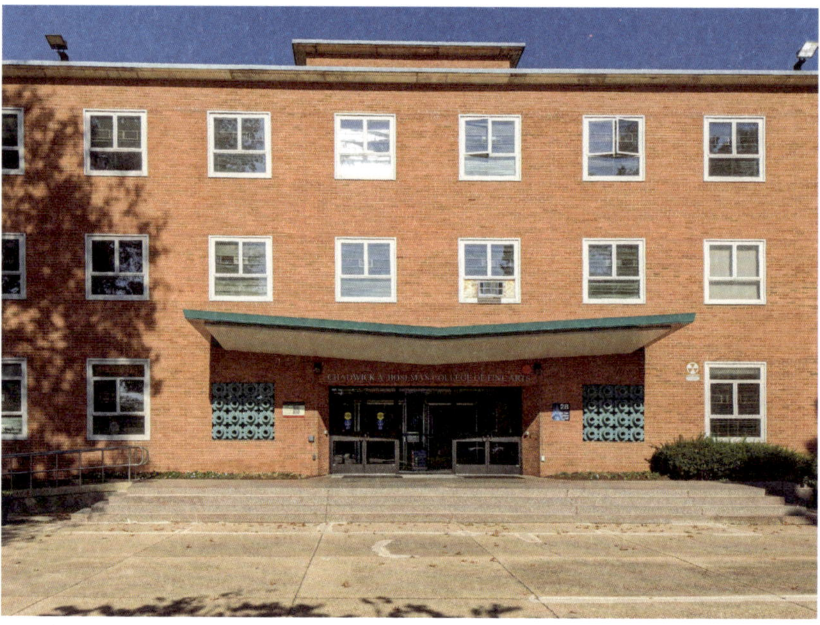

Chadwick A. Boseman College of Fine Arts, Lulu Vere Childers Hall, Howard University. Photo: the author

prints, contemporary Argentinian art, Chinese textiles and images of San rock art.[10] Henry Ossawa Tanner's prominence in 'The Art of the American Negro', where he was the most well-represented artist, also points to a contrast between Herring's and Locke's priorities. Shown was Tanner's last-painted work, *Return from the Crucifixion* (1936), one of the Howard Gallery's earliest acquisitions.[11] Locke, in 'Legacy of the Ancestral Arts', wrote discouragingly about the gap between Tanner's many achievements and the formation of a 'school of Negro art', as Tanner had 'never maturely touched the portrayal of the Negro subject'.[12] Although Locke was a force at the university and beyond, the gallery's agenda was set by Herring as director, with Alonzo J. Aden's support as curator.

In 1939, an exhibition of paintings and prints by African American artists, through the Works Progress Administration (WPA), went up at the gallery, which had also received approximately thirty works from the Federal government's art programmes.[13] A trend in the history of the gallery is this imbrication of permanent collection and exhibition history. Nearly all the artists in the 1939 exhibition are represented in the Gallery of Art's collection, including Samuel Brown, Eldzier Cortor, Allan Crite, Archibald Motley and Dox Thrash. The introductory essay in the exhibition pamphlet, by the WPA regional advisor, is self-congratulatory about the opportunities afforded by the New Deal programmes. The essay espouses a 'melting pot' ideology: 'No longer is Negro art apparent as such; human progress has assimilated in an exceedingly sound manner all that each race has to offer in a truly American Art.'[14] This statement, on one level, is inconsistent with the organizing principle of the show, featuring exclusively African American artists, but it was not altogether incongruous with Herring's goals and was a statement of a desired national unity in art during the decade of the Great Depression. Some of the

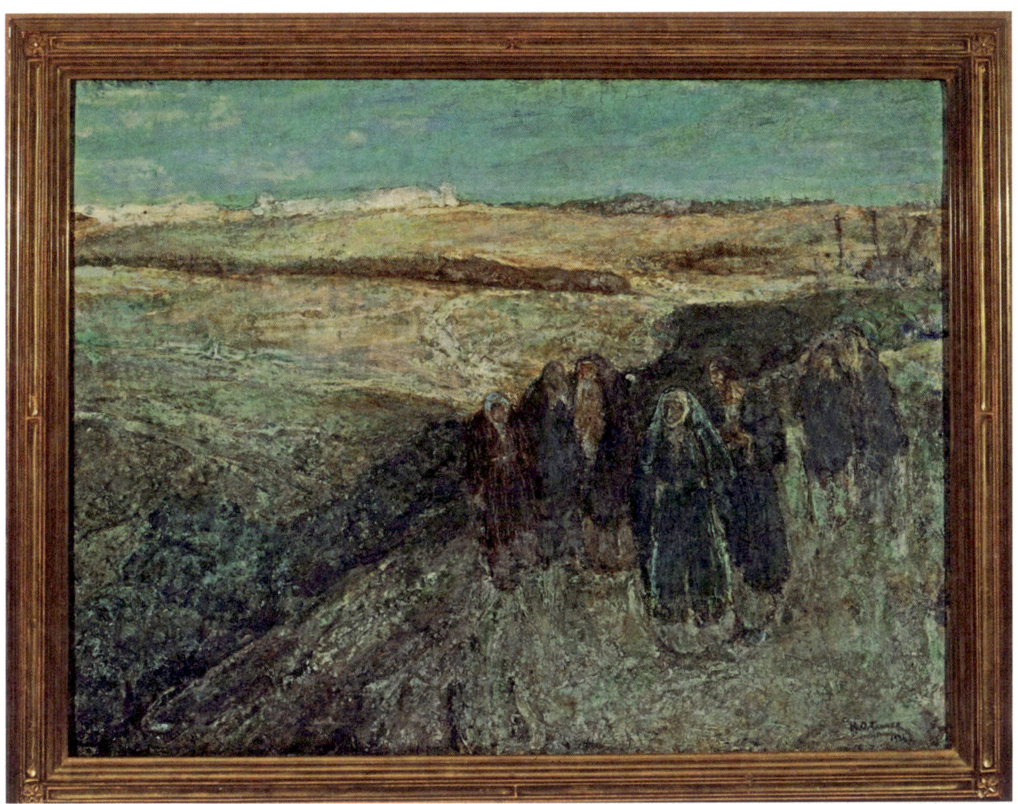

Henry Ossawa Tanner, *Return from the Crucifixion*, 1936, oil and tempera on board, 45.7 × 33cm. Howard University Gallery of Art. Photo: Gregory R. Staley. Courtesy Howard University Gallery of Art. Licensed by Art Resource, NY

Gallery of Art's exhibitions in this period highlighted African American artists exclusively, while others presented artists of different racial backgrounds.

The promotion of Black art and inclusivity, within the environment of segregated Washington DC, was also enacted in the programming of Herring and Aden's other joint venture, the Barnett Aden Gallery, founded 1943. Both galleries provided a platform for a cadre of influential African American professors whom Herring assembled to teach in the university's art department: Lois M. Jones, James A. Porter and James L. Wells (whose oeuvres are well represented in the gallery's permanent collection).[15] Their work featured in the gallery's 'Tenth Anniversary Exhibition' (1940), which Keith Morrison has called 'a major art event in the city'.[16] Morrison describes a grand opening reception attended by the university's president, faculty and prestigious guests, as well as 'all the art students'.[17] In this context, students would have seen their professors beyond the classroom, as models of exhibiting visual artists.

1960s and 70s

After moving from Rankin Chapel to Founders Library, an important moment for the gallery was finding its new (and current) home in Lulu Vere Childers Hall. The building, featuring three interconnected gallery spaces, was co-designed by Paul Williams.[18] The 1961 exhibition 'New Vistas in

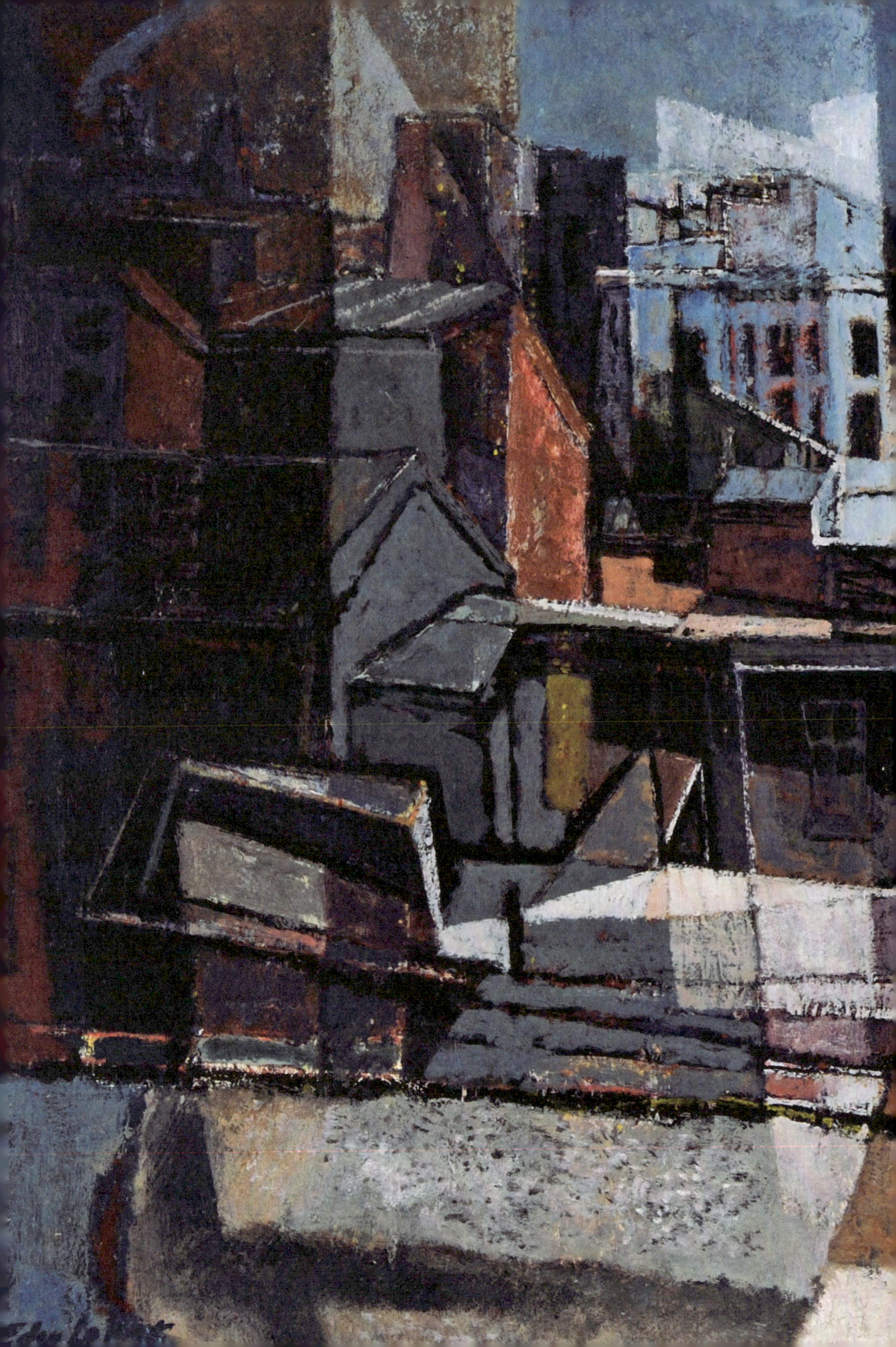

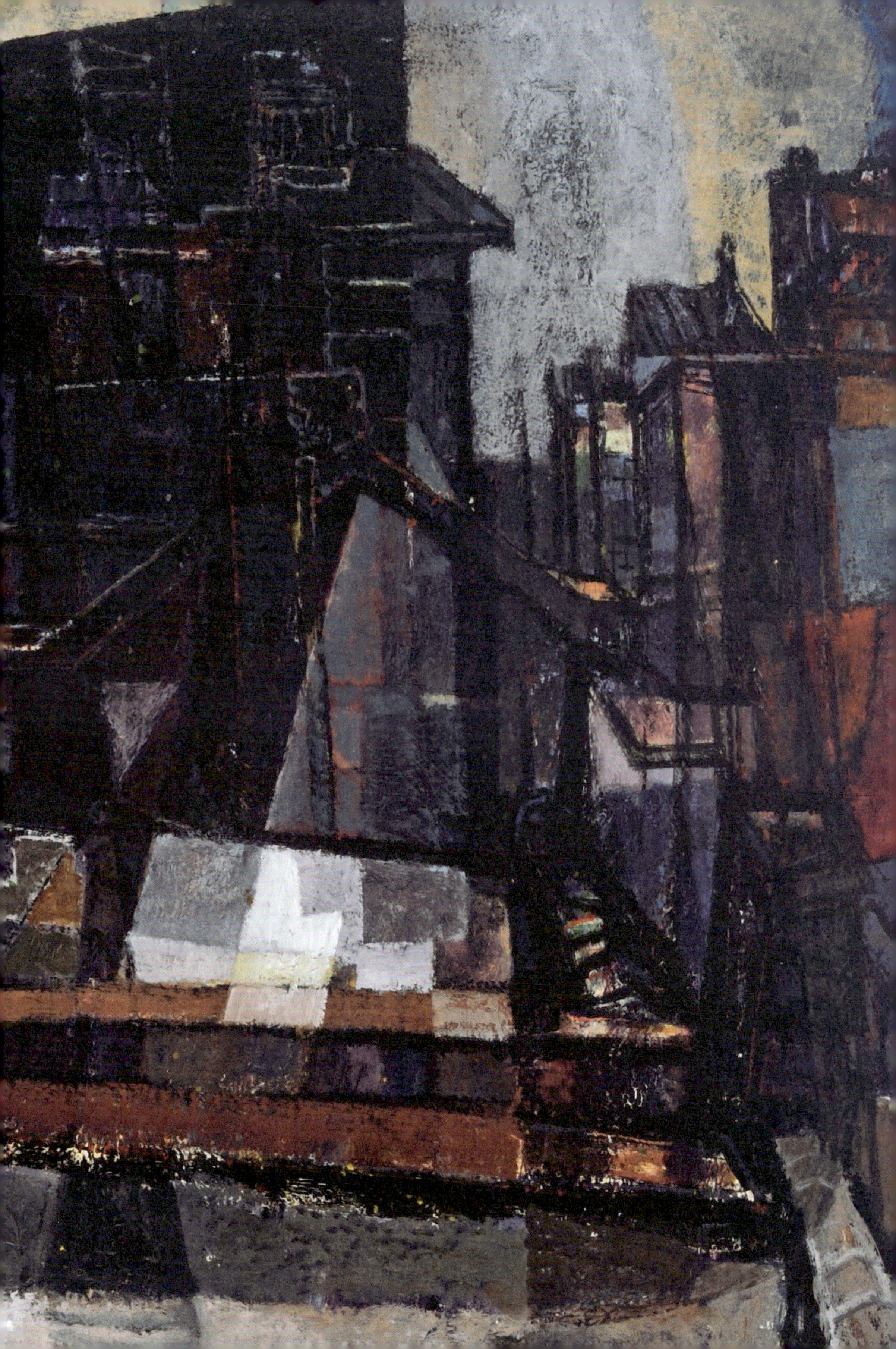

Alma Thomas, *Blue Abstraction*, 1961, oil on canvas, 86.4 × 101.6cm. Howard University Gallery of Art. Photo: Gregory R. Staley. Courtesy Howard University Gallery of Art. Licensed by Art Resource, NY

Previous spread: Edward Loper Sr, *Angry City*, c.1961, oil on board, 70.8 × 96.2cm. Howard University Gallery of Art. Photo: Gregory R. Staley. Courtesy Howard University Gallery of Art. Licensed by Art Resource, NY

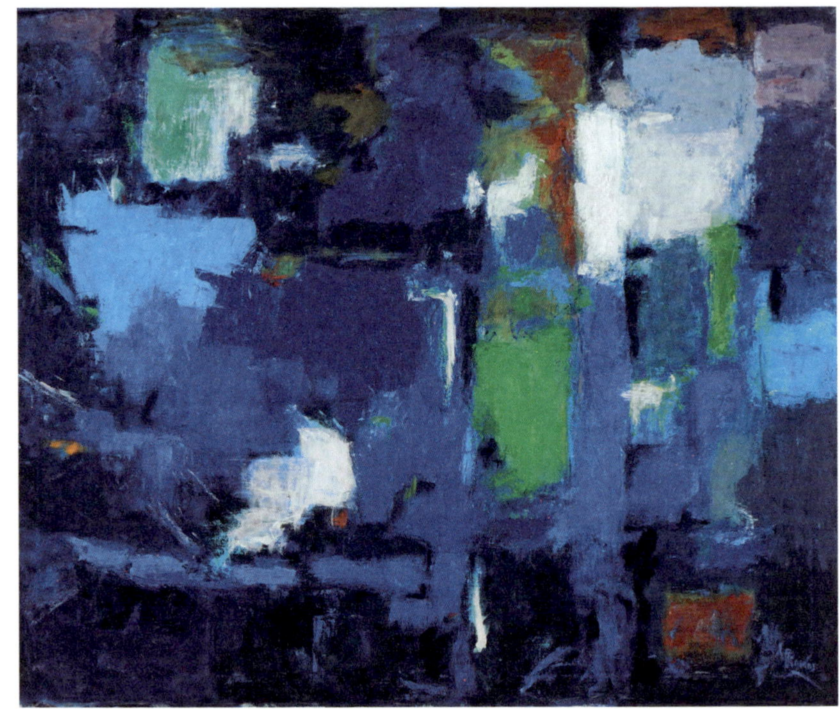

American Art' inaugurated the gallery's new location. Gallery leadership had changed by this point, but the trajectory had remained relatively stable. Albert J. Carter became curator in 1946, and Porter took up the mantle of director after Herring's retirement in 1953. Porter's foreword to 'New Vistas' echoes Herring in sentiment: '"New Vistas in American Art" includes the work of both white and Negro artists and incontestably proves that, regardless of racial or cultural bias, there is a vigorous unifying current of creativity in American art today.'[19] The main purpose of the exhibition was to allow the university to acquire new work.[20] Therefore, the artists who won top monetary prizes had their works brought into the permanent collection. Among the prize-winners were Edward Loper Sr's fractured, cubist cityscape *Angry City* (c.1961) and Alma Thomas's *Blue Abstraction* (1961), a non-figurative painting of soft, patch-like forms.[21]

Thomas was the Howard art department's first graduate, in 1924, and had her first retrospective at the Gallery of Art, in 1966. This exhibition has been cited for 'mark[ing] the start of Thomas's meteoric rise in the art world', leading to her solo show at the Whitney Museum of American Art in New York in 1972, the first there for a Black woman.[22] The Howard solo exhibition displayed Thomas's signature style, with individualized, semi-blocky paint strokes of bright colours organized into stripes and concentric circles. Driskell, who had just completed a period as acting director of the gallery during Porter's sabbatical, wrote the introduction to Thomas's exhibition pamphlet. Driskell would go on to curate another Thomas exhibition while serving at Fisk University in

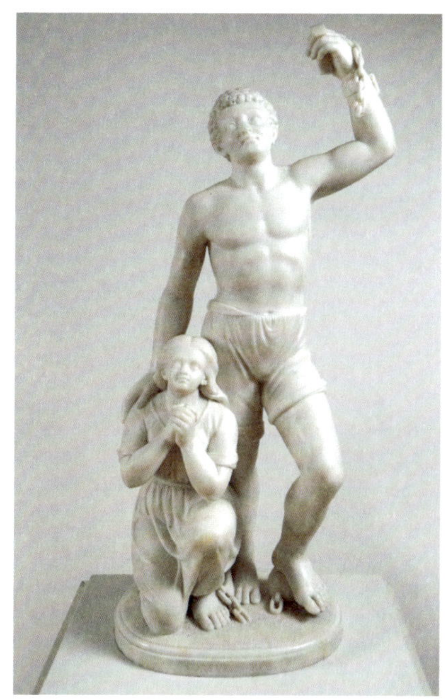

Edmonia Lewis, *Forever Free*, 1867, marble, 106 × 54.6 × 31.4cm. Howard University Gallery of Art. Photo: Gregory R. Staley. Courtesy Howard University Gallery of Art. Licensed by Art Resource, NY

Below: Newspaper clipping from *The Washington Afro-American*, 29 May 1954. Exhibition Files, Howard University Gallery of Art. Courtesy Scott W. Baker

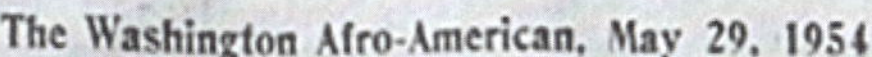

The Washington Afro-American, May 29, 1954

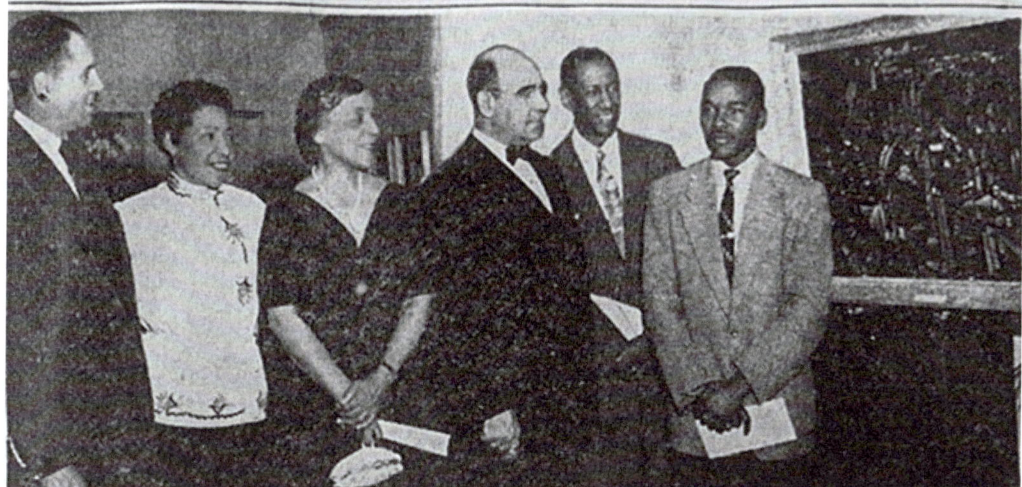

AT ART EXHIBIT—Dr. Mordecai W. Johnson, president of Howard University, was among the particippants at the opening exercises of the annual student exhibition in art at the University until June 30. The group is admiring one of the works of Davd C. Driskell who won the first prize in painting for the 1953-54 school year. Several of Mr. Driskell's works are on display. From left are James W. Jones, supervisor of art in the D.C. public schools; Lois V. Jones, associate professor of art at Howard; Mrs. and Dr. Johnson; James A. Porter, associate professor of art at Howard; and Mr. Driskell, a senior in the College of Liberal Arts.

Nashville, thereby furthering Thomas's ascent. Driskell himself, who would later curate the field-defining 'Two Centuries of Black American Art' (1976), which originated at the Los Angeles County Museum of Art, was inarguably indebted on a scholarly and artistic level to his time at Howard as a student and professor involved in the gallery.

On the university's centennial, in 1967, Porter's 'Ten Afro-American Artists of the Nineteenth Century' presented external loans and selections from the permanent collection in the Gallery of Art.[23] The scholarly spirit of Porter's foundational survey text *Modern Negro Art* (1943) is reflected in this exhibition's commitment to highlighting African American artists overlooked in dominant art historical narratives.[24] There were works in Porter's show by Edmonia Lewis, but her neoclassical masterpiece *Forever Free* (1867), which would be acquired later that year, was not among them. The exhibition anticipated that acquisition, as Porter's discussion of Lewis in the catalogue pointed to the scholarly work yet to be done on her and the rediscoveries of her sculpture yet to be made. In the decades since, scholarship on Lewis has blossomed and *Forever Free* has become the most well-known work in the Howard University Gallery of Art's collection.[25]

1970 marked a meaningful redirection. Porter passed away in 1970, and Jeff Donaldson was appointed the new chair of the art department and director of the gallery. Donaldson had co-founded AfriCOBRA, a group that gave striking visual dimensions to the Black Power movement. He had contributed to Chicago's Wall of Respect mural in 1967, and he coined the 'Trans-African' aesthetic.[26] His ideas coalesced with an environment of growing activism at Howard, an outgrowth of the broader struggle for civil rights. At the gallery, this was most dramatically expressed through a student 'seizure' stemming from the 1968 Washington DC riots, spurred by the assassination of Martin Luther King Jr.[27] Three paintings were stolen, and one was damaged in the episode.[28] In 1969, *The Hilltop* reported on 'a new wave of protest growing within the Art Department' and aimed at enlivening and 'desteriliz[ing]' the campus.[29] Taking issue with the gallery's choices, one student sculptor installed his own exhibition outdoors.[30]

Donaldson's leadership and the Black Arts Movement's inclination to making art publicly accessible, specifically to Black communities, furthered the momentum. Students' murals went up around Lulu Vere Childers Hall. They were illustrated in an article in *Ebony* magazine that described changes at the university during this period.[31] The *Ebony* journalist, Alex Poinsett, used mural-making as a metaphor by describing ideas burgeoning in the mid-1960s as the 'unpainted mural'; these ideas, concerning the university's Black identity, were now coming to fruition, as signalled by the large and energetic panels picturing Black figures that were reproduced on the first page of the article.[32] Donaldson oversaw curricular changes, so that art of Africa and the African diaspora became the emphasis of course offerings in the art department. He argued that students should 'get deeply involved in their own art', more so than in traditions from Europe.[33]

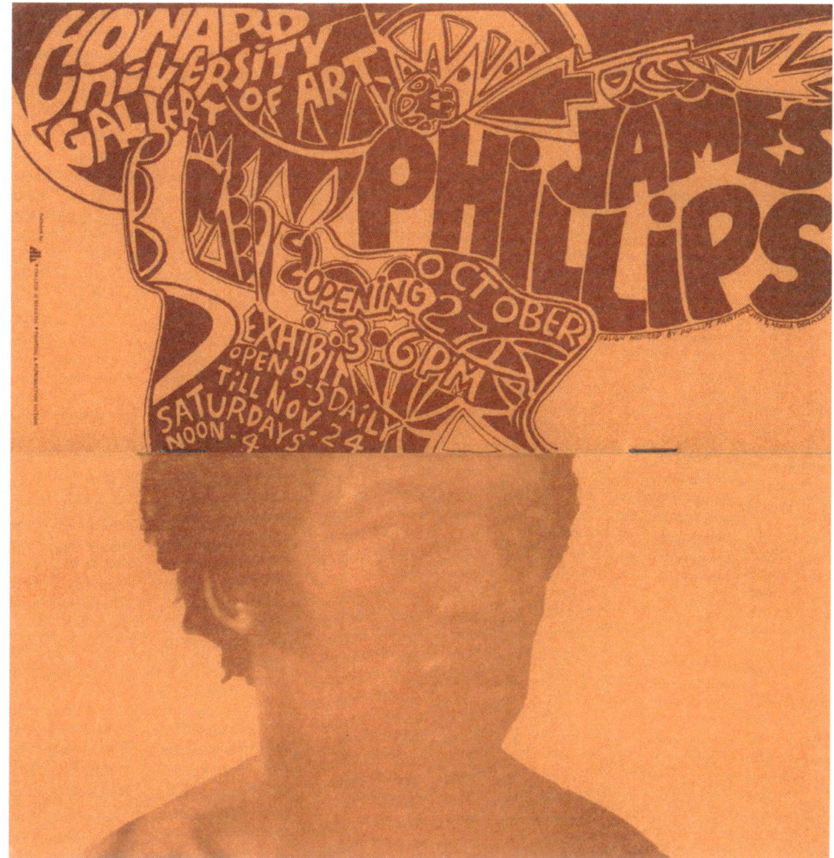

Jeff and Arnicia Donaldson, unfolded cover of the exhibition pamphlet for 'The Paintings of James Phillips', 1972. Exhibition Files, Howard University Gallery of Art. Courtesy Howard University Gallery of Art. Licensed by Art Resource, NY

The gallery's exhibitions corroborated these broader shifts, concentrating on art of Africa and the African diaspora.[34] Student shows emphasized Black community: 'We are exhibiting for all Black People', art students directly addressed the readership of *The Hilltop* in a 1971 exhibition announcement.[35] The announcement also indicated new and abstract ways of thinking about Black identity, encouraging readers to 'open your minds ... and show your Blackness'.[36] This call for open minds has a visual counterpart in the exhibition pamphlet for James Phillips's 1972 solo show, which unfolds to reveal a complete composition, an exuberance of psychedelic shapes and lettering crowning or sprouting forth from the artist's head. The design, by Jeff and Arnicia Donaldson, reflects the formal qualities of Phillips's abstractions. His large-scale, rhythmically colourful, multi-panel paintings would have encompassed the viewer's visual field, creating a powerful, all-over, and mural-like impact resonant with the zeitgeist of this era at Howard.

The Gallery of Art at Howard also hosted the shows 'AfriCOBRA II', in 1972, and 'AfriCOBRA III', in 1973.[37] The latter included a work entitled *Uhuru* by Nelson Stevens; the title of the work – meaning 'freedom' in Swahili – serves as a marker of Afrocentricity. *Uhuru* (c.1970), in the Howard collection, displays

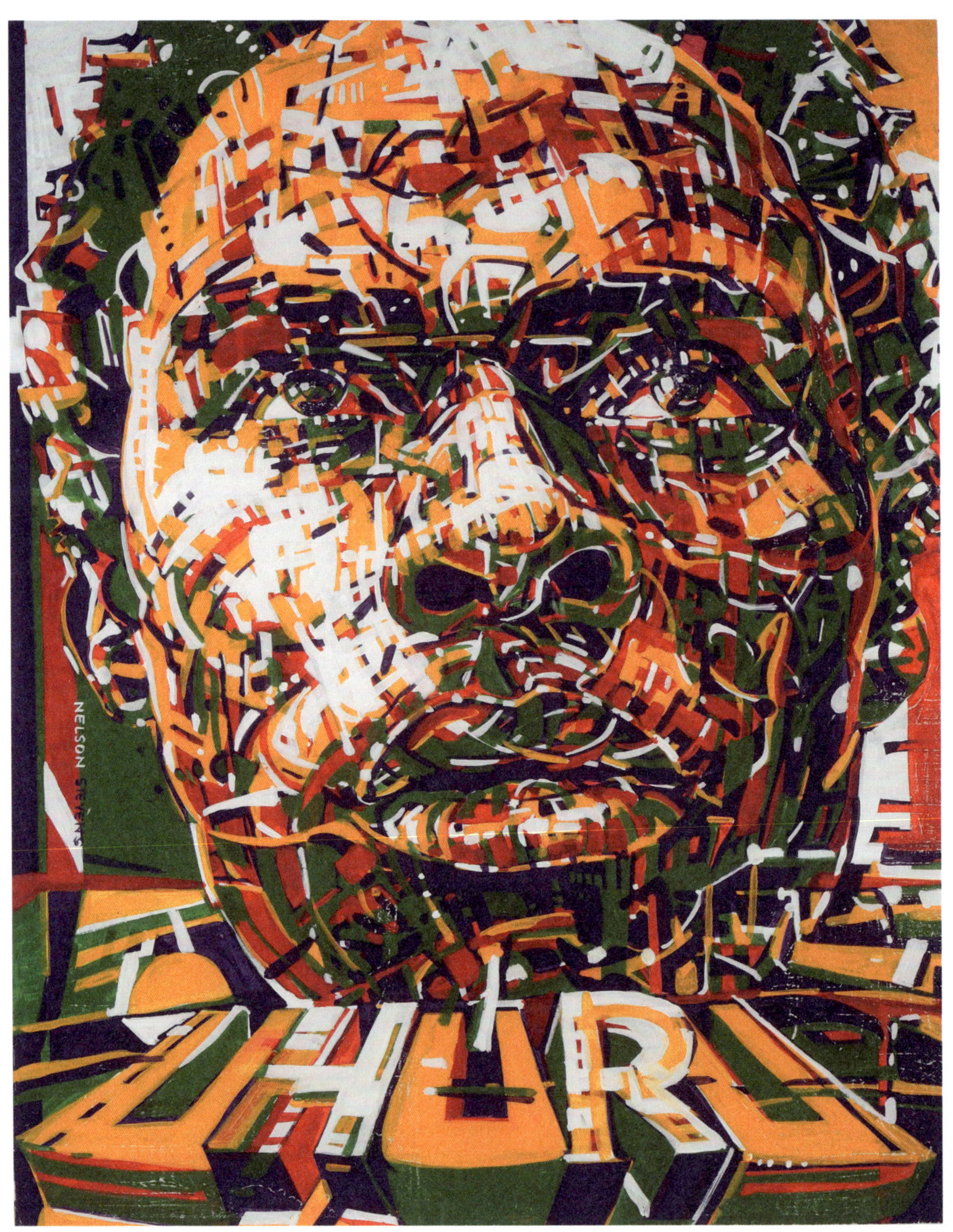

Nelson Stevens, *Uhuru*, c.1970, 106.7 × 78.7cm. Howard University Gallery of Art. Photo: Gregory R. Staley. Courtesy Howard University Gallery of Art. Licensed by Art Resource, NY emblematic AfriCOBRA style, with its incorporation of lettering, its dense and dynamic arrangement of pieces of colour to articulate form, its political call to action and its vibrant 'Kool-Aid' hues, in which the gallery walls were also painted.[38]

Washington Post critic Paul Richard reviewed several AfriCOBRA exhibitions at Howard. Emphasizing the group's global diasporic ambitions and positioning vis-à-vis the African continent, Richard wrote: 'Africobra is struggling to make African art for Africans only, not just those who live today between the Mediterranean and the Cape, but for anyone from Watts or Harlem, in Roxbury or Haiti, for anyone who's black.'[39] Richard so closely identified this Afrocentric style and point of view with the university that he referred to it as 'the Howard School'.[40] *The Hilltop* student journalist Calvin Reid reviewed the 1977 faculty exhibition as an example not only of the legacy of the Black Arts Movement but of 'its development and maturation', pointing to the faculty's use of African themes and symbols and emphasizing the connections made to 'our forefathers'.[41] The impact of this generation is apparent in the output of contemporary artists such as Bisa Butler, who has cited the teachings of her AfriCOBRA-affiliated Howard professors as fundamental to her ongoing practice.[42]

Conclusion

Into the twenty-first century, major exhibitions at the Howard University Gallery of Art have been retrospective in tone. Under the leadership of director Tritobia Hayes Benjamin, the gallery collaborated with five other HBCU museums and galleries on 'To Conserve a Legacy: American Art from Historically Black Colleges and Universities' (1999–2001). More than a travelling exhibition, this was a large-scale project to provide needed conservation interventions and train students in collections care.[43] 'A Proud Continuum: Eight Decades of Art at Howard University' (2005) showcased the work of 122 alumni, represented by one work each. The catalogue points to the reach of Howard alumni, who include the gallery's current leaders: Lisa E. Farrington, director, who contributed an essay on the impact that women have made on the art programme at Howard, and Scott W. Baker, chief curator, who contributed a historical essay and a work of art. After a period of closure for the Covid-19 pandemic, the gallery has restarted its in-person exhibition programming with selections from the permanent collection, new acquisitions and contemporary art. This is augmented by the permanent collection, which, through an active loan programme and digital presence, illuminates African American art history outside the gallery's physical walls. By providing a platform for student work and offering first-hand exposure to outstanding art by faculty and others, Howard Gallery exhibitions have helped launch careers and ignite passions for historical research and creative expression. The gallery's primary constituents – Howard University students – have contributed on a local, national and global scale. This dispersed impact, rippling outwards, lends immeasurable weight to the gallery's exhibition history.

Notes

[1] *Black Art: In the Absence of Light*, directed by Sam Pollard (HBO, 2021).

[2] It was preceded by the university's Historical Picture Gallery (1870–c.1873).

[3] See Ada Rainey, 'Art Schools are Showing their Work' and 'Two Exhibits of Negro Art Have Merit', *Washington Post*, 1 June 1930. Rainey's dually headlined review categorizes the Howard show with both other student shows and an exhibition at the National Gallery of Art in Washington DC that was co-sponsored by the Harmon Foundation. Bridget R. Cooks has discussed the first iteration of the latter show, and Rainey's review of it, as a 'sociological' presentation. African American art was kept separate rather than enabled to disrupt the canon perpetuated by American museums. See B.R. Cooks, *Exhibiting Blackness: African Americans and the American Art Museum*, Amherst: University of Massachusetts Press, 2011, pp.20–22.

[4] See Exhibition Schedules in College Art Association of America Records, The Frick Collection/ Frick Art Reference Library Collection. A figure of six to ten shows per year from the 1930s to 50s is cited in Keith Morrison, *Art in Washington and Its Afro-American Presence: 1940–1970*, Washington DC: Washington Project for the Arts, 1985.

[5] 'Negro Architects', *Opportunity* 9, no.5 (May 1931), p.155.

[6] Alain Locke, 'The Legacy of the Ancestral Arts', *The New Negro: Voices of the Harlem Renaissance* (ed. A. Locke), New York: Simon & Schuster, 1997 (1925), pp.254–67.

[7] A. Locke, 'The American Negro as Artist', *The American Magazine of Art*, vol.23, no.3, September 1931, pp.210–20; Corinne Prince, 'Dr. Alain Locke Discusses Art and the Negro', *The Hilltop*, 22 October 1931.

[8] A. Locke, 'The American Negro as Artist', *op. cit.*, p.220.

[9] James V. Herring, foreword to *The Art of the American Negro* (exh. cat.), Washington DC: Howard University Gallery of Art, 1937, photocopy of typescript, Exhibition Files, Howard University Gallery of Art.

[10] Ruby Moise Kendrick noted that 'the exhibits have been diversified in character'. R.M. Kendrick, 'Art at Howard University: An Appreciation', *Crisis*, vol.39, no.11, November 1932, p.348.

[11] See Connie Porter Uzelac, 'James Amos Porter Meets Henry Ossawa Tanner', *International Review of African American Art*, vol.20, no.3, June 2005, pp.3–11.

[12] A. Locke, 'The Legacy of the Ancestral Arts', *op. cit.*, p.264.

[13] A.G., 'Exhibition of Paintings by Negro Artists is shown at Howard University Gallery', *Washington Post*, 30 April 1939. Eleven works came from the Public Works of Art Project (PWAP). See letter from Aden to Frances M. Pollak, 12 June 1934, College Art Association of America Records. These holdings were augmented in 1947 with works dispersed from Fort Huachuca, Arizona.

[14] Russell C. Parr, *Oil Paintings, Watercolors & Prints by Negro Artists* (exh. cat.), Washington DC: Howard University Gallery of Art, 1939.

[15] This is especially true given the gallery's 2021 acquisitions of the Porter and Jones Collections.

[16] K. Morrison, *Art in Washington and Its Afro-American Presence*, *op. cit.*

[17] *Ibid.*

[18] He had met his co-designer, Hilyard Robinson, at the 1931 show, and together they received many commissions from Howard University. See American Institute of Architects, 'Gallery: Howard University, Washington, DC', Paul R. Williams Project, https://www.paulrwilliamsproject.org/gallery/howard-university-washington-dc-/.

[19] J.A. Porter, foreword to *New Vistas in American Art* (exh. cat.), Washington DC: Howard University Gallery of Art, 1961.

[20] The show also honored three African American sculptors: Meta Warrick Fuller, Selma Burke and John Rhoden. Locke's 1955 bequest of African art was shown in the first gallery space. See Leslie Judd Ahlander, 'Howard U. Opens New Art Gallery', *Washington Post*, 2 April 1961. The exhibition history of African art at Howard was outside the scope of the conference for which this essay was prepared but warrants in-depth study.

[21] While the modernist paintings are formally quite different, E. Hoffman interpreted Thomas's abstraction as a city skyline, thus paralleling Thomas's subject with Loper's. Ellen Hoffman, 'Colorful Abstracts Reflect Her Spirit', *Washington Post*, 4 May 1966. This article was written for Thomas's 1966 solo exhibition. Thomas mused to the reporter how 'lovely' *Blue Abstraction* remained, stating with good-humoured regret, 'I should have kept that one myself.'

[22] Rebecca VanDiver, 'Howard University's Orbital Pull: Alma and Her Alma Mater', in Seth Feman and Jonathan Frederick Walz (ed.), *Alma W. Thomas: Everything is Beautiful* (exh. cat.), New Haven: Yale University Press in association with the Columbus Museum and Chrysler Museum of Art, 2021, p.116.

[23] Tanner's *Gate of Tangier* was a loan to the show that became a gift to the gallery, again demonstrating the connection between exhibiting and collecting activities.

[24] James A. Porter, *Modern Negro Art*, New York: Dryden Press, 1943.

[25] Lewis's portrait appears on a January 2022 stamp by the United States Postal Service.
[26] See Tobias Wofford, 'Jeff Donaldson's Howard: A Center of Trans-African Art', *Callaloo*, vol.40, no.5, 2017, pp.29–35.
[27] Romare Bearden and Harry Henderson, *A History of African-American Artists: From 1972 to the Present,* New York: Pantheon Books, 1993, p.379.
[28] *Ibid.*
[29] Barbara Womack, 'Art student's work displayed', *The Hilltop*, 19 December 1969.
[30] *Ibid.*
[31] Alex Poinsett, 'The Metamorphosis of Howard University', *Ebony*, vol.27, no.2, December 1971, pp.110–22.
[32] *Ibid.*, p.114. The mural illustrated was by graduate student William Battle, according to the author's conversation with Scott W. Baker.
[33] A. Poinsett, 'The Metamorphosis of Howard University', *op. cit.,* p.112.
[34] Wofford has argued that while the department's 'cultural nationalism was, in some sense, a turn away from the diverse artistic community' of earlier times, it was also a 'turn to an expansive notion of Black community that looked beyond the American context'. Concomitantly, exhibitions showed work by artists hailing from the Bahamas, Brazil, Ethiopia, Haiti, Ghana, Senegal and many other countries, especially in the 'Exhibition of African Contemporary Art' (1977). T. Wofford, 'Jeff Donaldson's Howard', *op. cit.,* p.32.
[35] 'Art students exhibit works in gallery', *The Hilltop*, 5 November 1971.
[36] *Ibid.*
[37] Wadsworth A. Jarrell, *AFRICOBRA: Experimental Art Toward a School of Thought*, Durham, NC: Duke University Press, 2020. In 1989, an AfriCOBRA retrospective was mounted between the gallery space in Childers Hall and the neighbouring student centre. This time, the AfriCOBRA group exhibited with an artist collective from Martinique, and in so doing reinforced their kinship with the worldwide Black community.
[38] They were painted in this palette at least for 'AfriCOBRA II'. See *ibid.,* p.197.
[39] Paul Richard, 'Africobra: African Art for Africans Only', *Washington Post,* 27 February 1972. AfriCOBRA co-founder W.A. Jarrell has written about ambivalence surrounding Richard's writing. See W.A. Jarrell, *AFRICOBRA: Experimental Art Toward a School of Thought, op. cit.*, pp.201–14.
[40] P. Richard, 'A Bright New "School" with a Black Theme', *Washington Post,* 19 March 1976.
[41] Calvin Reid, 'Seventh Annual Faculty of Art Exhibition', *The Hilltop*, 18 March 1977.
[42] Sok.Vision, 'Quilting for the Culture: Bisa Butler', 6 June 2020, https://youtu.be/_P3_61nh3xo.
[43] See Jock Reynolds, 'Conserving a Legacy: Forging a Partnership', in *To Conserve a Legacy: American Art from Historically Black Colleges and Universities* (exh. cat.; ed. Richard J. Powell and J. Reynolds), Andover, MA and New York: Addison Gallery of American Art and the Studio Museum in Harlem, 1999, pp.31–76. The show travelled to the Corcoran Gallery of Art in Washington DC and a smaller, complementary exhibition was mounted at Howard.

Between Inclusion and Making Space

Bridget Cooks's 2011 publication *Exhibiting Blackness: African Americans and the American Art Museum* introduces a tension between two dominant modes for exhibitions of Black art: anthropological exhibitions organized via an ethnic signifier and exhibitions that aim at establishing art as universal. Within this tension, some Black artists have insisted on inclusion by organizing exhibitions outside mainstream museums, while others have worked with the museum, as David C. Driskell did, to highlight Black artists' contributions. This section explores the diverse ways that Black artists have organized, from activist and protest initiatives such as those mounted against the 1969 exhibition 'Harlem on my Mind' at the

Metropolitan Museum of Art in New York; to the establishment of Black spaces such as New York's Cinque Gallery and Acts of Art in the 1960s–70s; to the way Driskell, in landmark projects such as 'Two Centuries of Black American Art' at the Los Angeles County Museum of Art in 1976, strategically utilized the museum in order to transform the field.

Insisting on Inclusion and Making Space Downtown – Howard Singerman

On 18 November 1968, *The New York Times* reported that a 'group of some 30 black artists, their friends and supporters picketed the Whitney Museum yesterday afternoon' to protest the exclusion of Black artists from its expansive survey of American painting and sculpture in the 1930s.[1] On 12 January 1969, and again on the 14th and 16th, many of those same artists and supporters, now organized as the Black Emergency Cultural Coalition, mounted pickets against the Metropolitan Museum of Art's 'Harlem on My Mind', an exhibition devoted to the 'cultural capital of Black America', but that included no work by Black painters or sculptors. Earlier that same January, another group of activist artists staged an action at the Museum of Modern Art (MoMA); the artist Takis (Panayiotis Vassilakis) removed a work of his that the museum had acquired from a temporary exhibition, and, with a group of supporters, held it hostage in MoMA's sculpture garden. Later that month, under the banner of the Art Workers' Coalition, the activists presented the museum with a list of thirteen demands. Near the top of the list was the call for 'a section of the Museum, under the direction of black artists ... [and] devoted to showing the accomplishments of black artists', as well as for the extension of the museum's programmes into 'Black, Spanish and other communities' with 'exhibits with which these groups can identify'. The organized pressure on New York City's cultural institutions, whether for representational inclusion or more radical transformation, continued through the year, and through the first years of the new decade.

The demands that the Black Emergency Cultural Coalition posed to the Met in early 1969, and to the Whitney in meetings that extended from April 1969 through 1970, were for the desegregation of white museum walls and curatorial office spaces. The call by artists Faith Ringgold and Tom Lloyd, writing for the Art Workers' Coalition, for separate spaces for Black artists and for exhibitions organized for the Black community, echoed the Black cultural nationalism of groups like the Harlem-based Weusi Artists Collective and their belief in the political and social necessity of an avowedly Black art. But whether the demand was for representational integration or for a cultural separatism, there was a pragmatic, tactical understanding, across ideological lines, that in that moment the only visibility available for Black artists individually was as Black artists collectively and, most often, in Black spaces or white spaces temporarily claimed for Black representation.

Those alternatives and the situation at hand were in many ways embodied by two art galleries for Black artists that opened downtown in Greenwich Village in the fall and winter of 1969. Cinque Gallery, the better known of the two, was founded by Romare Bearden, Norman Lewis and Ernest Crichlow – all well-established artists who had known one another, and who had been engaged with various formations to support the work of Black artists, since the 1930s. Housed in Joseph Papp's Public Theater building on Lafayette Street, Cinque opened in December 1969 to show and support 'young minority artists'. The press release circulated for its inaugural exhibition, of works by the

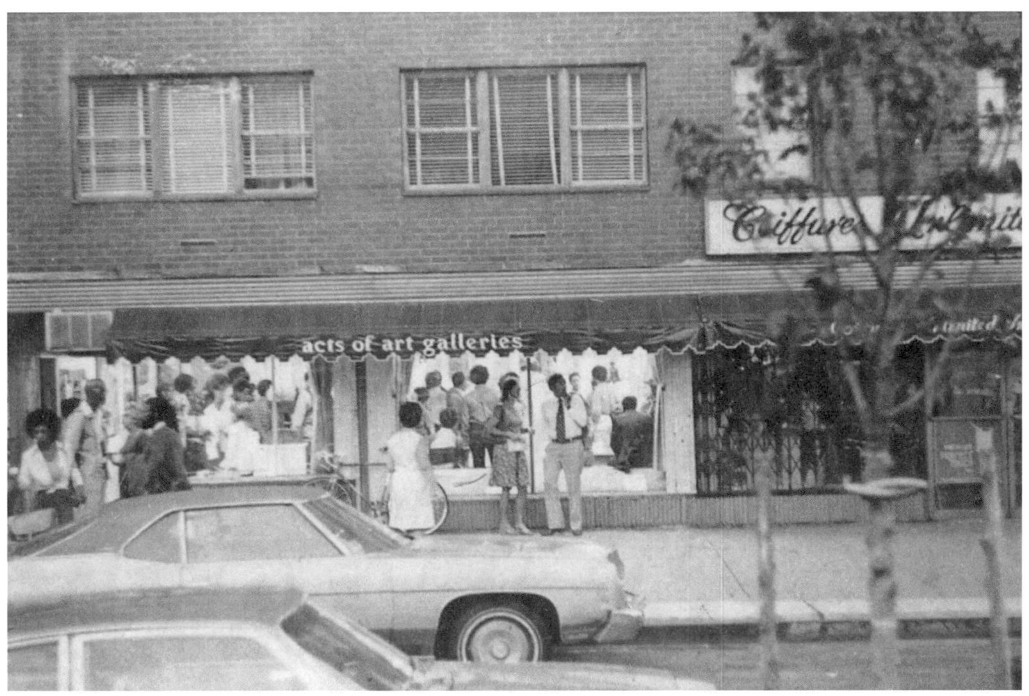

Acts of Art, 15 Charles Street, New York, on opening night of 'Black Artists in the New York Scene', 10 September 1974. New York University Tamiment Library and Robert F. Wagner Labor Archives, Daily Worker and the Daily World Negatives Collection. Photo: Nandi Guillame. Courtesy People's World

young, Pratt Institute–trained artist[2] Malcolm Bailey, explained the gallery's goals with an extended quote from Bearden, the best known of the three founders. Bearden envisioned Cinque as 'a bridge and a training center … in the hope that artists and personnel can move, should they desire, into the mainstream of the contemporary art world'. While the statement spoke to both artists and would-be administrators, artists were at the centre of Cinque's mission, and the stakes and expectations were high. 'The purpose of the gallery … is to provide that essential encouragement so vital to the artistic development of serious young artists who have already demonstrated marked ability as well as a deep concern for *universal* aesthetic criteria.'[3] The word 'universal' is underlined in the typescript; underlined or not, it was a charged word in contemporary debates among and about Black artists, as it long had been. In 1928, in an essay entitled 'The Dilemma of the Negro Writer', James Weldon Johnson cautioned that Black artists must reach beyond their 'racial foundation' for 'the universal in truth and beauty', and in 1946, Bearden echoed both Johnson's title and his argument, writing in 'The Negro Artist's Dilemma' that 'the true artist feels that there is only one art – and it belongs to all mankind'. But for many Black artists, writers and critics by the mid-1960s, such appeals to the universal were suspect, particularly as they were marshalled against urgent demands for a recognizably Black art. 'Some of us keep feeling that to be black is not to be universal, and to be black is to be limited. Why is black such a limiting idea?' asked the poet and playwright Adam David Miller in 1970, in a volume devoted to theorizing and promulgating a Black aesthetic. 'Johnson imagines that the "universal in truth and beauty" says something about a standard of aesthetics', but 'in reality, he is talking

GALLERY HOURS:
TUES THRU SAT 2-8PM

MAP OF GREENWICH VILLAGE AREA

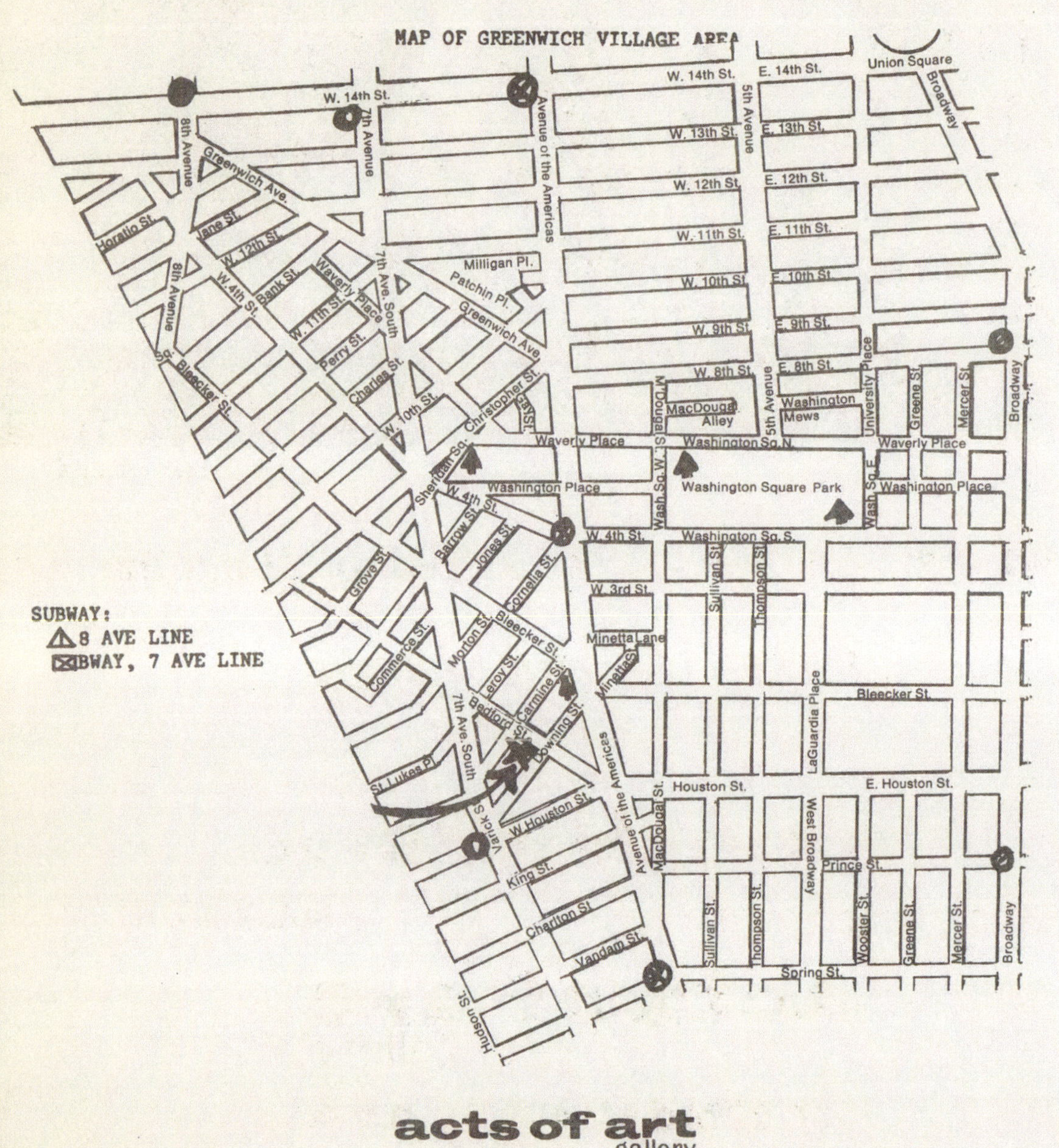

SUBWAY:
△ 8 AVE LINE
⊠ BWAY, 7 AVE LINE

acts of art
gallery

31 BEDFORD STREET, CORNER OF DOWNING STREET, NYC, 10014, (IN GREENWICH VILLAGE) 989-8335

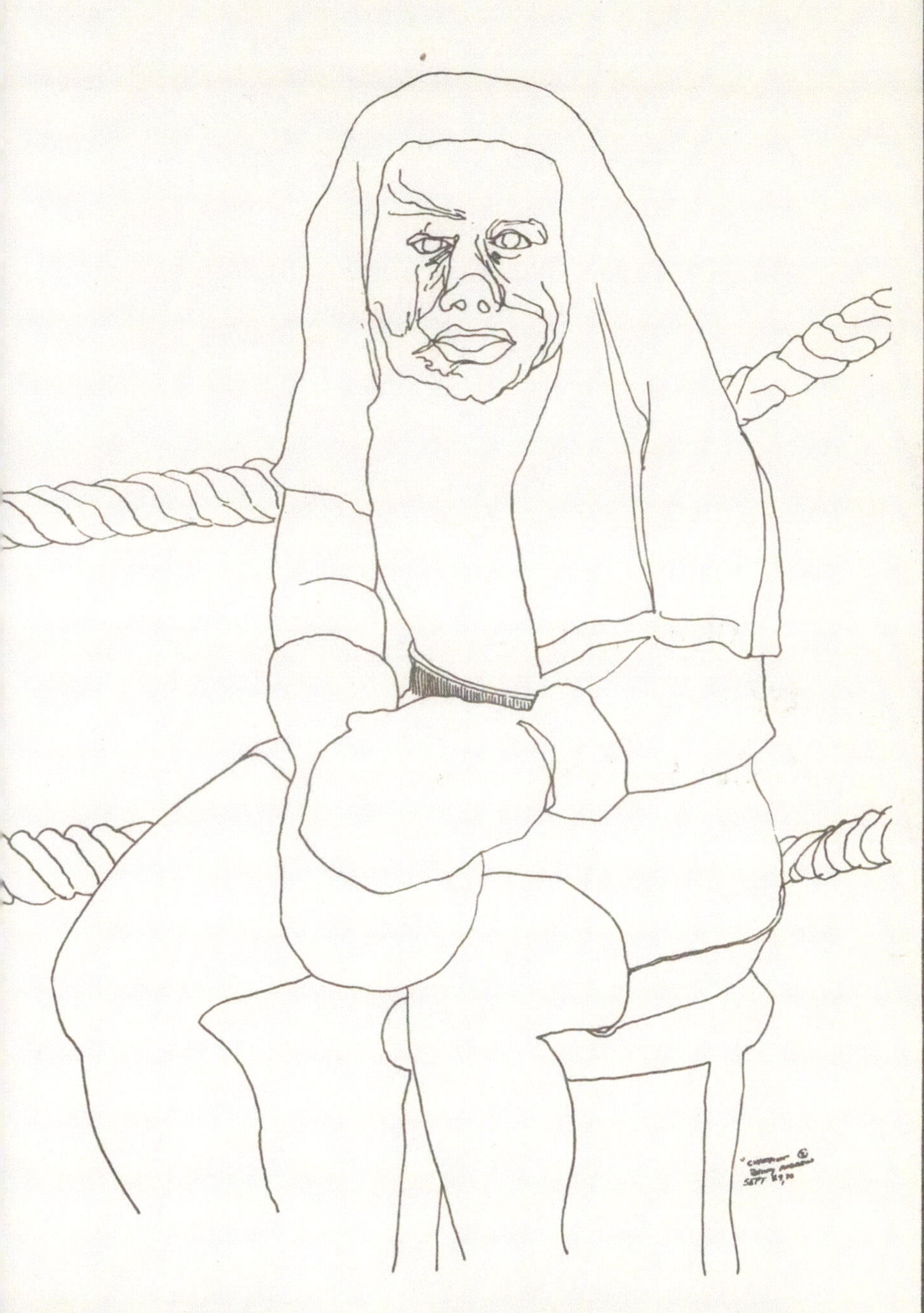

drawings
and
selected
works
by

BENNY ANDREWS

CT.31, *Thru* NOV.18, *1970*

acts
of
art

Hilton Kramer, '"Black Art" and Expedient Politics', *The New York Times*, 7 June 1970

Previous spread: Announcement for 'Drawings and Selected Works by Benny Andrews', Acts of Art, New York, 1970. Benny Andrews papers, Stuart A. Rose Manuscript, Archives, and Rare Book Library, Emory University, Atlanta. © Estate of Benny Andrews / VAGA at ARS, NY and DACS, London 2022

'Black Art' and Expedient Politics

By HILTON KRAMER

BOSTON.

WRITING last Sunday about the exhibition called "Afro-American Artists: New York and Boston," currently on view at the Museum of Fine Arts, I suggested that the concept of "black art" put forth by Edmund B. Gaither, the black organizer of the exhibition, was fundamentally a political conception. "Implicit in the distinctions Mr. Gaither has drawn in his Introduction to the catalogue of this show," I wrote, "is an assumption that 'black art' is to be exempted from the customary application of critical discriminations based on purely artistic values."

The Boston exhibition is not, to be sure, entirely devoted to "black art." Much of the work here belongs to what Mr. Gaither himself characterizes as "mainstream American art." The best of these "mainstream" artists are, in my opinion, the painters Norman Lewis, Alvin D. Loving Jr., Bill Rivers, Alma Thomas, and Feirath Hines—all abstractionists of various persuasions—and the sculptor Jack White. Others who are represented by work of notable "mainstream" quality are Marvin Brown, Thomas Sills, Frank Bowling, Ellen Banks, and the late Bob Thompson. There is also a fine drawing by Ronald Boutte.

•

Two of the best-known New York artists in the show—Romare Bearden and Benny Andrews—work in styles

or less in the manner of Kurt Schwitters, a handsome painted wall sculpture reminiscent of Arp (his best work, I think), and two political drawings that are little more than crass illustrations. Mr. Ryder is an artist of real gifts, and the division that is so dramatically evident in his work is, in some respects, the most important "message" which this exhibition discloses.

•

With the bulk of the "black art" in the Boston show, we are in the presence of political propaganda pure and simple. For the most part, this art displays a vivid, highly exacerbated black awareness of social problems and social aspirations, but an altogether depressing lack of awareness of artistic problems. Such art undoubtedly has its purposes—for the white public as well as for the black—but they are not artistic purposes. With the purposes of art, such work is not really concerned. No discernible artistic standards obtain in its creation. One is left with the unhappy impression that the practitioners of "black art" have been very largely content to draw upon the most moribund visual conventions of the white art world for the expression of black social grievances. Perhaps such work will serve, in Mr. Gaither's words, "to project the future which the nation can anticipate after the struggle is won," but I frankly doubt it. Its very style—and lack of style—looks to the past rather than the future.

holds a double appointment with both the Museum of Fine Arts and the National Center of Afro-American Artists, is, in effect, the only museum staff member who specializes in contemporary exhibitions, and his responsibility (as I understand it) is limited to "black shows." Thus, "Afro-American Artists: New York and Boston" is not just the largest but the *only* survey of contemporary American art the Museum of Fine Arts has initiated in many years.

•

Would a museum with a healthier, more knowledgeable and sympathetic interest in contemporary art have been in a position to handle the complex problems of a "black show" differently? I don't really know. For so long as political criteria are insisted upon in the selection of "black shows," and the imposition of rigorous artistic standards is regarded as simply one more form of white racism, I am not sure that any art institution—no matter what its past history may be—can deal with the "black" problem any other way. Yet I see no point in pretending that an exhibition such as the present one in Boston is anything but what it actually is: an art exhibition mounted under the pressures of political expediency that fails, by and large, to justify itself in terms of artistic accomplishment.

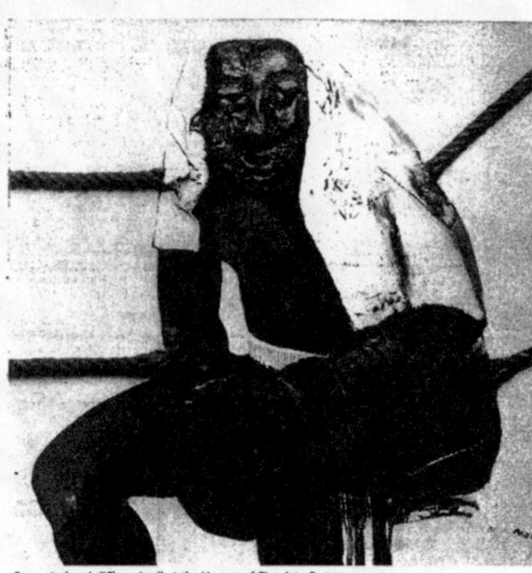

Benny Andrews's "Champion," at the Museum of Fine Arts, Boston
Are artistic standards simply a form of white racism?

about cultural judgments, and ultimately the way power is exercised in our society … . I would like to see the idea of "universal" laid to rest.'[4]

Two months before Cinque opened in the Village, the painter Nigel Jackson and the artist Pat Grey, his partner,[5] opened Acts of Art in a small storefront at 31 Bedford Street in the West Village, just above Houston, with an exhibition advertised in *The Village Voice* and *The Villager* as the gallery's 'first ethnic showing, featuring Black Art in America'.[6] According to an undated grant application draft, that first exhibition 'included 150 works by 15 Black artists' and 'attracted about two hundred people to the opening'.[7] The names of most of the fifteen artists have been lost, but we know that Benny Andrews was among them. While it had a couple of mentions early on in the *Amsterdam News*, New York's largest-circulation Black newspaper, the gallery would not come into its own until the late summer of 1970. In a feature article in *The Villager* that August, Jackson laid out his and Grey's vision for Acts of Art: it was to be less a bridge, as the founders of Cinque fashioned their gallery, than an intervention. Its site in the Village was a way of making, and taking, space. Jackson described Acts of Art as a 'gallery to promote black artists and provide a showplace for Black art outside the ghetto', and he pointed to the problem, the ideological confusion that mission engendered: 'If it's an all-Black thing, it doesn't belong outside the ghetto, people would say. If it's to go outside', Jackson continued, 'it must be integrated.'[8] He would underline the significance of Acts of Art's location in interviews with the press and in press releases and brochures throughout the life of the gallery. In a 1971 informational brochure, he stressed: 'If you're not a black artist, you cannot fully recognize the need for an art gallery specializing in fine art by black artists, LOCATED OUTSIDE THE GHETTO AREAS … . For the black artist to emerge at all, a gallery outside the ghetto must accept his work.'[9] Jackson's repeated stress on the word 'ghetto' is jarring now, and it was a heatedly contested term when Jackson wielded it in the early 1970s.[10] *The Villager* profile noted that Acts of

Art had scheduled an upcoming one-person exhibition for Andrews, who had been exhibiting in New York since the mid-1960s and had built a reputation. Andrews's solo show opened on 30 October 1970, and afterwards, in his journal, he set down his thoughts on the kind of space Acts of Art both represented and provided. His entry suggests the possibility of a different, more open, less alienating art world:

> *The exhibition was a realization of a wish I'd had for a long time, rhetoric aside, and that was to break through to several different groups and make a point of proving that with good artwork, a conscientious art dealer ... , a good exhibition can be put on. It does not matter that we are Black, that the gallery has only 500 square feet of exhibition space, that it is hard to find, etc. What does matter at this stage of art history in general and Black in particular, is 'heart and soul'. I was especially pleased to see Black people in regular Western dress, mingling with Black people in African dress, students Black & white, artists Black & white, collectors, friend[s], and passers-by, all were happy to be there. It was more than my show, it was a place to meet, talk, and relax for a while. The long term gains should be to establish in the minds of the art world that Black art expertise is coming of age.*[11]

The gallery was small and the promotional materials handmade; the image on the mailer would have been familiar to those who came out for the opening, situating the gallery quite explicitly in the middle of discussions about the spaces for Black art and artists. The work Andrews and Jackson chose to reproduce was *Champion 2*, a drawing after Andrews's 1968 painting of the same name that had been included in educator and curator Edmund Gaither's 'Afro-American Artists: New York and Boston', at the Museum of Fine Arts, Boston in the summer of 1970; the painting had ended up on the front page of the arts section of *The New York Times*, accompanying the second of Hilton Kramer's essay reviews of the Boston exhibition, which was titled '"Black Art" and Expedient Politics'.[12] *Champion* appears as the poster child for Kramer's question 'Are artistic standards simply a form of white racism?', a follow-up to the questions he posed in his earlier review: 'Must we go back to Social Realism?' and 'What, alas, is Black art?'[13] Two weeks later, *The New York Times* published 'On Understanding Black Art', Andrews's long defence of his painting and of the exhibition's focus on Black artists, along with Gaither's response, a call for a 'new criticism'.[14] Through the summer of 1970, Andrews and *Champion* were markers in a debate that Jackson was eager to enter, and to make a space for.

Andrews's show was a way to put the gallery on the map, and the map itself was a feature of almost all printed materials produced by Acts of Arts, even after the gallery moved from Bedford Street to a larger space on Charles Street, just off Seventh Avenue, at Waverly Place, in January 1971.[15] In the first year in the new space, Jackson mounted two exhibitions that served as manifestos: 'Rebuttal to the Whitney Museum Exhibition: Black Artists in Rebuttal', in April 1971, and 'Where We At: Black Women Artists', in June. Andrews and other members of the Black Emergency Cultural Coalition had been lobbying the Whitney since the spring of 1969 for greater representation of Black artists in the museum's long-established annual exhibitions; in its permanent collection; and in focused, one-person exhibitions. They lobbied, too, for a survey of Black artists and for Black representation on the curatorial staff to help bring that initiative, and all of the others, to fruition. In early January 1971, after still more heated negotiations, the Black Emergency Cultural Coalition pulled its support from the Whitney's survey 'Contemporary Black Artists in America' and began steps for a boycott and a counter exhibition. 'Rebuttal' opened the same night as the Whitney's show, with nearly fifty artists representing a broad umbrella of cultural positions and formations – as broad an array of artistic approaches as the Whitney's show, albeit differently balanced. As Bridget Cooks insists in *Exhibiting Blackness* (2011), there was, and is, a 'difference between the art museum's enforcement of the racially segregated show and the choice of self-representation by Black artists through exhibition'.[16] Jackson's commitment to 'self-representation', and his entrepreneurial push for greater visibility for the gallery as well as for Black artists, lay behind his openness to the proposal for an exhibition of women artists that Dindga McCannon brought to him soon after. McCannon's work was included in 'Rebuttal' and she was one of the women artists who formed the nucleus of Where We At, with Faith Ringgold, Kay Brown, Carol Blank and Pat Davis. Where We At began meeting in her East Second Street walk-up in the spring of 1971, as meetings for 'Rebuttal' were taking place.

Speaking with David Shirey of *The New York Times* in February 1972, about six months after the 'Rebuttal' exhibition and 'Where We At', on the occasion of an exhibition of works by Arthur Coppedge, Jackson repeated his insistence that Acts of Art was the 'only gallery in the city specializing in Black art outside the ghetto' – this despite Cinque's location, a fifteen-minute walk down Waverly Place – and he spoke about the gallery's purpose and audience. The gallery's 'first and foremost' purpose was to exhibit works of quality that might 'function as an inspiration to blacks', showing a Black audience 'what other blacks can achieve in art'. Speaking in the aftermath of the 'Rebuttal' exhibition, Jackson explained to Shirey that 'We use politics only to get an audience .... Once we've gotten that, we concentrate on the art.'[17] It was a provocative comment, particularly in a moment when art and politics seemed fully intertwined and artists increasingly politicized. Coppedge, for example, had been an active member of the New York Art Strike, mounted in the immediate aftermath of the shootings at Kent State University in Ohio and Jackson State College in Mississippi. It was strange, too, given the political and aesthetic issues sandwiched together in questions like those Hilton Kramer had posed: 'Must we go back to Social Realism?' and 'What, alas, is Black art?' Jackson's comment to Shirey about art and politics followed hard on the reviewer's description of the gallery as an 'educational center for Blacks, a meeting place for lectures, poetry readings and discussions on such questions as "Does Black Art Exist?"'

While Jackson would show a few Black artists who were working abstractly – he was committed to the young gestural painter Frank Wimberley and also showed, in the gallery's last years, older artists like Hale Woodruff, who turned to abstraction in the 1950s, and Harlan Jackson, who had been a student of painter Clyfford Still in California in the late 1940s – Acts of Art's programme was increasingly shaped by what art historian Darby English has termed 'Black representational space', the mutual and mirroring identification of artist and audience around the 'fact of Blackness'.[18] Let me leave the details of English's argument to one side; what I want his term for here is its descriptive, denotative clarity. Acts of Art stood out, quite literally, geographically: as Black representational space, set against a white field. Recalling the gallery on a panel in 1984 at the studio of artist Camille Billops and her husband, the historian James Hatch – one of two panels gathered there to focus on spaces for Black artists that emerged in the late 1960s, including Acts of Art, Cinque, the Studio Museum and the Weusi Artists Collective's Nyumba Ya Sanaa Gallery – artist James Denmark described Jackson's gallery as a 'hub' and 'focal point of what was then known as "the black art movement" in New York City'.[19] And indeed, most of the artists Jackson showed in the months between 'Rebuttal' and Arthur Coppedge's exhibition shared a broad engagement with the cultural nationalism that Denmark refers to, and with Harlem.

In November 1971, Jackson showed paintings, prints and drawings by Ademola Olugebefola, one of the founders of the Weusi Artists Collective, works that drew on his engagement with the Yoruba Temple in Harlem[20] and his education in Dogon and Yoruba cosmologies; performers who had appeared in Ed Bullins's *To Raise the Dead and Foretell the Future* (1970), at the New Lafayette Theater, sang and chanted at the opening.[21] Solo exhibitions of figurative assemblage by Denmark – 'sculptures [that] reflect the definite socially minded viewpoint this gallery has assumed'[22] – and Dindga McCannon followed. McCannon, too, was associated with the Weusi artists. She had begun to show alongside Weusi members at the Harlem Outdoor Art Show in 1965, while still a teenager; her one-person show at Acts of Art was titled 'From Harlem to Haiti and a few stops in between'. Jackson would feature Denmark in five solo shows in the gallery's history, and McCannon and Olugebefola both would be included in a number of two- and three-person shows and group shows at Acts of Art before the gallery closed in 1975.

I have used the words 'mission' and 'commitment' a few times as a way to insist on the legible intentions and purposefulness of this story's actors, but the narrative trajectory and the divisions that drive it may not be as clear as I have laid it out. Nor is the line between art and politics as sharp as Jackson would have wanted, that he insisted upon. In an interview with James Hatch and Camille Billops recorded at the gallery in December 1972, Jackson defended the formulation on art and politics he had offered to David Shirey in *The New York Times.* 'Many black people question me about that statement because they still feel that there is no difference between art and politics.' 'If you step on my art, I'll show you my politics', he continued. 'I'm an aesthetic artist, not a politician. But if you abuse my aesthetics, I'll certainly be a politician and show you that I too can be political.'[23] What Jackson does not speak to, at least at this moment in the conversation, is his role as a gallerist and the political positioning it entailed. In the same interview, he was clear-eyed, even cynical, about the role racial politics played in publicizing the gallery and in sales. Jackson noted that

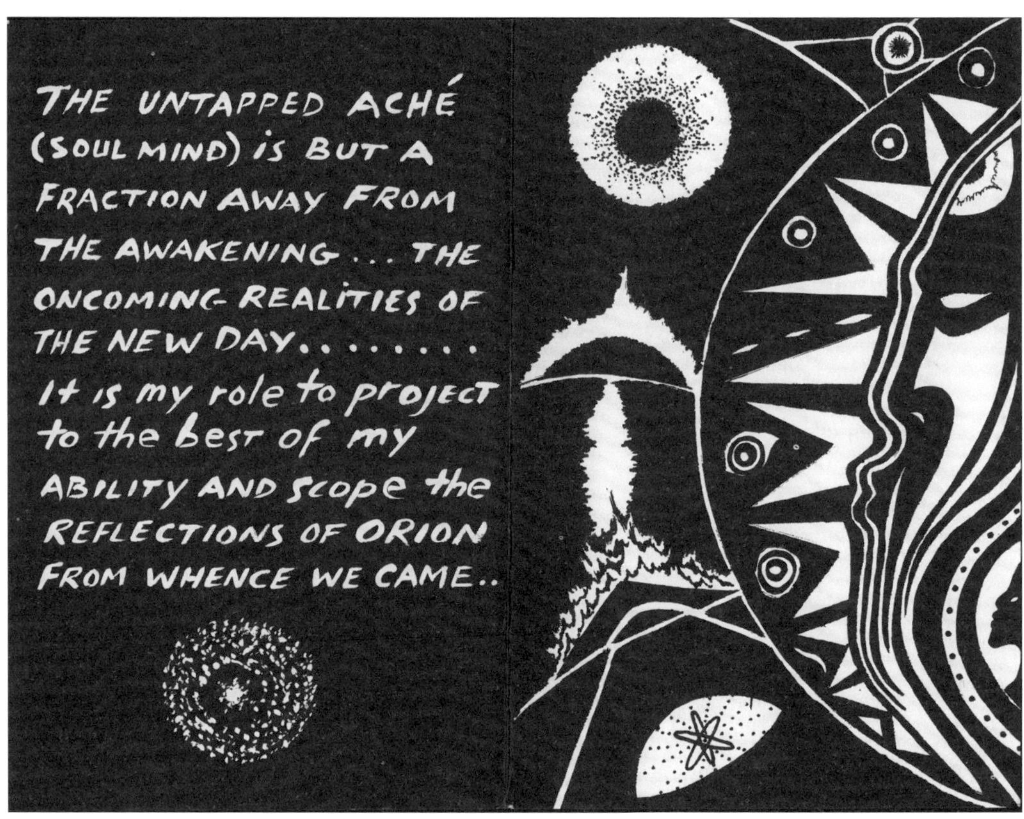

Announcement for 'Ademola Olugebefola: Reflections Orion, New Explorations', Acts of Art, 1971. Acts of Art, Inc. collection, 1970–75, Stuart A. Rose Manuscript, Archives, and Rare Book Library, Emory University, Atlanta

despite its location in overwhelmingly white Greenwich Village, the 'gallery is supported by blacks ... many whites still wish it would go away'. But speaking specifically about the press that came with the 'Rebuttal' exhibition, he commented that 'it was the first time many, many, many people – Black or white – became aware of the Black artist so, yes, we seized an opportunity there. And we got some publicity. At the expense of the Whitney. And that's really what it amounted to ... . Many of the artists who showed in the "Rebuttal" made some money.'[24] Jackson was maybe too blunt about the monetization of racial difference, but Benny Andrews also acknowledged it early on. In a letter to the painter Reginald Gammon, written in March 1971, on the evening of the opening of the Museum of Modern Art's double surveys of Romare Bearden and Richard Hunt – MoMA's first solo exhibitions of Black contemporary artists – and just after a contentious planning meeting for the Whitney boycott and Acts of Art's 'Rebuttal', Andrews laid out the intertwined political and economic calculus of their public action: 'Now I realize that there is no style that causes any of us to get the chance to exhibit but rather [it is] what has happened to us in connection with our Blackness that can be used to separate us from someone else that works exactly in the same style and time as we do.'[25] In the moment of 'Rebuttal' and the Whitney exhibition and in the aftermath, individual artists' professional and economic viability was linked to a visibility – a becoming-visible – that was always already racialized.

Jackson insisted in the Hatch-Billops interview that he was a painter – 'an aesthetic artist, not a politician' – so by way of an ending, I will address a couple of his paintings, albeit works I have seen only in reproduction and that may no longer exist. The first is a portrait titled *Harry Reading Fanon*, painted sometime before 7 February 1973, when it was reproduced in the *Asbury Park Press* to accompany an article on an exhibition Jackson organized for the Monmouth County, New Jersey chapter of Delta Sigma Theta Sorority. 'Every culture must have a structural foundation', he told the paper, 'and the black artist has a task at hand now.'[26] The reproduction of *Harry Reading Fanon* is in black-and-white and it is difficult to read the painting formally, but the accompanying caption offers some direction, noting that it 'recalls the expressive quality of the late Max Beckman[n]'s work'. The young man's features are angular and schematically rendered, and he is seated against what seems a quickly brushed and scumbled background. Wearing a knit cap and what appears to be a leather jacket, he reads Frantz Fanon's *Black Skin, White Masks* (1952), its cover easily legible and recognizable. The figure is likely Harry S. Huggins, a writer from New Haven, Connecticut who contributed texts to the *Raven Art Rap*, Jackson's short-lived newspaper of Black art in New York, and to the 'Rebuttal' catalogue. One imagines Jackson is making a point here, registering not only Huggins's interests and politics, but his own – suggesting how we might read him and the work of Acts of Art.

The second painting is a group portrait titled *The Businessmen,* reproduced in the *Amsterdam News* to illustrate a review of Jackson's first solo show at Acts of Art in May 1972. It, too, helps to situate the gallery and the political space it occupied, and it speaks to Jackson's sense of irony and possibility. The accompanying caption doesn't offer clues as to the painting's colour or characterize its style, but it does identify the work's three figures, who are more tightly rendered than Jackson's *Harry* and likely painted from a photograph rather than life: 'William Hudgins, Rodman Rockefeller and Darwin Bolden, two board members and the national executive director of the Interracial Council for Business Opportunity [ICBO]'.[27] In the centre is Rodman Rockefeller, the son of New York's governor Nelson Rockefeller. On the right is William Hudgins, a civic leader and the founder of two Harlem-based banks over two decades. Darwin Bolden, on the left, had been chairman of New York CORE, the Congress of Racial Equality, before becoming the ICBO's national executive. In the lead-up to 'Rebuttal', Jackson had curated an exhibition at the ICBO's offices on Park Avenue South that included Andrews, Denmark, McCannon, Vivian Browne and Ann Tanksley. In April 1972, just before his solo show opened, he was awarded a business achievement award by the organization. The *Amsterdam News* review records the comment of one clear-eyed viewer at Jackson's opening: 'That's a good picture of our economics. If that guy in the middle – Rockefeller – doesn't sign those papers, we can't do a thing.'

The skeptic may have been Jackson himself. In the 1972 Hatch-Billops interview, he makes the same point. 'I have a painting that's called *The Businessmen*. And there it shows two black guys reaching up to Rodman Rockefeller to get him to sign a piece of paper which would then mean funds coming down to the so-called Black community. This is significant because our growth and

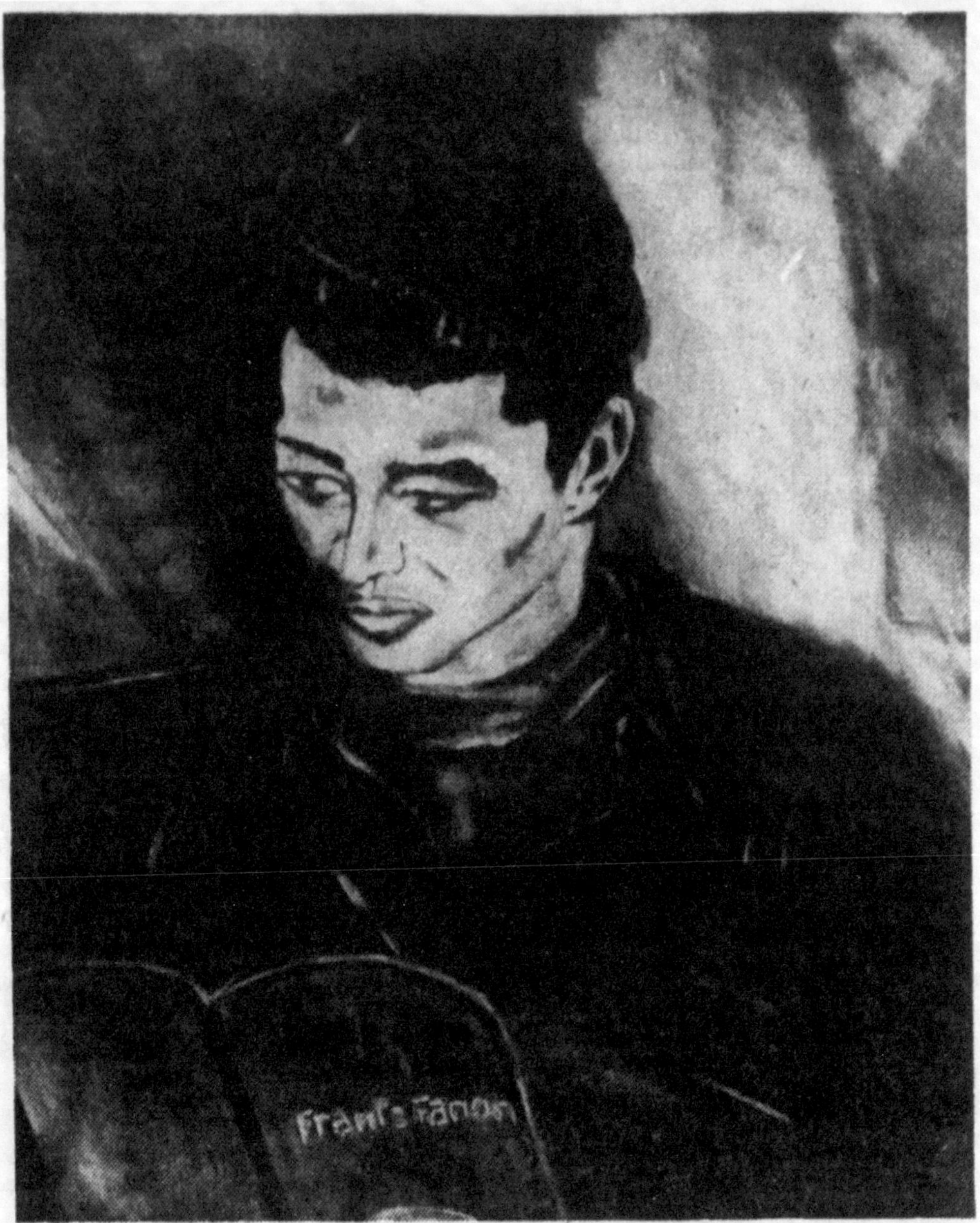

"Harry Reading Fanon," an oil portrait by Nigel Jackson, New York, recalls the expressive quality of the late Max Beckman's work. While Beckman related the chaos of his post-Warld War I Germany on the canvas, Mr. Jackson draws his subject matter from the culture of the Negro people. In this portrait, Mr. Jackson shows a young man reading Frantz Fanon, a Negro philosopher who died in 1961.

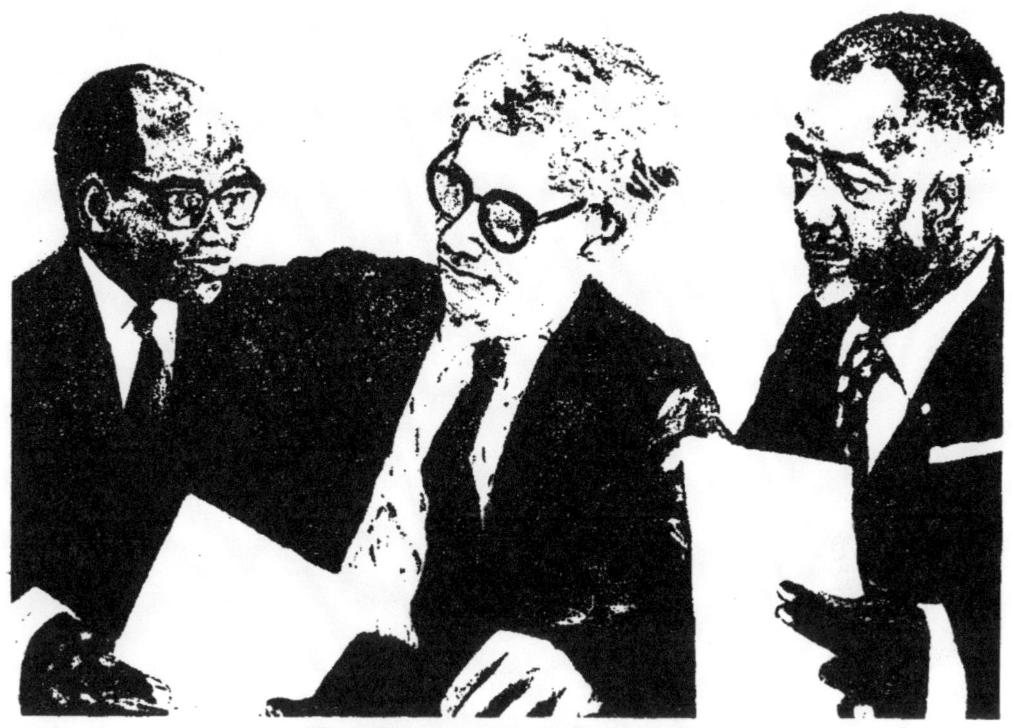
Business and the arts

Nigel L. Jackson's one-man show at the Acts of Art gallery, 15 Charles St. in Greenwich Village, includes "The Businessmen" (above), which depicts 3 VIPs of the Interracial Council for Business Opportunity. They are, left to right: Darwin Bolden, national director, and Rodman Rockefeller and William Hudgins, co-chairmen of the ICBO Board of Directors. Jackson, who is gallery director as well as an artist, will have his paintings and drawings on display until May 20th.

Nigel Jackson's *The Businessmen*, c.1972, reproduced in Mel Tapley, 'Strong Portraits in Jackson Art Show', *New York Amsterdam News*, 6 May 1972

Opposite: Nigel Jackson's *Harry Reading Fanon*, c.1973, reproduced in 'Negro Artists' Exhibit, Sale is Set', *Asbury Park Press*, 7 February 1973

our funds [are] still controlled in this fashion, so that keeps any growth or any ideas such as development from happening. It actually keeps it from happening.'[28] Jackson's position here is a Black nationalist one, an argument for economic as well as cultural autonomy. One might footnote it with something like Robert L. Allen's 1969 book *Black Awakening in Capitalist America*,[29] a book that could join *Black Skin, White Masks* on Jackson's reading list. As it happens, Bolden reviewed Allen's book for *The New York Times* in January 1970, rounded up with a handful of titles on economic development in Black communities. Bolden's summary of Allen's argument begins: 'Allen rejects the attempts of the capitalist power structure, led by the Ford Foundation, the Urban Coalition and the National Alliance of Businessmen, to coopt the black power movement.'[30] CORE, too, was on Allen's list, and it is likely that Bolden found himself and the ICBO implicated as well. While 'they drape themselves "in the mantle of nationalism"', Bolden continues, quoting Allen directly, '"Their strategy is to equate black power with black capitalism … [but] far from aiding in the achievement of black liberation and freedom from exploitation, [their programmes] instead weld the black community more firmly into the structure of American corporate capitalism"'.[31] This is the dynamic *The Businessmen* represents, the dependence that the *Amsterdam*

News' viewer saw right away. It was also the condition of existence for both Acts of Art and Cinque from the beginning. Cinque was founded with a $30,000 grant from Columbia University's Urban Center, itself an initiative wholly funded by the Ford Foundation, and received early support from a New York State Council on the Arts project that was born, in 1967, as the 'Ghetto Arts Program' to foster 'arts organizations serving predominantly black and Puerto Rican audience groups'.[32] Jackson and Acts of Art relied on the ICBO for visibility and assistance, and it too was dependent on direct government funding. Over the life of the gallery, its greatest single source of support was the Expansion Arts Program of the National Endowment for the Arts, targeted to 'groups which share a common location, ethnic origin or economic situation and which have been outside the reach of mainstream American culture'.[33]

Nigel Jackson closed Acts of Art in late November 1975, and left for Africa in early 1976, to live and work in Botswana. When he returned to New York two years later, he wanted no part of the art world, Black or white. He passed away in 2005. The last major exhibition Acts of Art mounted, in September 1974, was 'Black Artists in the New York Scene', an exhibition that once again demanded space and visibility – the acknowledgment that Black artists were here and had been working within the New York art world for decades, despite that world's refusal to see them. The exhibition's press release invited viewers 'to attend ... and do whatever you can to erase the ugly stigma on the New York art scene'. The release suggests Jackson's frustration and exasperation, and seems to foreshadow the gallery's closing: the project of making a viable space for Black artists downtown, and of opening spaces for Black artists within the 'mainstream of American art', had been 'ignored and passed over'.[34] For its part, Cinque Gallery soldiered on through 2004, moving uptown from Lafayette Street at the end of the 1970s, and back down to Soho in 1988. Over those years, it functioned only occasionally as the bridge its press release promised, to a white art world that was uninterested in holding up its end. Rather, to borrow James Denmark's description of Acts of Art, it became an important hub and focal point for a community of Black artists in New York that it helped to nurture and connect.[35]

Notes

1 Grace Glueck, '1930's Show at Whitney Picketed by Negro Artists Who Call It Incomplete', *The New York Times,* 18 November 1968.

2 Founded in Brooklyn in 1887, the Pratt Institute is a private professional school of art, architecture and design and one of the most important art schools in the city. Jacob Lawrence taught at Pratt from 1959 to 1970, as one of the school's few Black faculty members. A Black Student Union was formed at Pratt in the spring of 1969, just after Malcolm Bailey's graduation.

3 'Urban Center at Columbia University Funds Gallery for Young Minority Artists: Opening December 22', press release. Joseph Papp/New York Shakespeare Festival Collection, *T-Mss 1993–028, box 1–73, folder 19, Billy Rose Theatre Division, New York Public Library for the Performing Arts. Emphasis in original.

4 Adam David Miller, 'Some Observations on a Black Aesthetic', in *The Black Aesthetic*, ed. Addison Gayle, Jr, Garden City, NY: Doubleday & Company, 1971, pp.401–02.

[5] Pat Grey, a white artist and fellow student of Jackson's at the Art Students League in New York, is listed on Acts of Art letterhead as 'D. Patricia Grey, Vice-President' and sometimes as 'Treasurer and General Manager'. Grey showed in group exhibitions in the gallery in its very first months and is listed in a small brochure as Pat (Verdicchio) Grey. I refer to the gallery as Jackson's throughout as he was the public face and voice of Acts of Art. Grey and Jackson married in 1970; it is likely they separated before the gallery closed in 1975.
[6] See *The Village Voice*, 2 October 1969, and *The Villager*, 9 October 1969.
[7] Benny Andrews papers, MSS 845, box 18, folder 2, Stuart A. Rose Manuscript, Archives and Rare Book Library, Emory University, Atlanta.
[8] Nancy Burton, 'Gallery Has a People Following', *The Villager*, 27 August 1970.
[9] Acts of Art membership brochure, c.1971, Reginald Gammon papers, 1927–2007, bulk 1960–2005, Series 2: Correspondence, box 1, folder 20, Archives of American Art, Smithsonian Institution, Washington DC.
[10] The use of 'ghetto' to describe the densely populated Black communities of industrial cities in the northern US – enclaves with boundaries enforced by covenants, red-lining, legal statute and state violence – emerged with St. Clair Drake and Horace R. Cayton's *Black Metropolis: A Study of Negro Life in a Northern City*, a sociological study of Chicago's Bronzeville neighborhood in 1945. For Drake and Cayton, Bronzeville's boundedness resembled that of other urban ethnic enclaves, most often European immigrant communities, whose borders limited opportunity but offered protection and social cohesion. It was only in the 1960s that the word was linked firmly and nearly exclusively to Black communities, and to their decay. In Kenneth B. Clark's 1965 study of Harlem, *Dark Ghetto: Dilemmas of Social Power*, the image and the outcomes are much bleaker, and the role of state power and violence, clearer. 'The dark ghettos are social, political, educational and – above all – economic colonies. Their inhabitants are subject peoples, victims of the greed, cruelty, insensitivity, guilt and fear of their masters' (p.11). Clark's study insisted on the individual human costs of exclusion and stigmatization, and posited ghettoization as a process: 'Human beings who are forced to live under ghetto conditions and whose daily experiences tell them that almost nowhere in society are they respected and granted the ordinary dignity and courtesy accorded to others will, as a matter of course, begin to doubt their own worth' (p.64). Clark's description of the ghetto as a site of colonial subjugation and of the desire for dignity and respect that is refused there echoes in Nigel Jackson's statement. But it is Clark's description of the ghetto as a 'tangle of community and personal pathology' (p.106) – a phrase that Daniel Patrick Moynihan borrowed and amplified as a way of shifting blame from the colonizers to the colonized – that comes to dominate the popular image of the ghetto. See K.B. Clark, *Dark Ghetto: Dilemmas of Social Power*, 2nd edition, Middletown, CT: Wesleyan University Press, 1989; and Michael Duneier, *Ghetto: The Invention of a Place, the History of an Idea*, New York: Farrar, Straus and Giroux, 2016.
[11] Journal entry 983, 30 October 1970, Estate of Benny Andrews, Brooklyn, NY. See also Susan Cahan, *Mounting Frustration: The Art Museum in the Age of Black Power*, Durham, NC: Duke University Press, 2016, p.145.
[12] Hilton Kramer, '"Black Art" and Expedient Politics', *The New York Times*, 7 June 1970.
[13] H. Kramer, 'Trying to Define "Black Art": Must We Go Back to Social Realism?', *The New York Times*, 31 May 1970.
[14] B. Andrews, 'On Understanding Black Art', and Edmund B. Gaither, 'A New Criticism is Needed', *The New York Times*, 21 June 1970.
[15] Acts of Art's Charles Street location was a ten-minute walk from the original Bedford Street storefront, along Seventh Avenue in Greenwich Village. Like almost all of Manhattan below 110th Street, the Village was overwhelming white, but it had been home to a significant Black population in the nineteenth century, and had been a crucible for radical politics and avant-garde cultural practices, and their intersections, since the first decade of the twentieth century. Amiri Baraka pitted Greenwich Village and Harlem against one another as sites for Black transformation, writing of his abandonment of Greenwich Village in 1965, 'We had made a line of demarcation (we felt) between the artists we'd left downtown and ourselves ... . Working politically in Harlem, that became the badge of our sincerity.' A. Baraka, 'The Black Arts Movement: Meaning and Potential', *Nka: Journal of Contemporary African Art*, no.29, Fall 2011, pp.25, 27.
[16] Bridget R. Cooks, *Exhibiting Blackness: African Americans and the American Art Museum*, Amherst: University of Massachusetts Press, 2011, p.159. For an in-depth account of the negotiations between the Black Emergency Cultural Coalition and the Whitney Museum of American Art, see S. Cahan, *Mounting Frustration*, pp.109–70; and Howard Singerman, 'Rebuttal and Representation', in *Acts of Art and Rebuttal in 1971* (exh. cat.), New York: Hunter College Art Galleries, 2018, pp.8–45.
[17] David L. Shirey, 'Gallery in the Village Seeks to Inspire Black Artists', *The New York Times*, 5 February 1972.
[18] Darby English, *How to See a Work of Art in Total Darkness*, Cambridge, MA: MIT Press, 2007, pp.27–70.
[19] James Denmark, 'When That Time Came Rolling Down, part II', *Artist and Influence 1985*, ed.

Leo Hamalian and Judith Wilson, New York: Hatch-Billops Collection, 1985, p.144.

[20] Established in Harlem in 1960 by Oseijeman Adefunmi (born Walter Eugene King), the Yoruba Temple drew on West and Central African religious traditions and cosmologies and their echoes in the Black Caribbean, 'combin[ing] an Africanized Santería with an Americanized racial nationalism' (p.88). See Tracy E. Hucks, *Yoruba Traditions and African American Religious Nationalism*, Albuquerque: University of New Mexico Press, 2012.

[21] Interview with Ademola Olugebefola, 3 December 2020. See also '"Orion" at Acts of Art', *The Villager*, 2 December 1971, in Ademola Olugebefola papers, microfilm, reel 2, Schomburg Center for Research in Black Culture, New York Public Library.

[22] B[ill] B[eckley], 'James Denmark (Acts of Art)', *ArtNews*, vol. 70, no.8, December 1971, p.14.

[23] Nigel Jackson, 1 December 1972, Camille Billops and James V. Hatch archives, MSS 927, Series 6: Oral History Interviews, box 4 folder 441, Stuart A. Rose Manuscript, Archives and Rare Book Library, Emory University, Atlanta.

[24] *Ibid.*

[25] B. Andrews, letter to Reginald Gammon, 23 March 1971. Reginald Gammon papers, 1927–2007, bulk 1960–2005, Series 2: Correspondence, box 6, folder 3, Archives of American Art.

[26] '"Negro Artists" Exhibit, Sale is Set', *Asbury Park Press*, 7 February 1973. The one-day exhibition and sale included a number of artists associated with Acts of Art: James Denmark, Earl Hill, Enid Richardson, Robert Robinson, Ann Tanksley, Lloyd Toone and Frank Wimberley.

[27] Mel Tapley, 'Strong Portraits in Jackson Art Show', *New York Amsterdam News*, 6 May 1972.

[28] N. Jackson, 1 December 1972, Camille Billops and James V. Hatch archives, *op. cit.*

[29] Robert L. Allen, *Black Awakening in Capitalist America: An Analytic History*, Garden City, NY: Doubleday, 1969.

[30] Darwin W. Bolden, 'What Can Business Do About Watts?', *The New York Times*, 18 January 1970.

[31] *Ibid.*

[32] See *New York State Council on the Arts Annual Report 1970–71*, p.76.

[33] See *National Endowment for the Arts and National Council for the Arts Annual Report 1975*, p.32.

[34] Press release for 'Black Artists in the New York Scene', Acts of Art, Inc., Art and Artists Files, Smithsonian American Art and Portrait Gallery Library, Smithsonian Libraries, Washington DC.

[35] Cinque's role in building a community of Black artist in New York was the subject of the exhibition 'Creating Community: Cinque Gallery Artists', Phyllis Harriman Mason Gallery, Art Students League, New York, 3 May–4 July 2021, curated by Susan Stedman with Nanette Carter.

Revisiting *Exhibiting Blackness: African Americans and the American Art Museum* – Brittany Webb

Bridget R. Cooks's *Exhibiting Blackness* (2011) functions as a kind of mentoring text. It supports the intellectual work for scholars in the field who do not have well-placed institutional mentors, who are told that their projects don't have intellectual heft, or aren't properly art historical, or properly disciplined in the various programmes they're working in. This is a text that serves as a scholarly lighthouse, as proof of concept, as an affirmation, as an alibi, as a deeply rigorous foil to other scholars who serve as gatekeepers in so many ways to students trying to get out of their academic programmes with the credentials they came for. So many people are dependent on works like *Exhibiting Blackness* to support intellectual projects that are ahead of their time. It feels necessary to acknowledge how important this work is for students trying to clear the degree hurdles in their various institutions – just to be eligible to get into this field. I can say on behalf of myself and so many other colleagues who are pushing institutions to do better by Black visual producers: We are here because Bridget Cooks wrote this.

I want to revisit the lessons of *Exhibiting Blackness*. In particular, I want to focus on the pushback to two exhibitions in New York in the late 1960s and 1970s – 'Harlem on My Mind: Cultural Capital of Black America, 1900–1968' at the Metropolitan Museum of Art (1969), and 'Contemporary Black Artists in America' at the Whitney Museum of American Art (1971) – to historicize the past few years of upheaval in museums. I want to suggest that *Exhibiting Blackness* is not just a history of the present. To me, it represents the proverbial canary in the coal mine – it chronicles a history that should have put the field in a position not to repeat.

Exhibiting Blackness is a book that could have saved a lot of museums the trouble they got into in 2020. First, it demonstrates that many institutions misunderstand and underestimate their audiences. Most of the pushback by Black artists responding to these shows take the museums at their word when they present themselves as 'general' and cite their broad-based missions that insist they want the widest possible audience. The protests against the Metropolitan Museum in 1969 and the Whitney Museum in 1971 included demands to meet with the museums' leadership in order to work with them on future shows, reflecting a desire for deeper engagement with institutions. An alternative response could have just as easily been whole communities of artists and their publics abandoning these museums and leaving them to narrow audiences. The artists' deep engagement with museum staff was generous.

Second, *Exhibiting Blackness* shows that 'mainstream' 'encyclopedic' institutions are using those designations as euphemisms for *white* – presenting a very narrow view of art history as general when that view is actually particular. This makes it possible to understand the public criticism of such institutions, past and present, as a way of intervening in art history – providing correctives to existing limited frameworks. It is also why the establishment of community outreach positions, or diversifying public programming and education departments, has not always solved the problems of exhibiting art (or failing to exhibit art) by Black people. This is useful to note in light of contemporary conversations about diversity and inclusion, and of the ways that the pushback major museums have gotten from Black audiences and critics in the past few years has been based on similar criticisms, with calls for better exhibition ideas, sharper curatorial framing, more expansive collecting practices, better object labels and catalogue essays – essentially a call for the cultural competence that people like Benny Andrews and the Black Emergency Cultural Coalition (BECC) were demanding fifty years ago.

Following spread: Black Emergency Cultural Coalition protest at Whitney Museum of American Art, New York, 31 January 1971. Photo: Jan van Raay

It is important to remember that the protests of 'Harlem on My Mind' and 'Contemporary Black Artists in America' were based on the curatorial framing of the exhibitions – not just who was included or excluded, but how the works in the exhibitions were framed. This critique is both administrative and substantively art historical: the pushback to 'Harlem on My Mind' and 'Contemporary Black Artists in America' featured artists demanding to be included in planning processes because they found the exhibition planners culturally and intellectually incompetent. It was not just inclusion that artists wanted, but the same curatorial treatment that they felt white artists enjoyed. Learning these lessons helps us historically contextualize this contemporary moment and the press and social media attention on Black museum professionals in curatorial and leadership roles today.

Let us revisit some of the main reasons for the Metropolitan Museum to organize 'Harlem On My Mind'. As Cooks notes, 'the exhibition was conceived as an intervention into the growing cultural gap between Blacks and Whites. Through the exhibition, the Met attempted to be an ambassador of racial harmony.'[1] Furthermore, 'under the command of Allon Schoener, director of the Visual Arts Program of the New York State Council on the Arts and director of the Met's Exhibition Committee, and Thomas P.F. Hoving, recently hired director of the Met, the museum's new leadership hoped to mix current cultural issues with the traditions of the prestigious institution.'[2] This is not the only example of a museum making the case that an exhibition could *or should* bridge a racial gap and tackle cultural issues – but in this context the curatorial choices in the exhibition, and the refusal to consider the input of the community of Black artists in New York City, is especially egregious. Schoener studied at the Courtauld Institute of Art at the University of London and earned his MA in art history from Yale University.[3] One imagines that this is the kind of background that could inform an incredibly rich framing of 68 years of fine art produced by Harlem artists.

Despite this, the exhibition contained thirteen galleries organized into several decade-long sections, and consisted primarily of large-scale photomurals, unframed photographs, projected images of street scenes, speakers playing Harlem street sounds and reproductions of ephemera such as the National Association for the Advancement of Colored People (NAACP)'s *The Crisis* magazine. This was before arts institutions took photography seriously as

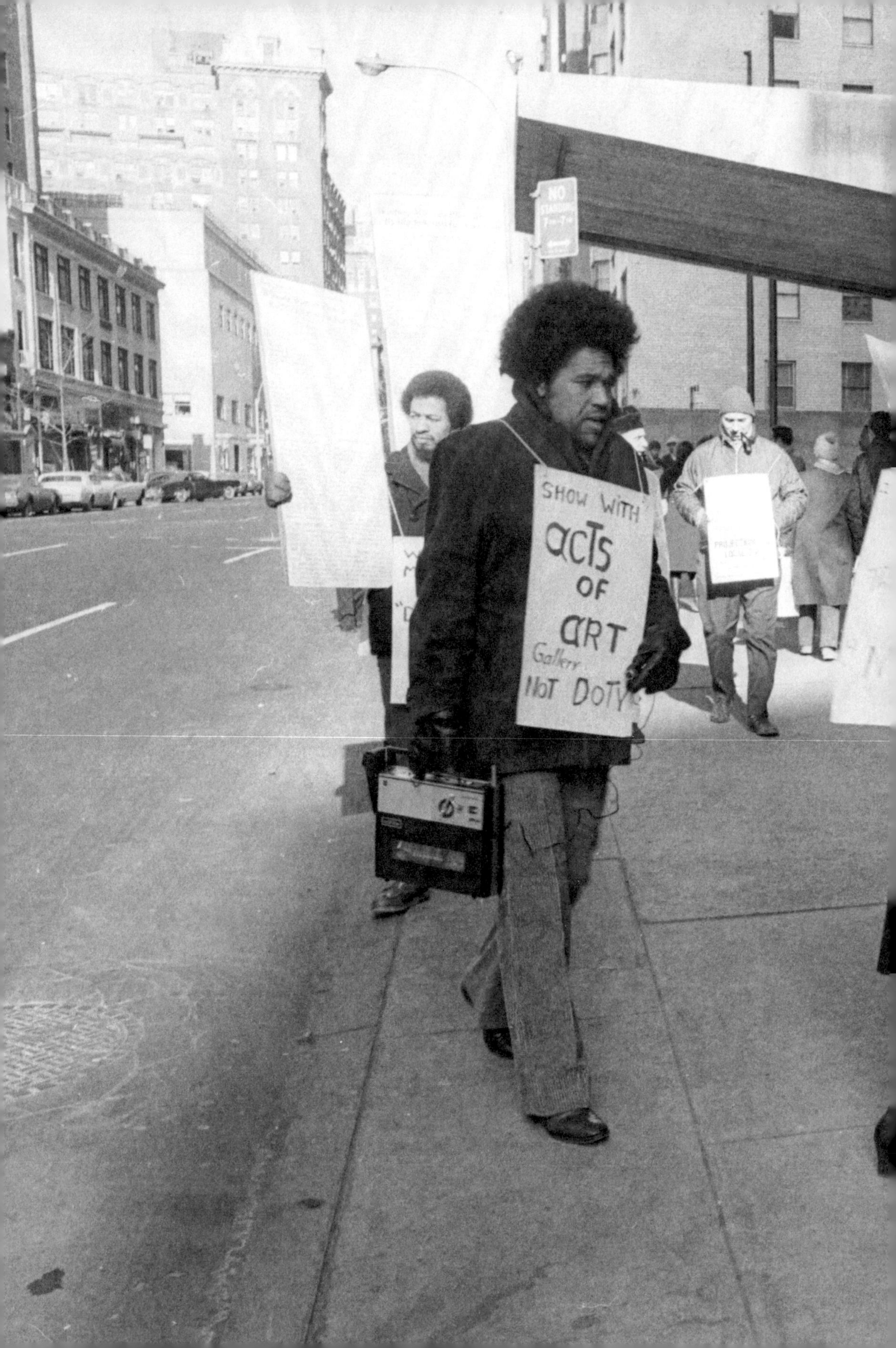
SHOW WITH
ACTS
OF
ART
Gallery
NOT DOTY
NO

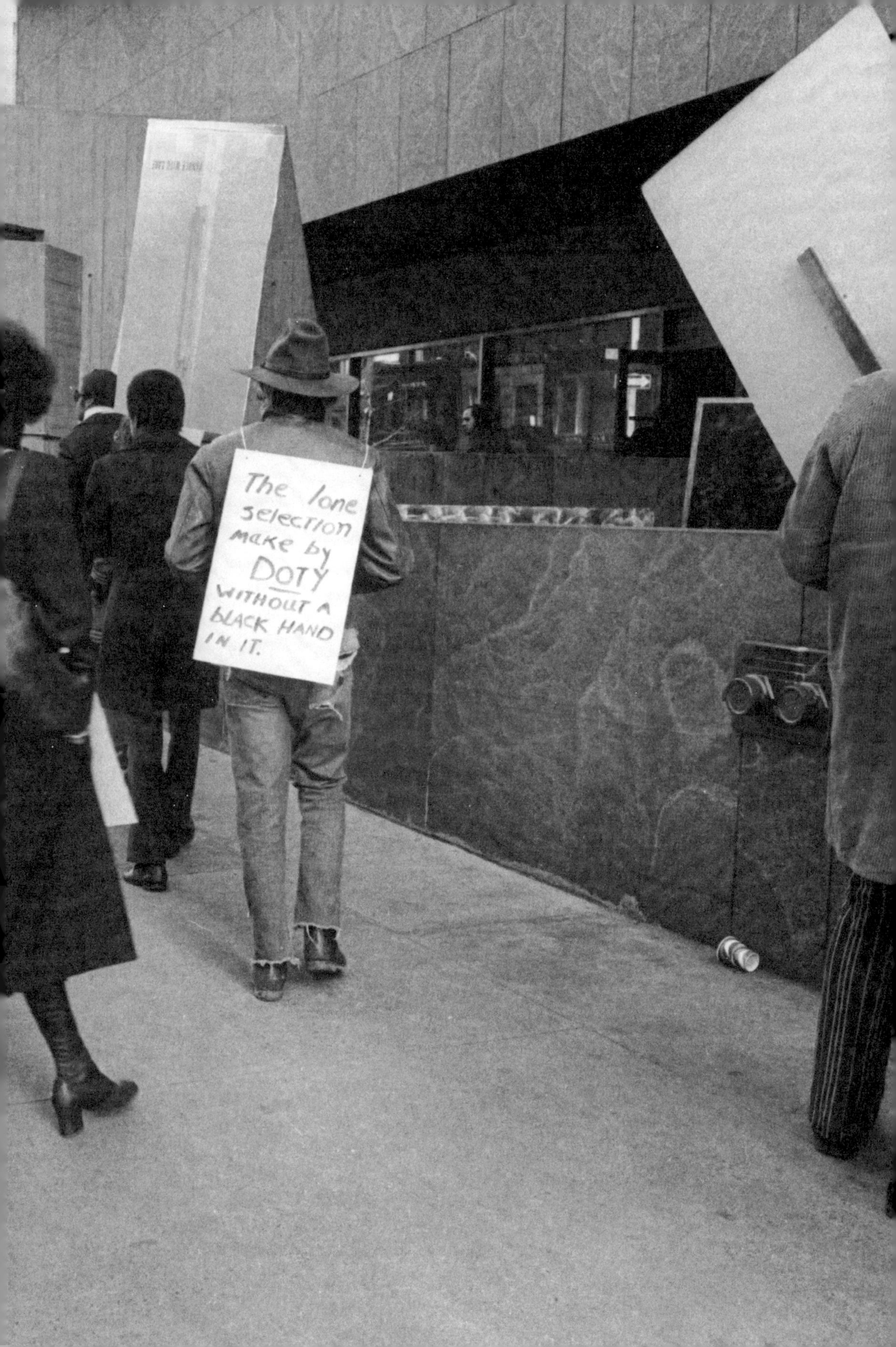
The lone
selection
make by
DOTY
WITHOUT A
BLACK HAND
IN IT.

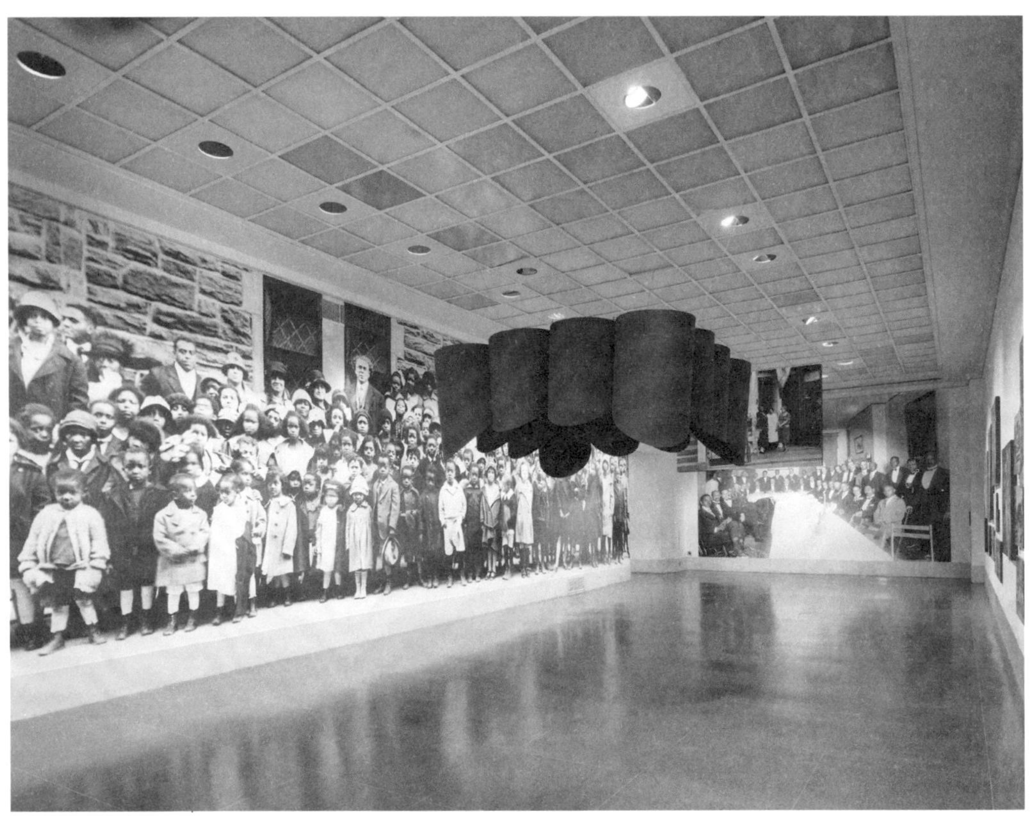

Installation view, 'Harlem on My Mind: Cultural Capital of Black America 1900–1968', The Metropolitan Museum of Art, New York, 1969. Photo © The Metropolitan Museum of Art/ Art Resource/ Scala, Florence

contemporary art, and the overall effect was to present Harlem in a way that has been described as anthropological, sociological or humanistic.[4] This presentation style was out of sync with the type of exhibitions the Met typically presented, and outside the expertise of the curatorial staff. The exhibition catalogue didn't even reproduce the exhibition's ephemera or the exhibition text. Instead, it contained newspaper articles about Harlem alongside essays from Schoener, Hoving, and Candice Van Ellison, a recent high school graduate of Roosevelt High School in the Bronx, whose expertise was described as 'Harlem resident', and who Schoener had asked to remove the footnotes and quotations so it would be less academic. One of the most delightful parts of Cooks's analysis of the exhibition is the way it quotes Hoving's preface, in which he 'elaborates on his personal relationship to Harlem by writing about what Harlem meant to him as a child':

> *Times change, bodies change, minds change. When I grew up in New York and when I was a boy of eight, nine, ten, eleven, twelve, there was a Harlem. And Harlem was with me and my family – a wonderful maid of sunny disposition and a thin, sour chauffeur who drove me to school in moody silence. To me and my family, living on 84th and Park Avenue, Harlem was a light-year away, uptown. And that was good. For behind the vague misty thoughts concerning* other people *that came through members of my family*

down to me, Negroes – colored people – constituted an unspoken menace, the tribe that must not be allowed to come down the Avenue.[5]

For an exhibition aimed at bridging a racial and spatial cultural gap, the decision to preface the publication with a director's framing of Harlem as the source for domestic labourers who served his family as a child is, as Cooks observes, a curious one.[6]

For all the critiques of how artless 'Harlem On My Mind' was, the exhibition wasn't even properly anthropological. It was not Harlem as conceived by anthropologist and *Black Metropolis* (1945) author St. Clair Drake.[7] And this is not the only exhibition we could make this observation about. (I often wonder what it might have looked like if New York's Museum of Modern Art (MoMA)'s first solo exhibition of work by a Black artist, the self-taught autodidact William Edmondson, had a publication featuring writing by Zora Neale Hurston – especially given Cooks's analysis of the exhibition, which notes that MoMA had framed Edmondson as an art world outsider, based on his lack of formal training, and also quoted him in Black dialect, as did the press.[8]) Given the contents of the exhibition, the criticism from artists and publics was understandable. Romare Bearden and Norman Lewis met with Schoener throughout 1968 and advocated for the real recognition of the contribution of Harlem artists (to no avail), and Andrews organized the BECC in 1969 to organize protests against the museum. The BECC widened their attention to other New York institutions, meeting with representatives from MoMA and the Whitney shortly after. They began meeting with Whitney director John Bauer in April 1969 about the whiteness of the museum's exhibitions, and the four demands they made to the Whitney were:

1. The Museum should put on an exhibition of Black artists with a Black guest curator.
2. Put more Black artists in the Whitney's Annual.
3. Hire a Black curatorial staff to coordinate these endeavors and other activities in the future.
4. Stage five or more solo exhibitions of Black artists during the year.[9]

The demands were ultimately rejected. In 1971, the Whitney curator Robert Doty organized 'Contemporary Black Artists in America', and when the BECC demands for the show weren't met, they protested the exhibition. Several artists pulled their works from the show, opting instead to show work in 'Rebuttal to the Whitney Museum Exhibition: Black Artists in Rebuttal' at Acts of Art gallery in New York, an exhibition that ultimately included 47 artists.

In *Exhibiting Blackness*, Cooks describes how the missteps of the Metropolitan Museum and the Whitney, and the pushback of the BECC, are partly to credit for shifts in how other white institutions went on to stage exhibitions featuring Black artists and how they hired Black museum professionals (such as curators Lowery Stokes Sims, at the Met in 1972, and Thelma Golden, at the Whitney in 1988). The lessons here are about the importance of Black curators and scholars in staging shows in these institutions, and in that sense, the way 'Harlem on My Mind' inspired a generation of artists, curators and institutional leaders as a 'how *not* to stage an exhibition' has been miraculous. In outlining the stakes and the impact of the 1976 landmark exhibition 'Two Centuries of Black American Art' for the Los Angeles County Museum of Art (LACMA), Cooks observes the way that curator David C. Driskell intended for the show to counter 'Harlem on My Mind'. 'Two Centuries of Black American Art' opened with a large photomural, which viewers would have seen at the entrance of the exhibition, before revealing over 200 works of art by 63 artists. The blockbuster exhibition was interpreted by art critics in mainstream press outlets as being too sociological to warrant serious engagement – a response Cooks rightfully notes the irony of, especially given its contrast to 'Harlem on My Mind'. Still, the exhibition's catalogue had a notably large print run of 5,000 copies. It has, since its publication, been treated as a textbook by many American art educators, and a foundational project in the history of exhibiting art by Black Americans:

> *Although the exhibition did not make lasting institutional change at LACMA, the life of the catalogue has made an impact in American art history. [...] The exhibition challenged art critics, some of whom admitted to having learned more about American art through the show and others who resented the artists' work in the art museum. These reviews demonstrated that the next step in understanding and valuing the work of Black artists was to have more exhibition models in art museums to feature work by Black artists and explore the diversity of their art in smaller focused shows rather than the survey format.*[10]

Recent debates around major New York institutions rehearse many of the critiques Black artists were making in the 1960s and 70s all over again. This adds some complexity to the idea that the culture wars happening now are just like those of the 1990s (which resulted in institutions acquiring more works by Black artists, but not necessarily in mounting more exhibitions of such works or targeting Black professionals for curatorial or senior leadership hires). The Whitney has been pulled into conversations about this more than once recently. For instance, the response to Black artists' critique of the inclusion of Dana Schutz's painting *Open Casket* in the 2017 Whitney Biennial – a critique of the curators' responsibility to appropriately assess the failure of the painting to adequately represent its historical source material (the 1955 murder of the Black teenager Emmett Till by Roy Bryant and J.W. Milam, a notorious act of white supremacist violence) – was frequently reported as a limitation of artistic freedom.[11] Or, a more recent case: 2020 saw the announcement (and subsequent cancellation) of an exhibition of artworks made by around eighty artists who had created work for fundraisers responding to the Covid-19 pandemic and Black Lives Matter demonstrations – yet these artists had no idea that anyone at the Whitney was collecting that work, or planning to exhibit it, until after it had already been announced publicly. The exhibition, 'Collective Actions: Artist Interventions in a Time of Change', was curated by the Whitney's director of research resources, who sent emails to the artists about the forthcoming exhibition weeks before it was set to open.[12] The debate that ensued over social media and in the press could be crudely described as a series of disagreements among some who thought the artists should just be happy to show work at the Whitney, and others concerned that artists who had not planned for their donated works to be included in a major museum show were newly finding out these works had been collected for the organization's archives (rather than permanent collection) and slated for exhibition without so much as a studio visit or conversation with museum staff about compensation, about the artists' practices, about whether or not they felt the work they had made for fundraisers was suitable for a show at the Whitney, or much of the information curatorial departments typically want from artists to be able to craft a competent extended exhibition label.

The currency of Black artists' critiques of major institutions in the 1960s and 70s now underscores the salience of those criticisms and the failure to apprehend them as properly art historical. Many contemporary conversations about the late-twentieth-century protests are framed as community responses that productively produced new institutions: artist-run spaces, Black museums and neighborhood arts centres among them. This conception has a kind of populist thread that suggests an expertise gap between the intellectual work that happens in those spaces and the work in major white museums, and we're seeing in these calls for increased cultural competence from the work in major museums that this expertise gap does not exist – at least, not in the direction many think it does.

This is an important historical note to keep in mind in our conversations about what's possible for the current supposed 'influx' of Black curators into large white institutions, and the diversity/equity/inclusion moves in the field, as a way to contextualize our expectations for what kind of institutional change is possible. As *Exhibiting Blackness* shows, the protests and exhibitions in the 1960s and 70s left lessons that impacted the production and reception of subsequent exhibition projects. As I mentioned, one of the lessons of the 'Two Centuries' exhibition was a need for smaller, more focused shows of Black artists – and many of the most celebrated art exhibitions featuring Black artists' work in the past decade have done this explicitly. Cooks does this work in her own curatorial practice. Her expansive scholarly output features exhibitions of contemporary and historical art, solo and group shows, and different kinds of institutions, including the survey show 'Grafton Tyler Brown: Exploring California', at the Pasadena Museum of California Art in 2018; a retrospective exhibition of the work of the artist Ernie Barnes, at the California African American Museum (CAAM) in Los Angeles in 2019; and the group show 'The Black Index', which travelled from 2021–22.[13] In these last two instances, exhibitions have been mounted in institutions with missions to speak specifically to Black audiences – which is especially significant given that not all museum professionals consider what care for Black audiences might require of them, even when they exhibit work that's about or in conversation with Black art and material culture. This underscores the importance of understanding the intervention that Cooks so astutely made a decade ago in *Exhibiting Blackness.*

Notes

[1] Bridget R. Cooks, *Exhibiting Blackness: African Americans and the American Art Museum*, Amherst: University of Massachusetts Press, 2011, p.56.

[2] *Ibid.*, p.58.

[3] See 'SFMOMA 75th Anniversary: Allon Schoener', interview by Lisa Rubens, 2007, Regional Oral History Office, The Bancroft Library, University of California, Berkeley, 2009, available at https://digitalassets.lib.berkeley.edu/roho/ucb/text/schoener_allon.pdf.

[4] See B.R. Cooks, *Exhibiting Blackness*, *op. cit.*, chapter 2.

[5] *Ibid.*, p.79.

[6] It is especially curious given that, as Hoving would later admit in his memoir, the maid never actually existed – this detail was pure fiction, invented for the purposes of the preface.

[7] See St. Clair Drake and Horace R. Cayton, *Black Metropolis: A Study of Negro Life in a Northern City*, Chicago: University of Chicago Press, 2015.

[8] See B.R. Cooks, *Exhibiting Blackness*, *op. cit.*, pp.24–33.

[9] Benny Andrews, quoted in J. Richard Gruber, *American Icons: From Madison to Manhattan, the Art of Benny Andrews, 1948–1997* (exh. cat.), Augusta, GA: Morris Museum of Art, 1997, p.144. Also quoted in B.R. Cooks, *Exhibiting Blackness*, *op. cit.*, p.181, n.93.

[10] *Ibid.*, p.109.

[11] See, for instance, Randy Kennedy, 'White Artist's Painting of Emmett Till at Whitney Biennial Draws Protests', *The New York Times,* 21 March 2017, available at https://www.nytimes.com/2017/03/21/arts/design/painting-of-emmett-till-at-whitney-biennial-draws-protests.html; and for a good critical overview, Aruna D'Souza, 'Who Speaks Freely?: Art, Race, and Protest', *The Paris Review,* 22 May 2018, available at https://www.theparisreview.org/blog/2018/05/22/who-speaks-freely-art-race-and-protest/.

[12] See Julia Jacobs and Zachary Small, 'Whitney Cancels Show That Included Works Bought at Fund-Raisers', *The New York Times*, 25 August 2020, available at: https://www.nytimes.com/2020/08/25/arts/design/whitney-museum-exhibition-canceled.html.

[13] 'Grafton Tyler Brown: Exploring California', Pasadena Museum of California Art, 17 June–7 October 2018; 'Ernie Barnes: A Retrospective', CAAM, Los Angeles, 8 May–8 September 2019. 'The Black Index' was on view at the University Art Galleries at the University of California, Irvine, 14 January–20 March 2021; Palo Alto Art Center, California, 1 May–14 August 2021; Art Galleries at Black Studies, University of Texas at Austin, 16 September–12 December 2021; and the Hunter College Art Galleries, New York, 1 February–3 April 2022.

More than Preamble: Anticipating 'Two Centuries of Black American Art' – Julie L. McGee

I: City Quartet

Artist and scholar David C. Driskell (1931–2020) was a lifelong advocate for the rightful place of African American art in global art histories. Actively curating from the mid-1950s onward, Driskell tailored his transformational practices to what lay before him, maneuvering through white and Black institutional and discursive frameworks. He formulated theory from lived experiences and created space into which his ideas and others' would flow. Understanding the precarious position of African American art in the American imagination, Driskell invested in the evidential power of exhibitions and their catalogues. He positioned African American art in relation to American, European and African aesthetics, drawing attention to affinities and distinctions as appropriate. While Black curation in Driskell's hands foregrounds his visionary practices, it predicates this liberatory work on his synthesized role as Black artist and scholar.[1] When Driskell writes about Black artists, he is also writing about himself, and a world that helped shape the field.

In the summer of 1953, David Driskell attended the Skowhegan School of Painting and Sculpture in Madison, Maine. He was a 22-year-old undergraduate at Howard University in Washington DC, pursing a degree in fine arts.[2] The Skowhegan experience was pivotal for his self-fashioning and confidence as a professional artist. Returning to Washington from Maine, he took the opportunity to visit New York City for the first time, and in the company of newly established artist-colleagues. One of the paintings he completed after his Maine summer is *City Quartet* (1953). Stylistically related to the work of American painter Jack Levine (1915–2010), an instructor at Skowhegan that summer, the iconography is personal and historical. Driskell was a young Black artist operating in an arena dominated by white histories and discourses. With a nod towards *City Quartet*, this essay imagines Black curation in Driskell's hands, casting his foundational work in African American art in its integrated historical context.

In the fall of 1953, post-Skowhegan, Driskell became head of Howard University's Daubers Club (aka Daubers Art Club), a student organization founded in 1928 by James A. Porter (1905–1970). Inactive for two years, the club's charge was to develop appreciation for the arts outside of the classroom; nurture contacts with contemporary artists; and 'bring art to the entire campus community by means of symposia, exhibitions' and other activities.[3] This was an astute move for Driskell, as the professional activities advanced by the Daubers Club furthered his own education and field exposure. This early arts activism and stewardship foreshadowed the work he would undertake as a professional artist, educator and curator.

Driskell's curatorial sensibilities were intertwined with his professionalization as an artist and educator. In the context of the symposium 'Reshaping the Field: Arts of the African Diasporas on Display', Driskell's contributions are

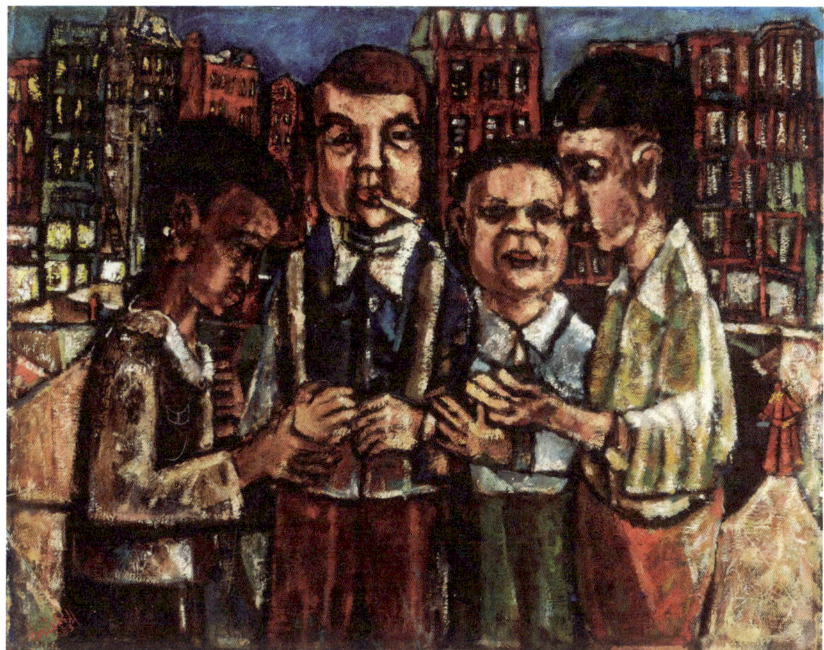

David C. Driskell, *City Quartet*, 1953, oil on canvas, 61 × 76.2cm. Purchased by the David C. Driskell Center at the University of Maryland, College Park, with funds from the C. Sylvia and Eddie Brown Arts Acquisition Fund. Photo: Greg Staley. Courtesy the David C. Driskell Center at the University of Maryland, College Park. © David C. Driskell/David C. Driskell Center, 2017. © Estate of David C. Driskell

widely celebrated. The field-defining work most often acknowledged is 'Two Centuries of Black American Art'. Curated by Driskell and opening at the Los Angeles County Museum of Art (LACMA) in September 1976, 'Two Centuries' marked a defining moment in American art history. A consequential exhibition that represented some 63 artists, it brought together more than 200 works, uniting painting, sculpture, drawing, graphics, crafts and the decorative arts. 'Two Centuries' attracted more than 88,500 visitors to LACMA and continued to excite American audiences through August 1977 at the High Museum of Art, Atlanta; the Dallas Museum of Fine Arts (now the Dallas Museum of Art); and the Brooklyn Museum. The illustrated exhibition catalogue, published by Alfred A. Knopf, includes principal essays by Driskell, short artist biographies and colour illustrations. A critical text for American art history, the catalogue (held by over 1300 libraries worldwide) has served as a key source of study for this exhibition phenomenon. As noted by scholar and curator Brittany Webb, Driskell 'wrote and taught the history of black artistic production in a cultural moment when many insisted it didn't exist'; Webb continues, 'David Driskell offered us lineages.'[4] The art historical and museological significance of 'Two Centuries' is undeniable. Yet, what preceded and readied David Driskell to deliver this audacious showcase?

II: Necessity is the Mother of Invention

> *I come out of the HBCU tradition, the historically Black college tradition, where one didn't have the luxury of being able to specialize. You really had to be able to teach almost everything.*
> – David C. Driskell[5]

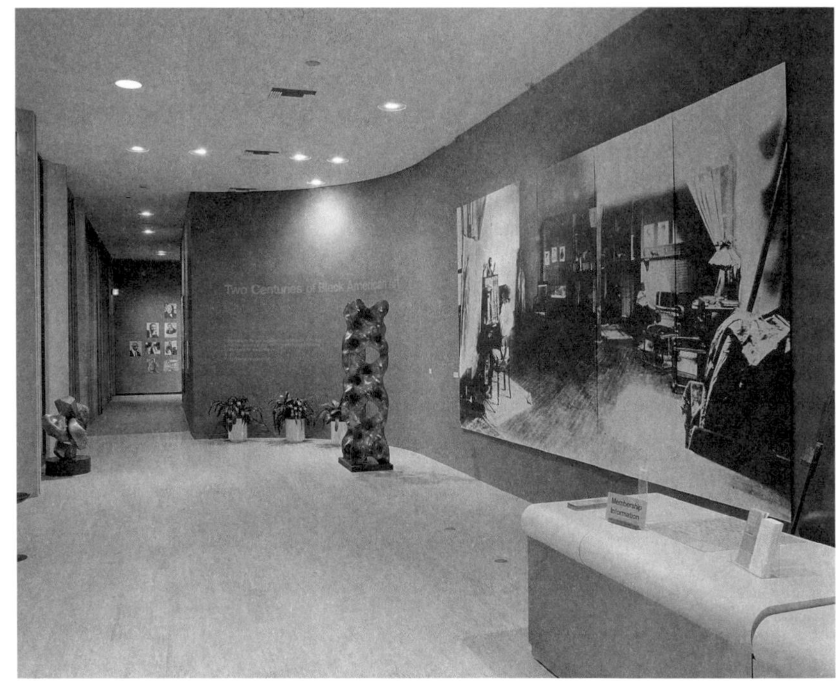

Installation view, 'Two Centuries of Black American Art', Los Angeles County Museum of Art, 1976, with enlarged photograph of Henry Ossawa Tanner's studio (right). Photo © Museum Associates/LACMA

'Two Centuries' was, for David Driskell, both anticipated and the realization of a vision. He had an extensive curatorial career by the time the exhibition opened. As he told *Atlanta Constitution* reporter Helen Smith in 1977, 'I could never have done it had I not had 25 years of research before then … . I knew what I wanted, what the key pieces would be. The format was very clear to me.'[6] Smith's article, with the unfortunate headline 'Black Art Sheds its "Primitive" Image', promoted the opening of 'Two Centuries' at the High Museum of Art, and positioned Driskell as a Black curator whose knowledge pertained to Black artists and exhibitions of African American art. In fact, Driskell's experience was much more expansive. Absent from the article are the enormous efforts he took to expose Historically Black College and University (HBCU) students and their communities to all manner of art – accomplishments foregrounded in more holistic considerations of Driskell's curatorial philosophy and audacity.

The antecedents of 'Two Centuries' are traceable and absorbing.[7] This essay introduces a small selection of Driskell's prodigious activities, first at Talladega College in Alabama and later at Fisk University in Nashville, to situate his reputation as a curator of African diasporic arts relative to a larger professional repertoire. As an act of Black curation, 'Two Centuries' was HBCU sown, emboldened by lessons gained from Driskell's mentors, among them James A. Porter, James V. Herring (1897–1969) and Alonzo J. Aden (1906–1961), and supported by Black institutions and the connections Driskell developed over time and across the United States. This includes the trust and support Driskell earned of artist peers and former students, many of whom loaned

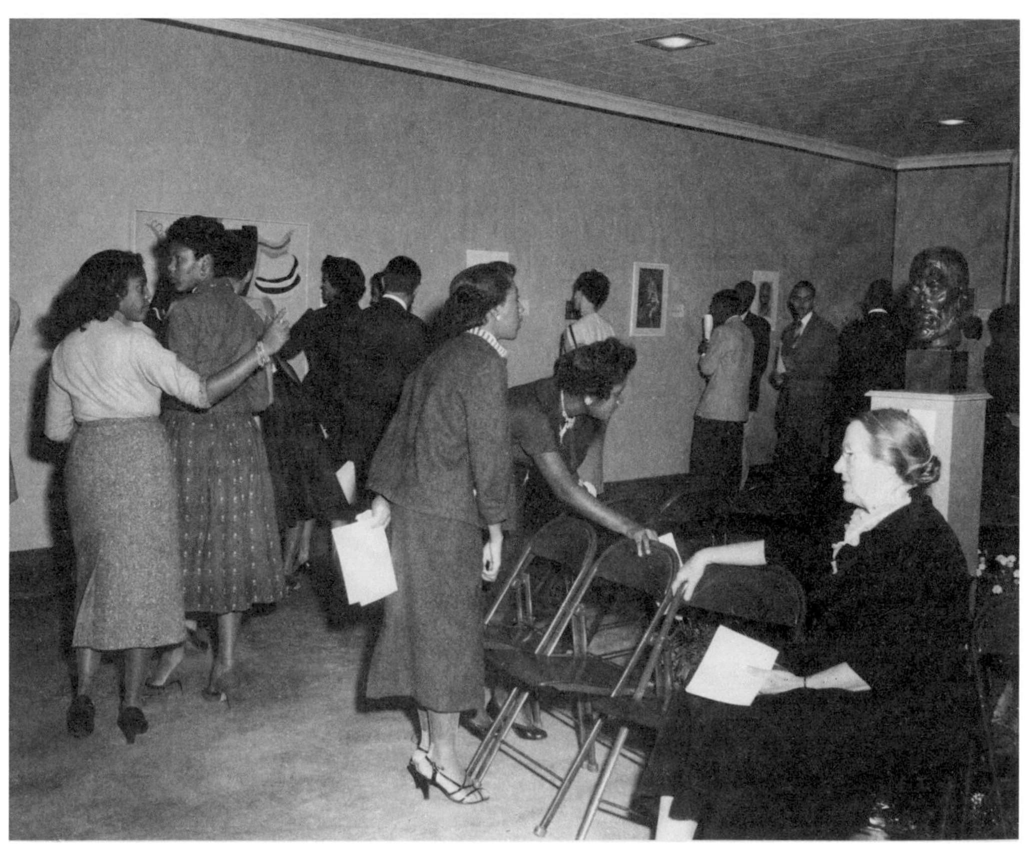

View of exhibition event at Talladega College, Alabama, c.1956. Courtesy the David C. Driskell Papers at the David C. Driskell Center at the University of Maryland, College Park. Gift of Professor and Mrs David C. Driskell

art for his exhibitions. Driskell's early curatorial efforts were also supported by his decades-long association with Mary Beattie Brady. Brady served as director of the Harmon Foundation from 1922 to 1967; Driskell met her through Porter and Aden. The Harmon Foundation was a frequent lender and occasional donor to the academic institutions where Driskell operated.

Driskell envisioned exhibitions as teaching tools that were equally useful for promoting the visual arts and developing arts communities. His teaching career commenced in 1955 at Talladega College, just after he completed his undergraduate studies at Howard University; he stayed through the 1961–62 academic year. Driskell began curating exhibitions and producing catalogues soon after his arrival. His curatorial perspectives were marked by his experiences in Washington, especially at Howard University and the Barnett Aden Gallery. Consequential parallels between the Washington nexus and what Driskell put into motion elsewhere point to a circulation of ideas, exhibitions and artworks among Black cultural leaders that helped shaped the field of American art from the South outward. This includes the College Art Service, founded by James Herring and operating out of the basement of the Barnett Aden Gallery, which provided loan exhibitions primarily to Southern HBCUs. This Black nexus did what few white-led museums would: circulate

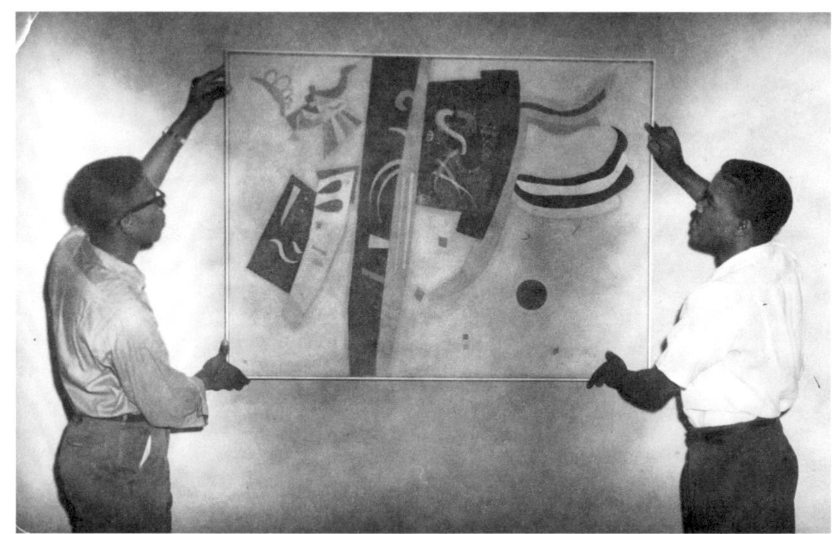

Richard English (left) and David Driskell (right) installing Wassily Kandinsky's *Violet–Orange*, 1935, in 'Paintings by Modern Masters', Callanan College Union Gallery, Talladega College, 1956. Collection of the Solomon R. Guggenheim Museum, New York. Courtesy the David C. Driskell Papers at the David C. Driskell Center at the University of Maryland, College Park. Gift of Professor and Mrs David C. Driskell

historic and contemporary African American art *and* international offerings, justifiably placing art by Black artists in a global creative continuum.

Exhibitions in Driskell's first year at Talladega include the annual student exhibition; a few solo artist exhibitions (including that of his predecessor, Claude Clark); and European and Japanese prints from the collection of Erich Nussbaum, Talladega professor of mathematics and philosophy.[8] Succeeding years saw increasingly robust offerings. In 1956, Driskell secured an extended loan exhibition from the Solomon R. Guggenheim Museum that included works by Wassily Kandinsky, Paul Klee, László Moholy-Nagy, Marc Chagall and others. The college was the first institution in the state of Alabama to receive a loan from the Guggenheim.[9] On view for six months (September 1956–February 1957), the exhibition 'Paintings by Modern Masters', as Driskell titled it, was accompanied by a small catalogue, also produced by Driskell. He augmented the loan with two exhibitions: 'Drawings by Young Americans' (November 1956) and 'Watercolors by Women Artists' (December 1956). The latter was on loan from the National Association of Women Artists, while 'Drawings by Young Americans' was drawn from Driskell's personal collection and included work by artists he knew from Skowhegan and Howard. Further exhibitions included an invitational for artists from Talladega County; 'Thirty-Eight Latin American Prints', on loan from the Fine Arts Collection of International Business Machines Corporation of New York City; a solo exhibition of Driskell's own work; and the annual student exhibition. Most exhibitions lasted less than a month, and Driskell produced an art calendar for the academic year, decorated by hand and topped with a quote from Johann Wolfgang von Goethe: 'The highest problem of any art is to cause by appearance the illusion of a higher reality.'

The exhibition schedule for successive academic years was no less busy, as Driskell secured loans from museums and exhibition agencies and showcased the work of local artists, students and faculty. The Guggenheim Museum, IBM, the National Association of Women Artists, Herring's College Art Service and the Harmon Foundation continued to provide loans, as did the National Gallery of Art and the Georgia Museum of Art at the University of Georgia. By 1961, Driskell had secured an 'indefinite loan' from the Harmon Foundation – several original artworks from their African American art collection – and 75 prints (reproductions) suitable for the 'Student Circulation Collection'. Talladega's robust art programme was possible because Driskell practically willed it into being: tapping art suppliers for prize money for students; securing loans at no cost to Talladega, save transport; and teaching students how to make, appreciate and, yes, install art. In a statement from the time, Driskell wrote: 'In addition to serving to help meet the educational needs of this institution, these exhibitions serve to enhance the cultural backgrounds of the community citizens as well.'[10]

Enrollment had tripled in the studio art classes by 1961, and Driskell felt he had exhausted the good will of his professional relationships to support exhibitions and the wider art programme at the college. As he wrote to the college's president, Arthur D. Gray, 'Teaching people to be creative and to have imagination now is teaching them to be creative during later years in their lives. This is a vital part of my job as artist-teacher. If sufficient tools are not available, I cannot do the kind of job required of me: To recognize this is to recognize failure.'[11] In his final year at Talladega, for the spring of 1962 Fine Arts Festival, Driskell secured the Jacob Lawrence retrospective organized by the American Federation of Arts.

Driskell secured loan exhibitions out of economic and geographic necessity, offering a visual education for students, staff and the surrounding Alabama community.[12] For Driskell, Black curating at that time meant creating opportunities to experience a range of art typologies: historic to contemporary, local, national and international – not unlike what he had experienced at Howard and at the Barnett Aden Gallery. Reproductions, facsimiles and originals were utilized; annual exhibitions of student, faculty and staff handiworks fostered an atmosphere in which the arts were seen as belonging to all. Talladega's first Spring Arts Festival emerged with Driskell's support in April 1960.[13] He was steadfastly advancing his agenda, albeit often through the agency and power of exhibition lenders. Notwithstanding the generosity of lenders, the circulation of art exhibitions is not a neutral endeavor.[14]

III: Circulation & Influence: The Division of Cultural Research

In the decade David Driskell spent at Fisk University in Nashville, Tennessee, from 1966 to 1976, exhibitions of African art and art by African American artists were part of an expanded exhibition programme, and one that included an artist-in-residence programme.[15] Most exhibitions had catalogues; many were designed by Driskell. As at Talladega, the display of arts of the African diasporas was placed within the larger goal of arts education, professionalization *and* Driskell's desire to showcase 'a common ethos which is born out of the human experience'.[16] On the whole, exhibitions emphasized variety and diversity of creative expression and media. For example, the 1966 exhibition '8

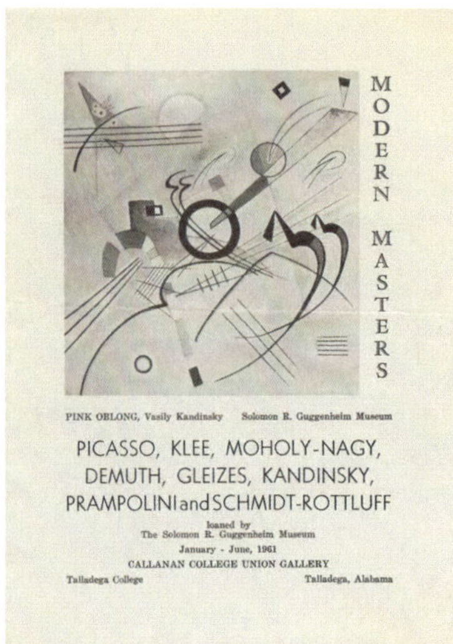

Cover of exhibition catalogue for 'Modern Masters', Callanan College Union Gallery, Talladega College, 1961. Courtesy the David C. Driskell Papers at the David C. Driskell Center at the University of Maryland, College Park. Gift of Professor and Mrs David C. Driskell

ART CALENDAR

NO.1 1956-57

DEPARTMENT OF ART
Talladega College
Talladega, Alabama

STATEMENT: The highest problem of any art is to cause by appearance the illusion of a higher reality.- GOETHE.

HEADLINES: AN EXTENDED LOAN from THE SOLOMON R. GUGGENHEIM MUSEUM of NEW YORK CITY comes to TALLADEGA COLLEGE for SIX MONTHS.

EXHIBITIONS FOR THE SCHOOL YEAR
1956-57

September, 1956 - February, 1957
PAINTINGS BY MODERN MASTERS
Loaned by The Solomon R. Guggenheim Museum.

October 14.
FORMAL OPENING of THE GUGGENHEIM EXHIBITION
2:30 P.M.

November.
THE GUGGENHEIM EXHIBITION and DRAWINGS by YOUNG AMERICANS

December.
THE GUGGENHEIM EXHIBITION and WATERCOLORS by WOMEN ARTISTS from THE NATIONAL ASSOCIATION of WOMEN ARTISTS, INC.

1957.
January.
THE GUGGENHEIM EXHIBITION

February.
THE GUGGENHEIM EXHIBITION (last month)

March 3.
''THE FARM'' . An Invitational exhibition from artists of Talladega County.

March 30.
''THIRTY-EIGHT LATIN AMERICAN PRINTS'' Loaned by the Fine Arts Collection of International Business Machines Corporation of New York City.

April 21.
PAINTINGS by DAVID C. DRISKELL , Assistant Professor of Art, Talladega College.

May 26.
ANNUAL STUDENT ART SHOW. Exhibition of drawings, paintings, ceramics, design, and crafts.

THE ART GALLERY
Savery Library
Talladega College

Art Calendar, no.1, 1956–57, Department of Art, Talladega College. Courtesy the Savery Library Historical Collection, Talladega College

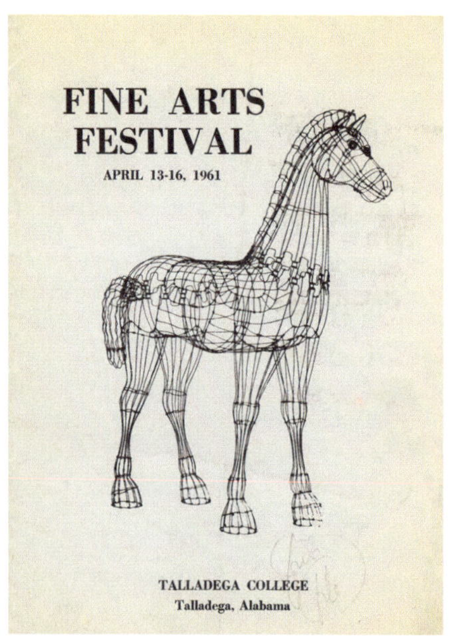

Hayward L. Oubre Jr's *Young Horse*, 1960, on cover of exhibition catalogue for Fine Arts Festival, 1961, Talladega College. Courtesy the David C. Driskell Papers at the David C. Driskell Center at the University of Maryland, College Park. Gift of Professor and Mrs David C. Driskell

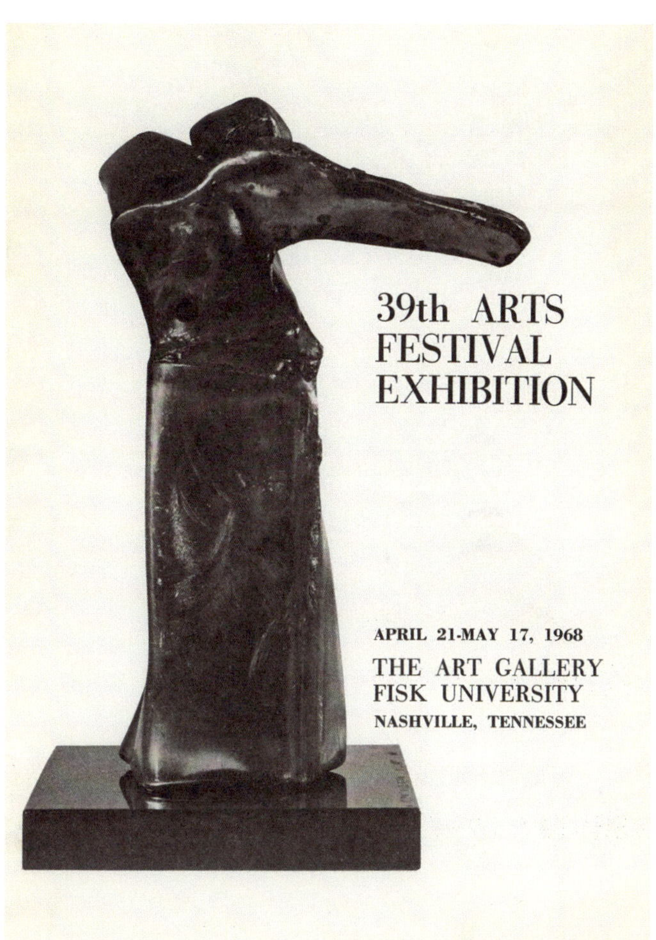

Richard Hunt's *Small Antique Study*, undated, on cover of catalogue for 39th Arts Festival Exhibition, 1968, The Art Gallery, Fisk University, Nashville. Courtesy the David C. Driskell Papers at the David C. Driskell Center at the University of Maryland, College Park. Gift of Professor and Mrs David C. Driskell

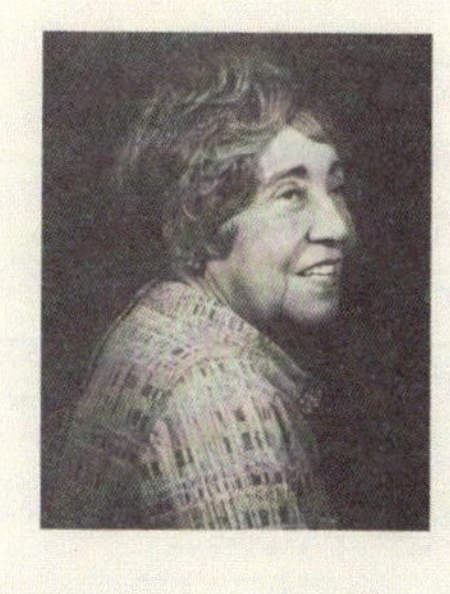

Cover of exhibition catalogue for 'Alma W. Thomas: Recent Paintings', Carl Van Vechten Gallery of Fine Arts, Fisk University, 1971. Courtesy the David C. Driskell Papers at the David C. Driskell Center at the University of Maryland, College Park. Gift of Professor and Mrs David C. Driskell

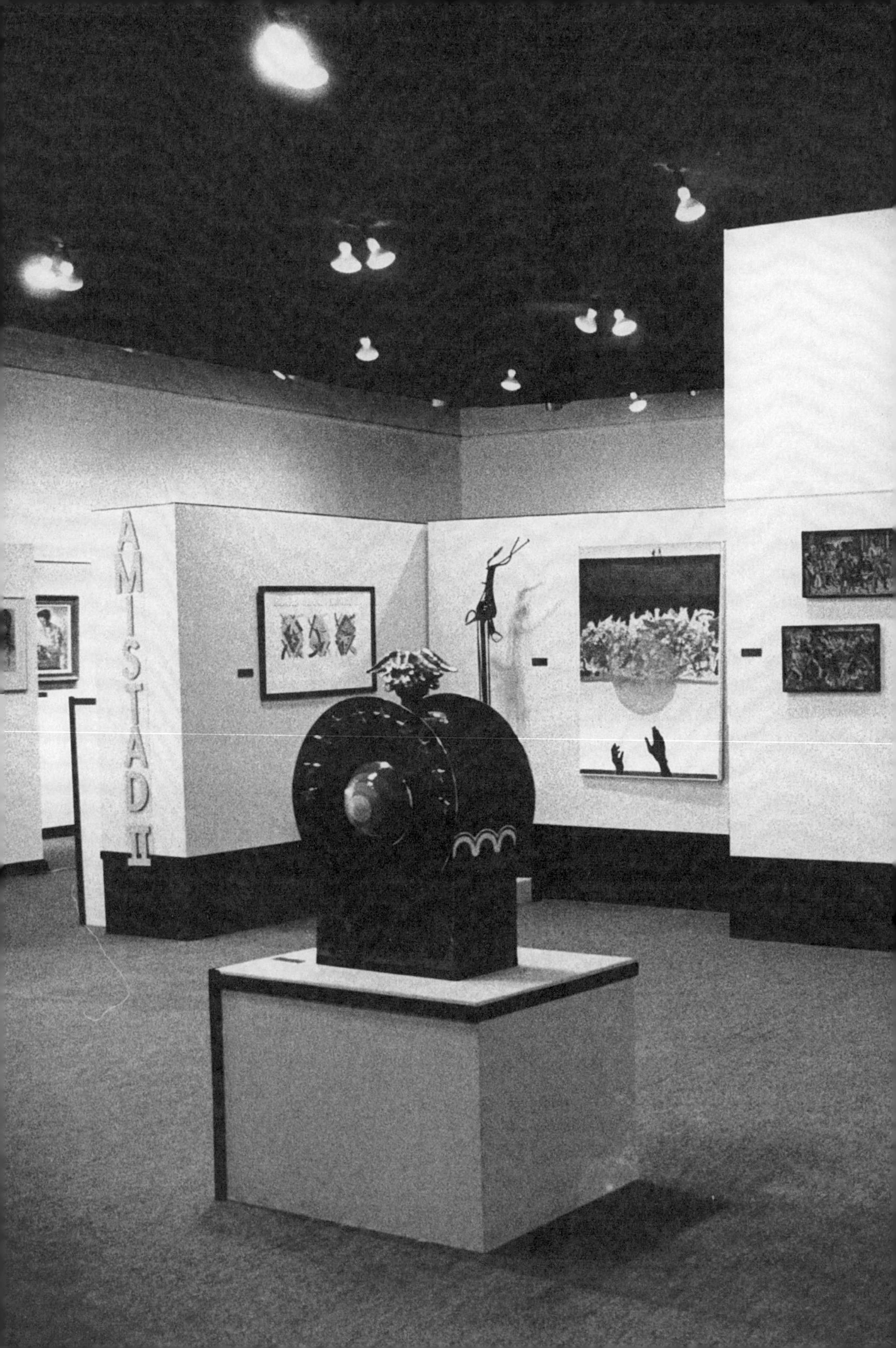
AMISTAD II

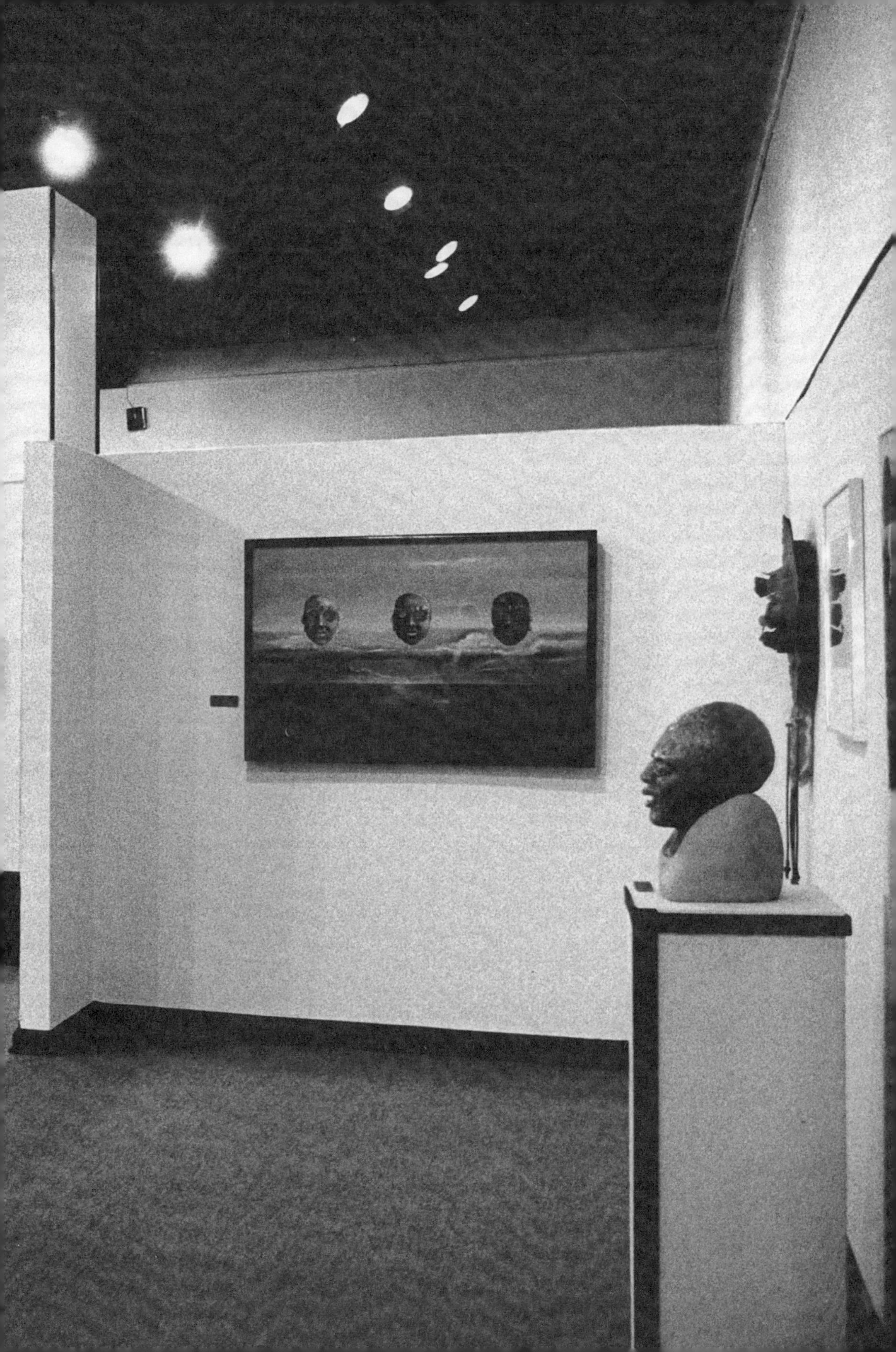

Image of 18th-century iron slave chains on cover of exhibition catalogue for 'Amistad II: Afro-American Art', Department of Art, Fisk University, in cooperation with the American Missionary Association and the United Church Board for Homeland Ministries, New York, 1975. © 1975 United Church Board for Homeland Ministries

Previous spread: Installation view, 'Amistad II: Afro-American Art', unidentified location, c.1975. Courtesy the David C. Driskell Papers at the David C. Driskell Center at the University of Maryland, College Park. Gift of Professor and Mrs David C. Driskell

Young Printmakers' featured woodcuts, engravings, etchings and lithographs by an international roster of artists. The catalogue cover featured a print by Pakistan-born artist Hans Bhalla (1927–1977). A former student of Driskell's at Talladega, Bhalla received his MFA at Cranbrook and then returned to Alabama to teach.[17]

The next advancement for Driskell was to become the agent with the power to circulate exhibitions; this materialized during his time at Fisk University and continued thereafter. Under the auspices of the Division of Cultural Research, housed in the department of art, Fisk became a hub for the production of travelling exhibitions and the distribution of cultural resources for teaching African diasporic art and culture, inclusive of slide kits, syllabi and bibliographies. Sample circulated exhibitions included: 'Small Paintings of Afro-American Artists', 'Contemporary African Art', 'Collages by Sam Middleton', 'Afro-American Prints' and 'Contemporary Trends in African and Afro-American Art'. Also among these was the 'Retrospective Exhibition of Afro-American Art', assembled by Driskell for the Ninth Annual Arts Festival at Talladega College in April 1968. Collectively, these exhibitions and accompanying texts paved the way for the material that shaped 'Two Centuries'.

The largest of the travelling African diaspora art exhibitions supervised by Driskell and generated from Fisk was 'Amistad II: Afro-American Art'. After the exhibition prototype opened at Fisk in April 1975, 'Amistad II' circulated through 1977, stopping at some 22 venues and thus overlapping with the better-known 'Two Centuries'.[18] Indeed, Driskell worked on 'Amistad II' and 'Two Centuries' simultaneously. Designed as a US Bicentennial exhibition, 'Amistad II' included documents related to the Amistad incident and nearly eighty works of art, dating from 1790 to 1975. The exhibition was part of the larger Amistad Art Project, which in concept form included a caravan of three tractor trailer units – two artmobiles and one mobile mixed-media theatre.[19] Representing six HBCUs affiliated with the American Missionary Association (AMA); the United Church of Christ, funded by the AMA; and the United Church Board for Homeland Ministries (UCBHM), 'Amistad II' also received substantial funding from the National Endowment for the Arts.[20] The exhibition catalogue included numerous black-and-white illustrations, a select bibliography specific to African American art and three essays. Clifton H. Johnson chronicled the Amistad incident; Driskell wrote on African American Art; and Allan Gordon provided an unusual essay on 'the phenomenology of a Black aesthetic'.[21]

Exhibitions are largely known and critiqued in their executed form and through their reception histories. Exceptional ones such as 'Two Centuries of Black American Art' – wellsprings for continuous study – take on measurable afterlives. No doubt there are many reasons why 'Two Centuries' became the exhibition of wonderment and curatorial measurement and not 'Amistad II'.

The selection of art, I contend, was not one of them. While there was significant overlap in the artists represented, 'Amistad II' was smaller in size than 'Two Centuries'.[22] Differently calibrated, the circulating agents – LACMA for

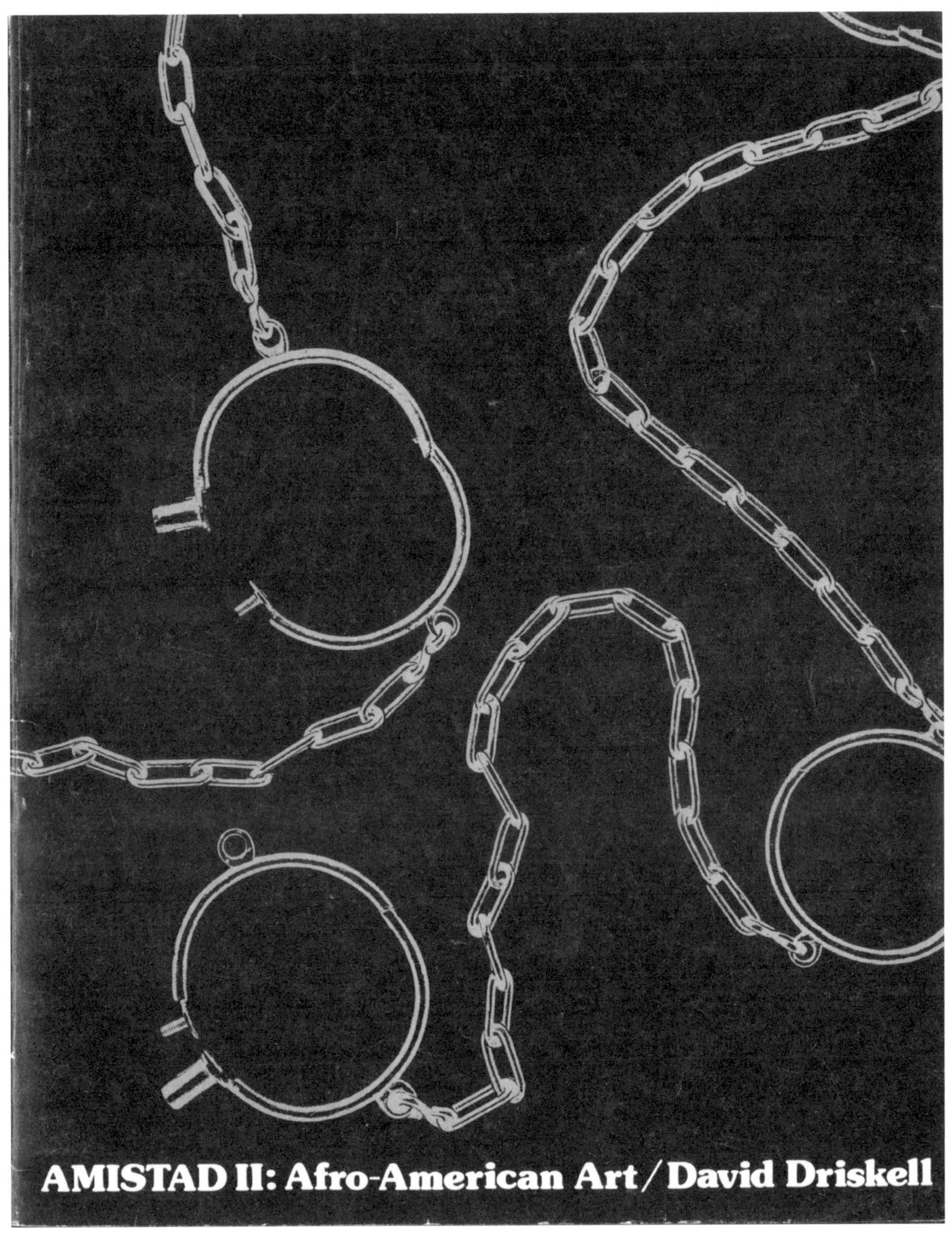
AMISTAD II: Afro-American Art / David Driskell

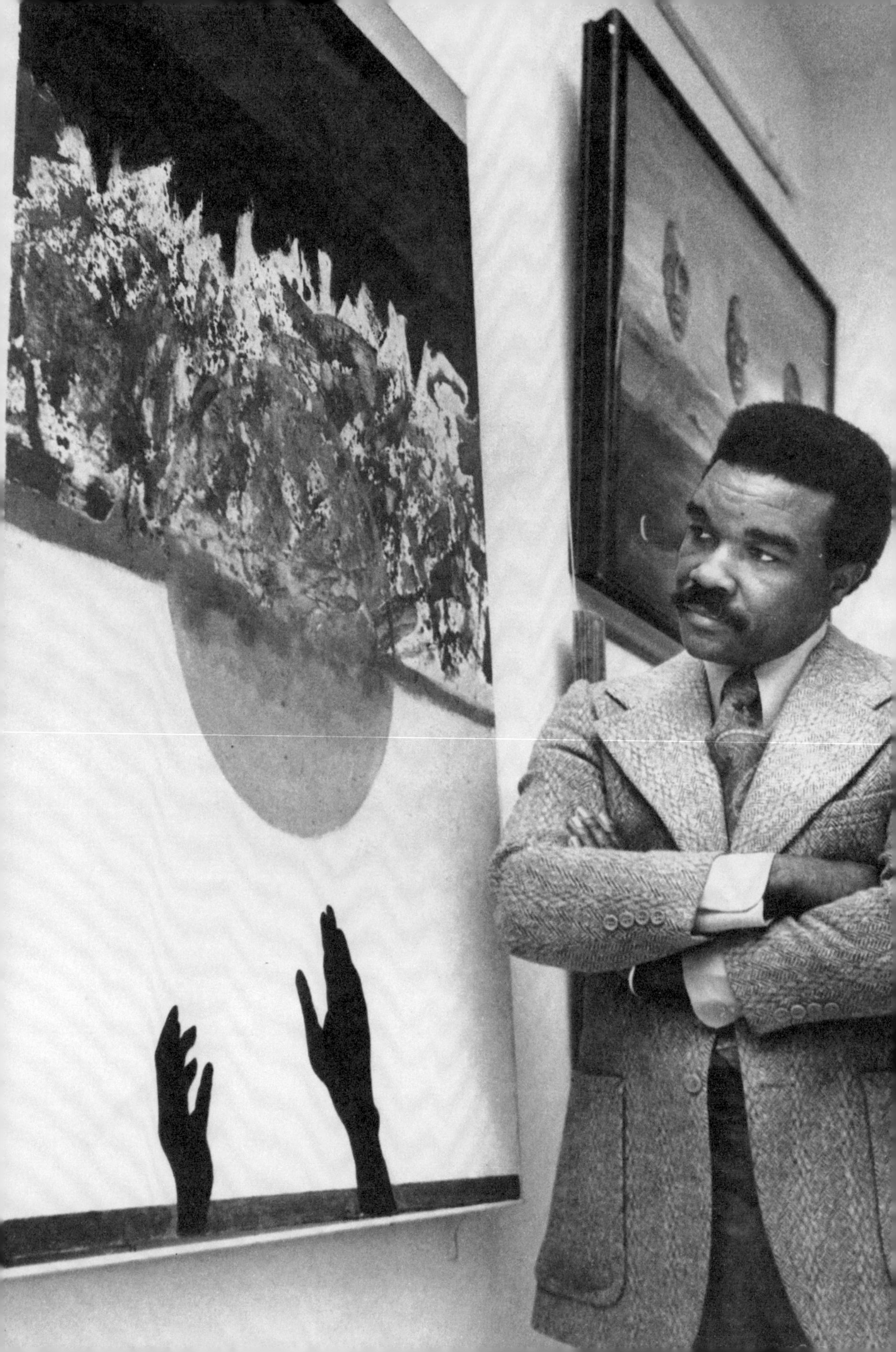

'Two Centuries' and the Fisk-AMA-UCBHM coalition for 'Amistad II' – surely held different places in the American imagination in the late 1970s. 'Two Centuries' appeared at American art museums in Los Angeles, Atlanta, Dallas and Brooklyn. The twenty-plus venues for 'Amistad II' included universities, religious venues, libraries and only a handful of art locations. Among these were the Studio Museum in Harlem, New York; the Birmingham Museum of Art, Alabama; the Brooks Memorial Art Gallery (now the Memphis Brooks Museum of Art), Tennessee; and the Columbus Gallery of Fine Arts (now Columbus Museum of Art), Ohio. The Studio Museum of Harlem was publicized as the exhibition's national or, in some cases, 'world premiere', thereby diminishing the importance of the two previous venues: Fisk University and the Minneapolis Auditorium and Conventional Hall, where it coincided with the Tenth General Synod of the United Church of Christ. Often on view for less than a month, 'Amistad II' lived up to its promotional spin as a 'travelling exhibit'. Perhaps it was too ambitious for American audiences. Promoted as 'a Bicentennial celebration for all, inspired by the struggle of the few', 'Amistad II' offered viewers more than an art exhibition. 'Amistad II' asked audiences to directly confront the injustices of slavery through the fate of 53 Africans bound for sale aboard 'La Amistad', and to learn the founding history of the AMA. In addition to the 'iron slave chains' used for the catalogue design, chains appear in installation views. The Chuck Davis Dance Company performed a 'multi-media portrayal of the Amistad epic in the context of contemporary U.S.A.' – a performance titled *Chains*.[23]

David C. Driskell with his painting *Swing Low, Sweet Chariot*, 1972, at 'Amistad II: Afro-American Art', unidentified location, c.1975. The painting is in the collection of Tougaloo College Art Collections, Tougaloo, Mississippi. Behind Driskell is a painting by Philip R. Dotson, *Anthropomorphic Psychosis*, 1975, in the collection of Memphis Brooks Museum of Art. Courtesy the David C. Driskell Papers at the David C. Driskell Center at the University of Maryland, College Park. Gift of Professor and Mrs David C. Driskell

'Two Centuries' did not shy away from the history of slavery, but it was not a thematic binder, and audiences entered the exhibition framed by the American art museum context. Yet comparisons of these productions must inevitably return to the historical lacuna that underpinned them – the 'paucity of critical recognition' of Black artists, to quote Driskell.[24] Applauding the arrival of Black shows timed for the Bicentennial, including 'Amistad II', Romare Bearden lamented the limited opportunities for Black artists: 'Yet today many museum curators who did a so-called "Black Show" in the 1960s feel their obligations to Black artists have been fulfilled. What can the young Black artist of today expect in a time of such retrenchment and prejudice?'[25] As the US approaches the semiquincentennial in 2026, Bearden's question resonates. Driskell's legacy bears witness to the necessity and significance of Black curation. To be sure, the liberatory praxes of Black curation will continue lead the way forward.[26]

Notes
[1] The significance of this conjunction to the field, while beyond the scope of this essay, is important.
[2] Howard University awarded the summer scholarship to Driskell. He received his BA in Fine Arts in 1955.
[3] Mildred Thompson, 'Driskell Heads Daubers Club', *The Hilltop*, 23 November 1953, p.8, available at https://dh.howard.edu/hilltop_195060/24. The listing for the club varied over time and by Howard publication, and include Dauber's, Daubers', and Daubers.
[4] Brittany Webb, 'Stories from PAFA: Remembering Dr. David C. Driskell (1931–2020)', 22 April 2020, Pennsylvania Academy of the Fine Arts website, https://www.pafa.org/news/remembering-dr-david-c-driskell-042220?gclid=EAIaIQobChMIwLz43dbc9AIVxa6GCh06TwBaEAMYAiAAEgJL-WPD_BwE.
[5] 'David C. Driskell: Life Among the Pines', interview conducted by Bridget Cooks and Amanda Tewes, 2019, Oral History Center, Bancroft Library, University of California, Berkeley, 2020, p.107, available at https://digicoll.lib.berkeley.edu/record/219400?ln=en.
[6] Driskell quoted in Helen C. Smith, 'Black Art Sheds its "Primitive" Image', *Atlanta Constitution*, 13 January 1977.
[7] This essay introduces material from my extended research project on Driskell's curatorial record. Important repositories include archives held by the Solomon R. Guggenheim Museum Archives, New York; the David C. Driskell Center at the University of Maryland, College Park; and Talladega College Savery Library, Special Collections. Special thanks to David Conway at the Driskell Center and Perry Trice at Talladega College.
[8] Claude Clark taught art at Talladega College from 1948 to 1955.
[9] Exhibition announcement prepared by Driskell, October 1956, Savery Library Historical Collection, Talladega College. Driskell met James Johnson Sweeney, director of the Solomon R. Guggenheim Museum, in 1955.
[10] Driskell, announcement of art exhibitions for the 1958–59 academic year, September 1958, Savery Library Historical Collection, Talladega College.
[11] Driskell, letter to Arthur D. Gray, 29 March 1961, Savery Library Historical Collection, Talladega College.
[12] 'We sincerely urge you to take advantage of these cultural opportunities which sometimes are not available to us because of our geographical location.' Driskell, exhibition announcement, October 1956, Savery Library Historical Collection, Talladega College.
[13] Driskell was a member of the Arts Festival Committee, chaired by Dr J. Roland Braithwaite. The festival included a film screening, concert, flower arrangement contest, intercollegiate debate, theatre performance and art exhibitions. Sculpture by John Rood and paintings and prints by Driskell and students were on exhibition for the first festival.
[14] Albeit beyond the scope of this essay, the agency inherent to exhibition circulation at this time in the US is an important area of inquiry.
[15] A selection of the many Black artists to have feature exhibitions under Driskell's tenure at Fisk include: Elizabeth Catlett, Elton Fax, Earl Hooks, Richard Hunt, Jacob Lawrence, Sam Middleton, Keith Morrison, Alma Thomas, Mildred Thompson and Victor Young.
[16] Driskell in '3 Afro-Americans', 40th Annual Arts Festival Exhibition, Fisk University, 20 April–15 May 15 1969. Paintings by Merton Simpson, sculpture by Earl Hooks and photography by Bobby Sengstacke were exhibited on the occasion of Simpson's visit to Fisk University as guest artist. Sengstacke's photographs were on display in the student union.
[17] When Driskell left Talladega for Fisk, he recommended that President Gray hire Bhalla. Bhalla taught as Talladega from 1963 to 1967 and at Spelman College, where he was chair of the art department, from 1967 to 1979.
[18] 'Black Artists Exhibit at Fisk', *Chicago Defender (Big Weekend Edition) (1973–)*, 26 April 1975.
[19] The art caravan or mobile museum and theatre appear to have not been realized. Press reports do not mention the caravan, but some did mention performances.
[20] The HBCUs were Fisk University, Talladega College, Tougaloo College, LeMoyne-Owen College and Huston-Tillotson College (now Huston-Tillotson University), in collaboration with Amistad Research Center at Dillard University and the AMA. Press reports list the NEA award at $20,000. The NEA Annual Report for 1975 lists awards of $15,000 to the United Church Board for Homeland Ministries (under General Programs) and $5,000 to Fisk University for catalogue publication. Driskell was on the NEA Museums Advisory Board in 1975. See the NEA annual report for 1975, available at https://www.arts.gov/about/publications/1975-annual-report.
[21] Historian Clifton H. Johnson founded the Amistad Research Center in 1966 as a division of the United Church Board for Homeland Ministries (UCBHM) Race Relations Department and was its executive director. Originally located on the Fisk University campus, the Center moved to New

Orleans in 1970. Art historian Allan M. Gordon was professor of art at California State University, Sacramento. Gordon's essay is constructed as an interview with himself.

[22] The 'Amistad II' catalogue checklist includes 79 works by 53 artists, but not all works from the prototype exhibition at Fisk were on view at each venue; moreover, object counts differ in the publicity and various reviews of the exhibition, from 90 to 100.

[23] 'Amistad II' publicity card.

[24] Driskell, *Two Centuries of Black American Art* (exh. cat.), Los Angeles: Los Angeles County Museum of Art, 1976, p.11.

[25] Romare Bearden, 'The Black Man in the Arts', *New York Amsterdam News*, 26 June 1976. Bearden was one of the many advisory board members for the 'Amistad II' project.

[26] I look forward to Fisk University's 'African Modernism in America, 1947–1967' and 'Art and Activism at Tougaloo College', travelling exhibitions (2022–23) focused on HBCU collections with Driskell imprints, and to the ongoing creativity, agency and audacity of successive generations committed to the arts of the African diasporas.

Ruptures

The 2001 exhibition 'Freestyle' at the Studio Museum in Harlem, New York, curated by Thelma Golden and Christine Y. Kim, heralded the term *post–black* as a shift in the positioning of Black artists who were born after the civil rights era. At the same time, *post–black* reintroduced ongoing debates on identity and art. 'Freestyle', as a group exhibition of early-career Black artists, emphasized the Studio Museum's role in fostering young talent and introducing them to the wider public, and it attempted to redefine the meaning of Blackness for the twenty-first century. This section explores these ruptures and the questions they provoke; the problematics of Black representation triggered by *post–black* and the art market; and the importance of post-structural discourses and transdiasporic connections as part of *post–black* discourse.

'Freestyle' – How *Post-Black* Ruptured Black Art – Nana Adusei-Poku

The 2001 exhibition 'Freestyle', at the Studio Museum in Harlem, brought the introduction of the term *post-black* art by curator Thelma Golden – a maneuver met with modest enthusiasm at the time.[1] Spotlighting a younger generation of artists of African descent whose works ranged in theme and style, 'Freestyle' has since proven a transformative event, for Golden, for the Studio Museum in Harlem and for the artists, as well as for Black art discourse.[2] 'Freestyle' travelled to the Santa Monica Museum of Art in California, and *post-black* travelled with it.

As the newly appointed deputy director (later chief curator) of the Studio Museum, Golden was no novice when she conceptualized the exhibition (which was followed by 'Frequency' in 2006 and 'Flow' in 2008).[3] Born 1965 in Queens, Golden's early interest in museum work led to a curatorial apprenticeship at the Metropolitan Museum of Art while she was still attending the New Lincoln School, an experimental private secondary school.[4] Her internship at the Studio Museum in 1985, during her undergraduate studies in art history and African American studies at Smith College in Northhampton, Massachusetts, grew into a curatorial position. Soon after, she became a curator at the Whitney Museum of American Art, where she organized two controversial, much discussed and highly successful projects: the 1993 Whitney Biennial (co-curated with John G. Hanhardt, Lisa Phillips and Elisabeth Sussman) and 'Black Male: Representations of Masculinity in Contemporary Art' (1994–95). Golden left the Whitney after the appointment of Maxwell Anderson as director, replacing David Ross, and a 'curatorial restructuring' that resulted in her removal from the 2000 Whitney Biennial curatorial team.[5] From 1998 to 2000, Golden worked as a special project curator for contemporary art collectors Peter and Eileen Norton, before rejoining the Studio Museum.

Golden's intimate understanding of how Black artists had been historically, institutionally and economically positioned; her knowledge of African American art history; and her understanding of cultural discourses all culminated in a game-changing survey show. 'Freestyle' was not a critique of the art world's exclusion of Black artists, nor was it a political manifesto, nor did it claim a post-racial reality. The curatorial approach taken by Golden and assistant curator Christine Y. Kim was straightforward yet effective: they spoke to artists, made studio visits and selected artists' work, for a group exhibition that took place in a fairly small gallery (750 square metres).[6] The catalogue's front cover showcases a blue-tinted still from Dave McKenzie's video *Edward and Me* (2000), and the back features Eric Wesley's sculpture *Kicking Ass* (2000); its ninety pages of texts and images feature short essays (one to two pages in length) each pairing an exhibiting artist with an early- to mid-career curator, art historian or artist.[7] In her contribution, 'Post...', Golden proposes that a shift occured in the practices of Black artists around the turn of the century, distinguishing Black artists born after 1960 from previous generations. Drawing on conversations with artist Glenn Ligon, Golden offers the term *post-black* as 'a description of artists who were adamant about not being

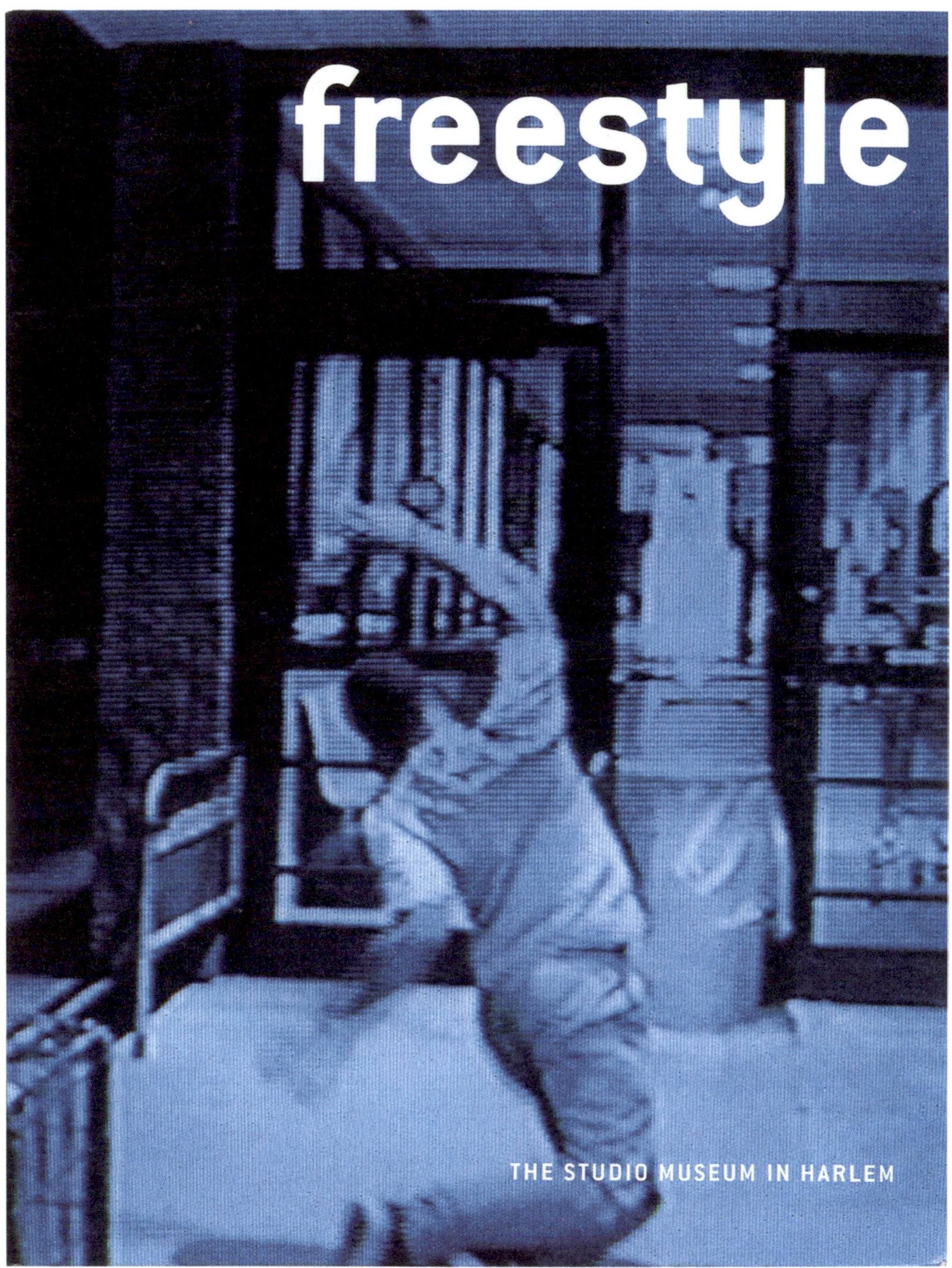
freestyle
THE STUDIO MUSEUM IN HARLEM

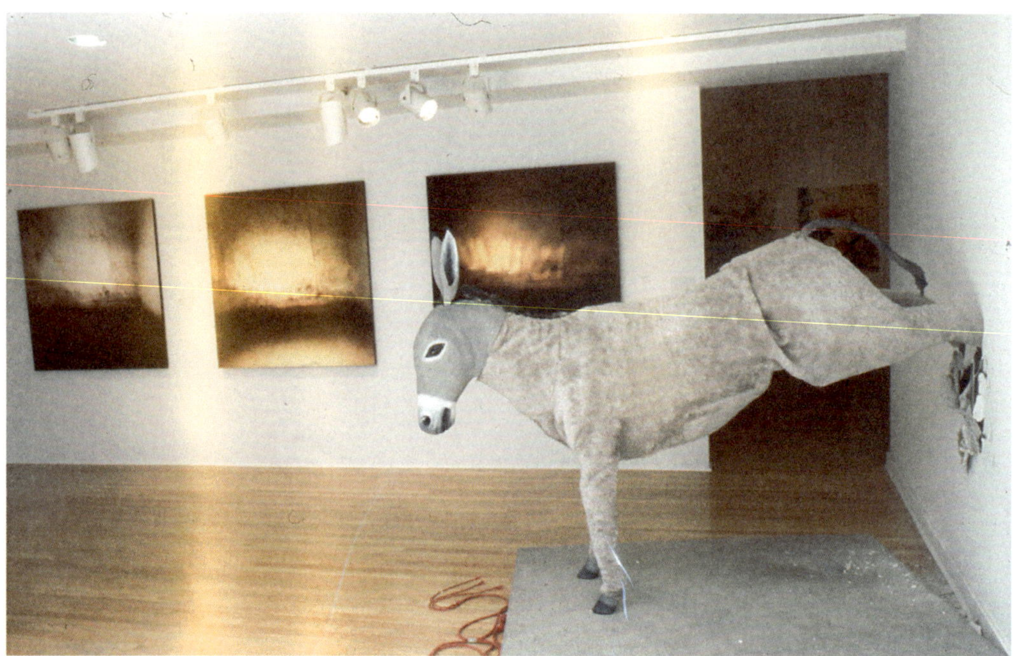

Installation views, 'Freestyle', the Studio Museum in Harlem, New York, 2001. Photo: Adam Reich. Courtesy the Studio Museum in Harlem Archives

Previous page: Cover of exhibition catalogue for 'Freestyle'. Courtesy the Studio Museum in Harlem Archives

labelled as "black" artists, though their work was steeped, in fact deeply interested, in redefining complex notions of blackness'.[8] Golden's use of *post-black* is fully aware of the conflicting politics it implies – the fixation on the term *black* and its simultaneous dissolution – and she highlights its chronological dimensions as well as its ideological repercussions.[9]

The curator and writer Hamza Walker's contextualizing essay 'Renigged' gives a critical account of his experiences of diversity politics and hyphenated identities. His observations capture succinctly the disparity between the potential of *post-black* and existing social realities. Walker emphasizes that hyphenated identities, which were introduced during the wave of multiculturalism in the 1980s and 90s, were artificial markers for the end of the civil rights movement and the Black Power era. He deliberately and proudly chooses not to embrace hyphenation, in order to stress the Black American experience as an open-ended narration rather than an (Aristotelian) story with beginning, middle (catharsis) and end.[10] Walker further elaborates on a 1989 newspaper article announcing the end of the integration era, and asks: 'So we had gone from post-segregation to post-integration. What happened to proper integration?'[11] In rightfully questioning the realization of what the article claimed had already taken place, Walker highlights his own observations of Black experience as not resonating with the proclamation of a post-integration era. He gives his experience of the deeply rooted, systemic racism manifest in institutions – whether at schools or in professional settings – as evidence of how multiculturalism, affirmative action and diversity politics had not yet delivered the promise of integration, equality and equity. Whilst pointing towards theoretical developments in cultural studies, Walker stresses the discrepancy between theory

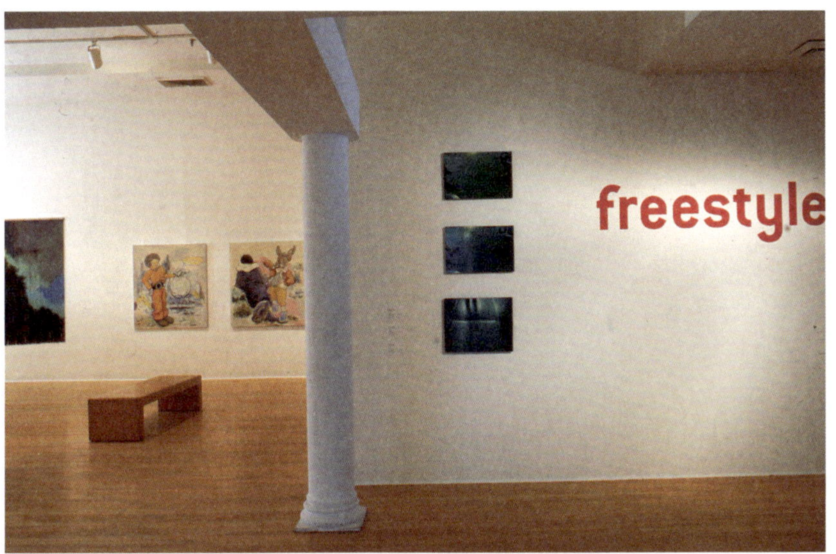
freestyle

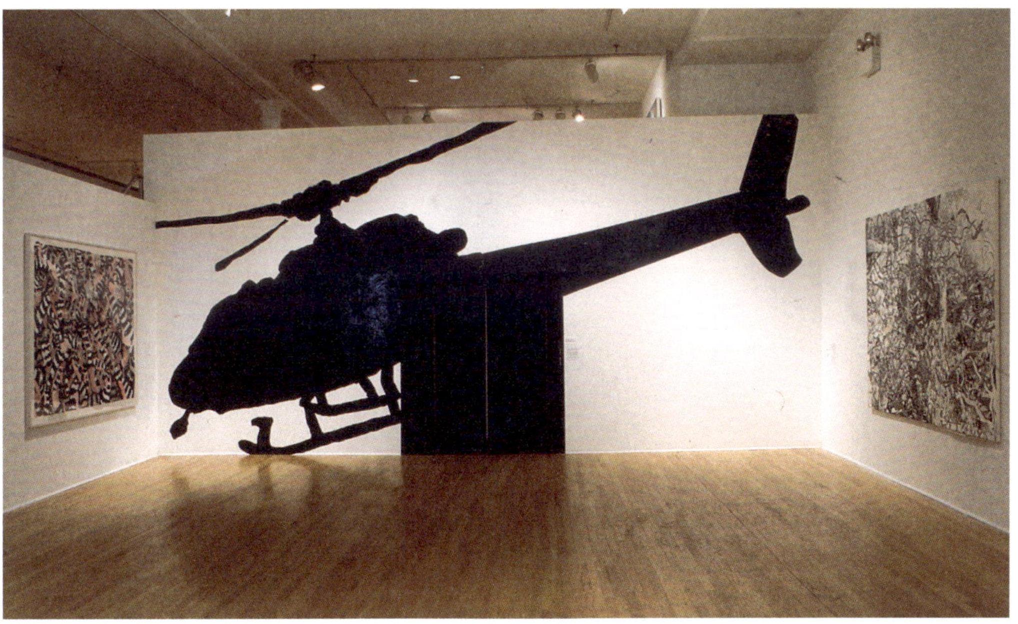

and practice. Hence, his insistence on claiming that *black* as a self-marker comes with an inconclusiveness as to what *black* means: 'I found discussions about race incredibly difficult to maintain because I had no idea for whom I was speaking, if anyone. The only voice I had was negational, one, I certainly could not imagine useful for constructively answering questions about an artist's relationship to his or her audience.'[12] Introducing the term 'renigged' in his closing remarks, Walker flags its use as exclusively for himself and as a catalyst to 'think about change and historical agency – questions that every generation will have to come to terms with, at some point'.[13] He emphasizes his generation's confrontation with a new set of questions.

For their part, Golden and Ligon use *post-black* in a sociological and art historical mode, as well as to describe a specific form of art by a specific group of artists. The questions that Golden's short essay highlights on *post-black* art include: 'How would this notion play out in the beginning of the twenty-first century? How would black artists make work after the vital activism of the 1960s, the focused, often essentialist, Black Arts Movement of the 1970s, the theory driven multiculturalism of the 1980s and the late globalist expansion of the late 90s?'[14] I argue that Golden's quandary can be effectively paraphrased in one short question: What does it mean to be Black in the contemporary and what kinds of aesthetics are produced as a result? 'Freestyle' was Golden's answer to that query.

Golden gave her most discussed and critically analyzed statement regarding *post-black* in a short interview she gave to the *Seattle Post*: 'There's no single way to think about it. I'm interested in its diversity and in bringing multiculturalism to the mainstream. I've become interested in younger black artists who are steeped in the postmodernist discourse about blackness but don't necessarily put it first. Glenn Ligon and I started calling it post-black. Post-black is the new black.'[15] Golden eloquently highlights two strategies while using provocation as a PR strategy. First, there is her emphasis on the potential of the term to transport notions of multiculturalism and thus make room for Black presence in mainstream art; second, she signals a change in the politics of representation by shifting away from post-modernist discourse. The provocation is the last sentence, as it somehow overwrites the sociohistoric dimension of the term *black* in the US context.

In 2009, I attended Golden's talk 'Post-Black Art Now' at Tate Britain in London, where she elaborated on 'Freestyle' and the *post-black* framing, in addition to offering insight into the Studio Museum exhibition 'Black Romantic: The Figurative Impulse in Contemporary African-American Art' (2002). After she delivered her talk, the Black British artist Raimi Gbadamosi, who was in the audience, asked Golden whether there is a desire to exhaust the word *black* in *post-black* as part of a new empowerment process? Her answer was a stringent 'No.' Quite the opposite, she said – she wanted to explore new boundaries, to be defined, of Blackness.[16] By insisting on the category of *black*, Golden clarifies that within the concept of *post-black* art, the political dimension still exists and identity politics are pitched against racism, with the desire to overcome a sociostructural fixity for Black individuals.

Gbadamosi's question would not have been possible if the concept didn't have so much room for interpretation. Golden's refusal to define *post-blackness* can be considered a provocation too. Asked to do so during a televised interview at the time of 'Freestyle', Golden explicitly raised the idea of 'provocation':

> *Well, that was a provocation of a sort. You know? I really with this exhibition wanted to sort-of open up a dialogue that would allow us to think about the kind of work that African American artists make a little bit differently. And there's a whole discourse of black art that emerged in the Black Arts Movement in the sixties, but of course has gone on as long as African American people have made work in this country. And I wanted to at least create what would even seem to be an artificial rupture because it comes from nothing but the fact that I did the show at this moment – but to create a rupture that would think about this body of work, this group of artists, this generation they represent, as being post-that. So, in the way that we speak about 'post-modern', 'post-feminism', 'post-anything', that this would set up a way to begin to talk about this a little bit differently.*[17]

My analysis of this is twofold: Golden's artificial rupture was necessary to bring much-overdue awareness to the multiplicity of practices that Black artists were engaged in during the early 2000s;[18] and secondly, this rupture potentially acknowledged, however indirectly, sociocultural and sociopolitical shifts. The 'sort of' in Golden's response reveals the spaces left open for misinterpretation – or better yet, free interpretation – of what these ruptures would bring into being. Rupture, from the latin *ruptura*, means to part by violence, as well as to create or induce a breakthrough. Whether in interviews or in her essay for the 'Freestyle' catalogue, Golden consistently leaves the reader with generalizations and yet insists on the process of redefining Black art and Blackness from the beginning of this century onwards: 'Most importantly, their (Black artists) work in all of its various forms, speaks to an individual freedom that is a result of this transnational moment in the quest to define ongoing changes in the evolution of African-American art and ultimately to an ongoing redefinition of blackness in contemporary culture.'[19]

The art historian and curator Courtney J. Martin has written that 'Freestyle' was oddly positioned in the art market calendar, having closed just two months prior to the monumental break that was 11 September 2001. That event would forcefully metamorphize the world as we knew it forever.[20] The 'War on Drugs', dating back to Republican US president Richard Nixon, transformed into the 'War on Terror', in the phrasing of Republican US president George W. Bush. Martin writes: 'Although no longer explicitly racial, the "color line" still runs through all these forms of domination. Paul Gilroy speaks of a "hemispheric order of racial domination", while Mills speaks of "the metaphysical infrastructure of global white supremacy".'[21] Systemic forms of racialization through the 'War on Terror' were magnified and the idea of multiculturalisms that had peaked in the 1990s slowly came to an end; neoliberal ideology – with its promises of endless growth, infinite wealth through entrepreneurship and market sovereignity – has continued to grow exponentially.

Group portraits of artists featured in 'Freestyle', in 'V-Gallery, The New Masters', *Vibe Magazine*, May 2001. Courtesy Jason Schmidt

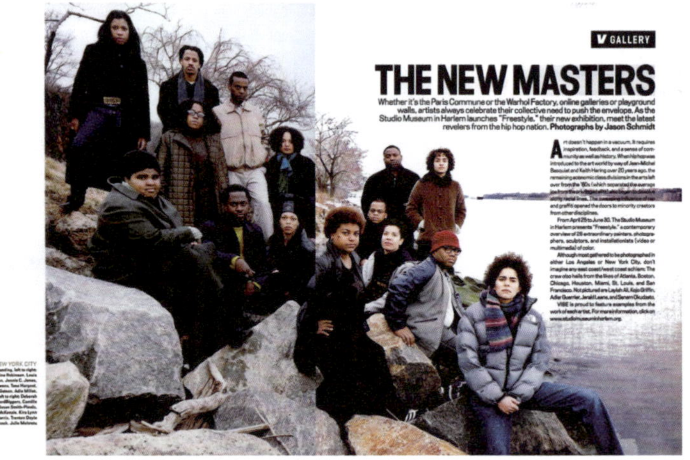

V GALLERY

THE NEW MASTERS

Whether it's the Paris Commune or the Warhol Factory, online galleries or playground walls, artists always celebrate their collective need to push the envelope. As the Studio Museum in Harlem launches "Freestyle," their new exhibition, meet the latest revelers from the hip hop nation. **Photographs by Jason Schmidt**

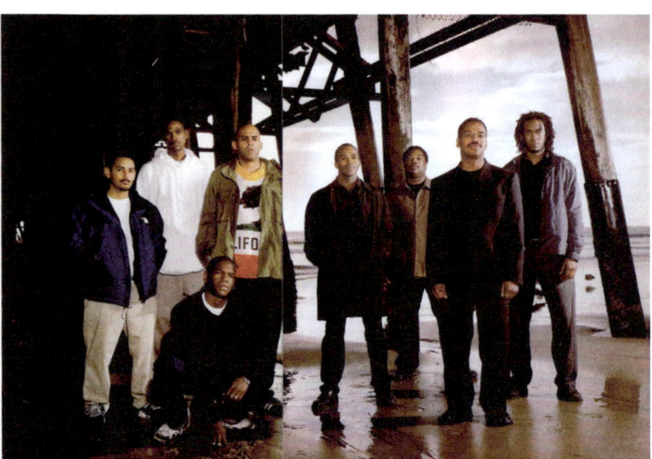

The idea of neoliberalism and its diversity politics may have had strength during the era of politicians such as Bill Clinton, Gerhard Schröder and Tony Blair, but their diversity politics and economic promises were shattered in 2008, exposing the widening gap between financial wealth and poverty. After its introduction by Golden and later discussion in Touré's publication *Who's Afraid of Post-Blackness?: What It Means to Be Black Now* (2011), for which he interviewed 105 individuals working in various fields and with a public profile, the term was seen as part of a neoliberal class discourse, where the individuals leading the discussion represent the Black American middle class and specifically those in power and able to talk about it.[22] But what about those who still operate on the margins of society? Neoliberalism operates by emphasizing an interest in personal growth, as opposed to forms of solidarity, and neoliberalism instrumentalizes ideas of Blackness. This is why it is important to highlight the questions that the artists in 'Freestyle' raised as they interrogated the 'global' network cultures and hybridity that neoliberalism stresses, as well as the conservative retreats it fosters. The moment when *post-black* emerged was one of great tension, but also of beginnings. If nothing is stable – including Blackness – we have to open our thoughts to ways of thinking that intrinsically include this instability.

In sum, the early 2000s dealt with a set of variables and glitches that opened up the possibility for a reconfiguration of what it means to be Black in the contemporary. Since art is an intrinisic form of knowledge production, the term *post-black*, as well as the exhibition 'Freestyle', did what art does best: it articulated sociopolitical as well as sociohistorical discourses to foreshadow conceptual and political changes that were a reality already present, but that hegemonic cultures were not ready to embrace. The 'messianic' position that Barack Obama would hold when he became, in 2008, the first person of African descent to be elected President of the United States, would connect 'Freestyle' forever with the changes it heralded.

I read *post-black* as a symptom of a discourse that was already in the making in Black studies (in the US) and cultural studies (in the UK) in the early 1990s, launched by the arrival of post-structuralism in the English-speaking world. Whether one engages with Hortense Spillers's close reading of Louis Althusser in *The Crisis of the Negro Intellectual: A Post-Date* (1994), listens to Stuart Hall's speech 'Race as a Floating Signifier' (1997) or thinks with Édouard Glissant's *Poetics of Relation* (1990; translated into English in 1993),[23] the time prior to the turn of the century was marked by a decisive shift in Black intellectual thought, towards a fusion and further integration of post-structuralist, post-Marxist and post-colonial theory. These frameworks make it clearly not possible to hold on to essentialisms and not possible to think about Blackness as exclusively African American.

With further investigation, one comes to understand the *post* in *post-black* as analogous to more established terms such as *post-modernism*, first introduced by Jean-François Lyotard in 1979 (and in English translation in 1984), and *post-feminism*, which emerged in 1985 in the writings of Toril Moi. Thus, a shift is signified, from one epoch into the next, indicating that different concepts, political frameworks and ideologies exist in synchronicity – not yet over, consistently about to become past if not countered or contradicted by the very same paradigms.[24]

Notes

A different version of this article was originally published in Nana Adusei-Poku, *Taking Stakes in the Unknown: Tracing Post-Black Art*, Bielefeld: Transcript, 2021.

[1] At the Studio Museum in Harlem, New York, 'Freestyle' was on view from 28 April–24 June 2001. 'Freestyle' traveled to Santa Monica Museum of Art from 29 September–18 November 2001. When Golden introduced the term *post-black*, she did not know that the art historian Robert Farris Thompson had noted in 1991: 'A retelling of Modernism to show how it predicts the triumphs of the current sequences would reveal that "the Other" is your neighbor – that black and Modernist cultures were inseparable long ago. Why use the word, "post-Modern" when it may also mean "postblack."' In so writing, Thompson highlighted the intertwined nature of the development of

modernism in the West and the inspiration borrowed from African and diasporic art. Robert Farris Thompson, 'Afro Modernism', *Artforum*, vol.30, no.1, September 1991, p.91.

[2] 'Freestyle' gathered 28 artists: Laylah Ali, John Bankston, Sanford Biggers (in collaboration with Jennifer Zackin), Mark Bradford, Louis Cameron, Rico Gatson, Deborah Grant, Kojo Griffin, Adler Guerrier, Trenton Doyle Hancock, Tana Hargest, Kira Lynn Harris, David Huffman, Jeral Ieans, Rashid Johnson, Vincent Johnson, Jennie C. Jones, Arnold Kemp, Dave McKenzie, Julie Mehretu, Adia Millett, Kori Newkirk, Camille Norment, Senam Okudzeto, Clifford Owens, Nadine Robinson, Susan Smith-Pinelo and Eric Wesley.

3 'Frequency', 9 November 2005–12 March 2006, and 'Flow', 2 April–29 June 2008, both at the Studio Museum in Harlem.

4 Golden's internship took place whilst Lowery Stoke Sims was the first African American curator at the Met.

[5] Okwui Enwezor, '"Elsewhere": A Conversation with Thelma Golden', *Nka Journal of Contemporary African Art*, issue 13–14, 2001, p.26.

[6] 'I came to the Studio Museum about seventeen months ago, when the museum underwent an amazing transition where the board hired Lowery Stokes Sims, who is a pre-eminent curator of modern art, who came to be the director. And Lowery hired me to come on. And the first thing I really wanted to do was to really do what I do best, which is to make an exhibition of emerging artists and art historical proposition.' Golden, interviewed on the *Charlie Rose* television programme, PBS, 2001.

[7] See *Freestyle* (exh. cat.), New York: The Studio Museum in Harlem, 2001. It is worth highlighting that many of the writers are now in leading positions in the field of African diasporic art and its related institutions, often in directorial roles. The pairings in the catalogue also created a dialogue that has since been carried by the 'post-black generation'.

[8] T. Golden, 'Post…', in *Freestyle*, *op. cit.*, p.14.

[9] *Ibid.*

[10] Hamza Walker, 'Renigged', in *Freestyle*, *op. cit.*, p.16.

[11] *Ibid*

[12] *Ibid.*, p.17.

[13] *Ibid.*

[14] T. Golden, 'Post…', *op. cit.*, p.15.

[15] Quoted in Regina Hackett, 'A Moment with ... Thelma Golden, Art Director', 31 March 2003, https://www.seattlepi.com/entertainment/article/A-moment-with-Thelma-Golden-art-director-1111034.php.

[16] 'The Status of Difference: Thelma Golden – Post-Black Art Now', 11 March 2009, available at https://www.tate.org.uk/audio/status-difference-thelma-golden-post-black-art-now.

[17] T. Golden, *Charlie Rose*, *op. cit.*

[18] For another argument with a strong focus on why multiplicity in Black art wasn't recognized, see Dawoud Bey, 'The Ironies of Diversity, or the Disappearing Black Artist', *Artnet*, 2014, http://www.artnet.com/magazine/features/bey/bey4-8-04.asp. Bey argues that the discourse of representation in the 1990s marginalized the variety of styles practiced by Black artists.

[19] T. Golden, 'Post…', *op. cit.*, p.15.

[20] Courtney J. Martin, 'Style, Influence, and the Freestyle Generation', in *Four Generations: The Joyner/Giuffrida Collection of Abstract Art*, New York: Gregory R. Miller, p.155.

[21] Robert Stam and Ella Shohat, *Race in Translation: Culture Wars around the Postcolonial Atlantic*, New York: New York University Press, 2012, p.63.

[22] Touré, *Who's Afraid of Post-Blackness?: What it Means to Be Black Now*, New York: Free Press, 2011. The book's interviewees include Michael Eric Dyson, Harold Ford, Jr, Henry Louis Gates, Jr, Malcolm Gladwell, Kamala Harris, Melissa Harris-Perry, Reverend Jesse Jackson, Glenn Ligon, Paul Mooney, Soledad O'Brien, David Paterson, Greg Tate, Kara Walker, Cornel West, Kehinde Wiley and many others. Many of these individuals are not from middle-class backgrounds but moved into the middle class through education or profession.

[23] Hortense J. Spillers, 'The Crisis of the Negro Intellectual: A Post-Date', *Boundary 2*, vol.21, no.3, 1994, pp.65–116; Stuart Hall, 'Race: The Floating Signifier', lecture at Goldsmiths College, London, 1997, available at https://www.youtube.com/watch?v=PodKki9g2Pw; Édouard Glissant, *Poetics of Relation* (trans. Betsy Wing), Ann Arbor: University of Michigan Press, 1997.

[24] On how 1970s and 80s feminisms are undermined by 'post-feminist' ideas of women's desires and rights, paired with an unrelenting neoliberalism, see Angela McRobbie, *The Aftermath of Feminism: Gender, Culture and Social Change*, London: Sage, 2009.

Does the Plantation End When the Market Begins? Personal Reflections and More Than a Few Questions in Personal and Public Practice Post-'Freestyle'
– Senam Okudzeto

For participating artists, 'Freestyle' (2001), was a moment of camaraderie, joy, excitement.[1] A broad range of artists, materials and media showcased a healthy dose of abstraction alongside notably tech-savvy digital and sonic works by women artists. Yet the current state of the art market throws up a reflection different from the sophisticated post-black imaginary promised two decades ago. Stepping into European art fairs, there are black bodies on sale everywhere – a strange over-representation of figurative painting, which is stark given the relative absence of black audience members. The ways in which these bodies are rendered, taken collectively, seems to flatten into imagery close to caricature. The disproportionate focus on two-dimensional analogue art is also notable in an art world where there are large numbers of black artists making abstract and digital art. As artists, we must ask ourselves if we have become complicit in some of the more sinister turns in popular representations of blackness? Is the same market that sold the ancestors in fact actively commodifying white guilt? Is there a process at hand, which is in fact colonizing the discourse of decolonization?

I want to question the history of the commodification of struggle in the Black Atlantic – and also maybe talk about ways in which I've looked for alternative forms of practice in the twenty years since 'Freestyle'. This response came up through visiting Art Basel in Switzerland in September 2021. I was shocked because the audience was very un-diverse, which is not always the case. But this year there were very few black people attending the fair. However, there was a disproportionately high amount of representation of black figuration. One felt that galleries were looking for representations of black people and black bodies, to hold up a kind of black figure in your booth as if it's some sort of talisman against the accusation of racism. Taken individually, it's not so disturbing, but when you repeatedly see galleries that have had no consistent relationship with people of colour over the last two decades suddenly showing these strange paintings of exaggerated blackness – where the works always show the black skin depicted in a very flat, two-dimensional way – without nuance, without context, often floating in an empty space it – I can only think of slaves on an auction block. And then, worse than that, realizing some of the depictions of black bodies produced in these strange ways were made by non-black artists.

My shock peaked at a work by Jenny Saville. Saville came to fame as part of the Young British Artists – the YBAs – in the mid-1990s, and herself once represented a desperately needed diversity in the art world, as a young, feminist painter who dealt with nonconforming representations of the female body. What I saw at Art Basel was an example of more recent work, these frightening paintings showing her body with the head of an African sculpture. Literally in blackface. What is even more traumatizing is the context, where every booth at the fair seems to have these strange two-dimensional portraits of black people.

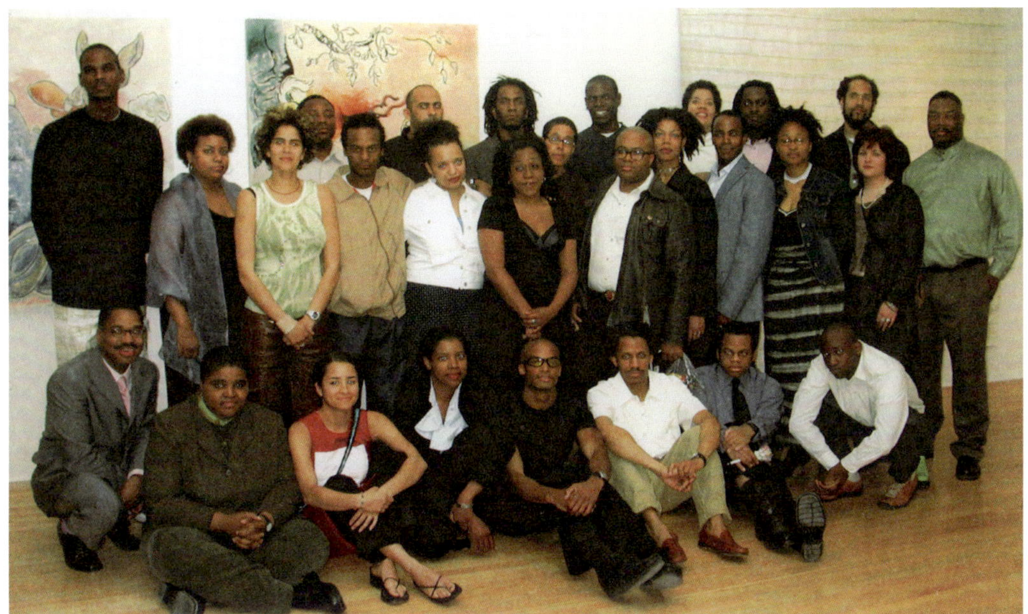

Group portrait of artists featured in 'Freestyle', the Studio Museum in Harlem, New York, 2001, including Senam Okudzeto (middle row, third from right). Courtesy the Studio Museum in Harlem Archives

To me, these images are a demand for a return to the moment in art history where the only position for people of African descent was as the unnamed authors of 'tribal art', as a source of inspiration for the (incorrectly presumed to be exclusively white) European early avant-garde; indeed, to a moment in the late nineteenth and early twentieth centuries when it was presumed that there should be no black protagonists. Even more problematic is that Jenny Saville named this series *Ancestors* – there is a body of work like this by her from around 2018, which clearly didn't sell at the time, and which made it to Art Basel. And I wondered, is this artist trying to insert herself into the discourse of blackness because it is such a strong currency?

So, it is in light of this context that I want to revisit what happened with 'Freestyle', twenty years ago. Because when 'Freestyle' came into the public eye, the work was cutting-edge for anybody from any background, whether black, white, blue or purple. You had women like Camille Norment making this incredible sonic digital work, which was very subtle and highly abstract. She presented a small, partially enclosed space full of highly polished metal poles that emitted a high-pitched resonant frequency, evoking disjunctive sensory spaces, where the only real direct reference to a black body was if you put your black body into this sonic space that she created.[2] Or someone like Tana Hargest, who was a computer programmer, and so was making this early, cutting-edge digital new media work and programming all the code herself.[3] Same with Nadine Robinson. I mean, Nadine and I were artists in residence at the Studio Museum in Harlem in 2000–01, at the same time as Julie Mehretu; and Nadine was always wiring up her sound installations – works that she called 'Boom paintings' – and her speakers in very complex ways. These 'paintings' often consisted of a large grid of canvases with embedded loudspeakers

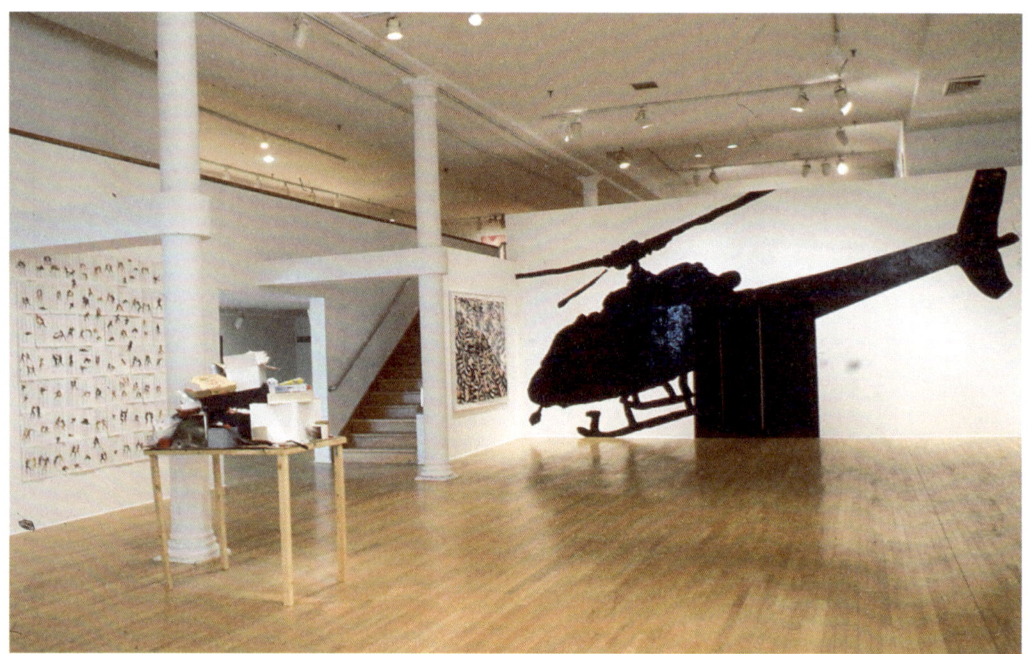

Installation view, 'Freestyle', the Studio Museum in Harlem, 2001. Courtesy the Studio Museum in Harlem Archives

in series, each broadcasting a different recorded sound piece which made a commentary on black emancipation movements. The works also subtly referenced the canon of American modernism – Nadine would always say to me, 'Senam, remember the three R's: Ryman, Rauschenberg and Robinson.' And we'd laugh, but she was serious. These works were also in part a nod to her Jamaican American heritage, turning the sound system into a modernist archive of political narrative.

What I produced for 'Freestyle' was my work *Long Distance Lover* (1999–2001). This was painted on 98 pages of my British Telecom bills from when I lived in London and had a boyfriend in New York. And this work was inspired very much by Paul Gilroy's *The Black Atlantic* (1993),[4] which really spoke to me because my mother is American and my father is from Ghana, but I am also British. My identity is between the poles of the Black Atlantic – between Nigeria, Ghana, the UK and the US. I feel like a lot of the ways in which we've been able to articulate ourselves in visual culture and within identity and politics comes through the discourse created through the African American experience.[5] I wanted to make a work which talked about that, but also talked about my own personal life. And this work also deals with figuration, so you can understand that my anxiety about the new commodification of black bodies – which really makes the market feel like a slave auction, when you have none of the black collectors present and you have no black audiences. This, as I said, causes particular anxiety to me (in Europe).

In the last few years, I've moved away from pure figuration unless it's used in the context of an installation, and I've started working more with counter-

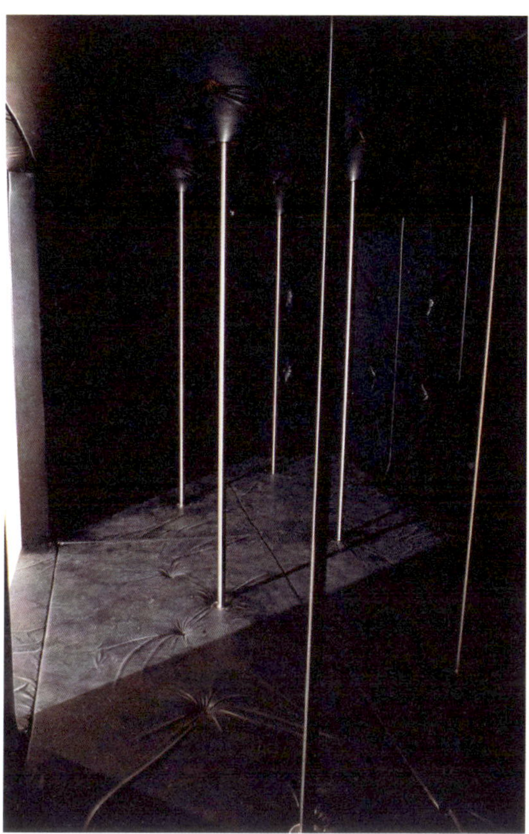

Camille Norment, *Notes from the Undermind*, 2001. Installation view, 'Freestyle'. Courtesy the Studio Museum in Harlem Archives

Nadine Robinson, *Americana*, 2001. Installation view, 'Freestyle'. Courtesy the Studio Museum in Harlem Archives

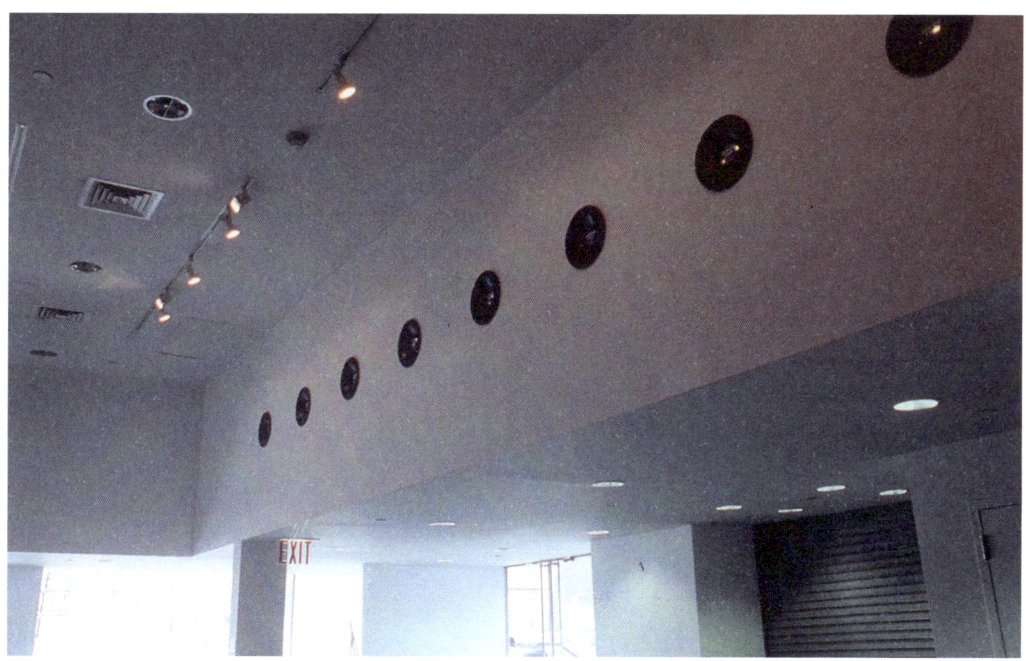

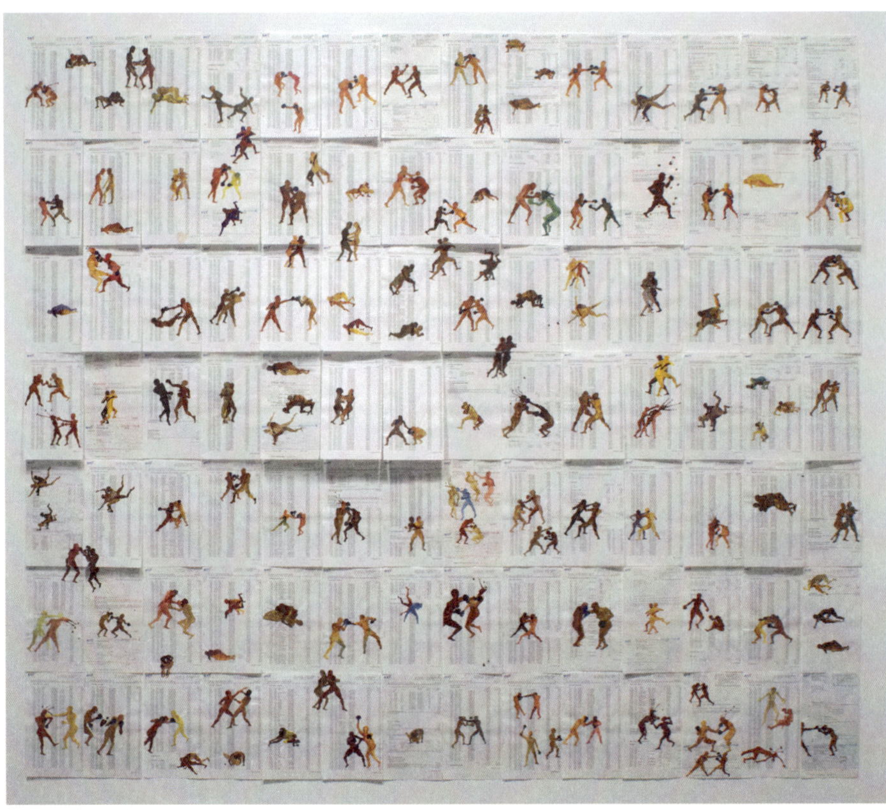

Senam Okudzeto, *Long Distance Lover*, 1998–2000, acrylic on 98 pages of British Telecom phone bills, 213.4 × 238.8cm. Photo: Paul Hester. Courtesy the artist

narratives – revisiting different moments in history that represent narratives of modernity and modernism, both artisically and politically to examine Black and African histories that have been overlooked. Take, for example, *The Frigidaires of Justice / She Was a Test Pilot in the Name of the King / I Command You the Chickens of Empire* (2018), which is about recovering feminist history in relation to architecture, modernity and memory in Ghana. Or *Disappearing Africans* (2020), a film installation I was commissioned to make for 'Exotic? Regarder l'ailleurs en Suisse au siècle des Lumières' ('Exotic? Switzerland Looking Outward in the Age of Enlightenment'). For this exhibition, a really young, dynamic group of Swiss curators came together with the idea that they wanted to question the history of Switzerland post-Enlightenment in a critical way – because Swiss people have the idea that they were not involved in the slave trade and the commodification of black people. Yet the exhibition argued that there are very clear links through the trade of fabrics like cotton, and that some Swiss people had invested and had interests in plantations. I discovered through researching the work of the eighteenth-century Enlightenment philosopher Anton Wilhelm Amo that there was a Swiss medical surgeon who wrote an 'important' manual on how to keep your slaves alive through the Middle Passage.[6] This actually wasn't known to the curators of 'Exotic?', and while dealing with the exhibition, I kept coming across texts which the curators and catalogue art historians felt uncomfortable

BT

Your Customer No. WE 8400 6072 Q004
Date (and tax point) 13 May 1998

Breakdown of information for 0171-723 8982 Page 27 of 38

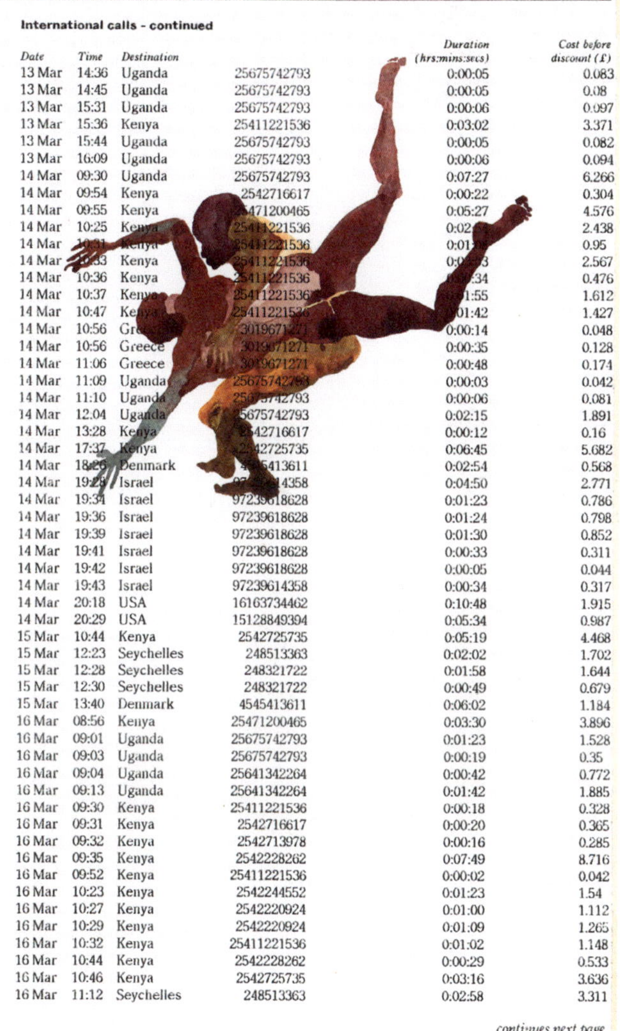

International calls - continued

Date	Time	Destination		Duration (hrs:mins:secs)	Cost before discount (£)
13 Mar	14:36	Uganda	25675742793	0:00:05	0.083
13 Mar	14:45	Uganda	25675742793	0:00:05	0.08
13 Mar	15:31	Uganda	25675742793	0:00:06	0.097
13 Mar	15:36	Kenya	25411221536	0:03:02	3.371
13 Mar	15:44	Uganda	25675742793	0:00:05	0.082
13 Mar	16:09	Uganda	25675742793	0:00:06	0.094
14 Mar	09:30	Uganda	25675742793	0:07:27	6.266
14 Mar	09:54	Kenya	2542716617	0:00:22	0.304
14 Mar	09:55	Kenya	[illegible]	0:05:27	4.576
14 Mar	10:25	Kenya	25411221536	[illegible]	2.438
14 Mar	[illegible]	[illegible]	25411221536	[illegible]	0.95
14 Mar	[illegible]	Kenya	25411221536	[illegible]	2.567
14 Mar	10:36	Kenya	25411221536	[illegible]	0.476
14 Mar	10:37	Kenya	25411221536	[illegible]	1.612
14 Mar	10:47	[illegible]	[illegible]	[illegible]	1.427
14 Mar	10:56	[illegible]	[illegible]	0:00:14	0.048
14 Mar	10:56	Greece	[illegible]	0:00:35	0.128
14 Mar	11:06	Greece	[illegible]	0:00:48	0.174
14 Mar	11:09	Uganda	[illegible]	0:00:03	0.042
14 Mar	11:10	Uganda	[illegible]	0:00:06	0.081
14 Mar	12.04	Uganda	[illegible]	0:02:15	1.891
14 Mar	13:28	Kenya	[illegible]	0:00:12	0.16
14 Mar	[illegible]	Kenya	[illegible]	0:06:45	5.682
14 Mar	[illegible]	Denmark	[illegible]	0:02:54	0.568
14 Mar	[illegible]	Israel	[illegible]	0:04:50	2.771
14 Mar	19:34	Israel	[illegible]	0:01:23	0.786
14 Mar	19:36	Israel	97239618628	0:01:24	0.798
14 Mar	19:39	Israel	97239618628	0:01:30	0.852
14 Mar	19:41	Israel	97239618628	0:00:33	0.311
14 Mar	19:42	Israel	97239618628	0:00:05	0.044
14 Mar	19:43	Israel	97239614358	0:00:34	0.317
14 Mar	20:18	USA	16163734462	0:10:48	1.915
14 Mar	20:29	USA	15128849394	0:05:34	0.987
15 Mar	10:44	Kenya	2542725735	0:05:19	4.468
15 Mar	12:23	Seychelles	248513363	0:02:02	1.702
15 Mar	12:28	Seychelles	248321722	0:01:58	1.644
15 Mar	12:30	Seychelles	248321722	0:00:49	0.679
15 Mar	13:40	Denmark	4545413611	0:06:02	1.184
16 Mar	08:56	Kenya	25471200465	0:03:30	3.896
16 Mar	09:01	Uganda	25675742793	0:01:23	1.528
16 Mar	09:03	Uganda	25675742793	0:00:19	0.35
16 Mar	09:04	Uganda	25641342264	0:00:42	0.772
16 Mar	09:13	Uganda	25641342264	0:01:42	1.885
16 Mar	09:30	Kenya	25411221536	0:00:18	0.328
16 Mar	09:31	Kenya	2542716617	0:00:20	0.365
16 Mar	09:32	Kenya	2542713978	0:00:16	0.285
16 Mar	09:35	Kenya	2542228262	0:07:49	8.716
16 Mar	09:52	Kenya	25411221536	0:00:02	0.042
16 Mar	10:23	Kenya	2542244552	0:01:23	1.54
16 Mar	10:27	Kenya	2542220924	0:01:00	1.112
16 Mar	10:29	Kenya	2542220924	0:01:09	1.265
16 Mar	10:32	Kenya	25411221536	0:01:02	1.148
16 Mar	10:44	Kenya	2542228262	0:00:29	0.533
16 Mar	10:46	Kenya	2542725735	0:03:16	3.636
16 Mar	11:12	Seychelles	248513363	0:02:58	3.311

0000015

continues next page

This page and following spread: Senam Okudzeto, *Long Distance Lover* (details). Photo: Adam DeCroix. Courtesy the artist

about, because they mentioned the words *nègre* or *Neger* ('negro' in French and German respectively). The curators and writers felt these words were offensive and should be deleted, so they would write *n****. And then they'd have a little asterisk: 'This word is offensive, we mustn't use it anymore.' So they'd try not to use it at all. And I said to them, 'Well, look, this is really problematic, because you can't erase this history or the fact that people said this. Furthermore, if I'm researching the history of racism and you remove all the racist words from the database, I'm going to have a hard time finding materials, because you have changed history to make your forefathers seem nicer than they actually were. Maybe there's a reason you've done this – because

Your Customer No. WE 8394 1746 Q011
Date (and tax point) 21 February 1999

Local calls - continued

Date	Time	Destination		Duration (hrs:mins:secs)	Cost before discount (£)
16 Feb	15:04	London	0171 724 5342	0:00:05	0.042
16 Feb	22:35	London	0171 266 5154	0:00:07	0.042
17 Feb	10:38	London	0171 266 5154	0:07:16	0.243
17 Feb	11:08	London	0171 263 4561	0:07:39	0.256
17 Feb	12:53	London	0171 937 8613	0:00:34	0.042
17 Feb	16:00	London	0171 385 5835	0:15:15	0.512
17 Feb	16:16	London	0171 911 8427	0:00:04	0.042
17 Feb	16:17	London	0171 911 8214	0:00:02	0.042
17 Feb	16:18	London	0171 937 8613	0:03:15	0.108
17 Feb	16:26	London	0171 911 8427	0:00:08	0.042
17 Feb	16:30	London	0171 737 6296	0:00:15	0.042
17 Feb	16:40	London	0171 385 5835	0:11:23	0.382
17 Feb	18:10	London	0171 373 3421	0:09:37	0.12
17 Feb	18:20	London	0171 499 8408	0:00:56	0.042
17 Feb	18:21	London	0171 499 8408	0:03:33	0.044
18 Feb	09:[illegible]0	London	0171 409 1900	0:07:31	0.252
18 Feb	15:1[illegible]	London	0171 385 5835	0:00:45	0.042

	Number of calls	Duration (hrs:mins:secs)	Cost before discount (£)
Total local calls	598	41:05:39	£ 63.12

Regional & national calls

Date	Time	Destination			Duration (hrs:mins:secs)	Cost before discount (£)
12 Dec	13:51	Eastleigh	01703 653[illegible]		0:00:26	0.042
12 Dec	15:41	Sevenoaks	01732 456775		0:00:38	0.042
13 Dec	21:46	Brighton	01273 703273		0:00:26	0.042
13 Dec	21:47	Brighton	01273 703273		0:07:47	0.195
13 Dec	23:07	Eastleigh	01703 653920		[illegible]2:23	0.812
18 Dec	15:16	Brighton	01273 70[illegible]		[illegible]:32	0.042
18 Dec	23:26	Brighton	[illegible]		[illegible]	0.14
28 Dec	16:24	Brighton	01273 675886		0:03:19	0.222
28 Dec	20:51	Bristol	0117 973 7167		0:01:34	0.055
30 Dec	15:48	Charsfield	01473 737272		[illegible]:13:02	0.876
1 Jan	14:17	Milland	01428 741219	!OFFER!	[illegible]:01	0.425
3 Jan	14:57	Sevenoaks	01732 456775		[illegible]31	0.514
3 Jan	15:49	Eastleigh	01703 653920		0:00:01	0.042
8 Jan	16:20	Manchester	0161 275 3711		0:00:45	0.049
10 Jan	15:29	Charsfield	01473 737272		0:12:44	0.319
12 Jan	15:13	Cardiff	01222 380003		0:05:30	0.369
15 Jan	22:31	Cambridge	01223 526311		0:36:59	1.312
19 Jan	09:51	Milland	01428 741219		0:01:24	0.093
11 Feb	12:54	Eastleigh	01703 653920		0:00:30	0.042

	Number of calls	Duration (hrs:mins:secs)	Cost before discount (£)
Total regional & national calls	19	[illegible]:45:30	5.633

International calls

Date	Time	Destination			Duration (hrs:mins:secs)	Cost before discount (£)
26 Nov	20:47	USA	19176868644	USA Plan	0:00:24	0.057
26 Nov	22:52	USA	12138765504	USA Plan	0:00:51	0.119

continues next page

0000017

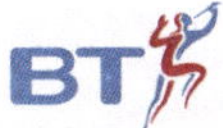

Your Customer No. WE 8394 1746 Q011
Date (and tax point) 21 February 1999

VAT zero-rated items

1 Charges

Reference number

Dates	*Description*	*Quantity*	*Quarterly rate (£)*	*Cost (£)*
22 Nov	430 BT TALKTIME MINS W/E LOCAL RATE From BT Chargecard			-4.30
Total charges				-£ 4.30

Amendments to a previous bill

1 For bill dated 22 November 1998

Description	*Amount (£)*
VAT Refund Correction Dec 98	2.69
ChargeCard VAT refund - Dec 98	-2.69
ChargeCard VAT refund - Dec 98	-2.69
Total amendments to a previous bill	-2.69
Total VAT zero-rated items	-£ 6.99

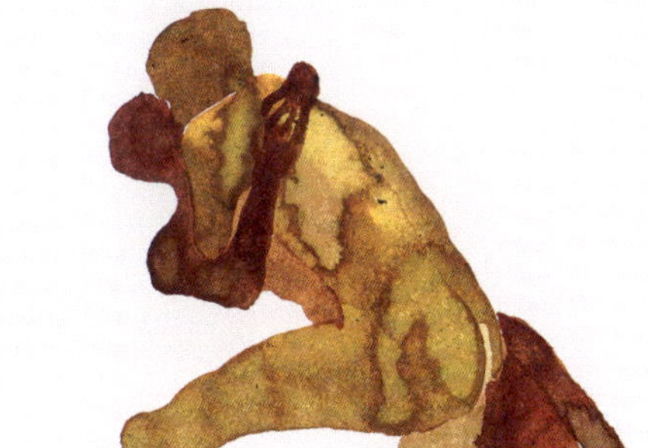

0000017

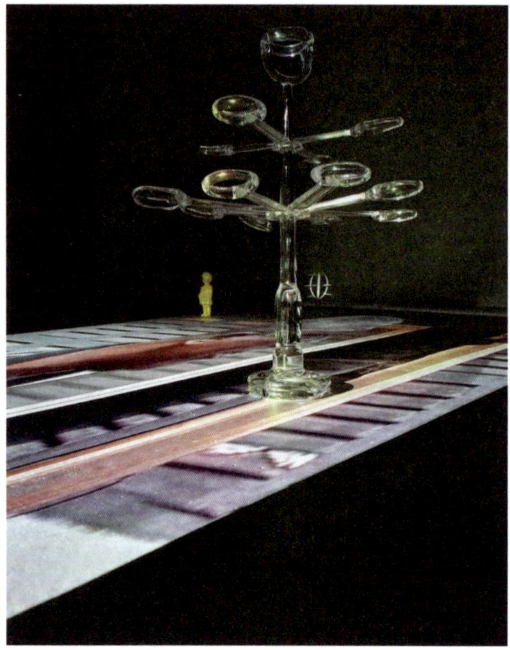

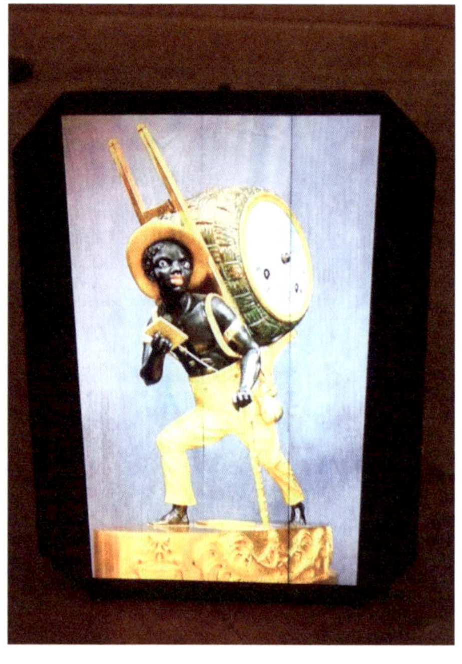

Left:
Senam Okudzeto, *The Frigidaires of Justice / She Was a Test Pilot in the Name of the King / I Command You the Chickens of Empire* (detail), 2018, multimedia installation (digital video, 15:22 min; lead crystal sculpture; iron sculpture; plastic dolls; antique silver coin; ceramic bowl). Photo: Lea Zeitman. Courtesy the artist

you don't trust your students to learn the nuance of why we can't forget these racist histories. But one of the problems is, we're constantly having people re-write history to suit their current positions. We're pretending that we haven't gone through these historic periods of erasure – apartheid, slavery, colonialism – which constantly erase black histories, black voices and black contexts.'

So *Disappearing Africans* does a kind of physical re-enactment of the erasures of history. It's based on these two clocks from a historic museum that are in the exhibition: so the one clock shows a slave with a bale of cotton on his back and a gilt timepiece; the other is a version of this that is fully gilt and shows a white peasant. And while the camera rotates around that, you have an image of me lit by a candle, which represents the failure of the Enlightenment. Then a hand comes out of nowhere, paints my face black, and I disappear. And then the same thing happens to a colleague of mine, Brendhan Dickerson, who is a white South African. And he also is painted, and as

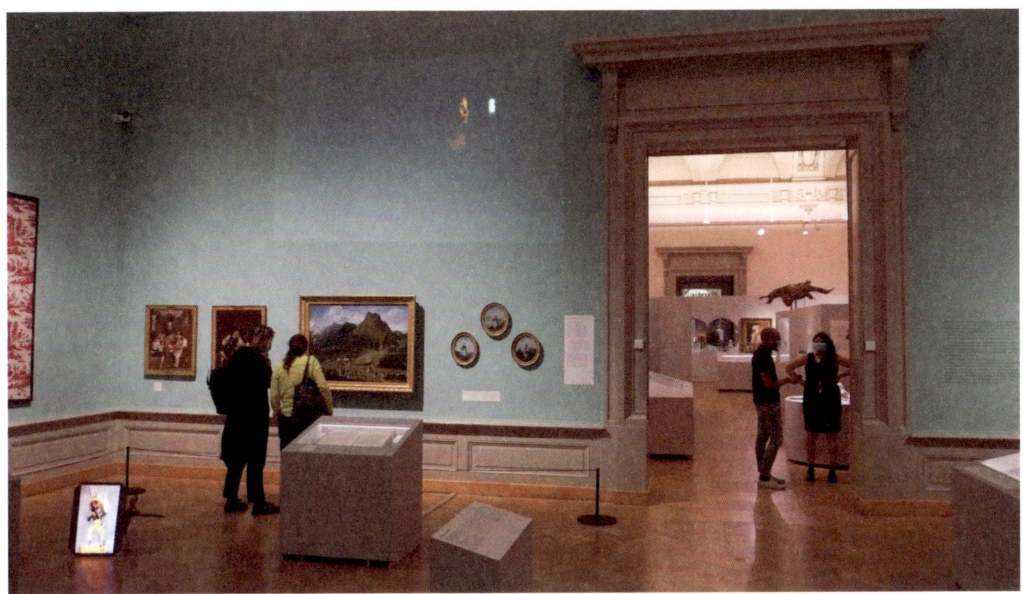

Senam Okudzeto, *Disappearing Africans*. Installation view, 'Exotic? Regarder l'ailleurs en Suisse au siècle des Lumières', Palais de Rumine, Lausanne, 2020–21. Photo and courtesy the artist

Opposite: Senam Okudzeto, *Disappearing Africans* (detail), 2020, multimedia installation (two-channel video projection, 16:56 min; antique wooden table). Photo and courtesy the artist

he's painted, he becomes this horrible caricature, and then he disappears. So it basically says that the dehumanization of racism suffered by black people really points to the dehumanization of society as a whole. In Europe in the last decades, I see more and more caricatures of black people, which people imagine are anti-racist – they're actually pulling up racist, stereotyped images of black people and presenting them as if they're doing us a favour in actually representing us, because so little nuance is available. The film ends with a text in French and in English, which calls for the designation of blackface as a hate crime, the idea that wherever it appears, it should be designated as a hate crime; and that, because of that, even *Disappearing Africans* will itself eventually have to disappear because these representations have to stop.

And this brings me back to my experience at Art Basel 2021 where the over-representation of black figuration really gave me a shock and changed my whole intention about what we should talk about post 'Freestyle'. Because it felt like all the ground that was won through 'Freestyle' had somehow been lost, because blackness has become a commodity that demands clear identification (rather than the ambiguous promise of 'post-blackness' the show so cleverly proffered). Whereas the premise of 'Freestyle' was that we were going to complicate blackness in such a way that our skills as artists were going to dominate the discourse. We were never abandoning blackness – it's one of the things that you can never undo – but we were going to make work that was so formally and technically brilliant that blackness was not the identifying final thing you took away from it.

We can forget that 'Freestyle' was also important because there was very little gallery representation for contemporary black artists in the early 2000s. I feel like Thelma Golden really worked overtime to try and erase this horrible

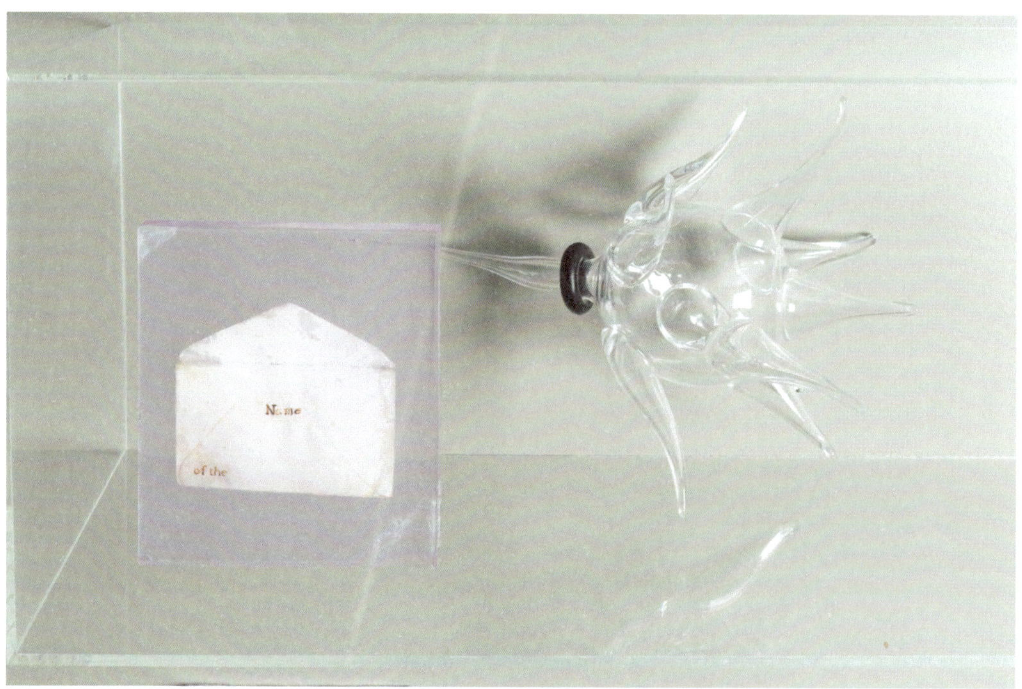

Senam Okudzeto, *Name of the Father* (left), 2019, resin, approx. 14.7 × 16.8 × 2cm; *The Meeting of Light and Earthly Gravitations; Crystal Currency no. 9* (right), 2017, lead crystal and black rubber cock ring, approx. 44 × 31cm. Photo: Margot Montigny. Courtesy the artist

legacy we had where, if you were successful, the market would want to say you're the one, the next Basquiat – you're not like the other people, you know? And she was like, 'I'm bombarding you with thirty artists who are equally brilliant. You cannot single them out.' You had artists who were working in the decades before and who were successful – Nari Ward or Kara Walker, for example – but in a way they were kind of isolated. Whereas Thelma really cracked the market for us once and for all. So it seems very strange that the majority of the artists from 'Freestyle' did not subsequently enter the market in the very strong way we are seeing younger artists in the market today, with the exception of Julie Mehretu and Mark Bradford – and it's for good reason that these two became very successful. But let's think about it. Where's that legacy of the larger group? Because the success of Mehretu and Bradford meant that we could revisit other black abstract artists, people like Jack Whitten and Sam Gilliam, because suddenly, in the world that didn't care about black artists in Europe or the USA, there was an interest in the forefathers who paved the way for contemporary successors. But that was forgotten, or the critical transition that 'Freestyle' represented has been forgotten.

Part of the problem is that blackness has become such a strong commodity. We're at a point where we don't have clear genres, and blackness has become one of the things that is very easily identifiable in the market, and it's also highly profitable. We're seeing artists go for millions – young emerging artists, most of them very good. However, because those works are out of reach, galleries are scrambling to find other work to sell. My gripe is that artists, before they mature, are being grabbed and flung into the market – and you're getting artists who aren't fully aware of or able to control the context of their work. Furthermore, I'm ranting from Europe. I think that in America a much richer frame exists. One of the things that annoys me is the work doesn't come with its intellectual frame when exported internationally. This rich, nuanced, complex discourse doesn't make it over the pond. So you get art without art history. You literally only get the commodity, these flat representations. And sometimes when you have complicated artists with very complex narratives, they'll get a solo show at a big museum and the museum will be like, 'Oh, we don't want to give any of that Black American history context. You know, it's so complicated. We respect the work formally, so we don't need the historical context.' And yet you have all this work – say, Theaster Gates or Kara Walker – which comes with very clear responses to very real historical experiences that are not a kind of fictive imagination or imaginary or memory. A real homage to the resilience of black people through civil rights, through slavery, through colonialism. To remove that – to remove those historical contexts – is a violence.

So what have I done to get over it? What have I been doing in the past twenty years? I've been making work and writing. But one of the things that's really nurtured me has been teaching, and also setting up Art in Social Structures, an NGO in Ghana, where we work on recovering lost forms of heritage and contemporary art and architecture. In 2019, I took six of my favourite French students to Nigeria for an exchange with two institutions there, the University of Nigeria, Nsukka and Yaba College of Technology. El Anatsui sponsored the trip and we got to visit El's studio to see his work just before the Venice Biennale, which was so inspiring. I want to highlight this teaching work as a counterpoint – because the market has become so strange and so frightening due to the immense corruption that large sums of money bring. I quit the commercial world because I was always catching dealers trying to steal from me, and when I caught them stealing I became angry, and then creatively and emotionally blocked. I have found that the most rewarding place is the classroom; I feel the importance of reclaiming history and creating complex narratives through education is coming up more strongly than ever now. It is very important that those of us who practice art teach and pass skills on, as well as our perspectives and context, because too many art schools have been handed over to administrators who do not practice.

When I was Visiting Professor at ENSAPC (École nationale supérieure d'arts de Paris Cergy) in Paris, I taught a seminar on recovering the positions of black protagonists in the canon of European artistic modernity. I think that among the things we need to recapture in art history, or rediscover, are the discourses between important white and black European figures in the 1920s onwards. In my experience Art Basel felt like a demand to return to a false impression of this earlier moment which incorrectly presumes there were no black European protagonists. Today, this should also prompt critical reflection on that milieu – Karl Einstein wrote for *Présence Africaine*, and a lot of the other people like him who were involved with George Bataille's *Documents*, working with Cheikh Anta Diop and others in anti-colonial publications like *Présence Africaine*. The black European founders of Negritude literally

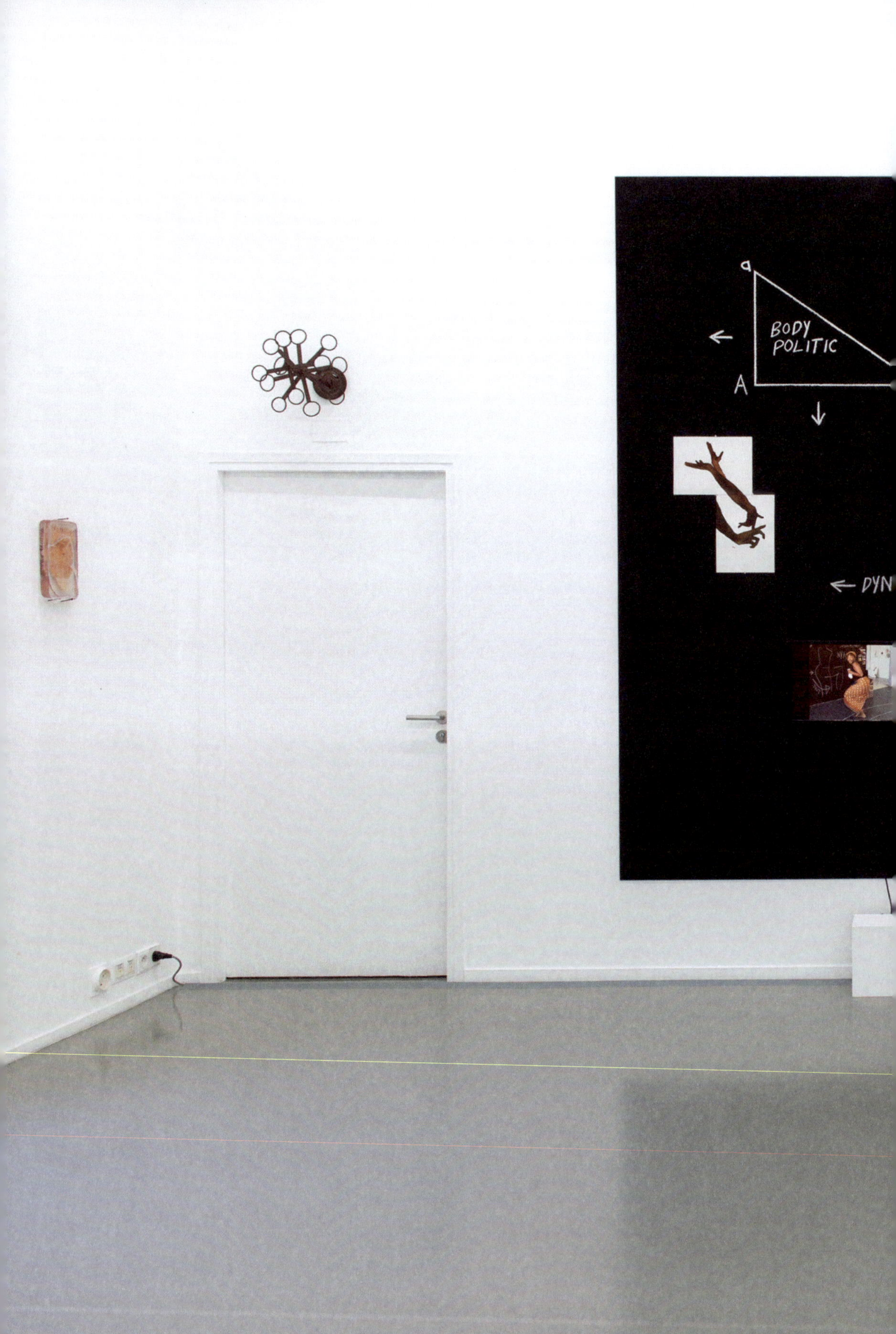
BODY
POLITIC
DYN

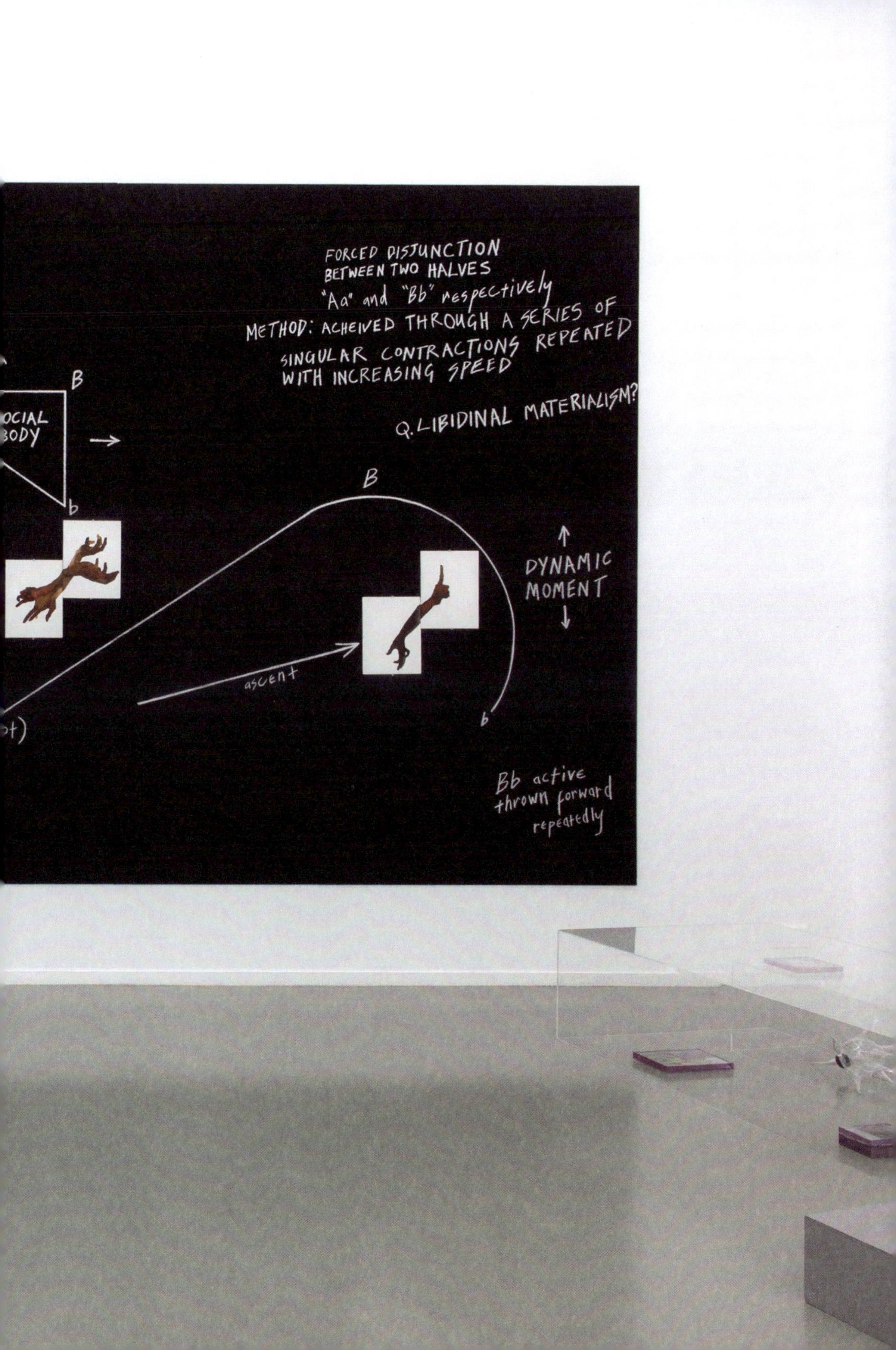

FORCED DISJUNCTION
BETWEEN TWO HALVES
"Aa" and "Bb" respectively
METHOD: ACHEIVED THROUGH A SERIES OF
SINGULAR CONTRACTIONS REPEATED
WITH INCREASING SPEED

B

OCIAL
BODY

Q. LIBIDINAL MATERIALISM?

b

B

DYNAMIC
MOMENT

ascent

b

ot)

Bb active
thrown forward
repeatedly

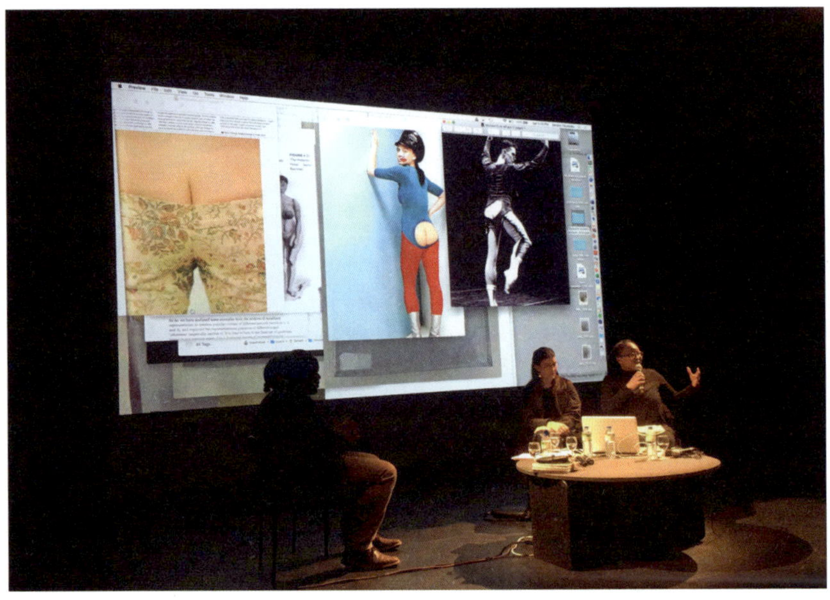

Senam Okudzeto (seated to the right) speaking at the symposium 'Afro-Modernity and Feminist Discourse', Centre Culturel Suisse, Paris, 15 February 2020. The on-screen images featured in Okudzeto's 2005 feminist Lacanian lecture performance accompanying the installation *The Dialectic of Jubilation*. Photo: Claire Hoffmann. Courtesy the artist

Previous spread: Senam Okudzeto, *The Dialectic of Jubilation; Afro Funk Lessons*, 2002–05, multimedia installation (video, 9:47 min.; acrylic on paper; paint and chalk drawings on wall), approx. 301 × 400cm. Installation view, 'We Wanted the Object to be the Subject (Before We Wanted the Reverse)', Centre Culturel Suisse, Paris, 2019. Photo: Margot Montigny. Courtesy the artist

commissioned important white European thinkers to write anti-racist works for publication. There are countless examples. And, you know, Jean-Paul Sartre was asked by Léopold Sénghor to write what became one of the most important historic texts for black emancipation and anti-colonial movements: 'Orphée Noir' ('Black Orpheus', 1948) as an introduction to his own book.[7] There was a collaboration, there was a discourse. So, we need to recapture the conversations they were having with each other, which are now out of date, and which maybe black people tolerated because they thought it was breaking down barriers – you know, thinking things would get better, not worse. They may have been better off back then than we are now.

I still feel there's a duty to art, which involves pedagogy, that I can't walk away from yet. Because, even if I'm teaching in West Africa, my students are getting the same material from the same art world. They get the same stereotype-based positions that need to be unlearned, and they need to be offered alternative positions. So unfortunately, we don't get to take a day off. The struggle is to demand diversity of practice. Diversity of practice means having the right to work on things – all the things that you care about: environment, gender, politics, economics and so forth. But one runs the risk that art history will then just erase all those other complicated narratives and reduce you to a discourse of blackness. How do we insist upon and create the grounds for diversity of practice and the right to have authority in diverse fields of practice? That is the great struggle.

Notes

[1] 'Freestyle', curated by Thelma Golden, took place at the Studio Museum in Harlem, New York, 28 April–24 June 2001. This text is adapted from the author's presentation at the online conference 'Reshaping the Field: Arts of the African Diasporas on Display', hosted by the Center for Curatorial Studies, Bard College, 4–6 November 2021.

[2] As Camille Norment describes it: 'You see, every material has a resonate frequency that will vibrate and allow it to make sound; with metal it is easy to bring out that sound and have the "voice" of the material itself be present in the space. In this piece, the dissonant ringing, for me, is symptomatic of a psychosis – a collapsing of seduction and repulsion that is further contemplated in other elements of the work. … Visually, I focus on juxtapositions of common materials with contradictions in the narrative, simultaneously evoking comfort zones, fetish coves and insane asylums'. *Freestyle* (exh. cat.), New York: The Studio Museum in Harlem, 2001, p.65.

[3] Tana Hargest's work was contemporaneous with the consumer critique of Naomi Klein's influential book *No Logo: Taking Aim at the Brand Bullies*, Toronto: Alfred A. Knopf Canada, 1999.

[4] Paul Gilroy, *The Black Atlantic: Modernity and Double-Consciousness*, Cambridge, MA: Harvard University Press, 1993.

[5] Although in recent years we have understood the urgent need to present Afro-European and other black histories which are highly under-researched.

[6] Amo is the only known African philosopher of the Enlightenment. He was taken as a slave from an area called Axim in contemporary Ghana and later trained in philosophy as the whimsical experiment of a European duke. See Senam Okudzeto, 'Refusing the Tautological Return', in 'JSAH Roundtable: Constructing Race and Architecture (1400–1800), Part 2', *Journal of the Society of Architectural Historians*, vol.80, no.4, 2021, pp.409–10.

[7] Sartre's text was originally written for the introduction of Senghor's book *Anthologie de la nouvelle poésie nègre et malgache de langue française*, Paris: Presses universitaires de France, 1948.

Blackness on Display: On Racial Fetishism and the Right to Opacity – Derek Conrad Murray

> *Of course, the whole thing is, once you cease to be a master, once you throw off your master's yoke, you are no longer human rubbish, you are just a human being, and all the things that adds up to. So, too, with the slaves. Once they are no longer slaves, once they are free, they are no longer noble and exalted; they are just human beings.*
> – Jamaica Kincaid[1]

I would like to consider the relation between black representation – as a form of recuperation and humanization – versus the ubiquity of racial fetishism in American visual culture. While examining the contradictions between black visibility (as a pathway towards vision and justice), contrasted by the desire to resist racial objectification, this essay endeavours to critically explore the consequences of constant visibility.

In the early 1990s, Édouard Glissant theorized this dynamic in terms of a right to opacity, championing the right to unknowability, while acknowledging the implicit failures of representation to actually *see* certain subjects; that is, to actually understand – which is more about reciprocity and empathy than simply observing. What Glissant located was a core tension, implicit to the representation of difference in social contexts, in which alterity is the nexus for forms of social discrimination. To that point, the fraught relation between visibility and invisibility, between being perpetually viewed and having social value, are contradictions subtending the perilous terrain of visual representation. In a recent interview in the journal *Radical History Review*, I addressed these concerns, because I have become increasingly alarmed that there may be perils implicit to both the hyper-visualization of black bodies in American culture and beyond, and the very limited set of critical themes and approaches that appear to dominate black intellectual life:

> *I have a lingering concern about the overexposure of African-descended folks worldwide, who find themselves the subject of a rapacious Western image culture that consumes black bodies for entertainment purposes ... as an affective visual spectacle. In many respects, that societal thirst – and the plethora of images it generates – is confused for racial progress, because it grants visibility and provides support and pathways to success for a select few. If we look at African American life as a totality, and not just the elite ... we obviously see a disjuncture between the deluge of images of black bodies, contrasted by rampant disenfranchisement.*[2]

This concern has many intersecting dimensions that must be addressed. As an art historian, critic and theorist of American art, I'm attuned to particular tendencies in artistic production, as well as historical, critical and theoretical considerations that have far-reaching implications. In many respects, both spheres are heavily impacted by liberal politics and institutional structures that are plagued by racial inequalities that are often bolstered by reductive and unsophisticated engagements with difference. The impact of this problem is well-known, though there is not enough critical reflection on tendencies that are potentially harmful. While there is a cultural thirst for images and narratives dealing with or depicting blackness – specifically black bodies and their traumas – there is also a tendency for black scholars to be limited to a few intersecting fields: African, African American and the African diasporas. My point is that we need to carefully and honestly look at the institutional value systems and financial structures that support the arts – paying particular attention to the ways in which black cultural producers are being encouraged to limit themselves to a reductive set of scripts. I often ponder if we are creating an accurate picture of who we are as black people, or are we simply creating depictions of ourselves that the dominant culture wants to see? This question equally applies to the histories we construct, the theories we advance and the general manner with which we approach culture. Art historian Eddie Chambers has discussed this thorny issue as a problem that plagues his discipline:

> *Looking around at the art history departments across the United States with which I had varying degrees of familiarity, I perceived that African American faculty were frequently, somewhat predictably, there to teach African American art. It was similarly apparent that African faculty were there to teach African art; Chinese academics taught Chinese art; and so on. In other words, there existed the appearance of a pronounced and decidedly unsubtle* stay in your lane*ness that was applied to art history faculty of colour.*[3]

Chambers is correct that Art History suffers from a deeply problematic form of racial categorization that segregates creative histories and restricts scholars of colour from engaging in research areas extending beyond those related (or at least perceived to relate) to their respective identities. Simply put, we are limited in the conversations we can engage in, the fields we discuss, and therefore there is a perception that our role in the academy is to teach in fields for which there is little institutional investment. For black scholars in the arts, their institutional presence and purpose, not to mention the perception of their breadth of knowledge and expertise, are limited to a damaging set of ideological reductions.

Needless to say, this absurdity is maintained both by structures of reward – in the form of funding, diversity mandates, publishing, fellowships and major awards – as well as intracultural mandates, a racial politics of authenticity and identity-based policing. In other words, there are spoils for staying nestled within one's prescribed racialized box, whether that pressure is exerted by institutional structures or from within one's own identity group. On the other hand, and as Chambers rightly points out, most black scholars choose their topics as a labour of love and a reflection of deep personal commitment:

> *A great many academics of colour love their scholarship and love their teaching on subjects that they may regard as growing out of, and having a direct correlation with, their individual personhood, identity, biography and so on. But this must not, does not and should not preclude aspiring or emerging art historians from a wide range of ethnicities – those undertaking programs at*

the BA, MA or PhD levels – from studying as their primary fields whatever areas of art history to which they are inclined [...] Our challenge is to see to it that faculty of colour teach on all sorts of specialist subjects, and not just on African art, African American art and African Diaspora art. White professors have jealously guarded that privilege – to research and teach on specialist subjects not constrained by their ethnicity. It is time to share that privilege and to make it more widely known to aspiring and emerging art historians of colour that they have every right to pursue whatever branch of art history interests them. That will surely mark a decisive step toward implementing genuinely antiracist, or nonracist, art history departments and the curricula they offer.[4]

These issues have always impacted my presence in the discipline, which has been anomalous, to say the least, as there are very few black art historians. That said, the diversity of my intellectual interests has consistently been a challenge for both the disciplinary establishment and among my black colleagues in the arts. My scholarly interests are broad and varied, yet the interrelation between black representation and art historical scholarship collided perhaps most meaningfully as a result of my critical interest in the term *post-black*. The origins of the term are now widely known in the arts and humanities, where it has gained a fraught yet persistent presence within the intellectual contemplation of black representation in the twenty-first century. Once articulated rather casually by curator Thelma Golden, it quickly ignited a firestorm of divisive debate. The irony, of course, is that despite the casual manner with which the term was initially introduced, it quickly became a dividing line among the black intelligentsia and a delineating terminology that, depending on its usage, became a fraudulent marker of one's racial fidelity. Many black intellectuals wilfully mischaracterized *post-black* as synonymous with fantasies of a post-racial America: as the naïve stance of individuals with little to no historical consciousness. Its usage was mocked by many and rendered as a sign of a certain immaturity around one's racial identity. In time, however, *post-black* became a thriving discourse, especially in the humanities, where the term was expanded beyond the arts and formed into a very generative conversation about black cultural representation. As is widely known, Golden used the term in response to her own groundbreaking exhibition 'Freestyle' (2001), in New York at the Studio Museum in Harlem. At the time of its mention, the term was never unpacked by Golden, but it still resonated with the intelligentsia and seemed to capture a collective consciousness that was deeply satirical and reflective of a contradictory engagement with the signifiers of blackness.

The concerns around black representation that emerged in the wake of 'Freestyle' opened up a much-needed conversation about the black-themed exhibition in general. Since the era of multiculturalism and the identity debates of the 1980s and 90s, American museums have become fond of the black-themed exhibition as a means to appease the representational demands of under-represented communities, while simultaneously protecting the European canon from the violence of historical revisionism. It was a strategy that worked, tout court. In the past, I have reflected on the black-themed exhibition as problematic –

while embracing the satirical troubling of post-blackness as a potential for a radical rethinking of black representation within the museum space:

> *The black-themed exhibition was once the staging ground for racial sermonizing, despite the works' ultimate status as commodity objects. In addition to 'Freestyle', the Whitney Museum's 1994 'Black Male: Representations of Masculinity in Contemporary American Art', the Studio Museum in Harlem's 2006 'Frequency' (both curated by Thelma Golden), and the Contemporary Arts Museum Houston's 2005 'Double Consciousness: Black Conceptual Art since 1970' (curated by Valerie Cassel Oliver) are each exemplars of major exhibitions dedicated to redefining our relationship to what historian Darby English has termed 'black representational space'. Each of these exhibitions explored the intricacies of black identity and its attendant politics and ideologies to various degrees, but since the 1993 Whitney Biennial exhibition ushered in a sense of legitimacy around identity politics in art discourse, there has been a broad shifting away from serious racial conversation toward an embrace of what could be termed a satirical turn in black art production.*[5]

This satirical turn in contemporary African American art that emerged in the early 2000s was filled with an oppositional optimism that was short-lived, primarily because it became a victim of its own success. For a short time, there was a self-critical tendency that took hold; a very cynical self-reflective engagement with the foibles of black culture that was influenced by the work of artists Michael Ray Charles and Kara Walker. This most recent iteration of satire was more aggressive and incendiary in its critique of homophobia in the black community and a more overt embrace of queer aesthetics and conceptual themes. But the mainstream success of openly gay artists like Glenn Ligon, Kehinde Wiley and Mickalene Thomas ultimately led to a more conservative, regressive retreat back into a politics of respectability and an embrace of market success. The rise of the Black Lives Matter movement, in many respects, brought with it an anti-racist politics rooted in nostalgia for 1960s and 70s radicalism. Pro-blackness has now become a brand as fashionably empty as any other – and the black body has emerged as a representational cliché that is almost bereft of polemical meaning. The black body is everywhere these days, especially within the worlds of fine art, where it has a fraught representational function in a culture where anti-blackness is still a predominating socio-economic, cultural and political reality. In so many ways, the black body in representation is trapped between fetishism, objectification, condescension, disdain and the pleasures of ennobled suffering. From art galleries and museums, to scholarship and popular visual culture, we see this reductive tendency towards the culturalization of blackness as entertainment.

Regardless of the cultural milieu, perhaps we need to expand what we mean when we say *black representation* beyond a visual rhetorics of the black body – and towards a consideration of the social function of blackness in institutional contexts. What we see all-too-often are black bodies as commodities within the logics of racial commerce, which is meant to take the place of a meaningful and substantive investment in ending racial inequity. The celebrations of black trauma within the realms of culture are often taken as corrective measures, while racial disparities only increase. What concerns many intellectuals of African descent is a tendency in black visual culture towards explicit, if not also gratuitous, depictions of racial struggle and violence inflicted upon black bodies – representations perceived to take on (or be deeply entangled with) the logics of power and social authority. Considering the representational entanglements between images of anti-black violence in American visual culture and an increased consumer demand for black bodies in contemporary art and popular culture, it is necessary to rigorously question how a visual culture of blackness is being received, consumed and interpreted.

There needs to be a very in-depth discussion about the proliferation of images of black suffering. What do these images mean? What is their social function? And who is permitted to mobilize them? In many respects, both the images and the very predictable response to their presence, have become *culture* – and therefore, I am beginning to question the larger social role that blackness (as an imago and a positionality) plays within the cultural landscape.

In popular visual culture, particularly within film and television, there has been a rise in programming that takes on the issue of black trauma. Inspired by Jordan Peele's films *Get Out* (2017) and *Us* (2019), a new genre has emerged in black visuality. The movies *Antebellum* (2020) and *Candyman* (2021) and the television series *Them* (2021) have each taken on the horrors of black trauma in the face of anti-blackness. But despite the popularity of this trend, there is a growing chorus of black critics who are rallying against what they perceive to be damaging representations. Angelica Jade Bastién, writing for the online magazine *Vulture*, is one such voice. In her scathing denouncement of Gerard Bush and Christopher Renz's debut horror film *Antebellum*, Bastién is outspoken about what she recognizes as the film's flippant engagement with the violence of slavery:

> *I am tired. I am tired of pop-cultural artifacts that render Black people as merely Black bodies onto which the sins of this ragged country are violently mapped. I am tired of suffering being the primary lens through which we understand Black identity. I am tired of being so hungry for Black joy and Black representation that scraps feel like a meal. I am tired of films about slavery refusing to acknowledge the interior lives of Black women even as their beings become tools for filmmakers to explore the horrors of the enslaved. I am tired of thin characterization and milquetoast social messaging being the kind of representation Black folks receive. I am tired of films like* Antebellum.[6]

Whether or not one agrees with Bastién's point of view, her questioning opens up a vital conversation about the social function of black representation. There tends to be a perception that images of black trauma may function as a means to generate empathy and compassion. However, there is also a kind of claimed cultural ownership over the black body that renders it into what could be characterized as a fraudulent conduit for empathetic engagement. Saidiya Hartman has spoken most eloquently about this absurd relation between pleasure and the possession of black bodies as property: 'Thus the desire to don, occupy or possess blackness or the black body as a sentimental resource and/or locus of excess enjoyment is both founded upon and enabled by the material relations of chattel slavery.'[7] The brilliance in Hartman's query lies in its location of a perverse conjunction within the racial melodrama: that pleasure can be gained from the masochistic fantasy of black pain, while simultaneously a sadistic enjoyment can be derived by the visual spectacle of sufferance.[8] But is there a reciprocity that is galvanized through this relation, or does it function purely as ideological entertainment?

In Sharon P. Holland's book *The Erotic Life of Racism* (2012), she ponders the contrast between the erotic dimensions of racism (which she characterizes as *the desire for the Other*) versus generosity, or the lack thereof. Inspired by Emmanuel Levinas's meditation on desire for the Other in the essay 'Meaning and Sense' (1964), Holland contrasts the French philosopher's question with a very similar sentiment expressed by the British Ghanaian cultural theorist Kwame Anthony Appiah: 'In our private lives, we are morally free to have aesthetic preferences between people, but once our treatment of people raises moral issues, we may not make arbitrary distinctions.'[9] Appiah similarly considers the contradictory relation between desire for the Other and a contempt that subtends that very longing. There is, as Appiah argues, a need to detach individual longing for the Other from racist desire – though in contrast to Appiah's more outward looking critique, Levinas's questioning is more contemplative or introspective in its engagement with individual desire: 'The movement toward the Other, instead of completing me and contenting me, implicates me in a conjuncture, which in a way, did not concern me and should leave me indifferent – what was I looking for here? Is the desire for the other an appetite or a generosity?'[10]

In Holland's reading, Levinas's pondering of whether desire for the Other is an appetite or a generosity is a generative means to unpack the underpinnings of an appetite for difference; not as a form of reciprocity, but as consumption, or as a devouring that is disinterested in mutuality and generosity. For Holland, Levinas's and Appiah's sentiments exist in relation to each other. But as the scholar elaborates, the stakes in this notion involve whether or not aesthetic preference can ever pass for moral practice. However, the words *appetite* and *generosity* are both compelling and generative for Holland, particularly when unpacked in tandem: 'In reading the words "appetite" and "generosity" together, one could surmise that what we need to do is turn an appetite – an (in other words an) "aesthetic preference" – into an antiracist stance.'[11]

The very notion of an aesthetic preference as a moral practice is a vexation that informs my writing about the complexities and contradictions of black representation. There is a pervasive sense that the representation of black subjectivity disrupts a lengthy and violent history of deprivation, devaluing and erasure: that the humanistic imaging of racialized difference holds the potential to both reimagine the black subject, but also foster a more empathetic and moral engagement with black life. The challenge to this notion resides precisely in Holland's question of whether or not it is possible for appetite and generosity to coincide in the racial imaginary. To what degree does the image challenge representational and ideological regimes of thought that are rooted in anti-blackness? Does that cultural thirst for blackness *in* representation (the appetite) hold the possibility to be anti-racist?

There is an obscenity, or a disturbing operation at the heart of this desire, which is a disjuncture between the accolades given to the black cultural elite versus a vicious (and often violent) degradation of black life that continues to plague the United States. At what point do we begin to question the logics of this relation, a condition upon which racialized blackness (and its perpetual recuperation, celebration and reification) becomes the sole leitmotif of black scholars and artists? Funding models, institutional set-asides, awards, publicity and diversity hires are seemingly generated with the sole purpose of maintaining the logics of intellectual, creative and professional segregation. In other words, the visual poetics of ennobled suffering has become de rigueur in the art world and other cultural spheres – yet there remains a steadfast adherence to the false notion that impassioned testimonials to black pain or images of black beauty will somehow reverse the hearts of the intolerant. Previous generations fought vigilantly to break down the walls of segregation; now there appears to be an equally rapacious effort to erect them, and all in the name of racial pride. There is a fashionable cultural politics of blackness that is steeped in grand essentialist expressions of racial pride that appear to represent a culture in deep conflict with itself ... and reckoning with a cultural positioning that demands a kind of intellectual and creative servitude within a racial culture game, where black cultural producers function as trauma griots for entertainment purposes.

This very performative form of black trauma sermonizing has, to put it simply, become culture. It's actually a very hip and popular positionality within the auspices of mainstream liberalism. The philanthropic support of major institutions has engendered a creative drought, defined by a deluge of representational and thematic clichés that have proven successful and lucrative for a select few. However, this strategy (as cynical as it may be) has a cost and that cost may be counterproductive to its aims. Black trauma is now a product that vigorously sells – and like any commodity, it is often plagued by shallowness. What does all this black representation mean? What toll does it take on a people fighting so hard to present a humanistic, dignified image of themselves to a dominant culture that is indifferent, or sees blackness as a cool trend?

The culture industries in the US are steeped in a kind of progressive bourgeois cynicism and a cosmetic liberalism that relies on disingenuous minoritarian victimhood for its very existence. Needless to say, what this leads to is an absurd, fake sympathy for the racialized Other that is (in a comically absurdist way) contradicted by inequitable cultural and institutional practices, not to mention the horrors of black inner-city life. Why is it that, in order to have thriving mainstream careers, black creatives and intellectuals must (or at least it appears they must) produce narratives, histories and images *only* about black deprivation, and within very limited themes, of which we are all abundantly familiar? And how is it that all-too-often very privileged black cultural producers, many of whom have attended elite academic institutions and who operate among the cultural and economic elite, cannot create narratives about themselves: about growing up within privileged or cosmopolitan circumstances and circumnavigating upper-middle-class environments throughout their lives?

Of course, to tell these stories would be to unveil the vicious types of institutional racism that define such spaces, and the pernicious forms of psychic violence engendered by the intolerances of supposedly sophisticated, highly educated and progressive whites, who self-present as politically committed and stridently against structural inequality. This again is the cynical relation that becomes the inevitable by-product of liberal institutions: a largely unspoken culture game whereby black intellectuals are compelled to perform ennobled victimhood, and progressive whites the role of empathetic ally. Neither of these positionalities are entirely honest, but they maintain a logic of peaceful separation and of power differentials that are rooted in a non-coercive brand of segregation. The relation of which I speak is a fantasy, and for many that fantasy is better than reality. That pleasing illusion is pervasive within the privileged spaces of cultural production. But, as we are all aware, that structural inequality is still very much in place within the social order, though it has arguably been replaced by a soft bigotry that encourages self-obsession, self-segregation and tribalism among those groups vying for reciprocity and recognition. James Baldwin knew that to embrace the fantasies heaped upon oneself – *to love one's wound*, so to speak – is to ultimately choose a pathway to destruction:

> *There is an illusion about America, a myth about America to which we are clinging which has nothing to do with the lives we lead and I don't believe that anybody in this country who has really thought about it or really almost anybody who has been brought up against it – and almost all of us have one way or another – this collision between one's image of oneself and what one actually is is always very painful and there are two things you can do about it, you can meet the collision head-on and try and become what you really are or you can retreat and try to remain what you thought you were, which is a fantasy, in which you will certainly perish.*[12]

To enjoy one's wound as social spectacle is indeed a losing gambit. And in our current cultural reality of constant exposure and visibility, the tendency to reveal is as pernicious as ever. As writer Akiko Busch has rightfully argued, maybe it is time to 'reevaluate the merits of the inconspicuous life, to search out some antidote to continuous exposure, and to reconsider the value of going unseen. Might invisibility be regarded not simply as refuge, but as a condition with its own meaning and power? Going unseen may be becoming a sign of decency and self-assurance.'[13] In the US, there has always been a cultural thirst for images of black bodies, but this desire to consume belies the very stark realities of structural inequality, criminalization and often death. But we need to carefully ponder how we look upon and display certain bodies, and be cognizant of the unique liabilities of these instances of revealing. The right to opacity is perhaps a means to resist the violence of this incessant unveiling: to defy the ideological reduction of which Glissant spoke. For the Other, the right to go unseen may function as a powerful means to resist the limiting scripts and clichéd tropes that overdetermine the representation of blackness.

Notes

[1] Jamaica Kincaid, *A Small Place*, New York: Farrar, Straus and Giroux, 2000, p.81.

[2] Alexis Boylan, 'The Cost of That Revealing: Interview with Derek Conrad Murray', in *Radical History Review*, issue 142, January 2022, pp.152–68.

[3] Eddie Chambers, 'It's Time to Share', colloquium, *Panorama: Journal of the Association of Historians of American Art*, vol.6, no.2, 2020, pp.1–4.

[4] *Ibid.*, p.3.

[5] Derek Conrad Murray, 'Post-Black and the Resurrection of African American Satire', in *Post-Soul Satire: Black Identity After Civil Rights*, Jackson: University of Mississippi Press, 2014, pp.6–8. See also Darby English, *How to See a Work of Art in Total Darkness*, Cambridge, MA: MIT Press, 2010.

[6] Angelica Jade Bastién, 'I Am Tired of Films Like *Antebellum*', *Vulture*, 14 September 2020, https://www.vulture.com/2020/09/antebellum-movie-review-i-am-tired-of-films-like-this.html.

[7] Saidiya Hartman, 'Innocent Amusements: The Stage of Sufferance', in *Scenes of Subjection: Terror, Slavery, and Self-Making in Nineteenth-Century America*, Oxford: Oxford University Press, 1997, p.21.

[8] *Ibid.*

[9] Appiah as cited by Holland in Sharon P. Holland, 'Desire: or "A Bit of the Other"', in *The Erotic Life of Racism*, Durham, NC: Duke University Press, 2012, pp.41–42.

[10] Emmanuel Levinas, 'Meaning and Sense', in *Collected Philosophical Papers* (trans. Alphonso Lingis), Dordrecht, Netherlands: Martinus Nijhoff Publishers, 1987, p.94.

[11] S.P. Holland, 'Desire: or "A Bit of the Other"', *op. cit.*, p.42.

[12] James Baldwin, 'Notes for a Hypothetical Novel', in *Nobody Knows My Name*, New York: Vintage, 1992, p.153.

[13] Akiko Busch, 'Introduction', in *How to Disappear: Notes on Invisibility in a Time of Transparency*, New York: Penguin Books, 2020, p.9.

'The Thin Black Line' (1985), curated by Lubaina Himid; 'The Other Story: Afro-Asian Artists in Post-War Britain' (1989), curated by Rasheed Araeen; 'Transforming the Crown: African, Asian, and Caribbean Artists in Britain, 1966–1996' (1997–98), curated by Mora J. Beauchamp-Byrd, are just three examples of the intense debates surrounding the ways Black artists have been exhibited across Black diasporas. Araeen advocated for an acknowledgment of African and South Asian artists' engagement with modernism and their contributions to post-War Britain, in place of the reduction of their work to their ethnic signifiers. Beauchamp-Byrd's 'Transforming the Crown', meanwhile took a corrective stance on the history of British art and continued activism for visibility and inclusion that Marlene Smith, Claudette Johnson and many other Black British artists fought for in the 1980s. This section explores this rich set of histories, considers some of the practitioners who have shaped the discourse and follows the paths of artworks across time, exhibitions and publics.

Moving Images, Exhibition Histories: *Dreaming Rivers* and *Handsworth Songs* – Lucy Steeds

Black Audio Film Collective and Sankofa Film/Video Collective made philosophically informed, ideologically and aesthetically powerful artworks in Britain during the 1980s. While not a part of the commercial mainstream for film, their works nonetheless shared the same conventional forms of distribution – thereby circulating more widely than, say, paintings and sculpture. In what follows, I wish to follow two particular works – *Handsworth Songs* (1986) by Black Audio Film Collective and *Dreaming Rivers* (1988) by Sankofa Film/Video Collective – into different settings. Reflecting on the 'exhibition histories' for these artworks, I will be asking: What have varying contexts of presentation brought out in the films? And how might that shape an appreciation of them now?

Dreaming Rivers may be seen as a tribute to women who came to England from the Caribbean as colonial subjects following the Second World War – and it is quietly devastating about the courage required and struggles involved. There is a main character, whom we learn bits about, but as palpable as any narrative is a slow, complicated mood: one that is both engaging and painful; one of tough beauty. As I shall go on to elaborate, the film is claustrophobic while elegiac. Thirty minutes in duration, it circulated as 'a short', with its premier hosted by the French Institute in the opulent London district of South Kensington in April 1988. *Dreaming Rivers* was the fourth work created by Sankofa Film/Video Collective.[1]

Handsworth Songs is rooted in footage of social unrest triggered by racism in the British city of Birmingham in the mid-1980s, yet ranges far wider than this to develop an intricate historical picture. A montage of audio elements sometimes entwines and sometimes leads astray the collaged visuals. There is a twice-spoken line, often quoted from the film, regarding the limits of journalistic reportage: 'There are no stories in the riots, only the ghosts of other stories.' Classed as a feature, given an hour's duration, *Handsworth Songs* had its theatrical release at the Metro Cinema in Leicester Square, at the heart of London's West End, in January 1987.[2] It was the first film made by Black Audio Film Collective.[3]

As described by Stuart Hall in London at the time, *Dreaming Rivers* and *Handsworth Songs* are films that address contemporaneous cultural contestation over Britishness. He highlights how the films bring the past to bear, while noting their evident awareness of the complex mediation at play in our relations with the past. Hall suggests that *Dreaming Rivers* may remind us of the role played 'by memory, fantasy and desire' and that *Handsworth Songs* flags 'inter-textuality', or makes explicit the mediation by news coverage, for example.[4] He remains one of the few cultural theorists to give the works equal weight and attention. To date, the exposure of and literature on *Handsworth Songs* has been more extensive than that for *Dreaming Rivers*.[5] To amplify Hall, then: as I aim to make clear in what follows, the historical mediation brought out in *Dreaming Rivers* is linguistic, material, figurative

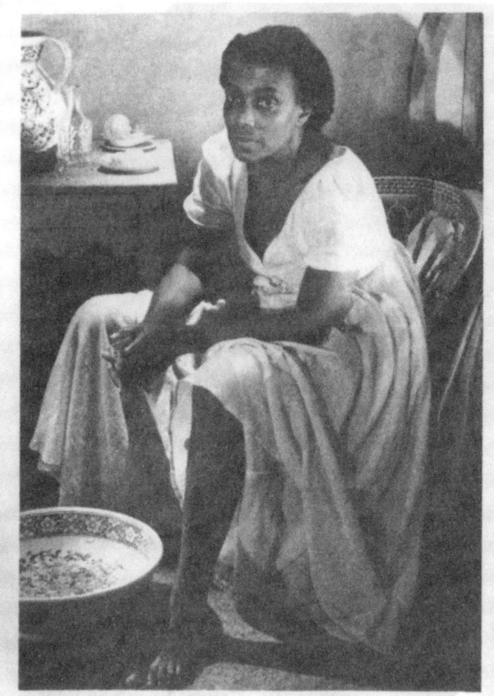
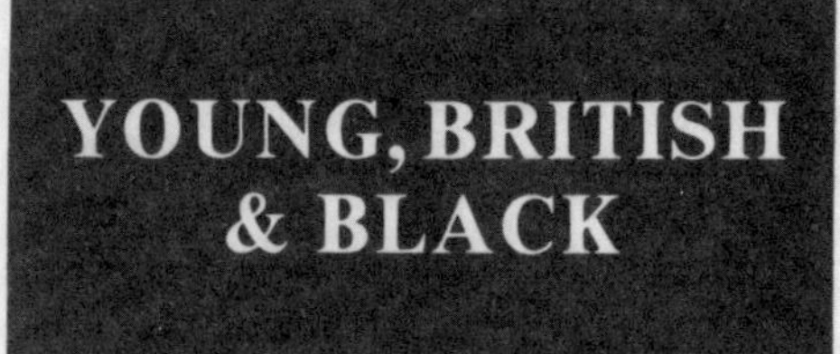

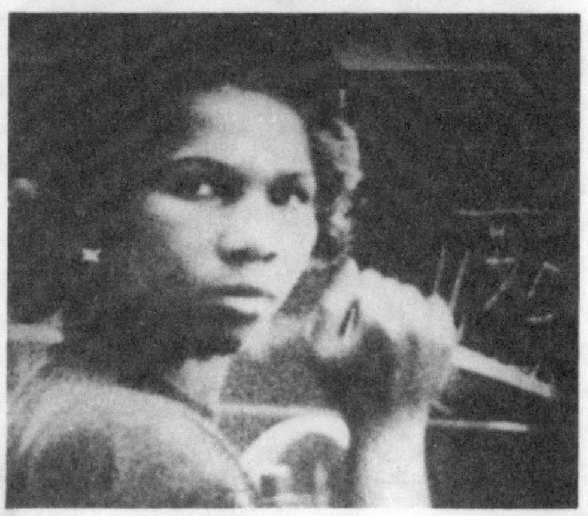

Invitation card for 'Young, British & Black', Hallwalls Contemporary Arts Center, Buffalo, New York, 1988, curated by Coco Fusco and produced by Ada Gay Griffin of Third World Newsreel. Left: frame enlargement from Sankofa Film/ Video Collective, *Dreaming Rivers*, 1988; lower right: frame enlargement from Black Audio Film Collective, *Handsworth Songs*, 1986

and intimate – as well as being, when it comes to memory, fantasy and desire – cognitive, affective and libidinous.

✡✡✡

I will start my situated thinking and imagining in New York City in the 1980s. Specifically, I invite you to join me at the Collective for Living Cinema, on White Street in Lower Manhattan, for a programme titled 'Young, British and Black'. Described as an avant-garde venue known for alternative film, the Collective for Living Cinema sits closer to the art establishment than to the mainstream cinema world.[6] It is May 1988, and people are gathering in an auditorium that can hold 125, for screenings and discussion. 'Young, British and Black', as curated by Coco Fusco and produced by Ada Gay Griffin of Third World Newsreel, conjoins recent work by Black Audio Film Collective and Sankofa Film/Video Collective, as two groups active in the UK at the time.[7]

We are in the decade of Ronald Reagan in the US and Margaret Thatcher in the UK. These heads of state cultivate the 'special relationship' across the North Atlantic on Republican and Conservative terms, respectively. Neoliberal financial growth – described at the time by Susan Strange as 'casino capitalism' – is cultivated between them.

Film-making, on the one hand, and artistic practice, on the other, are commonly dissociated in Britain in the 1980s – for instance by the Arts Council of Great Britain. The cultural might of the US in both domains of production

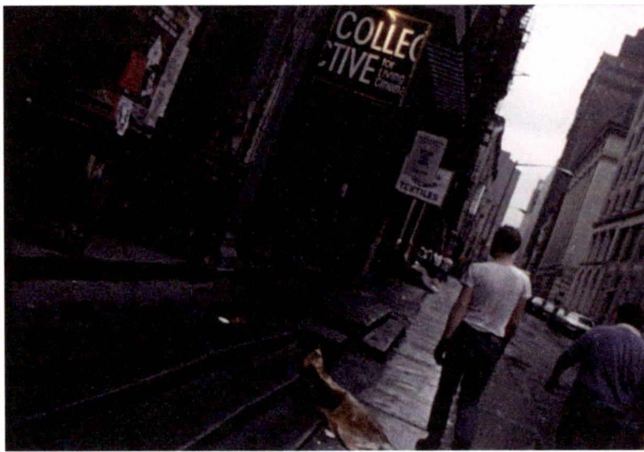

Still from Jeff Preiss's *CARS–A–POPPIN for Bob Fleischer*, 2019, showing the Collective for Living Cinema, White Street, New York, 1980s. Courtesy the artist

is evident, and at the same time there is interconnectivity within a European context. Many creative practitioners with African, African Caribbean or South Asian heritage are uniting as Black British in order to mobilize against the racism of the White cultural establishment.

To discuss their films, Martina Attille and Isaac Julien from Sankofa and John Akomfrah and Eddie George from Black Audio Film Collective have travelled to the US. Proceedings are reviewed in both *Cineaste* and *Film Comment*, as published in New York at the time. Armond White, an African American critic, opens his piece in the latter with this:

> *'Young, British and Black'... shows a different kind of filmmaking movement from the black independents in the United States. The difference is virtually the same that divides other European filmmakers from their American counterparts – an art versus entertainment approach to film. [...] [T]his was a tour of ideological cousins, if not brothers and sisters. A fascinating family squabble ensued.*[8]

The 'art approach' of the British film-makers is described as 'formalist'; involving 'academic' traditions that threaten to produce inaccessibility, indeed to exclude. Apparently, it risks suggesting to the gathered US audience 'an elitist detachment from the experience of racial oppression'.[9] Yet, all is apparently not lost. The review ends with this:

> *Attille spoke one phrase, with beguiling British precision, that struck a unifying note of good sense: 'Dominant culture'. That concept spears the British collectives' move into higher, artier realms. As blacks, and as intellectuals, they work against status quo filmmaking and any other restrictive agenda.*[10]

Here we find that *Dreaming Rivers* and *Handsworth Songs* are received in New York as unsettling, perhaps because they are wilfully anti-hegemonic. And this resonates with their cinematic reception in the UK, where they are seen to experiment with film form as well as engaging with politics.[11] Moreover, they

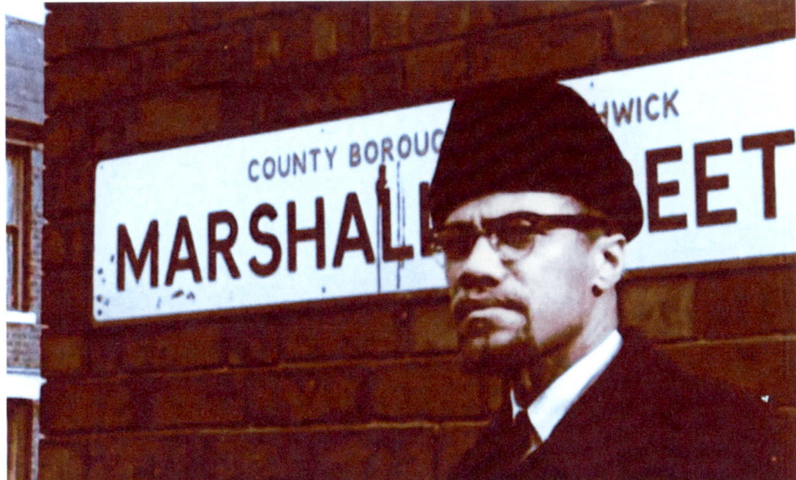

Still from Black Audio Film Collective, *Handsworth Songs*. Courtesy Smoking Dogs Films

are seen as taking up Third Cinema's task of pursuing cultural struggle – by rejecting both mainstream commercialism and individualistic auteurism – while simultaneously being shaped and informed by First World discourse, perhaps most notably by film theory, British cultural studies and French philosophy.[12]

✡✡✡

Terraced town houses of the industrial revolution – and the enduring urbanization of labour and lives – resonate through *Handsworth Songs*. In watching the film, my eyes swim with bricks; not only composing domestic houses but also courthouses, train stations and police stations, shops and cobbled roads. This Victorian fabric remains the scenery for many of us pacing along British streets or gathering on them today.

The nineteenth-century architecture of White Street in Manhattan highlights some of the grandeurs of industrialization. Metal fire escapes, snaking the buildings' exteriors, anchor this place resolutely in the US rather than the UK. And, in the 1980s, it was down at heel; film footage shot at this time, showing some of those involved in the Collective for Living Cinema outside on White Street, skims off the battered frontages of buildings, catching on strewn litter.[13]

In *Handsworth Songs*, a woman's voice recounts the visit of Malcolm X to the UK's Midlands in 1965 – in what would turn out to be shortly before his murder, back in the US, in New York. Malcolm X was invited to Birmingham and surrounding areas by the UK's Indian Workers' Association. Newsreel conveys his iconic presence on particular British streets then notorious for racism, while the narrator tells us he suggested to those gathered that 'we have a common struggle', in a voice that 'swooned over the ashes of decline'. A community of resistance, across widely scattered and aging cities, is given words again at the end of the work by Black Audio Film Collective. A female voice convenes this solidarity, uniting all those 'who live with the sorrows of defiance, who live among the abandoned aspirations which were the metropolis'.

The protagonist of *Dreaming Rivers* might easily have been summoned by this call, but more tangible in this film is the social isolation that prevents many in comparable conditions from coming together. Here, life as lived with others on the streets, with bricks as backdrop, is replaced by the solitary experience of being bricked into a domestic interior.[14] Although the line between confinement and refuge, prison and haven, may not be clear-cut.

✡✡✡

To extend the situated thinking and imagining, I will jump from New York's Collective for Living Cinema in the late 1980s to Tate, in London, two decades later – while also coming even closer to the present day and looking a little more widely across Europe.

Handsworth Songs enters the UK's national collection for modern and contemporary art, as hosted by Tate's galleries, in 2009. It is put on display at Tate Britain, where the work is positioned prominently, immediately off the grand central passageway through the ceremonial pomp of the Victorian building.[15] If we walk into the darkened room that has been constructed for the purposes of its display, we may take a seat on a bench. Perhaps we get lucky and walk in just at the beginning of the film; most likely we start part way through.

I cannot now recall any adjacent works: in my memory *Handsworth Songs* stands alone within – even uncontained by – Tate Britain. I believe this sense of exceeding the curatorial and institutional frame stems from my previously encountering the work as a part of Documenta 11, in Kassel in 2002. Indeed, I have a hunch that its exposure in Okwui Enwezor's lauded iteration of the German quinquennial may go some way to explaining its belated acquisition, as an artwork to be preserved for British cultural posterity, by Tate.

I visited Documenta 11 while a student in London and, travelling with a fellow student from another part of the world, we stayed in the local youth hostel. I remember being struck by how British *Handsworth Songs* seemed, in this particular exhibition context; yet how plausibly it was also so-called 'global contemporary art'. It both steadied me and questioned me, in the throes of an overwhelming show, the first of that scale I had visited. The prevailing visuals, voices and music were entirely recognizable to me as someone with lived experience of Britain, yet their combination – the cumulative picture and orchestrated arguments – were so considerably bigger than any narrow national claim. I found myself forced to identify with the anti-Black context of my upbringing, yet allowed to feel some solidarity in the ongoing and worldwide cultural struggle against racism.

As I recollect it, *Handsworth Songs* was installed close to *I only wish that I could weep* (2002) by the Atlas Group, and this seems surprisingly apposite: something is resonant in the conjuring of evocative fictions out of documentary footage at the same time that a sinister sense of political threat is manipulated out of imagery by power. Study of the installation plans for the KulturBahnhof in Kassel now remind me that in fact the closest physical adjacency was with another film, also from the mid-1980s: Trinh T. Minh-ha's *Naked Spaces: Living is Round* (1985). This pairing echoes programming under the banner of 'Third Cinema: Theories and Practices' – at the 40th Edinburgh International Film Festival of 1986.[16] The curatorial inclusion of another moving-image work within the KulturBahnhof, albeit digitally produced, as video rather than film, then becomes striking for dating from this same era: *Measures of Distance* (1988) by Mona Hatoum.[17] I am tempted to anchor the rise of 'global contemporary art', such as it was proposed in Documenta 11, in conceptually inflected moving images from the 1980s that are transculturally aware and coloniality conscious. These are artworks informed by political and economic migration into the wealthy and culturally dominant northwest of the world, offering inspired takes on the avant-garde marching historically from there.

Following spread: Black Audio Film Collective, *Handsworth Songs.* Installation views, Documenta 11, Kulturbahnhof, Kassel, 2002, as featured in *Kunstforum International*, no.161, August–October 2002

If, as already suggested, Tate's acquisition of *Handsworth Songs* – the entry of this film into the realm of possibility commanded in the name of a British art canon – is very much not a starting point for me, then certainly it is not an end point. As a work in the British national collection, it has been curated interestingly into shows since;[18] however, I want to briefly consider a more fleeting but powerful stand-alone presentation in the auditorium at Tate Modern. For this, then, we must leave Tate Britain and cross London onto the South Bank of the River Thames.

With a two-day turnaround, from initial idea to actual event, Stuart Comer – on the curatorial staff at Tate Modern – is screening *Handsworth Songs* on a Friday night, late in August 2011. The screening – and its hosted discussion – responds to live protests across the UK following the death of Mark Duggan, a British man with African Caribbean and Irish heritage, at the hands of the police. The Tate event is sold-out and Mark Fisher blogs about its importance for *Sight and Sound* courtesy of the British Film Institute.[19] Interestingly, a film celebrated at the time for rejecting 'nowness' in favour of 'historical depth', is here co-opted to a new now, 25 years after its initial moment. While its formal qualities remain fresh – still 'creating a space of critical reverie which counteracts the active ideological forgetting of England's colonial past in media discourses' – the relevance of its own historicity is a sharp reminder of how little has changed structurally in British society in a quarter of a century.[20]

In relation, I want to foreground another Tate screening, which takes place a few years later and gives space to a work that is *not* in their collection to date: *Dreaming Rivers.*[21] We are back in Tate Britain for this, at Milbank on the River Thames – only now in the auditorium housed within the Postmodern annex added in the late 1980s to the original nineteenth-century building. Films screened here never quite feel like they carry the sanction of works presented under Britannia's sculpted stony bulk next door. It is 2015 and *Dreaming Rivers* has been programmed by Zoe Whitley, on the curatorial staff at Tate Britain. Panellists in discussion after the screening include Sonia Boyce, given her role on set design for the film, but also a pertinent inclusion in this presentation context since a couple of her early pictures are in Tate's collection, as notably acquired in the 1980s.

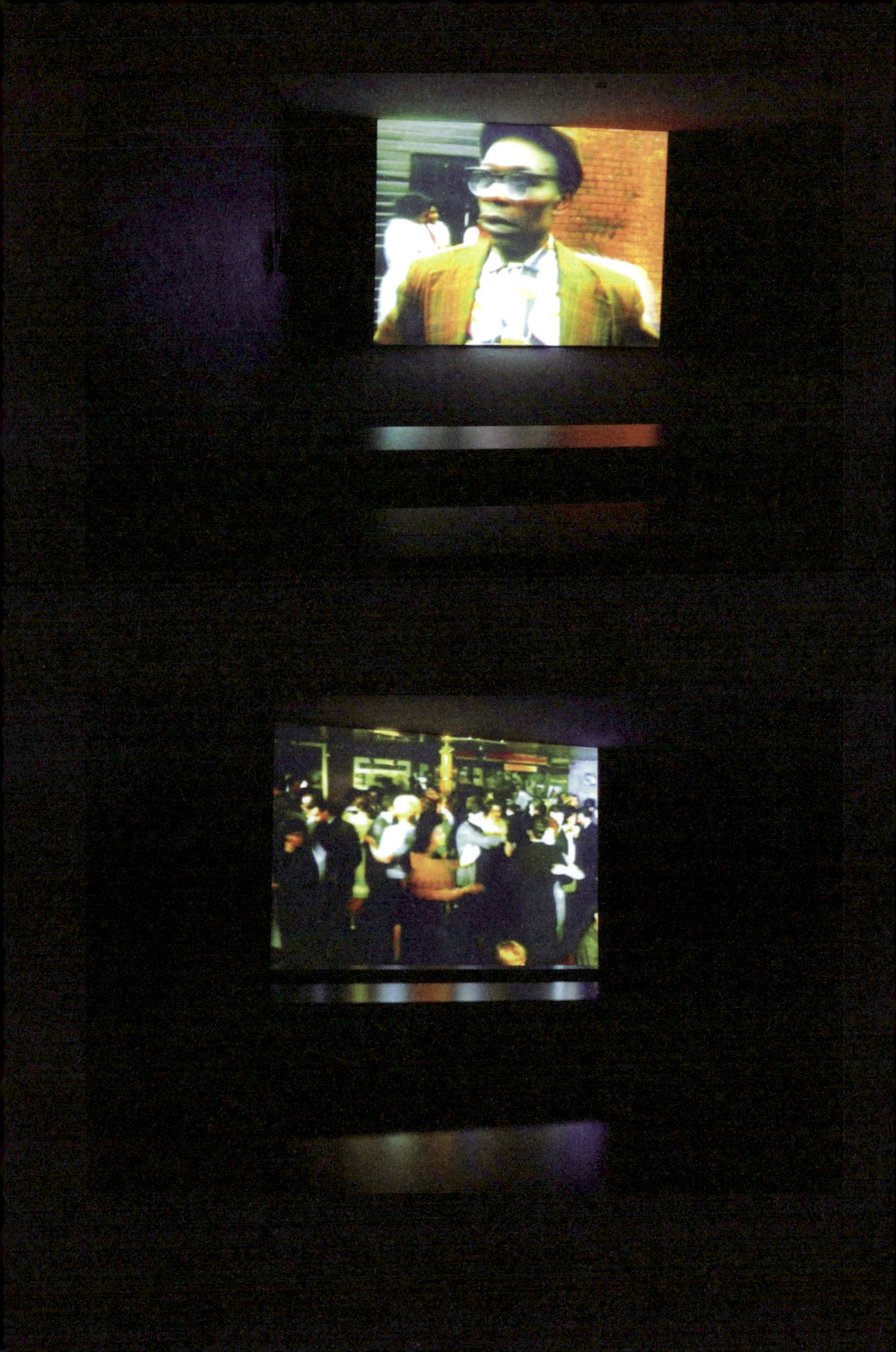

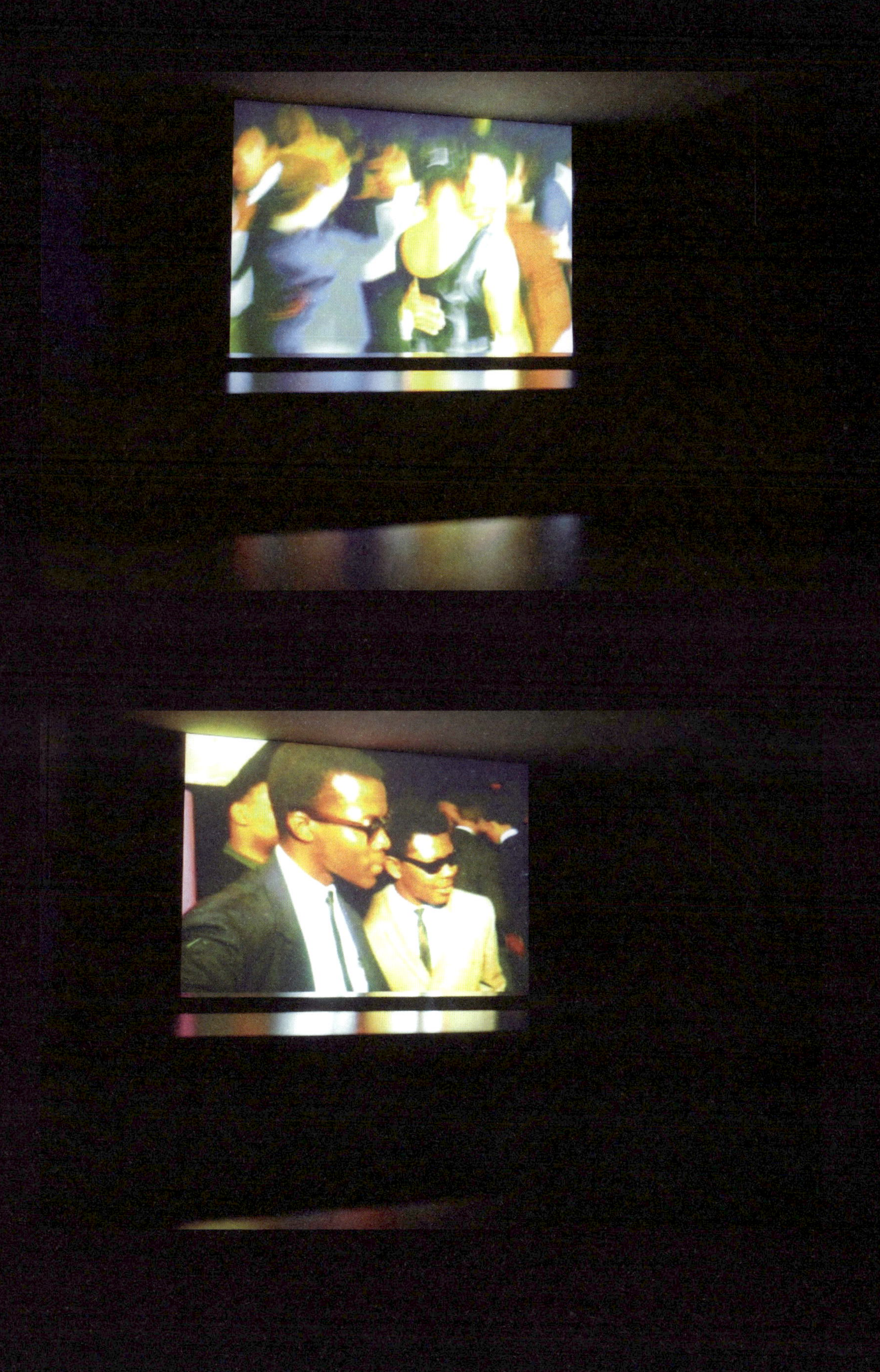

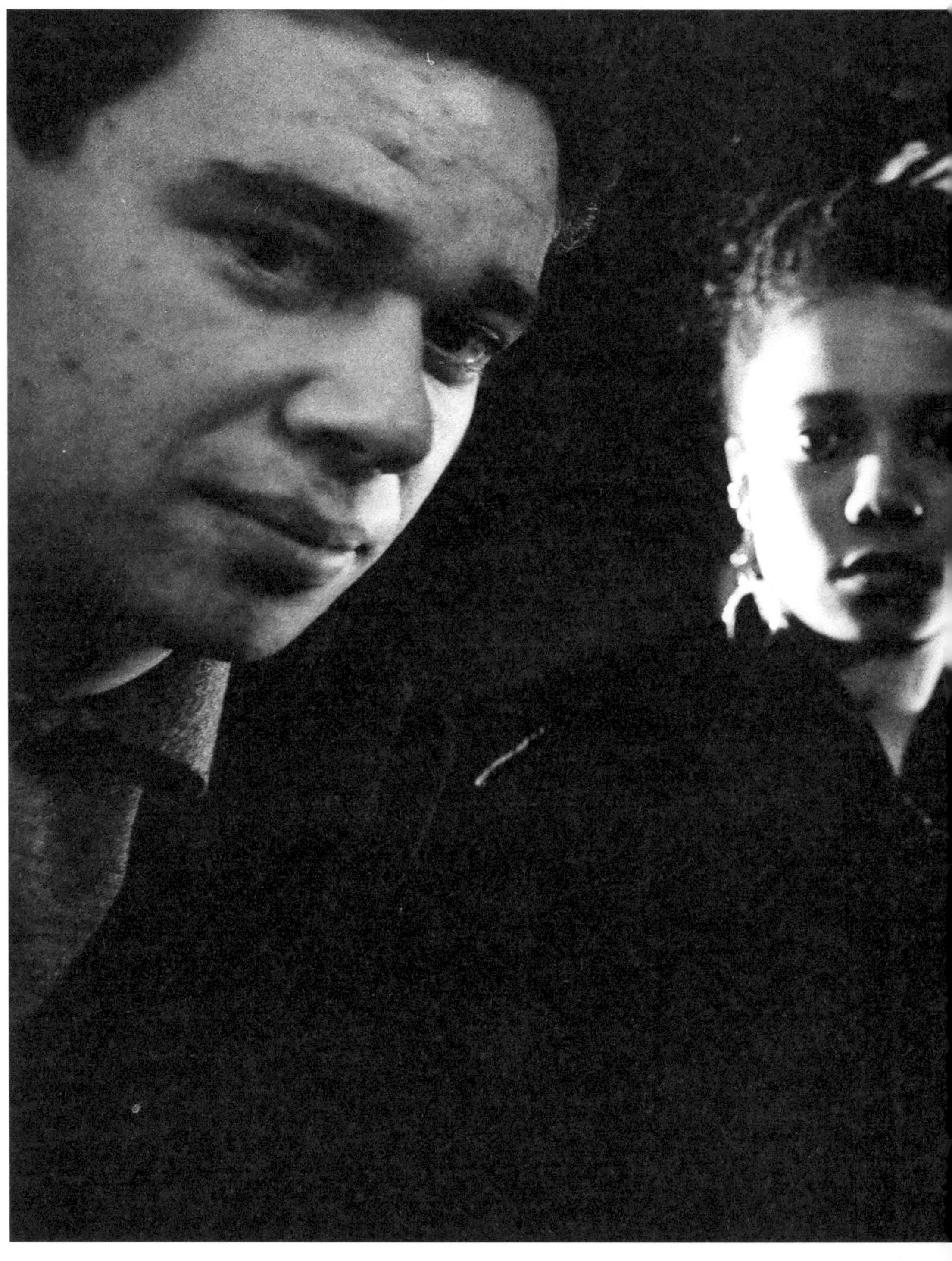

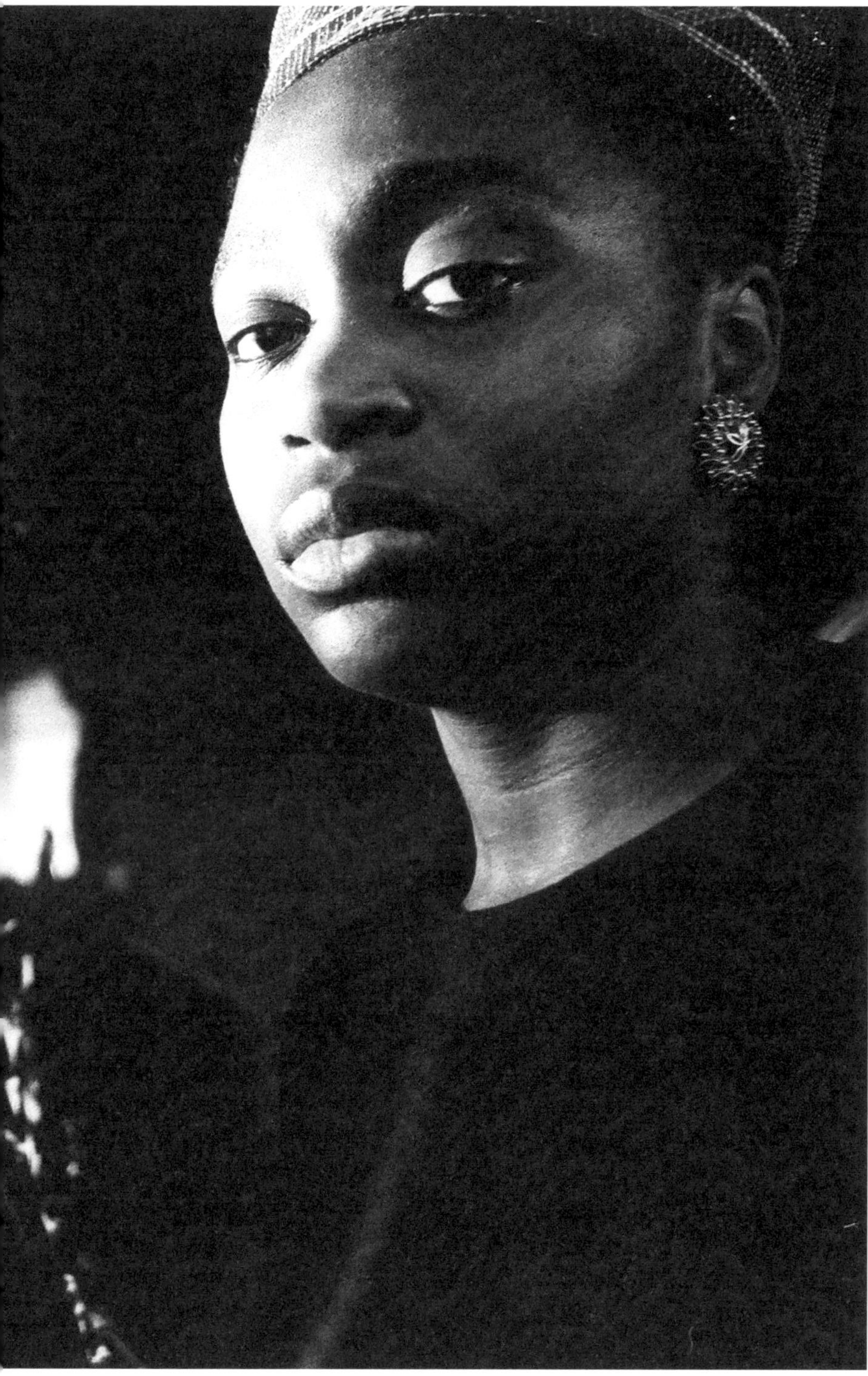

Still from Sankofa Film/Video Collective, *Dreaming Rivers*. Courtesy Lux and Judah Attille

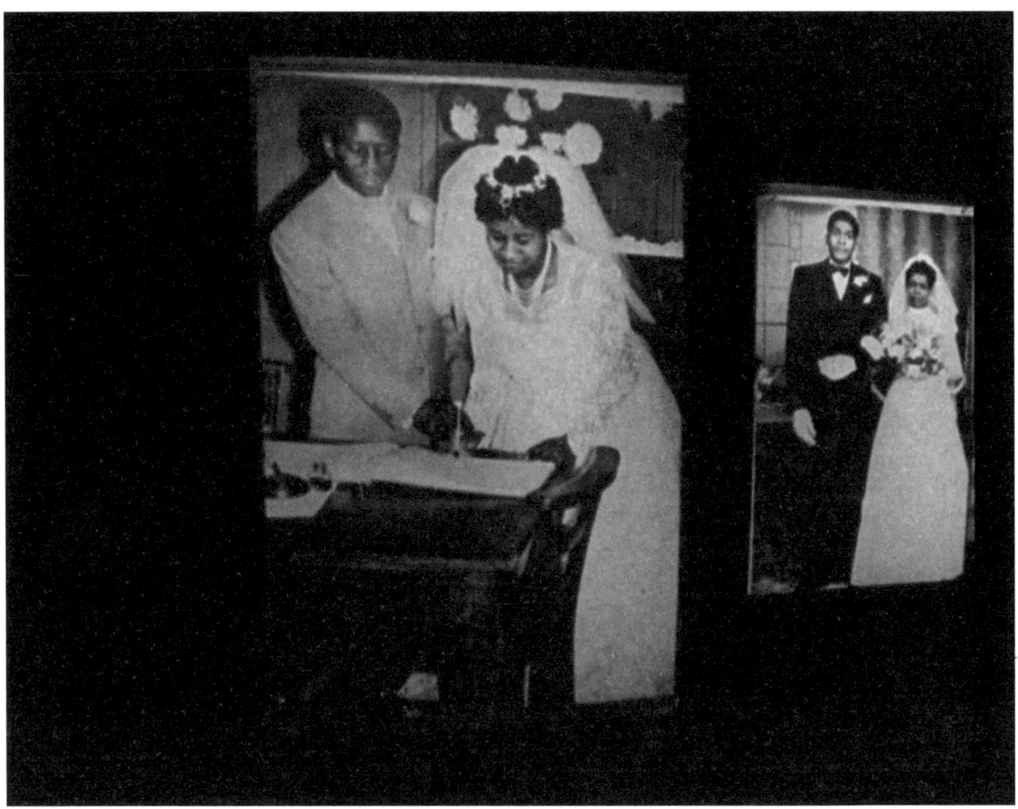

Still from Black Audio Film Collective, *Handsworth Songs*. Courtesy Smoking Dogs Films

The political import of this one-off screening, at this moment of time, is something we can only recognize fully in retrospect. Theresa May was British Home Secretary and Minister for Women and Equalities in this era. Serving under Conservative Prime Minster David Cameron, she instigated an avowedly hostile environment for immigrants. Legislation ensued that led to the deportation of people who had come to Britain from its colonies – like the protagonist of *Dreaming Rivers* from the Caribbean – on the basis of an invitation to legal settlement, one that did not necessarily protect rights to remain with paperwork. The shameful scandal would only hit the mainstream news in 2018, and it remains ongoing.

I do not seek to yoke *Dreaming Rivers* and *Handsworth Songs* to ongoing crises of racism and nationalism in the UK in order to reduce them in some way to politics. As I hope I have already gone some way to establish, their aesthetic registers are entirely central to their critical and ideological potential. However, I believe their politics should be celebrated in the apolitical desert of much celebrated European and US art of the 1980s; and their ongoing relevance, politically, is something that, formally articulated, keeps them painfully and powerfully alive in new contexts of exposure.

***

The staged presence of *Dreaming Rivers* – the use of a set, of pronounced gestures and stillness, delivered lines and pauses, foregrounded props and costumes – all underscore the drama of overwhelm conveyed in the film. If the threshold between a life and its ending is presented, then that transition is explored in the amplifying of more irresolute shifts, as made between disparate islands, between arriving and getting lost, disappearing and standing out, seeing and being seen, wakefulness and dreams. Beyond the theatricalization of life as it is routinely lived – conveying the regular tragedy of every death and the hammy power of love – there is a productive channelling of expressionist cinema's representation of social trauma in personal melodrama.

The protagonist never leaves her bedroom, but with her we traverse generations and continents – riding out their swirling together. In the intense privacy of this bedroom, the windows do not show us any views out, but the mirrors and framed pictures – like the other gathered objects and visitors – allow us further in. At the same time, these co-presences channel historical narratives and entangle geo-political contexts. As the individual engages and is engaged, there is both crisis and clarity, a mingling of longing with learning and reaching with falling.

There are surprising and disturbing resonances in *Handsworth Songs*. For instance, towards the end of the film, a female voice reads a letter attributed to a doll maker from East Bengal, writing to her sister in 1937: 'You asked me what I think of Birmingham. Sometimes I see myself floating at the centre of the earth, loving and loathing the city. In these moments I forgive myself for being alive.'

***

I would like to make a further situational move, shifting to the UK at large in the 1980s.

The average Briton is watching 25 hours of television per week. New, in this context, is Channel 4, which has something of the public service remit of the two BBC channels and something of the independence of ITV. In a two-pronged approach to supporting innovative work and reaching new audiences, Channel 4 is funding groups – including Sankofa and Black Audio Film Collective, among others – to operate as workshops producing films that it may then buy for television transmission.

On this basis, *Handsworth Songs* and *Dreaming Rivers* are both made with core funding from Channel 4 and then broadcast by it across the UK. As such, the films address a nation – and members of that nation in their eclectic private spaces. Yet TV presentation of such experimental works means a late-night slot. The medium provides only a small screen with poor visual definition, uncontrolled volume and domestic interruptions. It means a distributed audience that does not share a discursive forum. Nevertheless, there is the knowledge that an audience of more than 300,000 will routinely be reached.[22] And there is the magic of this number simultaneously sharing a focus of attention.

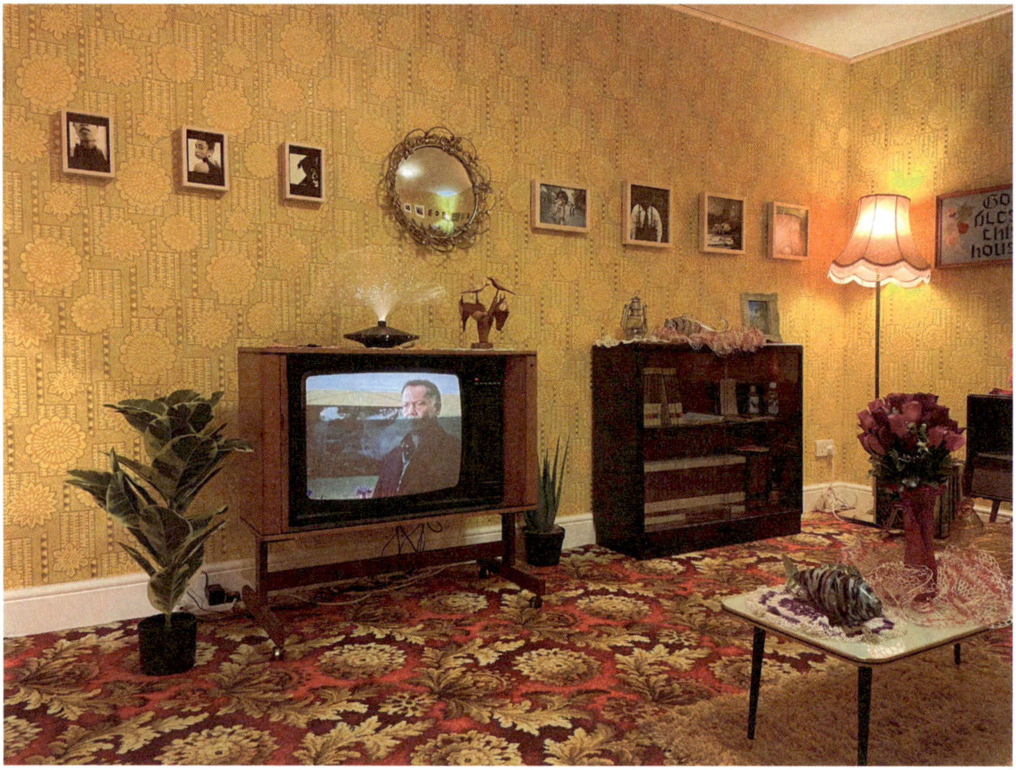

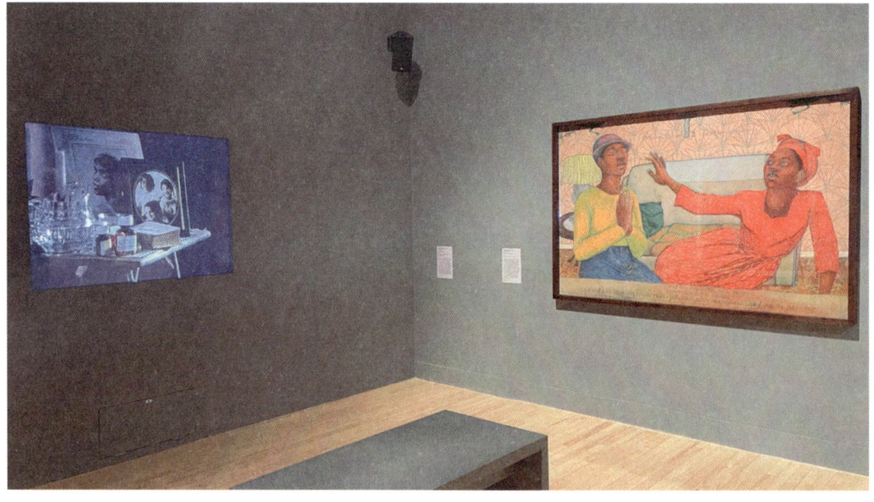

Handsworth Songs is screened on British television in July 1987, as part of a series titled 'Britain: The Lie of the Land'. Its inclusion, and deconstruction, of reportage regarding Black lives in the UK, both picks up on, and critically dilates, the regular fare of television news. Moreover, its momentary footage of photographic portraits of Britons of the African diaspora – shown as images suspended, large-scale, in a darkened room, reserved only for their display – cross-fertilizes the status sanctioned by public gallery exhibition, on the one hand, with domestic family pictures as hung on the walls of homes (complete with televisions), on the other. *Handsworth Songs* reaches 750,000 viewers on British TV.[23]

Opposite, above: Michael McMillan, *The Front Room*, 2021. Installation view, 'Life Between Islands: Caribbean-British Art 1950s–Now', Tate Britain, London, 2021–22. Courtesy the artist

Opposite, below: Sankofa Film/Video Collective, *Dreaming Rivers*, and Sonia Boyce, *Missionary Position II*, 1985. Installation views, 'Life Between Islands: Caribbean-British Art 1950s–Now', Tate Britain. Courtesy the artists

Dreaming Rivers is screened on Channel 4 in November of the next year, as a part of a season programmed by June Givanni with the title 'Black Cinema from Europe'. The British domestic domain – presented as both sanctuary and cell for the protagonist of *Dreaming Rivers* – resonates precisely, yet open-endedly, with the situation that the viewer, at home, watches the film within. Moreover, while *Handsworth Songs* puts into question the news programming typical of TV, *Dreaming Rivers* undoes the norms of classical TV drama, for instance, the BBC's *Play for Today* series.

John Akomfrah has reflected, looking back in an interview:

> *It was a new space, on your street! I would go out occasionally and stand on a different street from the one we lived on, just to see which lights were up. Were they watching Channel 4? Because it was the only thing that was going, late at night. Suddenly there were all these lights, on streets. A new community of the night was emerging… It was seismic.*[24]

I was fractionally too young – my family too White and remote from artistic practice – to know about that new community of the night. However, when I watch *Dreaming Rivers* now, I feel almost seismically connected to what I missed then. I am transported back to the kitchen where our TV lived, sharing the cooking surfaces; my feet are propped up on the cutlery drawer as I sit a mere metre from the screen for hours after school. The film powerfully reminds me today of hitting my teenage years back then – of the material culture my family gathered about us, held dear and shed; of the fickleness versus endurance of style, or the power of fashion and how it can betray us; of presence and loss as lived through migration; of matriarchy; and the awkward melodrama of growing up and aging.

☆☆☆

I am sitting on the sofa, glancing around the room hosting me. A moment of conversation bubbles up with the young women I find myself sitting beside, as we share respective stories of family members bringing back, from their travels, ornaments like those on top of the television opposite. We might be at a social gathering in someone's house, but instead we are in the latest iteration of Michael McMillan's *Front Room* project,[25] installed at Tate Britain in the exhibition 'Life Between Islands: Caribbean-British Art 1950s to Now' (2021–22). This artwork restages the Victorian parlour turned 1970s reception space for visitors to the home of someone living in England with African Caribbean heritage. In the exhibition catalogue, Gilane Tawadros describes the work as 'connecting private and public worlds, and presenting the enormous performative effort expended to bridge the "rupture of migration"'.[26]

Next door, *Dreaming Rivers* is projected in close proximity to contemporaneous pictures by Sonia Boyce, with the hushed grey of the walls drawing intense contrast with the vociferous wallpaper and ornamentation that constitutes McMillan's *Front Room* on the other side of the plasterboard partition. Here, on this side, Shirley Thompson's award-winning music, St Lucian folk songs sung in creole and the multiple speaking voices of *Dreaming Rivers* hold sway.

The director of *Dreaming Rivers* has quoted Abondance Matanda on culture as it is lived at home as opposed to that outside of the domestic sphere. In her essay 'The First Galleries I Knew Were Black Homes', Matanda writes: 'We learnt to vocalise our thoughts about visual media long before we started stepping in white cube galleries, wondering why nobody laughs out loud or runs their mouths in there.'[27]

***

Through film festivals and screening programmes in the 1980s, *Handsworth Songs* and *Dreaming Rivers* addressed many parts of the world: representing contemporaneous Britain and channelling the attendant ghosts, while entering into dialogue with other places.[28] Belatedly recognized within Britain as British *art* – partly on the back of exhibition elsewhere – these films continue to speak to the present moment in the country.

However, the work probably reaches most audiences now through online streaming – for instance through MUBI or courtesy of LUX, via Vimeo. In fact, *Handsworth Songs* currently awaits you on YouTube whenever you want it. While I regret the move these platforms have made away from collective recognition for the teams responsible – something that Tate, at the point of accessioning the work of Black Audio Film Collective and following the lead perhaps of Documenta, did not perpetuate – I welcome the return to a domestic viewing context. Certainly, through the films being online, even if only for a limited period, we have lost the precisely synchronized domesticity that prompted seismic tremors for some watching television in 1980s Britain. However, exhibitions have usually operated through durational fields, aggregating dispersed attendees – rather than as singular events, with a unified audience – and new discursive forums have opened up technologically that, at their best, enable a convening of debate between widely distributed individuals.

If you watch these films online at home, their screening history on UK television in the 1980s would seem important to remember. As a result of that history, they might address you *in your home*, while asking renewed questions. After *Handsworth Songs*: What enters into your private space, quasi neutrally, via news coverage or archival footage on your screen? After *Dreaming Rivers*: What might you keep on or around you, to anchor you, or as ballast for flight?

Notes

I wish to thank the following for keying me into different parts of the material covered here: Karen Alexander, David A. Bailey, Steven Ball, Sonia Boyce, Wing Chan, Stuart Comer, Lauren Cornell, Ben Cook, Coco Fusco, Lena Kühnel, Michael McMillan, David Morris, Filipa Oliveira, Jeff Preiss, William Raban, Karin Schneider, Sunil Shah, Teka Selman and Rod Stoneman.

[1] The roles among members of Sankofa on *Dreaming Rivers* are attributed as follows: Martina Attille, director; Isaac Julien, assistant director; Nadine Marsh-Edwards, production manager; and Maureen Blackwood, production assistant. Additional credits on the film go to Sonia Boyce as set designer, Nina Kellgren as cinematographer and Shirley Thompson for composition of the musical score, for example. All the actors are named, of course, as are three individuals responsible for 'St Lucian Voices'.

[2] Kobena Mercer notes that '*The Passion of Remembrance* [by Sankofa, also 1986] and *Handsworth Songs* were the first black-directed feature films to begin theatrical exhibition at a West End London venue, a standard *rite-de-passage* in film culture.' See K. Mercer, 'Recoding Narratives of Race and Nation', the introduction to his edited volume *Black Film, British Cinema*, London: Institute of Contemporary Arts, 1988, p.6. Coco Fusco describes the Metro Cinema as 'occup[ying] a place analogous to that of the Film Forum in New York City'. See C. Fusco, 'Black Filmmaking in Britain's Workshop Section', in Michael T. Martin (ed.), *Cinemas of the Black Diaspora: Diversity, Dependence, and Oppositionality*, Detroit: Wayne State University Press, 1995, p.316, n.2.

[3] The roles among members of Black Audio Film Collective on *Handsworth Songs* are attributed as follows: John Akomfrah, director; Lina Goupaul, producer; Reece Auguiste, production assistant; Trevor Mathison, sound; Avril Johnson, assistant sound; and Edward George, camera assistant. Additional credits for the film list, for instance, Sebastian Shah on camera, voiceovers by Pervais Khan, Meera Syal and Yvonne Weekes, also numerous interviewees and archival sources.

[4] Stuart Hall, 'New Ethnicities', in K. Mercer, *Black Film, British Cinema*, *op. cit.*, p.30.

[5] See, in particular, however, Almna Malik, 'Migratory Aesthetics: (Dis)placing the Black Maternal Subject in Martina Attille's *Dreaming Rivers* (1988)', in R. Victoria Arana (ed.), *"Black" British Aesthetics Today*, Cambridge: Cambridge University Press, 2007.

[6] Bérénice Reynaud, who was involved with the Collective for Living Cinema, described the venue at the time as 'a 125-seat alternative film showcase, which is a not very well-endowed "avant-garde organization", and does not exactly qualify as being a part of the art establishment' ('Response to Coco Fusco's "Fantasies of Oppositionality"', *Screen*, vol.30, no.3, Summer 1989, p.80). She wrote this in response to Coco Fusco's description of the organization as being 'until quite recently' among the 'bastions of overwhelmingly white avant-garde cultural practices' ('Fantasies of Oppositionality: Reflections on Recent Conferences in Boston and New York', *Screen*, vol.29, no.4, Autumn 1988, 'The Last "Special Issue" on Race?', p.80).

[7] Described as a 'touring film exhibition', 'Young, British and Black' moved from the Collective for Living Cinema to a community centre in the Queens borough of New York City and upstate to Hallwalls Contemporary Art Center in Buffalo, where an accompanying publication was produced: C. Fusco, *Young, British and Black: A Monograph on the Work of Sankofa Film/Video Collective and Black Audio Film Collective*, Buffalo, NY: Hallwalls Contemporary Arts Center, 1988.

[8] Armond White, 'Journals: Young Guns and Old Masters', *Film Comment*, vol.24, no.4, July 1988, p.2.

[9] *Ibid.*

[10] *Ibid.*, p.4.

[11] Kobena Mercer perhaps offers the most extensive analysis of the work of Sankofa and Black Audio Film Collective at the time, although he rarely considers *Dreaming Rivers*. See, for example: 'Third Cinema at Edinburgh: Reflections on a Pioneering Event', *Screen*, vol.26, no.5, Autumn 1986; 'Recoding Narratives of Race and Nation', in *Black Film, British Cinema*, *op. cit.*; and 'Diaspora Culture and the Dialogic Imagination: The Aesthetics of Black Independent Film in Britain', in Mbye B. Cham and Claire Andrade-Watkins (ed.), *Blackframes: Critical Perspectives on Black Independent Cinema*, Cambridge, MA: MIT Press, 1988, and republished in Mercer's anthology *Welcome to the Jungle: New Positions in Black Cultural Studies*, London: Routledge, 1994, p.97.

[12] In the late throes of the Cold War, the First World, as anchored in the US and Western Europe and opposed to the Second World of the USSR, had managed to undermine the political statement of non-aligned nations gathered together under the banner of the Third World. In this context, Third Cinema played a complex and contested role culturally, with ambiguous status when invoked in relation to film-makers of the African diaspora working in the US and UK. See discussion between contributors to K. Mercer, *Black Film, British Cinema*, *op. cit.*, notably texts by Judith Williamson and Coco Fusco; and Jim Pines and Paul Willemen (ed.), *Questions of Third Cinema*, London: British Film Institute, 1989.

[13] Jeff Preiss shot this footage and transformed it into the artwork *CARS-A-POPPIN for Bob Fleischer* (2019).

[14] Perhaps the clearest evocation of a domestic interior in *Handsworth Songs* comes when listening to the words of Patricia Jarret from 1985. With both composure and rending compassion, she describes the recent death of her mother following a police raid on their London home. We have already seen something of the media frenzy over Cynthia Jarret's funeral, and glimpsed the wreathed words at the back of one of the slowly progressing black cars which spell, as intimately as publicly, 'GRAN'.
[15] *Handsworth Songs* was first presented under Tate's auspices as a part of 'The Elusive Sign: British Avant-Garde Film and Video 1977–1987', which then toured the UK and internationally. However, this was seen an education initiative, as much as a curatorial one, and 'staged in gloomy basement lecture rooms', as recalled (in general for Tate's film programmes of the era) by David Curtis. See D. Curtis, '"In the Bloody Basement Again" – Three Observations about British Conceptual and Structural Film', *Moving Image Review & Art Journal* (*MIRAJ*), vol.6, nos.1–2, December 2017, p.261. Curtis got *Handsworth Songs* into the galleries at Tate Britain as a part of his year-long presentation of screenings 'A Century of Artists' Film in Britain' (2003–04). However, here too there was apparently a sense that the exhibition was marginalized from the collection displays and relative to newly commissioned art, with a lack of sufficient darkness and ongoing educational overtones rather than artistic centring.
[16] Offering 'Some Critical Reflections' on 'Art and Cinema' for the catalogue published in conjunction with the Documenta 11 exhibition, co-curator Mark Nash would write: 'The Edinburgh International Film Festival Conferences from the 1970s until 1986 were probably the most important single location in the anglophone world for the development of theoretical debates on cultural production, with a specific focus on film.' In Okwui Enwezor (ed.), *Documenta11_Platform 5* (exh. cat.), Ostfildern-Ruit: Hatje Cantz, 2002, p.134. The 1986 'Third Cinema' edition was programmed by Jim Pines and Paul Willemen, co-ordinated by June Givanni and led to the publication *Questions of Third Cinema*, *op. cit.*
[17] Hatoum's videos constituted the only moving-image works featured in the landmark exhibition 'The Other Story: Afro-Asian Artists in Post-War Britain' (Hayward Gallery, London, and touring to Manchester and Wolverhampton, 1989–90). Hatoum's videos were united with the work of Black Audio Film Collective at the Tate Gallery in 1987 for 'The Elusive Sign' (see n.15). Hatoum's *Measures of Distance* entered Tate's collections in 1999.
[18] *Handsworth Songs* featured strikingly in 'Migrations: Journeys into British Art' at Tate Britain in 2012. This was not unproblematic as remarked, for instance, by Hammad Nasar in 'Notes from the Field: Navigating the Afterlife of "The Other Story"', *Field Notes 04: Publics, Histories, Value: The Changing Stakes of Exhibitions*, Hong Kong: Asia Art Archive, 2015, p.55.
[19] Mark Fisher, 'The land still lies: *Handsworth Songs* and the English riots', 6 June 2012, http://old.bfi.org.uk/sightandsound/newsandviews/comment/handsworth-songs-london-riots.php.
[20] K. Mercer, 'Diaspora Culture and the Dialogic Imagination', *op. cit.*, p.97.
[21] Tate's brochure for the screening of *Dreaming Rivers* on 2 November 2015 is available at https://www.tate.org.uk/file/martina-attille-dreaming-rivers-screening-notes.
[22] This statistic is given by Alan Fountain, Channel 4's commissioning editor for independent film and video at the time. See his 'Channel 4 and Black Independents', in K. Mercer, *Black Film, British Cinema*, *op. cit.*, p.43.
[23] This statistic is quoted in Lynne Jackson and Jean Rasenberger, 'Young, British and Black', *Cineaste*, vol.16, no.4, 1988, p.24.
[24] John Akomfrah in conversation with Ashley Clark, in *Neither/Nor, Chimeric Cinema, Black Audio Film Collective, 1980s–1990s*, Los Angeles: Academy of Motion Pictures of Arts and Sciences, 2018, pp.24–25, available at https://issuu.com/truefalsefilmfest1/docs/neithernor_2018_final.
[25] Compare the contemporaneous installation of this project as part of the collection displays at the Museum of the Home in London. The historical development of the project is connected with this institution, where it opened as *The West Indian Front Room*, a temporary show, in 2005 (the institution was known as the Geffrye Museum at the time).
[26] Gilane Tawadros, 'Home and Away: Odysseys, Entanglements and Acts of Resistance', in David A. Bailey and Alex Farquharson (ed.), *Life Between Islands: Caribbean-British Art 1950s–Now*, London: Tate Publishing, 2021, p.82. With 'rupture of migration', Tawadros quotes Stuart Hall, 'The "West Indian" Front Room', in Michael McMillan (ed.), *The Front Room: Migrant Aesthetics in the Home*, London: Black Dog Publishing, 2009.
[27] Abondance Matanda, 'The First Galleries I Knew Were Black Homes', in Nathan Connolly (ed.), *Know Your Place: Essays on the Working Class by the Working Class*, Liverpool: Dead Ink, 2017, p.14.
[28] *Handsworth Songs* was screened in several film festivals in 1986, the year prior to its cinema release and TV broadcast, for instance in Birmingham and London in the UK, and also Stockholm and Havana. In 1987 it won prizes at film festivals in Burkina Faso and Los Angeles, and also documentary awards from the British Film Institute and the National Black Programming Consortium in Columbus, Ohio. For more details, see Kodwo Eshun and Anjalika Sagar, *The Ghosts of Songs: The Film Art of the Black Audio Film Collective*, Liverpool: University of Liverpool Press, 2007,

pp.217–18. *Dreaming Rivers* notably won an award at the 35th International Film Festival in Mannheim in October 1988 and was screened alongside work by Gurinder Chada, Mona Hatoum, Ngozi Onwurah and Pratibha Parmar in a UK programme as part of the feminist Third Cinema festival 'In Visible Colours', curated by Zainub Veerjee and Lorraine Chan in Vancouver in November 1989.

The Afterlives of 'Transforming the Crown': Black British Art and the Survey Exhibition – Mora J. Beauchamp-Byrd

Introduction

In November 2019, my article 'Cut-outs and "Silent Companions": Theatricality and Satire in Lubaina Himid's "A Fashionable Marriage"' was published online in the art journal *Burlington Contemporary*.[1] Its publication marked a pivotal moment in my exploration of Himid's work over the decades, including scholarship that has addressed both the feminism and diasporic narratives in her art as well as her curatorial initiatives. On an even more personal note, the article represents a key moment in the afterlife of 'Transforming the Crown: African, Asian and Caribbean Artists in Britain, 1966–1996' (1997–98, hereafter 'Crown'), my early curatorial project that stands out as a key art historical moment, shaped as it was by tremendous conceptual and logistical challenges.

In late 1993, in New York City, I began organizing 'Crown', which eventually featured the work of more than fifty artists. I envisioned it as a form of introduction, for North American audiences, to the fullness and diversity of late-twentieth-century British art. 'Crown' was shaped by a multiculturalism-inspired curatorial strategy that was fairly commonplace in the 1980s and 1990s, and informed by my interests in a broad range of interdisciplinary scholarly approaches: psychoanalysis; global modernisms; cultural studies; Black Atlantic thought; diasporic themes in art and literature; and feminist, postmodernist and queer studies.[2] The exhibition opened at three separate venues – the Bronx Museum of the Arts, the Caribbean Cultural Center and the Studio Museum in Harlem – in mid-October of 1997, and has been viewed as the largest US-organized survey of Black British art. While the show and its catalogue received a flurry of global critical attention that was largely positive, its reception was also marked by a broader critique of similar group shows – such as 'The Decade Show' (1990), also in New York and co-organized by the New Museum, the Museum of Contemporary Hispanic Art and the Studio Museum in Harlem – that were viewed as shaped by 'identity politics'. 'Crown' has been the subject of ongoing analysis and assessment, from a lengthy *New York Times* review by art critic Holland Cotter that appeared soon after the show opened, to artist and scholar Eddie Chambers's fairly recent *Nka* discussion of the show, in 2019.[3]

In this essay, I will ask: What does the continued discussion regarding 'Crown' reveal about the 'usefulness' of the survey exhibition as curatorial strategy? I will consider my aims in developing 'Crown', involving diaspora-related questions and the interest in global modernisms that has fuelled my curatorial practice. I will also explore a few of the critical responses. Using my own scholarly trajectory after 'Crown' as a case study of sorts, I wish to make a defence of the survey exhibition format, envisioning it as a seed – one that will ideally generate later monographic exhibitions and publications, as well as other examples of long-form scholarship. I argue for the survey's continuing relevance as we deal with the hierarchies and omissions that continue to shape our field.

The Caribbean Cultural Center and Precedents for 'Crown'

I began developing 'Crown' at the Caribbean Cultural Center, an institution established by Dr Marta Moreno Vega in 1976, where I became curator and director of special projects in 1993. When 'Crown' opened, the Center had been actively producing programmes that emphasized the global manifestations (and impact) of Africa-based cultural and spiritual traditions for twenty years. These initiatives included 'Carnival in New York', an annual tribute to African diaspora women; conferences; dance and musical performances; exhibitions; lectures; school programmes; and scholarly publications. These events attracted loyal audiences that were often drawn from the city's African American, Latino and Caribbean communities, while Center programmes featured artists, performers and scholars from throughout the world. My Caribbean Cultural Center projects included social history exhibitions such as 'CUBOP! The Life and Music of Mario Bauza' (1993); 'Transcending Silence: The Life and Poetic Legacy of Audre Lorde' (1994); and 'The Worldview of Katherine Dunham' (1994), which examined the life and work of the pioneering anthropologist and choreographer. I also developed projects centred on the visual arts, such as 'Struggle and Serenity: The Visionary Art of Elizabeth Catlett' (1996), a mini retrospective that included a near-complete group of the artist's paintings, most of which had never before been exhibited publicly.[4] In early 1997, I organized 'When I Am Not Here/Estoy Alla: Photographs by Maria Magdalena Campos-Pons', an exhibition that presented a series of striking, conceptually rigorous, large-format Polaroids by the Cuban artist.[5]

For 'Crown', I was inspired by the art historian and curator Kellie Jones's highly influential projects, among them 'US-UK Photography Exchange' (1989), organized in collaboration with David A. Bailey, and 'Interrogating Identity' (1991), a travelling exhibition co-organized with Tom Sokolowski, which also included British- and US-based artists.[6] My curatorial path was also fuelled by British precedents such as the pioneering 'The Other Story: Afro-Asian Artists in Post-War Britain' (1989), developed by Rasheed Araeen, and 'From Two Worlds' (1986), whose curators, Nicholas Serota and Gavin Jantjes, focused on 'a fusion of European and non-European visions'.[7] 'Crown' also emerged from my 1980s intrigue with Hanif Kureishi's *My Beautiful Laundrette* (1985); Isaac Julien's *Looking for Langston* (1989) and other films produced in the UK; and music, album covers and music videos by Culture Club, Fine Young Cannibals, Loose Ends, Sade, Simply Red, Soul II Soul and Tears for Fears. While I was still an undergraduate at NYU, a student work-study trip to London in the summer of 1989, organized through the university's international offices, further cemented my interest in the UK. During that visit, I was able to see curator Dawn Ades's 'Art in Latin America: The Modern Era, 1820–1980' exhibition at the Hayward Gallery, which also had an impact on my development of 'Crown'.[8]

One of my guiding questions was: 'How have artists of African, Asian and Caribbean descent in Britain engaged with ideas of home and nationality, particularly in periods of heightened racism and xenophobia … ?'[9] In the early to mid-1990s, we were witnessing increasing media coverage of anti-immigration legislation in the US. I was also considering how British artists

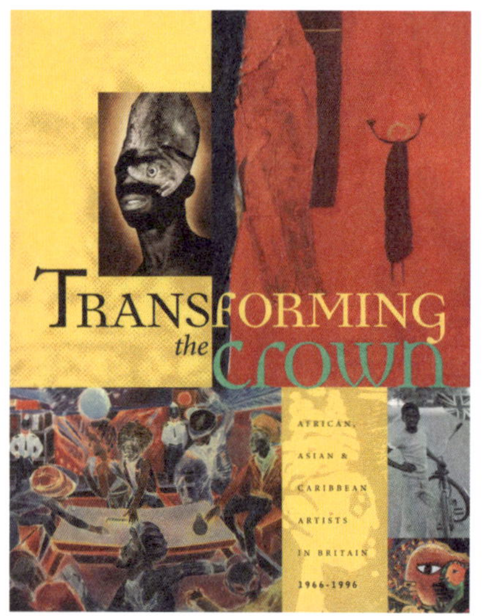

Cover of exhibition catalogue for 'Transforming the Crown: African, Asian and Caribbean Artists in Britain, 1966–1996', The Bronx Museum of the Arts, the Studio Museum in Harlem and The Caribbean Cultural Center, New York, 1997–98

Curator Mora J. Beauchamp-Byrd, artist Ingrid Pollard and Kinshasha Holman Conwill, executive director of the Studio Museum in Harlem, at the opening reception for 'Transforming the Crown', the Studio Museum in Harlem, October 1997. All images courtesy the author

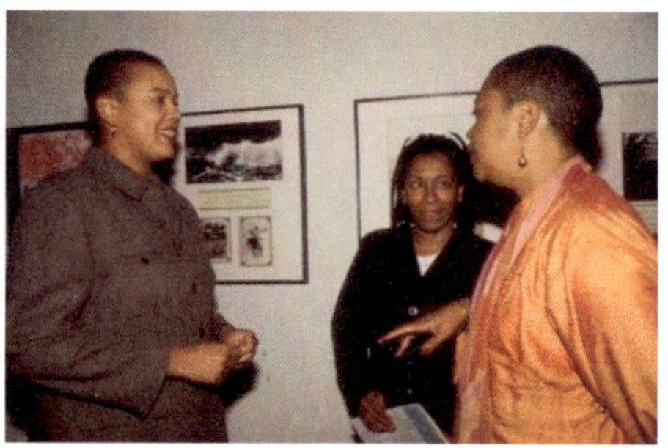

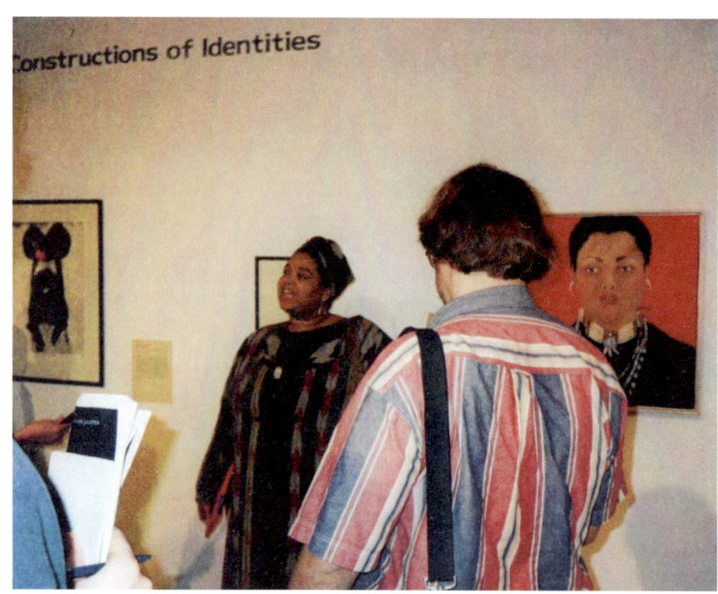

Rita Keegan discussing her work at press preview for 'Transforming the Crown', The Bronx Museum of the Arts, October 1997

Cover of exhibition catalogue for 'The Worldview of Katherine Dunham', The Caribbean Cultural Center, 1994

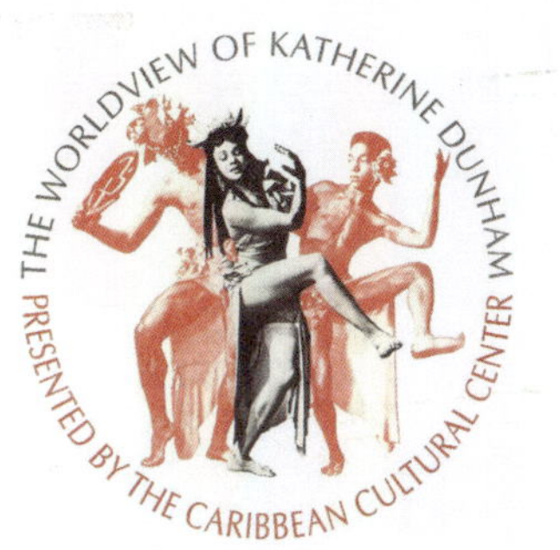

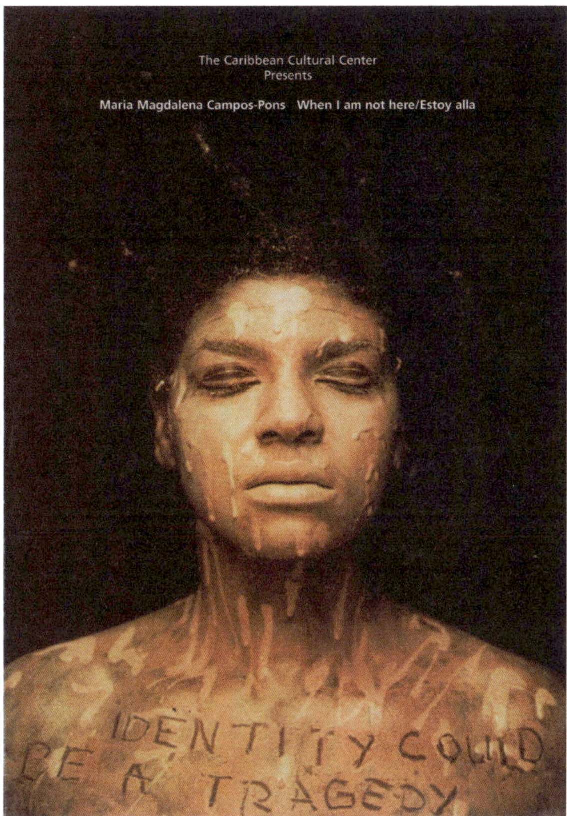

Cover of exhibition brochure for 'Maria Magdalena Campos-Pons: When I Am Not Here: Estoy Alla', The Caribbean Cultural Center, 1997

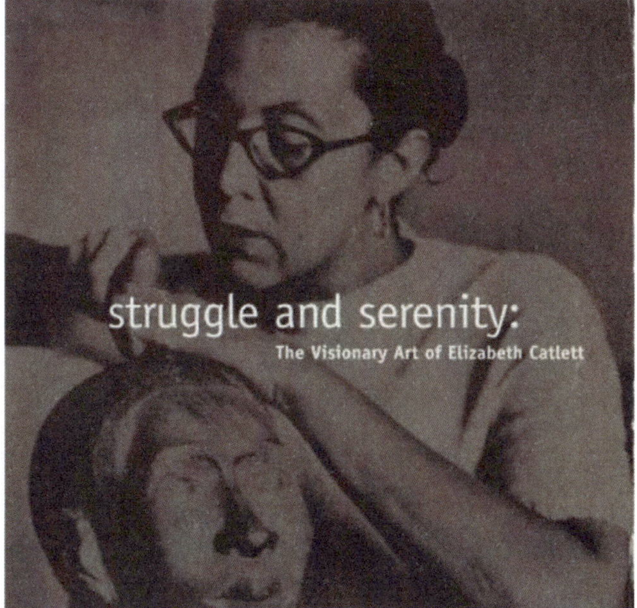

Cover of exhibition catalogue for 'Struggle and Serenity: The Visionary Art of Elizabeth Catlett', The Caribbean Cultural Center, 1996

defined themselves, and how they were being defined – if they were mentioned at all – in British art historical scholarship. Questions of identity had long been part of my upbringing in the US state of Louisiana, where everyday discussions often evoked the complex nuances that define Cajun, Creole and Creole of colour identity.[10] By 1994, I had begun conducting studio visits in the UK for the show, photographing artists, documenting works of art and gathering exhibition brochures regarding their previous shows. I remember wondering: Why hadn't these artists' intriguing works been discussed in the texts that were assigned in my art history courses?

Structuring the Exhibition

After each of my curatorial research trips to the UK, I was consistently asked when I returned home, 'Are there Black people in England?'[11] – this despite earlier curatorial initiatives like 'Interrogating Identity', and despite the popularity, in the US, of British musicians like Sade, Soul II Soul and Loose Ends. And so 'Crown' was meant, in part, to introduce US audiences to its featured UK-based artists. I initially planned a small show of eight to ten artists, but soon began developing a much more expansive project that ultimately presented the work of 55 artists and nearly 220 paintings, sculptures, photographs, prints, installations and video works. I had worked at both the Studio Museum in Harlem and the Bronx Museum of the Arts at the earliest stages of my career, and I proposed a partnership between the three venues. After discussions with each executive director (Marta Moreno Vega at CCC, Kinshasha Holman Conwill at the Studio Museum and Jane Delgado at the Bronx Museum), I organized a joint meeting with all three as well as curatorial staff. I was most intrigued about possibilities for merging the distinct audiences of these three important New York City institutions.

I decided on a thirty-year survey that would begin with the Caribbean Artists Movement (CAM) – a literary, visual and performing arts movement (1966–72) established in Britain by the novelist Andrew Salkey, of Jamaica; poet Edward Kamau Brathwaite, of Barbados; and poet and activist John La Rose, of Trinidad.[12] With the exception of the CAM section, which was at the Studio Museum, I structurally divided the plan of the exhibition into thematic sections. In addition, the CCC site was devoted to thirty years of work by photographer Vanley Burke; 'Picturing England: The Photographic Narratives of Vanley Burke' included a series of life-sized, framed prints documenting the Afro Caribbean and Asian communities that were recruited to work at factories in Birmingham and elsewhere in the UK's Midlands after World War II.[13] The other sections delved into themes that had emerged from my numerous visits to artists' studios: 'The Flag: Evocations of Home and National Identity'; 'The Eternal Question: Spirituality, Myth and Ritual in Art'; 'Written on the Body: Contemporary Constructions of Identity'; and 'Visualizing Resistance: Artists and Activism in Britain'. In structuring the show, I also had to remain mindful of spatial needs and challenges. For example, it was clear that the Bronx Museum's higher ceilings would work best for large-scale installations like Bhajan Hunjan's *Red Piece* (1994) and Faisal Abdu'Allah's *Last Supper* (1995). The Bronx Museum also had a raised, stage-like area that was ideal for the 'Written on the Body' section, which featured self-portraits. In a similar fashion, Denzil Forrester's monumental *Red Room* (1983) was best suited to the first-floor space at the Studio Museum in Harlem, while David Medalla's collaborative and resplendent *A Stitch in Time* (1968–) was perfect for the second floor/mezzanine area.

I knew that I needed a major focus on the Black Arts Movement in the UK, highlighting how artists of African, Asian and Caribbean descent established galleries and developed exhibitions as well as exhibition catalogues and other publications in the 1980s. Since many of the artists had been born in England, as opposed to the Caribbean-born generations of CAM, I wanted to know: What had been the impact – culturally, politically, stylistically – of these quite distinct organizing efforts at two periods of time?

My early research was greatly assisted by the exhibition catalogues for the numerous projects organized by Eddie Chambers, including 'Black Art an' done' of 1981, co-organized with Keith Piper at Wolverhampton Art Gallery in the UK. It was one of numerous projects undertaken by Chambers and the group of artists that would later be called the Blk Art Group, whose members included Chambers, Piper, Marlene Smith, Donald Rodney and Claudette Johnson. I also researched projects developed by Panchayat, founded by Bhajan Hunjan, Shaheen Merali, Symrath Patti, Allan deSouza and Shanti Thomas in 1998 to promote the work of South Asian artists. I knew that these initiatives would need to be documented in the exhibition and/or the catalogue. I also had access to *Passion: Discourses on Blackwomen's Creativity* (1990) edited by Maud Sulter; Chambers's exhibition catalogues; and *Polareyes,* a jewel-like magazine developed by photographer Anita Jeni McKenzie that featured a rich and broad selection of photographs by Black and Asian women photographers. I also returned to the 'Critical Decade' issue of *Ten.8* on a regular basis.[14]

Of particular interest to me were the groundbreaking exhibitions organized by Himid to focus on women artists, including the seminal 'The Thin Black Line' (1985) at the Institute of Contemporary Arts (ICA), London. I wanted to emphasize how, through her curatorial and publishing projects as well as her establishment of a gallery called The Elbow Room, Himid brought heightened visibility and attention to then-emerging artists such as Sutapa Biswas, Sonia Boyce, Chila Burman, Rita Keegan, Ingrid Pollard, Veronica Ryan and others. In recent years, this generation of artists have increasingly been the subject of retrospectives and other major surveys.[15] Himid's *Between the Two My Heart is Balanced* (1991), from her *Revenge* series; Sonia Boyce's *She Ain't Holding Them Up, She's Holding On (Some English Rose)* (1986); Jeni McKenzie's *Untitled (from the exhibition 'Blood Ties' with Geraldine Walsh)* (1991); and Vanley Burke's *Boy with Flag* (1970) captured the attention of potential funders in the run-up to the show, and would feature in media coverage later on. The 'Crown' team at CCC also planned a full complement of public programmes for each site, including a film series called 'Colour Screens: Film and Video by African, Asian and Caribbean Artists in Britain'.[16]

Assessing the Reception of 'Crown'

During the 1990s, multiculturalism-inspired curatorial projects were often vilified, particularly as they sought to counter hegemonic, racist, sexist and

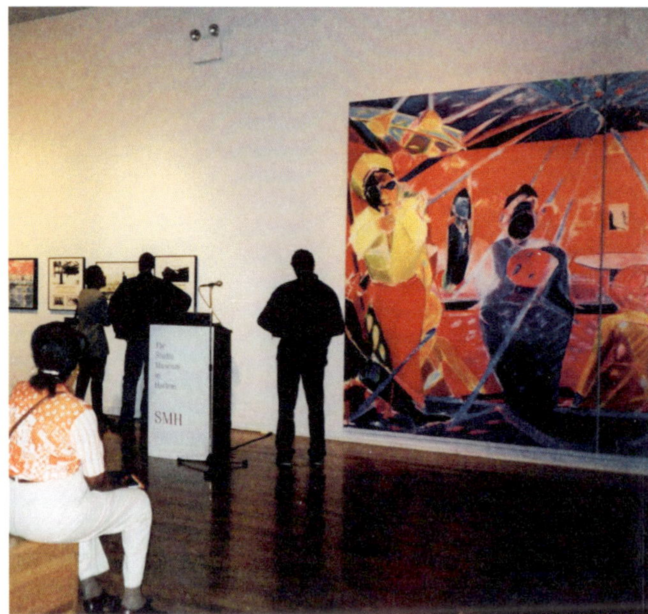

Denzil Forrester, *Red Room*, 1983. Installation view, 'Transforming the Crown', the Studio Museum in Harlem. To the left of Forrester's painting is a work by Ingrid Pollard

Opening reception audiences engaging with David Medalla's *A Stitch in Time*, 1968–, at 'Transforming the Crown', the Studio Museum in Harlem, 14 October 1997

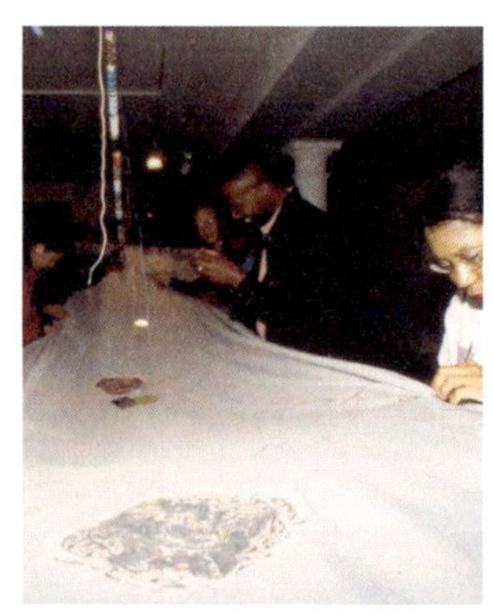

Exhibiting artists Hassan Aliyu, Lesley Sanderson, Winston Branch, Juginder Lamba and Emmanuel Jegede at opening reception for 'Picturing England: The Photographic Narratives of Vanley Burke', The Caribbean Cultural Center, 16 October 1997, a component of 'Transforming the Crown'

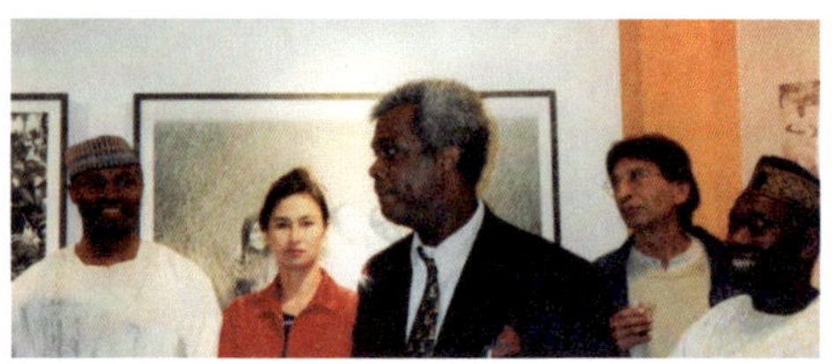

Curator Mora J. Beauchamp-Byrd and artist Rita Keegan at press preview for 'Transforming the Crown', the Studio Museum in Harlem, October 1997

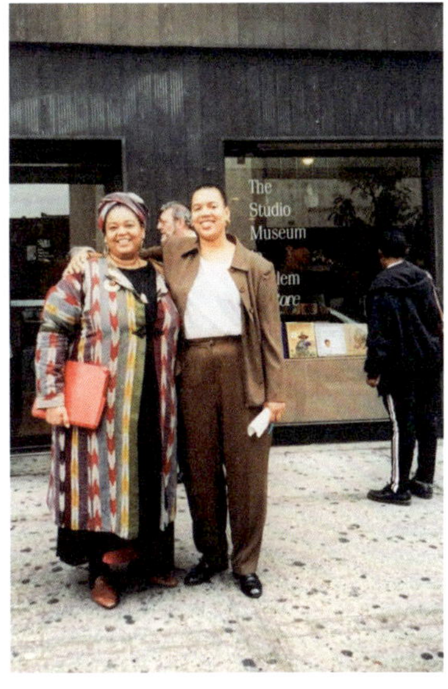

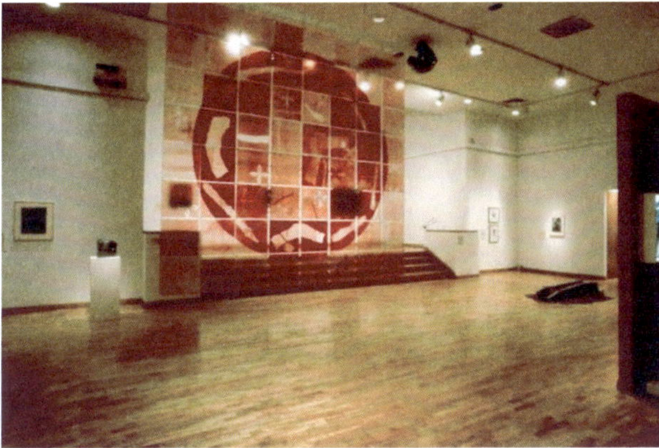

Bhajan Hunjan, *Red Piece*, 1994. Installation view, 'Transforming the Crown', The Bronx Museum of the Arts, 1997–98

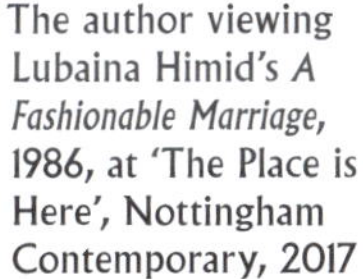

The author viewing Lubaina Himid's *A Fashionable Marriage*, 1986, at 'The Place is Here', Nottingham Contemporary, 2017

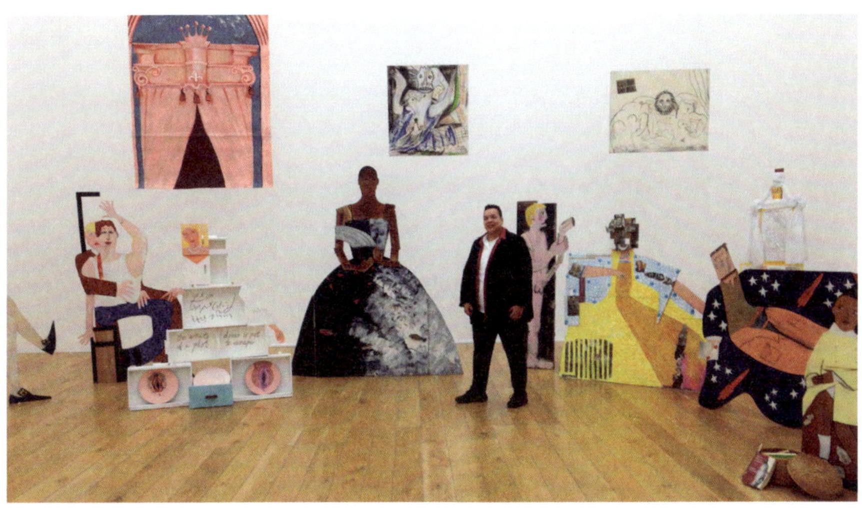

homophobic practices in the art world.[17] Group exhibitions were routinely attacked by art critics for their strategic inclusion of African American, Asian American, Latino and Native American artists, and for their efforts to examine, engage with and sometimes celebrate the work of artists of colour, women and LGBTQ artists. The 1993 Whitney Biennial, often deemed the 'multicultural' or 'political' edition of that event, was a prominent flashpoint, targeted by critics like Robert Hughes as 'a fiesta of whining'.[18] I was decidedly *not* in agreement with these critics, having emerged from an art historical grounding that I knew was too rarely diverse in scope. Were artists expected to merely wait for mainstream 'validation', or one-person shows, from institutions that continued to ignore them?

Soon after 'Crown' opened, Holland Cotter's *New York Times* review appeared. Spread over four pages, it included several full-colour images and highlighted numerous works. Cotter was certainly positive about aspects of the show, but he zeroed in on several criticisms that would later be echoed by others: he questioned a thematic structure rather than a chronological framework for the thirty-year period covered by the show, and he raised a lack of focus on the 1970s. Cotter's review concluded by stating that 'Crown' was 'a success, not just in the A-for-effort way but as the real thing: a group exhibition that projects a unified force field of energy as palpable as it is hard to define'.[19]

In the spring 1998 issue of *African Arts*, Elizabeth Harney conceded that the exhibition 'introduced an American audience to a plethora of artistic talents rarely seen on this side of the Atlantic', but she lamented the focus on 'identity politics', expressing her wish for a 'stronger historical framework' and noting that the CAM section was 'tucked away in a back room and unable to interact with other works'.[20] Harney concluded with a desire that cultural organizations 'move beyond identity-driven group shows to enable individual talents the opportunity to present a fuller story of their own practice'.[21]

Other coverage appeared in *African Arts*, *American Visions*, *Flash Art International*, *India Today International*, *Nka* and elsewhere, and I was invited to submit an article regarding the show to *The International Review of African American Art* (*IRAAA*).[22] A 1998 episode of *In the Life*, a television news magazine that aired on public television stations in the US, documented the show in a segment that primarily focused on the inclusion of LGBTQ-themed works.[23] In 2005, Judith Wilson (who also contributed to the 'Crown' catalogue) provided an overview of the show's reception as well as that of 'Disputed Identities: U.K./U.S.' (1990), at San Francisco Camerawork, and 'Interrogating Identity' (1991), at the Grey Art Gallery at New York University.[24] Wilson made the distinctions that 'Crown' was the only project of the three that was focused solely on British artists, that it was organized by an institution of colour and that it was a non-travelling show. Like other critics, she noted the lack of a 1970s focus and that both US and UK reviewers criticized the non-chronological format; but she also questioned the harsher criticism of 'Crown' that emerged from the UK, citing an 'antipluralist backlash' that had become prominent by the 1990s.[25]

The Progress of 'Crown': A Defence of the Survey

In considering the reception of 'Crown', I have often returned to the question of the role and impact of survey exhibitions. Due to their monumental scale and the scholarly gaps that they often propose to fill, survey exhibition projects are often conceived with lofty curatorial briefs and expectations that are nearly impossible to achieve. Yet the reception of a group survey often evolves dramatically through the years, as perception is shaped by the passage of time, ever-shifting waves of scholarly thought and the continuing emergence of fresh scholarship, including exhibitions and publications that traverse similar thematic paths.

My perspective has certainly been shaped by my experience of researching in preparation for 'Crown'. Beyond my discussions with the artists, survey exhibition catalogues were essentially *all I had.* These highly treasured and formative publications provided me with a tremendous fount of knowledge, enabling me to complete preliminary lists of artists and checklist items in the earliest stages. Through them, I developed artists' files that enhanced my preparation for studio visits, resulting in much more fruitful and mutually meaningful conversations with the artists. Also during studio visits, both before and after 'Crown', I photographed the artists and their works extensively, amassing a rich body of archival material. I was driven by the idea that my documentation of these artists was critical to a more expansive British art history, to the charting of global modernisms and to the study of contemporary artists' practices. This also informed my development of the exhibition catalogue of 'Crown' as a crucial part of the project, in the hope that it would inform and even inspire future researchers.[26]

Will we always require the survey? We will certainly need introductory texts as a foundational reference point, or an armature, or a skeletal framework, for later studies. 'Crown' was a pre-internet project, but even today the concentration and focus of research found in a survey can offer more to the researcher than the undifferentiated abundance of information to be found online. In teaching, I often use textbooks as a foundation, and I believe that survey exhibitions should be viewed in the same way – as ever-imperfect, never-meant-to-be-complete narratives; foundations that provide portals, or openings, for further research and scholarship.

Conclusion

As I have attempted to outline here, the various afterlives of 'Crown' include its critical reception; its appearance on course syllabi and in libraries internationally; and its ongoing life in scholarly and curatorial activities as a point of reference and debate. On a more personal note, these afterlives also include my own scholarship since 'Crown', including my lengthy examination of Lubaina Himid's work, and the friendships and professional relationships that I have established with the other artists, as well as my frequent incorporation of these artists and their work into my art history and museum and curatorial studies lectures.[27] It is certainly my experience that a survey exhibition such as 'Crown' can be highly generative for future research, writing, exhibitions and projects – and it is my hope that this may hold true for others.

Twenty-five years after the presentation of 'Crown', I recall my primary curatorial brief: to explore and present a broader and fuller view of late-twentieth-century British art, highlighting the varied and formally and conceptually rich work of the exhibiting artists. These histories have become even more valuable as we witness a rise in museum and curatorial studies programmes, and as museums become increasingly called upon to focus on DEAI (Diversity, Equity, Accessibility and Inclusion) initiatives. Perhaps one day I will assign a modern or contemporary art textbook to my students that includes the work of Sutapa Biswas, Rotimi Fani-Kayode, Sunil Gupta and Veronica Ryan. Until then, we can draw sustenance and contextual grounding from survey exhibitions and their indispensable catalogues, through afterlives that bear fruit for generations to come.

Notes

I extend my sincere and heartfelt thanks to Nana Adusei-Poku for inviting me to participate in this highly significant, exciting and much-needed project. I also appreciate Tracy Pollock, Ramona Rosenberg and all of the organizers at CCS Bard that facilitated the project. I thank my fellow panellists, Marlene Smith and Lucy Steeds, and discussant Kobena Mercer. I also appreciate the diligence and efforts of David Morris and Wing Chan at Afterall. Finally, I must also acknowledge the incredible and enthusiastic support of the following treasured friends and colleagues: LaNitra Berger, Christa Blackwood, Kendra Frorup, Cristina Cruz Gonzales, Erica Moiah James, Brandy Thomas Wells and Robin Vander.

[1] See Mora J. Beauchamp-Byrd, 'Cut-outs and "Silent Companions": Theatricality and Satire in Lubaina Himid's "A Fashionable Marriage"', *Burlington Contemporary*, issue 2, November 2019, https://contemporary.burlington.org.uk/journal/journal/cut-outs-and-silent-companions-theatricality-and-satire-in-lubaina-himids-a-fashionable-marriage-35. My article highlights Himid's use of the cut-out form, as inspired by dummy boards or 'silent companions': flat, often life-size painted wood figures that originated in the seventeenth-century in the Netherlands and were used as decorations or advertisements. Himid's appropriation of works by white European artists includes her well-known, large-scale installation *A Fashionable Marriage* (1986), drawn from William Hogarth's *Marriage A-la-Mode* (1743–45). My article primarily addresses Himid's engagement with theatricality, emphasizing her early grounding in set design at the Wimbledon School of Art and stylistic affinities with David Hockney's paintings and set designs, aspects not fully explored in previous scholarship on Himid.

[2] While working on 'Crown', I was an MA student in the art history department at Columbia University in New York, where we actively engaged with all of these approaches during my graduate studies.

[3] See Holland Cotter, 'This Realm of Newcomers, This England', *The New York Times*, 24 October 1997; and Eddie Chambers, introduction to 'Black British Art Histories' (special issue), *Nka Journal of Contemporary African Art*, no.45, November 2019, pp.4–6.

[4] See M.J. Beauchamp-Byrd, 'An Aesthetic of Survival: The Visionary Art of Elizabeth Catlett', in *Struggle and Serenity: The Visionary Art of Elizabeth Catlett*, New York: Caribbean Cultural Center, 1996.

[5] See M.J. Beauchamp-Byrd, 'Interview with Maria Magdalena Campos-Pons', in *When I Am Not Here/Estoy Alla: Photographs by Maria Magdalena Campos-Pons* (exh. cat.), New York: Caribbean Cultural Center, 1997.

[6] See Kellie Jones and David A. Bailey, *US-UK Photography Exchange* (exh. cat.), New York: Jamaica Arts Center, 1989; and K. Jones and Thomas W. Sokolowski, *Interrogating Identity* (exh. cat.), New York: Grey Art Gallery and Study Center, New York University, 1991.

[7] Gavin Jantjes and Nicholas Serota, introduction to *From Two Worlds* (exh. cat.), London: Whitechapel, 1986, p.5.

[8] See Dawn Ades, *Art in Latin America: The Modern Era, 1820–1980* (exh. cat.), New Haven: Yale University Press, 1989.

[9] See M.J. Beauchamp-Byrd, 'Introduction', in M.J. Beauchamp-Byrd and Franklin Sirmans (ed.), *Transforming the Crown: African, Asian and Caribbean Artists in Britain, 1966–1996* (exh. cat.), New York: Caribbean Cultural Center, 1997, p.13.

[10] Texts that define these distinctions include: Arthe Anthony, *Picturing Black New Orleans: A Creole*

Photographer's View in the Early Twentieth Century, Gainesville: University Press of Florida, 2012; Virginia Dominguez, *White by Definition: Social Classification in Creole Louisiana*, New Brunswick, NJ: Rutgers University Press, 1986; and Sybil Kein (ed.), *Creole: The History and Legacy of Louisiana's Free People of Color*, Baton Rouge: Lousiana State University Press, 2009.

[11] M.J. Beauchamp-Byrd, introduction to *Transforming the Crown*, *op. cit.*, p.12.

[12] See Anne Walmsley, 'The Caribbean Artists Movement, 1966–72: A Space and a Voice for Visual Practice', in M.J. Beauchamp-Byrd and F. Sirmans (ed.), *Transforming the Crown*, *op. cit.*, pp.46–52.

[13] I would later write about Burke's work in 2005. See M.J. Beauchamp-Byrd, 'Everyday People: Vanley Burke and the Ghetto as Genre', in *Back to Black: Art, Cinema and the Racial Imaginary* (exh. cat.), London: Whitechapel Gallery, 2005.

[14] See David A. Bailey and Stuart Hall (ed.), 'Critical Decade: Black British Photography in the 80s' (special issue), *Ten.8*, vol.2, no.3, 1992.

[15] These projects included the major solo exhibition 'Sutapa Biswas: Lumen', Kettle's Yard, University of Cambridge, October 2021–January 2022, with a companion exhibition at Baltic, Gateshead, June 2021–March 2022; the exhibition 'Mirror Reflecting Darkly: The Rita Keegan Archive', South London Gallery, with an accompanying publication edited by Matthew Harle and Keegan (Goldsmiths Press and MIT Press, 2021), to which I contributed the essay 'Black People Dressed Up is What I Knew: Rita Keegan's Performative Self-Portraiture'. Veronica Ryan's solo exhibition at Spike Island, Bristol, opened in 2021; also that year, her installation representing the UK's first public monument honoring the Windrush Generation, a series of stunning, large-scale sculptures in marble and green patinated bronze, was unveiled on Narrow Way Square in Hackney, London.

[16] At the Caribbean Cultural Center, I had the diligent and much-appreciated support of Jerry Philogene and Rocio Aranda-Alvarado, both serving as Project and Curatorial Coordinators; Patricia Blanchet, Development Consultant; and Cylena Simonds, who oversaw the film and video series. Organized in partnership with NYU's Africana Studies Program and Institute of Afro-American Affairs and held at NYU, these film series events were introduced by film-maker Isaac Julien and cultural studies scholar May Joseph.

[17] For an insightful overview of 1980s works of art, their critical reception and the social and political environment that produced them, see Helen Molesworth (ed.), *This Will Have Been: Art, Love, and Politics in the 1980s*, New Haven: Yale University Press, 2012.

[18] See Robert Hughes, 'Art: The Whitney Biennial: A Fiesta of Whining', *TIME*, 22 March 1993; and Hilton Kramer, 'The Whitney Biennial: Closed for Deconstruction', *New York Observer*, 29 March 1993.

[19] H. Cotter, 'This Realm of Newcomers, This England', *op. cit.*

[20] See Elizabeth Harney, 'Transforming the Crown', *African Arts*, vol.31, no.2, Spring 1998, pp.81–83.

[21] *Ibid.*

[22] See Bruce King, 'Review: *Transforming the Crown*', *Flash Art*, vol.33, no.1, p.210; Laura Melwani, 'Shades of Colour', *India Today International*, 2 March 1998; Sally Price, 'Artists In and Out of the Caribbean', *NWIG*, vol.73, no.4, 1999, pp.101–09; and M.J. Beauchamp-Byrd, '"New" England: Notes on Art, Migration and National Identity', *International Review of African American Art*, vol.15, no.3, 1998, pp.30–41.

[23] The segment, part of episode 704 ('*In the Life* Goes Global'), includes clips from an interview with me that was videotaped at the Bronx Museum and also interview clips with Isaac Julien and Pratibha Parmar. *In the Life*, produced by In the Life Media, aired on PBS and other public television stations from 1992 to 2012.

[24] See Judith Wilson, 'Triangular Trades: Late-Twentieth Century "Black" Art and Transatlantic Cultural Commerce', in D.A. Bailey, Ian Baucom and Sonia Boyce (ed.), *Shades of Black: Assembling Black Arts in 1980s Britain*, Durham, NC: Duke University Press in collaboration with the Institute of International Visual Arts (inIVA) and the African and Asian Visual Artists' Archive (AAVAA), 2005.

[25] *Ibid.*, p.99.

[26] I provided an introductory essay and invited Eddie Chambers, Anne Walmsley, Kobena Mercer, Gilane Tawadros, Deborah Willis, Judith Wilson and Okwui Enwezor to contribute texts. I also invited Krista A. Thompson to chart British art-making practice from 1966 to 1996, and she produced a meticulously researched and comprehensive timeline. Franklin Sirmans served as co-editor for the catalogue, providing exemplary copy-editing skills for the publication.

[27] As well as the essays I have mentioned in previous notes, 'Crown' certainly led to critical aspects of my dissertation, 'Hogarth's Progress: Modern Moral Subjects in the Work of David Hockney, Lubaina Himid and Paula Rego', which I completed in 2011 at Duke University under the guidance of my dissertation advisor, Richard J. Powell.

Finding the Room Next to Mine – Marlene Smith in conversation with Claudette Johnson

Marlene Smith invited painter Claudette Johnson to look back together through a sequence of images that speak to their shared life experience and art practices. This is the edited transcript of their conversation, which took place in London on 26 April 2022.

Claudette Johnson: We're looking at an image of a poster for the exhibition 'The Pan-Afrikan Connection: An Exhibition by Young Black Artists' in 1982.

Marlene Smith: I don't remember the show that clearly, but it really was a game changer for me. It was where I was recruited to join the Blk Art Group by Keith Piper. When I saw the poster, I remember the hairs on the back of my neck standing up because it was so powerful. I'd never heard words like that related to Black art in Britain. I'd only come across African American artists who made very political statements. The first line is Eddie Chambers: 'Black art must respond to the realities of the local, national and international black communities.' And Dominic Dawes: 'Since then I became, and still am becoming more aware of how Black people have become victims of this fascist and racist white brutality.' I'd never really encountered anything quite like it.

CJ: What did 'Pan-Afrikan' mean to you at that point?

MS: I think by the time I saw this poster, it meant people of African origin living all over the world. At seventeen, that was a really important message for me to understand, because I was looking for something in terms of my own identity and making sense of my place in the world. I was still in school, doing my A-levels, and I had decided to do a project on Black artists in Britain. I hadn't met any yet. I remember that my tutors at school were very worried for me, because they were absolutely convinced there were no Black artists. So luckily for me, I did find a group of artists based in Birmingham, including Vanley Burke. And then one of my tutors brought me this clipping from one of the Sunday papers, about an exhibition of Commonwealth artists at London School of Economics, 'Third World Art Exhibition' [1981]. I managed to get myself to London to see the exhibition, and then, through the gallery, I managed to write to some of the artists. They included Frank Bowling and Ronald Moody, who wrote back to me. They were really generous in their responses to my seventeen-year-old questions.

The next 'Pan-Afrikan Connection' exhibition was at the Herbert Art Gallery & Museum in Coventry. This was the first time I actually exhibited with the Blk Art Group. This is a bittersweet memory for me, because when you look at the names on the poster, you don't see my name there. I was still quite nervous about showing my work publicly. And so, by the time I decided I was ready to show, I had missed the deadlines for the print. I did actually have work in that show, but there's no record of it. There was a review written by Lubaina [Himid], and because my name wasn't in the publication, she overlooked me. I spoke to her later and she was very apologetic about it. And then there was a critical review from Joseph Olubo, who mentioned my work, but in a very negative way. When I look back to the 1983 show, I have very mixed feelings. But it was, I think, on the whole a positive experience for me, because it was the first time I had the courage to show my work in public.

CJ: And you were nineteen. I just can't get my head around how precocious you were...

MS: How precocious we all were. We were basically eighteen to twenty-three years old, writing to galleries and demanding that they show our work, and making some very vibrant, strident statements within the work. The Blk Art Group wasn't the reason why I went to art school, but it kept me there. Because I felt very isolated in the art college, and the Blk Art Group and the wider community that it introduced me to enabled me to feel part of something bigger than what was happening on my campus.

CJ: It reminds me of the excitement of that time. The incredible rush of emotion, seeing the work in a proper gallery for the first time, and all talking about Black issues or featuring Black people. And those big declarative statements within the work.

MS: I think it was received as confrontational. It was unapologetic about its confrontation. The fact that it wasn't just one exhibition but a series of exhibitions – in which we were repeating ourselves in terms of strident statements about race and racism – is really important.

'The Thin Black Line' was organized by Lubaina Himid at the ICA [Institute of Contemporary Arts] in London in 1985. Lubaina had been invited to use the gallery space, but she'd been given quite restricted access. So there was a very thin corridor, called the Concourse Gallery. She invited eleven Black women to make work. She had five or six of us on one side of the wall, and then she grouped the photographers together on the opposite side. She invited us to bring in our family photos and fill the wall above the professional photographers' work with images of our homes, our families and our lives.

CJ: It reminds me of all the gatherings with so many different women coming together at our houses, at galleries, at event spaces. That sense of a cornucopia of Black women bursting out into what was a very white space, and submerging it with images of our realities. The daring and the energy really come across to me.

MS: *Good Housekeeping I* is the piece I made for 'The Thin Black Line'. *Good Housekeeping II* was on the wall around the corner, and for that I used the pages from *Good Housekeeping* magazine – literally took the pages out. There was a fashion shoot that had been done with Maasai warriors as the backdrop. I'm saying that out loud now and I cannot believe that anybody thought it was a good idea to take a whole bunch of white models to Africa

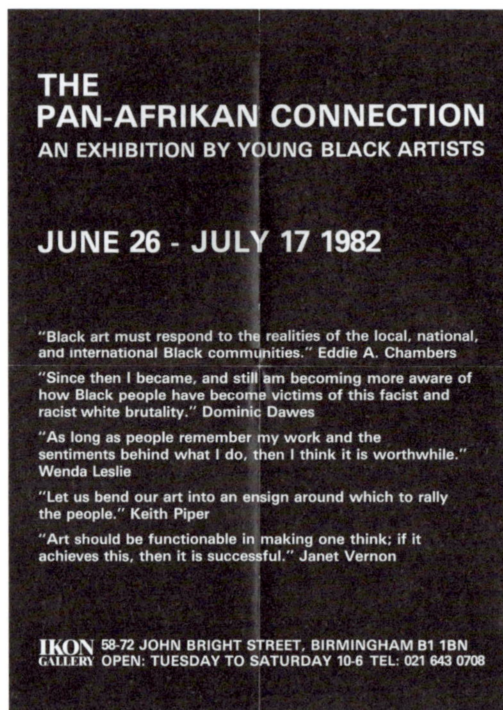

Poster for 'The Pan-Afrikan Connection: An Exhibition by Young Black Artists', Ikon Gallery, Birmingham, 1982

Cover of exhibition catalogue for 'The Thin Black Line', Institute of Contemporary Arts, London, 1985. Courtesy Lubaina Himid

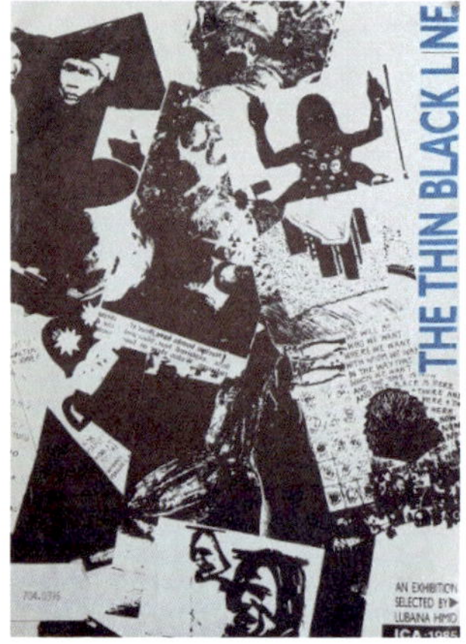

Marlene Smith, *Do, Please! A Happy Ending*, 1987, poster paint and pastel on paper. Courtesy the artist

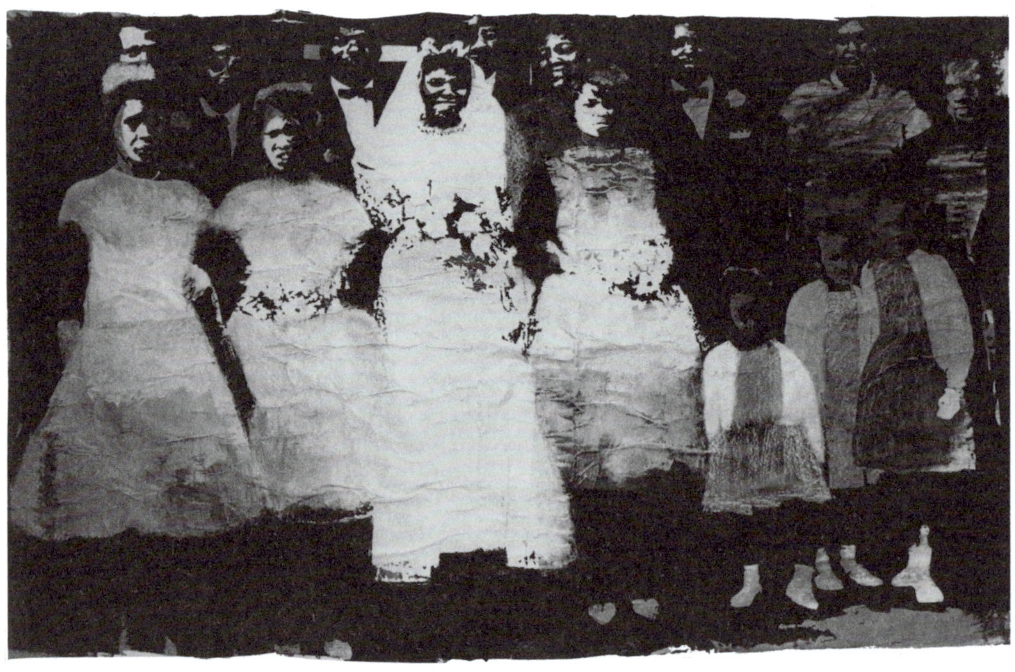

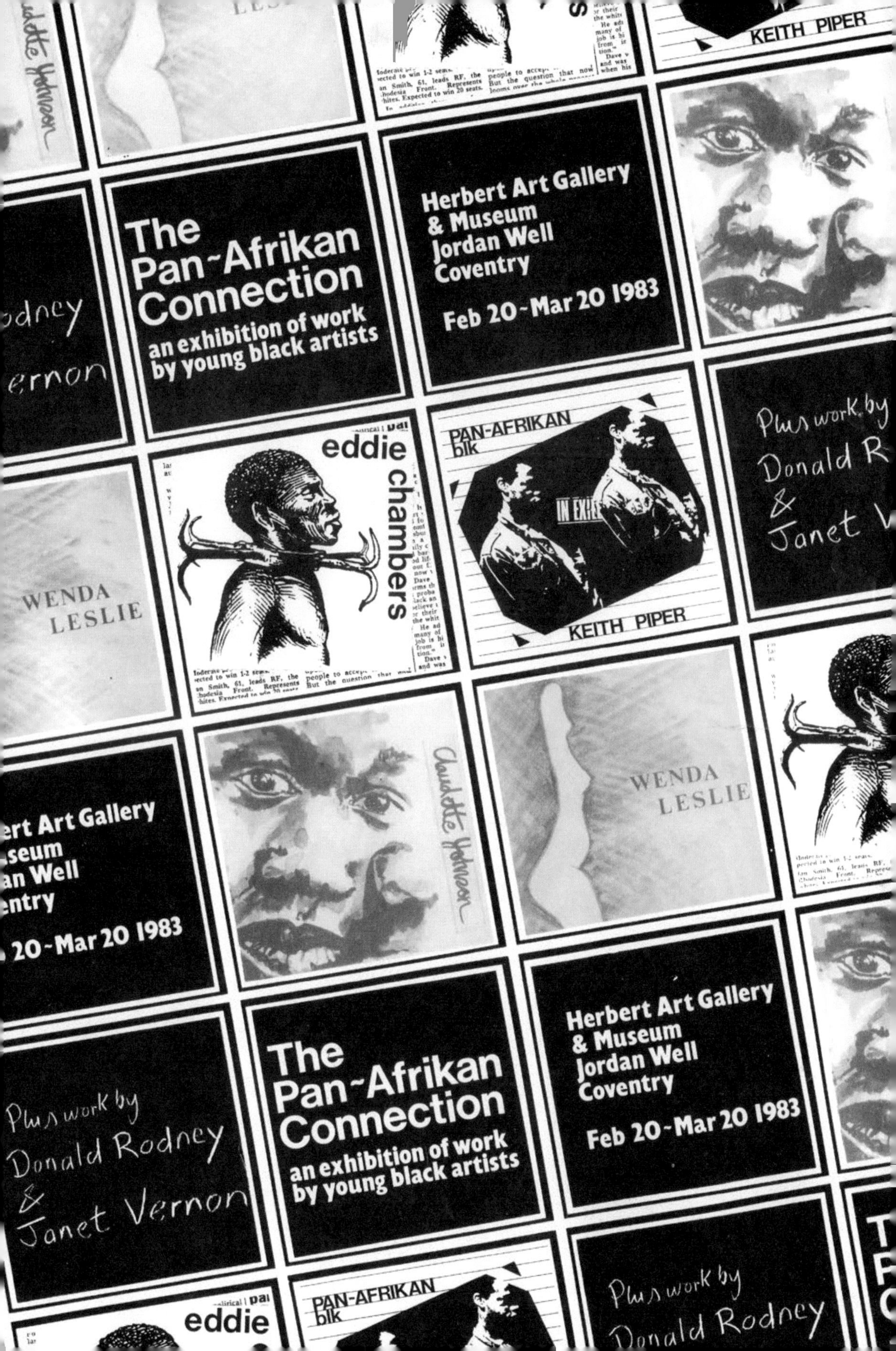

The Pan~Afrikan Connection
an exhibition of work by young black artists
Herbert Art Gallery & Museum
Jordan Well
Coventry
Feb 20~Mar 20 1983
eddie chambers
PAN-AFRIKAN blk
IN EXILE
KEITH PIPER
WENDA LESLIE
Claudette Johnson
Plus work by
Donald Rodney
&
Janet Vernon

Previous page: Poster for 'The Pan-Afrikan Connection: An Exhibition by Young Black Artists', Herbert Art Gallery & Museum, Coventry, 1983

so that they could film some ethnic-looking clothes... But they did. It must have cost them a fortune. I think when I picked up that magazine and saw those images, I just didn't know what to add. So I literally just took the pages from the magazine and pasted them onto the wall in the ICA. But anyways, in *Good Housekeeping I*, at the top there's a figure leaning against the corner, and just behind her left shoulder is an image of a family gathering. At the top of the image the lettering says: 'My mother opens the door at 7am. She is not bulletproof.' And I made this piece shortly after Cherry Groce was shot in her home. What happened was that the police were looking for her son, and they called at her house early in the morning, hence the reference to 7am. And somehow, in whatever happened in that space, they managed to shoot her. This woman was left paralyzed. It was an infamous case of police brutality. And I remember that I had already been asked to take part in 'The Thin Black Line' when I decided what I was going to make a work about. I remember going to a rally or a long march that was in protest at this outrage. Around the same time, Cynthia Jarrett's home was also searched by police, and she had a heart attack and died. So having put up with lots of stop-and-search, we were now entering a realm where our mothers weren't safe in their own homes.

This is *Mr. close-friend-of-the-family pays a visit whilst everyone else is out.* Sonia Boyce, 1985.

CJ: An absolutely incredible piece. This was Sonia's piece for 'The Thin Black Line'. I remember it arriving and I remember being speechless.

MS: There's the pristine wallpaper. And then there's this arm reaching across, from somebody with a slightly paunchy belly. He's got his shirt unbuttoned halfway down his chest.

CJ: Very 70s.

MS: I think it's poignant that he's got a cross hanging around his neck. And all the hands on the border of the piece. And then that look from that young woman. She's looking straight out at us from the canvas. I don't even know what to call that expression.

CJ: It just stops you. It holds you. You can't look away. His hand is reaching for her breast. She's asking us to witness this. She's asking us to bear witness. The hands around the border are almost morphing into a chain, a protective chain encircling the scene. It makes me think about the impact of works by Alice Walker or Toni Morrison, *The Color Purple* [1982], *The Bluest Eye* [1970], and the backlash they got for talking about abuse in the Black community, because it was seen as betrayal.

MS: Betrayal, or washing our dirty linen in public. Women are always accused of that.

CJ: So again, the courage was really startling.

MS: When I took part in 'The Thin Black Line', I had decided to take a year out of my art studies. I was studying in Bradford, but I was so impatient to get involved in what was happening in London. And I was lucky in that one of the artists that I'd met back in 1982 was Shakka Dedi. By 1985 he had opened The Black-Art Gallery in Finsbury Park. When I came to London for my year off, not only were he and his wife kind enough to sublet me their flat, but he also found a job for me working as his assistant at The Black-Art Gallery. I was lucky enough to have the space to organize a show myself, called 'Some of Us Are Brave, All of Us Are Strong'. The title is referencing an anthology of Black American women's writing, which I remember was edited by Barbara Smith. It was the first time I'd ever organized an exhibition on my own. It felt very much like it was my show.

CJ: Yeah, I thought of it as your show.

MS: I still love the poster. I love that image because they just look so … on the one hand angelic, and on the other mischievous.

CJ: There's something about little Black girls as bridesmaids. I think lots of us, our parents and our parents' friends, they'd come over to the UK. And in the UK, they had these big weddings and got married in ways that wouldn't have happened in the same way were they at home in Jamaica, Trinidad, Barbados or wherever. There was the whole cycle of Black girls at weddings, in these beautiful wedding outfits, with the white gloves and the long white socks, patent leather shoes and the rosette of flowers on their heads. I felt like there was some desire to see us in those roles. My sister was almost a professional bridesmaid, regularly booked for my parents' friends' weddings.

MS: It was a desire for, I don't know … the kind of lives you see on magazine covers. It's something that tried to get away from the reality. I have very mixed feelings about my bridesmaids in their gowns. I like the juxtaposition of the title 'Some of Us Are Brave, All of Us Are Strong' alongside the little pretty girls.

CJ: Like a fable.

MS: I'm always stunned by how much we managed to pack into such a short period of time. Lubaina opened The Elbow Room, which was her private gallery, in the mid-1980s. What I remember about 'Unrecorded Truths', this show I was in, is that it was an exciting development for Lubaina to have her own space rather than having to negotiate with other venues. And it was stunning – a beautiful, beautiful show. I do remember this show much more clearly than I remember some of the others, because the work was so striking. I remember Simone Alexander's beautiful, allegorical paintings, like she was painting nursery rhymes. And I remember Sonia Boyce. That was the show that she did *She Ain't Holding Them Up, She's Holding On (Some English Rose)* [1986].

CJ: And the title, it's so powerful, isn't it? 'Unrecorded Truths'. Lubaina was mapping out, again, that our voices had not been heard before.

MS: Around that time, the Cornerhouse, which was an art gallery in Manchester, invited myself and Keith Piper to curate a show for them – 'the image employed', in 1987. We tried to make a show about the use of narrative in Black art.

CJ: I remember making the work for that show in my kitchen, on the kitchen wall, and being excited to be part of that show. It was in Manchester, where I'm from. We'd all planned to be at the opening and we all went down. There was a bit of a party. But 'the image employed' – you know, this actually was Britain in the 80s, high levels of young Black people unemployed. We kind of accepted that there wasn't going to be an income from our practice. But our practice is what we're committed to doing, so the only way to have any money was to...

MS: Have an alternative income.

CJ: And you're also making a statement about the practice – *employing* the image.

MS: And the subtitle was 'the use of narrative in Black art'. I remember we didn't want it to be a survey exhibition of Black artists. We wanted it to be a thematic exhibition. So we did try to talk about what the work is doing. But I don't think we had the language. We didn't have the tools to really interrogate the images. I wrote the essay in the catalogue that tries to do that. But it's just not enough words.

CJ: That show may have generated work. It certainly did for me...

MS: One of the things that I find most exciting when I look back on my selection of shows is that we were so industrious. It wasn't just that we were showing frequently, we were also making new work. And one of the things that the curating of that time did was really help to bring forth new work, because it created contexts in which the work could be seen. And 'the image employed' was only the second time I'd curated an exhibition. Although we didn't call it 'curating' at that time – we called it 'organizing'.

CJ: Yeah, it says 'selected by' but it was quite a collaborative process that we were all interested in and excited by each other's work. In that sense it was a movement. We wanted to support each other to make the work visible. I am reminded of Keith Piper's epistle for 'The Pan-Afrikan Connection' poster, which reads: 'Let us bend art into an ensign around which to rally the people.' For a long time, I would have put that on a banner or a T-shirt. Because it was perfect. A rallying cry. It was the belief that we all carried with us: we could change things through the work.

MS: We did change things with the work, but not quite in the way we probably expected.

Now this is a 1987–89 piece of work I made called *Do, Please! A Happy Ending*. I'm still obsessed with weddings. I think one of the things that I've done throughout my career is I've mined and utilized my family albums. And this is absurd. This is an image of my uncle's wedding. When I started making this in 1987, my parent's generation were probably around the same age that I am now, maybe even slightly younger. It's funny how time passes and how the meaning of a piece of work can change because of that context of time, that temporality.

Following spread: Sonia Boyce, *Mr close-friend-of-the-family pays a visit whilst everyone else is out*, 1985, charcoal on paper, 109.2 × 150cm © Sonia Boyce. All Rights Reserved, DACS/Artimage 2022. Photo © Arts Council Collection, Southbank Centre

CJ: I find it a poignant image, it has a fugitive quality, partly because of the materials and the way the pastels sit on the paint and partly because it is highlighting the fleeting nature of childhood. The image feels fragile, with some parts harder to read than others. For me there's something clandestine about it, perhaps because it reminds me of how my sisters and I would sneak up to our parents' room, find the photo albums buried in my mother's chest of drawers, and pore over the wedding photos of family members and strangers. There was always a sense of them fading away slightly – that they belong to a past we weren't part of, when our parents were young and adventurous. Your image is full of hope, isn't it?

MS: Absolutely. Well, that's in the title. It's hoping, asking, pleading for a happy ending. It's partly also my cynicism about these kinds of ... that there's such a thing that our parents had, such a desire in them for a happy ending. My cynicism about marriage as an institution comes across in this image.

CJ: It makes me think of so much work that's processional – Frida Kahlo, Diego Rivera, you know, these sweeps of people emigrating, having crossed from there to arrive here, trying to establish themselves.

MS: One of the first solo exhibitions I organized at The Black-Art Gallery was your show 'In This Skin' [1992]. When I came to the gallery, one of the things that I wanted to do – again controversially – was widen who was showing there. I wanted to show a lot more women. I wanted to do solo exhibitions rather than group shows, because I thought that the scale of the gallery lent itself to solo exhibitions – especially first-time solo exhibitions. And I wanted to show artists whose work was being excluded or had been overlooked. I feel like 'In This Skin' was an opportunity to do a number of those things. And I love this image on the poster. It's so concentrated, it's beautifully rendered. I just love the engagement of those eyes and the fact that the protagonist is looking at you, and that she's quite defiant. And she does have her own business in the skin on this planet – there's no doubt that she does.

CJ: Yes, because it's a torso. It's a woman seated, naked, and mostly it's her torso that's visible, her face is visible from the eyes down. Her arms and legs are cut off by the edge of the frame. There is very spare use of tone and

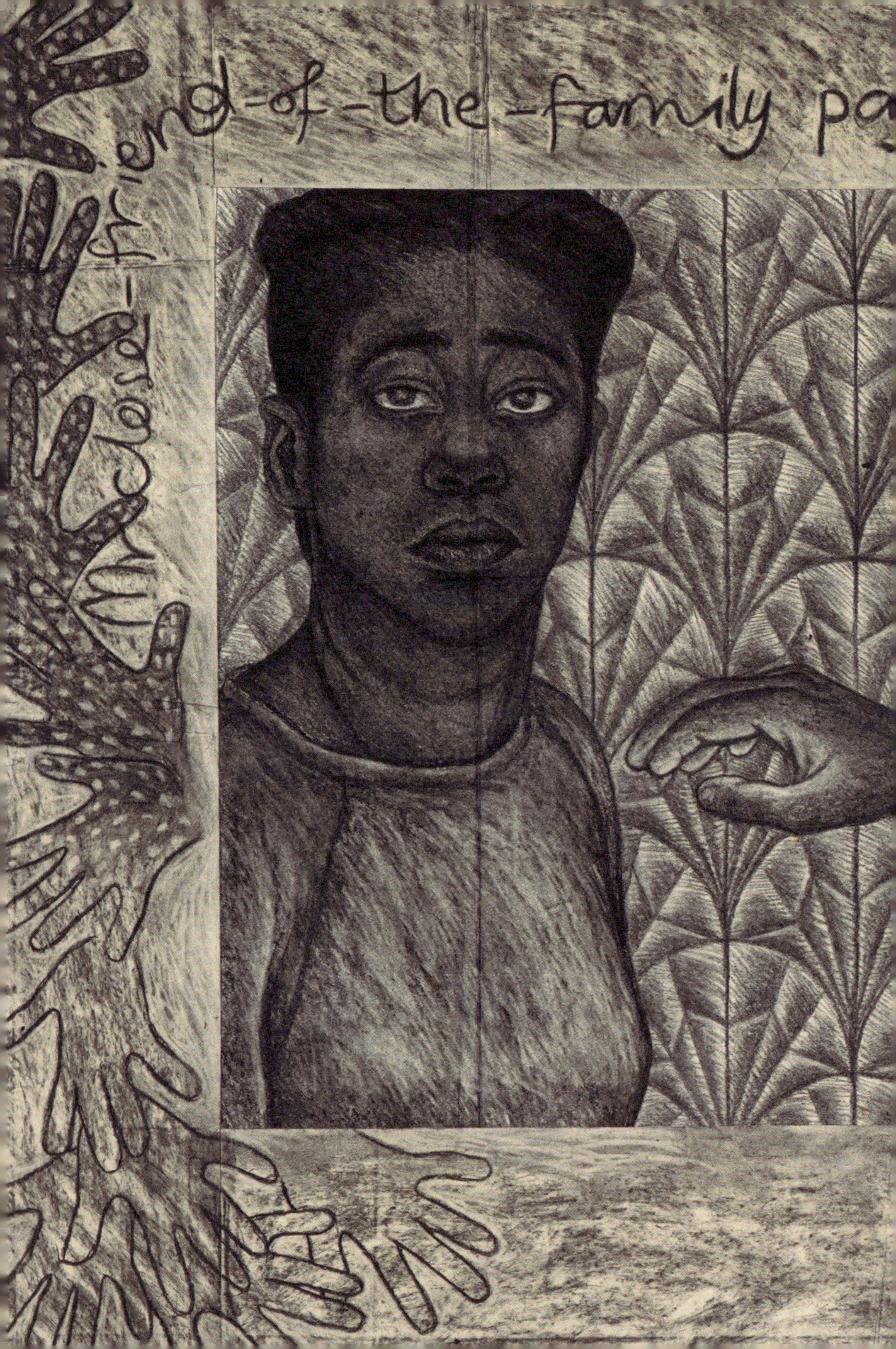
Mr-Close-fri
end-of-the-family pa

a visit whilst everyone else is out

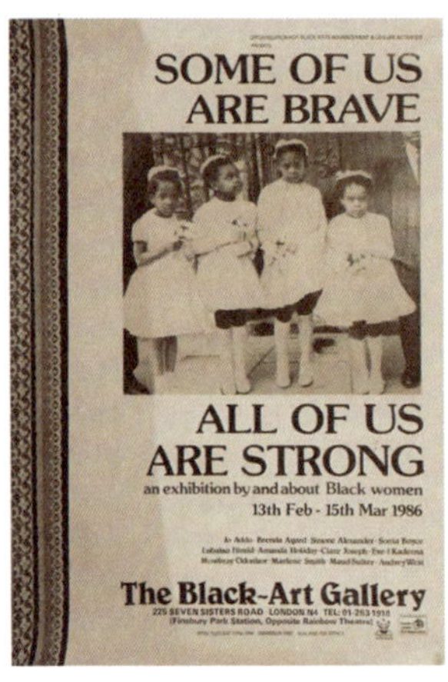

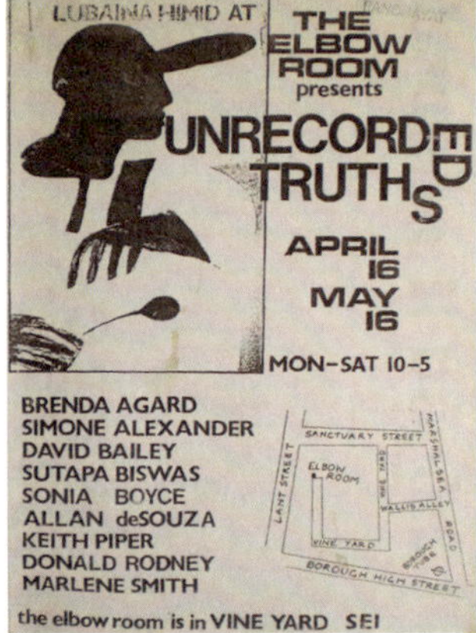

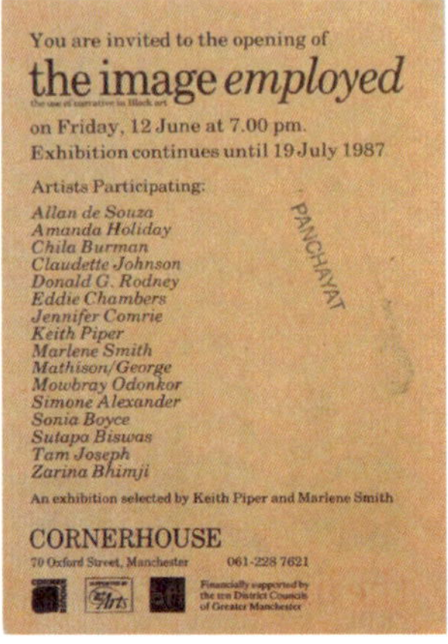

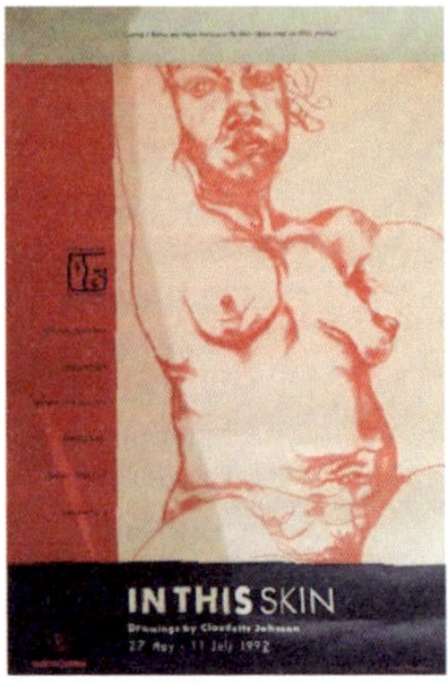

Clockwise from upper left:
Poster for 'Some of Us Are Brave', The Black-Art Gallery, London, 1986; Cover of exhibition pamphlet for 'Unrecorded Truths', The Elbow Room, London, 1986. Courtesy Lubaina Himid; Private view invite for 'The Image Employed', Cornerhouse, Manchester, 1987. Courtesy Marlene Smith and Keith Piper; Poster for 'In This Skin', The Black-Art Gallery, 1992

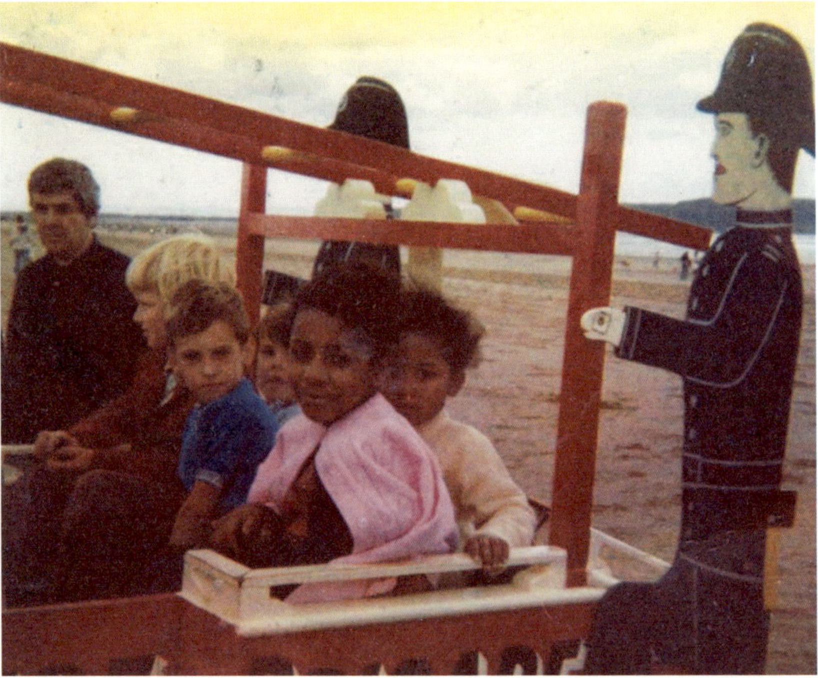

Family photograph of daytrip to Weston-super-Mare, North Somerset. Courtesy Marlene Smith

Keith Piper, *Reactionary Suicide: Boys Keep on Swinging*, 1983, mixed media. Courtesy the artist

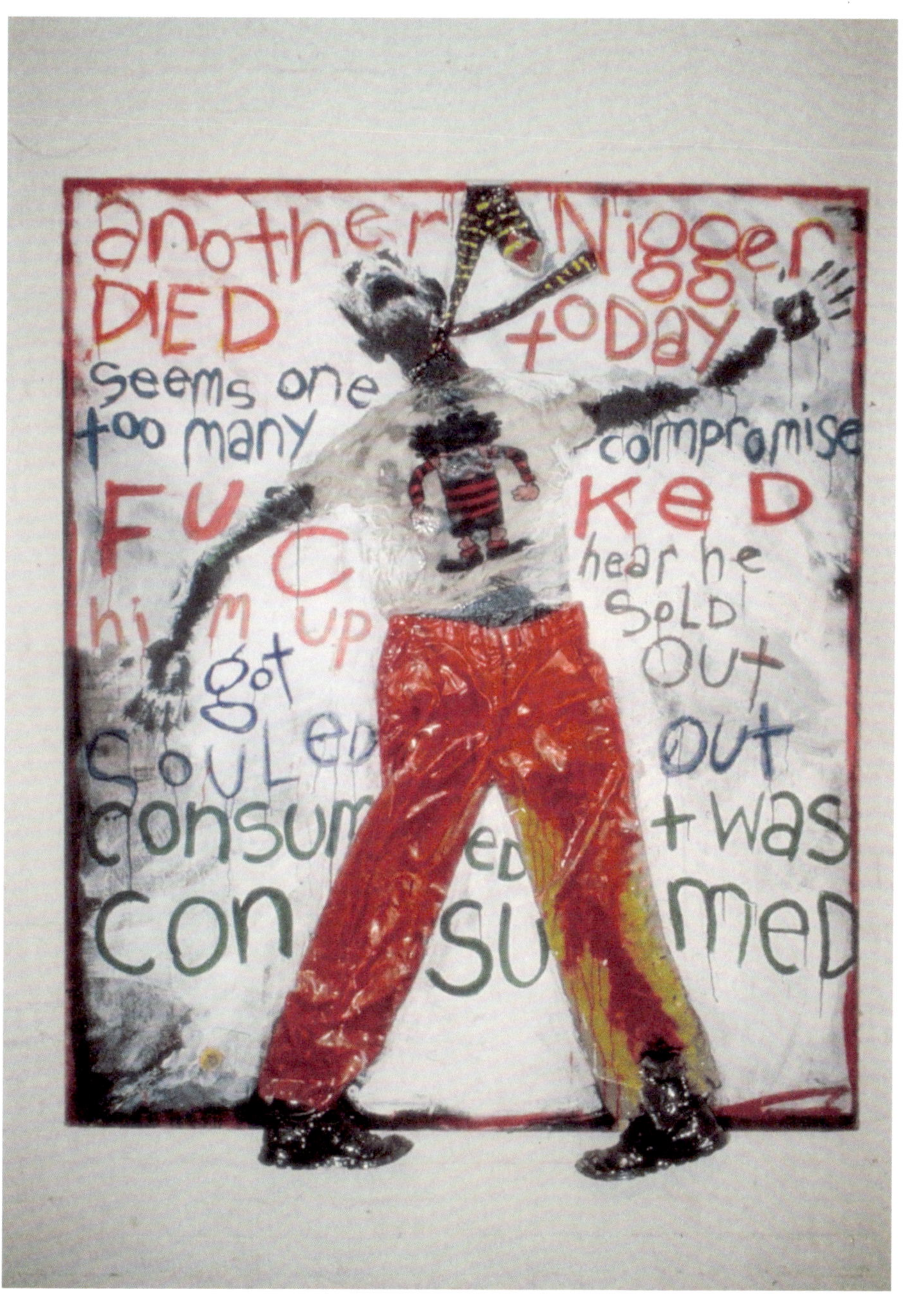

largely linear description. I later called it *Afterbirth* [1990]. Because it was made shortly after the birth of my second child. I still find it an almost embarrassingly intimate image of that post-partum moment. I remember the thrill of having that solo show at The Black-Art Gallery that you had so generously afforded me, because I had felt that I was never going to exhibit there. I'd never been able to be part of any of the shows there.

MS: I do remember feeling very strongly that I went to The Black-Art Gallery with a list of people that I wanted to show. And I wasn't able to show everybody that I wanted to show. I wanted to show Frank Bowling, for example, and Tam Joseph, and I hadn't been able to do that. What I was able to do was a Lubaina Himid show and a Claudette Johnson show, and I felt that those were long overdue. One of the things that I did controversially with The Black-Art Gallery was that I showed the work of African and Asian artists, and that's something that the gallery had not been doing previously. So that was all very important to me.

CJ: Yes, at the time, and as reflected in films like *Handsworth Songs* [1986] by Black Audio Film Collective, 'Black' was an umbrella term that was used by African, Caribbean and Asian people to recognize how similar our struggles and experiences as settlers in Britain were. 'In this Skin' is very significant for many reasons, it was not only my first solo show in London, it was also the first time I'd been reviewed by the *Guardian*. Furthermore, this show was visited by a young Black art student, Steve McQueen, who reviewed the exhibition for a grassroots newspaper that he was working for at the time. So again, the ripples from a show... You can never anticipate how far they are going to reach.

MS: Now that you raise that, it reminds me of your presentation at the Wolverhampton conference [The First National Convention of Black Art, organized by the Blk Art Group at Wolverhampton Polytechnic, 1982]. I remember how beautifully and poignantly you spoke about your strategies for doing something different with the Black female body. I think that people who dismissed the work on the basis that they can see nakedness hadn't really looked very hard. I remember that you spoke about making the woman central to the image – how you cropped the images so that they filled up the space. You talked about other people's images of Black women and bodies, and how in certain artists' work every single inch of the canvas is treated in the same way, and how you tried to do that differently.

CJ: To leave open space, yes, and not work every part of the image.

MS: This is a photograph from 1972, of me and my little sister on a day at the seaside. I put this in because I wanted to just take a moment to situate myself, to talk about my viewing position as it were, to remind everybody that I was a child of the Windrush generation. There's something about the little pink and yellow cardigans and the hair that's a bit messed up by the sea winds... What I see in this image is that myself and my sister are sitting in this vehicle, which tries to look like a fire engine. Right next to us is a little boy and he's giving dagger eyes. He's not very happy about us sitting next to him. There's a gentleman in the far-left corner who is also scowling. It just reminds me of what it was like to be growing up in the 1970s in the UK. You go out for an innocent visit to the seaside and you are still not welcome. Again, it's a mixed bag of emotions that this brings up. For me, it summarizes quite nicely what it's like to be of that generation. My expression is a bit more resolute. It is like, oh God, when is this going to be over, the torture of it? But it means so much has changed. Racism is still something that we feel and we know about, but it doesn't feel quite so overt these days.

The Blk Art Group's work was shown widely back in the early 1980s, and then it kind of went into abeyance in the 1990s. So I just wanted to take a moment to look at some of it. This is from Donald Rodney's series *How the West Was Won* [1982]. It is quite kind of 'abstract expressionist' in style, wouldn't you say?

CJ: It is, but it's also pop art. It's deceptively playful, isn't it? Yet we know he's deadly serious. It's loose and ragged at the edges. Each feature is really exaggerated, with the eyes and the mouths articulated with broad brush strokes.

MS: This is *Untitled I and II.* It's a 1983 work. It's gouache, ink, chalk on paper. It's two images of Akua'ba doll. On the left-hand image, there's text which follows the right-hand side of the doll, and it says: 'the most sacred commandment'. Then there's larger text that says: 'violated'. So you can see 'violated' before you get to see 'the most sacred commandment'. And there's an image of a Portuguese merchant, and there's a big red cross. In the next image, the Akua'ba doll has lost its head. The Portuguese merchant moves to the top of the canvas and it says, 'violated' – so violated and violated again. It was just a really shorthand way for me to talk about Black female femininity and Black womanhood by using the Akua'ba doll as a stand-in for all of that.

CJ: This is also speaking about collections such as the British Museum's, and appropriation. The other thing that strikes me on the first image of violation is the big red cross that slashes across the lower half of the Akua'ba figure. It's across the stomach and genitals. So we have the idea of a double rape: first your body and then your mind...

MS: Going back to Coventry, 1983, this is the piece called *Reactionary Suicide*, with defamatory language: 'another nigger died today seems one too many compromise fucked him up hear the sold out and was consumed'. And 'sold' is spelt in two ways: s-o-l-d on one side and s-o-u-l-e-d on the other.

CJ: So the moment you're reading vertically you're pulled across to read horizontally again ... 'got consumed'. This piece unnerved me when I first saw it. It is so raw and so profound. It continues to resonate down the decades: the deaths, the indifference, the tragedy and the fury continue.

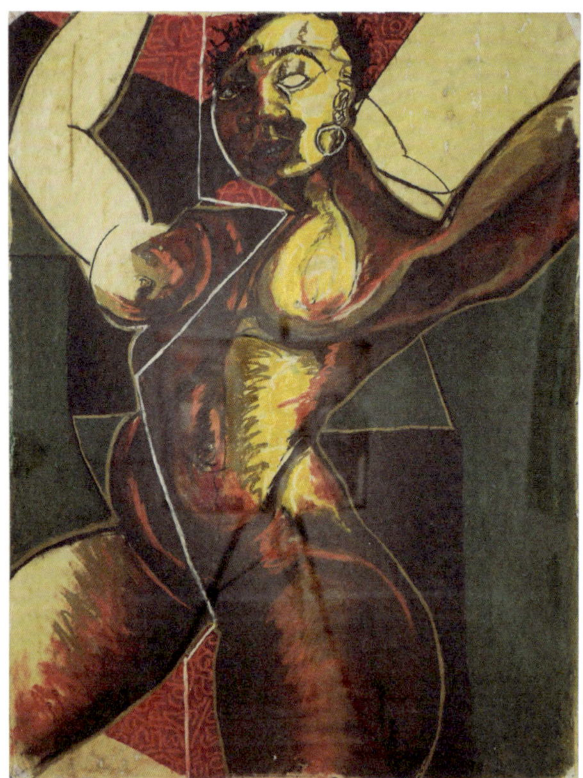

Claudette Johnson, *And I Have My Own Business in This Skin*, 1982, pastel and gouache on paper. Courtesy the artist

Donald Rodney with his painting *How the West Was Won*, 1982, acrylic paint on canvas. Courtesy Donald Rodney Estate

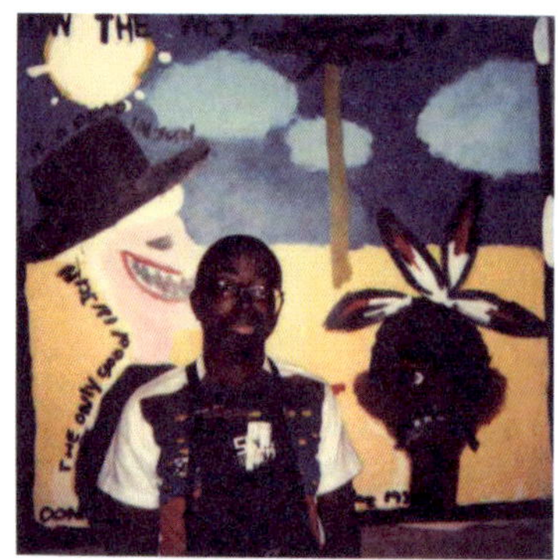

Eddie Chambers, *How Much Longer You Bastards*, 1983, mixed media. Courtesy Sheffield Museums and the artist

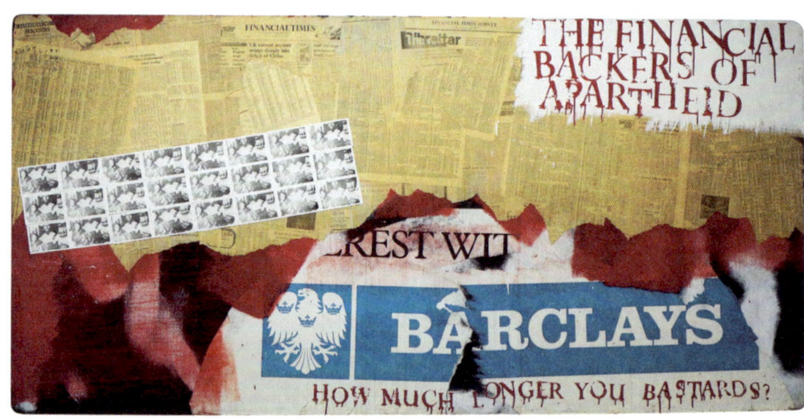

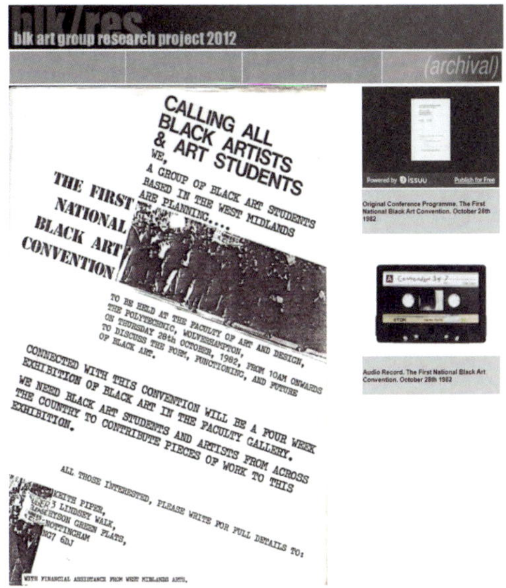

Handbill and audio recording for the First National Black Art Convention, Wolverhampton Polytechnic, 1982. Screenshot of online archive of Blk Art Group, https://www.blkartgroup.info/oct82archive.html

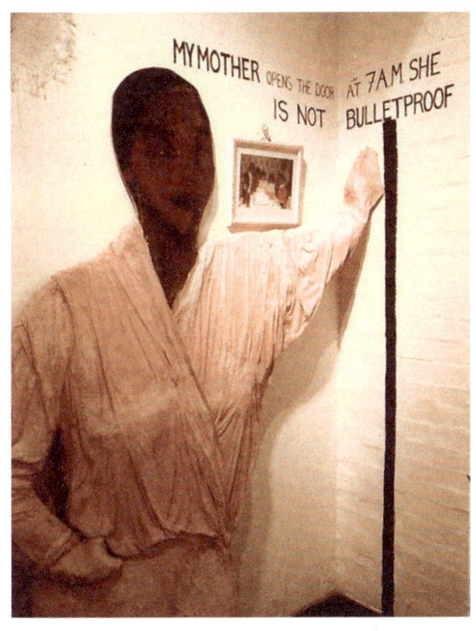

Marlene Smith, *Good Housekeeping I*, 1985. Installation view, 'The Thin Black Line', Institute of Contemporary Arts, London, 1985. Courtesy the artist

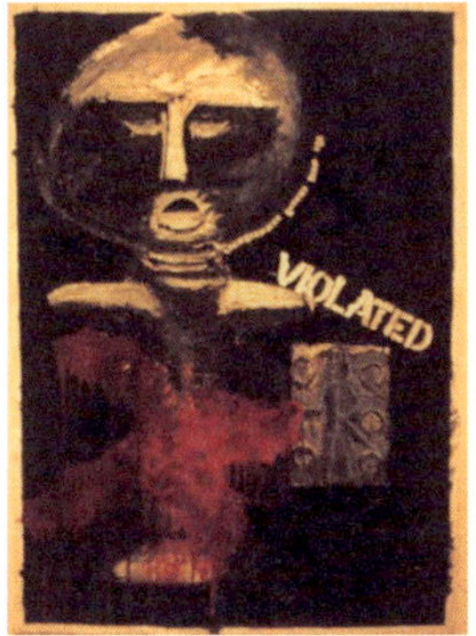

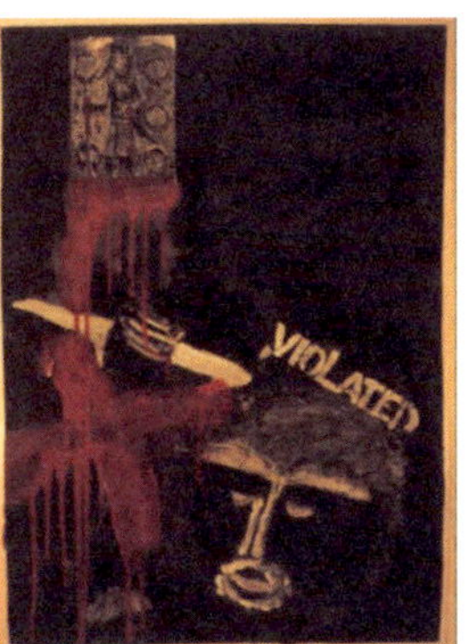

Marlene Smith, *Untitled I and II*, 1983, gouache, ink and chalk on paper. Courtesy the artist

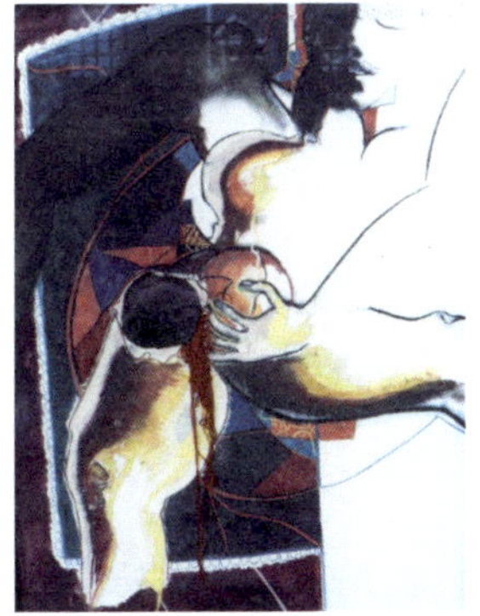

Claudette Johnson, *Untitled (with wool & leather)*, 1982, wool, leather, pastel and gouache on paper. Courtesy the artist

MS: The next is a piece that was shown in the 2011 exhibition at Sheffield Museums. It's *How Much Longer You Bastards?* [1983] by Eddie Chambers. It makes reference to Barclays as the financial backers of Apartheid. I think of Eddie as a printmaker, but I do get reminded from time to time that he did make collages and other types of image-making.

CJ: That image is mounted on sheets from the *Financial Times*. A whole swathe appears across the top of the image, taking up almost half of the canvas.

MS: It's very striking that it's red, white and blue – referencing the British flag.

CJ: Very clearly saying, 'What do these institutions stand for?' That was so on all of our minds at the time, as in, 'How are we involved in this?' And, 'How can we make a difference?'

MS: The whole story of Apartheid was really written large in the 80s, when we were students and young people, because it was a seemingly unending torture being played out in a land far away. But we still, because of our Pan-Afrikan connection, were really thinking about ourselves, putting ourselves in the shoes of the victims of Apartheid. I think it's already been documented that lots of Conservative MPs and maybe a couple of our prime ministers were anti-ANC [African National Congress], pro-Apartheid. Thatcher and Reagan and Botha were a triumvirate that were trying to shore up Apartheid.

CJ: I made this piece, *And I Have My Own Business in This Skin* [1982], as part of my degree show. I remember it got the tutors talking to me. I had had months in 'the wilderness' where it seemed the tutors just didn't spend any real time with me. However, when they saw this piece, they did become interested. They were interested in the references to Modernism, Cubism and specifically Picasso's *Les Demoiselles d'Avignon* [1907]. After seeing Picasso's work, I knew I could reconfigure the women to say something about Black female experience. I felt I'd found my language. I knew what I had to do.

MS: There are some remnants. There are some things in this piece that I see in your current work, in terms of the way that you break up the space and the surface.

CJ: Taken apart and put back together again. That's exactly because I felt that was what our identities were made up of – these disjointed stories that we're trying to make sense of, and that we have to, somehow, create a whole from these fragments. I talked about this in the catalogue for 'In This Skin', and about working from life again.

MS: It's not striving for that epitome of beauty, but it's still free and self-determined.

CJ: Yes, my Baudelairian moment! When I read of Charles Baudelaire titling his poetry volume *Les Fleurs du Mal*, it struck a chord with me. I understood him to be protesting about the resistance that artists faced from the establishment when trying to reflect the darker side of Parisian life in writing or art. He suggested that the absence of this darker side led to work that was anodyne. His 'flowers of evil' were the prostitutes and poverty that had been expunged from the work of artists and poets. He said: there's beauty in this, there's beauty in the urban life. I wanted to explore some of the darker myths about black identity, some of the stuff buried in my psyche and it gave me new form. It gave me a form of black Cubism, if you like.

MS: Yes. What's in this is that it's an androgynous image that is very powerful, and there's beauty in that power. It's a very different type of beauty to the idealized womanhood.

CJ: *Untitled (with wool & leather)* [1982]. What do you think is going on in this piece?

MS: I think that this is a woman enjoying her femaleness. It feels almost orgasmic. Half-open mouth, and where her hand is exploring her body. It's somebody who is at home in their enjoying themselves and having an ecstatic moment.

The First National Convention of Black Art, organized by the Blk Art Group at Wolverhampton Polytechnic, was in 1982. It took us thirty years – until 2012 – to start commemorating what the Blk Art Group had already done. I think we were so 'in the moment'. What happened in the 2010s was that yourself, myself and Keith Piper decided that we would set up something called the Blk Art Group Research Project. And we decided that we would try as far as possible to put all the documents related to the Blk Art Group into the public domain, so that they could be made available to people interested in the history.

CJ: The 2000s have been called the 'wilderness years' for many of us. This seemed to be marking the end of it. The beginning of the end of it.

MS: Yeah. 2011 was also the year that Tate did 'Thin Black Line(s)'. There was a revisiting of the exhibitions that Lubaina curated during the 1980s. It does feel as if 2011, 2012 were pivotal years.

CJ: Part of the brilliance of reimagining 'The Thin Black Line' into 'Thin Black Line(s)' was that Lubaina created that Underground Railroad piece, where it showed the unfolding story of the connections between Black artists, it showed the interconnection and interdependence between us.

MS: I don't know how it was for you, but for me, after the euphoria of the 1980s, the 1990s were really difficult years. The politics had moved to the right and lots of the institutions that had been supporting Black art were no longer doing so. The Black-Art Gallery lost its funding from Islington

Council in 1993, I think. I managed to keep it going till 1994 – just about – but they were very difficult times. Then, by the time we came to do this project in 2011, I'd come full circle. I'd spent a lot of years – in the 1990s, in particular, and the early 2000s – in complete denial that I was ever involved with the Blk Art Group. I didn't want to talk about it, I didn't want to revisit those times. And when people suggested that I might, I ran in the opposite direction. Then a colleague of mine, Jason Bowman, invited me to take part in an event 'About DIY Culture'. And so, for the first time in ages, I went up into my attic and got down my cardboard boxes of documents and images related to the Blk Art Group. And I was so struck by how beautiful that work was. It's almost as if I'd forgotten how powerful it had been. And how necessary and how timely.

Curating Black Futures

When we look at the history of Black exhibitions, we look at more than just the intricacies of artistic display and inclusion or exclusion. Black exhibitions tell cultural histories and are a tremendously rich resource for understanding artistic movements, political shifts and aesthetic developments. They allow for debates to emerge that reveal our current moment and collective future(s). The following section turns to this notion of futurity, foregrounding the voices of contemporary Black curators and practitioners working within the field of African diasporic art. As part of this dialogue, the shared yet often isolating experience of predominantly white institutions is problematized as a historical through line, as the contributors gathered here articulate their visions, experiences and hopes for the field. What influences their work? Within which historical dialogues do they see their practices? How do they see the future of the field?

Black Girl: A Plot and a Promise – Amber Esseiva

I come to this, as I come to most things, as a Black girl. I come to this as a curator whose work has been dedicated to institution building and commissioning works of art.[1] I started this work with vision, ethics and purpose. I started without reverence for existing hierarchies of institutional power in the art world; without a firm sense of how an institution's administrative arms should surround the work of artists and curators. I moved through this work and arrived at a crossroads where I was confronted with the reality that not all governing structures were in place to support the goals and desires of artists and curators. I found myself confused, trying to reconcile how the function of an institution sometimes worked against its own mission; against its own publicly stated values. Herein lies the disappointment that follows a hopeful institution; that follows hope in general. Hope can only be carried out by the many people who make an institution; yet hope can be held within conflicting personal, political or collective goals that render institution building as complicated as the democratic project.

What I encountered across many institutions were old habits and fixations as to how work should be organized and implemented. Relics of old institutionalism, old administrative governance. Control and interference. A system of silos that keeps good work from happening and allows mediocrity to persist in its old ways.[2] It's almost as if built into the logic of an institution are checkpoints meant to remind you who is really in power. I never knew *why* this was, but I became committed to uncovering *how* it is.

I am reminded that the time between coming to know and beginning to articulate might include a gulf so large that the moment might pass. The possibility for change exists any time fresh eyes are brought to what is stuck and broken, but the opportunity may be too brief, since eyes quickly grow tired when looking closely at such things.[3] Maybe this is how the inequities of governance work are designed to reveal themselves – slowly and once the decisions have already been made. Writing from this perspective, one of loss and bewilderment, makes me think of Saidiya Hartman's notion of the subjunctive mood, describing that which 'should' or 'might' be. She explains its role to 'both tell an impossible story and to amplify the impossibility of its telling'.[4] Institutions, and those who benefit from their legacies, know they must appear to take on the mantle of struggle towards change. We are constantly engaging with institutions that seem to be transforming when, really, they are shapeshifting so as not to be detected.[5]

I've come to realize that my initial naïvety was a gift; it allowed me access to energy and ambition that was necessary at the time. Naïvety works this way for most of us, until we reach the point where the things that are broken become so clear that scepticism is needed to move forward, to begin to question all the aspects of our work that were traditional but are no longer applicable. Through the years, as I created an exhibition programme prioritizing young Black artists, I grew increasingly aware of the work that needed to be done

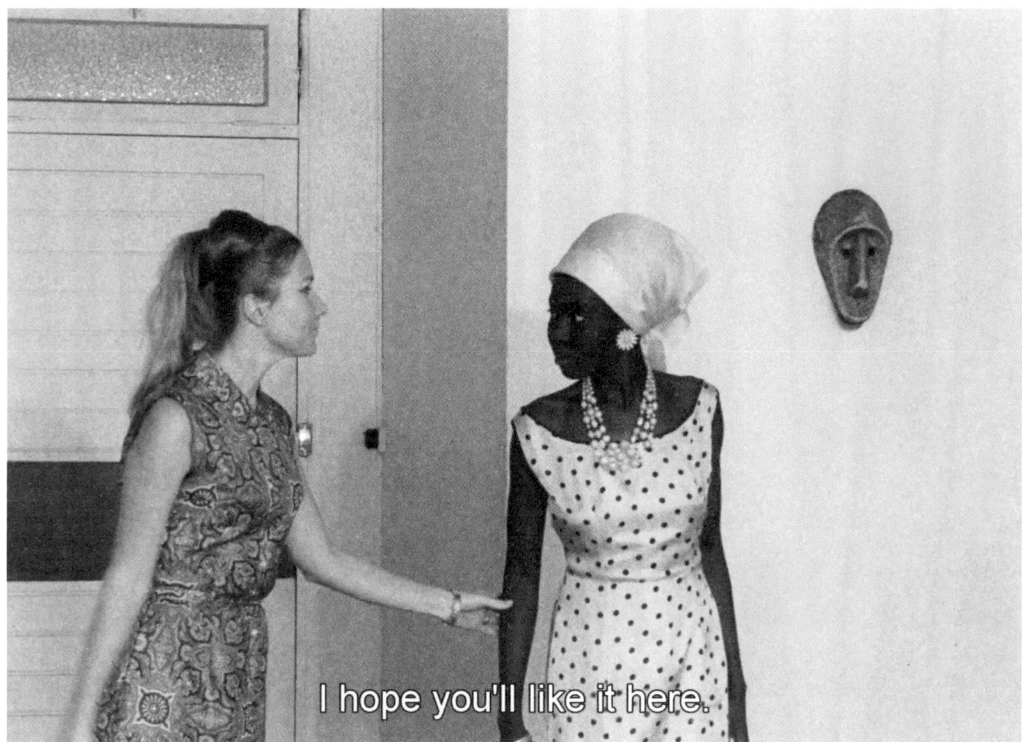

An opening scene of *Black Girl* (1966, directed and written by Ousmane Sembène): The madame of the house (Anne-Marie Jelinek) welcomes Diouana (Mbissine Thérèse Diop) to her home to begin her stint of servitude. There is subtle violence in her greeting as she welcomes Diounna with a force that is shielded by performative kindness. Her hope is an order, triggered by her unwelcomed physical touch, and Diounna's first sense of unease on-screen. Both Diouana and the mask behind are captive to this household.

beyond the galleries. I felt it was no longer enough to put on an exhibition. I wanted to understand how I could incorporate the demands of artists within the structure of the institution. How can the institution respond to the premises of the work it shows? If an artist's work is concerned with piracy and accessible educational practices – take, for example, Kandis Williams and Cassandra Press[6]– how can the institution be instrumental in the removal of paywalls around its knowledge holdings?

When considering the future of Black artists and curators within contemporary arts institutions, I choose to use imagery from the past as a reminder of the institutional tensions that many of us are still working so hard to dismantle. In times like ours, conservative reaction tends to follow the need for revolution with the persistence of a shadow. Sometimes the impulse to temper one's stridency is so subtle and convincing that the slight shift of one's own position might obscure the most offensive parts of one's grievance, vanish its presence all together – making you forget what it is you set out to do in the first place altogether.

Ousmane Sembène's French-Senegalese film *Black Girl* was released in 1966, a year in which a cultural revolution was burgeoning, bubbling to the surface. It was produced during an era in the grip of multiple wars, the rise of youth culture and the struggle for human and civil rights. This revolutionary period leading to 1968 reminds me of the promise institutions insist on dangling; a

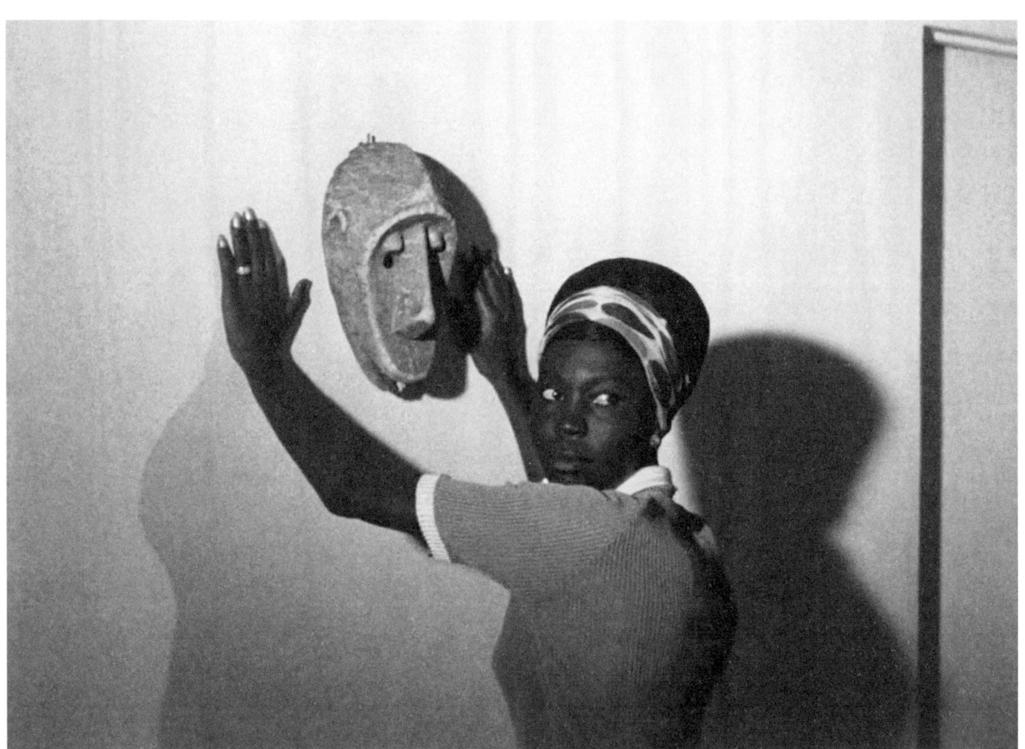

A weary and fed-up Diouana faces the mask. In a voice-over, she speaks: 'Back in Dakar, they must be saying: "Diouana is happy in France, she has a good life." For me, France is the kitchen, the living room, the bathroom and my bedroom.' This scene illustrates the irony of her circumstance. Where most assume that because of her place in France with a well-to-do white family she must be fulfilled, when in fact she is isolated in her servitude to this home and family – a sentiment she can share with this African mask – a symbol of her displacement.

promise that suggests that there is in fact a revolution to be had, change to be made. This promise ignites us, oftentimes inspiring us to take on roles that are then met with the opposite of revolution: fixity and suppression.

Black Girl, Sembène's first feature, has the visual power to accompany a retelling of struggle within an American arts institution today; a struggle sold as work in service to revolutionary ends but that doesn't quite feel as such, especially when the work continues to be impeded and entangled with historically grown structures of power. It explores the nature and effects of cultural domination. It is the story of arriving in a place where you are meant to work, where you are not asked to enact change – a story of defiance and the persistence of selfhood in spite of it all. A Black girl in a white house, or a house run by white supremacy and Black labour. A house where Black art is on the walls and Black food on the table, but where Blackness has more visual presence and reduction to thingliness than structural agency and command.

I want to know what it looks like when the people whose faces are used as a representation of change can actually enact structural transformations. I want to know how the desires of each and every artist who comes through the institution can be adapted as part of the institution's logic; how governance too can become a practice of desiring, through the lens of the artist. *Desire* is the will to want, enact and be open to the unknown or the repressed. I want to know what it feels like for institutions to be flexible, scalable and dynamic;

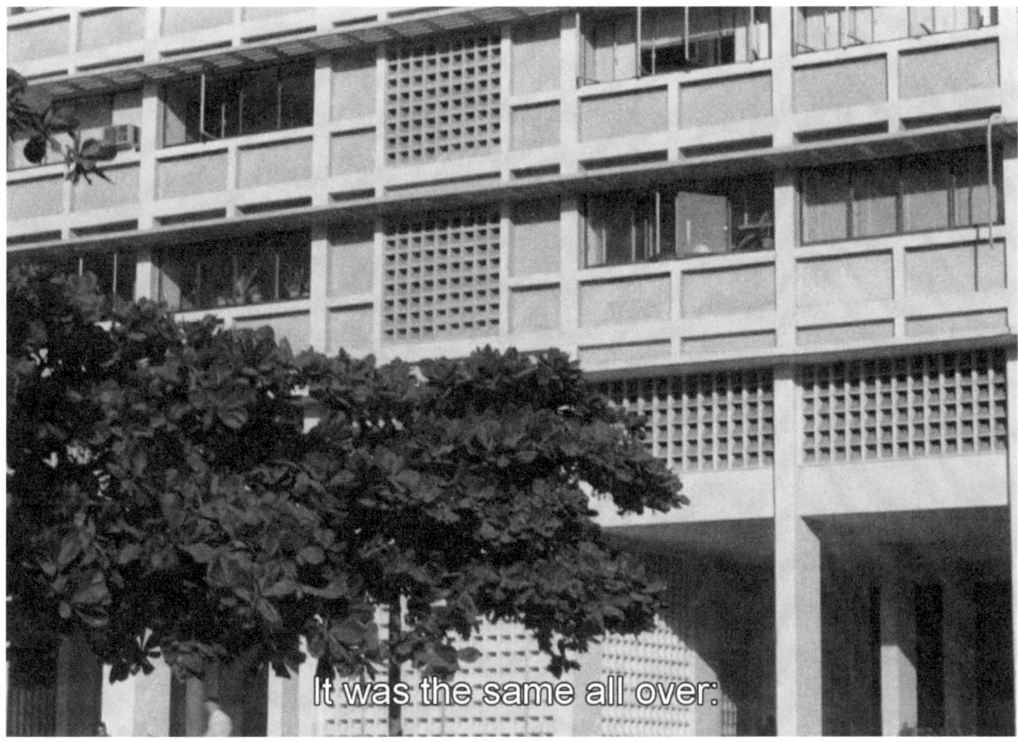

what it means to have a mission that changes as quickly as desires form. Most of all, I want to know what it's like to derive pleasure from developing a project, as well as having it received by the public, because even a successful project is rarely pleasurable to realize. They have borne the weight of so much institutional pressure that artists, arts educators and curators leave it under a pallor of secrets and isolation, having come to hate the thing they give out of love. These feelings are often too shameful to express as the result of both a protective instinct toward the institution and a fear of being perceived as ungracious or even insubordinate.

Tired of her circumstance, Diouana wanders the town in search of new employment within a building filled with similar families, where she is met with familiar rejection time and again. She recognizes a pattern within an architectural element meant to hold the tradition of family, ownership and wealth. In doing so, the sameness she describes becomes an institutional quality that she cannot escape.

A Plot and a Promise

'Black Girl: A Plot and a Promise' is a reassessment of the complicated relationship between Black practitioners and the museum. This limited scope is not to exclude other experiences but simply to speak from a position that is my own. I'd like to think of this as a reflection on my experiences with and observations of artists and institutions over the past five years, which will be continually revisited and reassessed as time goes on – as things change, as we make change. A plot recognizes that, whether the institution is newly founded or centuries old, we are entering into a structure that is somewhat predetermined, despite all promises; that is designed to function in ways that are not always revealed. According to the plot, a sequence of events transpires, and I end up somewhere. But I won't be buried there. I'm not dumb enough to believe I can change the plan altogether, but the promise of its transformation is invoked everywhere. This is the uncomfortable bind we find ourselves in. Lured by promise, trapped by plot.

Bridget Cooks's seminal work *Exhibiting Blackness: African Americans and the American Art Museum* (2011) serves as the catalyst that allows me to put these thoughts to page. The book speculates on the future of Black people in the museum, in any role, and leads me to ask the following questions: Has the field of museum administration changed enough for the institution to appropriately reflect the contributions of Black people? Do exhibitions serve a symbolic function in the museum, attempting to prove that the United States is a democratic project?

The term and concept of a plot is inspired by Sylvia Wynter's 1977 essay 'Novel and History, Plot and Plantation', wherein she describes how predetermined logics and narratives are designed by those outside the labour force – a logic akin to that of a plantation.[7] She describes modes of production, from crops to literary forms, ruled by external authors who shape the logics of production. In the logic of empire, effectively a plantation logic, the frameworks in which we produce are dictated by external factors that seek to create profit; a plot that benefits the few without reciprocity for the many.

Since 2015, I've been thinking about this within the context of cultural production, particularly through institutions that are benefiting from the labour of Black creatives. A plot can be thought of as a sort of scaffold that dictates how institutions think and operate. It speaks to how institutions rationalize and manage those who work within them; how institutions standardize and make efficient the myriad people who come through their doors. Standardization is the business of how institutions process difference, fitting it into a procedural machine: the business of institutionalizing.

The plot encompasses how institutions treat difference with hegemonic strategies of assimilation; strategies that are intended to create efficiency, safety and uniformity – standardization. When you apply formulae to artistic expression, however, you lose qualities that are essential to the work, you confuse the artistic intent and you fail to convey to the public what the artist set out to achieve.

If 'the plantation was the superstructure of civilization; and the plot was the roots of culture', where is the locus of the plantation system that lingers in the American art institution?[8] Where do instances of control, management and profit thread through and interrupt the work that we do? It seems to me that constraints are the work of the executive, administrative and financial arms of an institution – with those arms responsible for implementing austerity measures. I think the institutional representatives enacting such measures often convince themselves of their morality. They transform themselves into believers of a severe and anti-humanist cult, maintaining that the dogma they espouse and enforce is self-evidently good and true because it enforces procedural law.

When we consider the plot in this way, as something that's predetermined, it

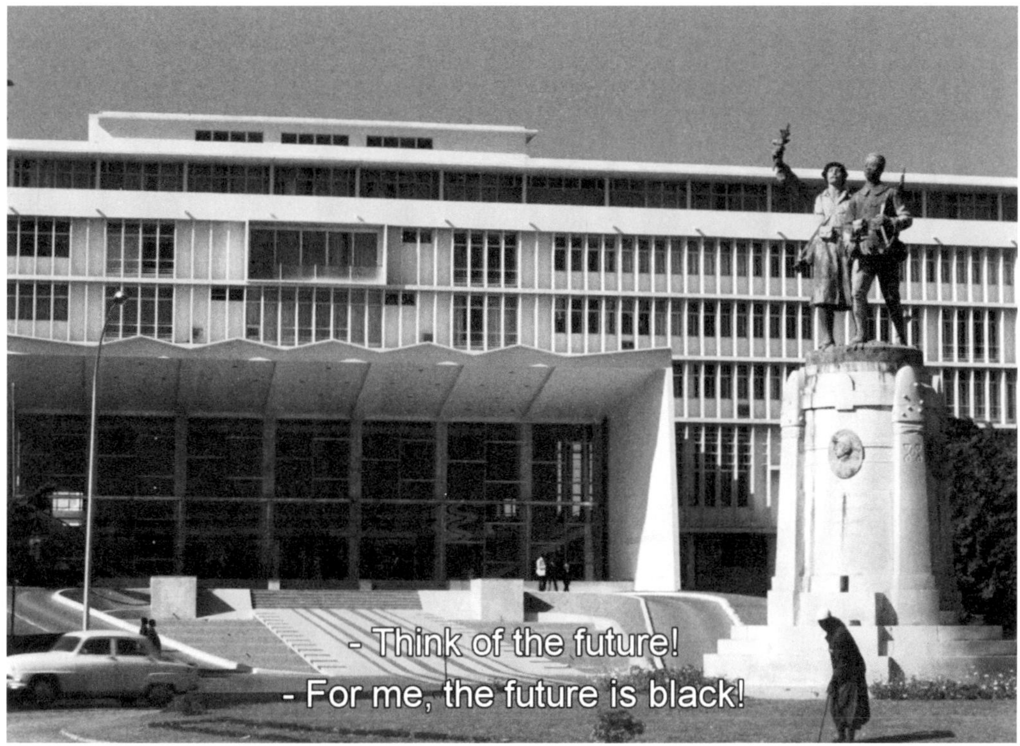

becomes hard to think of it as a scaffold, since that implies support. It functions instead as a series of ladders with trap doors. Here is a distinction, perhaps the hardest to navigate and even to put into words: the disharmony between the way something looks and how it feels. We can compare it to the gulf between intentions and actions, something that comes up a lot in adjudicating microaggressions. The articulated intentions of a person can feel nothing like the substance of their actions. Likewise, an institution's mission is everywhere contradicted by its operational procedures. The actions are where the plot is revealed, and the intentions are where the promise lies. The plot keeps us buried in the machine, and its promises keep us hopeful and working.

Following Diouana's search for new employment she makes the announcement that the future is Black and by doing so speaks to the impossibility of institutional advancement without Black labour. Yet with this statement she hints at a future that is not merely fuelled by contributions via labour but is instead constructed in entirely new ways.

The antidote lies in the artists, the curators and the people the institution is meant to serve. Change can only be realized when those who the institution promotes become the architects of its internal logic. This would require an incredible amount of flexibility and vulnerability on the part of the institution. It would be a step toward eliminating those abovementioned trapdoors, creating a bridge between the plot and the promise, so that they become one and the same. A sort of merger between intent and action.

This surrender would amount to a sort of revolutionary action, potentially even a political mess. Though if we've learned anything since 2016, it is that politics as they are do not work. So we should welcome the mess. I often think about how Fred Moten characterized the politics of the mess when he said,

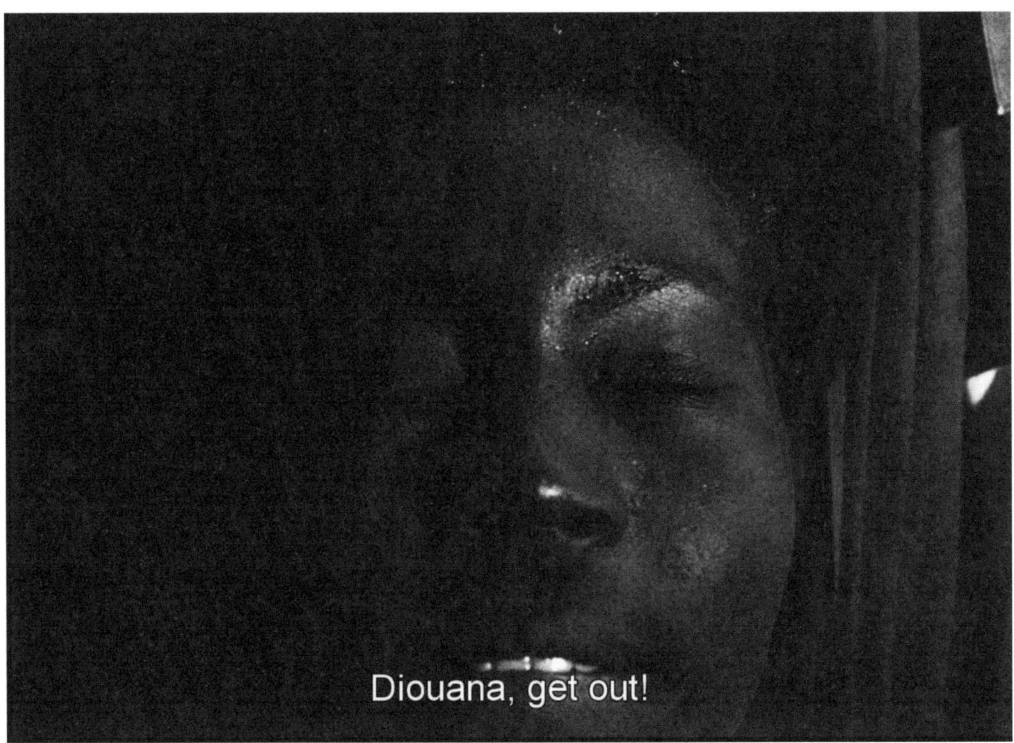

Diouana locks herself in the bathroom while the madame pleads for her to exit and work. The demand that she gets out narrates Diouana's desire to escape to places much further than the confines of the madame's bathroom.

Stills of *Black Girl*, 1966, directed and written by Ousmane Sembène, black-and-white film, 59 min.

> *Revolution and anti-colonialism (as per Fanon), is a program of total disorder, and museums and academic institutions clean up messes. The history of the modern subject is about cleaning up a mess – the eradication of business and fuzz. And politics is meant to regulate the mess. What if museums chose to present rather than clean up?*[9]

I believe in the potential of the mess. It need not have a negative influence on our psyches, but should rather have a positive one, a generative one. What this idea commands is a move away from corporate models of governance wherein everything is standardized and made into formulae. Instead, we approach each project we produce with the intention, ethic and creativity that the artist brings to the institution, bearings which of course change every time. This would radically change how we are supported in the matter of creative production; how our ideas are reflected in the ethics and culture of the institution, thereby transforming the institution itself.

The promises institutions make are the lure that drives our work. They'd like me to believe that this time will be different; this time our research will be valued and its ethics will be implemented. The last time the issue was circumstantial, not the entire field – a bad apple. Lines like these prolonged my initial naïvety, but today they reveal themselves as fallacies with a scorching clarity. The metaphor of a marriage feels appropriate here: a pact is forged through promises that callous over time.

How to believe in the promise that the plot continually foils? It leads me to ask: *What are we being promised and what is being asked in return?* I grapple with what the wave of Black inclusion means during years that have produced an overwhelming volume of material culture evidencing racism and inequality. When institutions give the lie to what a society says it believes, then Black artists and curators get used as tools in the management of unresolved conflicts. We are tasked with supervising the space between the fictions and realities of living in this country.

When I hear the term 'Black future' I imagine a future composed of resilient strategies, creativity, hybrid solutions, collaborative come-ups, new models, new standards committed to never becoming stale. I envision a collective that can move seamlessly; action that takes place within and through desire and reality. For the future of Black practitioners to be viable and enjoyable we need to ask how artists and institutions might revise this corrupt sociopolitical contract. How do we compose new relationships to power structures and modes of production? Artists, arts educators and curators can absolutely complicate our relationship to the world and propose new models for relating to promise. It's up to the institution to take these proposals up as a viable logic, to be positioned so that they can pivot continuously and non-defensively, as a matter of practice.

We are disciplined to manufacture and present, but I want us to move toward the type of discipline that Stuart Hall described when he said, 'The only discipline worth having is the discipline of purpose, in the context of love.'[10] I invoke love not to suggest anything hokey, but to insist that our modes of production be fuelled by mutual desire driven by the producers through flexible institutional strategies. When we do this, we can render desire within a structural environment where bureaucracy is propelled toward supporting creative work.

The future is when being Black in an institution doesn't feel like complete isolation. The future is when the workers inside an institution are empowered to set its course. The future is when the mission of an institution can be demonstrated in its action, in the public eye as well as behind closed doors.

Notes

[1] The term *institution building*, to me, is characterized by the various efforts to build ethical institutions. Whether the project be the founding of a new institution or redefining an established one, this work is committed to amending the aspects of an institution – from its internal make-up to its programmes – that no longer serve its staff, audiences or collaborators.

[2] My use of the term *old* here does not suggest the capitalistic obsession with the idea of 'the new'. It acknowledges that at times new is worse. Old instead refers to attitudes towards governing that are stuck in paradigms that no longer serve the progression of an institution towards newly defined goals.

[3] *Tiredness* meaning exhaustion towards the resistance to the actions that would lead to change.

[4] Saidiya Hartman, 'Venus in Two Acts', *Small Axe: A Caribbean Journal of Criticism*, vol.12, no.2, 2008, p.11.

[5] *Detection* here characterizes being subject to public scrutiny carried out by a culture that is committed to calling out institutions that refuse to adapt to change.

[6] See https://cassandrapress.org/.

[7] See Sylvia Wynter, 'Novel and History, Plot and Plantation', in *Savacou,* no.5, 1971, pp.95–102. The term *plot* here is inspired also by Saidiya Hartman's essay 'The Plot of Her Undoing', which appeared in the Feminist Art Coalition's online series *Notes on Feminisms,* available at https://feministartcoalition.org/essays-list/saidiya-hartman.

[8] S. Wynter, 'Novel and History, Plot and Plantation', *op. cit.*, p.100.

[9] Fred Moten, quoted in Johanna Burton et al., 'An Ongoing Conversation', in *Trigger: Gender as a Tool and a Weapon* (exh. cat.), New York: New Museum, 2017, p.274.

[10] Stuart Hall, 'Absolute Beginnings: Reflections on the Secondary Modern Generation', in Paul Gilroy and Ruth Wilson Gilmore (ed.), *Selected Writings on Race and Difference*, Durham, NC: Duke University Press, 2021, p.24.

Creating the Histories We Think We'll Need: Thoughts on Black Futurity – Brittany Webb

I'll begin with a text that's been on my mind this fall.[1] Tina Campt's *A Black Gaze: Artists Changing How We See* (2021) charts the emergence of what she calls a 'Black gaze' in the work of contemporary artists such as the lens-based artists Arthur Jafa, Kahlil Joseph, Jenn Nkiru, Dawoud Bey and Deana Lawson and the multimedia artists Okwui Okpokwasili, Simone Leigh and Luke Willis Thompson. In Campt's articulation:

> *A Black gaze is a structure of visual engagement that implicitly and explicitly understands blackness as neither singular nor a singularity; it embraces instead the multiplicity of blacknesses these artists simultaneously grapple with and personify. Here my choice of the indefinite article is intentional, for I am proposing that we think about a Black gaze (rather than the Black gaze) and understand it as both multiple and polyvalent. It is at once a critical framework, a reading apparatus, a term that describes an artist's practice, and a spectatorial mediation that demands particularly active modes of watching, listening, and witnessing.*[2]

For the past few weeks, I've been thinking with this passage at the end of the opening section, 'Prelude to a Black Gaze':

> *I must cop to the fact that I've been drawn to counterintuitive concepts for a long time, as they have always offered me a powerful source of inspiration. Counterintuition requires us to think beyond our comfort zone, to think oppositions in tandem, and to think them in a different grammar – not the grammar of the declarative ('this is'), but in the grammar of my favorite tense: the subjunctive tense of the future real conditional. It is not a provisional tense, but one premised on the realization of a different future. It is the tense of 'as if'. It is an intentional deployment of aspiration that strives toward a multitude of possibilities. The future real conditional or* that which will have had to happen *is proceeding 'as if'. It proceeds 'as if' our aspirations were being or had already been realized. It is a radical provocation to see blackness differently and, in so doing, to create a path to* living *blackness differently – not in the future, but now.*[3]

I've been sitting with this section, '*that which will have had to happen …* proceeds "as if" our aspirations were being or had already been realized'. It articulates a kind of work I think many of us are doing, or are trying to do, in the varied modes of working in this field. In my panel yesterday, Bridget Cooks asked us why we had this intense interest in the 1970s, and while I've been thinking about the new insights that are available to us based on critical distance and new archives (resources where the assembly or the public access is new), I also think about the fact that our students and publics are constantly demanding new histories from us. We're frequently reckoning with pasts we cannot change and using that as a springboard for thinking about how to move differently in the future.

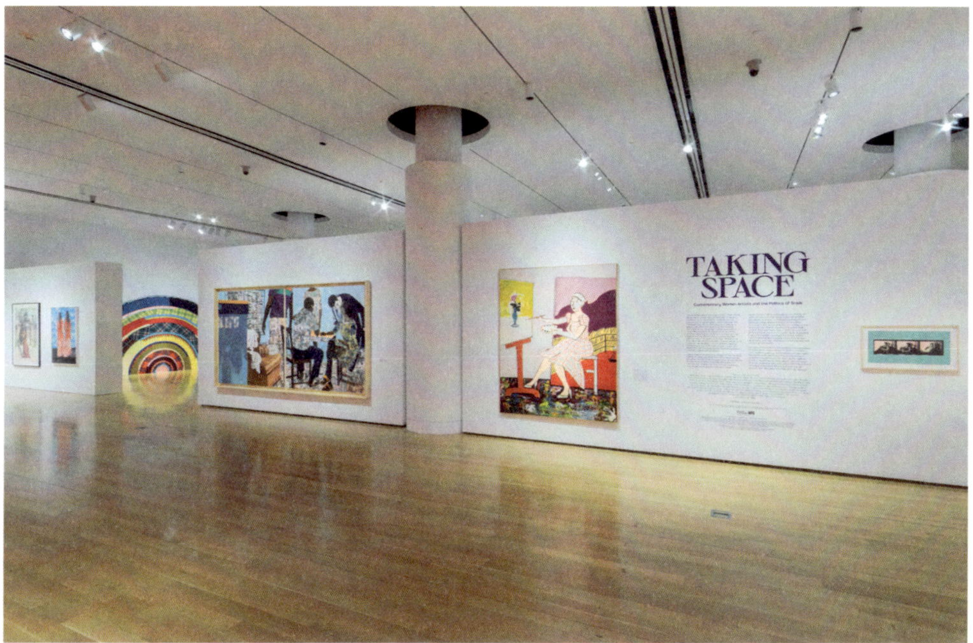

Installation view, 'Taking Space: Contemporary Women Artists and the Politics of Scale', Pennsylvania Academy of the Fine Arts, Philadelphia, 2021. Photo: Adrian Cubillas. Courtesy Pennsylvania Academy of the Fine Arts

I'm thinking here of the occasion where Nana Adusei-Poku and I met at Cooper Union in New York, where she was giving a brilliant paper on the sculptor Augusta Savage and melancholy. She provoked the audience to think about what it meant to have an enlarged photo of Savage's sixteen-foot sculpture *Lift Every Voice and Sing* (1939) on view with its miniature, and whether it would be productive for us to sit in melancholy with the reality that this sculpture was destroyed, rather than preserved, and that the form of the exhibition meant that might require a curatorial strategy that emphasizes that absence by *not* reproducing a large-scale photo, by letting audiences be uncomfortable that we're only left with miniature replicas. It strikes me that this is one of the tensions many of us are managing, on the one hand wanting to proceed as if our aspirations have already been realized – in our art, our exhibitions, our writing projects – and on the other hand knowing that there's still so much work to do to create new histories, which requires us to take this kind of speculative, anticipatory stance, to predict the histories we think we'll need in the future, to do that work now. Many of our institutions are in upheaval, so it has me frequently wondering, how do we get to the future from here?

I'll briefly mention two shows that have occupied much of my 2021, both of which are permanent collection projects based at my own institution in Philadelphia, the Pennsylvania Academy of the Fine Arts (PAFA). First I'll mention 'Taking Space: Contemporary Women Artists and the Politics of Scale', which just closed in the autumn of 2021 and considered the use of size, seriality and repetition as strategies of scale-making across 62 works of art by women.

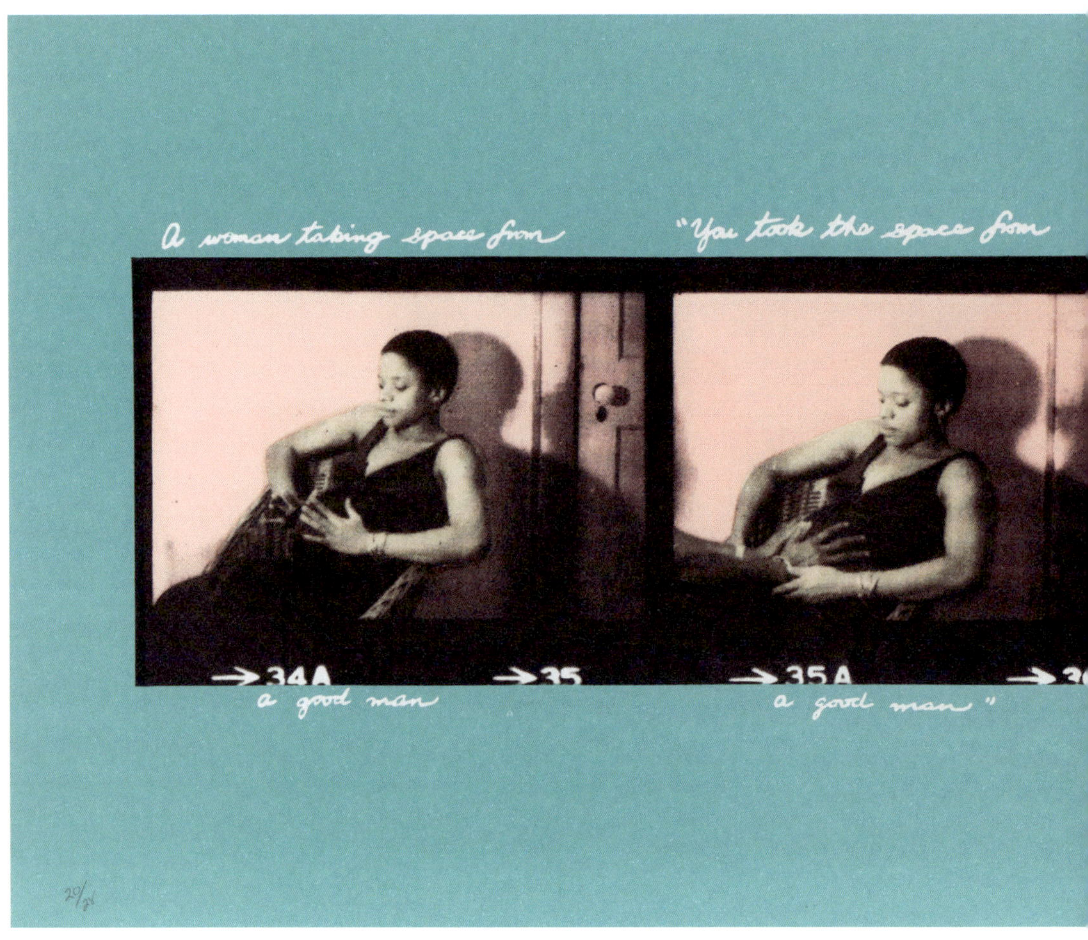

Deborah Willis, *I Made Space For a Good Man*, 2009, lithograph, ed. 20/28, 37.5 × 74.9cm. Courtesy the artist

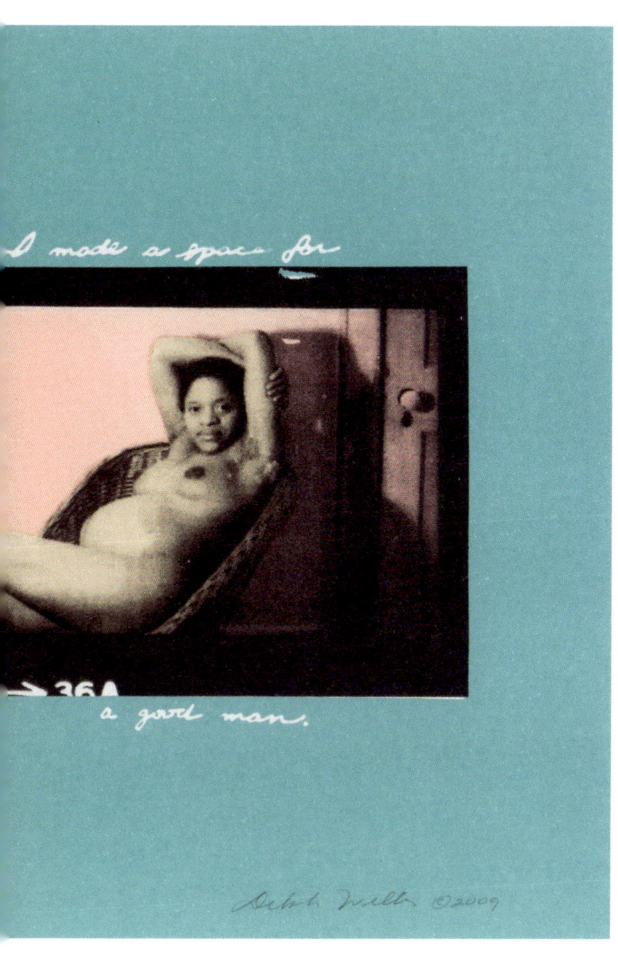

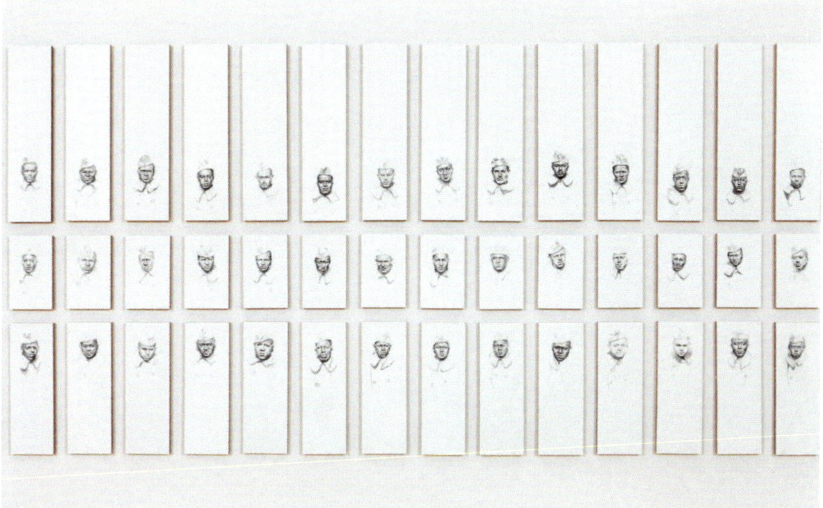

Debra Priestly, *somewhere listening: Company B, 365th Infantry Regiment, 92nd Division, A.E.F. 1918–1919* (detail), 2014, charcoal pencil on paper mounted on 212 board panels, 71.1 × 746.8cm. Collection of Pennsylvania Academy of the Fine Arts. Courtesy the artist

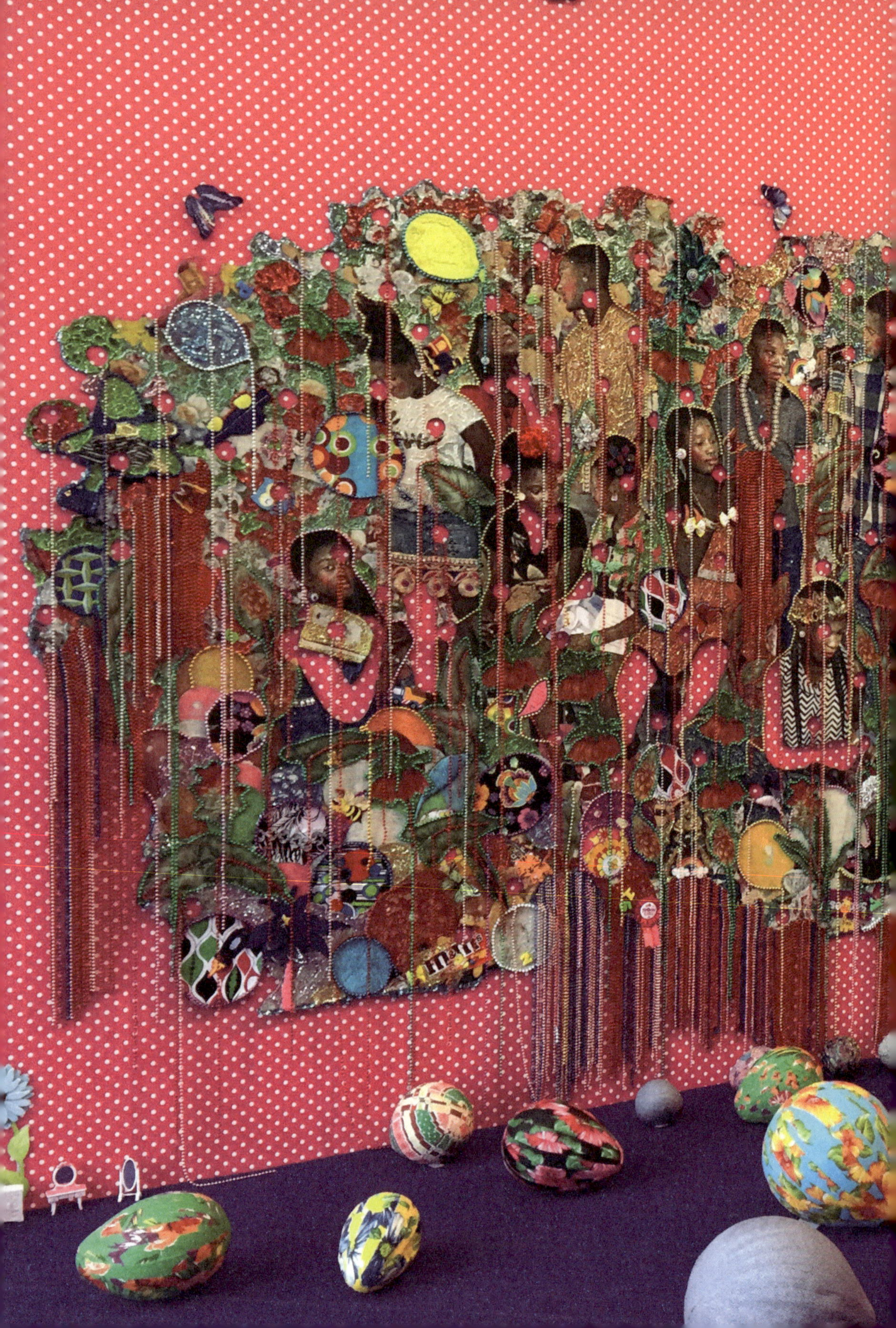

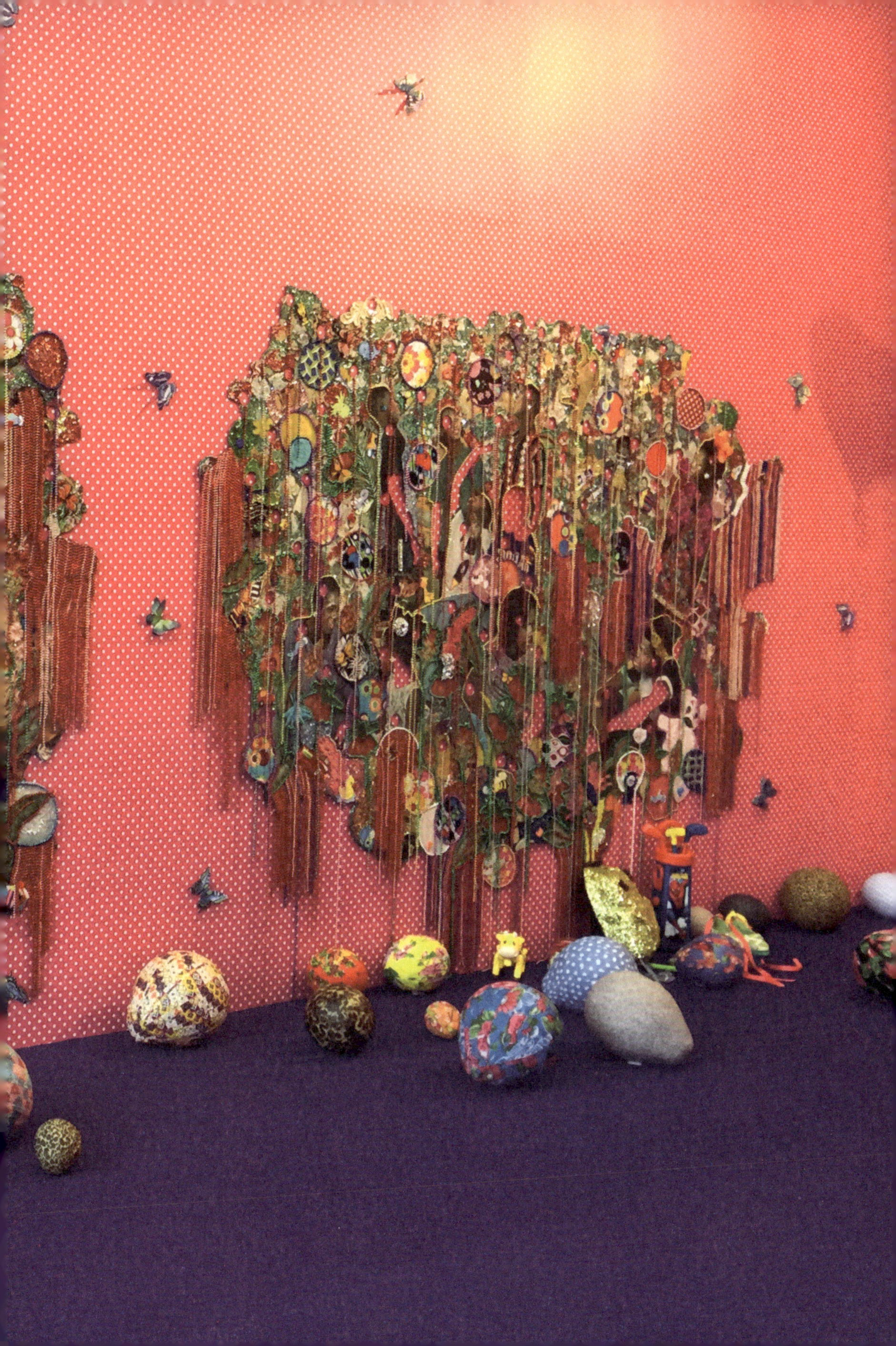

Previous spread: Ebony G. Patterson, *... doing what they always do... (when they grow up...)*, 2016, mixed media on hand-cut jacquard woven tapestry with beads, appliques, embellishments, broaches, plastic, glitter, fabric, embellished knapsack, books, plastic toys, handmade shoes and wallpaper fabric, 315 × 1092.2 × 30.5cm. Courtesy the artist

The exhibition was anchored by the lithograph *I Made Space For A Good Man* (2009) by the great art historian, curator, pathbreaker and MacArthur Genius Dr Deborah Willis, which features three 1970s self-portraits in a row with captions in cursive script: the left one reads 'A woman taking space from a good man'; the centre, '"You took the space from a good man"'; and the right, 'I made a space for a good man'. In the lithograph, Willis reclaims an earlier history, of being told by a professor that it was a shame that she was a student in his class 'taking up a good man's space'. The presumption behind this interaction was that a young Black woman was not going to have a future art career of any consequence, and that just by being in the classroom, or in the art programme, she was in a space that could have gone to a good man who would have had the kind of career one expected an artist to have if they aren't getting married and raising children.

What is incredible about this work is that it becomes a triumph narrative, both in the sense that Dr Willis has made great space for many of us in this field, having gone on to be the 'dean' of African American photography and a mentor to many. In the image, she's pregnant with her child, who will become the contemporary artist Hank Willis Thomas. This became a great work to think about the space of the body, the psychic space of imagining futures, the space of the classroom, who has the right to be in a programme, to dream a particular kind of future? So many artists told us, when we walked them through the exhibition, that they had a similar kind of story. This was a great piece to open the show, to tackle ideas about the space of the body, the natural and built environment, and seriality as a practice of physically enlarging the space an artwork takes up.

Again, the show tackled ideas of space and the body, space and environment (both natural and built environments), psychic space, seriality as a practice of taking up space, and there was also incredible material diversity across the artworks. My co-curator, Jodi Throckmorton, and I were sort of staking a claim about the audacity and the material needs required for so many formidable women to be working in large scale, and we were interested in these conversations our field frequently has about whether or not to dispense with the idea of group shows of all women, all artists of colour, etc. We ended up getting such interesting feedback. We had some young visitors who said these types of exhibitions were sort of old school and unnecessary, and at the same time they would point out all these women whom they'd never heard of (which is sort of the point). We also had visitors our age and older who said that they wished they'd seen more projects like this when they were in school, and – my favourite – artists in the exhibition who told us about all the social networks among the women on view that weren't visible even to us as curators, or who said they were told 'no museum will ever show your work' when they had studio visits with art world gatekeepers two or three decades ago.

It was interesting to reflect on the idea of not just showing work by Black artists in shows about Blackness. People kept finding ways to ask me, as a Black curator, how many African American artists had work in the show – in 2021 – and at first I would have to go through the checklist and count.

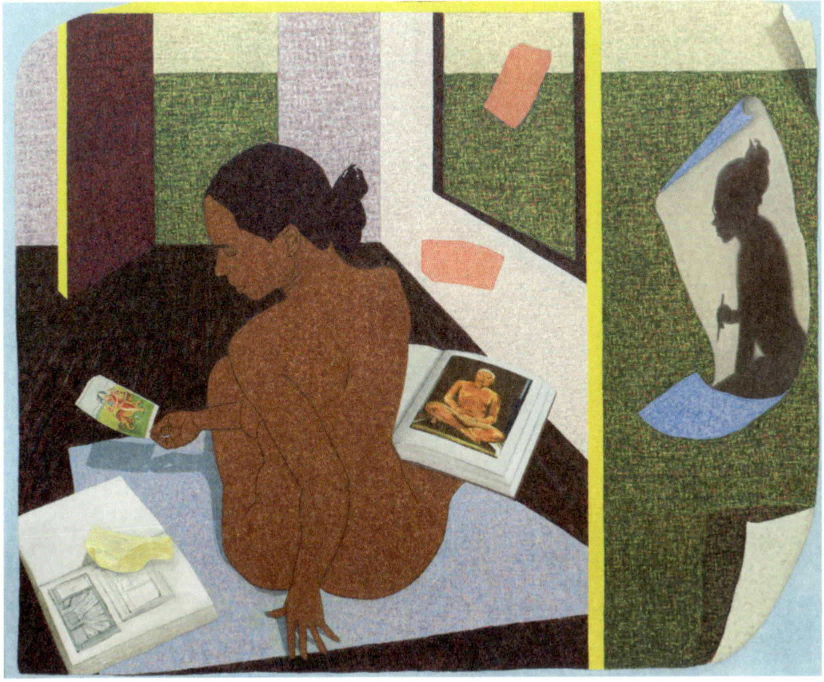

Mequitta Ahuja, *A Real Allegory of Her Studio*, 2015, oil on canvas, 203.2 × 243.8cm. Courtesy the artist

Then I'd have to respond with a complicated answer about how Blackness and racialization works, and how Deborah Willis and Debra Priestly and Faith Ringgold and Mickalene Thomas and Betye Saar are Black Americans, but Wangechi Mutu is Kenyan American and Ebony G. Patterson is Jamaican and Mequitta Ahuja is Black American and South Asian, and these details are important because of the kinds of visual cultural histories and materials that are syncretized brilliantly in their work, despite how that might confound any demographic headcount someone is trying to take.

The other project I want to think with as we consider Black futures is an upcoming retrospective exhibition featuring the work of Birmingham-born, Brooklyn-based sculptor John Rhoden (1916–2001), an exhibition that he never really got during his life. The exhibition will open in Fall 2023 at PAFA, and will tell the story of Rhoden, who 'nobody really knew' despite the fact that he is embedded in the Harlem Renaissance network legacies. He attended Talladega College and met Hale Woodruff at Atlanta University, who advised him to go to New York. When he got to New York, he met people like James Weldon Johnson, Cab Calloway, Bill Robinson and Augusta Savage – who introduced him to Richmond Barthé, the most celebrated Black sculptor of the day, who became his mentor and someone with whom he shared living and studio space. He served in the army in World War II and enrolled at Columbia University on the GI Bill, where he studied with sculptors Oronzio Maldarelli, Hugo Robus and William Zorach. He got into the American Academy in Rome and became the first

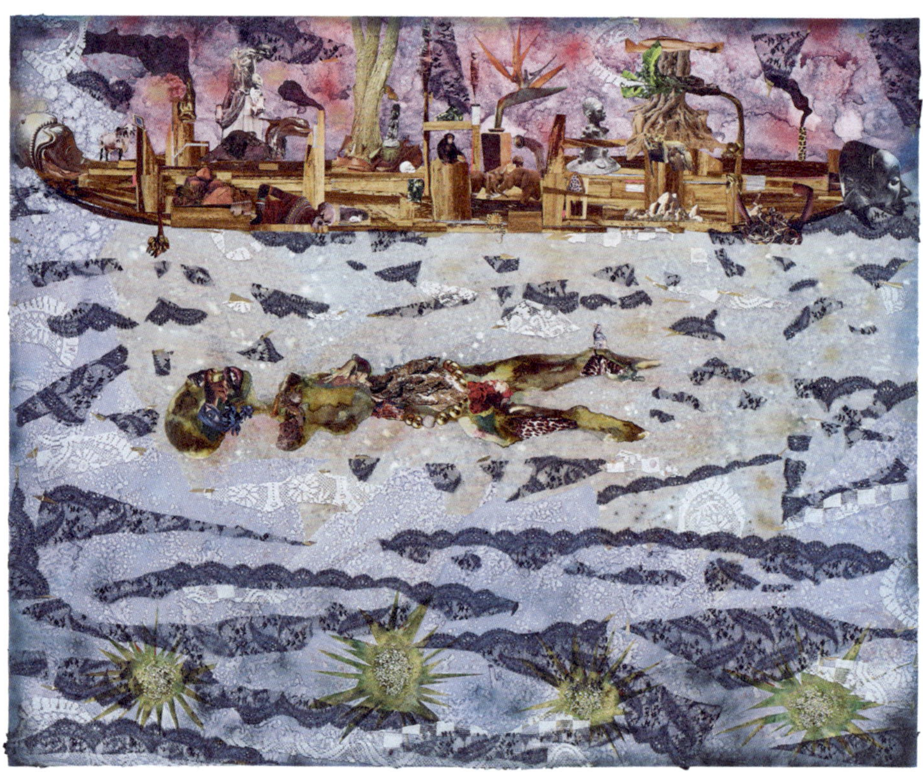

Wangechi Mutu, *If we live through it, She'll carry us back*, 2014, paint, paper, lace, wood, beads and collage on vinyl, 152.4 × 182.9cm. Courtesy Victoria Miro Gallery and the artist

Black visual artist ever in residence, and he also won the Rome Prize. This became a springboard for him to become an artist tapped by the US State Department to eventually tour twenty countries between 1955 and 1959. This expanded the visual influences on his work, and a fellowship from the Rockefeller Foundation supported his spending two years in Indonesia, where he started working in large-scale wood.

Rhoden also has an incredible exhibition history, including in gallery spaces and HBCUs. He was written about in the press all over the world and covered by the Black press in the United States. He was in some of the most storied Black exhibitions of the twentieth century, including 'Contemporary Black Artists in America' at the Whitney Museum in 1971, and 'Two Centuries of Black American Art', curated by Dr David Driskell, which started at the Los Angeles County Museum of Art in 1976 and toured to five venues. He also did a number of public commissions, including *Nesaika* (1976), for the African American Museum in Philadelphia; the Reverend Shuttlesworth statute, completed in 1992 for the Birmingham Civil Rights Institute; and a number of New York commissions, including the *Mitochondria*, in 1970. All of this confounds the idea of Rhoden as an 'unknown' sculptor. This is someone whose papers are archived with the Smithsonian Archives of American Art in Washington DC and whose records there helped us identify titles of sculptures that came to PAFA without an illustrated inventory or checklist.

In looking at images of what the work looks like when it comes to us, needing to be processed, I want to emphasize that this is physical and administrative labour. Someone has to move sculptures out of a home and onto shelves. Someone has to take papers out of bins and figure out how to put them into archival files, into boxes, on shelves to make it searchable, to create an archive that makes it possible for us to mount a retrospective where we can show and contextualize works on view like Rhoden's *Slave Ship* (1989). So in some ways, thinking about this group show and this solo artist retrospective has had me wondering about the research and curatorial strategies we all might be better deploying to get to the future from here.

Notes

[1] Editors' Note: This text is adapted from the author's presentation at the online conference 'Reshaping the Field: Arts of the African Diasporas on Display', hosted by the Center for Curatorial Studies, Bard College, 4–6 November 2021.

[2] Tina M. Campt, *A Black Gaze: Artists Changing How We See*, Cambridge, MA: MIT Press, 2021, p.21.

[3] *Ibid.*, p.24.

No Real Closure: Curating Black Futures Now – Languid Hands (Imani Mason Jordan and Rabz Lansiquot)

You could say that our curatorial interest comes from the very earnest (naïve?) place of simply being black artists who are interested in working with other black artists, in sustaining the practices of those who sustain us. Through interdisciplinary public programming, exhibition-making, political study and collaboration, we have sought out opportunities large and small to honour many incredible artists making work today. Our work, naturally, takes place within the broader context of our lives, which means it is formed both reactively and proactively in our contemporary world. Who we are as people, our identities and predilections, and our idiosyncrasies, shape our shared practice. So too does the political moment we find ourselves in, and the historical dialogues and legacies that have paved our way.[1]

The first three years or so of our curatorial output were focused almost exclusively on public programming, primarily through our work within the larger collective sorryyoufeeluncomfortable (SYFU). We developed discursive, interventionist forms of responding to institutions, and if we were lucky, responding to the art held inside them. In this sense, we spoke to, about and around black art before we were ever in a position to commission it. This is perhaps why our curation as Languid Hands, the artistic and curatorial project we began in 2019, is so often attentive to a kind of aesthetics of study, to work that recalibrates how we think as well as how we feel. Though we know well the perils of privileging academic knowledge over other forms, we respect the rigour of political thought, the challenge of dense texts meant only to be understood in relation, in collectivity. Our influences, then, come from a range of disciplines both formal and informal, practical and theory-based. We have always felt it important to demonstrate that black artists are not a monolith, that there are enough contemporary black artists (and enough difference between them, aesthetic, geographical and otherwise) to engender lifelong commitment to such separatism in our practice. Our audiences are invited into our way of seeing, to commune with us in deep appreciation of black art, black life and black people.

No Real Closure

Our curatorial programme 'No Real Closure' was presented at Cubitt gallery in London between September 2020 and April 2022 as part of their unique curatorial fellowship structure. 'No Real Closure' was conceived as a platform for experimentation and development of black artistic practice across exhibitions, moving image, text, performance and public programming. Absent was the disproportionate emphasis on surface-level survey-style programmes and representational focus: when we gathered, we wanted to do so in order to manifest collaboration, exchange, dialogue and relationships – a sum greater than its individual parts. In our 2020 world of pandemics and insurrections, with closures abounding, 'No Real Closure' took on somewhat of a deeper meaning. It spoke to the persistent and ever-present wounds of anti-blackness that are always and already open. It was a reminder that there is no closure to our ongoing work of dismantling the violent structures within which we

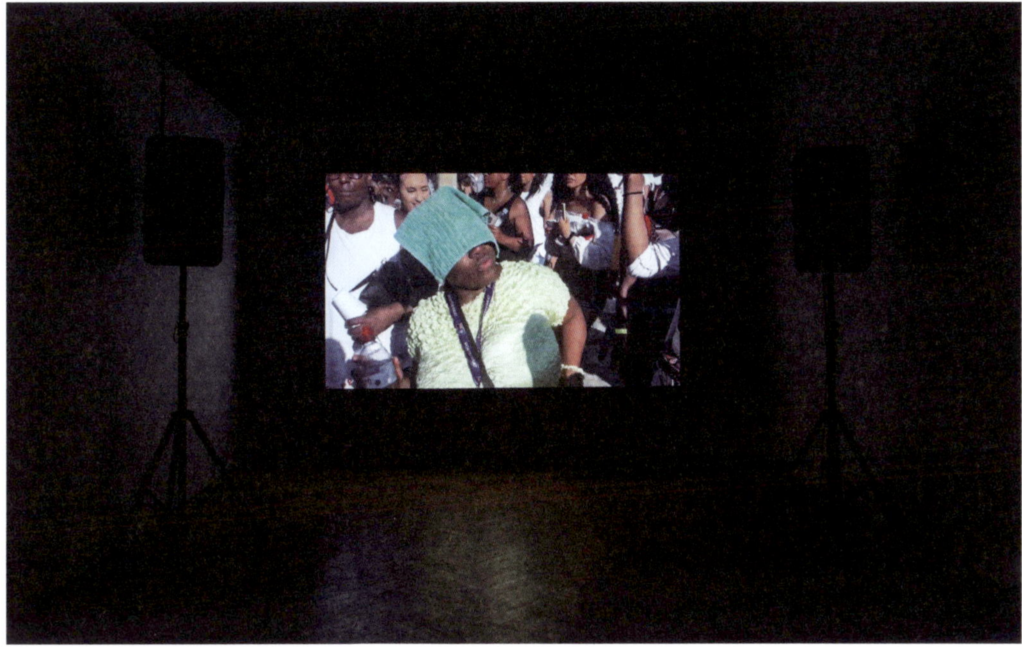

Languid Hands, *Towards A Black Testimony: Prayer/Protest/Peace*, 2019, film, 40 min. Installation view, 'Towards A Black Testimony, Part 2: Terrain', Display, Prague. Photo: Peter Watkins. Courtesy Display

cannot breathe. No closure to our collective resilience, nor to our communal grieving. 'No Real Closure' became acknowledgement and refusal, commitment and surrender.

Just as the world around us had shifted the meaning of our curatorial framing before we were even able to open the gallery doors, each invited artist brought a new dimension to our collective theorizing. In the following sections, we illustrate this phenomenal shifting in scope and breadth, exploring how the artists in our programme have taught us to think and feel, and to live with and in no real closure. With gratitude, we are held because of it.

Towards a Black Testimony: Prayer/Protest/Peace

Our first planned exhibition in 'No Real Closure', which was cancelled as a result of the Covid-19 pandemic, was to be a group show featuring new commissions from artists Barby Asante, Christopher Kirubi, Derica Shields, Rebecca Bellantoni and mayfly. It was framed as an extension of our ongoing artistic/curatorial project *Towards a Black Testimony: Prayer/Protest/Peace (TABT:P/P/P)*, which takes our 2019 film of the same name as both an artwork in its own right and curatorial prompt – a call that allows for a range of creative responses. Our film, originally commissioned by Jerwood Arts in London, examines black testimony as obscured, ignored and undermined. Drawing on archival imagery, black geographies and the dying declarations of black martyrs, it explores the complexities of truth, empathy, justice, the law, life and death for what Imani Mason Jordan has referred to as 'Black Mass'.[2] The work borrows its subtitle – *Prayer/Protest/Peace* – from the third track on jazz drummer and composer Max Roach's 1960 album *We Insist! Freedom*

Now Suite, featuring jazz vocalist Abbey Lincoln. Using this composition as an underlying structure, *TABT:P/P/P* presents three chapters, or meditations, on death and dying, considering the im/possibility of black testimony through evidentiary and legal forums. The script draws from a variety of well- and lesser-known texts, weaving the audience through a performance/narration composed and delivered by Imani Mason Jordan, and carefully annotated by Rabz Lansiquot's incisive archival exploration.

Throughout the course of *TABT:P/P/P*, we have commissioned responses from upwards of 25 geographically diverse practitioners working in performance, text, sound, painting, critical theory, academia and public programming. We have also ourselves made new work in response to the film, notably our 2021 work *Detritus!*, for Cypher Billboard, a site in Bounds Green, London, which consisted of a large-scale public artwork, sound mix and accompanying text. We have been in conversation about the work, and the project overall, on numerous occasions. At the time of writing, we are in the process of self-publishing an edited collection of responses to the project. *TABT:P/P/P* has allowed us to experiment with the concept of multiplicity in relation to both art-making and curatorial practice, utilizing a non-binary method of both/and, refusing to settle for either/or. It has become apparent to us that whilst curatorial and artistic practice do have some distinctions, the combined practice of artist/curator allows us to be fully present with all sides of ourselves. Our curatorial practice is discursive; as artists we have a deep love and appreciation for our fellow artists. It is not surprising, then, that our favourite artists make us want to make work, and vice versa. As Languid Hands, we have sought to weave our multiple sensibilities together, blurring the distinctions between artistic and curatorial work as we have traditionally understood them. You could say we have developed a kind of double consciousness: hybrid, multitudinous ways of looking, knowing, working; two eyes, two hats, two hands – *languid hands*.

Curatorial Tactics

In June 2020, we hosted the first in a series of semi-regular meetings to establish Curatorial Tactics (CT), a network of black curators and artists dedicated to ethical modes of working and collective strategies for a black curatorial praxis. The aim of CT has become to foreground the complex, precarious conditions of marginalized and vulnerable art workers. We want to support one another logistically, to transform informal and unstructured relationships between peers into an effective network of mutual support.

Our objectives for CT are:

> *1. to share and distribute knowledge, skills and resources towards collective standards of practice;*
> *2. to develop an ethics of black curatorial practice through language and action;*
> *3. to establish sustainable frameworks for peer support and collective curatorial tactics that honour the historical legacy of black curators and artists;*
> *4. to provide peer mentorship and critical feedback in curatorial and artistic practice.*

We embrace the opportunity to utilize our fellowship beyond its enabling us to showcase work. We embrace our capacity to be advocates for ethical, liberatory praxis and to develop a shared understanding of what that means in our current context; and to know how to move forward in (seemingly everlasting) times of uncertainty, both within the art world and in our lives at large.

We have some questions:

> *What becomes of our jobs as curators when the artists we work with are poor, or sick, or unable to survive racial capitalism, let alone make work? What is our duty to those within our field, and those outside of it? How can black curators build an ethic of care in relation to the black artist? What might a radical, liberatory black curatorial praxis look? Or in what ways might a practice compound or reinforce oppressive structures, and how can we oppose these?*

And some guiding principles:

> *Our aim is not to be didactic in building a framework for black curatorial praxis and ethics, but to challenge ourselves to create a framework in our collective image. This could happen through a variety of meeting formats, such as masterclasses, discussions and study groups, as well as by workshopping ethics and planning collectively agreed-upon working practices. CT resists the individualism, competition and scarcity that white supremacist, ableist, capitalist working conditions encourage, instead celebrating collectivity, abundance and solidarity. CT values the interdependence needed in such precarious contexts and recognizes the often unbalanced, parasitic and exploitative relationship that curators have to artists; CT seeks to resist such models. The need for a curatorial ethics in defence of black life is clear.*

Three Exhibitions

Languid Hands has curated three solo exhibitions as part of 'No Real Closure': R.I.P Germain's 'Dead Yard', Ajamu X's 'Ajamu: Archival Sensoria' and Camara Taylor's 'a rant! a reel!'. Each commissioned artist was invited to respond in whatever way they felt best to the shared prompt of 'no real closure'. Though quite different, aesthetically speaking, each of the following artists created exhibitions that had a deep attentiveness to black people found in the archive, as well as to the embodied archives held in people, places and communities.

R.I.P. Germain: 'Dead Yard'

R.I.P Germain is a visionary artist. To work with him, to join him in the process of creating an exhibition, is to be in awe of intricate detail, to learn new meanings for specificity and intention. In 'Dead Yard', our first exhibition in the 'No Real Closure' programme, audiences were welcomed into a space for mourning. The exhibition contained four main works: a sound work comprised of multiple voices reflecting on their own experiences of grief, and various sculptural installations, each with multiple symbolic elements, and each dedicated to and named after a person who had passed away

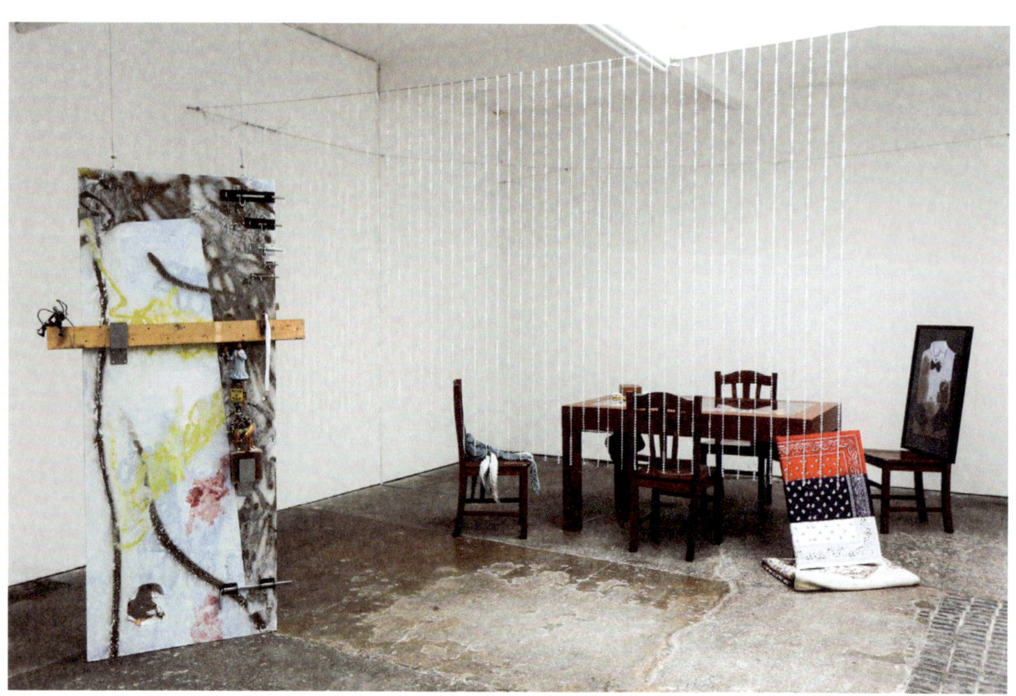

R.I.P Germain, *Imarl* and *Sonny*, 2020. Installation view, 'Dead Yard', Cubitt Gallery, London, 2020. Photo: Vanessa Peterson. Courtesy Cubitt Artists and Languid Hands

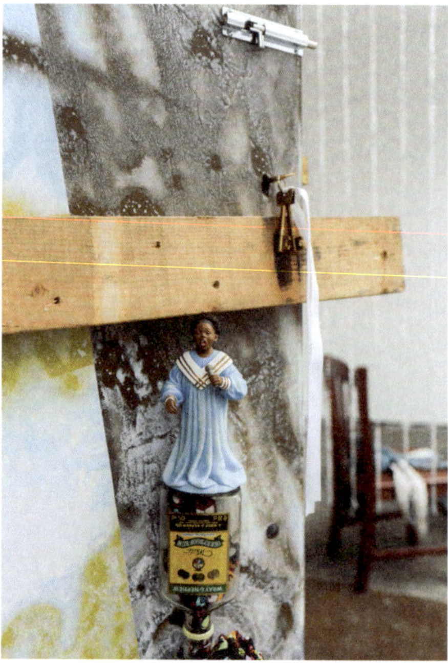

Left:
R.I.P Germain, *Imarl* (detail). Photo: Vanessa Peterson. Courtesy Cubitt Artists and Languid Hands

Right:
R.I.P Germain, *Lloyd*, 2020. Installation view, 'Dead Yard'. Photo: Vanessa Peterson. Courtesy Cubitt Artists and Languid Hands

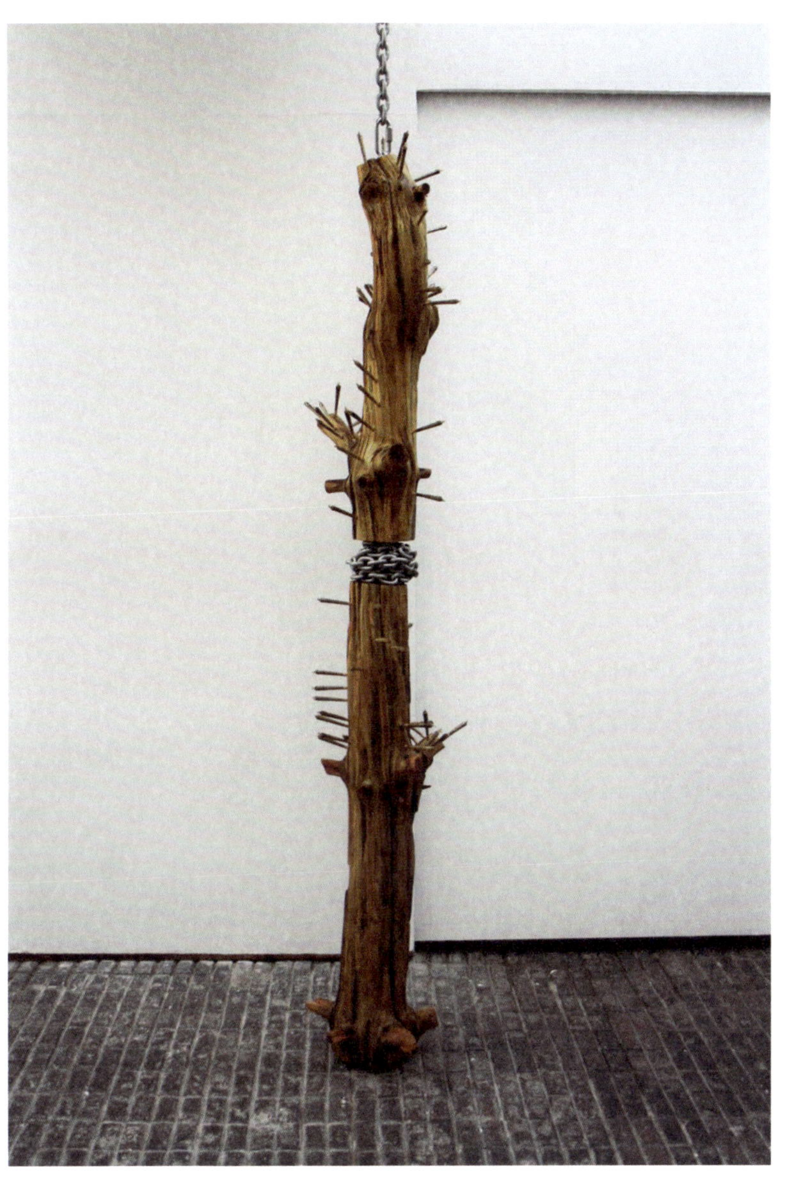

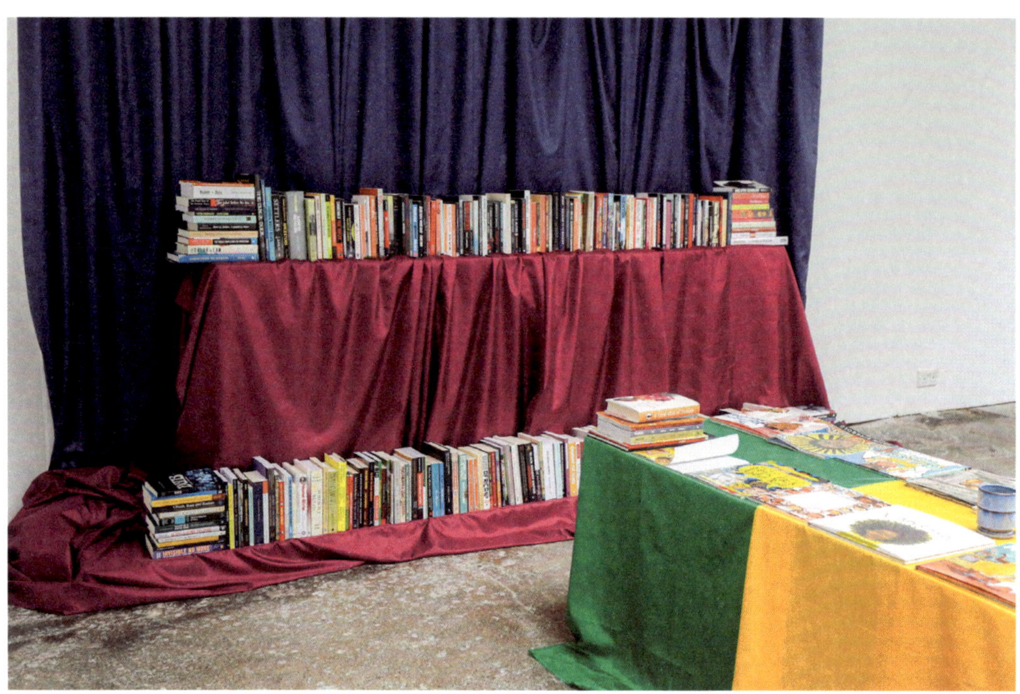

R.I.P Germain, ______, 2020. Installation view, 'Dead Yard'. Photo: Vanessa Peterson. Courtesy Cubitt Artists and Languid Hands

and who was close to the artist in some way. Through these converging parts, the artist honoured those he has personally lost, lamenting the various ways in which black people are denied the right to mourn, even as we are forced to confront death and dying in a world aggressively indifferent to our safety. Audiences were invited to engage with these intimate works, which referenced Caribbean mourning rituals, hip-hop and UK drill lore. Loosely arranged around the space were an altar of objects to ponder, a vitrine upon which to play a game of dominos, a tree stump suspended from the ceiling and a library of radical black literature from which to learn and question.

Aesthetically speaking, R.I.P. Germain leans into maximalism, which he describes as specifically rooted in his Jamaican heritage. 'Dead Yard' was a show full of colour, and numerous domestic and quotidian objects were carefully placed in and around each work. Beads and satin drapery adorned its structures, with each element referencing intimate stories or collective practices of lamentation. The maximalism of this exhibition, for us as curators, spoke to the complex and uninhibited nature of emotions as they relate to death and dying, and the intentions of the artist who draws more from his own personal experiences and cultural references than from any canon of art history or trend of minimalist aesthetics in contemporary art. While some reviewers of the show described this as a curatorial failure to edit, we are significantly inspired by Clyde Taylor's argument that the notion of aesthetics is in fact 'synonymous with western aesthetics [...] alienat[ing] those outside of the western bourgeoisie from their own creativity and the socio-political knowledge embedded therein'.[3]

We believe that our job as curators is to best reflect artists' work and intentions to an audience, regardless of (perhaps in spite of?) dominant aesthetic ideology. 'Dead Yard' felt like an exhibition opening at just the right time in September 2020 – between strict lockdowns, when visitors could quietly poke their heads out from isolation and spend time sitting with the collective grief of the prior seven months. The maximalist aesthetics of 'Dead Yard' felt like an ode to the overwhelm of grief, which can't always be pulled apart or understood in distinct parts. The *too full*-ness of the space felt like the *too close*-ness of grief's shame. *Oh, the no real closure of it all!* Besides, who are we to edit the untidy organization of black grief?

Ajamu X: 'Ajamu: Archival Sensoria'

Our second exhibition opened in May 2021, after a long and dark second lockdown in the UK. More so than previously, there was much waiting and many logistical stops and starts. The gracefully patient and unflappable force of nature that is Ajamu made these difficult times joyful in ways that we could not have anticipated.

Drawing on the personal archive Ajamu has collected over his 30-year career as well as previously unexhibited contact sheets, personal photos and community documentation, 'Ajamu: Archival Sensoria' was a celebration of black queer life and a visual tribute to the generative creativity of LGBTQ+ and gender-nonconforming lives. Pumping through the gallery was DJ Biggy C's mix of classic disco and house music, which has defined black queer nightlife for decades, and there was a sense of celebration among audiences who were excited to feel surrounded, after so long, by reflections of their community, and to feel a part of the historical legacy of black queer life in the UK. Throughout his practice, and in an ongoing capacity, Ajamu has used portraiture to document key figures in black British queer life, ensuring their visibility in the archive – a living, breathing lineage.

For the newly commissioned body of work, a series of 22 portraits taken with the theme of reverence in mind, Ajamu photographed an intergenerational group of people of black queer artists, photographers, DJs, activists, campaigners, writers, thinkers and more. In addition, a series of three upright vitrines entitled *Archiving Sideways*, first shown in 2015, were restored and updated with ephemera from throughout Ajamu's life and work. As wallpaper, his contact sheets of photography from community events such as UK Black Pride, as well as playful self-portraits and images of fellow artists, lovers and friends since the 1980s, were displayed publicly for the first time. In a separate, red-lit, darkroom-like space with a leather bench and music ever-so-slightly bleeding in from the gallery, a reel of his works – explicit, erotic and otherwise – were also presented for the first time in a gallery setting. We wanted to emphasize, not cower away from, the explicitly sexual aspects of Ajamu's practice, and of queer life at large. 'Ajamu: Archival Sensoria' paid homage to the passion, intimacy, sex, desire and love that exists within black queer communities.

Ajamu X, *Portrait: Onyeka Igwe*, 2020. Installation view, 'Ajamu: Archival Sensoria', Cubitt Gallery, London, 2021. Photo: Vanessa Peterson. Courtesy Cubitt Artists and Languid Hands

'Ajamu: Archival Sensoria' celebrated Ajamu's incredible impact as a photographer, documenter, archivist and radical sex activist and brought attention to the artist's process in and among community. As young black queer curators, we want to ensure that those of our generation who follow our practice are aware of Ajamu's, and his subjects', contribution to their lives today. We want to signal to the art world at large that it is past time to give him his proverbial flowers. Ajamu continues to document our lives and care for us, and he does so with reverence and awe. 'Ajamu: Archival Sensoria' was both a study of black queer archival practice and a display of an ever-growing archive. In Ajamu's work, there is a sense of unbound freedom, of an expressive capaciousness. 'No Real Closure' became no real enclosure: always, 'life lived otherwise' – to borrow phrasing from Gail Lewis, whose portrait was included in the exhibition, and who inspired the theme of reverence.

Camara Taylor: 'a rant! a reel!'

Camara Taylor's 'a rant! a reel!' leant directly into the 'platform for experimentation' aspect of our intentions for the 'No Real Closure' programme. The exhibition, which stemmed from Taylor's ongoing research project exploring black presence in Scotland, used 'silt'[4] and the process of 'desilting'[5] as both metaphor and methodology in examining the country's intimate entanglement and key role in the development of the current global order, specifically through slavery and colonialism. Negotiating flimsy cultural memories, illegible archives and black gestures – think gossip, rumour, whispers and conspiracies; those forms of history-making which resist the stoicism and austerity of the typical historical archive – the exhibition acted as a repository for Taylor's current 'Transfixions' (after Shola von Reinhold)[6] as they work towards a film they have described as 'currently situated in the gut'. The multiple registers of the exhibition's title invoke the various definitions of *a rant* among Scots, meaning to romp, to roister, a shout, a lively tune or dance, a gathering or great noise, while *a reel* takes up the artist Hannah Black's reading of 'a word that means both a dance and the preparation for a fall'.[7]

Works in the show operated more as experiments, demonstrations of a research practice or threads leading to other threads, than as objects bound for purely aesthetic or artistic consumption. On the floor, shallow, open-topped vitrines housed reproductions of Scottish landscape paintings by the African American painter Robert S. Duncanson submerged in water and white rum and left to decay and grow multicoloured spores. On the walls, there was a tiny reproduction of overlapping threads of online searches, in addition to a gold zipper lighter embossed with the phrase 'Noodles who rave for abolition', augmented stills from the 1930 film *Borderline* by Scottish film-maker Kenneth Macpherson, starring Paul and Eslanda Robeson, and a poetic text obscured slightly by an overlay of black acetate. Behind a precariously hung wall, a slide projector displaying images the artist has gathered in their research into black presence in Scotland. On this wall's opposite side were two images: a close-up photograph of an intimate family moment, and a tiny reproduction of an eighteenth-century painting of slaveholder and sugar planter John Taylor, likely the source of the artist's surname.

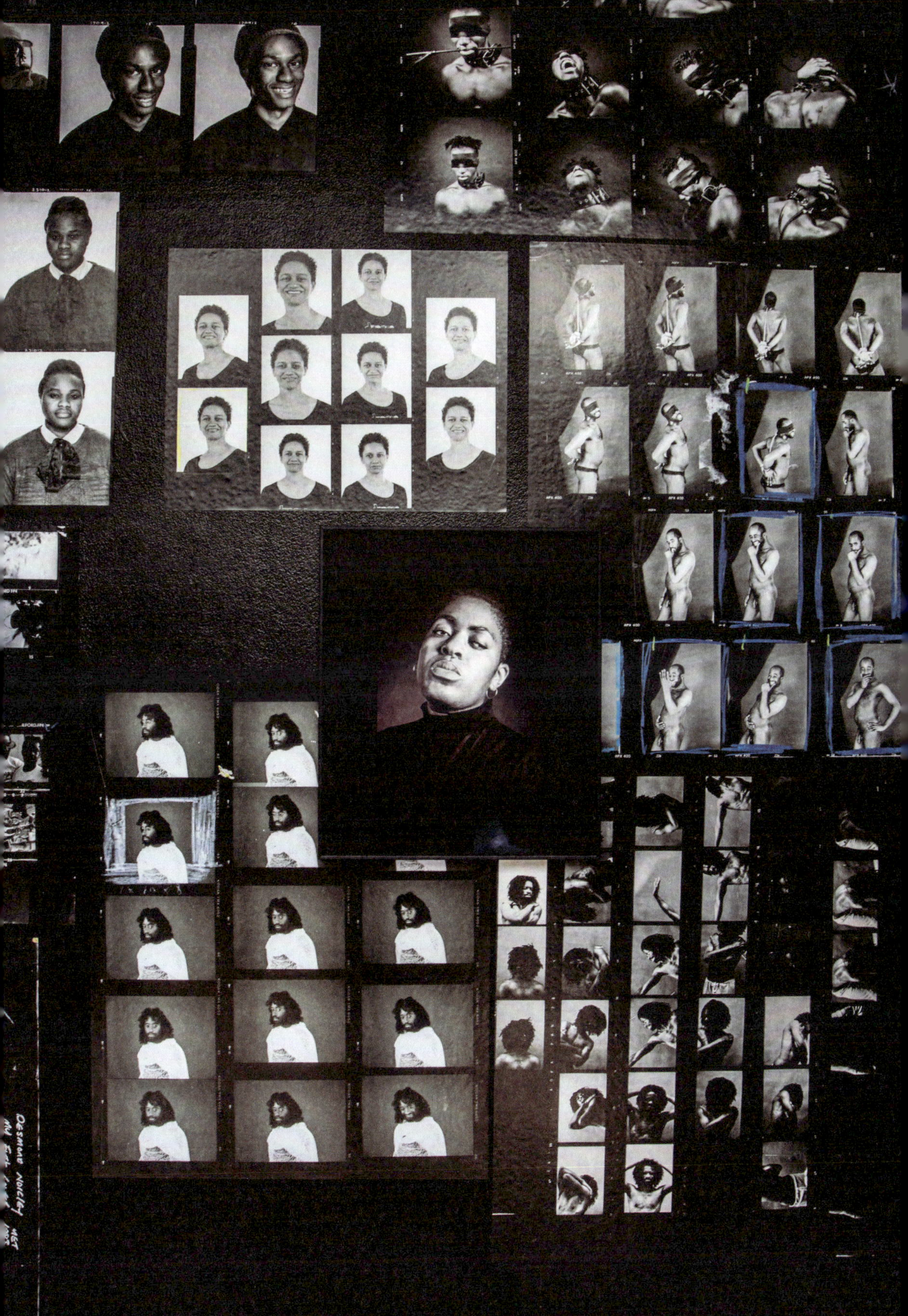

Ajamu X, *Dark Room: Aura*, 1992. Installation view, 'Ajamu: Archival Sensoria'. Photo: Vanessa Peterson. Courtesy Cubitt Artists and Languid Hands

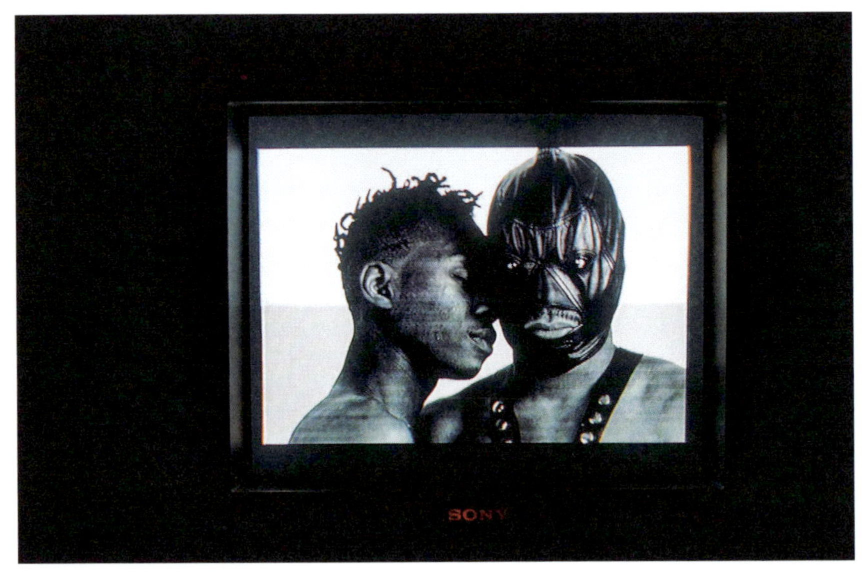

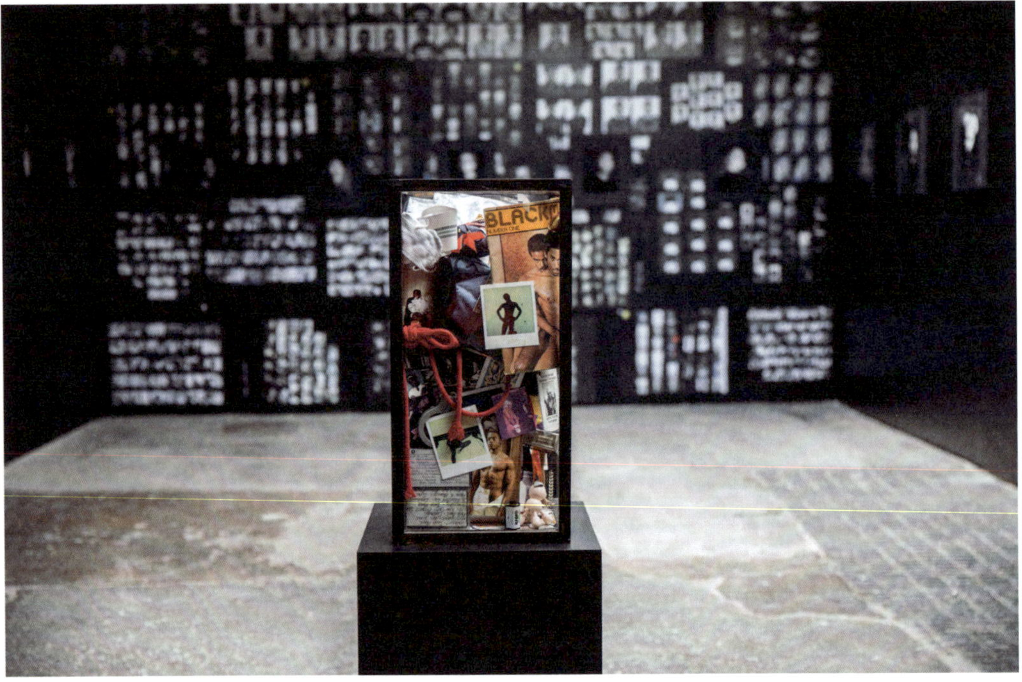

Ajamu X, *Archiving Sideways*, 2015/2021. Installation view, 'Ajamu: Archival Sensoria'. Photo: Vanessa Peterson. Courtesy Cubitt Artists and Languid Hands

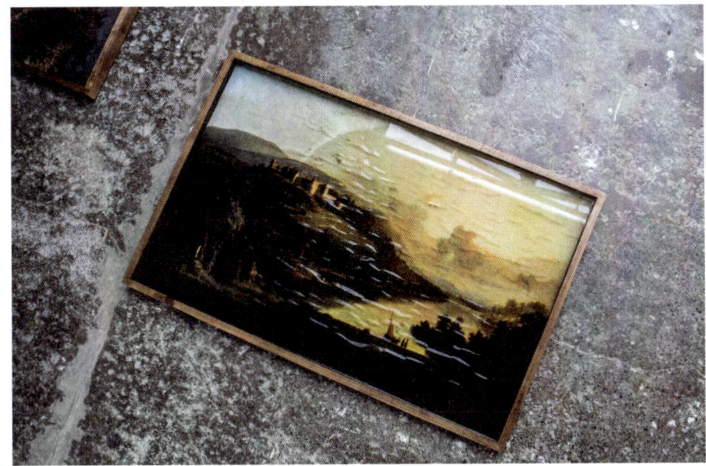

Camara Taylor, *untitled (the submerged paintings of African American painter Robert F. Duncanson)*, 2021. Installation view, 'a rant! a reel!', Cubitt Gallery, London, 2021. Photo: Vanessa Peterson. Courtesy Cubitt Artists and Languid Hands

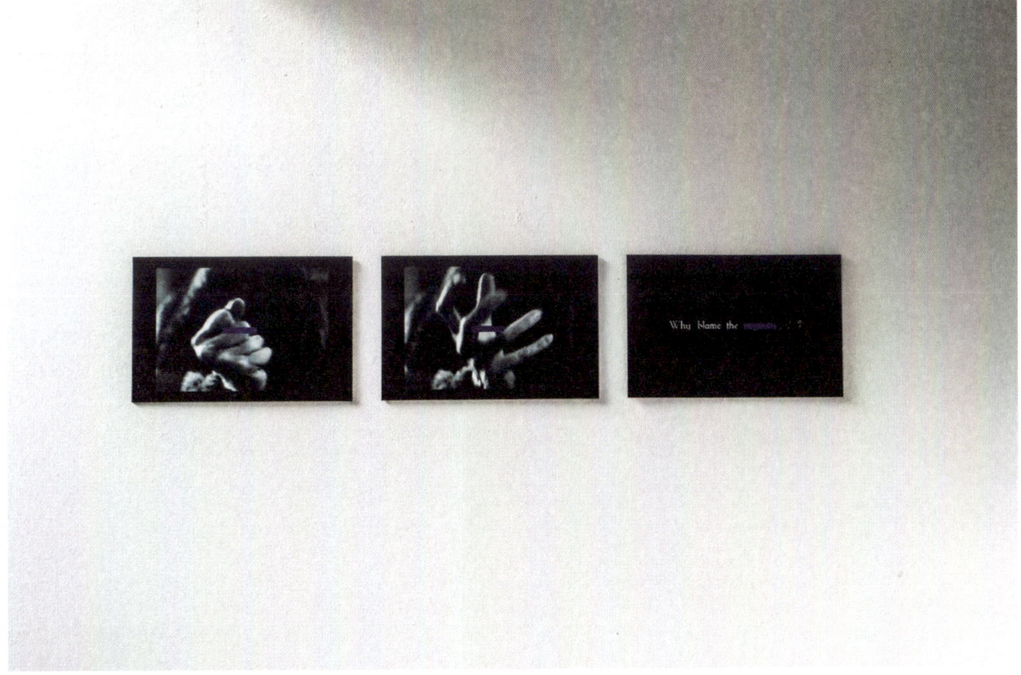

Camara Taylor, *untitled (why blame the _______ ?)*, 2021. Installation view, 'a rant! a reel!'. Photo: Vanessa Peterson. Courtesy Cubitt Artists and Languid

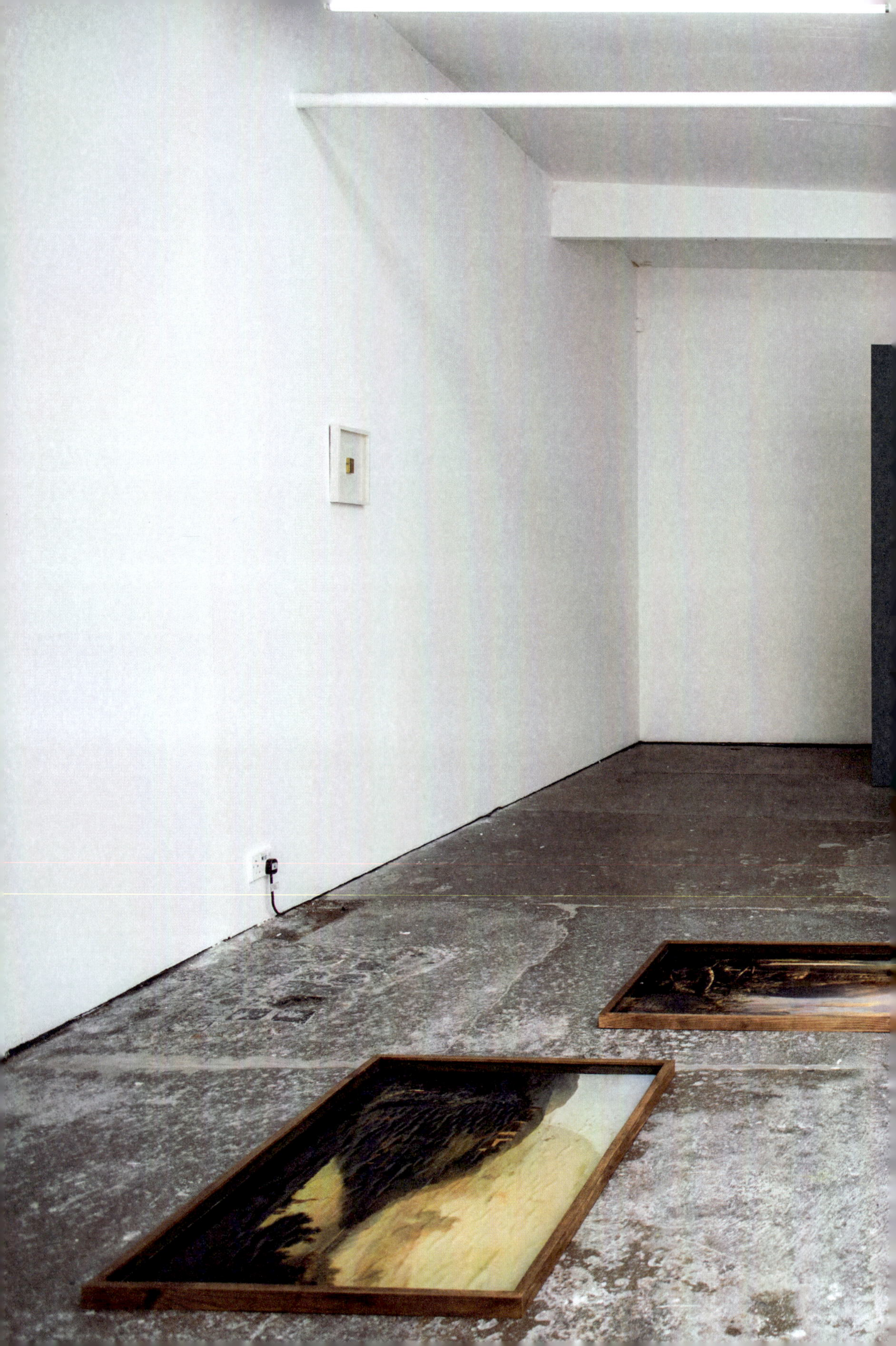

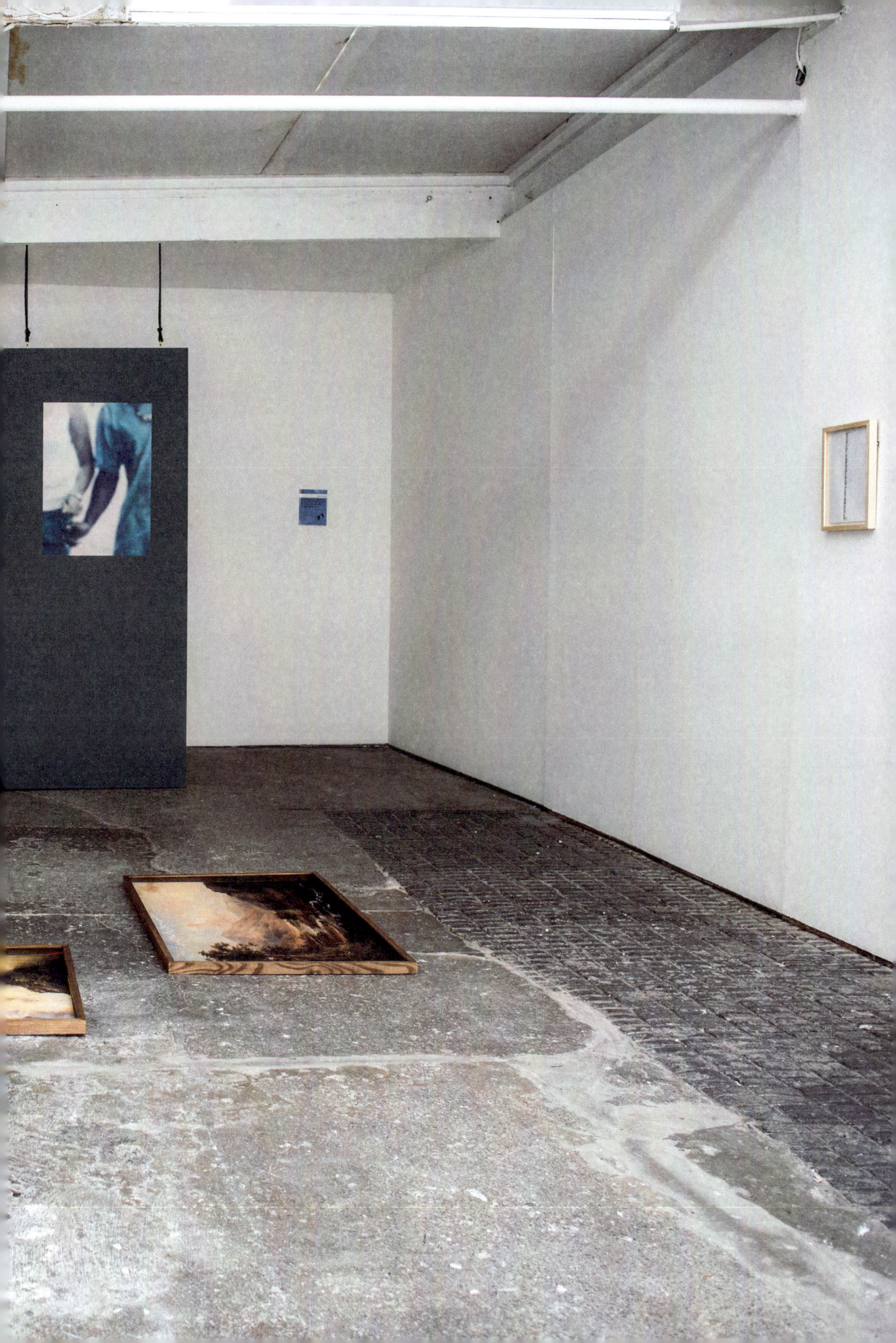

Previous spread: Installation view, 'a rant! a reel!'. Photo: Vanessa Peterson. Courtesy Cubitt Artists and Languid Hands

Zarina Muhammad, writing as The White Pube, described the power of Camara Taylor's exhibition so perfectly that we wish to share a passage here:

> *How can art engage with history? I feel like that is such a loaded and febrile question, especially now, especially as a political question. But remove that. What is art capable of doing in relation to history? Does it have to be a tool; a way to construct narrative, linear, productive? Does it have to be a buckle, a staple, holding things together? I think in this show, art is a container. If I want to link the things up, like join the dots, then I am only joining them together with the wave of my hand, with a gesture. I'm not leaving any marks, I am only pointing. Like a critical vessel through which other shapes are warped, pressure is released, and things can be held closer to us. No longer just history, or object to interpret, understand; now it's got character for you to meet on level terms, palpable atmosphere to move through, experience, relate to. It, whatever ~it!~ is, can be transformed, widened. Ahh ahhhh ahhhhhhh – exhibition can be soft, mid-point, art can be liquid!*[8]

Of course, the ongoing research process can and does have *no real closure*, but more so, Taylor's practice necessitates an acknowledgement of archival loss, or of the false dwelling places of truth, fact and evidence. 'A rant! a reel!' enabled the artist to explore and experiment with imagination and gossip in the archive, with false truths, with perhaps not knowing and so, inventing. Call it wayward life and critical fabulation, after Saidiya Hartman – always already ongoing, this is how we create our ways of being.

At the time of writing, we have one month left of 'No Real Closure' at Cubitt. We are about to close 'Reel: Axis, Not Poles', a screening programme of moving-image works by S*an D. Henry-Smith, Dita Hashi, Kadeem Oak, Che Applewhaite and Kondo Heller, and will next install the final project in the gallery, 'Ah So It Go, Ah No So It Go, Go So!', a listening space exploring belonging, land, growing and grounding by Shenece Oretha. Very soon we will have a moment to properly take stock of all that this fellowship has generated, to reflect on all that went right and all that went wrong and to allow those lessons to guide our languid hands forth. But first, rest!

Notes
[1] There are many historical dialogues and lineages that we feel akin to, and as we continue to study the archives available to us we seek out new threads that bind. In the UK, we are deeply indebted to the work of many black artists and collectives in Britain, including the Blk Art Group, Black Audio Film Collective, Ajamu X, Ingrid Pollard, Menelik Shabazz, Judah (Martina) Atille, Isaac Julien, Rotimi Fani-Kayode, cultural theorist Stuart Hall, scholar and activist Gail Lewis and our long-standing mentor Barby Asante.
[2] See Imani Robinson, *Objects Who Testify*, London: PSS, 2019.
[3] Clyde Taylor, 'We Don't Need Another Hero: Anti-Theses on Aesthetics', in Mbye B. Cham and Claire Andrade-Watkins (ed.), *Blackframes: Critical Perspectives on Black Independent Cinema*, Cambridge, MA: MIT Press, 1988.
[4] Fine sand, clay or other material carried by running water and deposited as a sediment, especially in a channel or harbour.
[5] The removal of silt from a body of water, a process undertaken in Glasgow's River Clyde in the 1800s in order to increase shipping profits coming from encounters in the Americas and the Caribbean.
[6] See Shola von Reinhold, *LOTE*, London: Jacaranda Books, 2020.
[7] Hannah Black, 'New World Disorder', *Artforum*, 27 February 2017, available at https://www.artforum.com/slant/hannah-black-on-the-new-world-disorder-66897.
[8] The White Pube, 'a rant! a reel!, Camara Taylor @ Cubitt', 8 January 2021, available at https://thewhitepube.co.uk/art-reviews/arant-areel/.

Harmattan Dust[1]
– Serubiri Moses

> *The egrets are the color of waterfalls,*
> *and of clouds. Some friends, the few I have left,*
> *are dying, but the egrets stalk through the rain*
> *as if nothing mortal can affect them, or they lift*
> *like abrupt angels, sail, then settle again.*
> – Derek Walcott, from 'White Egrets'[2]

Dear Ayrson Heráclito,
In this poem by Derek Walcott, life and death are connected through the complex symbol of the white egret. The image of these birds as 'abrupt angels' makes me think of what philosopher John Mbiti described as the separation between the visible and invisible worlds.[3] I imagine the egrets as travellers across the binary, becoming mediums between these two worlds. Ayrson, this reminds me of how our meeting in June 2015 in Dakar set me on a path to find a curatorial language for how we, on each side of the sea, remain connected. Even as I am currently a US resident, I arrived here via Brazil, Hong Kong, South Africa, Senegal, Kenya, Ghana, Germany and elsewhere. Rather than addressing the conceptual territory demarcated as US-UK, therefore, I want to return to Senegal in particular as a point of engagement with the diaspora. In this way I want to reflect on the many lessons that your art – which highlights the links between West Africa and South America – imparted on me at an early stage of my career as a curator, and how exhibition-making may address both the displacement of slavery and the epistemic erasure of colonization.[4]

In our very first meeting, you gave me a lesson that would reverberate for years afterward. You spoke of the seasonal winds that blow across West Africa – during Harmattan season, between the end of November and the middle of March. You told me that, during Harmattan, sand from the Sahara may reach as far as Brazil, feeding and providing nutrients to the Amazon forest.[5] Admittedly this did not make sense to me at the time, but it became clearer to me a year later, in August 2016. I had moved to Ghana to work on the *Cultural Encyclopedia*, an education and exhibition platform founded by film-maker and curator Nana Oforiatta Ayim, which echoes the yet-incomplete *Africana Encyclopedia* by W.E.B. Du Bois (who died in Accra in 1963). While visiting Cape Coast Castle in the south of Ghana, I would think about the Harmattan movement across the ocean, and indeed of this planetary relation. I have studied the Atlantic and the Indian Ocean slave trades since high school, and visited the former slave hub of Mombasa, yet in August 2016, while in Ghana, your statement spoke to me with a new force and urgency.

I began to reflect on the Atlantic slave trade with the tools you gave me. That the desert had been a life-giving force, rather than mere barren land. That, if only we looked at the world at a planetary scale, we might see how interconnected and interdependent our worlds have been. Paul Gilroy's book *The Black Atlantic* (1993) has no doubt shaped your thinking. Like that book's description of the Middle Passage – which comes, arguably, from Homer –

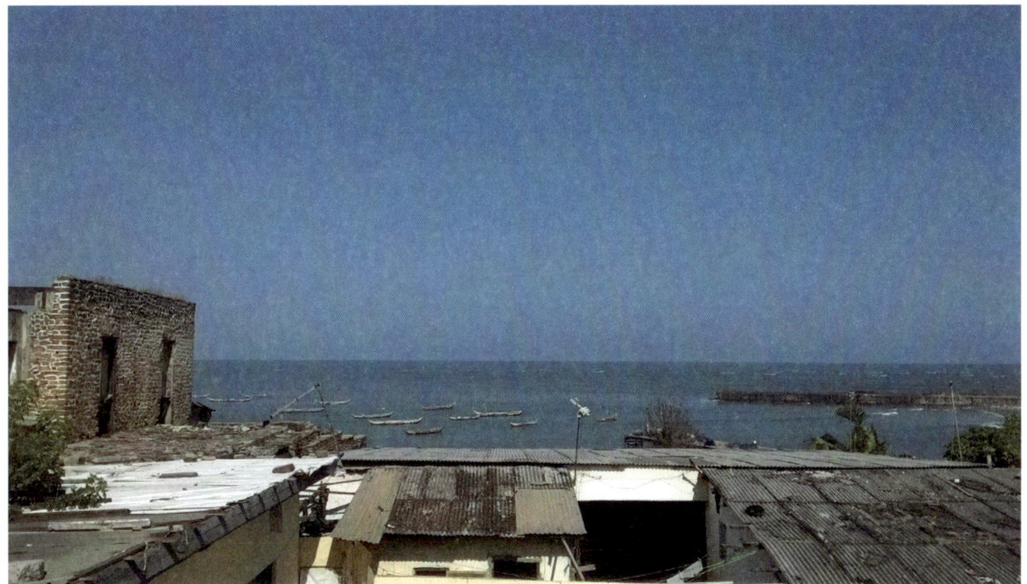

The sea from Ghana. Photo: the author

your story rooted itself in poetic and historical metaphors.[6] In 2018, when you curated the exhibition 'Histórias Afro-Atlântica' at the Museo de Arte São Paulo (MASP), you brought together the work of artists in Africa and its diasporas – in the Americas, the Caribbean and Europe – using memory and poetic metaphor as the umbilical cord of a shared heritage.

In 2016, I visited Brazil House in Jamestown, Accra for the first time. I encountered an architecture that solidified the Afro-Brazilian presence. The house, which stood out next to the ocean, was both a home and a community space. I remember its large façade with the words 'Brazil House' displayed prominently, its extremely large windows, its elaborate staircases. The bright yellow paint on its exterior walls resembled houses in Salvador de Bahia. These design aspects have been termed 'neo-baroque', in that the masons and builders who constructed these grand houses modelled them after the neocolonial buildings on which they had laboured in Brazil before their forced remigration to West Africa.[7] While the architecture of Brazil House appears rather European in its origin, my encounter was a lesson in understanding – or rather, beginning to articulate – this mixed cultural heritage that many in the African diaspora inherited and still possess today.

This point would become clearer to me through the perspectives of important writers from Martinique and Guadeloupe, among them Maryse Condé. Condé helped me understand that despite her migration from Guadeloupe to Guinea-Conakry and later Ghana, and regardless of her participation in Ghana's decolonization movement (she knew both feminist author Ama Ata Aidoo and political theorist and Pan-African leader Kwame Nkrumah), she remained an outsider, audibly marked by the fact that she did not speak an African language. This may be why her satirical first novel, *Hérémakhonon*

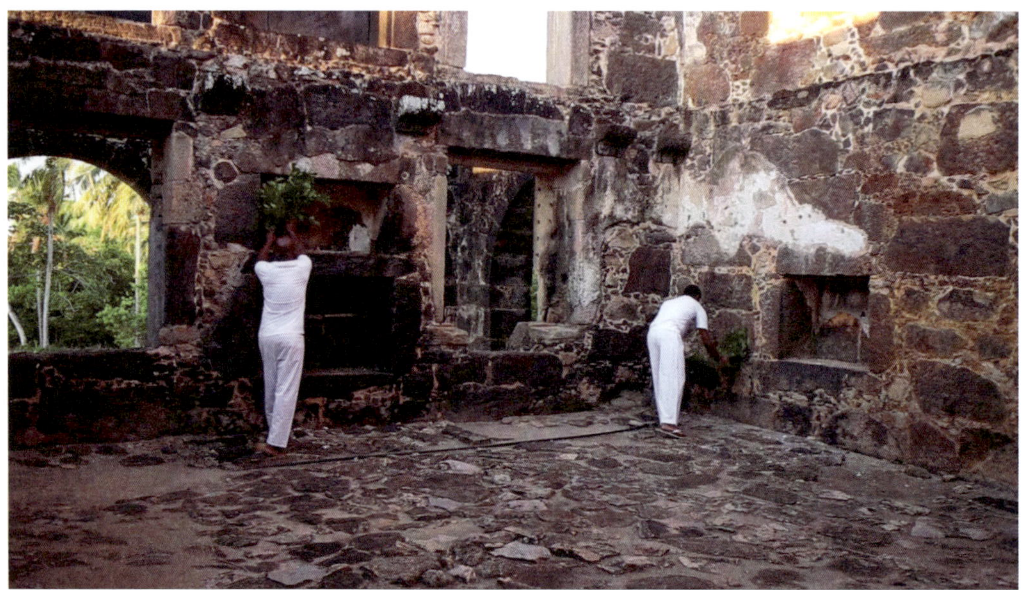

Stills from Ayrson Heráclito, *O Sacudimento da Casa da Torre*, video, 2015. Courtesy the artist

(1976) – translated as 'Welcome House', from a Mande language of Guinea – presents a fairly pessimistic view of postcolonial Africa.[8] More recently, Saidiya Hartman's *Lose Your Mother: Journey Along the Trans-Atlantic Slave Route* (2006), which follows Hartman's various research trips to Ghana and Britain in the late 1990s, echoes Condé's pessimistic argument by revealing that African Americans in Ghana were called *obruni*, which translates as 'foreigner' in Akan.[9]

In any case, at Cape Coast Castle in 2016, I recalled your words about Harmattan, and this perhaps triggered that deep longing sometimes called *saudade*. I distinctly remember the trip back to Accra from Cape Coast. I felt a wave of sickness looking at the ocean that is hard to put into words. How might a yet-to-come curatorial and exhibition-making practice account for this feeling of sickness and longing? If – and this is difficult to imagine – these practices were to incorporate African languages including Akan and Mande, as well as Afrodiasporic languages like Haitian Kreyòl, Black American English, Guyanese Creole and Afro-Brazilian Portuguese, how might the exhibition of contemporary art become a ritual of reorientation or recognition? Could the exhibition become reparative in its address of displacement across the ocean, and epistemic erasure in the recognition of culture?

Ayrson, I want to address your powerful notion of Saharan dust providing nutrients to the forests of Brazil, and to address the lessons that you and your work have imparted on me since that time. The work that you made on that trip to Senegal in 2015, when we met, is titled *Sacudimentos* – a word that translates as 'shaking' and a sacred practice of cleansing in Afro-Brazilian culture. According to a recent book that explains the religious practice: 'It seeks to remove evil spirits and bad influences from a place or a person.'[10]

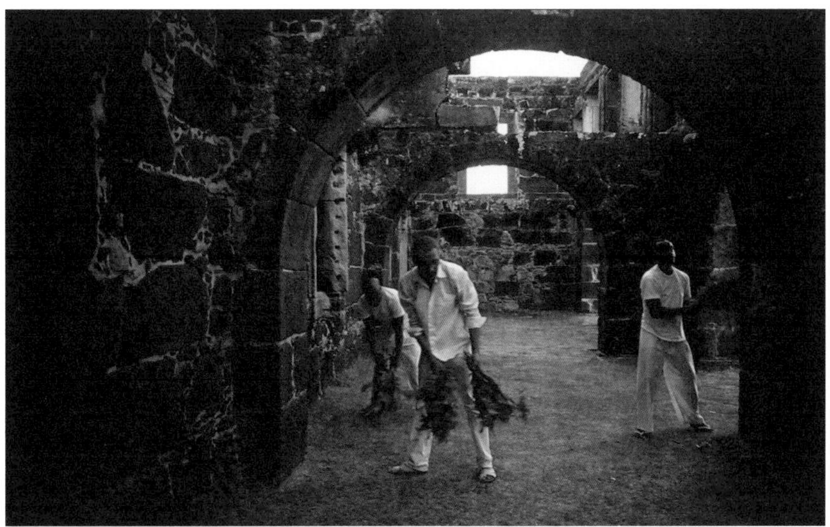

Presented as a two-channel video and photographic installation, the work was included in the Venice International Art Biennale ('Viva Arte Viva') in 2017, and then shown at MASP in 2018. In it, one video depicts the ritual of Sacudimento performed at Gorée Island, Senegal, at the Maison des Esclaves (House of Slaves), and the other shows the same ritual performed in Brazil at Casa da Torre, a former colonial administration office in Bahia.[11] In the photographs, we see you, Ayrson, with two other men, all holding bunches of plants. Subsequently, we see you hitting these plants on the walls of the slave house. Even without direct familiarity with the religions or the ritual, it is clear that what is being done reverberates through time: in search of something that no longer exists, but which could potentially be called back.

Ayrson, after you finished the ritual of Sacudimento at the colonial administration building Casa da Torre in Bahia, you reported:

> *When I 'shook' the Tower House, the only* egun *that was there, that those walls were pregnant of even after so many years, was the slave master; more, the only* egun *that there was, that haunted me for remaining among us, because there, from the Tower House, his castle or fortress, he migrated and seeped into the whole social fabric of Bahia; but not only that: it was the coming violence of slavery and the old colonial system, which bequeathed to us an extreme inequality and also as its fruit, poverty.*[12]

On cleansing rituals in African religions, John Mbiti wrote: 'Washing in the river is a ritual act of cleansing from the pollution caused by death.'[13] Often during cleansing the person is requested to abstain from sexual contact. A common technique is to seek places in nature for healing. Herbs have a medicinal quality, and in my youth I learned about specific shrubs and green herbs that were used to treat malaria. Herbs were used to bathe a newborn in order to dispel any bad luck or disease. At home, aloe plants lined one of

Stills from Ayrson Heráclito, *O Sacudimento da Maison des Esclaves em Gorée*, video, 2015. Courtesy the artist

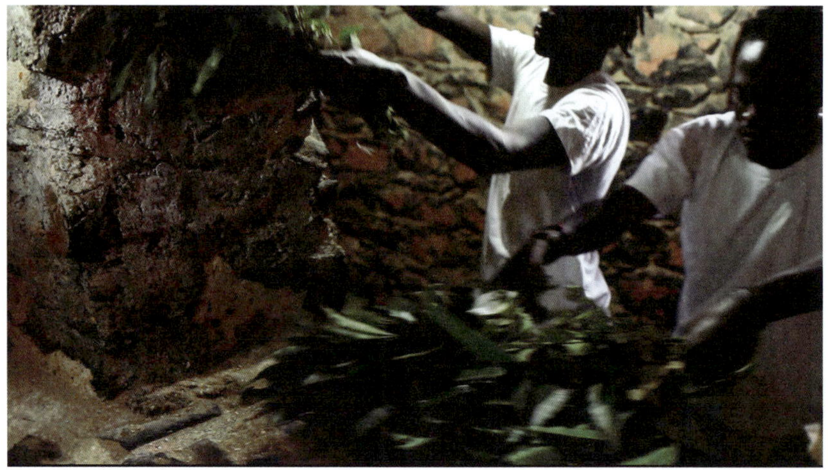

our yard fences. I learned that these plants had a double function: to dispel malevolent spirits and to heal disease. Because of these experiences, I recognized the meaning of ritual in your artwork, because it recalled these many medicinal and cleansing practices in Uganda.

Your work draws, of course, from the histories and imaginaries of Candomblé. Historian João José Reis notes that the organized houses of the Candomblé religion that first emerged in Bahia in the nineteenth century were metropolitan and run by free Africans.[14] This is crucial because, as he explains, it is in the context of Black revolution that Candomblé emerged. This mirrors established accounts of the Haitian Revolution of 1791–1804, where Vodou festivals and celebrations took place for long stretches of time prior to the revolt.[15] Yet the context of nineteenth-century Bahia is a surprising one. Yes, there was poverty. But according to Reis, there was effectively a *quilombo* (a free African settlement) in the urban space of Bahia. There were vibrant markets for fish rigorously administered by free African women.[16] There were Muslim imams and their followers. The Yoruba and Hausa Muslims could read and write in Arabic. Reis notes that this literacy and correspondence was one of the ways that organized revolt took place. There were Catholic brotherhoods, and there were manumission societies from which African slaves borrowed funds to buy their freedom.[17] The other significant moment in nineteenth-century Bahia, aside from the founding of Candomblé, was the Malê revolt of 1835. This had far reaching consequences, most notably leading the effort towards establishing freedom for Africans and Brazilian-born Black people. It was during this moment that the majority of Yoruba Muslims who took part in the revolt were expelled from Brazil and sent to Lagos and Accra.[18]

Ayrson, what spirits – or *egun* – were present when you 'shook' the Maison des Esclaves on Gorée Island? Which ones have remained with you afterwards? Is it the slave master who lived above the slave houses? Or is it the enslaved Africans underneath the twin grand staircases? The photograph *O Sacudimento da Maison des Esclaves em Gorée* (2015) that you took of yourself with two other

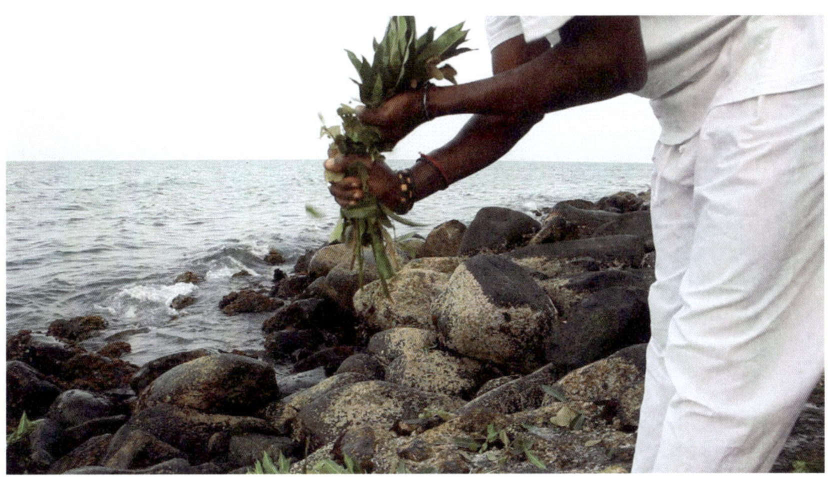

Black men holding the plant bunches for the ritual in front of this building, still haunts me. You stand in the middle of the staircase. The two men who joined you in the ritual stand at the foot of the staircase on either side, against the two separate gates for enslaved men or enslaved women. Often it is said that the memory of slavery is repressed or erased in present-day Africa. Let me briefly challenge this single story. When I studied the history of the Indian Ocean slave trade in high school, I read about Arab slave raids in the Congo, and about slave trading hubs such as Bagamoyo, in present-day Tanzania. Guided by my history teacher, I read brief excerpts of the Scottish missionary David Livingstone's account of the slave trade route to the East African coast.[19] My history teacher pointed out the participation of traditional ruler, the Buganda king, during the nineteenth-century slave trade. I learned that the Buganda kingdom had affinities with the sultan of Zanzibar, a major hub for the Indian Ocean slave trade. I also learned that the lingua franca of trade along the East African coast was Kiswahili, a Bantu language that incorporates Arabic. I also learned that circa 590 AD the first muezzin to call Muslims to prayer from the minaret was called Bilal, and was an African man who had converted to Islam in order to gain his freedom from slavery.

I recently rewatched Botswana-born artist Kitso Lynn Lelliott's video-poem *Transatlantic Saudades* (2013), filmed at Sacatar in Brazil. In this work, we encounter again the sea, and the artist connects Africa and Brazil through the notion of memory, which becomes ever-elastic, constantly changing. A shoreline vista emerges, and we see a Black woman, dressed in Victorian clothing, walking along a jetty towards the sea. Her image is transparent, ghostly. The sea in the distance 'grows' to cover the beach as the light becomes darker. A poem is spoken, describing the situation of being 'between continents' and noting the 'insurmountable body of water between two islands'. This short video-poem does much with a few gestures: the ghost, the Black woman, the island, the sea. Drawing from both South Africa and Brazil, Lelliott engages a complex network of remembering, erasure and loss. What has been lost on either side of the Atlantic haunts the viewer. The same woman reappears in another of Lelliott's works, *By and By a Trace Remains* (2015), where she is seen scrubbing the walls and floors of an old assembly house: Constitution Hill in Johannesburg. In this context, the focus on the Black woman reflects the continuing disenfranchisement of Black women in South Africa since the colonial era. It was, after all, Black female domestic workers in apartheid South Africa who protested in 1956 against the pass laws that required Black people to carry internal passports that limited their free movement.[20] As I watched Lelliott's 2015 work, shown in the context of the tenth edition of Bamako Encounters – African Biennale of Photography, I could imagine these ghosts emerging from its Sacudimento, or 'shaking', of the Constitution Hill building.

Can exhibitions respond to such historical erasures? For the edition of Bamako Encounters at which Lelliot's work was shown, curator Bisi Silva adopted a self-reflective and questioning approach to its exhibition histories. Silva reflects that the exhibition 'allow[ed] us to reflect on the twenty years that Bamako Encounters ha[d] existed as the principal platform for photography on the African continent and to assess the new developments that have characterised that period. It allow[ed] us to chart a new beginning that [took] cognisance of today's realities.'[21] It was through this approach that Silva and her team – including Antawan Byrd, Yves Chatap and publication researcher Hansi Momodu-Gordon – developed a focus on lusophone Africa and its diasporas, which ultimately led you, Ayrson, to receive a monographic exhibition survey in Bamako – your first solo exhibition on the continent.

Funfun (2012), the work you showed at the tenth Bamako Encounters, has come back to me. In this work, the title of which means 'white' in Yoruba, you show a large tree in the middle of a stream. The tree has a large group of white egrets nesting on it. The video was dedicated to Estelita de Souza Santana, one of the leaders of the Sisterhood of Our Lady of the Good Death, Cachoeira, Salvador de Bahia. When I looked at the image of the white egrets sitting on the large tree in the river, I was stunned. It triggered the memory of a similar tree, with thousands of white egrets, near my childhood home. In African religions, it is a bad omen to cut down large trees or destroy a nesting of birds, despite the noise they make and their soiling of the ground underneath. This ethical respect for trees and birds echoes in the Yoruba religion, in which birds are understood to be custodians that carry messages from the visible into the invisible world. When designing the crown of the Oba, Yoruba artists often include small figures of beaded birds as a way to depict wisdom, insight and the connection to time – past, present and future.[22] The temporal nature of the bird's symbolism in Yoruba art is illustrated by Derek Walcott when he writes that birds witness 'that peace beyond desires and beyond regrets at which I may arrive eventually', and that they 'will be there after my shadow passes with all its sins into a green thicket of oblivion'.[23]

Yours sincerely,
Serubiri Moses

Notes

[1] I would like to acknowledge my debt to Ayrson Heráclito and to the organizer Arts Collaboratory and host Raw Material Company who made our meeting in June 2015 possible. I also thank Bisi Silva, Kitso Lynn Lelliott and Rosana Paulino, all of whom I met during Asiko, the Pan-African roaming academy in Dakar in June 2014, organized by Center for Contemporary Art, Lagos. I also acknowledge my conversations with my dear colleagues Thiago de Paula Souza, Bernardo Mosqueira and Julián Sanchez Gonsalez. Special appreciation to Maryse Condé, without whose work I would feel lost in the diaspora.

[2] Derek Walcott, *White Egrets*, London: Faber & Faber, 2011, p.9.

[3] John Mbiti, *Introduction to African Religions*, Long Grove, IL: Waveland Books, 2015, p.35.

[4] Ayrson Heráclito is a Brazilian artist, curator and professor based in Salvador de Bahia. His work often deals with the African presence in Brazil. Together with Adriano Pedrosa and Helio Menezes, he curated the exhibition 'Histórias Afro-Atlântica' at the Museo de Arte São Paulo (2018). His work has been shown at the 2017 Venice Biennale and is in the permanent collection of Museum Kulturen der Welt, Frankfurt.

[5] Conversation with A. Heráclito, June 2015. I referred to this conversation in my text 'City Boys', published in the Invisible Borders Collective publication *The Trans-African* (issue 9, September 2016).

[6] Paul Gilroy, *The Black Atlantic: Modernity and Double-Consciousness*, Cambridge, MA: Harvard University Press, 1993.

[7] Adédoyin Teríba writes: 'Over a period of seven decades, thousands of Afro-Brazilians landed on the shores of the Bight of Benin and in Lagos, they deployed an idiosyncratic neo-baroque architecture, which was inspired by the churches and houses that they worked on, repaired or saw in city centers in Brazil.' A. Teríba, 'Afro-Brazilian Architecture in Southwest Colonial Nigeria (1890s–1940s)', PhD dissertation, Princeton University, June 2017, p.i.

[8] Maryse Condé, *Hérémakhonon*, Paris: Union generale d'editions, 1976. The novel's central character, Veronica Mercier, is a teacher by profession and lives in Paris. She decides to leave Europe to resettle in a West African country. Her pursuit of Africa is set in the context of the political movement for decolonization on the continent.

[9] 'As I disembarked from the bus in Elmina, I heard it. It was sharp and clear, as it rang in the air, and clattered in my ear making me recoil. Obruni. A stranger. A foreigner from across the sea. Three children gathered at the bus station shouted it, giggling as it erupted from their mouths, tickled to have spotted some extraterrestrial fallen to earth in Ghana. They summoned me, "obruni, obruni," as if it were a form of akwaaba (welcome), reserved just for me.' Saidiya Hartman, *Lose Your Mother: Journey Along the Atlantic Slave Coast*, New York: Farrar, Straus and Giroux, 2008, p.3.

[10] 'Ele visa afastar os maus espíritos e as mas influencias de um lugar ou de uma pessoa.' Janaina Azevedo, *Tudo o que voce precisa saber sobre Umbanda*, São Paulo: Universo dos Livros, 2010, p.54.

[11] Alexia Tala, 'Ayrson Heráclito: The Place of the Sacred', *SP-Arte 365*, 3 December 2018, available at https://www.sp-arte.com/en/editorial/ayrson-heraclito-the-place-of-the-sacred/.

[12] A. Heraclito, 'O Sacudimento da Casa da Torre and O Sacudimento da Maison des Esclaves em Gorée', *Art Rabbit*, available at https://www.artrabbit.com/events/ayrson-her%C3%A1clito-o-sacudimento-da-casa-da-torre-and-o-sacudimento-da-maison-des-esclaves-em-gor%C3%A9e.

[13] See J. Mbiti, *African Religions and Philosophy*, London: Heinemann, 1990, p.148. For a more recent account of various acts of ritual cleansing in the African context, see J. Mbiti, *Introduction to African Religions*, *op. cit.*

[14] João José Reis, 'African Nations in Nineteenth Century Salvador de Bahia', in *The Urban Black Atlantic in the Age of the Slave Trade* (ed. Jorge Canizares Esguerra et al.), Philadelphia: University of Pennsylvania Press, 2013, pp.63–82.

[15] C.L.R. James, *The Black Jacobins: Toussaint L'Ouverture and the San Domingo Revolution*, London: Vintage, 1989, p.18.

[16] J.J. Reis, 'African Nations in Nineteenth Century Salvador de Bahia', *op. cit.*

[17] *Ibid.*

[18] *Ibid.*

[19] David Livingstone, *Narrative of an Expedition to the Zambesi and its Tributaries; and the Discovery of the Lakes Shirwa and Nyassa, 1858–1864*, New York: Harper and Brothers, 1866.

[20] See Gabi Ngcobo and Virginia MacKenny, *Second to None*, Iziko: South African National Gallery, 2006; and Center for Historical Reenactments, *PASS-Ages: References & Footnotes*, 2010, available at http://historicalreenactments.org/images/projects/Passages/15-1.pdf.

[21] Bisi Silva, 'Telling Time', *10th Rencontres de Bamako: Biennale Africaine de la Photographie* (exh. cat.), Heidelberg: Kehrer Verlag, 2015.

[22] Moyo Okediji, 'Art of the Yoruba', *Art Institute of Chicago Museum Studies*, vol.23, no.2, 1997, pp.165–98.

[23] D. Walcott, 'White Egrets', in *White Egrets*, *op. cit.*, p.6.

Roundtable Conversation: Curating Black Futures Now – Nana Adusei-Poku, Amber Esseiva, Languid Hands (Imani Mason Jordan and Rabz Lansiquot), Serubiri Moses and Brittany Webb

Nana Adusei-Poku: Amber took us on a beautiful journey about isolation; Moses revealed the South-South connection; Imani and Rabz built dialogue with the previous UK panel about the 'collective' and suggested the digital as a curatorial conversation; and Brittany highlighted the silences in art history. I wanted to give you all the opportunity to talk to each other, in the collaborative spirit.

Amber Esseiva: The notion of isolation might affect all of us in different ways, but for me it's a very confusing conundrum. Especially now, when there's a ton of opportunities, but you are stuck with this notion – or rather this reality – of isolation. That's a very specific kind of confusion to arrive in when you're pleased with an exhibition or a collaboration with an artist, but something still is missing. Which led me to thinking about the infrastructural deficiencies that lead to this.

NA-P: If we persuade ourselves that our aspirations have already been realized, this almost puts us into a schizophrenic position. As if to say, 'for the greater goal I'm not going to engage with what actually is infuriating, but I know that putting this on display will do something that I want to see in the world ... '

Brittany Webb: That resonates with me. I'm often in all kinds of spaces where I just want to upturn the table and leave. And the thing that keeps me from doing that is that if you're often the only Black person in the room, the thing that is infuriating goes unchecked when you leave the room. Also, as somebody who is heavily dependent on history and archives, I constantly remind myself that what I'm working on is only possible because Dorothy Porter Wesley – who was an archivist and a historian at Howard University – put papers into files, into boxes and on shelves. We were not alive at the same time long enough for me to tell her how much I appreciate her work. But her work is the root of so many intellectual projects that she probably could not have imagined. If you're somebody who loves books or feels like a book saved your life or a work of art saved your life, then pay it forward. The idea that people are able to find our work after we're not alive anymore is sometimes the thing that keeps the project going for us.

Serubiri Moses: I wanted to complicate this idea of the South-South. If I think of art in the African American context, Alain Locke seems to be forgotten now. Jeffrey C. Stewart has written a wonderful biography (*The New Negro: The Life of Alain Locke*, 2018) about the lengths to which he went to expose African American artists to African art. The biographer tries to explain what Africa really means to Locke in a philosophical moment and what African art specifically meant to Locke. He really wanted the Harlem Renaissance painters to start looking at Africa because, in his words, European artists were already looking at African art. So I don't know if it's only me evoking this connection that is South-South. Saidiya Hartman too has tried to evoke the Black Atlantic South-South conversation. Her work resonates with me.

Rabz Lansiquot: I've definitely been struggling with the physical sense of isolation – due to the Covid-19 pandemic our recent work has largely taken place exactly where we're sitting right now, at our kitchen table – but also with what happens when a curator becomes a perceived position of power within groups of peers. That can create its own kind of isolation. In the previous panel, Marlene Smith described being an artist who curates; in our case, we talk about being artists who like to work with other Black artists. We're lucky to have been immersed from a young age in the legacies of the people who are already doing this work and knowing that that's already there. Whereas a lot of our peers have to fight for that space and the ability to be in that space.

Imani Mason Jordan: A sense of belonging.

RL: Right. I think this is where this kind of return to the 'collective' is coming from. It is remembering that we can make that space for each other, whether it be funded or taken into institutions or not. I think that's where our practice comes from.

IMJ: In terms of isolation, there's also something liberatory perhaps in isolating particular groups of artists with whom we wish to work, in isolating ourselves from institutions, remaining independent and trying to find a way on our own, for ourselves, for each other. To do the work that we want to do. I also wanted to say administrative labour, infrastructural deficiencies, these are the things that will have to be dealt with, in part because being a curator or an archivist is extremely admin heavy and extremely laborious. I think there is perhaps a perception that it is not that way. I've often thought, What is my job? What is our role as curators? Is this what everybody else is doing?

NA-P: Yes, this is the crux. If the infrastructure around a project is so close to a colonial paradigm, right? It's like it's all administration. It's also possible through administration that it actually enables us to do our work. Another connection that came up is the notion of 'travelling theory', or how we share references across different curatorial practices. What kind of role does theory play to you or for you?

AE: The way that I access theory is that there is a certain point in which it makes sense to me in lived experience. For instance, with Stuart Hall. If you'd have showed me his notion of relating through love a couple of years ago, I would have been like – What? How does that work? It wasn't until I was in positions where there was such a lack that it made sense to me. Working with theory is complicated because it's like a door, and sometimes the information comes through, and sometimes it just can't because you're not ready to confront it.

SM: For me, it always goes back to who we think we are talking about. Who do you think you're talking about when you talk Frantz Fanon? Which Fanon are you talking about? Is it Fanon in Algeria, or Fanon in Martinique? Fanon in France, the Freudian or Lacanian Fanon? Which Fanon are you engaging with? African and Black feminism is also something that I've continued to try to understand and work with. Audre Lorde. She was at FESTAC (The Second World Black and African Festival of Arts and Culture) in 1977. No one says anything. She was part of a kind of independence movement in the Caribbean and in her home country, was teaching Fanon to police officers and was talking about open confrontation at Hunter College in New York, where I teach now, but in the 60s. Or Hortense Spillers, whose thinking on psychoanalysis and race is arguably the centre of her research and practice – and she established herself in that realm by thinking about about jazz, and Senegal, and thinking about psychiatry in Senegal. I think there's a way of assuming in the curatorial sphere that the theorists who we're talking about do not have the reach, do not have the experience of understanding, the complexity that is happening. I think it is a blindsightedness on our part as curators to not know that, for instance, Lorde knew Africa, knew New South Africa, had an NGO in South Africa, was engaging with police officers, etc.

NA-P: It feels like I directly carry her with me when I call myself an Afro-German, because she was so influential. Another question – at a time when more contemporary Black artists are entering museum collections, how can curators at institutions engender future care of these works, thinking of archiving the future?

BW: I have a very unsexy administrative answer. I will say that that question makes me think of the acquisition processes of the institutions that I have been affiliated with and have colleagues at, and the importance of compensating contemporary artists appropriately. If the only people who cannot continue to live well in this art world are the artists at the centre of all of it, someone has gotten something wrong. That is such a fundamental thing that so many really well-placed, well-endowed, very wealthy institutions are surprisingly not always good at.

The other thing I think is important is the kind of paperwork that goes along with acquiring work by an artist. Doing an oral history and writing a really robust, expansive sense of the importance and the significance of that artist's work is incredibly important. It is incredible how much ink has been spilled around artists that we see in exhibition over and over and over again every year for the past hundred years. And yet for Black artists, the institutions that have the work sometimes can only produce basic tombstone information for you. And you think, No one thought to interview this person about all of these rich visual, symbolic and iconographic things that are happening with their work? Nobody thought to talk to them about their influences or what they were reading? So this is another kind of administration that makes our work possible or impossible. It's really unsexy, because this kind of writing doesn't necessarily see the light of day, it doesn't necessarily end up in a book. But it's so important for those who want to find it later, in the future.

AE: An experience that I had could tie a bow around what institutions do. I've been recently spending time in an archive at an HBCU in Virginia. Usually there is a sense of control in an archive that I don't love. You have to control your every move: where your drink is, where your hands are, what you're doing. But I had this experience at Virginia State University that made me realize how infrastructural differences make a huge difference. From the second that I walked in the door to the library, there was care and love, from the *hey baby*s to the personable conversations. No policing nor control of my movement through the archives. It allowed me to go from box to box without having to check things out and without having to feel that I was being watched and policed. I had never felt that in an archive. And I was like, okay, this is the difference when the logic and the rationale around controlling and protecting something is done differently. That just blew my mind. I kept wanting to go back. And I think the reason why is because of where that archive was and who was caring for it.

NA-P: I think it's important that we return to something that Bridget Cooks touched on in her opening and that keeps coming back, that is, there is always a moment of crisis. And I'm curious how you've been experiencing this.

SM: The crisis we're in politically, geopolitically, socially and nationally, etc. – wherever we are in our institutions and whatever crisis we're facing – I want think of this also on a very personal level of crisis. Emma Wolukau-Wanambwa, a British-Ugandan artist, is really the person who made me into a curator. I went to see her work in 2012, when it was shown in Uganda, and I became a curator by virtue of understanding how she was dealing with the crises that had made or unmade her. Being born in the UK with parents from Uganda and understanding herself, through her art and research, in relation to a certain kind of memory of displacement. A crisis is what brings you back to Africa, to answer your question, Nana. In trying to understand Emma's work, I think I could tap into what it means to work with artists who have experienced a real sense of crisis. How do I become an artist? Why do I become an artist? Why research? I think for me, the crisis is understanding what kind of challenges artists have conceptually, but also why they do what they do. How do they position themselves in a way that makes them effective? In Emma's case, she is an artist who chose to become a researcher, write historical papers and intervene in art history. Many art historians are very wary of some of her ideas, even though she is not an art historian, because they challenge the kind of scholarship they produce.

RL: We've had the approach of building upon what has come before us, and acknowledging that the crisis is ongoing. That there is *no real closure* – no end to the crisis in the foreseeable future. But there is this sense of life in between all of that. In June 2020, our inbox exploded. We had already outlined 'No Real Closure' as this platform for Black experimentation, and suddenly everyone wanted a piece and everyone was interested. There's something uncomfortable about that; it can feel exploitative or it can feel complicated. But if you take the approach that the crisis is ongoing, and that certain people just don't pay attention at certain times, it allows for a slowness that is necessary to do the work that we're all talking about. It doesn't happen at flashpoints. It happens in a long term, more laborious way. I think this is both difficult and exciting. It's okay if we can't see the end point. There's a relief in not having to be the first or the biggest or the most. I find that comforting, to think of myself as a part of this lineage as opposed to having the pressure of the lineage on my back.

IMJ: I was thinking about the meaning of *crisis*: 'turning point'. We are always turning. We're always figuring a way round. We're always trying to get out of this cycle, yet the cycle keeps returning. I think what is so generative about theory is that it offers us ways out of that cycle and particularly, of course, abolition offers us a way out of this particular crisis in relation to the Black Lives Matter movement, in the sense of tackling police violence, and whether our strategy is reform or revolution. Abolition gives us the tools to be able to think, and do our way out of this, in practice. It's an ongoing crisis, but let's find a different cycle to find ourselves in. I think that this also goes back to the labour of administration, the labour of archiving and the kind of imaginative critical fabulation that might get us somewhere new.

RL: I like to think of theory as a form, one of many forms. Like, theory is no more important to me than music or art or all of these forms. We can think about it not as the way that we've been taught to think about it, as a hierarchical thing, but as form or type of thing, among others. We don't ask poets to be more legible, because it's about what do we do with that form and how do we offer it to a public and create a space.

NA-P: Is there anything else you would like to share in the last few minutes that we have? How does a flexible institution look like? What exactly is that flexibility to you?

AE: For me, it's about taking on – from the top to the roots – the ethics of the art, especially when you're working with living artists. It's not just about presenting the ethics in language in the gallery. It's about being about doing that on the level of administration. If the show is about radical politics, that's how the show should be produced and brought into the world. And that's going to require constant change and a lot of frustration. But I think that is the only way that institutions can grow and expand and that we can incorporate fully the things that we believe in and champion.

RL: Something that happens quite a lot with the Cubitt fellowship is that someone leaves a policy behind and brings it back to the programme. We tried to do something similar in a small way. We invited the artists to choose an organization which they wanted to support. We put in the copy, 'Please donate whatever you would pay for this exhibition to this place.' What we can do really easily as curators is to implement organizing strategies or mutual aid strategies within what we do with the artist, including what they're interested in.

IMJ: I think when we think about curating Black futures, it's really important for us to be invested in Black futures beyond the art world, beyond our roles in our institutions, because we're Black people and our future is not promised.

And in many ways, it's created and co-created. So this is also a shift that we've tried to commit to in our work: to be like, it's my job as a curator and as an artist, to be cognizant of all the ways I can contribute to the dismantling of racial capitalism, to the building of something new.

SM: I do want to speak to this question of the future very briefly. I have been reading a lot about Africa and its epistemology and religions, and I understand that the future does not really exist in some of these philosophical writings. The fascination with the future, especially in, say, German philosophical traditions, has to do with cause and effect, the consequences or whatever is produced and projected into. There is a Marxist notion or an accumulative basis of the future, which I think I'm trying to respectfully step away from. Instead, I'm thinking I should borrow from Ugandan philosopher Okot p'Bitek, thinking about the burden of responsibility: the burden of looking after the people whom one loves, the burden of looking after not only your children but your family, and how your friends actually begin to pull you out of really drastic moments. The crisis of our time may not be resolved by anticipating and accumulating and projecting into the future. It may actually be resolved by those whom we entrust with our secrets. Those who are able to share with us and to come to us in moments of most need.

Author biographies

Nana Adusei-Poku, PhD, is Assistant Professor in African Diasporic Art History in the Department of History of Art at the University of California Berkeley. She was previously Associate Professor and Luma Foundation Fellow at the Center for Curatorial Studies, Bard College, Annandale-on-Hudson, New York. Her research includes Cultural Shifts and how they articulate themselves through the intersections of Art, Politics and Popular Culture; Artistic productions from the Black Diasporas, and curatorial practice as a research tool to shape art historical discourses. Her book *Taking Stakes in the Unknown: Tracing Post-Black Art* was published in 2021 with Transcript Verlag and her articles have been published in *Nka: Journal of Contemporary African Art*, *e-flux*, *Kunstforum International*, *Flash Art*, *L'Internationale* and *darkmatter*. She curated the event 'Performances of Nothingness' (Academy of Arts, Berlin, 2018) and 'Black Melancholia' (Hessel Museum Bard College, Annandale-on-Hudson, New York, 2022).

Mora J. Beauchamp-Byrd, PhD, is Visiting Assistant Professor of Art and Design at the University of Tampa, where she teaches Modern and Contemporary Art and Museum Studies. An art historian, curator and arts administrator, she specializes in the art of the African diasporas, American art and modern and contemporary art, with a focus on late-twentieth-century British art; museum and curatorial studies; and representations of race, class and gender in American comics. She has organized numerous exhibitions, including 'Transforming the Crown: African, Asian and Caribbean Artists in Britain, 1966–1996' (Bronx Museum of the Arts, Studio Museum in Harlem and Caribbean Cultural Center, New York, 1997), 'Picturing Creole New Orleans: The Photographs of Arthur P. Bedou' (Xavier University of Louisiana, 2019) and 'Little Nemo's Progress: Animation and Contemporary Art' (Oklahoma State University Museum of Art, 2019). Beauchamp-Byrd is presently completing a manuscript that examines the appropriations of William Hogarth's eighteenth-century satirical narratives by David Hockney, Lubaina Himid and Paula Rego. She is Vice President for Publications, an Executive Committee member, of the Board of Directors of the College Art Association (CAA) in the US.

Bridget R. Cooks is Associate Professor in the Department of Art History and the Department of African American Studies at the University of California, Irvine. Her research focuses on African American artists, Black visual culture and museum criticism. Cooks has worked in museum education and curated exhibitions including 'Grafton Tyler Brown: Exploring California' (Pasadena Museum of California Art, 2018), 'Ernie Barnes: A Retrospective' (California African American Museum, Los Angeles, 2019) and the nationally touring exhibition 'The Black Index' (2021–22). She is the author of the book *Exhibiting Blackness: African Americans and the American Art Museum* (University of Massachusetts Press, 2011). Other texts by Cooks can be found in *Afterall*, *Afterimage*, *American Studies*, *Aperture* and *American Quarterly*.

Abby R. Eron works as Registrar at Howard University Gallery of Art, Washington DC. She received her PhD from the University of Maryland, College Park, in 2020; her dissertation considered the symbolist impulse in American art across media circa 1900 by exploring the work of Henry Ossawa Tanner, Gertrude Käsebier, Alice Pike Barney and George Grey Barnard. Eron earned her MA also from the University of Maryland; her MA thesis concerned public sculpture in the United States in the 1930s and the New Deal. Eron has worked at the Rose Art Museum, Brandeis University, Waltham, Massachusetts; the Association for Public Art, Philadelphia; and the Conservation Center for Art & Historic Artifacts, Philadelphia. She has been an intern or fellow with the National Museum of American Jewish History, Philadelphia; the National Gallery of Art, Washington DC; and the Philadelphia Museum of Art. Before coming to Howard, she served as Registrar and Curatorial Assistant at the University of Maryland Art Gallery, where she curated an exhibition on the multi-disciplinary modernist Djuna Barnes.

Amber Esseiva is a Swiss-Senegalese-American curator and educator who specializes in producing contemporary art exhibitions and programmes by national and international mid-career and emerging artists. Esseiva is currently Curator at the Institute for Contemporary Art at Virginia Commonwealth University. Since joining ICA VCU, she has been essential to the institution's programming and has curated 'Great Force' (2019–20), an exhibition exploring how art can be used to envision new forms of race and representation freed from historical constructs. Most recently, Esseiva curated the first solo museum exhibition by Los Angeles-based artist Kandis Williams ('A Field', 2020) and solo exhibitions by South African artist Dineo Seshee Bopape ('Ile aye, moya, là, ndokh … harmonic conversions … mm', 2021) and New York–based composer, performer and artist Jeremy Toussaint-Baptiste ('Set If Off', 2021–22). Esseiva received her MA in 2015 from the Center for Curatorial Studies, Bard College. She is co-founder of the interdisciplinary curatorial journal *aCCeSsions*. In 2022, she was appointed Curator-at-Large at the Studio Museum in Harlem.

Cheryl Finley is Director of the Atlanta University Center Art History + Curatorial Studies Collective and Distinguished Visiting Professor of Art History at Spelman College, Atlanta. As a visionary leader committed to engaging strategic partners to transform the art and culture industry, she leads an innovative undergraduate programme at the world's largest Historically Black College and University consortium in preparing the next generation of African American museum and visual arts professionals. She is a curator, contemporary art critic and award-winning author noted for *Committed to Memory: The Art of the Slave Ship Icon* (Princeton University Press, 2018), the first in-depth study of the most famous image associated with the memory of slavery – a schematic engraving of a packed slave ship hold – and of the art, architecture, poetry and film it has inspired since its creation in Britain in 1788.

Claudette Johnson is an artist living and working in London. She started her career as a member of the Blk Art Group, which she joined in 1981 whilst a second year Fine Art student at Wolverhampton University. She took part in the group's second exhibition 'The Pan-Afrikan Connection' at The Africa Centre in 1983. In the 1980s, Johnson showed her work in significant shows including 'Five Black Women' (Africa Centre, London, 1983), 'Black Women Time Now' (Battersea Arts Centre, London, 1984), 'The Thin Black Line' (Institute of Contemporary Arts, London, 1985) and 'In This Skin: Drawings by Claudette Johnson' (The Black-Art Gallery, London, 1992). Together with Marlene Smith and Keith Piper, she started the Blk Art Group Research Project in 2011. Johnson's recent solo exhibitions include 'Claudette Johnson: I Came to Dance' (Modern Art Oxford, 2019) and 'Still Here' (Hollybush Gardens, London, 2021). Recent group shows in 2022 include: 'Drawing Closer' (RISD Museum Rhode Island), 'Me, Myself and I: Artists Self Portraits' (Royal West Academy, Bristol), 'Life Between Islands: Caribbean British Art 1950s – Now' (Tate Britain, London). Works by Johnson are held in numerous public collections in the UK, including Tate; the British Council Collection; the Arts Council Collection; Manchester Art Gallery; Wolverhampton Art Gallery; Rugby Art Gallery & Museum; and Herbert Art Gallery & Museum. In 2022 she was awarded an Honorary Doctorate of the Arts at Wolverhampton University.

Languid Hands are the collaborative London-based artistic and curatorial duo of Rabz Lansiquot (DJ, film-maker and programmer) and Imani Mason Jordan (writer, artist and editor). Languid Hands were Curatorial Fellows at Cubitt, London until the spring of 2022 and Curators of Frieze London LIVE 2021. Their practice explores collaboration; curation; Black studies; and experimentation across exhibitions, moving image, text, performance, publications and public programming as well as peer-led artist development and residencies.

Julie L. McGee is Associate Professor of Africana Studies and Art History and Director of the Interdisciplinary Humanities Research Center at the University of Delaware, Newark, where she is Interim Director, Special Collections and Museums. As an art historian and curator, she focuses on African diasporic art history and contemporary South African art. She has curated exhibitions for the David C. Driskell Center, College Park, Maryland; Bowdoin College Museum of Art, Brunswick, Maine; the Visual Arts Center of New Jersey, Summit; and Guga S'Thebe Community Arts Centre in Langa, Cape Town. With Vuyile C. Voyiya, McGee co-produced the 2003 documentary film *The Luggage Is Still Labeled: Blackness in South African Art*. In addition to the exhibition 'David Driskell: Icons of Nature and History' (Portland Museum of Art, Maine, 2021), her scholarship includes the monograph *David C. Driskell: Artist and Scholar* (2006), curatorial essays, artist interviews and analyses of Driskell's writings. McGee's research is simultaneously focused on Driskell's curatorial legacy and American art history and on American Dutch artist Sam Middleton and transnational art history.

Derek Conrad Murray is an interdisciplinary theorist specializing in the history, theory and criticism of contemporary art and visual culture. He is Professor of History of Art and Visual Culture at the University of California, Santa Cruz. He works in contemporary aesthetic and cultural theory with particular attention on technocultural engagements with identity and representation. Murray is Co-editor of the journal *Visual Studies*, Associate Editor of *Nka: Journal of Contemporary African Art* and a member of the editorial advisory board of *Third Text*. His books include *Visual Culture Approaches to the Selfie* (Routledge, 2021), *Mapplethorpe and the Flower: Radical Sexuality and the Limits of Control* (Bloomsbury, 2020) and *Queering Post-Black Art: Artists Transforming African-American Identity After Civil Rights* (I.B. Tauris, Bloomsbury, 2016).

Serubiri Moses is an independent writer and curator who lives in New York City. He co-curated the fifth edition of the contemporary art survey 'Greater New York' at MoMA PS1 in 2021. From 2020–21, he was Adjunct Assistant Professor in the Department of Art and Art History at Hunter College, New York, where he taught contemporary African and Black art history. Since 2018, Moses has been a faculty member of independent art education platforms such as Dark Study (US), Digital Earth Fellowship (Netherlands) and New Centre for Research and Practice (US and Germany). Between 2017–18, he was part of the curatorial team for the Tenth Berlin Biennale of Contemporary Art, titled 'We Don't Need Another Hero'. Recent and forthcoming essays, books and conference talks include: 'Which Art History in Africa?: A Question of Method', in *Critical Interventions: Journal of African Art History and Visual Culture* (2021); 'The Problem of Mastery: Criticism from Kampala', in the exhibition catalogue *Here and Now: Dynamic Spaces* (Museum Ludwig, 2021); 'Death as a Premonitory Sign', for the Singapore Biennial Symposium (2020); 'Counter-Imaginaries: Women Artists on the Move', 'Second to None' and 'Like a Virgin ...', in *Afterall* (2019); and *FESTAC '77: Second World Black and African Festival of Arts and Culture* (Afterall Books, 2019). He co-edited *Forces of Art: Perspectives from a Changing World* (Valiz, 2020).

Senam Okudzeto is a British American artist of US and Ghanaian descent. Her work incorporates writing, scholarly research and art practice within a wide range of media, including painting, film, installation and social sculpture. Her methodological practice of Afro-Dada is a critical response to previously overlooked socioeconomic and political histories. Okudzeto has taught across diverse fields, ranging from African studies, material culture and architectural and art history, through to practical and theoretical approaches to drawing. She was the 2018–19 Visiting Professor at Ecole Nationale Supérieure d'Arts de Paris-Cergy (ENSAPC) and has taught at art schools and universities in West Africa, the US and Europe. Selected exhibitions include: 'Exotic? Regarder l'ailleurs en Suisse au siècle des Lumières' (Palais du Rumine, Lausanne, 2020); 'We Wanted the Object to Be the Subject (Before We Wanted the Reverse)' (Centre Culturel Suisse,

Paris, 2019); 'Dada Afrika' (Museum Rietberg, 2016); 'Saltwater' (Fourteenth Istanbul Biennale, 2015); 'The Progress of Love' (The Menil Collection, Houston, 2012); 'Portes-Oranges' (MoMA PS1, New York, 2007); 'Africa Remix' (Center Pompidou, Paris, 2005); and 'Freestyle' (Studio Museum in Harlem, New York, 2001). Okudzeto's latest writing includes 'Race as Trope of Erasure, Refusing the Tautological Return', in *JSAH Roundtable: Constructing Race and Architecture, 1400–1800* (2021), and 'Remembering African Cities: Rethinking Urban Conservation as Radical Public History', in *Historic Cities: Issues in Urban Conservation* (Readings in Conservation Series, Getty Conservation Institute, Los Angeles, 2019).

Richard J. Powell is John Spencer Bassett Professor of Art and Art History at Duke University, Durham, North Carolina, where he has taught since 1989. After receiving his BA from Morehouse College, Atlanta, he earned his MFA from Howard University, Washington DC. Shortly thereafter, Powell completed a Rockefeller Foundation Fellowship in Museum Education at New York's Metropolitan Museum of Art; after a brief teaching stint in Virginia, he entered Yale University, New Haven, where he received an MA in African American Studies and an MPhil and PhD in the History of Art. It was during Powell's time at the Metropolitan Museum of Art that he became interested in art criticism and organizing art exhibitions. In 1979, the Studio Museum in Harlem enlisted Powell as guest curator for 'Impressions/Expressions: Black American Graphics', one of the first art museum surveys of works by African American printmakers. Powell, a recognized authority on African American art and culture, has organized numerous art exhibitions, including, most notably, 'The Blues Aesthetic: Black Culture and Modernism (1989); 'Rhapsodies in Black: Art of the Harlem Renaissance' (1997); 'To Conserve a Legacy: American Art at Historically Black Colleges and Universities' (1999); 'Back to Black: Art, Cinema, and the Racial Imaginary' (2005); and 'Archibald Motley: Jazz Age Modernist' (2014). Among the major museums where his curated exhibitions have been presented are the Art Institute of Chicago; Los Angeles County Museum of Art; New Orleans Museum of Art; Whitechapel Gallery, London; and the Whitney Museum of American Art, New York. Along with teaching courses in American art, the arts of the African diasporas and contemporary visual studies, he has written extensively on topics ranging from primitivism to postmodernism, including such titles as *Homecoming: The Art and Life of William H. Johnson* (Rizzoli, 1991), *Black Art: A Cultural History* (Thames & Hudson, 1997, 2002, 2021), *Cutting a Figure: Fashioning Black Portraiture* (University of Chicago Press, 2008) and *Going There: Black Visual Satire* (Yale University Press, 2020).

Jamaal B. Sheats is Director and Curator of Fisk University Galleries and Assistant Professor in the Department of Art at Fisk University, Nashville. Since joining the institution in 2015, he has curated nineteen exhibitions, established the Fisk Museum Leadership Program, expanded and nurtured partnerships and implemented innovative programs to foster access to and engagement with the collections. Sheats is a Trustee of the Frist Art Museum and a member of the Boards of Directors of the Alliance of HBCU Museums and Galleries, the Association of Academic Museums and Galleries and the Dan and Margaret Maddox Fund. He earned his MFA from Tufts University, Medford, Massachusetts and BS in Art from Fisk University.

Howard Singerman is the author of *Art Subjects: Making Artists in the American University* (University of California Press, 1999), *Art History, after Sherrie Levine* (University of California Press, 2012) and *Sharon Lockhart: Pine Flat* (Afterall Books, 2020). He has contributed essays to numerous exhibition catalogues over the past four decades, including on canonical Los Angeles artists Chris Burden, Charles Gaines and Mike Kelley, as well as on the sprawling surveys 'A Forest of Signs: Art in the Crisis of Representation' and 'Public Offerings', both at the Museum of Contemporary Art, Los Angeles, where he served as Museum Editor from 1985–88. Singerman is currently the Phyllis and Joseph Caroff Chair of Art and Art History at Hunter College, New York, where he has curated 'Robert Motherwell and the New York School at Hunter' (2015) and 'Acts of Art and Rebuttal in 1971' (2018). Before his appointment at Hunter, he was Professor of Art History at the University of Virginia, Charlottesville, and he has also taught at the University of California, Los Angeles; ArtCenter College of Design, Pasadena; and the California Institute of the Arts, Valencia. Singerman holds a BA from Antioch College, Yellow Springs, Ohio; an MFA in Studio Art from Claremont Graduate University, California; and a PhD in Visual Cultural Studies from the University of Rochester, New York. In 2020, as Mellon Visiting Senior Fellow at the Center for Advanced Visual Studies at the National Gallery of Art, Washington DC, he researched his upcoming book, tentatively titled *"Black Artists in the New York Scene": Acts of Art and Cinque Galleries, 1969–1975*.

Marlene Smith is an artist who curates. In the early 1980s, she was a member of the BLK Art Group and Assistant Curator at The Black-Art Gallery, then newly founded in London. During her year in London, Smith exhibited at the Institute of Contemporary Arts, as part of Lubaina Himid's 'The Thin Black Line' (1985), and in The Elbow Room's 'Unrecorded Truths' (1986). That same year, Smith had her first solo curatorial project, 'Some of Us Are Brave', at The Black-Art Gallery. Smith was Director of West Midlands Minorities Arts until 1991, when she returned to The Black-Art Gallery as Director. Solo exhibitions she curated there include Zarina Bhimji, Claudette Johnson and Lubaina Himid. In 2001, Smith joined the team that created the Public Gallery Ltd., an exhibition space at the heart of a regeneration project dedicated to examining collaborative and socially engaged practice; she became Director in 2003. In 2008, she took up a NESTA (National Endowment for Science Technology & Art) International Cultural Leadership fellowship in Shanghai. She initiated The Room Next to Mine, an ongoing collection of events, in 2014. From 2015–17, she was UK Research Manager of the Black Artists & Modernism project, led by Sonia Boyce, and she enrolled as a PhD candidate at Chelsea School of Art, London. Her research subject was women's exhibition practices during the British Black Arts Movement of 1979–92. In 2017, Smith became Associate Artist at the contemporary art gallery Modern Art Oxford and an Associate at Making Histories Visible, an archive created by Lubaina Himid at the University of Central Lancashire, Preston.

Lucy Steeds is a writer, teacher and occasional curator, based at Edinburgh College of Art. Her research centres on art in its public moment, historically and around the world, where this has challenged norms in ways that are useful to reflect on here and today. She is a Series Editor for the *Exhibition Histories* books and, together with Bo Choy, Charles Esche and David Morris, co-edited the previous volume in the series, *Art and Its Worlds: Exhibitions, Institutions and Art Becoming Public* (2021). With other collaborators, Steeds has co-edited *Curating after the Global* (2019), *How Institutions Think* (2017) and *The Curatorial Conundrum* (2016) (all MIT Press). She is responsible for *Exhibition* in the 'Documents of Contemporary Art' series (MIT Press, 2014).

Brittany Webb is the Evelyn and Will Kaplan Curator of Twentieth Century Art and the John Rhoden Collection at the Pennsylvania Academy of the Fine Arts, Philadelphia. She is currently working on a retrospective exhibition of John Rhoden's work that includes an initiative to gift more than 250 sculptures by the African American sculptor to museums around the country. Webb came to PAFA from the African American Museum in Philadelphia. She holds a PhD in Anthropology from Temple University, Philadelphia and a BA in Political Science from the University of Southern California, Los Angeles.

Bibliography

Since the number of publications with a focus on Black exhibition histories is rather scarce, what follows is a list of books that allow deeper investigation into African diasporic art histories. This list includes very early titles, such as Freeman Henry Morris Murray's *Emancipation and the Freed in American Sculpture* (1916), Alain Locke's *Negro Art: Past and Present* (1936) and James A. Porter's *Modern Negro Art* (1943). These publications represent only a few of the rich sources that allow us to trace the ways in which African diasporic art has been thought and exhibited.

David A. Bailey, Ian Baucom and Sonia Boyce (ed.), *Shades of Black: Assembling Black Arts in 1980s Britain,* Durham: Duke University Press, 2005

Romare Bearden and Harry Henderson, *A History of African-American Artists: From 1792 to the Present*, New York: Pantheon Books, 1993

R. Bearden, Sam Gilliam, Richard Hunt, Jacob Lawrence, Tom Lloyd, William Williams, and Hale Woodruff. 1969. "The Black Artist in America: A Symposium." The Metropolitan Museum of Art Bulletin 27 (5): 245–61

Eddie Chambers, *Black Artists in British Art: A History Since the 1950s*, London: I.B. Tauris, 2014

E. Chambers (ed.), *The Routledge Companion to African American Art History*, New York: Routledge, 2019

Judith Wragg Chase, *Afro-American Art and Craft*, New York: Van Nostrand Reinhold Co., 1971

David C. Driskell and Leonard Simon, *Two Centuries of Black American Art* (exh. cat.), Los Angeles: Los Angeles County Museum of Art, 1976

Samella S. Lewis and Ruth G. Waddy (ed.), *Black Artists on Art*, vol.1, Los Angeles: Contemporary Crafts Publishers, 1969

S. S. Lewis and R. G. Waddy (ed.), *Black Artists on Art*, vol.2, Los Angeles, CA: Contemporary Crafts Publishers, 1971

Alain Locke, *Negro Art: Past and Present*, Washington DC: Associates in Negro Folk Education, 1936

Kobena Mercer, *Welcome to the Jungle: New Positions in Black Cultural Studies*, New York: Routledge, 1994

Rianna Jade Parker, *A Brief History of Black British Art*, London: Tate Publishing, 2021

Sharon F. Patton, *African-American Art*, Oxford: Oxford University Press, 1998

James A. Porter, *Modern Negro Art*, New York: Dryden Press, 1943

Richard J. Powell and Jock Reynolds (ed.), *To Conserve a Legacy: American Art from Historically Black Colleges and Universities*, Andover, MA and New York: Addison Gallery of American Art and The Studio Museum in Harlem, 1999

R. J. Powell, *Black Art and Culture in the 20th Century*, London: Thames & Hudson. 1997

Deborah Willis (ed.), *Picturing Us: African American Identity in Photography*, New York: The New Press, 1994

Acknowledgements

The editors would like to thank the authors, artists and photographers for their contributions to this book.

For support in the research process that led to this publication we are additionally grateful to: Mequitta Ahuja; Sarah Applegate, LACMA | Los Angeles County Museum of Art; Bea Bradley, Victoria Miro Gallery; Starasea Camara, Studio Museum in Harlem; Eddie Chambers; Bo Choy; David Conway, The David C. Driskell Center, University of Maryland; Edward Deluca, DC Moore Gallery; Martina Dodd, Atlanta University Center Robert W. Woodruff Library; Elvira Dyangani Ose; Megan Foy, Monique Meloche Gallery; Ayrson Heráclito; Habiba Hopson, Studio Museum in Harlem; Bhajan Hunjan; Rita Keegan; Sabeena Khosla, DC Moore Gallery; Lena Kühnel, documenta archiv; David Lawson, Smoking Dogs Films; Trevor Mathison; Michael McMillan; Rodney Miller; Wangechi Mutu; Ebony G. Patterson; James Phillips; Tracy Pollock, Center for Curatorial Studies, Bard College; Jeff Preiss; Debra Priestly; Ramona Rosenberg, Center for Curatorial Studies, Bard College; Stuart Semple; Holly Smith, Women's Research & Resource Center, Spelman College; Diane Symons, Estate of Donald Rodney; Perry H. Trice, Special Collections/Archives, Savery Library, Talladega College; Emily Winslow Tucker, Hallwalls Contemporary Art Center; Jan van Raay; Deborah Willis; and Andrew Wilson.

Nana Adusei-Poku: 'I would like to thank David Morris and Wing Chan for their thoughtful, incredibly productive, and mindful support during the editing process of this publication; it is due to them that *Reshaping the Field* has come so quickly and beautifully into being. A special thanks go to Bridget Cooks, whose groundbreaking book *Exhibiting Blackness* (2011) paved the way for the scholarship in this publication. I also would like to express my deepest gratitude to all the authors who have despite full schedules managed to send their brilliant and excellent articles including rich visual materials that manifest a Black presence in the field of Exhibition Histories. Many thanks for the support of the publication also go to Tom Eccles, Lauren Cornell and the larger Afterall team for their unwavering support for this project.'

The Exhibition Histories research and publishing project is made possible through generous support from: Asia Art Archive; Central Saint Martins, University of the Arts London; the Center for Curatorial Studies, Bard College; the Faculty of Fine, Applied and Performing Arts, University of Gothenburg; and public funding through Arts Council England.

Index

U

V

W

Y

Z

Notes